The Resolution of Family Conflict
Comparative Legal Perspectives

The Resolution of Family Conflict

Comparative Legal Perspectives

edited by
JOHN M. EEKELAAR
Fellow of Pembroke College,
Oxford, England

SANFORD N. KATZ
Professor of Law,
Boston College Law School,
United States of America

BUTTERWORTHS
TORONTO

The Resolution of Family Conflict: Comparative Legal Perspectives
© 1984 by Butterworth & Co. (Canada) Ltd.
All rights reserved. No part of this publication may be reproduced, stored in a retrieval system, or transmitted, in any form or by any means: photocopying, electronic, mechanical, recording, or otherwise, without the prior written permission of the copyright holder.

Printed and bound in Canada.

Canadian Cataloguing in Publication Data
Main entry under title:
The Resolution of family conflict

Papers presented at the fourth annual conference of the International Society on Family Law, Harvard University, 1982.
Includes bibliographical references.
ISBN 0-409-83984-1

1. Domestic relations – Addresses, essays, lectures.
I. Eekelaar, John. II. Katz, Sanford N., 1933 –
III. International Society on Family Law.

K670.A55 1982   346.01'5   C84-099022-7

The Butterworth Group of Companies
Canada
Butterworth & Co. (Canada) Ltd., Toronto and Vancouver
United Kingdom
Butterworth & Co. (Publishers) Ltd., London
Australia
Butterworths Pty. Ltd., Sydney, Melbourne, Brisbane, Adelaide, and Perth
New Zealand
Butterworths (New Zealand) Ltd., Wellington and Auckland
Singapore
Butterworth & Co. (Asia) Pte. Ltd., Singapore
South Africa
Butterworth Publishers (SA) (Pty) Ltd., Durban and Pretoria
United States
Butterworth Legal Publishers, Boston, Seattle, Austin, and St. Paul
D & S Publishers, Clearwater

Acknowledgements

This book is the end product of a gathering of specialists in family law from all over the world. In June of 1982 Harvard University permitted us to convene in its law school the Fourth Annual Conference of the International Society on Family Law. We owe a debt of gratitude to the conferees who enriched the meeting with their papers and discussions. The papers offered by the speakers represent a worldwide, state-of-the art approach to the theme of the conference: Toward Alternative Methods of Resolving Conflicts Within the Family. We heard of laws and viewpoints as far apart as those of Japan, Tasmania, India, Africa and all the nations of the Western World. From those papers we culled and edited the articles that appear in this volume.

We are deeply grateful to Dean Richard G. Huber of Boston College Law School who supported the months of work spent at first in arranging the conference and then the long and arduous editing of the papers that make up *The Resolution of Family Conflict: Comparative Legal Perspectives*. The book would not have been possible without his enthusiastic advocacy, both intellectual and financial, of our projects. And the scrupulous attention to detail and endless patience of Butterworth & Co. (Canada) Ltd., our publisher, and especially of Linda Kee in working through the minutiae of the format, must not go without an expression of warm gratitude.

At Boston College Law School the editorial expertise of Melba McGrath and the research assistance of Scott Birnbaum, who is a third-year law student, were of invaluable assistance in the final result.

Contents

Introduction   Towards a Functional Analysis of Family Process, *Frank E. A. Sander*   **xi**

PART ONE   THE SETTLEMENT OF DISPUTES — HISTORICAL AND THEORETICAL PERSPECTIVES   1

Chapter 1   Questioning the Delegalization Movement in Family Law: Do We Really Want a Family Court? *Michael D. A. Freeman*   **7**

Chapter 2   Negotiated Settlement of Family Disputes, *Donald J. MacDougall*   **26**

Chapter 3   Wife Sale and Desertion as Alternatives to Judicial Marriage Dissolution, *Katherine O'Donovan*   **41**

Chapter 4   Some Aspects of Mediation and Conciliation in the Settlement of Matrimonial Disputes in Tanzania, *Barthazar Rwezaura*   **52**

PART TWO   EMERGING PROCEDURAL MODELS   71

Chapter 5   The Scandinavian Law of Procedure in Matrimonial Causes, *T. Svenné Schmidt*   **77**

Chapter 6   Mediation Conferences — The New Zealand Family Court's Alternative to Litigation, *J. M. Priestley*   **99**

Chapter 7   The Role of Mediation in Yugoslav Divorce: Court Versus Out-of-Court Mediation, *Petar Šarčević*   **107**

Chapter 8   Procedural Aspects of Marriage Dissolution in Japan, *Ichiro Shimazu*   **116**

Chapter 9   The Role of the Expert in Judicial Divorce Procedures, *Frank Bates*   **123**

Chapter 10   Divorce in South Africa — Principles and Practice, *June Sinclair*   **142**

Chapter 11   Divorce Proceedings: Ends and Means, *Henrik H. H. Andrup*   **163**

Chapter 12   The Completed Reform: The Family Office, *Henrik H. H. Andrup* and *Klaus A. Ziegert*   **179**

PART THREE   MEDIATION AND PROFESSIONAL ROLES   189

Chapter 13   Divorce Mediation — The Emerging American Model, *H. Jay Folberg*   **193**

Chapter 14   Divorce Mediation, Private Legal Practice and Legal Ethics in the U.S.A., *Richard E. Crouch*   **211**

Chapter 15 Arbitration and Mediation of Disputes Involving Children and Matrimonial Property in Canada, *Alastair Bissett-Johnson* **233**
Chapter 16 Custody Mediation in Denver: Short and Longer Term Effects, *Jessica Pearson* and *Nancy Thoennes* **248**
Chapter 17 A Study of Conciliation Counselling in the Family Court of Toronto: Implications for Socio-Legal Practice, *Howard H. Irving* and *Michael Benjamin* **268**

PART FOUR THE SCOPE FOR PRIVATE AGREEMENT 291

Chapter 18 Financial Agreements on Divorce and the Freedom of Contract in Continental Europe, *Marie-Thérèse Meulders-Klein* **297**
Chapter 19 Agreements Regarding the Financial Aspects of Divorce: How Free? How Binding? *J. M. Grossen* **313**
Chapter 20 Financial Agreements on Divorce in France, *J. P. Peigné* **322**
Chapter 21 Compromise as the Aim of Danish Divorce Procedures, *Noe Munck* **328**
Chapter 22 Judicial Control of Divorce Settlements in Belgium, *Walter L. Pintens* **341**
Chapter 23 The Legal Response to Private Financial Arrangements in Divorce, *Eric Clive* **347**
Chapter 24 Divorce Bargaining: The Limits on Private Ordering, *Robert H. Mnookin* **364**

PART FIVE THE SPECIAL POSITION OF CHILDREN 385

Chapter 25 Decision Making Relating to Children in the Republic of Ireland — Restraints on Introducing New Models, *William Duncan* **389**
Chapter 26 Representation of Children: Does More Mean Better?, *Henri Giller* and *Susan Maidment* **405**
Chapter 27 Decision Making: The Roles of the Judge and the Guardian *Ad Litem* in England, *Judith M. Masson* **421**
Chapter 28 Towards a Natural History of Access Arrangements in Broken Marriages, *Adrian L. James* and *Kate Wilson* **436**

PART SIX THE FINANCIAL DILEMMA — THE SEARCH FOR A SOLUTION 457

Chapter 29 Equity and Equality in Divorce Settlements: A Comparative Analysis of Property and Maintenance Awards in the United States and England, *Lenore J. Weitzman* **461**

Chapter 30 The Economic Consequences of Divorce for Families with Children, *Mavis Maclean* and *John Eekelaar* **488**

Chapter 31 Maintenance and Family Support: The Social Reality in England and Wales, *Colin S. Gibson* **505**

Chapter 32 Alternatives to Judicial Child Support Enforcement: A Proposal for a Child Support Tax, *Marygold Melli* and *Sherwood Zink* **516**

Chapter 33 New Zealand's Nonjudicial Parental Income Attachment Scheme, *G. J. Thomas* **534**

Chapter 34 Child Support in the United States: Reporting Good News, *Harry D. Krause* **543**

PART SEVEN FAMILY DECISIONS AND MEDICAL ETHICS 553

Chapter 35 Decision Making about Health Care and Medical Treatment of Minors, *Madzy Rood-de Boer* **557**

Chapter 36 Medicine and Human Rights: Emerging Substantive Standards and Procedural Protections for Medical Decision Making Within the American Family, *Charles H. Baron* **575**

Introduction

Towards a Functional Analysis of Family Process

Frank E. A. Sander

Harvard Law School, U.S.A.

While perusing the rich variety of family processes described in this volume, one is likely to be impressed by the dominant roles played by cultural context and historical evolution. Rarely does a country explicitly examine the broad range of choices available and opt clearly for one process or another because of some specific goal served by that process. The development of different kinds of procedures for handling various family controversies is often quite haphazard.

This, therefore, is a plea for a functional, purposive analysis of process in family proceedings. Although culture and history will inevitably still play their parts, we should constrain those forces by a sophisticated analysis of the goals we seek to achieve, and then develop a process that is likely to attain them.

Consider, for example, the case of divorce. Over time, these proceedings have taken the form of ecclesiastical concessions, royal writs, legislative acts, and finally, judicial decrees. Moreover, in recent years, while the courts have been dispensing divorces, there have been dramatic changes in the applicable substantive law, reflecting a major shift from fault to no-fault grounds. Yet the procedural framework has not changed commensurately. There has been little attempt, either by legislatures or by legal scholars,[1] to ask basic questions such as: What goals are sought to be achieved by this particular type of proceeding? What types of procedures are available that might achieve those particular goals? It is to questions like these that this Introduction is devoted. My aim throughout is not to develop specific solutions for particular problems but rather to set forth a general framework that might be useful in the analysis of family process.[2]

Before undertaking that inquiry, however, I would like to identify the special characteristics of family disputes that may point us towards one or another specific dispute settlement procedure. We will then look at the range of available dispute settlement mechanisms as well as the various goals that we might wish to achieve in setting up any particular procedure. Our ultimate objective will be to seek to develop a rational dispute settlement procedure for any particulr type of family dispute on the basis of an analysis of the primary goal or goals to be attained.

THE SPECIAL CHARACTERISTICS OF FAMILY DISPUTES

If one looks at family disputes through a process-oriented lens, a number of points seem particularly noteworthy. First, in family relations, we are usually dealing with continuing and interdependent relationships. This is true even where the family is seeking to dissolve itself (i.e., in the case of divorce). Even in that case there will be continuing relations between the parties over financial and child-rearing questions. Hence it is important that any dispute settlement system help to facilitate constructive relations in the future, rather than leading to the exacerbation of existing relations. Another way of putting that point is Lon Fuller's observation that many of the questions that arise in family controversies call for "person oriented" rather than "act oriented" interventions.[3]

There are also some particular characteristics of family disputes that need to be taken into account. Because these disputes often involve a complex interplay of emotional and legal complaints, it is sometimes dfficult to discover the "real" issue in dispute. Thus there may be a great need for an open-ended, unstructured process that permits the disputants to air their true sentiments. In addition, disputants frequently have such intense feelings that a question arises whether the formal legal processes will be effective. Not infrequently disputants are prone to take the law into their own hands if they are dissatisfied with the results that the adjudicatory system gives them. This suggests the desirability of using to the greatest extent possible consensual processes (such as negotiation and mediation) that reflect maximal commitment by the parties to the undertaking.

Another important point is the fact that some family disputants (such as children and the mentally disabled) are not fully competent. Obviously that requires special procedures and protections.

Finally it is essential to note that the family itself represents a private ordering system that has the capacity for resolving its own disputes. In fact many, if not most, family disputes are resolved in precisely that way, and the state has a strong interest in supporting the family as an indigenous dispute resolution mechanism. Hence the question arises when and to what extent that system should be deferred to, and what should be its relation to the general societal "official" dispute resolution system.

AVAILABLE MODES

Let us now look briefly at the range of available dispute resolution processes. The most familiar by far is court adjudication. It has the virtue of giving the disputants a formal opportunity to present their arguments to the neutral presider and assuring them of a definitive decision that will not only resolve their particular case but may also cast a "shadow" (in the form of general principles) to guide future disputants.[4] But adjudication (whether by a public judge or by a private arbitrator) involves the imposition of a decision upon the parties by an outsider. In that important respect it differs from negotiation (the parties' own attempt to resolve their disputes) and mediation (a process whereby a third party helps the parties to resolve their dispute).

In view of the common characteristics of family disputes that were previously discussed, mediation deserves special emphasis. There are several reasons for this. First and foremost, mediation is an open-ended, problem-solving process that looks to the future and that has as its principal goal the repair of a frayed relationship between the disputants. Second, mediated solutions are more flexible than those brought about by adjudication because they are crafted by the parties themselves, with the help of the mediator. Third, mediation avoids the winner-loser syndrome, a point that assumes special importance where there is an ongoing relationship. Fourth, the mediation process involves a wide-ranging inquiry into what the interested parties want to talk about; it is not dominated by what the judge wants to hear about. Although mediation is not therapy,[5] it can certainly be a therapeutic experience. It can also be an important learning experience. There is evidence that people who go through mediation learn how better to handle conflicts that may arise in the future. Obviously this dispute-prevention aspect is critically important if one is dealing with continuing relationships. Finally, mediation gives an enhancing sense of participation to the disputants. Thus, they have a strong commitment to the result that is reached. It is not surprising therefore to learn that compliance with mediated solutions is greater than with adjudicated solutions.[6]

Although adjudication is normally performed by a judge or an arbitrator, mediation may be provided by a great variety of public or private individuals, ranging from the police to friends of the family (or sometimes even family members themselves). But that very fact might imply that anyone can be a successful mediator. Nothing could be further from the truth. The art of mediation is an exceedingly difficult one, requiring immense sensitivity, insight, and creativity.

Although the noted differences between adjudication and mediation are particularly critical in family disputes, these are simply points on a spectrum of disputant "ownership" and control. Since, at least in the

United States, most disputes that are filed in court are in fact resolved, or "settled," by the parties themselves through negotiation, many of the benefits that attend mediation are present in these cases as well.

In addition to the primary processes of negotiation, mediation, and adjudication, there are also a number of other processes that should be briefly mentioned. Because of the psychological complexities of many family issues, there is a common tendency to involve experts of some kind (physicians, psychiatrists, or social workers) in the decision making. These experts may be cast as the sole decision makers (as where a child custody decision is submitted to a specially created tribunal),[7] or they may simply play some designated role in the adjudicatory or mediative processes. Examples of the latter might be expert witnesses in court — sometimes even brought in by the judge — and mediation performed by individuals possessing special behavioural skills (like the conciliators whose role is mandated by law in disputed child custody cases in California).[8]

Another totally different type of specialized dispute resolution is represented by the jury in Anglo-American law and by community-based mediation in China.[9] Here the goal presumably is to bring to bear community sentiment in the settlement of family disputes. In the American legal system, which places such heavy emphasis on individual rights, there is relatively little place for such input. But in countries like China or Japan, where subordination of the individual to collective goals is much more common, such mechanisms are frequently utilized.

Finally there is the possibility of some type of bureaucratic/administrative determination, like that used for consent divorces in Japan. Such a mechanism may be far cheaper and faster than the more elaborate adjudicatory mechanism.

To this brief list of individualized dispute resolution mechanisms should be added the legislature as a mechanism available for generalized rule formulation.

FUNCTIONAL ANALYSIS

Now that we have seen the wide array of possible dispute resolution mechanisms, each with its particular characteristics, it may be useful to look at some typical family disputes with a view to seeing whether we can suggest specific mechanisms for particular types of disputes on the basis of the goal or goals that are sought to be achieved. The purpose of this exercise, it must be reemphasized, is to illustrate a suggested method of processual analysis rather than to arrive at any definitive universally applicable answers. Such analysis might be utilized by a legislature in setting up an appropriate mechanism form resolving a particular type of family dispute, or it might be looked to by two private individuals seeking to design their own method of dispute resolution. As suggested below, it could even be used by a court when faced by the question whether it should decide a dispute itself or whether it should "remand" that question to an indigenous dispute resolution tribunal such as the family.

Disputes in the Ongoing Family

An interesting example of such a dispute is the case of *McGuire v. McGuire*,[10] involving a Nebraska couple in which the husband was considerably older than the wife. After many years of marriage the wife brought suit to have the court order adequate support from a husband who clearly did not treat her in the manner that his means would justify. Although he had $200,000 or more of assets, he did not provide her with indoor plumbing and did not afford her many of the amenities suitable to one of his station. But the court rejected the suit on the ground that it was inappropriate for the courts to get involved in this kind of dispute. If the court did so, it would have more business than it could handle, and besides, it was exceedingly difficult for the courts to monitor this kind of disagreement.

The obvious need in such cases is for some type of conciliation or therapy that will seek to explore what is fundamentally a relational dispute. That would point to the use of mediation or family therapy, possibly coupled with ultimate recourse to some form of adjudication if the matter could not be resolved consensually. Although the court in the *McGuire* case thus reached the right conclusion, the more persuasive reason is not that the courts would be flooded if such cases were presented to them. It is rather that they are really incompetent to deal with the essential problem being presented to them and poorly equipped to monitor the ongoing relationship. In such cases the state should provide ready access to an agency furnishing family counselling or mediation.

Of course disputes cannot be analyzed merely in categorial terms if one is to match them to the appropriate dispute resolution mechanisms. Because some intrafamily disputes, though in form suggest a need for conciliation, may in fact raise issues of personal protection. If Mr. McGuire not only denied Mrs. McGuire appropriate support but also abused her physically, a strong case could be made for sanctioning and deterrence rather than counselling and dispute settlement. While in China such sanctioning might be effectively carried out by a neighbourhood mediation committee, in the Anglo-American system we would insist on a court, with appropriate procedural protections for the defendant.

The same issue arises with respect to parent-child disputes in the ongoing family. While mediation has great promise for dealing with various types of domestic disputes about rights and obligations of parents and children,[11] cases of serious child neglect may require the full adjudicatory panoply, with appropriate legal protections for the parents who may be deprived of their legal rights to a child in such a proceeding.

Dissolution

In simple divorce cases where there are no children and no substantial assets, and both parties desire a divorce, there is really no dispute. Hence it it wasteful to utilize an elaborate adjudicatory mechanism like a court to handle such cases. Even though such cases are typically processed very routinely in court, the net result of this mismatch of dispute to process is to squander the court's valuable resources and to breed disrespect for the court on the part of the litigants. Presumably some type of administrative proceeding (such as is used in Japan) would serve the primary goal of registration.

But where there is a dispute about custody or support, it would make sense initially to utilize some form of mediation — for all the reasons earlier advanced — and to employ adjudication only as a last resort. Although there has been increasing recognition of this fact with respect to custody and visitation disputes, there is relatively little use of mediation for support issues. This seems ironic in view of the widespread disregard of support obligations that have been imposed by divorce courts. Greater use of mediation in such cases would seem to be a promising avenue to explore.

Medical Procedures for Minors or Other Incompetents

One type of case under this rubric involves parents who refuse to authorize a medical procedure for a child. In such cases it may be important to distinguish situations involving threats to the life of the child from others where such urgency is absent, and some outsider (e.g., a child welfare department) simply disagrees with the parents' proposed course of conduct. In the former situation, issues of child protection are at stake, and therefore court adjudication is indicated. But in the latter type of case, it would seem desirable for the court to "remit" the problem to the family for its own appropriate disposition.

A somewhat different situation is presented, for example, where parents seek to have a retarded child sterilized because of her inability to take appropriate contraceptive measures or to handle the trauma incident to conception and birth of a child. Such cases raise issues of child protection just as sharply as do those where the parents are accused of inaction that threatens the child's life. Moreover, here there is a danger that no one will articulate the case against taking such drastic action and that, in the nature of the situation, the child's own views will not be brought to bear. Hence the courts have commendably established both procedural protections (such as appointing a guardian for the child) and substantive criteria (such as requiring medical necessity or the exercise of "substituted judgment" for the incompetent child).[12]

CONCLUSION

The preceding examples are simply illustrative of the type of analysis suggested here. The essential point is that we have too long tended to emphasize substance over process. In fact, as I have tried to show, there exists a rich variety of processes, each with its own special strengths and weaknesses. Only if we make the choice of process a deliberate and informed one, by seeking to match the process to the problem, can we get optimal results.

NOTES

1. For notable exceptions, see Mnookin, "Child Custody Adjudication in the Face of Indeterminacy," 49 *Law & Contemp. Probs.*, 226 (1975), and Weyrauch and Katz, *American Family Law in Transition*, (Washington, D.C.: Bureau of National Affairs, 1983) 505. These authorities point to a fundamental distinction between those child custody disputes (e.g., neglect cases) where the goal is child protection, as distinguished from the typical divorce custody case, where the primary goal is private dispute settlement. Obviously the process in the two types of cases needs to be very different to accommodate those different goals. See also Goldstein and Katz, *The Family and the Law*, (New York: The Free Press, 1965).

2. See Sander, "Varieties of Dispute Processing," in *The Pound Conference: Perspectives on Justice in the Future* (Levin and Wheeler eds. 1979) 65. Also reprinted in Feeley and Tomasic, *Neighborhood Justice: Assessment of an Emerging Idea*, (New York: Longman, 1982) 25. In this paper, delivered at the 1976 Pound Conference, I tried to develop a similar typology for disputes generally.

3. Fuller, "Mediation — Its Forms and Functions," 44 *So. Calif. L. Rev.* 305, 328 (1971).

4. Mnookin and Kornhauser, "Bargaining in the Shadow of the Law: The Case of Divorce," 88 *Yale L.J.* 950 (1979).

5. Compare Kelly, "Mediation and Psychotherapy: Distinguishing the Differences," 2 *Mediation Quarterly* 33 (1983).

6. McEwen and Maiman, "Small Claims Mediation in Maine: An Empirical Assessment," 33 *Maine L. Rev.* 237 (1981); Pearson and Thoennes, "Divorce Mediation:

Strengths and Weaknesses Over Time," in American Bar Association, *Alternative Means of Family Dispute Resolution* (Davidson, Ray and Horowitz, eds., (Washington, D.C.: American Bar Association Press, 1982).

7. See Kubie, "Provisions for the Care of Children of Divorced Parents: A New Legal Instrument," 73 *Yale L.J.* 1197 (1964).

8. See California *Civil Code* § 4607.

9. Consider also the tripartite conciliation panels in the Japanese Family Courts, consisting of a judge and two prestigious citizens (often elders) from the community.

10. *McGuire v. McGuire,* 157 Neb. 226, 59 N.W. 2d 336 (1953).

11. See for example the Scottish Children's Hearings described in Martin and Murray, Children's Hearings, Edinburgh: Scottish Academic Press (1976); Bruce and Spencer, "Face to Face with Families — A Report on the Children's Panel in Scotland," Loanhead, Scotland: Macdonald Publishers (1976). See also *Roe v. Doe,* 29 N.Y. 2d 188, 272 N.E. 2d 567 (1971) (daughter unsuccessful in suit against father to compel him to pay for her to live off campus rather than in college dormitory).

12. See, e.g., C.D.M., 627 § 2d 607 (Alaska 1981).

Part One

The Settlement of Disputes — Historical and Theoretical Perspectives

"Disputes" wrote the great American jurist, Karl Llewellyn, "are the eternal heart and core of law. They do not mark its circumference, but they will always mark its centre. It is when two people are in dispute, it is especially when they are in a dispute not otherwise settled, that law shows its first societal value."[1] In this formulation, Llewellyn not only recognizes the centrality of conflict resolution to the task of law, but also the truth that resort to law is not the only way of resolving disputes. It is only when a dispute is "not otherwise settled" that resort is had to law. This is, he says, because "so many disputes are settled in one way or another, by argument or by wrangling or simply by self-assertion on the one side and submission on the other, or by bargaining or compromise or mediation. The primary business of law is not with this. Law on its dispute side is the machinery of last resort, when these others have failed."[2]

It has long been apparent to legal anthropologists that societies have available to them a wide variety of mechanisms for averting or resolving disputes. Retributive violence, often conventionalized or ritualized, shaming, and ostracism may be preferred to mediation or adjudication.[3] Within families, it is particularly apparent that there are a multiplicity of ways in which conflicts may be resolved. "Assertion, submission and compromise" are part of the very dynamics of family living. Family members characteristically resort to relatives or friends for support or potential mediation during such conflicts. What is new is the current wave of interest by lawyers in "extralegal" modes of conflict resolution. The distinction made by Llewellyn between dispute resolution by law and other forms of problem solving has been blurred. Legal rules, we now say, can influence, even determine, the way disputes are settled outside the courtroom, whether by the application of social or economic pressure or through bargaining and mediation. Legally constituted institutions may actively intervene in and perhaps control the course of such processes. It has been this movement in the direction of the focus of analysis that has prompted the present volume. But why has it happened?

The answer to that question must, at present, be incomplete. It might be seen as part of a (possible) more general movement away from formalized justice. This could have significant implications. Formalized justice, in the sociology of Max Weber, is associated with the growth of bureaucratic institutions, their regulation by law and the depersonalization of entitlements.[4] Seen in these terms, informalism can be characterized as a threat to individual rights, an extension of state power into the lives of individuals.[5] These issues are addressed in the opening chapter, where Freeman links them to a critique of the expansion of power by "welfare professionals." If we move from court-centred adjudication, based on rules and rights, to controlling or supervising the other means of settling disputes, we may be abandoning the regulation of the law, with its susceptibility to democratic oversight, to the tyranny of the nonlegal professional. This introduction does not wish to prejudge that issue. But it must prompt regular questions in the light of which almost all the subsequent contributions should be read.

Whatever view is taken of these large issues, certain features seem to be specific to family law. The moments of most extreme conflict in family living occur, of course, when families break apart. Until relatively recently, it was rare for the conflicts which then occurred to be resolved by court adjudication. They were "otherwise settled." The reason, as indicated by MacDougall in the second chapter, is not difficult to discover. The rules settled the issues with comparative certainty and simplicity. Each party would keep their separate property (if any) and there were few opportunities for its redistribution. The apparent matrimonial guilt might be taken to settle the issue of maintenance, and simple preference rules governed the question of custody of the children. But the substantive law of divorce, maintenance and custody has undergone a profound revolution.[6] The question of whether a divorce should be granted and, if so, to whom, formerly the major question for adjudication, is now rarely litigated. The dispute is increasingly over how the assets of the spouses should be divided, how the parties should organize their postdivorce life, especially with regard to their children.[7] The means for doing this have greatly increased with the expansion of judicial powers in this area. The problems this raises have thrown legal systems into complete confusion. As the discussion in Part Six will show, as far as family support after divorce is concerned, there is little agreement even about what the basic goals should be. There is still greater uncertainty over what kinds of mechanisms are best suited for dealing with these novel issues.[8] What appears to be happening is a reversal of Maine's famous aphorism that substantive law was secreted in the interstices of procedure. We are searching for a procedure to accommodate the about turn of substantive law. Need it be court-centred at all?

So how do we answer this question? MacDougall (Chapter 2), who offers no regrets for the growth in litigation-based conflict here, suggests that the various techniques of conflict resolution should be assessed by reference to four criteria: their effectiveness in ending the dispute; their cost; their justice; and, their promotion of independent social goals. By these criteria, negotiation is seen as an "effective, relatively inexpensive procedure for the just resolution of family disputes" and MacDougall explains how negotiation theory might be applied to family disputes. But even if negotiation is a suitable technique for the resolution of family disputes, is it the only one? Furthermore, are all solutions reached by this method acceptable? Negotiation may need to be put within some framework, perhaps simply rules of substantive law, perhaps also some institutional setting. It may need to be supplemented or accompanied by mediation. These are all matters which will be addressed in subsequent chapters. But the importance of these further questions is brought out by the chapters by O'Donovan (Chapter 3) and Rwezaura (Chapter 4). The "private ordering" (delegalization) of divorce arrangements is not new. In England, it was practised as wife sale for over a thousand years. Even today it persists in the form of simple desertion: the wife is "thrown" on to the state. In the past, the official law of marriage and divorce had little relevance for the bulk of the population. Wife sale, believed to be valid, was a device resorted to as a means of regulating the termination of a marriage. It was true private ordering, untrammelled by legal rules. The lesson we learn from it is that, without true equality of bargaining power, uncontrolled private ordering opens the way for domination and exploitation.

It may be that negotiation can be placed within an institutional context which inhibits its adverse potential. Mediation is often offered as such a device. The use of mediation in traditional societies is represented here by the discussion by Rwezaura of mediation in pre- and post-independent Tanzania. The significance of mediation lay in the society's perception that the maintenance of good relations between the disputants was essential to its economic or kinship system. The mediator (and the wider community) would thus have an interest in settling the dispute rapidly. He would normally be recognized by both disputants as a person of status and authority. The tradition of mediation has survived strongly into postcolonial Tanzania, where the function may be exercised by relatives, leaders of a political party cell, state instituted arbitrarian tribunals and Church leaders. Indeed, there are strong social pressures against disputants, especially wives, from taking their matrimonial grievances to the courts. Contrasting the degree of litigiousness between two groups, the Haya and the Kuria, Rwezaura attributes the difference to the fact that whereas a Haya man has little to lose by not going to court because he can remarry without obtaining a divorce and there is little bridewealth to reclaim, a Kuria man pays heavily for his wife and will not hesitate to sue for recovery.

Rwezaura's account suggests that the dominant position of men in

Tanzanian society diminishes the value of mediation from the point of view of the women. However, some women are beginning to have recourse to the courts for remedies appropriate to their changing economic position. Studies of traditional societies have tended to underscore the limits of mediation. In a study of four such societies, Merry[9] identified at least eight features characteristic of mediated settlements:

1. successful mediation needed to take place promptly;
2. mediation tended to be a lengthy process;
3. successful mediation resulted in concrete redress rather than vague promises;
4. mediators tended to be of higher social status than the disputants;
5. mediation was most likely to succeed where the parties needed to deal with one another in the future;
6. mediation should be accompanied by some measure of coercion, such as social pressure, for it would be in the community's interest to resolve the dispute;
7. where the parties were unequal, mediated settlements tended to reflect the inequality; and
8. mediators represented the norms and values of their communities.

If mediation is, as has been claimed,[10] basically an attempt to influence parties by appealing to their own interests, it is difficult to resist the conclusion that mediated settlements are likely to reflect the inherent power relationship between them. If, as Merry also argues, a mediator should possess authority to equalize this balance, questions about the source of this authority and how it is controlled need to be confronted. Obviously, conclusions from data drawn from nonindustrialized societies cannot be applied to western societies without qualification. But they may be instructive, nevertheless, and of relevance when assessing the discussion of conciliation and mediation in subsequent chapters.

NOTES

1. Karl N. Llewellyn, *Jurisprudence: Realism in Theory and Practice* (University of Chicago Press, 1962) 79.
2. *Ibid.*
3. Simon Roberts, *Order and Dispute* (Oxford, Martin Robinson, 1979) 53-55.
4. Max Weber, *Wirtschaft and Gesellschaft.* 660-65.
5. See de Sousa Santos, "Law and Community: The Changing Nature of State Power in Late Capitalism," in Richard L. Abel (ed.), *The Politics of Informal Justice* (New York, The Academic Press, 1982) vol. 1.

6. These changes have been fully described in works such as Max Rheinstein, *Marriage Stability, Divorce and the Law* (University of Chicago Press, 1972); Mary Ann Glendon, *State, Law and Family* (Amsterdam, North Holland, 1977) and *The New Family and the New Property* (Toronto, Butterworths, 1981); and John M. Eekelaar and Sanford N. Katz (eds.), *Marriage and Cohabitation in Contemporary Societies* (Toronto, Butterworths, 1981).

7. Walter O. Weyrauch and Sanford N. Katz, *American Family Law in Transition* (Washington, D.C., Bureau of National Affairs, 1983) 227–28.

8. *Ibid.,* at 316.

9. Sally E. Merry, "The Social Organization of Mediation in Non-Industrial Societies: Implications for Informal Community Justice in America," in Richard L. Abel (ed.), *The Politics of Informal Justice* (New York, Academic Press, 1982) vol. 2.

10. Torstein Eckhoff, "The Mediator, the Judge and the Administrator in Conflict Resolution," *Acta Sociologica* 10, 158 (1966).

Chapter One

Questioning the Delegalization Movement in Family Law: Do We Really Want a Family Court?

Michael D.A. Freeman

University College,
London, England

Open almost any family law treatise, any report on an issue of family policy, and you will find that it contains at some point a plan for the family court ideal. I too have frequently stressed the need for the establishment of a family court. Indeed, I was a member of the Justice Committee on Parental Rights and Duties and Custody Suits[1] which recommended that a family court be set up in England. As to the structure of the court we were content to adopt the Finer Report's recommendations[2] as our own. That report had noted that submissions to it in favour of the family court ideal offered "more by way of enthusiasm than elucidation,"[3] but that is hardly surprising.

Critics of the existing system seem to agree on what is wrong. Inglis put it well when he said in a public lecture, which was subsequently published,

> Matrimonial litigation is simply one phase in a relationship which must continue in a variety of aspects once the litigation is over. Few matrimonial disputes ever completely end the parties' relationship. It is simply redefined for the future.[4]

We are all, I think, agreed that the adversary system has very severe limitations in the area of family law. Manchester will have spoken for many when he wrote,

> Yet surely we are now agreed upon the basic premise of the family court system...a "caring court" with social and welfare services integrated within it as part of a total team operation.[5]

Words constantly repeated are "civilized" and "humane." Very few have cautioned against the family court. The English law lord and former chairman of the English Law Commission, Lord Scarman,[6] is one to have done so. Rereading his address to the Institute of Judicial Administration in Birmingham, nine years after it was given I am struck by the complacency of its tone and the thinness of its argument. I would not expect Lord Scarman to agree with the thesis that I am about to present. We are, however, agreed that the family court concept contains its own dangers. It is easy to be swept along on a tide of euphoria. It is rather more difficult to stand back and take a cool look at what has happened to the family in the twentieth century and to place moves towards the family court ideal within these welfare-oriented policies. This is what, in part, I attempt to do.

I am not concerned with describing in detail or analysing any particular family court or any posited ideal. Proposals are legion and there are in existence in different parts of the world a number of family courts. In my own country, the United Kingdom, proposals for a family court (but not the same one) have come from Royal Commissions,[7] from the Law Society,[8] from the Justices' Clerks' Society[9] and from the Conservative Party.[10] One of the fullest discussions of the concept emanates from Judge Jean Graham Hall.[11] One of the most articulate and sensitive, from Mervyn Murch,[12] a social administration lecturer. But it is accepted in England that we will not get a family court in the foreseeable future. As much divides current proposals and models as unites them. What does, however, unite all critics of the existing system is a desire to render the legal order more "efficient" and more responsive to the perceived needs of the family. These critics, though ideologically poles apart, share with radical critics of the legal order generally a concern over the impersonality, insensitivity and remoteness of law, not to say its excessive rigidity and formality.

This brings me to the second of my themes. Debates about the appropriateness of adversary justice, about the value of integrating adjudicative and welfare roles in the family court, are discourses about the form of law. These are debates with a long heritage and distinguished pedigree: the classical source is, of course, the sociology of Max Weber.[13] There are pervasive delegalization trends in contemporary advanced capitalist societies.[14] It was Weber who first noted that movements towards greater informalism contained the seeds of their own self-contradiction and were ultimately doomed. If this is right, what effect will the move to the family court have? The annals of legal history are strewn with examples of institutions and practices which have had unintended consequences.[15] Programmes which seem to weaken hierarchies of power may actually establish new channels through which they can be expressed or even strengthened. These new programmes may be rendered necessary by, or be more responsive to, technological or economic change. They may be by-products of new patterns of social administration. Observe the way the decline in the criminal sanction[16] has been matched by the growth of the regulatory sanction[17] spawned by the "new property"[18] state; note the way that the therapeutic state has medicalized deviance.[19] The effect is, what Cohen has called, a "dispersal of social control."[20] State involvement may be less, but intervention is more pervasive. We may be moving away from the era of total institutions only to find ourselves enmeshed in total societies.

This is, I think, a likely scenario for the family court. Few of the family court advocates see it this way and many would not find the consequences I describe distasteful. To some, what I am saying will appear far-fetched. But this is where part one of my thesis reemerges. The twentieth century has witnesses, what Philip Rieff has called, the "triumph of the therapeutic."[21] The emphasis on the family has resulted in its greater surveillance and more intensive supervision. The rhetoric is about family autonomy;[22] the reality is of a more pervasive control than existed one hundred years ago. The two parts of my thesis thus converge.

THE FAMILY AND THE STATE

The family has not always been as it is now.[23] The current ideal, which attained its fullest flowering in late Victorian times and now seems to be slowly decaying, rests on the companionate marriage, in which the union is one of two individuals rather than two lineages; on the child-centred household; on the quasi emancipation of women; and on the structural isolation of the nuclear family from the kinship system and the community.

In precapitalist societies and in the early stages of capitalism, work and family life overlapped. The household was the basic unit of production: the home was a place of work. There was no clear distinction between the role of worker and of family member. With industrialization and capitalist production the nature of work and family life changed radically. Productive work now took place in the factory. It became increasingly routinized. The factory system at first used women and children but increasing industrialization brought unemployment and women were driven into dependence upon men. Work done in the home was increasingly restricted to looking after husband-workers and producing children. Eli Zaretsky[24] has described how at the same time the family became idealized, as did the familial role of women. The home became a refuge from the demands of capitalist society. In Lasch's graphic phrase the family became a "haven in a heartless world."

> The family found ideological support and justification in the conception of domestic life as an emotional refuge in a cold and competitive society.[25]

The family became a private place to which people, but especially men, could withdraw.

The family was thus exalted. A "cult of domesticity"[26] was engendered, according to Carl N. Degler,[27] by women themselves. It confined women to the home but at the same time it made them the moral arbiters of the family and of whatever else touched its interests. He argues[28] that demands for the recognition of married women's property rights, for divorce laws favourable to women, for sexual self-control on the part of men, for acknowledgment of women's greater stake in regulating pregnancy, as well as for reforms in the larger social sphere, particularly in relation to "social purity" all arose out of the logic of domesticity itself.

The connection between the "cult of domesticity" and the emancipation of women has also been observed by Jacques Donzelot in his *La Police des Familles*. He sees that:

> Birth control and the "liberation" of women rested on women's old social vocation, and on their function as ambassadresses of culture.[29]

Donzelot also sees what Degler does not, *viz.*: that women's roles as cultural missionaries was to some extent the deliberate creation of doctors seeking to make wives and mothers agents of medical influence. Ideas were spread by "promotional goading and attendant blaming of families who, through their resistance, were ruining the members' chances."[30]

The emotional intensification of family life had, as one of its inevitable consequences, conflict. This, the nascent psychological sciences sought to explain and, of course, to prevent and solve. But, as Lasch has argued:

> To enlightened members of the professional classes — and this includes most feminists — knowledge of this kind, promised a preventive science of sexual and social control, which could be used among other things to civilise the poor, to subject them to new controls sincerely disguised as benevolence, and thus to integrate them more fully into the emerging industrial order.[31]

Women saw the advantage of professional intervention in family life. It undercut patriarchal authority. However, it also eroded the traditional prerogatives of women. Thus, as Ehrenreich and English[32] have also demonstrated, women welcomed the substitution of doctors for midwives in childbirth. The overall result was that professionals continually expanded their jurisdiction over family life. Patriarchal authority may have suffered but so did the authority formerly exercised by women themselves. Lasch makes the point that

> in allying themselves with the helping professions, women improved their position in the family only to fall into a new kind of dependence, the dependence of the

consumer on the market and on the providers of expert services, not only for the satisfaction of her needs but for the very definition of her needs.[33]

It is easy to see how society came to be governed by doctors, social workers, psychiatrists, juvenile court judges, criminologists, etc., in short, by the modern apparatus of resocialization. The "helping professions" during the first third of this century came to see themselves as doctors to a sick society. This is graphically portrayed in fictional form in D.M. Thomas's *The White Hotel*.[34] Many have written of the growth of the "therapeutic state."[35] Its influence, its impact on the family has been profound. What the cathedral was to medieval times and the legislative chamber was to the nineteenth century, the hospital, the clinic is to our day.[36]

It is all too common to read of the family losing its functions,[37] as if these had formerly been unproblematic and static. In reality what these commentators have observed is the takeover of society playing the nurturing mother of certain roles played by the family, nuclear and extended, at earlier times in history. I think Lasch has grasped this better than anybody. To socialization of production, he believes, we should add "socialisation of reproduction."[38] This, he claims, "proletarianised parenthood, by making people unable to provide for their own needs without the supervision of trained experts." Early proponents of children's rights typify this approach.[39] Contemporary advocates of rights for children, Holt[40] or Farson[41] for example, would not see the child-saving movement as bedfellow to theirs at all. It stressed protecting children while they emphasize the importance of protecting children's rights. The divergence between the two comes out distinctly if we examine the early philosophy in practice.[42] The development of a system of compulsory education fits the turn-of-the-century ethos very well.

> If the state is to have good citizens ... we must begin to teach the children in our schools, and begin at once, that which we see they are no longer learning in the home,

wrote Ellen Richards[43] in 1910 in a book intriguingly entitled *Euthenics: The Science of Controllable Environment*. Children were to achieve independence from parental control but they fell increasingly, instead, under the control of the state. In Donzelot's words, "family patriarchalism was destroyed at the cost of a patriarchy of the state."[44]

A second example, which is particularly well-documented, though not beyond controversy, is the development of a system of juvenile justice. The juvenile court substituted prevention for punishment, and close surveillance for judgment. It treated the child's or adolescent's crimes as symptoms of an unhealthy, unhygienic home environment, thus justifying enquiries into the morality of his family and his removal from home if this was deemed necessary. Donzelot describes how parents who called in the police or social workers in the hope that outside intervention would strengthen their authority over a wayward child found instead that their authority was tranferred to an outside professional authority.

> Instead of the desired admonition, however, the juvenile judge, after reviewing the results of the social inquiry, decides in favour of an educative assistance that has another purpose altogether, since it brings the adolescent into the sphere of the tutelary complex, leading to his detachment from family authority and transferral to a social authority... all in order to prevent him from contaminating his brothers and sisters and to enable his parents to devote themselves to the younger children.[45]

Architects of juvenile justice justified their creation on humanitarian grounds. They may have intended to be humanitarian. They saw themselves as replacing the undoubted barbarities of the criminal law with something better. They argued that the juvenile court was to be a friend of the juvenile offender as well as a confederate of his family. Donzelot describes this reasoning as "pious representations... of reasons that are much less 'democratic'."[46] Rothman admits that conscience may have played its part but so, he insists, did "convenience."[47] Donzelot is not the first to have questioned the motives of the reformers. Platt,[48] Fox,[49] Ryerson,[50] and Schlossman[51] have all rejected the orthodox interpretation of the development of the juvenile court. Like Platt, Donzelot sees intervention in the family as a "depoliticising strategy." It was inspired by a fear of class conflict: it belonged to a general attempt to control the poor. It was the liberal state's answer to socialist propaganda. It aimed to convert political debates into administrative procedures. The language used may have been that of hygiene and health, but political considerations were never far below the surface. The parallels between the rhetoric about the juvenile court at the turn of the century and the family court in the last decade are so striking that it is surprising that the implications for the family court ideal have not been drawn, but I would suggest that they are there for all to see.

I have given examples from two areas. Others could be cited. I resist that temptation in order to return to the general issue. Liberals tried to steer a course between what they saw as the Scylla of conservative paternalism, which upheld the family as the foundation of the social order, so that every change was seen as a threat to social integrity, and the Charybdis of socialism, which wanted to replace parenthood with the state. But, "in the end," to quote Lasch once again, "they outflanked their adversaries by creating a therapeutic state which left the family more or less intact yet subjected to non-stop supervision."[52] The liberal state as a result has a system of indirect controls which preserves the appearance, even some of the reality, of private initiative within an overarching structure of professional supervision. The therapeutic state leaves the family "'always' 'justified' in theory and always suspect in practice."[53]

PROFESSIONAL EXPERTISE

The victory of the medical model has meant the elevation of the expert. The effects of this can be seen starkly in the juvenile court. Even where a child has committed a criminal offence, there is reason to believe, and any examination of social enquiry reports reinforces this belief, that in the minds of decision makers the seriousness of his behaviour, what he has *done*, takes a back seat behind an interpretation of what he, and his family, *is*.[54] Individualized justice, the goal of welfare-oriented processes, has been said to result "in a frame of relevance so large, so all inclusive, that any relation between the criteria of judgment and the disposition remains obscure."[55] The social enquiry report is the linchpin of the juvenile court process. Anderson describes it as "the product of an application of social work ideology to the court context."[56] Social enquiry reports are apt to contain value judgments, to make unsubstantiated assertions and often to be based on assumptions which are not supported by the evidence.[57] Writers of the reports, who know no more about the causes of misbehaviour than the rest of us, tend to assemble information which reinforces stereotypes of "causes of trouble" such as broken homes, working mothers, etc., and often to put it into language loosely drawn from psychoanalytic theory.[58] Concepts such as personality disorder, psychopath, impaired bonding, dependency needs are pervasive. The use of theory is random and eclectic.

It is easy to criticize the welfare professionals, social workers, psychologists, child psychiatrists, to attribute this to bad practice. But the problem is deeper than this. As Andrew Sutton has argued, in a recent outstanding article,[59] there has been an unjustified professionalization of issues that are "in fact beyond the present reach of expert understanding."[60] He is not alone in questioning the expertise used by welfare professionals. It would take me too far away from the subject of this paper to give further details of this. Suffice it to say that Sutton, Morgan[61] and others[62] provide considerable evidence of the inadequacy of the knowledge base upon which assessment and treatment of children, the writing of social enquiry reports and similar tasks proceed. There has been, Sutton concludes, an "unjustified reliance on premature professionalism."[63] In Britain the most detailed investigations into social work practice have followed the deaths (or serious injuries) of children at the hands of parents or other caretakers. A common theme running through all the reports[64] of such enquiries is found in the assertion that the system of child care has failed: there has been a lack or ineffectiveness of communication and liaison between welfare professionals, and between them and the police and medical profession. None of these enquiries appears to have grasped the fundamental nettle, the problematic nature of professional expertise.[65] Such is the power of professional mystique.

I have not seen a single proposal for a family court which comes to terms with these issues at all. Take the fullest discussion of the family court in Britain. This is to be found in the Finer report on one-parent families, published in 1974.[66] Though disdainful of American family courts which, it says, are "committed to a social work philosophy which regards family breakdown as a phenomenon to be dealt with primarily by diagnosis and treatment" and which are as much a "therapeutic agency as a judicial institution,"[67] it advocates the use of court social workers. The welfare part of the court would be expected to "demonstrate a commensurate degree of professional integrity and expertise,"[68] commensurate that is with the integrity and formal expertise of the court. But we are talking of different types of expertise: lawyers have formal expertise; social workers aspire to expertise based on empirical knowledge. If Sutton, Morgan and the others are right, the operative words are "aspire to," for it is doubtful whether the knowledge base has as yet been obtained. The Finer report envisages court welfare services providing "assistance for people with marital problems."[69] If by assistance is meant conciliation,[70] so as to civilize the consequences of breakdown, then it is difficult to quarrel with the proposal. The report does not expand on the work tasks it expects welfare services to undertake. It does not, for example, see social workers taking part in the "family court conference," the convening of which it recommends where a maintenance or administrative order has been in operation for two years and the marriage still legally subsists.[71] It does not see social workers as decision makers but rather as handmaidens.[72] They will make social and welfare enquiries and the reports. But the line between informed (or not so informed) opinions and recommendations is a thin one and the experience of juvenile courts, and indeed adult criminal courts which commission reports on defendants, is that they expect, get, and act on recommendations of social workers and probation officers.[73] Indeed, similar evidence is available in the case of courts dealing with family matters where refusals to follow social workers' recommendations are rare and where the courts feel themselves obligated to articulate their reasons for so doing.[74]

DELEGALIZATION

Moves away from adversary justice and towards a family court are in effect moves towards the delegalization of family dispute settlement. Delegalization can take place on a number of levels and can be motivated or inspired by different goals. The simplification of divorce processes with the introduction in England in 1973[75] of the "special procedure" effected a limited measure of delegalization. It was a response to research which had shown that judicial hearings in divorce were perfunctory.[76] It was motivated also by a desire to rechannel money spent by the state through legal aid subsidizing divorce into other areas of unmet legal need.[77] Much discussion of delegalization[78] is in the context of wresting law away from remote authorities and allowing the masses to participate in the processes of justice. Obviously, movements towards deformalization (as indeed towards formalization) take on different meanings depending on cultural, political and historical contexts. Contemporary moves away from formality in the West may well reflect, in part, the decline in the market system and the growth of monopoly capitalism. A consequence of the decline of the market has been the rise of state redistribution as a dominant mechanism for allocation (including the growth of the so-called "new property").[79] The rise of monopoly capitalism has meant that the law does not have to be used to promote the ideal of a self-regulating market.

The temptation to approach formalism and informalism as if the effects of each were opposite to the other must be resisted. Weber saw this. He wrote:

> The position of all "democratic" currents, in the sense of currents that would minimize "authority", is necessarily ambiguous. "Equality before the law" and the demand for legal guarantees against arbitrariness demand a formal and rational "objectivity" of administration, as opposed to the personally free discretion flowing from the "grace" of the old patrimonial domination. If, however, an "ethos" — not to speak of instincts — takes hold of the masses on some individual question, it postulates *substantive* justice oriented toward some concrete instance and person; and such an "ethos" will unavoidably collide with the formalism and the rule-bound and cool "matter-of-factness" of bureaucratic administration. For this reason, the ethos must emotionally reject what reason demands. The propertyless masses especially are not served by a "formal equality before the law" and a "calculable" adjudication and administration, as demanded by "bourgeois" interests. Naturally in their eyes justice and administration should serve to compensate for their economic and social life-opportunities in the face of the propertied classes. Justice and administration can fulfil this function only if they assume an informal character to a far-reaching extent. It must be informal because it is substantively "ethical" ("Kadi-justice"). Every sort of "popular justice" — which usually does not ask for reasons and norms — as well as every sort of intensive influence on the administration of so-called public opinion, crosses the rational course of justice and administration just as strongly, and under certain conditions far more so, as the "star chamber" proceedings of an "absolute" ruler has been able to do.[80]

What Weber is saying is important. To the extent that law is set up to protect the weak, it must be formalistic and impersonal and confined by rules. Yet when it is invoked especially to achieve social justice, to protect the weak against the powerful, it is typically an expression of informal "substantive justice."[81] But this can be very easily subverted by the powerful to their advantage. Both law as form and law as substance may be equated with social justice but neither is able to deliver what it promises.[82]

This should alert us to the danger of falling into the trap of thinking that having created a particular structure, it will operate as we expect it to do. Both movements toward formalism and informalism contain within themselves the capacity to turn into something very different from what they appear. Weber depicted the rise of Western capitalism as a movement towards the dominance of formal rationality over substantive rationality.[83] This destroys popular justice. Instead we get bureaucratic centralization and protest against rational legal authority is seen as "irrational." This is why Weber can conclude that any trend toward greater informalism is doomed. "It is by no means certain," he wrote, "that those classes which are negatively privileged today, especially the working class, may safely expect from an informal administration of justice those results which are claimed for it by the ideology of the jurists."[84]

Further insight into what Duncan Kennedy has called[85] a "regime of rules" may be sought in the contemporary Marxist historian, E.P. Thompson. He is writing of eighteenth century England but some of the comments in his coda are of general application.

> ... People are not as stupid as some structuralist philosophers suppose them to be. They will not be mystified by the first man who puts on a wig. It is inherent in the especial character of law, as a body of rules and procedures, that it shall apply logical criteria with reference to standards of universality and equity. It is true that certain categories of person may be excluded from this logic ... and that the poor may often be excluded, through penury, from the law's costly procedures. ... But if too much of this is true, then the consequences are plainly counterproductive. Most men have a strong sense of justice, at least with regard to their own interests. ... The essential precondition for the effectiveness of law, in its function as ideology is that it shall display an independence from gross manipulation and shall seem to be just. It cannot seem to be so without upholding its own logic and criteria of equity; indeed, on occasion by actually *being* just . . .[86]

This is an important qualification to what Weber argued and it comes from an unexpected source. By stressing the equivocal character of formal law, Thompson is able to argue for the preservation of the "forms and rhetoric of law ... which may, on occasion, inhibit power and afford some protection to the powerless."[87] His is a plea not to throw out the "baby" with the "bathwater" and it is one we should heed. We must not let our concern about the rigidity, remoteness, insensitivity of traditional legal mechanisms turn us away from the unqualified good in the rule of law. We may find adversary processes inappropriate, even dehumanizing or alienating. Yet the formalism and rule of law which accompanies them provide a measure of protection to the powerless. In our context they are not, as in Thompson's or Weber's arguments, the working classes, but rather women, and especially, children. The rule of law also inhibits power, not least of welfare professionals. Our experience with the juvenile court provides abundant evidence of what is lost when informal procedures and treatment institutions replace traditional court structures and processes.[88] In the United States, realization of this led to the reintroduction of certain rights for juveniles,[89] in effect a partial relegalization of the juvenile court. But at about the same time in Britain, the decriminalization of "children in trouble" was reaching its high-water mark with the *Social Work (Scotland) Act* of 1968[90] and the English *Children and Young Persons Act* of 1969.[91] The British legislature, it seems, had not noticed *Re Gault*.[92] Are those who hanker for a family court similarly blinkered? The hyperbolical language which greets the family court ideal today is so very reminiscent of descriptions of the juvenile court half a century ago.[93]

Too much must not be read into this analogy with moves to the juvenile court earlier this century. To do so would be to divorce the movements from their historical contexts. The juvenile court emerged during the heyday of classical capitalism. The relationship between capitalism and formalism has been so thoroughly analysed[94] that it need not be elaborated upon further here. Capitalism needed certainty, calculability, stability, and formalism promoted this. In this sense the juvenile court was something of an anomaly, perhaps explained by excepting policies concerned with wayward youth from state initiatives generally.[95] But the economic organization of society has changed in the course of the twentieth century. A postindustrial society, a "third wave"[96] has different needs and expectations. To what extent these have been shaped by legal institutions and ideas and themselves influence legal developments are questions which have exercised the minds of a number of contemporary thinkers.[97] Classical capitalism stressed the division between public and private law and, though many jurists resisted the dualism,[98] the pervasive influence, some would say mystification, of the distinction remains deeply embedded in much liberal legal thinking even today. The separation is not easy to defend today and it is in fact widely under attack.[99] Once again legal rights of the individual are becoming dependent on status.[100] There are any number of manifestations of this trend: the rise in administrative law,[101] "the death of contract"[102] and the "therapeutic state"[103] are some of them. The historical setting for the family court is thus one in which status and hence particularistic relationships have reemerged. It is also one in which the patterns of decision making have shifted. Where once they were determined by reciprocal obligations or the wisdom of the market,[104] now they are centralized. There has been a shift, as Kamenka and Tay put it,[105] from *Gesellschaft* law[106] to bureaucratic administrative regulation. They see

> the contemporary crisis of law and legal ideology ... [as] a crisis of *Gesellschaft* law, a crisis in its capacity to deal with what are seen as the urgent problems of our time and, consequently in its claim to legitimacy.[107]

Whatever the reason and however one characterizes it, there has been an injection of substantive rationality into the formalized law of advanced capitalist societies. The attenuation of the market has necessitated reliance on other extraeconomic mechanisms to extract and redistribute surplus value. It has led to the rise of state redistribution. The "law" thus plays an affirmative role. Under classical capitalist conditions the law played almost a negative part. It promoted the ideal of a self-regulating market and it afforded a measure of protection to the weaker party. The rule of law has often been said to be a precondition of capitalist competition. With the growth of monopoly capitalism the protection offered by the law becomes a barrier in the way of the expansion of economic power. As capitalism becomes less of a market system the structure and content of law, its institutions and practices, undergo a profound change. For example, general rules give way to vague standards.[108] If we examine what is going on in advanced capitalist societies we can understand why formalism has declined. But this does not mean that we can hope to realize the goals (justice, equality, autonomy or whatever) in whose name formalism was attacked. Formalism has declined but not because of intellectual onslaughts upon it. Can delegalization succeed?

There are many delegalization projects of which those concerned with family dispute settlement make up only a small number. There are initiatives to involve the community in policing[109] and to introduce or strengthen the role of lay personnel in the administration of the lower, usually criminal, courts.[110] All these movements share in common a desire to promote the autonomy and self-sufficiency of local social units, whether these be communities, neighbourhoods[111] or, in our case, families, at the expense of the impersonal, bureaucraticized professional power centres. But the dispersal of control into local and traditional structures is perfectly consistent with the support, indeed the expansion of forms of social control which emanate from these power centres. Prison reform is an apt illustration of the process. The increased involvement of medicine and psychiatry in prisons has meant that

> No longer must such institutions be justified purely in terms of vengeance and punishment but as agencies of positive change the prison becomes a "correctional" institution . . . The scientists and the technicians are beginning to win out, not because of some inherent superiority in their paradigm of crime, but by showing that they have the power to be more effective custodians.[112]

The days of prisons as "human warehouses"[113] may be numbered, for,

> In the very near future, a computer technology will make possible alternatives to imprisonment. The development of systems for telemetering information from censors implanted in or on the body will soon make possible the observation and control of human behaviour without actual physical contact. Through such telemetric devices it will be possible to maintain 24-hour-a-day surveillance over the

subject and to intervene electronically or physically to influence and control selected behaviour. It will thus be possible to exercise control over human behaviour and from a distance without physical contact.[114]

Looked at superficially such changes (it is better not to call them "reforms") might appear to weaken hierarchies of power. In reality what they do is to make control more intrusive, more pervasive and more effective. The river may have burst its banks and the water may now flow in new channels. The water now comes at us from a number of directions and its total force may well be stronger than was the original river. The accepted view has been that control, certainly control within capitalism, required formality and impersonality, bureaucraticization and centralism. But today's advanced capitalism is compatible with decentralized social control. Penal developments draw attention to this in striking fashion but what they tell us can be generalized.

Even where the impetus for reform comes from below, from grass-roots sentiment, as to a large extent it does with moves to delegalize family dispute settlement, there is considerable likelihood that developments will be co-opted by the powerful, so that "bad" form takes over "good" substance. Adorno's remarks seem most pertinent.

> Whatever raises from within itself a claim to being autonomous, critical and antithetical — while at the same time never being able to assert this claim with total legitimacy — must necessarily come to naught; this is particularly true when its impulses are integrated into something heteronomous to them, which has been worked out previously from above — that is to say, when it is granted a space in which to draw breath immediately by that power against which it rebels.[115]

Is the result, as Cohen suggests, a "dispersal of social control"? Is the effect, as he argues it is,

> to increase rather than decrease the *amount* of intervention . . . and, probably, to increase rather than decrease the total *number* who get into the system in the first place[?][116]

He is writing of the criminal justice system but the parallels are too close to ignore. We can appreciate the proximity of the two when we return to and examine twentieth century policies towards the family.

We find rampant interventionism, a system of indirect controls and pervasive reliance on professional expertise. We find, in other words, policies which the family court legitimates. I believe, and I think my belief is shared, that the family has suffered from these policies. I believe that the family, particularly its weaker members, will suffer further from delegalization. And yet, if my thesis is correct, the move to a deformalized dispute settlement system in family matters has an air almost of inevitability about it. My article is written in the hope of opening our eyes to what we have been doing to the family and what the thrust of contemporary developments will do to the family in the future. Too much has been taken for granted that should be openly debated. Too much that is problematic has been glossed over. I hope my article raises the questions, even if it does not provide the answers.

NOTES

1. London: Justice, 1975, paras. 85 *et seq.*
2. Report of Committee on *One-Parent Families,* Cmnd. 5,629, 1974, London: H.M.S.O., part 4, sections 13 and 14.
3. *Idem,* para. 4.280.
4. "The Family, the Law and the Courts," 47 *Australian Law Journal* 647, 652 (1973).
5. "Reform and The Family Court," 125 *New Law Journal* 984 (1975).
6. In *The Domestic and Matrimonial Jurisdiction of Magistrates' Courts and County Courts,* Institute of Judicial Administration, University of Birmingham, 1973, 56-64, reported in *The Times,* 16 April 1973. See also Sir Leslie Scarman, *Family Law and Family Reform,* University of Bristol, 1966.
7. Finer, *op. cit.,* note 2, and Houghton, Report of Departmental Committee on the *Adoption of Children,* Cmnd. 5,107, 1972, London: H.M.S.O., paras. 276-279.
8. *A Better Way Out,* London: Law Society, 1979, parts III and VIII.
9. *The Case for a Local Family Court — Reform of the Family Jurisdiction of Magistrates,* 1978.
10. *The Case for Family Courts,* London: Conservative Political Centre, 1978.
11. *Proposal for a Family Court,* London: National Council for the Unmarried Mother and Her Child, 1973.
12. *Justice and Welfare in Divorce,* London: Sweet and Maxwell, 1980. I discuss this in "Towards a More Humane System of Divorce," 145 *Justice of the Peace* 1973 (1981).
13. See *Economy and Society* (eds. Guenther Roth and Claus Wittich) Berkeley: University of California Press, 1968, vol. II, pp. 641-900.
14. As to some of these are Richard L. Abel, *The Politics of Informal Justice,* 2 vols., New York: Academic Press, 1982. These volumes were not available in Britain when I wrote this article. Having now seen them, I realize how much my article would have profited from a study of them.
15. *Cf.* R. Merton (ed.), *Unanticipated Consequences of Social Action: Variations on a Sociological Theme,* New York: Academic Press, 1981.
16. See M. Spector, "Beyond Crime: Seven Methods to Control Troublesome Rascals" in (ed.) H. Laurence Ross, *Law and Deviance,* Beverly Hills: Sage, 1981, 127.
17. See Robert Kagan, *Regulatory Justice,* New York: Russell Sage Foundation, 1978.
18. See C. Reich, "The New Property," 73 *Yale L.J.* 733 (1964); M.A. Glendon, *The New Family and the New Property,* Toronto: Butterworths, 1981.
19. See N. Kittrie, *The Right to be Different: Deviance and Enforced Therapy,* Baltimore: Johns Hopkins U.P., 1971; P. Conrad and J. Schneider, *Deviance and Medicalization: From Badness to Sickness,* St. Louis: Mosby, 1980.

20. "The Punitive City: Notes on the Dispersal of Social Control," *Contemporary Crises* vol. 3, 339 (1979).
21. *The Triumph of The Therapeutic: Uses of Faith After Freud*, Harmondsworth: Penguin, 1966.
22. As in J. Goldstein et al., *Beyond The Best Interests of The Child*, New York: Free Press, 1973.
23. See L. Stone, *The Family, Sex and Marriage in England 1500-1800*, London: Weidenfeld and Nicolson, 1977 and E. Shorter, *The Making of the Modern Family*, London: Collins, 1976.
24. *Capitalism, the Family and Personal Life*, London: Pluto Press, 1976. See also A. Foreman, *Femininity As Alienation*, London: Pluto Press, 1977.
25. *Haven in a Heartless World*, New York: Basic Books, 1977, 6.
26. The term is Aileen S. Kraditor's. See *Up from the Pedestal: Selected Writings in the History of American Feminism*, Chicago: Quadrangle Books, 1968.
27. *At Odds: Women and the Family in America from the Revolution to the Present*, New York: Oxford U.P., 1980.
28. Following Nancy Cott, *The Bonds of Womanhood*, New Haven, Yale U.P., 1977 and Aileen Kraditor, *The Ideas of the Women's Suffrage Movement, 1890-1920*, New York: Columbia University Press, 1965.
29. Translated as *The Policing of Families*, New York: Pantheon Books, 1979, 221.
30. *Idem*. See the interesting critique by M. Barrett and M. McIntosh *The Antisocial Family*, London: Verso, 1982, 95 *et seq.*
31. "Life in the Therapeutic State," *The New York Review of Books*, vol. XXVII, no. 16 (12 June 1980) 24 and 27.
32. *For Her Own Good: 150 Years of the Experts' Advice to Women*, Garden City, New York: Anchor Press Doubleday, 1978.
33. *Op. cit.*, note 31, 27.
34. London: Gollancz, 1981.
35. See particularly N. Kittrie, *The Right To Be Different: Deviance and Enforced Therapy*, Baltimore: Johns Hopkins U.P., 1971.
36. *Cf.* P. Rieff, *Freud: The Mind of a Moralist*, London: Gollancz, 1960, 390.
37. See R. Fletcher, *The Family and Marriage in Britain*, Harmondsworth: Penguin, 1973 ch. 5. See also M. Nissel, "The Family and the Welfare State," *New Society*, vol. 53, no. 925 (7 August 1980), 259.
38. *Op. cit.*, note 25, 19.
39. See, e.g., Charlotte Perkins Gilman, *The Home: Its Work and Influence*, New York: McClure, Phillips, 1903, and Jenkin Lloyd Jones, quoted by Christopher Lasch in *Haven in a Heartless World, op. cit.*, note 25, p. 16.
40. *Escape From Childhood*, Harmondsworth: Penguin, 1975.
41. *Birthrights*, New York: Macmillan, 1974.
42. For the distinction, see C. Rogers and L. Wrightsman, "Attitudes toward Children's Rights: Nurturance or Self-Determination," *Journal of Social Issues*, vol. 34(2), 1978, 59. See also M. Wald, "Children's Rights: A Framework For Analysis," *University of California Davis L.R.*, vol. 12, 255, (1979) and M.D.A. Freeman, "The Rights of Children in the International Year of the Child," *Current Legal Problems*, vol. 33, 1980, 1; and *The Rights and Wrongs of Children*, London: Frances Pinter, 1983, ch. 2
43. Boston: Whitcomb and Barrows, 1910, 74.
44. *Op. cit.*, note 29, 219.
45. *Idem*, 158.

46. *Idem*, 100.
47. *Conscience and Convenience*, Boston: Little, Brown and Company, 1980.
48. *The Child Savers*, Chicago: University of Chicago Press, 1969 (a second edition was published in 1977).
49. "Philosophy and the Principle of Punishment in the Juvenile Court," 8 *Family Law Quarterly* 373 (1974).
50. *The Best-Laid Plans: America's Juvenile Court Experiment*, New York: Hill and Wang, 1978.
51. *Love and the American Delinquent: Theory and Practice of "Progressive" Juvenile Justice 1825-1920*, Chicago: University of Chicago Press, 1977.
52. *Op. cit.*, note 31, 30.
53. *Idem*.
54. See J. Lofland, *Deviance and Identity*, Englewood Cliffs: Prentice Hall, 1969, 150. See also E. Schur, *Labeling Deviant Behaviour*, New York: Harper and Row, 1971.
55. *Per* D. Matza, *Delinquency and Drift*, New York: Wiley, 1964, 115.
56. R. Anderson, *Representation in the Juvenile Courts*, London: Routledge and Kegan Paul, 1978, 25.
57. See L. Taylor et al., *In Whose Best Interests?* London: Cobden Trust/Mind, 1980; A. Morris et al., *Justice For Children*, London: Macmillan, 1980.
58. It is significant that little serious or sustained attention has been given by professionals to J. Goldstein et al.'s *Beyond the Best Interests of the Child*, revised edition, New York: Free Press, 1980 (first published in 1973), particularly to its idea of the "least detrimental alternative," despite the fact that the book is explicitly psychoanalytical in orientation.
59. "Science in Court" in (ed.) M. King, *Childhood, Welfare and Justice*, London: Batsford, 1981, 45-104.
60. *Idem*, 48.
61. Patricia Morgan, *Child Care: Sense and Fable*, London: Temple Smith, 1975 and *Delinquent Fantasies*, London: Temple Smith, 1978.
62. For example, G. Pearson, *The Deviant Imagination*, London: Macmillan, 1975.
63. *Op. cit.*, note 59, 95.
64. The most famous is the Department of Health and Social Security report into the Maria Colwell case (the Field-Fisher report) published by H.M.S.O., London, 1974. There have been some twenty other reports of enquiries. Eighteen reports are looked at in a new DHSS document, *Child Abuse — A Study of Inquiry Reports 1973-1981*, London: H.M.S.O., 1982. There is a fuller list in D.A. Jones, *Understanding Child Abuse*, Sevenoaks: Hodder and Stoughton, 1982, 290-92.
65. A rather similar point is made by J. Howells, *Remember Maria*, London: Butterworths, 1974.
66. *Op. cit.*, note 2.
67. *Idem*, para. 4.281.
68. *Idem*, para. 4.325.
69. *Idem*, para. 4.328.
70. There is a good description of the Bristol service, the most fully developed in England, in Lisa Parkinson, "Bristol Courts Family Conciliation Service," 12 *Family Law* 13-16 (1982).
71. See, *op. cit.*, note 2, para. 4.390.
72. I use this sexist expression deliberately since I believe it is within the spirit of the report. Also, I am not aware of a neutral term.

73. See J. Thorpe, *Social Enquiry Reports*, London: H.M.S.O., 1979.
74. See generally 9 *Family Law* 50 (1979), particularly the case of *Re C* (1973) discussed therein. See also *R v. R* (1978) 8 *Family Law* 169 and *J v. J* (1979) 9 *Family Law* 91.
75. Extended to all undefended cases in 1977. See Matrimonial Causes Rules, r. 33(3), 48. See S.M. Cretney, *Principles of Family Law*, London: Sweet and Maxwell, 1979, 159-63.
76. E. Elston et al., "Judicial Hearings of Undefended Divorce Petitions," 38 *M.L.R.* 609 (1975).
77. See M.D.A. Freeman, "Divorce Without Legal Aid," 6 *Family Law* 255 (1976).
78. For example, R.L. Abel, "Delegalization: A Critical Review of Its Ideology, Manifestations and Social Consequences," in E. Blankenburg et al. (eds.), *Alternative Rechtsformen und Alternativen Rechtssoziologie und Rechtstheorie*, Opladen: Westdeutscher Verlag, 27-47 (Jahrbuch fur Rechtssoziologie and Rechtstheorie Band 6). See also now, *op. cit.*, note 14, particularly vol. 1, chs. 7 and 10.
79. *Op. cit.*, note 18.
80. *From Max Weber: Essays in Sociology*, edited and translated by H. H. Gerth and C. Wright Mills. Copyright 1946 by Oxford University Press, Inc., renewed 1973 by Hans H. Gerth. Reprinted by permission of the publisher.
81. *Cf.* M. Horkheimer, *Eclipse of Reason*, New York: Seabury, 1974, 6.
82. See M. Galanter, "Legality and Its Discontents" in (ed.) E. Blankenburg et al., *op. cit.*, note 78, 11, and R. Abel, "Conservative, Conflict and Informal Justice," *Int. J. of Sociology of Law*, vol. 9, 245 (1981).
83. That is why "England" was such a problem for him. See A. Hunt, *The Sociological Movement In Law*, London: Macmillan, 1978, 122-28 for a discussion of this.
84. *Economy and Society*, (eds.) Guenther Roth and Claus Wittich, Berkeley: University of California Press, 1968, vol. II, 893.
85. "Form and Substance In Private Law," [1976] 89 *Harvard Law Review*, 1,685-1,778.
86. *Whigs and Hunters*, London: Allen Lane, 1975, 262-63.
87. *Idem*, 266.
88. See M.D.A. Freeman, "The Rights of Children Who Do 'Wrong'," (1981) 21 *British Journal of Criminology*, 210-29; A. Morris et al., *Justice for Children*, London: Macmillan, 1980.
89. See generally W. Vaughan Stapleton and Lee H. Teitelbaum, *In Defense of Youth*, New York: Russell Sage Foundation, 1972.
90. See P. Brown and T. Bloomfield (eds.), *Legality and Community*, Aberdeen: Aberdeen People's Press, 1979 and A. Morris and M. McIsaac, *Juvenile Justice*, London: Heinemann, 1978.
91. Never fully implemented. The current trend is increasingly punitive though a veneer of welfarism remains. The *Criminal Justice Act 1982* reverses some of the trends embodied in the 1969 legislation.
92. 387 U.S.I. (1967). See also *Breed v. Jones* 421 U.S. 519 (1975) and *cf. McKeiver v. Pennsylvania* 403 U.S. 538 (1971).
93. Juvenile courts were once hailed as the best plan "for the conservation of human life and happiness ever conceived by civilised man" *per* C.W. Hoffman, "Organisation of Family Courts, with Special References to the Juvenile Courts," in J. Addams (ed.), *The Child, the Clinic and the Court*, New York: New Republic, 1927.
94. Notably by M.J. Horwitz, *The Transformation of American Law 1780-1860*,

Cambridge: Harvard U.P., 1977. See also D. Kennedy, "Legal Formality," 2 *Journal of Legal Studies* 351-98 (1973) and R.M. Unger, *Law in Modern Society*, New York: Free Press, 1976, 203 *et seq*.

95. Those who propagated the juvenile court may have been moved by other considerations. See Anthony Platt's analysis in *op. cit.*, note 48.

96. Alvin Toffler's phrase (see *The Third Wave*, London: Collins, 1980). In using his expression, I am falling in with his description of a trend, not adopting his agenda, about which I make no comment.

97. See D. Sugarman, "Theory and Practice in Law and History" in (ed.) B. Fryer et al., *Law, State and Society*, London: Croom Helm, 1981, 70.

98. For example, Hans Kelsen, Léon Duguit and Yevgeny Pashukanis.

99. See R.M. Unger, *Law in Modern Society*, New York: Free Press, 1976; Karl Klare, "Law-Making as Praxis," 40 *Telos* 123-35 (1979).

100. Thus reversing the trend from status to contract depicted by Sir Henry Maine in *Ancient Law*. It hardly needs emphasizing that today's "status" is very different from the feudalistic motion in Maine's historical analysis. See, further, A. Fraser, "The Legal Theory We Need Now," *Socialist Review*, no. 40-41, 147-87 (1978).

101. See the two very different treatments of P. Nonet, *Administrative Justice: Advocacy and Change in a Government Agency*, New York: Russell Sage Foundation, 1969 and L. Scarman, *English Law — The New Dimension*, London: Stevens, 1974.

102. See G. Gilmore, *The Death of Contract*, Columbus: Ohio State University Press, 1974.

103. See N. Kittrie, *op. cit.*, note 19.

104. *Cf.* K. Polanyi, *The Great Transformation*, Boston: Beacon Press, 1944, ch. 4.

105. "Beyond the French Revolution: Communist Socialism and the Rule of Law" 21 *University of Toronto L.J.* 109-40 (1971).

106. There had previously been a move from *Gemeinschaft* law. The terms, of course, derive from Ferdinand Tönnies (see translation as *Community and Association*): similar ideas are found in the writing of Karl Renner.

107. "Beyond Bourgeois Individualism: the Contemporary Crisis in Law and Legal Ideology" in (eds.) E. Kamenka and R.S. Neale, *Feudalism, Capitalism and Beyond*, London: Edward Arnold, 1975, 140. *Cf.* D. Neiken, "Is there a Crisis in Law and Legal Ideology?" 9 *J. Law and Soc.* 177 (1982).

108. See R.M. Unger, *op. cit.*, note 94, 216 and F. Neumann, *The Democratic and Authoritarian State*, New York: Macmillan, 1957. Unger refers also to German writing by Friedrich Dessauer, Justus Hedemann and Rudolf Echterholter (see 292-93).

109. See, for example, J. Alderson, *Policing Freedom*, London: Macdonald and Evans, 1979 or "The Case For Community Policing" in (eds.) D. Cowell, T. Jones and J. Young, *Policing the Riots*, London: Junction Books, 1982, ch. 8, *cf.* C. Moore and J. Brown, *Community Versus Crime*, London: Bedford Square Press, 1981.

110. See Z. Bankowski and G. Mungham, "Laypeople and Lawpeople and the Administration of the Lower Courts," *Int. J. of Sociology of Law*, vol. 9, 85-100 (1981).

111. See, for example, D. McGillis and J. Mullen, *Neighbourhood Justice Centers: An Analysis of Potential Models:* Washington D.C.: Govt. Printing Office, 1977; Frank Sander, *Report on the National Conference on Minor Dispute Resolution*, Chicago: American Bar Association, 1977 (also his "Varieties of Dispute Processing," 70 F.R.D. 79 (1976)); L. Nader, *No Access to Law: Alternatives to the American Judicial System*, New York: Academic Press, 1980. See also Benson Royal Commission on Legal Services, London: H.M.S.O. 1979, Cmnd. 7,648, ch. 43. On the concept of "neighbourhood" see

R. Danzig, "Toward the Creation of a Complementary Decentralised System of Justice," 26 *Stanford L.R.* 1 (1973).

112. *Per* Stanley Cohen, "Human Warehouses: The Future of Our Prisons?", *New Society*, vol. 30, no. 632 (14 November 1974), 407 at 410.

113. Stanley Cohen's expression. See "Human Warehouses: The Future of Our Prisons?", *New Society*, vol. 30, no. 632 (14 November 1974), 407.

114. *Per* Barton L. Ingraham and Gerald W. Smith, "The Use of Electronics in the Observation and Control of Human Behaviour, and Its Possible Use in Rehabitation and Parole," *Issues in Criminology* 35–53 (Fall Issue, 1972).

115. "Culture and Administration," 37 *Telos* 93, 101–102 (1978).

116. *Op. cit.*, note 20, at 347. See also Stanley Cohen, "Prisons and the Future of Control Systems: From Concentration to Dispersal," in (eds.) M. Fitzgerald, P. Halmos, J. Muncie and D. Zeldin, *Welfare in Action*, London: R.K.P., 1977, 217–28.

Chapter Two

Negotiated Settlement of Family Disputes

Donald J. MacDougall

University of British Columbia,
Vancouver, Canada

INTRODUCTION

The twentieth century has experienced a significant increase in the volume of family disputes as previously repressed, or unrecognized, grievances are transformed into claims for relief. Most family disputes are resolved by negotiation. This article develops the thesis that negotiation should continue to be the primary method for resolving conflicts within the family, examines some of the contributions that modern research has made to our understanding of the negotiation process, and concludes with a call for further research and education to improve the skills of those involved in the negotiation of family disputes.

DISPUTES ARE NORMAL

Sociologists have suggested[1] that the predispute period can be analysed into three stages:

1. the perception of injurious experience;
2. the grievance — when the individual attributes the injury to the fault of another individual or social entity; and
3. the claim — when the individual with a grievance asks for some remedy.

"A claim is transformed into a dispute when it is rejected in whole or in part"[2] or "a dispute exists when a claim based on a grievance is rejected either in whole or in part."[3]

But what factors cause the transformation of a perceived injury into a grievance or claim? Should we not be concerned about the prevention, as well as the resolution, of disputes? Is our twentieth century too contentious? Do we manufacture too many grievances, claims and disputes? In particular, do lawyers foster grievances, claims and disputes that would not exist apart from their intervention? It is difficult, if not impossible, to answer these questions because there are not standards for determining what is a healthy, or proper, level of disputing.

Consider, for example, matrimonial property. Under the common law separate property system both the husband and wife were entitled to maintain their separate property interests and possessed few, if any, rights against the property of the other spouse. In many of the former separate property jurisdictions, matrimonial property reform has been effected by legislation which provides for some form of community property or the equitable sharing of family assets. This legislation has resulted in a significant increase in both the level of disputing and the amount of litigation. Is this a development to be deplored?

The following comment, by Miller and Sarat, was made in another context but it seems to be equally applicable in this context:

> Our own belief is that where there are grievances there ought to be claims, and that where there are claims, conflict is not necessarily an undesirable or unhealthy result. Those who fear conflict or who advocate acquiescence in the face of grievances fear threats to the social status quo. They bear a substantial burden in showing how people benefit from lumping or enduring injurious experiences or the denial of rights or how the status quo is served in the longer run as frustrations increase and legitimacy decreases.[4]

DISPUTE RESOLUTION

The traditional legal techniques for resolving family conflicts have been (i) negotiation or (ii) adjudication. Many critics of the legal system have minimized the importance of negotiation and exaggerated the importance of adjudication. In fairness to the legal profession it must be emphasized that most family conflicts are settled by agreement between the parties with the assistance of their lawyers.

There is more substance to the criticism that lawyers have not fully explored other alternatives to adjudication in cases where negotiations are unsuccessful. Experts in conflict resolution have developed a wide variety of alternative techniques. Conciliation, mediation and arbitration are techniques that are familiar to everyone. Indeed Crouch recently commented:

> It is as difficult today to be against mediation as it once was to be against motherhood. This dispute-resolution process is riding the crest of an immense wave of fad appeal, within both the professions and the media.[5]

However these familiar techniques do not exhaust the list of possible alternatives. Other forms of third party intervention, even less intrusive than conciliation, may lead to an agreement. For example, in a disputed custody case the parties may agree to appoint an expert to prepare a report for the court. In theory, the expert's role is merely to investigate and report. In fact, the clarification of perceptions that may flow from such a report may result in an agreement that was previously unattainable. This will not surprise anyone familar with the importance of information to decision making and persuasion. Similarly, experience in British Columbia suggests that the appointment of an independent advocate for the child often facilitates the settlement of custody disputes prior to trial.[6]

Given that there are a wide variety of techniques for resolving conflicts, what are the advantages and disadvantages of each? How are we to evaluate the various possibilities? Not surprisingly, legal academics have given more thought to the adjudicative process than to other procedures for resolving conflicts. Their comments about the adjudicative process suggest criteria that can be adapted for evaluating other techniques. Weinstein, for example, noted:

> Adjudication is a practical enterprise serving a variety of functions. Among the goals — in addition to truth finding — which the rules of procedure and evidence in this country have sought to satisfy are economizing of resources, inspiring confidence, supporting independent social policies, permitting ease in prediction and application, adding to the efficiency of the entire legal system, and tranquilizing disputants.[7]

Similarly, James commented:

> The full pursuit of the ... facts and applicable law in any dispute may ... be limited by the need for efficiency and finality. The hardest and most important job of a procedural system is to keep striking a wise balance throughout the various points of conflict.[8]

All techniques for resolving disputes have a practical purpose. They seek a variety of goals — sometimes overlapping, sometimes conflicting. At the risk of some oversimplification it is suggested that the following criteria can be used to evaluate different methods of resolving disputes:

1. effectiveness in ending disputes;
2. cost;
3. justice; and
4. promotion of independent social goals.

Effectiveness in Ending Disputes

The primary, but not the sole, goal of any conflict resolution technique is to end the dispute between the parties. What is involved in ending the dispute? Theoretically a judgment or an arbitration award ends a dispute but it is not unusual, especially in family disputes, to find one or both parties seeking to avoid the consequences of the judgment or award. Consequently, the real test of a conflict resolution technique is whether it produces a result or decision that both parties will accept as a satisfactory settlement of the dispute. Moreover, the settlement must be durable because many settlements in family law disputes will entail a continuing relationship between the parties. These considerations suggest that techniques which involve third parties in a minimal, and supportive, role (such as negotiation, conciliation and mediation) are to be preferred to techniques which involve third parties in more intrusive roles.

Cost

Direct negotiation between the parties, without assistance, is the least expensive technique and adjudication is usually the most expensive. It is hard to generalize about the other alternatives because the total cost in a particular case will depend on the length of time that third parties are involved in the process, their effectiveness, and their fees. For example, the use of nonlegal professionals in conciliation and mediation may reduce the total cost of resolving a dispute if their skills result in lower demands for legal assistance and smaller legal fees. Although mediation is promoted as a low-cost alternative to adjudication it is possible to envisage a situation where an extended, albeit ultimately successful, attempt at mediation would be more expensive than adjudication. No doubt similar anxieties can be expressed about the cost of other alternatives. A major concern is the cost of *unsuccessful* attempts to resolve the dispute.

Because family disputes cover a wide range (from simple — hardly requiring professional involvement — to complex — requiring the involvement of several professionals) and because different projects use different techniques, varying reports on the cost effectiveness of particular projects are to be expected.[9] Many are aware of the inherent difficulties in evaluating the provision of social services by any organization and will approach a laudatory report about a particular project with sympathy, but some suspicion. Unfortunately, politicians may not be equally critical.

A subsidiary issue arises around the question of who pays for the professional assistance. Conciliation or mediation services may be provided at public expense at little or no cost to a particular couple. This *de facto* subsidization of a particular technique of conflict resolution may distort the pattern of dispute resolution that would otherwise occur. Usually this subsidization is deliberately planned to provide an attractive alternative to litigation. Unfortunately, it may also have an unplanned impact on other nonsubsidized procedures, such as the negotiated settlement of family disputes.

There are noneconomic, as well as economic, costs involved in the resolution of family disputes. There is general agreement that litigation puts significant psychological and emotional demands on the parties although, in a few cases, it may provide a necessary catharsis. Presumably disputing parties will be more comfortable with processes over which they exercise some control (i.e., negotiation, optional counselling and mediation) and less comfortable with coercive alternatives (i.e., mandatory counselling and mediation, adjudication).

Justice

If a dispute proceeds to adjudication, the parties will receive justice according to the set of normative standards established in the particular legal system. However, we are all familiar with the tension that can arise between the need to administer justice according to law and the need to do justice in the particular case.

Other conflict resolution techniques give disputing parties the power, within broad limits, to determine what would be a just solution to their difficulties. Only the disputing parties have an intimate and detailed knowledge of the particular circumstances that should be weighed in the scales of justice. Unfortunately, experience teaches us that there are people who will take advantage of this freedom from normative restraints. The problem is not unique to negotiations within the family. It is common, for example, in commercial transactions. However, it is a particularly serious problem in the resolution of family conflicts because of the emotional stress that the parties may experience as a result of the breakdown of the marriage. Some will become angry and exploitative. Others, because of feelings of guilt, will be particularly vulnerable.

The intervention of a third party (conciliator, mediator, arbitrator) can operate as a check on possible abuse, but where there is only a single intervenor there is the continuing problem of conscious, or unconscious, bias. The basic argument for the common law adversarial system of justice (as contrasted with an investigative, or inquisitorial system) is that justice is more likely to result when each disputant has the opportunity to present his or her claim to an independent judge. Other procedures are not necessarily unjust but they involve greater risks. Moreover, those risks may increase where the intervenor is provided at public expense and therefore vulnerable to subtle pressure to pursue policies which may have little to do with the dispute between the parties. Even if the third party intervenor is legally trained, and thus likely to refer to legal norms in resolving the dispute, there is the possibility of injustice resulting from a misperception of the facts.

Courts traditionally attach great weight to settlements where both parties in dispute received independent legal advice. This is because judges recognize that such an agreement probably constitutes a just determination of the dispute. The following passage, from the judgment of Anderson J. in the case of *Dal Santo v. Dal Santo*[10] has been frequently quoted in subsequent Canadian cases:

> It is of great importance not only to the parties but to the community as a whole that contracts of this kind should not be lightly disturbed. Lawyers must be able to advise their clients in respect of their future rights and obligations with some degree of certainty. Clients must be able to rely on these agreements and know with some degree of assurance that once a separation agreement is executed their affairs have been settled on a permanent basis. The courts must encourage parties to settle their differences without recourse to litigation. The modern approach in family law is to mediate and conciliate so as to enable the parties to make a fresh start in life on a secure basis. If separation agreements can be varied at will, it will become much more difficult to persuade the parties to enter into such agreements.[11]

Of course, the courts will not lightly disregard agreements reached by the parties without professional assistance, or with the assistance of only one professional (whether legally trained or not). But there is not the same assurance that justice has been done in such circumstances.

Promotion of Independent Social Goals

Traditionally, family law has been concerned with the protection of public, as well as private, interests. However, there has been a major shift in the nature of the public interest in family law.[12] With the advent of simple no-fault divorce the state has clearly surrendered most of its concern with matters of marital statutes. But the current instability in family relationships has had a significant impact on social programs designed to help the less fortunate and to improve the quality of life. Legislators have begun to appreciate the financial and social burden that the state has had to assume in order to provide a minimal standard of living for economically dependent spouses and their children. The cost of these programs has affected the ability of legislatures to proceed with other social programs. The result has been a flurry of legislative and administrative activity designed to reduce the burden on public funds.

Programs are put in place to ensure better enforcement of maintenance and support judgments. Spouses are told that they must be self-supporting. Today the state's interest in family law is directed towards ensuring that other family members bear the primary responsibility for supporting any dependent spouse or children and, to a lesser extent, that the noneconomic interests of any children are protected.

It cannot be said that any of the existing dispute resolution techniques adequately promote these interests. Many would argue that society is still adjusting to the phenomenon of marriage as a transient state and that there is no agreement on the extent to which these interests should be protected. Sociologists have noted that the development of remedies almost inevitably lags behind the recognition of rights.[13] If these social interests are to be protected, new institutions or procedures may have to be developed to protect them.

Within the negotiation process there exists a mechanism that could be further developed. Lawyers already operate under a code of ethics which puts them, as members of a profession, under obligations to society as well as to their clients. In theory it would be possible, although in practice it might be difficult, to define the ethical obligations of a lawyer involved in the negotiation of a family dispute to include the protection of these social interests. If this proposal seems unrealistic, consider the alternatives. If the private ordering processes cannot be modified to ensure the protection of the public interest, it may be necessary to develop extensive administrative processes to protect those interests.

To summarize, the negotiation process is an effective, relatively inexpensive procedure for the just resolution of family disputes. It does not adequately protect the public interest in the terms of settlement, but there is a possibility of modifying the negotiation process to give greater recognition to the public interest. Moreover, none of the existing processes protect that interest adequately.

NEGOTIATION: GENERAL BARGAINING THEORY

Few lawyers have any formal training in the theoretical aspects of negotiation. Most, however, have extensive practical experience in negotiation and many have developed significant skills in negotiation — especially in dealing with certain familiar and standard situations.

General bargaining theory is concerned with how parties negotiate within the constraints imposed by the circumstances. It is convenient to divide those who have written on negotiation theory into two broad groups: (*a*) those who are concerned with the analysis of the negotiation process and the identification of factors that affect it; and (*b*) those who are concerned with the psychological aspects of negotiation.

The Analytical Approach

One of the major contributions of the analytical group was the identification of different types of negotiation. A situation imposes real constraints on the negotiating parties. Those constraints are like the rules of the game — they set the limits within which the negotiation must proceed. One obvious constraint arises from the financial resources of the parties. Another is the possibility of formal adjudication if agreement is not reached. To illustrate the importance of identifying different types of negotiation, let me give you two examples.

1. John and Mary are married but both continued to work during their marriage. They have no children. They are separating and a dispute has arisen about the division of their matrimonial property. This is very close to a "zero-sum" type of negotiation where the interests of the two parties are diametrically opposed. Any gain won by one spouse is a loss to the other. Contrast that with the following situation:
2. Bob and Barbara are married and have three young children. They have limited financial resources. Recently, however, Bob received a promotion to a position with a higher salary and Barbara returned to work in a part-time clerical position. Both Bob and Barbara have warm, affectionate relationships with their children. They are separating and a dispute has arisen about their financial obligations to each other, their future relationships with the children and the support of the children. In this situation the interests of the parties are partially opposed and partially coincident. To obtain the best possible agreement and to maximize their separate, individual interests, the parties need to cooperate to some extent. It is common to compare negotiation to the division of a pie. But in some cases the parties have the capacity to expand, or diminish, the pie to be divided. This type of negotiation is referred to as a "mixed motive" or "non-zero-sum" negotiation.

Why is it important to distinguish between different types of negotiations? Research indicates that certain tactics and skills that are likely to be successful in one type of negotiation may be unsuccessful in another type of negotiation.[14] Indeed some research indicates that negotiators with certain personality traits are more likely to be successful in certin types of negotiation than others.[15]

Analytical theory also provided certain basic negotiation concepts — the interplay between (i) information; (ii) goals; and (iii) strategy.[16] Game theorists pointed out that there was an analogy between the game — such as chess or bridge — and negotiations. Assuming that you have a clear goal in mind, your ability to determine your best possible move (or your optimal strategy) depends on the information that you have acquired. In a game like chess, where a player has perfect information, determination of the best possible move can be expressed in some complex mathematical calculations. In real life negotiations, when a negotiator is working with imperfect information, judgments about strategy cannot be made with the same assurance. But the basic principle holds. The more complete and accurate your information base, the more effective you will be in negotiating. Of course the relationship between information, goals and strategy is a dynamic, rather than a static, relationship. New information may affect your goals and strategy. Your choice of a tentative strategy may cause you to seek additional information on particular points. This interrelationship seems so simple, basic and self-evident that there is a tendency to underestimate its importance. A negotiator to be effective, needs (i) to be clear on the goals that he wishes to achieve in the negotiation, and (ii) to have as much information as possible about factors that will affect the negotiation. A corollary of that proposition is that a negotiator who has clear objectives, developed on a sound information base, is unlikely to be vulnerable to the negotiating tactics of his opponent.

Some theorists go even further. They attempt to quantify the various aspects of the negotiation so that the negotiation becomes almost a mathematical exercise. The problem, of course, is to identify *all* the factors and then give each of them a mathematical value. While these theorists have produced some interesting models, most negotiators consider that the more complex attempts to construct models of the negotiating process lose touch with reality.

The Psychological Approach

There is a danger in approaching negotiation from a purely psychological perspective. The psychologist might not appreciate the extent to which a negotiator's attitude and behaviour is a rational and planned response to the situation. As Anne Douglas wrote in her seminal article on industrial disputes:

> Some of the most misleading interpretations about the behaviour of this first stage [of negotiation] have been contributed by psychologists.[17]

Nevertheless there is general agreement that, as negotiations progress, psychological considerations begin to assume a critical role. Nierenberg has commented:

> Negotiating has often been compared to a game... In games the rules show the risks and rewards. However rules of this sort are not available in the unbounded life

process of negotiations. In negotiating any risks that are known have been learned from broad experience not a book. In a life situation, the negotiator ordinarily has little or no control over the complex variables, the innumerable strategies that the opposer may bring into the struggle.[18]

There have been attempts to identify the qualities or attributes that an ideal negotiator should possess. But negotiation involves an interaction between two, or more, individuals in a specific situation. The history of the interaction becomes more important than the parties initial orientation. As Hermann and Kogan suggest:

> It would seem to be a more prudent use of research time and funds to consider how personality characteristics interact with role characteristics and situational phenomena in affecting negotiations.[19]

The primary interest, therefore, is in tactics or strategies that will exert psychological pressure towards agreement. Some of the more common techniques (e.g., whipsaw, anger, false demand) are now conveniently catalogued and explained.[20] In theory, of course, there are an indefinite number of tactics that can be used in an effort to persuade your opponent to agree to a settlement. One of the major problems is the question of credibility. One party often has difficulty in persuading the other party to a dispute about his or her commitment to a particular claim. In such a situation a lawyer-negotiator has considerable advantages. Claims asserted by a lawyer on behalf of a client carry added weight because of the parties' perception of the role of the lawyer in our society and their knowledge of the coercive processes that he can invoke if negotiations are unsuccessful.

FAMILY NEGOTIATIONS: SPECIAL CONSIDERATIONS

It is not uncommon to find a distinctive superstructure built on the foundation provided by general negotiation theory. This is true, for example, of labour negotiations and international negotiations. The special character of these negotiations results, in part, from the special structures that have been created to deal with labour, and international, disputes. A skilled labour negotiator needs to have a specialized knowledge of labour law and practice as well as a knowledge of general negotiation theory. By those standards the procedures for dealing with family disputes are still relatively unsophisticated and not particularly distinctive.

Nevertheless, there are some areas of special concern to a lawyer negotiating a family dispute.

Establishing the Goals

In a typical lawyer-client relationship, the client has certain goals that he wishes to achieve. The lawyer advises him of any relevant law and the client and the lawyer agree on any necessary, or desirable, modification of the client's original goals. In most civil cases, the client's goals can be assigned a monetary value and, while proceedings may involve the client emotionally as well as intellectually, this involvement rarely affects his ability to discuss and make a sensible judgment about his objectives.

A client involved in a family dispute may have considerable difficulty in making a sensible judgment about his goals. He may be angry and vindictive. Or he may be vulnerable because of feelings of guilt. Or he may deny the reality of what is happening. There have been several attempts to describe the stages of divorce.[21] While they differ in detail, they all agree that a client's responses may be unstable until he accepts the reality of the divorce and begins to rebuild his life.

This poses a severe problem for the lawyer-negotiator. Ultimately, it is the client who must make the choice of goals. If the client's decision seems ill-advised the lawyer must give some thought to his own protection. At some future date the client may appreciate that his earlier decisions were unwise and criticize the lawyer's performance.

What are the options available to the lawyer? He can, of course, wait until the client is capable of making consistent and rational judgments about his objectives. But circumstances may force the lawyer to act at an earlier stage. If so, the lawyer should advise his client to seek professional counselling because it is extremely difficult for anyone to act as an effective negotiator if (i) the client is unclear about his objectives, or (ii) there is any misunderstanding between the client and his lawyer about those objectives.

Certain Strategies Inappropriate

There are some standard negotiating tactics which should be used with caution, if at all, in family negotiations. In this emotionally charged context the tactics may produce unanticipated responses and seriously jeopardize the chances of reaching a satisfactory agreement.

Consider, for example, the use of threats. In extreme cases the person making the threat may find himself charged with criminal misconduct, or unethical behaviour.[22] But even lesser threats (e.g., by the husband to move to another state or province, or by the wife to take the children to another city) may have negative consequences.

Another questionable procedure in this context is the use of commitment (i.e., where one spouse makes a firm commitment and *then* advises the other spouse). For example, a spouse may sell certain assets, or quit work, or spend money on some expensive object or activity. Similarly, Boulwareism, where a spouse makes a single offer on a "take it or leave it" basis, may produce a negative reaction as well as being largely ineffective having regard to the alternatives available to either spouse.

It may be argued that these tactics are inappropriate in those cases where there are children, there will be a continuing relationship between the parties and the parties will maximize their individual pay-offs by cooperating with each other, but that they may be appropriate and effective in cases where there are no children and a "clean break" is possible. Even in such situations, however, there is a danger that, because of the emotional factors involved in the negotiation of family disputes, aggresive tactics may produce an unanticipated and undesired response.

The Role-playing Advocate

There is evidence that many clients "hand-pick" their lawyers because of their reputations. An angry and frustrated spouse may choose a lawyer who is known for his ability to express that anger and frustration in the courtroom. Others may flinch at the damage he inflicts on the other spouse and any children of the marriage and question whether he is really effective in protecting his own client's interests. The lawyer is unlikely to change. He has found a role and he will continue to play it while the demand exists. Clearly negotiations with such a lawyer will be difficult. Nevertheless opposing counsel should not assume that a negotiated settlement is impossible. The benefits of negotiation are substantial and it may be possible to convince even a litigation-minded lawyer that this is one case in which negotiation could be preferable to litigation.

Should there be disincentives to such intransigent behaviour? In jurisdictions such as Canada, where one party may be required to pay the other party's costs, a refusal to accept a reasonable offer to settle can be punished by requiring the unreasonable spouse to pay a significant part of the other spouse's legal fees.[23] In other jurisdictions consideration may have to be given to alternative procedures (e.g., compulsory mediation,[24] pretrial conferences). There is the danger that the role-playing lawyer will treat these procedures as additional opportunities to display his manipulative skills. Moreover, lawyers may take advantage of such services to expedite settlement even in cases where they confidently expect to negotiate a settlement in any event. Given these risks, and the additional costs involved in establishing the procedures, it becomes a practical question whether the results achieved by these procedures justify the effort. The answer may vary from jurisdiction to jurisdiction. It must be accepted that adjudication is the most practical way of resolving some family disputes and a realistic objective for law reformers is a reduction in, rather than the total elimination of, the number of family disputes proceeding to litigation.

Impact of Alternative Processes

In labour and international negotiations the pattern of negotiations is affected by the legislative structure and the alternative institutions for resolving disputes. The negotiation of family disputes is affected by the same factors. The continuing increase in family disputes has led courts and legislatures to devise new mechanisms for resolving such disputes prior to trial. To the extent that these procedures provide attractive alternatives to litigation they reduce the pressure on the parties to negotiate their own settlement. On the other hand, a skilful lawyer may be able to exploit these new procedures as part of his negotiation strategy (e.g., to force his opponent to consider seriously a reasonable offer to settle). So the development of alternative processes will affect both the extent to which the parties settle their differences by private agreement and also the pattern of the negotiating process in a particular jurisdiction.

CONCLUSION

Most family disputes are settled by direct negotiations between the parties with the assistance of lawyers in more serious or difficult cases. As a technique for resolving family disputes, negotiation has proved to be effective and relatively inexpensive. Moreover, the resulting settlement is likely to be fair to both parties, especially if they have access to independent legal advice. Other conflict resolution techniques (e.g., conciliation, mediation and arbitration) should be developed but it would be unfortunate if these techniques interfered with the normal practice of settling family disputes by direct negotiation. Rather, these conflict resolution techniques should be developed as alternatives, or supplements, to the litigation process.

Meanwhile, efforts should be made to improve the negotiation process itself. There is a need for both research and education. Scholarly interest in the negotiation process is a recent phenomenon. There is a continuing debate about the nature and structure of the negotiation process, the classification of different types of negotiation and the factors which facilitate or impede successful negotiations. There is a growing body of research on general negotiation theory and practice but there has been little research on the specialized categories of (i) legal negotiations, and (ii) the negotiation of family disputes. At this stage our knowledge is incomplete. Indeed, negotiation may be more of an art than a science. It may never be possible to analyse completely the negotiation process. But further research will advance our general understanding of the negotiation process and its usefulness in specialized areas (e.g., family disputes). Moreover, such research will have a "spill over" effect in that it will advance our knowledge of other conflict resolution techniques.

Even our current imperfect and incomplete knowledge of the negotiation process can be used to improve negotiation skills. Many lawyers have developed considerable skill in negotiation because of their extensive practical experience in the negotiation of disputes or agreements. But, lacking a theoretical understanding of the process, their performance is likely to be erratic and they may use tactics that are inappropriate to the circumstances of a particular case. Law schools are beginning to offer courses in negotiation and continuing legal education authorities are offering programs for practising lawyers. It seems likely that negotiation will remain the primary method of resolving disputes, especially family disputes, in our society, and there is every reason to hope that the next decade will witness a dramatic increase in our skilfulness in using negotiation techniques.

NOTES

1. W. L. Felsteiner, R. A. Abel and A. Sarat, "The Emergence and Transformation of Disputes: Naming, Blaming, Claiming . . .," 15 *Law and Society Review* 631 (1981).
2. *Ibid.*, 636.
3. R. E. Miller and A. Sarat, "Grievances, Claims and Disputes: Assessing the Adversary Culture," 15 *Law and Society Review* 525 (1981).
4. *Ibid.*, 561-62.
5. R. E. Crouch, "Mediation and Divorce: The Dark Side is Still Unexplored," 4 *Family Advocate* 27 (1982).
6. F. Maczko, "Some Problems with Acting for Children," 2 *Canadian Journal of Family Law* 267 at 279-82 (1979) *cf.* R. Mnookin and L. Kornhauser, "Bargaining in the Shadow of the Law: The Case for Divorce," 88 *Yale Law Journal* 950 at 988-90 (1979).
7. J. B. Weinstein, "Some Difficulties in Devising Rules for Determining Truth in Judicial Trials," 66 *Columbia L.R.* 223. Copyright © 1966 by the Directors for the Columbia Law Review Association, Inc. All rights reserved. This quotation from the article, "Some Difficulties in Devising Rules for Determining Truth in Judicial Trials," originally appeared at 66 Colum. L. Rev. 241 (1966). Reprinted by permission.
8. F. James Jr., *Civil Procedure* (1965) 2.
9. Compare the following reports: J. Pearson and N. Thoennes, "Mediation and Divorce: The Benefits Outweigh the Costs," 4 *Family Advocate* 26 (1982) (on the Denver Custody Mediation Project), H. McIsaac, "Mandatory Conciliation Custody/Visitation Matters: California's Bold Stroke," 19 *Conciliation Courts Review* 73 (1981) (mandatory) mediation in California) and G. Davis, A. MacLeod and M. Murch, "Divorce and the Resolution of Conflict," 79 *Law Society's Gazette* 40 (1982).

10. (1975), 21 R.F.L. 117 (B.C.S.C.).
11. *Ibid.*, 120.
12. H. Finlay, "Defining the Informal Marriage," 3 *University of New South Wales Law Journal* 279 (1980).
13. Miller and Sarat, *supra*, note 3 at 564.
14. *Newsweek*, December 2, 1968, 90.
15. *Ibid.*, 92. See also note 19, *infra*.
16. See M. Shubik, *Readings in Game Theory and Political Behavior* 1-11 (1954), O.R. Young, *Bargaining* (1975).
17. A. Douglas, "The Peaceful Settlement of Industrial and Intergroup Disputes" (1957), 1 *Journal of Conflict Resolution* 69, at 74.
18. G. Nierenberg, *The Art of Negotiating* 19 (1968).
19. M. G. Hermann and N. Kogan, "Effect of Negotiators' Personalities on Negotiating Behavior" in D. Druckman (ed.) *Negotiations* (1977). See also J. Z. Rubin and B. R. Brown, *The Social Psychology of Bargaining and Negotiation* Ch. 7, 158-96 (1975).
20. H. T. Edwards and J. J. White, *The Lawyer as a Negotiator* Ch. 3 "Negotiating Techniques," 112-41 (1977).
21. R. S. Weiss, "The Emotional Impact of Marital Separation" in G. Lovinger and O. C. Moles (ed.) *Divorce and Separation* (1979), F. W. Kaslow "Stages of Divorce: A Psychological Perspective" (1979), 25 *Villanova Law Review* 718; N. Perlberger "Marital Property Distribution: Legal and Emotional Considerations" (1979), 25 *Villanova Law Review* 662.
22. J. M. Livermore, "Lawyer Extortion," 20 *Arizona Law Review* 403, (1978).
23. *Biafore v. Biafore* (1980), 20 R.F.L. (2d) 409 (O.S.C.); *Andrews v. Andrews* (1980), 120 D.L.R. (3d) 252 (O.C.A.); *Vance v. Vance* (1981), 128 D.L.R. (3d) 109 (B.C.S.C.).
24. H. McIsaac, "Mandatory Conciliation Custody/Visitation Matters: California's Bold Stroke," 19 *Conciliation Courts R.* 73 (1981).

Chapter Three

Wife Sale and Desertion as Alternatives to Judicial Marriage Dissolution

Katherine O'Donovan

University of Kent
Canterbury, England

The current period of change in legal regulation of marriage and divorce has been described as "a return to forms of social control other than legal rules concerning the formation, dissolution and organization of married life."[1] If this is correct, and the case has been persuasively made out, then it may be that lessons can be learned from previous experiences of informal marriage dissolution in England. The specific examples are the custom of wife sale which was practised over a period of about a thousand years, and desertion which continues today. A recent ethnographic study of sale of wives has brought together cases, including some from the twentieth century, in a comprehensive volume.[2] The custom was known to scholars in the nineteenth century, who regarded it with a mixture of horror and amusement.[3]

This article does not intend to suggest that there will be a return to earlier customs in the course of future delegalization of marriage and divorce; each age has its own ways of handling its trouble cases. Conditions which produced a custom such as wife sale are not likely to be reproduced. Nevertheless, the past can be a guidance to the future, and the aim of this article is to point to certain constant features of human behaviour and the human psyche, which must be taken into account in any future movement towards extrajudicial marriage dissolution.

THE CHANGE

Professor Glendon has argued that the current process of dejuridification and deregulation of marriage is gradual, and has involved a long period of discontinuity between social and legal phenomena. The state is redefining what is law and what is non-law. Social conduct has "gradually been pulling away from the law, treating the law as irrelevant. Now the law is pulling away from social conduct, leaving questions ... increasingly in the private order."[4] What the historical evidence suggests is that the period when social conduct and law were in harmony was a relatively short period in the mid-twentieth century.

Private ordering of marriage by contract *per verba de praesenti* or *per verba de futuro* was recognized in England until 1753, and lived on in folk custom for much longer.[5] The current practice of cohabitation outside legal marriage, with or without contract, is a return to this custom.[6] There is a major difference, however, between the unlegalized past and the delegalization of today. At present, cohabiting couples can fall back on the law to regulate the breakdown of their relationship, if they cannot do so by private negotiation. On matters such as custody of children and property division the courts can be relied upon to settle a dispute between cohabitants. So it is also with divorce. In the case of customary institutions of the past, such as wife sale, there was private ordering to a degree unknown today. Wife sale was outside the law; indeed a few participants were subjected to criminal sanction.[7] Today's private ordering of divorce takes place above a legal safety net. Despite this major difference, I think that certain cautionary lessons can be learned from the past.

WIFE SALE AS PRIVATE ORDERING

"Let the husband send her packing" was advocated as the remedy for adultery in the eighteenth century.[8] The practice of walking out on an unsatisfactory spouse and of remarrying without further ado seems to have been common in the unregulated England of the past.[9] Some sought a more public, more explicit termination of their union. The classic example, from Thomas Hardy's *Mayor of Casterbridge*, was the sale by Michael Henchard of his wife for five guineas.[10] Sale at a fair or a market is the most common form of sale recorded. Usually this was an auction conducted by a cattle dealer. The practice appears to have resulted from the unavailability of divorce to the people: either prior to the introduction of judicial divorce in 1857, or because of the cost thereafter.[11] But there was also a tradition of self-regulation of personal relations, as can be shown by looking at marriage contracts.

A variety of forms of marriage was available in England until the passing of *Lord Hardwicke's Act* in 1753. Although the state, through the agency of the church, eventually succeeded in gaining control over marriage, self-regulated marriage was accepted as valid prior to 1753.[12]

Marriage contracts *per verba de futuro* or *per verba de praesenti* were made by the spouses themselves, without outside supervision or interference. Where the transmission of property was not the major object of the marriage, regulation by authority was unnecessary. What was desired was community acceptance of the union, and the opinion of neighbours was the important factor.[13] Even after 1753 couples continued to "marry" privately. In many cases this was because of ignorance of the law. Some cases arose for religious reasons, for instance where dissenters and catholics continued to marry according to their consciences, rather than according to law. There were also those who did not wish to be bound by the legal effects of marriage. Some women maintained common-law practice as a way of retaining a separate legal identity.[14] The view is expressed by Gillis that the legal regulation of marriage by the state through legislation represented "an undisguised triumph of property, patriarchy, and male dominance generally."[15]

Was wife sale self-regulated divorce similar to common-law marriage? Let us look at some instances:[16]

> *The Times,* March 30, 1796:
> On Saturday last, John Lees, Stellburner, sold his wife for the small sum of 6d. to Samuel Hall, a fell-monger, both of Sheffield. Lees gave Hall one guinea immediately, to have her taken off to Manchester the day following by the coach: she was delivered up with a halter round her neck, and the clerk of the market received 4d. for toll.
>
> *The Times,* July 18, 1797:
> On Friday a butcher exposed his wife to sale in Smithfield Market, near the Lane Inn, with a halter about her neck, and one about her waist, which tied her to a railing, when a hog-driver was the happy purchaser, who gave the husband three guineas, and a crown, for his departed rib.
>
> *The Times,* September 19, 1797:
> An Hostler's wife, in the country, lately fetched *twenty-five guineas*. We hear there is to be a sale of wives soon at Christie's. We have no doubt they will go off well.

The first recorded instance is of gift rather than sale. During the reign of Edward I, Sir John de Camoys made a gift, by grant under seal, of his wife with her goods and chattels, to Sir William Paynel, "spontanea voluntate mea." On Sir John's death the couple married, and the wife then claimed dower from the estate of her former husband. This was denied by the King's courts in 1302, on grounds of the wife's adultery.[17] From this early example of informal ordering of personal relations, we can establish that the courts did not accept wife gift or sale as dissolution of legal marriage. And there is no evidence to suggest that the courts subsequently accepted such a contractual ending of marriage. So, in the cases of the propertied persons, who had recourse to the King's courts on matters of dower and land, evidence of institutional supervision of the dissolution (and celebration)[18] of marriage was insisted upon.

Despite this lack of legal recognition, wife sale flourished as an informal custom in England, indeed in the British Isles generally, for a period of about five hundred years. Ecclesiastical prosecutions became evident in the sixteenth and seventeenth centuries. In 1696 Thomas Heath came before the ecclesiastical court, presented by the churchwardens of Thame, for living in sin with the wife of George Fuller, "having bought her of her husband at 2¼d. the pound."[19] Wife sales at inns were prevalent for about a hundred and sixty years from 1730 to 1890.[20]

In what sense can wife sale be said to be private ordering? In a divorceless society it enables self-termination of marriage or of cohabitation, without supervision by the law, and with little expense. Current discussion of private ordering by Mnookin and Kornhauser is of a different nature.[21] It presupposes a regulation of the postdivorce state by laws concerning custody of and access to children, property relations and financial support. In Mnookin's world of private ordering, the role of the law is to act as a safety net where the negotiations between the parties fail. In that past world, there was no legal back-up for the institution of wife sale, no arbitrator for the couple to refer their differences to; it was genuine private ordering.

Mnookin gives the term "private ordering" to the "process by which parties to a marriage are empowered to create their own legally enforceable commitments."[22] This bargaining takes place against a legal backdrop. Legal provisions which give guidance to the divorcing couple as to how to order their affairs are crucial to the agreement that is reached. It is true that the law does not attempt to minimize private ordering, as it did earlier in this century, but nevertheless the outcome of the bargaining process is influenced by the "legal rules that allow the imposition of a particular allocation if the parties fail to reach agreement."[23] Thus, each party's bargaining position depends on its beliefs about how the matter would be decided in court. The question of belief was also crucial to wife sale, as the evidence suggests that most participants believed in the legality of the transaction. But before turning to specific features of similarity between modern private ordering and wife sale, such as belief and bargaining power, general explanations of the institution must be considered.

EXPLANATIONS

The most frequently offered explanation for wife sale is that it legitimated, in social terms, an adulterous relationship. The author of *The Laws Respecting Women* of 1777 stated:

> if the man has a mind to authenticate the intended separation by making it a matter of public notoriety, thinking with Petruchio, that his wife is his goods and chattels,

he puts a halter around her neck, and thereby leads her to the next market place, and there puts her up to auction to be sold as though she was a brood-mare or a milch-cow. A purchaser is generally provided beforehand on these occasions; for it can hardly be supposed that the *delicate* female would submit to public indignity, unless she was sure of being purchased when brought to market.[24]

Pillet, a French observer of the custom, agreed: "The purchaser, always a widower or a youth, is usually a connoisseur of the merchandise for sale, who knows her; one only presents her at market as a matter of form."[25] But many examples are available of sales where there was no purchaser,[26] of sales where the purchaser was a stranger,[27] and of sales where the purchaser was married.[28]

The transaction was perceived by the participants as the equivalent of divorce. In a society where divorce was unobtainable by ordinary people, it is not surprising that such a practice should have developed. Civil divorce was introduced only in 1857 and remained unobtainable to the mass of people until much later. Recourse to the ecclesiastical courts was hedged about with formal requirements, evidence and expense, and in any case, divorce as such was not granted. For rich men, a private Act of Parliament could be obtained in order to divorce.[29]

There is also evidence of a rejection by ordinary people of the conventions of the law. As earlier stated, common-law marriages in the form of folk customs such as "besom weddings" or "living tally" persisted long after they had been outlawed by statute.[30] Henry Mayhew found that legal marriage was exceptional among London costermongers.[31] Besom weddings provided for both self-marriage and self-divorce. The couple to be married jumped over a besom broom into the open door of the house in front of witnesses. If divorce was desired the couple jumped backwards over the broom.[32]

Economic motives can also be discerned in the accounts of wife sale: "the husband ... as he imagines, at once absolves her and himself from all the obligations incident to marriage," according the *The Laws Respecting Women.*[33] It was commonly believed that the sale transferred the wife as an economic burden from her husband to the purchaser. Kenny's view was that the purchaser insisted on the transaction in order to protect himself from an action for damages from criminal conversation by the husband. The sale was evidence of condonation of adultery by the husband which was a defence against later legal suit.[34]

Public sale also served the purposes of a *rite de passage* for the parties. Mnookin tends to discount the importance of ceremony to the parties, but other research shows that spouses were taken aback and disappointed at the lack of ceremony and speed of divorce.[35] In the case of desertion by a spouse there was no ceremony, but that does not seem to have impeded the formation of a new relationship. Yet ceremonial rites were considered necessary to those couples who had married during the

Napoleonic wars thinking that the soldier-husband of the wife had been killed in action. On the original husband's return a sale took place to legitimate the new relationship. This practice was frequent during 1815 and 1816; the authorities closed their eyes to it.[36]

Engels laid down a distinction between bourgeois marriage, in which the wife sells herself for financial security, and proletarian relationships based on love:

> The proletarian family is no longer monogamous in the strict sense, even where there is passionate love and finest loyalty on both sides and maybe all the blessings of religious and civil authority. Here, therefore, the eternal attendants of monogamy, hetaerism and adultery, play only an almost vanishing part. The wife has in fact regained the right to dissolve the marriage, and if two people cannot get on with one another, they prefer to separate. In short, proletarian marriage is monogamous in the etymological sense of the word, but not at all in its historical sense.[37]

This might be taken as a description of contemporary marriage in the West, but the point is that in Victorian England freedom to desert a spouse was possessed by the working class.

BELIEFS

In *R. v. Delaval* Lord Mansfield stated:

> I remember a cause in the Court of Chancery, wherein it appeared that a man had formally assigned his wife over to another man: and Lord Hardwicke directed a prosecution for that transaction, as being notoriously and grossly against public decency and good manners. And so is the present case . . . .[38]

Notwithstanding this direct statement of the illegality of wife sale, and other prosecutions of the practice, the participants seem to have believed in its legality. The *Record* newspaper of Dudley for August 26, 1859 reported a case where the "husband, in his ignorance thinks — and this repeated three times — she has actually no claim on him."[39] Mrs. Dunn of Ripon in Yorkshire in 1881 said: "Yes I was married to another man, but he sold me to Dunn for twenty-five shillings and I have it to show in black and white, with a receipt stamp on it, as I did not want people to say I was living in adultery."[40] Some believed that sale was the equivalent of legal separation. Others saw it as a transfer of partner, the new husband "stepping into the shoes" of the old.[41]

> August 31, 1773, Samuel Whitehouse of the parish of Willenhall, in the country of Stafford, this day sold his wife Mary Whitehouse in open Market, to Thomas Griffiths of Birmingham, *Value One Shilling*. To take her with all faults.
> Signed   Samuel Whitehouse
> Mary Whitehouse.[42]

Some agreements were signed by witnesses. The amount of the toll was occasionally disputed and the *Brighton Herald* of May 27, 1826 gives the following entry in the Brighton Market Book:

> May 17, 1826, Mr. Hilton of Lodsworth publicly sold his wife for 30/= upon which the toll of one shilling was paid.

The Magistrates sent for the toll collector to justify the toll charge and he at once referred the bench to the market by-laws as follows: "Any article not enumerated in the by-laws pays one shilling."[43]

In the private ordering of personal relations beliefs are crucial to the parties' scope of action. Although Mnookin tends to dismiss the argument that the spouses may lack knowledge of rights and entitlements under the law, yet this is a real possibility; and so is the problem of the knowing spouse who takes advantage of the other's ignorance.[44]

BARGAINING

Rules, it is agreed, are bargaining counters in private negotiations. We have already seen that beliefs about rules are crucial to the scope of argument before the bargain is struck. Without rules, will not the strong overpower the weak? Should not the rules protect the weak and create an equality of bargaining power? If so, then the rules, as standards for the negotiation process, are essential. But just as the parties do not bargain in a vacuum, but rather in the shadow of the law, so too the rules do not exist in a vacuum. The rules are a reflection of policy decisions, public opinion, the values of the community, etc. They exist in a cultural context. It is to an examination of that cultural context that we next turn. This will be done by looking at the context of wife sale and then at the context of those legal bargaining counters of today.

The Victorians expressed shock, horror and outrage at Hardy's novel. They denied the existence of wife sale, in spite of newspaper reports.[45] Yet Menefee has discovered nearly four hundred reported cases and, given the lack of interest in the ways of the common folk, these were surely not all.[46] The custom was regarded as degrading and brutal. As a reflection of the powerlessness of the wife, even where she agreed to the sale, the practice clearly shows vulnerability and economic dependence.

In Islamic law, a wife who does not please her husband can be sent back to her own kin. Islamic marriage dissolution is one of the great examples of extrajudicial divorce. In countries such as Egypt, Tunisia and Somalia which have reformed the law of divorce, the direction taken has been towards legislative and judicial control.[47] This change in family law has been away from individual control and private ordering toward state control. It is not intended to suggest that increased private ordering in

English or American divorce would result in an institution such as wife sale or *talaq*, but it is being suggested that a genuine bargain presupposes equality of bargaining power. Equality of bargaining power on divorce depends on a range of matters including preferences of the parties, their economic resources, financial incentives or disincentives, legal constraints, and the cultural context in which the bargaining takes place.

If we consider the cultural context in which wives were sold in the market place or at inns, inequality soon becomes apparent. A man at Baylham, Suffolk, "having a disagreement with his wife" sold her to a local farmer.[48] The *Gentleman's Magazine* reported the exchange of a wife for an ox at Parham fair, in Norfolk; the wife "was delivered to the grazier with a new halter round her neck, and the husband received the bullock, which he afterwards sold for six guineas."[49] In this case the sale was the result of a chance encounter. In East Lothian a sale was explained thus:

> they being together in John Wood his house drinking and speaking anent fieing of shearers; in the mean tyme James Steill his wife came in, and they fell to speaking anent her; but they all deponed that they cannot tell how that purpose began, but grants that in ane idle toy or merriment the one did sell his wife . . .[50]

The advertising that accompanied the sale is another indication of the powerlessness of the merchandise. An advertisement in 1796 stated:

> To be sold for *five shillings*, my wife, Jane Hebland. She is stout built, stands firm on her posterns, and is sound wind and limb. She can sow and reap, hold a plough, and drive a team and would answer any stout able man, that can hold a *tight rein*, for she is damned *hard mouthed* and headstrong; but, if properly managed would either lead OR drive as tame as a rabbit. She now and then, if not watched, will make a *false step*. Her husband parts with her because she is too much for him. — Enquire of the Printer. N.B. All her body clothes will be given with her.[51]

The halter was the symbol of the yoke of servitude. Its use parallelled the manner in which cattle and other animals were sold at fairs. The following report from the *Doncaster Gazette* of March 25, 1803 confirms the association with livestock property:

> The lady was put into the hands of a butcher, who held her by a halter fastened round her waist. "What do you ask for your cow?" said a bye-stander. "A guinea" replied the husband. "Done" cried the other, and immediately paid the money, and led away his bargain. We understand that the purchaser and his cow live very happily together.[52]

But it seems that public opinion swung against such practices, for ten years later the *Doncaster Gazette,* reporting another sale informed its readers that the populace pelted the participants with snow and mud.[53]

One husband "with the greatest satisfaction and good humour imaginable, proceeded to put the halter which his wife had taken off, round the neck of his Newfoundland dog. . . ."[54] A French visitor to Smithfield, in 1816, reported that a husband who was holding his wife by a cord around her neck allowed her to be inspected by a prospective purchaser "comme il avait examiné quelques instants auparavant une jument que je l'avais vu marchander."[55]

Not all wives were powerless or complaisant. *The Farmer's Journal* of May 5, 1810 tells the following tale:

> A young man in Bewcastle, Cumberland, who was not on good terms with his wife, resolved a few days ago to dispose of her by auction. Not being able to find a purchaser in the place where they resided, she persuaded him to proceed to Newcastle for that purpose. Accordingly they set out, and this modern Dalilah laid her plan so well, that immediately on his arrival a pressgang conveyed him on board frigate preparing to get under weigh for a long cruise.[56]

The context in which bargaining prior to termination of marriage or cohabitation takes place is also one of inequality. Cultural attitudes influence the outcome of the issue of child custody, with mothers obtaining custody, care and control in the great majority of cases. In England, at least, this is so marked a feature that the uninformed observer might reasonably conclude that there is a maternal preference rule.[57] At the same time a myriad of structures in tax law, social security law, and family law impose on the husband the role of family breadwinner.[58] A great deal has already been written on gender inequality within the family and it is unnecessary to prove the case again.[59] It must be emphasized that this is not just a matter of legal structures, but also real inequalities deeply embedded in the way in which we live.

Before we proceed too far along the road of private ordering of family relationships, we need to examine the structures and the constraints which surround it. Otherwise there will be a perpetuation of existing inequalities of bargaining power. These will merely move from the public gaze into the shadows.

NOTES

1. Glendon, Mary Ann, *State, Law and Family*, Amsterdam: North Holland Publishing Co., 1977, 321.
2. Menefee, Samuel Pyeatt, *Wives for Sale*, Oxford: Basil Blackwell, 1981.
3. See *Notes and Queries*, Vol. 175, Series 15, 1938, 314 for a list of all the references to wife sale in *Notes and Queries* for the nineteenth and twentieth centuries.
4. Glendon, *op. cit.*, note 1, at 321.

5. Gillis, John, "Resort to Common Law Marriage in England and Wales, 1700-1850" in *Law and Human Relations,* Past and Present Society, 1980.
6. E.g. Bottomley, A., Gieve, K., Moon, G., and Weir, A., *The Cohabitation Handbook,* London, Pluto Press, 1981. For an example from the past see *Notes and Queries,* Series 1, Vol. 7, 1853, 602.
7. *Notes and Queries,* Vol. 176, Series 15, 1939, 95.
8. Anon., *A Treatise Concerning Adultery and Divorce,* 1700, 38, quoted by Mueller, *infra.,* note 9, 563.
9. Mueller, G.O.W., "Inquiry into the State of a Divorceless Society," 18 *U. of Pittsburgh L. Rev.,* 1957, 545.
10. Hardy, Thomas, *The Mayor of Casterbridge,* London: Macmillan, 1920. At 9: "Will anybody buy her?" said the man. "I wish somebody would", said she firmly. "Her present owner is not to her liking!"
11. See McGregor, O.R., *Divorce in England,* London: Heinemann, 1957.
12. Helmholz, Richard, *Marriage Litigation in Medieval England,* Cambridge: University Press, 1974, ch. 2.
13. Laslett, P., *Family Life and Illicit Love in Earlier Generations,* Cambridge: University Press, 1977, 108.
14. Gillis, *op. cit.,* note 5, at 12.
15. *Ibid.*
16. See Ashton, John, *Old Times,* London: Nimmo, 1885, 342-43; Ashton, John, *The Dawn of the Nineteenth Century in England,* London: Fisher Unwin, 1886.
17. Kenny, Courtney, "Wife Selling in England," 45 *Law Quarterly Review,* 1929, 494; Rot. Parl. I, 140; Pollock and Maitland, *The History of English Law,* Vol. II, Cambridge: University Press, 1968, 395.
18. For dower to be payable, the marriage had to be celebrated *in facie ecclesiae.* Other marriages were recognized as valid but there was no dower. Pollock and Maitland, II, *op. cit.,* note 17, at 374.
19. Peyton, S.A. (ed.), *The Churchwardens' Presentments in the Oxfordshire Peculiars of Dorchester, Thame and Banbury,* Oxford Records Society, 1928, 184; quoted by Thomas, Keith, "The Double Standard," *Journal of the History of Ideas,* 1959, 213.
20. Menefee, *op. cit.,* note 2, at 46.
21. Mnookin, Robert and Kornhauser, Lewis, "Bargaining in the Shadow of the Law: The Case of Divorce," 88 *Yale L.J.,* 1979, 950.
22. Mnookin, Robert, "Bargaining in the Shadow of the Law," (1979) *Current Legal Problems,* at 65.
23. *Ibid.,* at 76.
24. Anon., *The Laws Respecting Women,* reprinted from the J. Johnson edition, London 1777, New York: Oceana, 1974, 55.
25. Pillet, R., *L'Angleterre Vue à Londres et dans ses Provinces,* Paris: Alexis Eymery, 1816; quoted by Menefee at 78.
26. *Notes and Queries,* Vol. 176, 1939, 95.
27. *Notes and Queries,* 3rd Series, Vol. 3, 1863, 486.
28. *Notes and Queries,* 1st Series, Vol. 7, 1853, 602; 6th Series, Vol. 3, 1881, 487.
29. Crouch, H., "The Evolution of Parliamentary Divorce in England," 52 *Tulane L. Rev.,* 1978, 513; McGregor, *op. cit.,* note 11, Ch. 1.
30. Gillis, *op. cit.,* note 5, at 2.
31. Mayhew, Henry, *London Labour and London Poor,* London, Griffin, 1864, Vol. 1, at 22.

32. Gillis, *op. cit.,* note 5, at 3.
33. Anon., *op. cit.,* note 24, at 55.
34. Kenny, *op. cit.,* note 17, at 495.
35. Elston, E., Fuller, J., and Murch, M., "Judicial Hearings of Undefended Divorce Petitions," 38 *Modern L. Rev.,* 1975, 609.
36. *Notes and Queries,* 3rd Series, Vol. 4, 1863, at 450; 3rd Series, Vol. 10, 1866, at 29.
37. Engels, F., *The Origin of the Family, Private Property and the State,* London: Lawrence and Wishart, 1972, 135.
38. (1763), 3 Burr. 1434, 96 E.R. 234.
39. *Notes and Queries,* 2nd Series, Vol. 8, 1859, at 258.
40. *Notes and Queries,* 6th Series, Vol. 4, 1881, at 133.
41. *Notes and Queries,* 4th Series, Vol. 10, 1872, at 469.
42. *Notes and Queries,* 3rd Series, Vol. 2, 1862, at 186.
43. *Notes and Queries,* 6th Series, Vol. 5, 1882, at 58.
44. In *Eves v. Eves,* [1975] 3 All E.R. 768, the plaintiff was a minor at the time of the purchase of the home for cohabitation. The defendant told her that, although he would have put the house in joint names had she been of full age, that because of her minority it would be conveyed into his name only.
45. Winfield, C., "Factual Sources of Two Episodes in *The Mayor of Casterbridge*," 25 *Nineteenth Century Fiction,* 1970, 224; Scudder, H.L., "Selling a Wife," *Notes and Queries,* Vol. 188, 1945, 123.
46. Menefee, *op. cit.,* note 2, appendix.
47. Pearl, David, *A Textbook on Muslim Law,* London: Croom Helm, 1979. Anderson, J.N.D., *Islamic Law in the Modern World,* Conn.: Greenwood Press, 1975.
48. Menefee, *op. cit.,* note 2, at 73.
49. *Notes and Queries,* 3rd Series, Vol. 3, 1863, 486.
50. Menefee, *op. cit.,* note 2, at 73.
51. *Ibid.,* at 75.
52. *Notes and Queries,* 2nd Series, Vol. 1, 420.
53. *Ibid.,* reporting from the *Doncaster Gazette* of February 3, 1815, on a sale at Pontefract.
54. Menefee, *op. cit.,* note 2, at 113.
55. Quoted in *Notes and Queries,* 4th Series, Vol. 10, 1872, at 469.
56. *Notes and Queries,* 3rd Series, Vol. 3, 1863, at 486.
57. See Eekelaar, J., and Clive E., *Custody After Divorce,* Oxford: Centre for Socio-Legal Studies, 1977.
58. See O'Donovan, K., "The Male Appendage — Legal Definitions of Women" in S.B. Burman (ed.) *Fit Work for Women,* London, Croom Helm, 1979.
59. A good summary is provided in Law Com. No. 103 *The Financial Consequences of Divorce: The Basic Policy,* London, HMSO, 1980, Cmnd. 8041.

Chapter Four

Some Aspects of Mediation and Conciliation in the Settlement of Matrimonial Disputes in Tanzania

Barthazar Rwezaura

University of Dar es Salaam, Tanzania

THE SOCIAL AND ECONOMIC CONTEXT OF DISPUTE PROCESS

Before considering mediation as a mode of dispute settlement in precolonial Tanzania, it is proper to state first what is meant by the term mediation, and how it will be used in this context. By mediation we mean the processing of disputes between two parties or groups whereby a third party intervenes in a dispute by invitation or at his or her own initiative to bring about the resolution of a dispute outside of state courts. This occurs through the application of a variety of skills which may range from a mere seeking of the basis of an agreement between the disputing parties to the imposition of a settlement through the invocation of political, moral, and or religious authority.

According to Gulliver (1969, 17) there are two major categories in which divers modes of dispute processes in precolonial Africa could be grouped. The first is what he calls "dispute settlement by negotiation between disputants each assisted by socially relevant supporters, representatives and spokesmen." Whether such negotiations are conducted on a face-to-face basis or through an intermediary, i.e., a mediator, the usual practice is for each side to seek to "exert what strength it can against the other, such strength ranging from forensic argument and skill to the threat of physical force, from moral pressure to offers or denials of other advantages" (1969, 17).

The second mode is dispute settlement "by adjudication" whereby an authoritative and binding decision is given by a third party. An adjudicator could be an individual or a group of people who have both the authority to settle a dispute brought before them, and the relative ability to enforce the decision. The coercive power to enforce an adjudicator's decision need not be overwhelming. As noted by Gulliver, "the ability to enforce may range from the virtually absolute to the little more than the effective public expression of accepted norms and standards of expectations in their application to a particular dispute." Thus, whatever degree of authority and power an adjudicator may have, enforcement of his decision is often reinforced, "to a greater or lesser extent by the additional pressures of diplomatic persuasion, inducement, moral stricture, and appeal to the supernatural."

Although Gulliver properly puts the two modes of dispute settlement into two discrete categories in order to analyse them, he recognizes their overlapping character. This is true particularly in respect of the enforcement methods. No such distinction is drawn here between the two modes of traditional dispute process. These two modes are in turn distinguished from adjudication procedures imposed by the colonial and later postcolonial states and enforced by official courts. The latter's decisions rely for enforcement upon the deployment of organized force, using state power. I emphasize the difference between the two modes of enforcement — i.e., the traditional and the externally imposed modes, mainly because certain important consequences flow from the invocation by parties of one or the other method of dispute settlement. Their expectations also are usually different. This distinction will become clear when I examine the social and economic context underlying disputes in precolonial Tanzania.

An understanding of the nature of disputes requires that a full grasp be had of the social, economic and political context out of which disputes arise. This is so because disputes are a product of human interaction and necessarily reflect the nature of a society. For some years now, some legal anthropologists have stressed that in order to understand a given dispute, one has to have some idea of both the social context out of which the dispute arises and the background to the dispute itself. Gulliver (1969, 15) has noted for example, that in order for a dispute to be meaningful, and particularly where such a dispute arises among societies in which status relations of a multiplex kind are dominant, "it is necessary to understand as fully as possible the previous development and the state of relations between the two parties, both dyadically and in their interconnection with other involved persons." According to Gulliver, this contextual understanding is essential because disputes which are "seemingly simple cases of theft, adultery, or slander may often be shown to be more complex, and more understandable in the context of prehistory."

Secondly, apart from understanding the "prehistory" of a case or cases, it is essential also to appreciate the wider social and economic context out of which various disputes emerge. Roberts (1979, 45-48) has argued, in support of the wider context approach, that issues about which people dispute depend largely "upon the beliefs that are held, the values subscribed to . . ., the forms of organization prevailing in the society" and the dominant economic activities in which such a society is engaged. Roberts stresses that within a group of nomadic hunter-gatherers, for example, "there may be little beyond questions of sexual access and the distribution of consumer perishables; whereas in other kinds of society tracts of scarce land, hoards of grain and large herds of stock may set the scene for significant quarrels over property."

In short therefore, the importance of the "context" in its wider social and political sense, and its narrow sense of a "prehistory" of a dispute, is extremely relevant for a correct understanding of disputes in any society at a given historical moment.

DISPUTES IN PRECOLONIAL TANZANIA

A significant aspect of the social and economic context of precolonial Tanzania is the kinship system and its organizational principle. Kinship ties provided a framework for production, allocation of essential resources, the recruitment of new members into the group and the care of the young and the infirm. Group consciousness and solidarity was considered to be the most important goal for all members, and status relations influenced the rights and obligations accruing to various members of the group. An individual "was important primarily as a member of a family or clan, bound by a web of reciprocal duties and obligations to the other members of the family or clan" (Tanganyika 1957, 2). Thus whether a given society was politically centralized or otherwise, (Gulliver 1963; Moore 1978, 181-213) kinship links were still important and were regularly deployed to legitimize or give weight to an individual's claims over others and vice versa.

Disputes emanating from such a social system often reflected important values held in that society as did the methods and procedures for settling such disputes. For example, the main principle underlying the settlement of disputes was to restore the equilibrium disturbed by a wrong committed against any member of the group. Herein is to be found the principle of conciliation which informs many precolonial legal systems throughout most of Africa. The aim of reconciliation was to restore wherever possible the good relations disrupted by the wrong or any act giving rise to the dispute. Such reconciliation was usually effected by applying the principle of compensation, the main aim of which was to try as much as possible to put the injured party back to his original position.

This also applied to intergroup disputes where the wrong was considered to have prejudiced the interests of all the members of the group.

The maintenance of good relations between parties in such societies was essential because important economic activities depended upon the understanding of all the members or at least the majority of them. Strained relations between groups threatened the outbreak of a war or any large-scale conflict, while interpersonal quarrels undermined essential activities of the group, such as production, ritual and defence. Speedy resolution of disputes was therefore seen to be the best way of maintaining social harmony.

To some extent the desire to achieve speedy settlement of disputes and the absence of specialized organs for the settlement of disputes encouraged the use of alternative dispute settlement institutions, all of which were *ad hoc* and informal. Disputes could be graded in terms of what was considered most serious in a given society. Disputes between husband and wife being perhaps the most frequent in any society were dealt with at the lowest level of society while those involving death of a family member and such like required the attention of higher institutions.

Family members are in particularly great need to resolve their disputes quickly in order to get on with the business of living together and managing their family affairs. Dispute settlement among spouses may be undertaken by the spouses themselves through negotiation, failing which some close members of the household group may be contacted for mediation. A clan or household head performed these functions as part of his overall responsibility for his household, and his authority and influence was often used to help him in the settlement of disputes among his family.

Conflicts between people outside the family or clan organization were submitted to mediators selected by using other criteria, such as membership to an age-grade, a dancing group, a chiefdom or a work party. Ruel (1955, 137) has noted, concerning the Kuria system of social control, that "in order to understand how law and order was maintained in Kuria society we have to look at the indirect and sometimes subsidiary activities of the clan segments, of local 'gossip' groups, of the conclave and so on . . ." all of which process a variety of disputes from individual members or groups.

It may be said, therefore, that the status relationship of the potential parties to a dispute had influence on their choice of forum and very often the forum selected for mediation was one to which both parties or groups were associated. This mode of selecting a forum suggests, firstly, that the institution or person selected for the settlement of a dispute was likely to have an interest in resolving the dispute as amicably as possible. Secondly, his effectiveness depended often upon the influence he could exert upon the disputants, his skill in identifying the scope of the dispute and his ability to suggest a settlement acceptable to all parties. Thirdly, failure to have a dispute settled always led to the use of an alternative forum and possibly a change in the various negotiating tactics. In all cases, however, the parties tended to select a forum to which they were both associated. Thus, as Gulliver has argued, in societies where status relations of a multiplex kind dominate, the selection of a forum for the settlement of disputes follows very closely existing alliances and status relations, and any person possessing sufficient social influence is a potential mediator among groups or individuals associated with him in a particular way.

DISPUTES IN COLONIAL TANZANIA

Colonial rule had significant impact on existing structures of dispute settlement and on the disputes themselves. By transforming the traditional economy from one based on subsistence production to one geared towards production for the world markets, the colonial state transformed social and property relations. Politically, the colonial state reduced the power of the traditional political institutions by abolishing them or by incorporating them into the colonial state structure and thus regulating their activities. The imposition of colonial courts with a monopoly over the deployment of organized force further reduced the influence of traditional dispute institutions while enhancing that of the colonial state.

An assessment of the changes caused by the intervention of the colonial state in dispute settlement processes in Tanzania must consider in particular the response of the various people to these changes. Some researchers working on the effects of social change in Africa have viewed it as a process leading to the breakdown of traditional social relations and the adoption of western models and values. Others have viewed African social systems and economic structures as unchanging and resistant to change. Such approaches, however, have not fully considered the totality of the contemporary situation in Africa. For indeed African social systems contain both elements of change and stability which cannot be reduced to their former condition nor to the western European models from where the major forces of change have emanated (see Fitzpatrick, forthcoming). A new approach therefore, has to be found for understanding change in Africa and most of the Third World.

Lloyd's earlier assessment of social change in Africa has stressed an important dimension which is relevant to a study of the transformation of disputes and dispute processes in colonial and postcolonial Tanzania. He argues that we must see "traditional institutions in terms of conflicts and competitions between individuals and groups as changing conditions are exploited to achieve [either] the goals of the indigenous society . . . [or those of the world beyond the traditional sphere]" (1972, 93–94).

In trying to understand the transformation of disputes and dispute processes in the colonial period and after, I apply the approach suggested by Lloyd. The imposition of the colonial legal system on indigenous societies, for example, must not be seen as necessarily supplanting the traditional dispute settlement institutions, but rather as providing additional and alternative institutions capable of performing the same functions. According to this approach, parties are viewed as deploying both traditional and state institutions to gain tactical advantages in the course of a single dispute. For example, a dispute taken to a state court, where sanctions are feared to be heavy, may be soon withdrawn for settlement in a traditional forum. The purpose of taking such a dispute to state courts in the first place could be designed to compel the other party to agree to settle out of court. Even the mere threat of taking a dispute to court may be used to settle the same dispute informally because of the fear of the costs and other consequences of adjudication in state courts. In an age of science and world religions, where traditional sanctions such as the fear of witchcraft could be easily ignored, a difficult disputant may be readily moved by a suggestion that state courts might be utilized. In such cases state courts may be used not only to gain rights in the traditional judicial field, but also may be combined with other traditional sanctions to gain an edge over the opponent in a dispute. Thus the creation of state courts during the colonial period widened the options of individual disputants under conditions where the traditional and the modern institutions were viewed by parties as a single and somewhat integrated arena.

But as the intervention of the colonial state in the economy and social life intensified and the local people became more familiar with the colonial officials, they saw them as suitable arbiters in their various interpersonal disputes (Joelson 1920, 160–72; Baker 1935, 111). Also the colonial officials agreed to hear these disputes mainly as a means of getting to know the people they governed. A District Commissioner visiting a remote part of his district, not having stationery or the services of a secretary would be met by a number of people anxious to present their disputes to him for mediation. He had to settle these disputes in the "traditional" way. And those disputes he could not hear were subsequently taken to his *boma,* i.e., the district office. Eventually people came to believe that the district office was a place to go to if one had a dispute to settle. As DuBow has noted, the coalescence of judicial and political power in the administrative officer led to the "popular impression that the *boma* was the place to go to if one wanted something done" (1973, 191).

THE INSTITUTIONAL FRAMEWORK FOR THE SETTLEMENT OF DISPUTES IN THE POST-INDEPENDENCE PERIOD

The post-independence state officials took over a practice which had started during the colonial period. They became involved in mediation not because it was part of their official duties but as a simple response to an existing need (DuBow 1973, 204). In the eyes of the local community, mediation by state officials was a continuation of the practice begun in the colonial era; the government official, however, found this to be a diversion from duties. He nonetheless offered the needed services because it was hard to resist the request to mediate by people who had shown such trust in him. In Arusha area, for example, DuBow (1973) found that "[t]he Area Commissioner who holds the highest administrative and political position in the district, estimates that forty percent of his time is taken up with inter-personal and inter-group disputes." Officials below him spent even much more time on these disputes.

In order to save the valuable time of the senior state officials the state moved into the arena of mediation with the intention of regulating what had hitherto been a free area from which individual disputants selected their *fora* as they saw fit. The exercise of regulation was begun by creating institutions specially designed for the functions of mediation. Although other institutions, such as the party cell, were formed to discharge party functions in the rural areas, they soon became incorporated into the arena of informal mediation. These institutions constitute the basic framework of state sponsored bodies concerned with mediation. They are considered below in chronological order.

The Party Cell

The ten-house cell system came into existence following a decision of the National Conference of the ruling party — TANU, as it was then called. The cell consists of ten households and is headed by an elected chairman popularly known as *Balozi*. It is the party's primary organ and its chairman is a delegate of his cell at the party branch annual conference.

The functions of the cell chairman are twofold: on the one hand he performs duties essentially involving the party activities such as keeping record of all party members in his cell, collecting party subscriptions, and encouraging nonmembers to join the party. The cell chairman is expected to explain to the people the policies of the party and the government and to encourage them to observe these policies and directives. On the other hand he articulates the views and opinions of his members and communicates them to the party branch and the government.

Apart from representing the party at this level, the chairman has other duties of general importance to all the cell members. He ensures that law and order is observed in his cell by seeing to it that all laws and regulations are observed. To discharge this function, the cell chairman is assisted by all the cell members who are expected to report to him all important matters affecting the cell. As succinctly put by Moore, the cell chairman "is supposed to be informed of all events of importance in his cell: birth, death, marriage, divorces, crimes, altercations of all kinds, and the like" (1978, 73).

From the nature of their duties the cell leaders are expected to, and do in fact, mediate in almost all disputes involving the people they represent. Researches conducted in parts of Tanzania concerning the activities of the cell leader have shown that "[o]f all the functions performed by the cell leaders, the one which takes most time is handling disputes between cell members" (Njohole 1975, 4; see also DuBow 1973, 197–8; Quorro 1975, 54; Mshangana 1975, 25; Kawago 1975, 58; Kokwebangira 1975, 47). As Njohole has noted, it is "a common practice now all over mainland Tanzania that all cases, minor and major, must first be reported to one's cell leader before they reach the courts." Similar observation has been made by DuBow in his study of Arusha. He states that "[t]here can be little doubt that the hearing of disputes by cell leaders is widely accepted."

The Arbitration Tribunals

The Arbitration Tribunals were established in 1969 under the *Magistrates Court (Amendment) Act, 1969*. The Act empowers the Minister for Justice to establish one or more Arbitration Tribunals in each ward throughout Tanzania. The Tribunal consists of up to five members appointed by the local branch of the ruling party. Any Tanzanian aged thirty years or older, and not being a member of parliament, the judiciary, civil service or the local authorities, may be appointed to the Tribunal for a renewable term of one year. The appointment or reappointment of the Tribunal members may be vetoed by the Regional Party Secretary who also has powers to remove any member if "he is satisfied that it is undesirable for such appointee to remain a member of the Tribunal." The Tribunal members are free to elect a chairman from among themselves.

The function of the Arbitration Tribunal is to hear all disputes submitted to it by any person residing in the ward and to assist the disputants in arriving at an amicable agreement. Its jurisdiction is derived from the parties' consent, which is also an essential condition to the enforcement of the final settlement. Once the parties have consented to the terms of the settlement, the Tribunal shall issue a certificate to the parties setting out the terms of the settlement. Once this certificate has been issued it cannot be challenged by either party to the dispute unless such challenge is based on the ground that either party did not consent to the terms of the final settlement. The local primary court has jurisdiction to determine any disputes concerning this aspect of the Tribunal's work.

In such cases the court has powers to set aside the settlement and hear the dispute *de novo*. Where the dispute brought before the Tribunal cannot be resolved, the Tribunal shall report that fact to the primary court or advise the parties to do so themselves.

There are no set procedural rules to be observed by the Tribunal in discharging its functions, but its hearings must be public unless good cause exists to hold them *in camera*. Any member of the Tribunal having pecuniary or other interest in the dispute is automatically disqualified from participating in the proceedings.

The Marriage Conciliatory Boards

Under section 102 of the *Law of Marriage Act,* the Minister is empowered to establish in every ward one or more Boards to be known as "a Marriage Conciliatory Board." Where the Minister is satisfied that any community in Tanzania has established for itself a committee or body of persons to perform the functions of a Marriage Conciliatory Board and that it is desirable that such committee or body of persons be designated to be the Board having jurisdiction over members of that community, the Minister may so designate such committee.

Every Board is headed by a chairman assisted by two or more persons. Under section 103 of the Act, the membership of the Board must not exceed six members including the chairman. In parts of the country where a Board does not exist, a local Arbitration Tribunal (already considered) is authorized to act as the Board and may exercise all powers as if it were a Board formed under the Act (GN 196/71; GN 211/71).

The Board has jurisdiction to hear matrimonial disputes between couples residing within the local ward. In the case of a community Board, including those formed by various religious groups, jurisdiction is based on membership of that community or religious body. The Board to which a matrimonial dispute has been referred has power to require the attendance of the parties and their witnesses. Where a person is summoned by the Board but fails to appear, the Board may apply to the primary or District court to issue a summons requiring such person to appear before the said Board. And further failure to appear before the board, "shall constitute contempt of court and be punishable accordingly."

The Board's duty is to attempt to reconcile the parties using all the mediation skills at its disposal. It may adjourn the proceedings as often as circumstances demand. Should the Board fail to resolve the matrimonial dispute referred to it to the satisfaction of the parties, "it shall issue a certificate setting out its findings" and may attach to the certificate such recommendations which are relevant to the dispute, as it may think fit.

This certificate constitutes necessary evidence and a condition to the institution of divorce proceedings in any court in Tanzania. The Boards, like the Arbitration Tribunals, are not expected to observe any predetermined procedural rules, and no advocates are permitted to appear before them for purposes of representing any disputant.

Since the post-independence period, the operation of the above institutions was buttressed by a policy of encouraging disputants to use the lowest institution first before moving on to a higher forum. It has now become a practice for all disputants to begin the process of mediation at the cell level and then to move on to the party branch and later to the district office. The Arbitration Tribunals are much used and their intermediate location between the cell and the primary court means that parties have an additional forum for mediation before they go on to court. In most cases disputes of a political nature are handled by the party organs up to the district and regional levels and those which are personal are referred to the Arbitration Board. Before the establishment of the Marriage Conciliatory Boards there were no separate institutions concerned with matrimonial disputes. Consequently, some marital disputes were processed by the Arbitration Tribunals, and other non-adjudicatory institutions. Since 1971 however, spouses have been strongly advised to use these Boards.

The legal importance of these Boards is that spouses wishing to obtain a decree of divorce or any matrimonial relief after divorce, cannot do so without first referring their dispute to these Boards. Under section 106(2) of the Act, "[e]very petition for a decree of divorce shall be accompanied by a certificate of the Board issued not more than six months before the filing of the petition." Where spouses select an out of court forum other than the Board for the settlement of their dispute, they are not subsequently exempted from this requirement if they should later wish to petition for divorce. In the case of *Isack Mwakyisyala v. Bupe Thomas,*[1] the wife, Bupe, successfully petitioned for divorce in a Dar es Salaam primary court without first referring the dispute to the Board. The couple had earlier on asked their families to reconcile them but this had failed. On appeal by the husband against the decision of the primary court, it was argued that the lower court lacked the jurisdiction to hear the petition for divorce since the wife had not referred the dispute to the Board. The High Court upheld the husband's ground of appeal and further criticized the lower court for failing to observe this requirement, adding that reference to the families of the couple was not sufficient to dispense with the Board. The appellate court stressed that there were "no family tribunals as such under the *Law of Marriage Act.* Nor could their purported role be implied."

The creation of the Boards had the effect of formalizing mediation procedures. Thus mediation at the level of the family, though still popular today, is not recognized by law as being adequate to enable the parties to petition for divorce without the support of a Board's certificate. Other mediation institutions such as the party cell and the local party branch which do settle many disputes between spouses are also not recognized as Boards. They may reconcile parties but they cannot issue valid certificates and they do not possess legal powers such as those granted to the Boards.

But since not all spouses desire to dissolve their marriages at the inception of a dispute their failure to use the Boards has not caused them much problem. For such spouses, the Board is one of many institutions to which matrimonial disputes are taken. A study I made in five regions of Tanzania, from 1975 to 1978, showed that most spouses living in rural areas took their marital disputes to relatives, friends, cell leaders, Arbitration Tribunals, and Church leaders. A few more referred their disputes to the local party branch but usually after having been to the cell chairman. Those residing in urban or semiurban areas used friends, employers, cell leaders, religious leaders and the Social Welfare office. The Social Welfare office has trained staff with limited powers to summon parties and to induce a settlement. Spouses who go to the Social Welfare office do so after having failed to resolve their disputes at the lower levels. In a sense these disputants consider the Welfare office as a stage much closer to the court and are often referred there when the dispute cannot be settled. This pattern of forum selection has been confirmed by a more recent study of Tarime District (Rwezaura 1982).

MEDIATION AS AN IDEAL PROCEDURE FOR THE SETTLEMENT OF MARITAL CONFLICTS IN CONTEMPORARY TANZANIA

Most people in Tanzania still consider mediation as an appropriate method for settling interpersonal disputes. This is shown by the extent to which even the state-sponsored institutions are heavily used. Indeed, it has been suggested that in some parts of the country state-sponsored institutions are currently handling many more disputes than traditionally based institutions (DuBow 1973, 197–99; Moore 1978, 203). This is certainly the case in Kuria society where, as far back as 1963, Chacha found that

> ... nowadays many people do not accept the decisions of the elders at first instance because they are not sure if justice has been done. That is why the Kuria people are so keen to appeal to higher authority so that no single tribe in Tanzania can surpass them (trans. BAR).

Mediation, whether conducted under the auspices of the state institution or under that of an indigenous-based institution, or indeed, by a village rich man, church leader or friend, has many advantages which appeal to many people. These advantages include the procedural informality which often distinguishes mediation from adjudication in state courts. However, I do not contend here that traditional procedures were not formal or even esoteric; I am merely suggesting that the procedure was known to all people and those who did not know it had spokesmen representing them at no cost. Secondly, the accessibility of the informal procedures has the advantage of sparing parties the expense of travelling long distances to appear before a court. They do not have to pay court fees and, very often, are not irrevocably bound by the settlement, as they are expected to participate in its formulation. Thirdly, in parts of the country where people do not speak the language of the court fluently, that is, Swahili, they are often reluctant to use courts, being unsure of the way of presenting their cases. This is true even though court interpreters are often employed; the procedure can be cumbersome and nerve-wracking.

To all this we must add the social cost of choice of forum. It has been suggested that "there is a general preference in all societies for settling disputes informally whenever possible" (Kawashima 1963, 41). This is true of many Tanzanian people. But, as noted by DuBow, adjudication in state courts in some societies is contemplated only with the greatest reluctance while in others it is more readily accepted. Thus the desire to settle out of court is dependent upon many factors, such as the parties involved, the nature of the dispute, the extent to which it has been going on, and the remedy desired.

What has been said above applies with greater relevance to matrimonial disputes that occur between spouses who are intimate and close to one another. The decision by one party to take a dispute to a forum beyond the family circle is done with great reluctance and only after initial attempts to mediate at the family or clan levels have failed utterly. Where one of the parties decides to take a dispute to a forum which is considered to be socially unacceptable, the other may refuse to appear, either as a protest against the other spouse's action or for fear of disclosing marital "secrets" in public — what has sometimes been called "washing one's dirty linen in public." Among the Haya people, for example, social pressure against a wife taking a dispute beyond the family is very great. My study of cases registered in two primary courts selected from two districts in Kagera region showed that over a nine-year period (1971–79), matrimonial disputes accounted for a small average of 5 percent. Where a Haya wife has children during her marriage, she usually fears that her husband will retaliate by prohibiting her from seeing them if she divorces him in court. She also fears gaining the reputation of a "court-goer" as such women are feared as well as hated. They are said to be "home-breakers" *(abatemi baamaka)* and their chances of remarriage could be very slim indeed. Thus, Haya wives keep away from state courts and try to resolve their disputes through mediation. When informal mediation fails, they quietly separate from their husbands wihtout a court divorce and, as a result, there are many women who, technically still married to their "former" husbands, are probably living with other men in the firm hope that their first marriage was dissolved under traditional law.

In contrast to the Haya situation, the Kuria study shows a different picture altogether. For example, cases examined in two primary courts in the area showed that over an eight-year period (1970–78), matrimonial disputes accounted for an average of 40 percent of all the disputes submitted to the two courts. About half of these involved claims for unpaid bridewealth between the father-in-law and son-in-law and claims for refund of marriage cattle in cases of divorce. The remaining half involved matrimonial disputes between spouses such as petitions for divorce, division of property and custody of children.

The differences between the Haya and the Kuria peoples over the use of courts in matrimonial disputes does not emanate entirely from the absence of social pressure in Kuria society against women taking disputes to the state courts. The major difference, in my view, is that in both cases, while men play a predominant role, in Haya society most men do not seek state court intervention in their marital disputes, while in Kuria society they do. This is partly because Haya men do not have a lot to lose by not going to court because in practice they can remarry without obtaining a divorce and usually do not claim refund of bridewealth as this is, on the average, negligible. The social pressure to settle disputes by mediation that is exerted on women extends to men who are expected to enforce it. Haya men think it is disgraceful (that is, *okugooka*) to take a wife to court. The desire not to spoil one's reputation acts as a deterrent against men using the court in matrimonial disputes. Even suing a former father-in-law for refund of bridewealth is considered disgraceful and could ruin the reputation of both the son-in-law and his family. A family which rushes to court to sue relatives is feared as well as hated. But this is only in the context of matrimonial disputes. For indeed, the Haya people, both male and female, are extremely litigious in land disputes and there is no social stigma attached to a man or woman suing for their land. Indeed, relatives sue one another more often than strangers on land matters. This is justified differently by saying that the protection of land rights is a supreme duty of every individual and more so when such land belongs to the clan.

On the other hand the Kuria who pay rather heavily for their wives, do not hesitate to sue in court. In the 1970s, the average bridewealth given for a Kuria wife was thirty head of cattle. Although this figure has fallen slightly in recent years, the amount of property transferred on marriage is large enough to create an irresistible temptation for husbands to seek court intervention in order to recover all or part of it. This is more so considering that very few fathers-in-law are prepared to give back any cattle on divorce without an order of the court. (Baker 1935, 113).

Kuria men, therefore, initiate divorces because they want to recover their cattle, whereas Haya men keep themselves and their wives out of court largely because little economic interest is involved. It is useful to add that Haya men can afford to be philosophical about the undesirability of court intervention in marital life, but if the law were to provide that on divorce a Haya wife should be given part of her husband's land, the Haya husband would be as eager to go to court as the Kuria.

FACTORS FAVORING THE USE OF THE ADJUDICATION PROCESS

There are three main factors that favour or encourage the use of the adjudication process in matrimonial disputes. The first is that most of the informal mediation institutions do not possess enforcement powers. This means that all settlements agreed upon depend mainly for their enforcement upon the willingness of both parties. Where one of the parties does not honour the terms of the settlement, courts are usually asked to intervene. Secondly, certain mediation institutions apply either traditional principles to the settlement of a dispute or are generally (and sometimes unconsciously) sympathetic to the traditional dominance of men. This makes such institutions unpopular with some women whose concern is to obtain equal rights in marriage. Such women find it oppressive that their marital relationship should continue to be governed by values and ideals which originated from the traditional society and are now largely inappropriate for the contemporary period. Finally, as mediation institutions are concerned with reconciling disputants, where this goal cannot be achieved and the dispute remains unresolved, a court of law appears to be the only possible legal alternative.

In order to illustrate this point, I shall take the example of marital disputes over property and show how courts in this context are viewed by women as the ideal forum for deciding disputes. Under most traditional laws, a man has no obligation to provide economic support for his former wife. This rule is based on the assumption, traceable to the precolonial period, that a woman should remarry soon after divorce. But should she remain unmarried, her economic needs must be met by her father's lineage who are expected to allocate to her sufficient land on which to grow food crops. Such a rule was not unreasonable in precolonial times when land was relatively abundant, and when subsistence needs were secured from agriculture and animal husbandry. Secondly, since there was little accumulation of property under subsistence economy, there was not much property to divide between spouses on divorce. Thirdly, as women were traditionally the main producers (Boserup 1970), the wife's departure resulted in the economic loss to the husband and it was considered wrong to require a man to support a divorced wife whose labour power was being transferred to her natal lineage or to that of her new husband.

Contemporary economic changes, however, have reduced the importance of the assumptions on which the rule exempting a man from providing economic support to his former wife were based. First, some women do not wish to remarry and yet they cannot obtain sufficient land at their natal homes upon which to grow food. In most societies women lack inheritance rights and hence face serious economic difficulties on divorce. The alternative of going into an urban centre to look for unskilled employment may be tolerable to a young woman but elderly divorced wives have very limited options of gaining an independent economic living. This situation makes many women aware of their economic insecurity and they are therefore more determined to obtain economic support from their former husbands.

Some recent cases concerning disputes over property between spouses show this trend very clearly. Some women state at the time that they should not be divorced without economic support from their husbands because they are too old to be useful to themselves. Others are keen to stress the purely economic aspect of their relationship, thus suggesting that the position of a husband is analogous to that of an employer. For example, Martha Robi sued her former husband Augustino Kinogo,[2] in a local primary court in Tarime district, claiming what she described as "a salary due to her as a former wife." The court awarded her a sum of Tshs. 180 but the former husband appealed against this order. In his memorandum of appeal, Augustino Kinogo expressed surprise as to why "the respondent should ask [him] to pay her a salary while she was [his] former wife." The couple had lived together for two years during which time the petitioner assisted her husband in running a family shop.

In another case, Silimina Aila[3] successfully sued her former husband, Odeny Okeny, claiming a sum of 800 shillings, estimated as the value of agricultural crops grown by the couple and left behind by the wife. She also claimed an additional 100 shillings for what she described vaguely as "the hard work she had been doing with her husband." Upon appeal against the lower court's order, the district court found that the additional claim was based on the wife's monetary evaluation of the marital sexual relations enjoyed by the couple during their two-year marriage. This claim was dismissed by the court, who noted that "every woman has a duty to ... share her love with her husband . . . [and] to perform all necessary domestic [duties] and she cannot claim payment when their marriage collapses." The third case concerns a wife who sued her former husband claiming "compensation of two head of cattle in respect of services she rendered as a wife."

What must be noted in all three cases is the fact that the applicants, all of whom were women, were applying for division of matrimonial property and maintenance after divorce. Due to lack of legal advice, however, most women do not know how to present their cases and, consequently, they appear to be claiming remedies which are not known at law, or if known, are not properly presented. But these wives were well aware that the economic undertakings in which they entered with their husbands usually led to the accumulation of assets and a share of such resources could only be obtained by applying to state courts. They were conscious of the fact that traditional dispute settlement institutions and others based in the local community were not appropriate bodies for this kind of dispute. Thus, although in the two preceding cases state courts did not grant the remedy, there is sufficient data on which to base the statement that courts are more willing to grant "nontraditional" remedies such as those wives were claiming than mediation *fora*.[4]

CONCLUSION

This chapter has shown that disputes and dispute settlement institutions are closely related to the social, economic and political context of a society. In precolonial Tanzania, interpersonal and group disputes were settled primarily through mediation. There were no specialized institutions for this function and disputants usually selected their forum on the basis of kinship relations or other status criteria.

Economic, political and social changes which were mainly the consequence of the process of colonization, affected the nature of disputes and the institutions concerned with dispute settlement. The colonial state intervened more intensively in social relations at a time when kinship relations were undergoing rapid transformation. The imposition of state courts and the takeover of indigenous political institutions by the colonial state created favourable conditions for a shift in the pattern of dispute settlement. Thus although most disputants continued to favour mediation as a more familiar and convenient mode of settlement, they increasingly invited the state agencies to mediate.

In the postcolonial period, the state intervened much more deeply into dispute settlement. It created special agencies for mediation and hence institutionalized the process which had hitherto not been externally regulated. In the sphere of marriage, special Boards were created to mediate between spouses and bring about a reconciliation. Indeed mediation through the Boards was made compulsory for spouses wishing to divorce. Furthermore state courts took over all the important matrimonial disputes such as divorce, separation and the granting of other matrimonial reliefs.

Although mediation as a process for the settlement of disputes continued to be the dominant mode throughout the colonial and postcolonial periods, there was a change in the pattern of dispute settlement. The major change was that traditional institutions lost most of their mediation functions to state agencies. This was inevitable given the extent of state intervention in social and economic relations and the loss of political power of the indigenous leadership.

Two significant features of this transformation are worth identifying. The first is that traditional institutions were not completely abandoned despite the changes. People may have utilized traditional organs less frequently than in the precolonial or early colonial periods, but they were used for mediation particularly at a lower stage of a dispute. Secondly, mediation as an indigenous mode of dispute settlement remained effective, albeit in a modified condition, and can be said to have partially survived up to the postcolonial period when the state decided to incorporate this mode into specialized structures. Thus the contemporary characteristic of mediation process, though increasingly becoming a function of state agencies, must be seen as a complex product of a dynamic interaction between an indigenous and an imposed political and legal system.

NOTES

1. Dar es Salaam High Court (PC) Matrimonial Appeal No. 25 of 1975, decided by Mwakibete J., 11 February 1976 (unreported).
2. Tarime District Court, Civil Case 130/68.
3. Tarime District Court, Civil Case 130/68.
4. For example, in 1973 a former wife was awarded Tshs. 4,400 by the High Court as a share of joint assets. The couple had been engaged in a fishing business since 1942, to which the wife had contributed Tsh. 200. In another case the High Court upheld an order granting a divorced wife Tshs. 3,300 "representing her contribution to the costs of erecting two houses and a hut during the subsistence of the marriage." *Abdallah Shante v. Mussa* (1972) H.C.D. n. 9.

REFERENCES

Baker, E.C. 1935. *The Bakuria of North Mara Tarime, Tanganyika Territory,* Manuscript available in the Library of the East African Institute of Social Research. Kampala, Uganda. Also available at Rhodes House, Oxford.
Boserup, E. 1970. *Women's Role in Economic Department.* Allen and Unwin.
Chacha, G.N. 1963. *Historia ya Abakuria na Sheria zao,* East African Literature Bureau, Dar es Salaam.
DuBow, F. L. 1973. *Justice for the People: Law and Politics in the Lower Courts of Tanzania,* Ph.D Thesis, University of California, Los Angeles.

Fitzpatrick, P. 1981. "Law, Plurality and Underdevelopment" in David Sugarman, Ed. *Legality Ideology, and the State*. Academic Press, London (Forthcoming).

Gulliver, P.H. 1969. "Case Studies of Law in Non-Western Societies" in Laura Nader, Ed. *Law in Culture and Society*. University of California, Berkeley.

Joelson, F.S. 1920. *Tanganyika Territory: Characteristics and Potentialities*. T. Fisher Unwin, London.

Kawago, K.S. 1975. "The Operation of TANU Cells in Iringa" in Proctor J. H., Ed. *The Cell System of the Tanganyika African National Union*, Tanzania Publishing House, Dar es Salaam.

Kawashima, T. 1963. "Dispute Resolution in Contemporary Japan" in A.T. von Mehren, Ed. *Law in Japan*, Harvard University Press, Cambridge.

Kokwebangira, R.M. 1975. "Cells in Dar es Salaam and Bukoba" in Proctor J.H., Ed. *The Cell System of the Tanganyika African National Union*. Tanzania Publishing House, Dar es Salaam.

Lloyd, P.C. *Africa in Social Change*. Penguin Books Ltd. Harmondsworth.

Moore, S.F. 1978. *Law as Process: An Anthropological Approach*. Routledge and Kegan Paul, London.

Mshagama, A.H. 1975. "TANU Cells: Organs of One-Party Democratic Socialism" in Proctor, J.H., Ed. *The Cell System of the Tanganyika African National Union*. Tanzania Publishing House, Dar es Salaam.

Njohole, B. 1975. "Building Party Cells in Tanzania" in Proctor J.H., Ed. *The Cell System of the Tanganyika African National Union*. Tanganyika Publishing House, Dar es Salaam.

Quorro, J.S. 1975. "Cell Leaders in Mbulu Mbulu and the Problems of Effectiveness" in Proctor J.H., Ed. *The Cell System of the Tanganyika African National Union*. Tanzania Publishing House, Dar es Salaam.

Roberts, S. 1979. *Order and Dispute: An Introduction to Legal Anthropology*. Penguin Books Ltd., Harmondsworths.

Ruel, M.J. 1958. *The Social Organization of the Kuria*. Fieldwork Report. (Available at the University of Nairobi.)

Rwezaura, B.A. 1982. *Social and Legal Change in Kuria Family Relations*, Ph.D. Thesis, University of Warwick School of Law.

Tanganyika, 1957. *Memoranda* (No. 2) (Local Courts) Government Printer, Dar es Salaam.

Part Two

Emerging Procedural Models

All through the industrialized world — and in some cases among African tribes — the movement, in one form or another, is sweeping toward escape from court proceedings into more humane and less painful methods of obtaining a divorce and settling the other problems attached to it: property division, maintenance, and the custody of children. The basic arguments for private ordering through mediation rest on the benefit to the spouses, who will be spared the cold and often intimidating atmosphere of a court room; and on the benefit to the courts, whose crowded dockets will be reduced to manageable proportions.

In the first chapter of this section on emerging procedural models (Chapter 5), Svenné Schmidt of Denmark writes about the Scandinavian procedures in matrimonial causes. Because of the political unity in earlier centuries between Denmark and Norway, and between Sweden and Finland, and with twentieth century deliberate legal cooperation, the substantive laws on grounds for divorce and separation and the rules governing the dissolution of marriage have been largely unified. Recently, Sweden has even further eased the access to divorce. That country, parenthetically, has an approach so liberal that in 1974 an Act was passed incorporating a provision for mediation by request between cohabitors who wish to separate. In detail the procedures in the four countries show some differences: in Sweden and Finland, as in most western countries, separation and divorce decrees are granted only by the courts, while in Denmark and Norway an administrative authority, the County Governor, has the final power. However, after a detailed review of the rules governing both methods, Svenné Schmidt concludes that the differences between them are not as wide as might be expected. The County Governor never has to decide in contentious cases, and thus spouses who seek an administrative decree must reach agreement not only on the dissolution of the marriage but also on the ancillary issues, after which the administrative officer will scrutinize the agreement for the fairness and reasonableness of its terms. If the spouses cannot agree, the officer will try through mediating counsel for an amicable settlement of the disputed issues — but when this is not attained the decree is denied, and the spouses must apply to the courts. Since most divorces and separations are noncontentious, the court most often acts only as a rubber stamp on the prior agreement, in which case the court's role is much like that of the Danish or Norwegian County Governor.

In Sweden voluntary mediation is offered both to legally married persons and to cohabitors who wish to separate; in the other three countries mediation is obligatory for divorcing spouses. Mediation may be by either ecclesiastical or secular counsellors. There is a minimum of "lawyering" and publicity, and in Sweden particularly, there exists a strong reliance on family counselling experts — psychiatrists, social workers, lawyers experienced in the field, and even gynecologists. All the countries have a well-developed system of free legal aid. But in spite of such advantages, the value of compulsory mediation is being seriously questioned, and has often been categorized as an "empty and delaying formality."

Continents away, in New Zealand, the element of conflict in the dissolution of marriage has also decreased, although judicial proceedings must still be employed. Priestley (Chapter 6) writes about the subsidiary problems of divorce, such as the financial arrangements, custody and access, with particular reference to the *Family Proceedings Act* of 1980. Among the changes this Act introduced was a separate Family Court (still absent in the mother country), with specialist judges and trained staff. Counselling service, sometimes voluntarily accepted but often made mandatory, must precede divorce application to the Family Court: the trial itself is the first step. Once litigation has commenced, the next step is the mediation conference, either requested by one of the parties or arranged by the Family Court Judge at any stage in the proceedings. The objectives are those common to all such mediation attempts — to identify and clarify the disputed issues and to try for agreement on them between the spouses. But the New Zealand mediation conference does have an unusual feature: the chairman must be a Family Court judge. He is not acting in his judicial capacity, but his position as a judge lends authority to his chairmanship and distinguishes mediation from a counselling session. Moreover, he can later revert to his position as judge to make consent orders and thus implement without delay any agreements reached at the conference. The role of lawyers is here again, as in the Scandinavian countries, extremely limited, although counsel appointed to act for children in disputed custody cases may make recommendations to the mediation chairman. The conference is, of course, private and its proceedings are privileged. Priestley makes a strong case for the effectiveness of the New Zealand Family Court's alternative to litigation.

In Yugoslavia, mediation has long been traditional. It has been considerably reformed in recent years, and is usually mandatory in the republics and provinces of that country. Unlike the situation in the United States, where there is considerable debate about the constitutionality of mandated mediation, the legality of the process has never been questioned in Yugoslavia. In Chapter 7, Šarčević compares the results of mediation offered by the court, required by the court, or out of court. Whatever the type, initial mediation seems to be cast in the modality of American marriage counselling, and has as its aim, seldom it may be noted successful, the preservation of marriage. One of the reasons for the failure of such mediation is that if one or both of the parties fail to appear, the court may consider this fact as indicating that the individual or joint petition for divorce has been withdrawn. Moreover, court mediation, according to some commentators, depends largely on the personality of the judge, who is rarely qualified to act as a professional marriage counsellor. Šarčević believes that out-of-court mediation is a much better method for reconciling the spouses or at least helping them reach an agreement about custody and support of the children that will serve the interests of the children. Such mediation requires professional counsellors who will provide therapy instead of imposing sentence, according to the author. This view of divorcing spouses as patients, however, is considered by many mediators in the United States and other western countries as questionable or indeed objectionable. Perhaps there is an aura of the People's Court in *The Caucasian Chalk Circle* about the concept, although Šarčević does cite the success of fully staffed institutions in Croatia, where results have been much better than in previous court mediation.

In Chapter 8, Shimazu describes the institution of divorce by mutual consent, adopted in 1898, and widely supported and used in 90 percent of all cases in Japan. In practical terms it consists of simply notifying the chief representative of the residents' town. The required signatures may even be by a third person, but there can be no divorce unless both spouses wish it. This simplification of the divorce process has advantages, but it still leaves open such questions as property division and child custody. In 1937 court provision was enacted for conciliation of personal affairs, a measure which formalized the old custom of having the village leader settle community disputes, and which was refined after the Second World War to incorporate current sociological advances. Divorce actions are handled by District or Civil Courts, conciliation by Family Courts. The first step for a person wishing to divorce is to apply to the Family Court for conciliation, a requirement which seems close to the Yugoslavian procedure. Again we find compulsory conciliation, and again this fails when the other spouse is unwilling to accept it. Conciliators are lay people, must be over forty years of age (a different slant from that in the United States), and have had some lectures or training as counsellors in vocational schools. In Japan, a judge is part of the conciliation committee but does not usually attend each session, and serves basically as an advisor. The personal background of each spouse is investigated (retroactive, sometimes to infancy); encouragement is given to the parties to think through their own problems and solutions. If divorce seems the right decision, discussions are held with the aid of the committee to arrange for division of property, which may, rather startlingly, include compensation for mental distress. Custody of children is most frequently awarded to the mother, with no visitation rights to the father.

When divorce intentions are firm but there is dispute on financial settlements, the Family Court determines both the divorce and the settlement, although if one of the spouses objects to the decision it loses effect. This decision, accordingly, without the ultimate power of enforcement, is infrequently rendered. The civil court still handles some divorces, with open hearings and public decisions. Here there are grounds: adultery, desertion, missing for more than three years, irreversible mental illness. The Supreme Court still adheres to rules of recrimination, and while only a minority of cases is decided on this principle, Shimazu feels that Japan's divorce laws need considerable improvement to bring them into line with the more liberal practices of most industrialized nations.

Australia has created a new court for judicial divorce proceedings, and a new law with an interdiciplinary approach. Perhaps the most important section of the 1975 *Family Law Act* specifies that, to be eligible for the role, a judge of the family court must have training and experience in this branch of law. More weight is given to the testimony of welfare offiers under the 1975 Act, and more sympathy to the opinions of psychiatrists. There is still, however, some question as to the limits of admissible evidence from welfare officers. These limits have been broad in the past and are even broader now; but Bates, who writes in Chapter 9 about the role of the expert in Australian court procedures for divorce, urges that the officers themselves exercise care not to cross the boundaries, and that cross-examination of the officers should be permissible. The court, with perhaps more extensive knowledge of all the relevant facts, will not always fully accept proposed solutions by the court officers.

The use of psychiatric evidence in Australia is still debated. The traditional view of the courts is that they must not have their adjudicative function usurped by experts. The more progressive approach considers that expert evidence is an extension for the judge's comparatively narrow experience. The situation is complicated by the frequent contradictions between the testimonies of psychiatrists, and between their attitudes toward their roles in court. The legal profession as a whole continues to harbor suspicions about interventions and contributions from psychiatric experts, although welfare officers seem to be more or less exempt from such hostility. Bates believes that much must still be done to clarify the position of the expert and to utilize his skills, and suggests that the law schools can take the lead in preparing its graduates to overcome the professional barriers between law and the other helping disciplines.

From South Africa, Sinclair (Chapter 10) describes the emerging practices of the divorce courts there, under the recently reformed divorce law in that country. The chapter raises interesting questions which may serve as a focus to draw together the strands of the preceding contributions. Perhaps the major theme is the uncertainty of the judicial role in modern divorce. With the collapse of fault-based divorce, which at least accorded well with traditional adjudicatory techniques of (retrospectively) "finding facts" and assessing behaviour, a more active role in the divorce process has been found for administrative officials (as in Denmark and Norway), professional counsellors (as in Japan and Yugoslavia), and "expert" witnesses (as in Australia). Where the judge's role remains important, we find frequent references to the significance of the personality of the judge, a matter highlighted in Sinclair's description of the South African experience, especially in relation to the contrast between the Black and White courts. There, as elsewhere, the present procedural dilemmas have been precipitated by reform of the substantive law and the introduction of no-fault divorce. But Sinclair noticed that the judge plays a more active role in the Black divorce court than in the White court: he is more likely to question the parties closely about their relationship and intentions than the judge in a "White" case.

Why should this be? The answer seems to lie partly in the social circumstances of the parties. With limited resources and precarious housing and residential entitlements, more is at stake for the black parties. But Sinclair considers the fact that Whites are more likely to be legally represented also important. The lawyers can, to a large extent, safeguard the parties' interests. These observations raise at least the following issues: How appropriate is it, as in the South African Black courts and as encouraged by the New Zealand procedures, to cast judges in the role of mediators? Is there a danger that the authority of the judge, even if formally suspended for the occasion, may impel a party into an agreement that has only the illusion of true consent? Can this be corrected by the presence of lawyers? The role of lawyers, and the profession, in the evolving processes of dispute settlement raises a new set of problems which are directly addressed in the next Part. We might perceive a further issue. The exhortations of judges to the parties in the Black South African courts to honor their family obligations might be represented (not necessarily critically) as the expression of the state interest that certain obligations be met primarily within the community. On the other hand, the readiness to accept the proposals of White parties may seem to concede to those individuals the right to arrange their own affairs and to give them priority over their perception of the interests of third parties (the children, or even the state). This tension between supervision and nonintervention underlies many of the issues arising from the procedural developments that are discussed in other sections.

In Chapter 11 Andrup offers a functional analysis of divorce proceedings that measures the advantages of various approaches in terms of how well they accomplish four goals: the preservation of the family; moral direction by society; the best interests of children; and support for the broken family in crisis. Andrup and Ziegert (Chapter 12) apply these criteria to several traditional and newly minted systems. They conclude that the most effective is the family court movement where the court combines its role as an administrative agency providing support with its juridical function of implementing society's beliefs about the family.

Chapter Five

The Scandinavian Law of Procedure in Matrimonial Causes*

T. Svenné Schmidt

University of Aarhus, Denmark

INTRODUCTION

Historical Survey

To understand legal development in the Scandinavian countries, it is necessary to consider their political history. From the beginning of the fourteenth century Finland was under the Swedish crown, and this lasted until 1809 when Finland was annexed by Russia. However, Finland was granted a limited internal autonomy as a Grand Duchy with the Czar as Grand Duke, and this meant that Swedish law to a great extent remained in force. At the end of the First World War, Finland became an independent republic. Similarly, since 1380, Denmark and Norway were united under the Danish crown. This union, which brought close together the countries' legal systems, continued until 1814 when Norway was united in a personal union with Sweden, although keeping its separate constitution, government and legislature. The personal union lasted until 1905 when Norway became a wholly independent constitutional kingdom. However, the result of the 400 years of union with Denmark meant that the present Norwegian legal system is closer to the Danish than to the Swedish legal system.

---

*This article is based on written contributions from Mr. Matti Savolainen, legal counsellor at the Finnish Ministry of Justice; Mrs. Kirsti Bull, associate professor at the University of Oslo, Norway; and professor, dr. jur Ake Saldeen, University of Uppsala, Sweden. The article does not cover Icelandic law.

In the sixteenth century, before the Reformation, marriage was considered a sacrament and indissoluble. The ecclesiastical courts might grant separation from bed and board but not divorce. After the Reformation this was changed. Following the teachings of Luther, the Danish and Norwegian courts could no longer grant separations whereas this was still possible in Sweden and Finland but only after the ecclesiastical and secular authorities had tried, often by rather severe means, to reconcile the spouses. On the other hand, statutes were passed in all the countries permitting divorce by court decree in cases of adultery and desertion. In Denmark and Norway the desertion had to have lasted for at least three years, but a similar time limit was not required in Sweden and Finland where only a desertion to a foreign country was acknowledged as a ground for divorce. The Danish and Norwegian statutes also provided for divorce in case of prenuptial leprosy, prenuptial and incurable impotence, and a sentence of exile for life (in 1750 this ground was extended to cover a sentence of life imprisonment). Similarly, a Swedish statute in 1810 provided for divorce by court decree in cases of exile or imprisonment for life, an attack on the life of the other spouse, and incurable insanity lasting for more than three years.

It will be seen that these statutory grounds for divorce, which continued in force until the new legislation at the beginning of this century, were very limited and primarily based on a gross violation of the marital duties. However, in practice this rigid system was gradually mitigated through exemptions made by the absolute Danish and Swedish kings. Possibly the kings were influenced in this respect by a widely accepted German protestant doctrine according to which a sovereign could dissolve a marriage by rescript. Already in the seventeenth century the Danish King had granted some decrees of divorce. At first the reason for this was either that it was found reasonable to spare a spouse, who had a statutory ground for divorce, the expenses and trouble of going to the courts or that the statutory limits for divorce had not expired. Later on, and especially from about 1770, royal decrees were granted as well in cases where no statutory ground for divorce existed.

The Danish King also started to grant separations by royal decree, for instance, where a husband, through intemperance, had severely neglected his duty to support his family or maltreated his wife or where both spouses applied for the separation, pleading that on account of deep incompatibility they found it impossible to continue their married life. This practice became so common that in 1768 the King delegated the authority to grant such separations to the Chancellery, and in 1790 a new and important step was taken as the King agreed to convert a separation decree into a divorce when the separation had lasted for three years. It was not a condition for such conversion that both spouses applied for the divorce. If no separation decree had been granted but the spouses *de facto* had lived apart for about six years each of them could also expect to obtain a royal decree of divorce.

As the rules for obtaining royal decrees of immediate divorce became more defined, the King gradually delegated the authority to grant such decrees to the Chancellery. Furthermore, by a royal ordinance in 1800 the County Governor was authorized to grant a separation decree when both spouses applied for it and it was established that they could not be reconciled; in 1827 the County Governors were authorized to grant decrees of divorce based on previous separation decrees when the separations had lasted for three years.

After the fall of the absolute monarchy, the first Danish Constitution of 1849 provided that the King either directly or through the relevant authorities might grant such exemptions from the statutes which had been made before 1849. This meant that, besides judicial divorce, divorce or separation by administrative decrees was retained and in the second half of the nineteenth century administrative divorce far exceeded the judicial. The dual system became so deeply rooted in Denmark that it has been preserved in the *Marriage Act* of 1922 and in the present *Marriage Act* of 1969.

After the separation from Denmark in 1814, Norway continued to follow the old Danish rules but from about 1825 the Norwegian Ministry of Justice assumed that immediate divorces by decree could not be granted and that separations by decree could only be granted when both spouses applied for the separation. This state of affairs continued until 1894 when the Ministry again started to grant both decrees of immediate divorce and decrees of separation based on the application of one spouse when the other had violated his or her marital duties.

In Sweden (and Finland) the King intervened in a similar way. From the end of the seventeenth century the King granted divorces by so-called dispensation although there were no statutory grounds for divorce. Until 1734, when the jurisdiction in matrimonial causes in Sweden was transferred from the ecclesiastical courts to the ordinary courts,[1] the King's dispensation took the form of authorizing the court to decide the case according to its "conscience." Later on, the King's right to grant such dispensations was recognized by Parliament in the statute of 1810, which gave examples of when the King could grant a divorce by dispensation.

In practice the most important of these instances was that the King could grant a divorce when the marriage had broken down (incompatibility). This presupposed, however, that the spouses had gone through different stages of reconciliation and warning before the church authorities, and if this did not help, had been separated for more than one year by court decree on account of "hate and bitterness" (*odium implacabile*). This method of obtaining a divorce was in the nineteenth century called "the long way" whereas "the short way" consisted in a misuse of the statutory ground of desertion. As mentioned above, the Swedish law did not prescribe a time limit for the desertion but requested that the deserter had gone abroad; this resulted in the so-called Copenhagen divorces where spouses who both wanted a divorce agreed that one of them would feign a desertion by going to Copenhagen for a couple of weeks whereupon the other spouse could obtain a divorce from the courts because of the "desertion." Similarly, Finnish spouses, who both wanted a divorce, obtained a so-called Haparanda-divorce, named after a town in Northern Sweden situated on the border of Finland. It is noticeable that, at the turn of the century, desertion was the most frequent ground for divorce in Sweden.

Although the connection between Finland and Sweden was severed in 1809, the Finnish authorities still followed the Swedish law and practice. Partly guided and inspired by the Swedish statute of 1810, the Finnish Supreme Court, which administered the dispensations from 1919 to 1929, laid down the foundations of the present divorce law. In a recent study by Sami Mahkonen[2] it is shown that between the years 1920 and 1929, the year before the dispensation practice was finally abolished, the rate of divorce by dispensation went up from 31 percent to 87 percent of all divorces. The grounds for a dispensation divorce could either be the gross fault or mental illness of the other spouse or the "permanent discord" between the spouses which usually required that there was a *de facto* separation for at least one year and that neither of the spouses objected to the divorce.

From this short survey it will be seen that although the very strict statutory rules for divorce by court decree were almost unchanged for about 350 years, the Scandinavian countries had by the beginning of this century, through royal intervention, become some of the most liberal countries regarding divorce and separation and that these were no longer soley based on the offence doctrine but to some extent also on the mutual consent of the spouses.

In 1909 Norway passed a *Divorce Act* which was partly a codification of the former practice. However, the new Act went further as it permitted separation on the request of one of the spouses if he could prove that the marriage had broken down *(Zerrüttungsprinzip)* although the other spouse did not agree to the separation. This led in 1910 to the appointment in Norway, Sweden, and Denmark of Marriage Commissions which worked closely together. The result was that almost identical *Marriage Acts* were passed in the three countries (Sweden 1915, Norway 1918, and Denmark 1922) and in 1929 Finland adopted a similar *Marriage Act* which came into force in 1930. On two important points there were, however, differences between the four Acts. Denmark and Norway decided to preserve the dual system with both judicial and administrative handling of the cases, whereas Sweden and Finland went over to a unified system with only judicial jurisdiction, and unlike the other countries, Finland did not adopt the system allowing divorce when the spouses had lived apart for a prescribed time after a judicial separation. In 1948, however, Finland reintroduced the judicial separation system partly due to the rapid growth of divorce rates which necessitated the introduction of less rigid no-fault divorce rules.

The Present Substantive Grounds for Divorce or Separation

In the middle of the 1950s, new Marriage Committees were set up in Denmark, Norway and Sweden. Their cooperation resulted in 1969 in the present Danish *Marriage Act* and a Norwegian Act which amended the old *Marriage Act* of 1918. The report of the Swedish committee was severely criticized and a new committee was appointed which in 1972 presented its report. This led to the present Swedish *Marriage Act,* which came into force on January 1, 1974, and which differed substantially from the common Scandinavian law at that time. Accordingly, it is necessary in presenting the present grounds for divorce and separation to distinguish between Denmark, Norway and Finland on the one hand, and Sweden on the other.

Denmark, Norway and Finland

Legal separation may be obtained by spouses who find that they cannot continue their marital life and agree to the separation. Furthermore, a spouse has a right to a legal separation when the other spouse grossly neglects to support the family or grossly violates other duties towards the spouse or the children,[3] or when, for other reasons, the relationship between the spouses may be considered as destroyed. Under the Danish Act, the separation cannot be granted if the breakdown of the marriage is mainly due to the petitioner, and in Finland the court may take the conduct of the petitioner into consideration. However, it is very seldom that Danish or Finnish courts refuse separations on this account as the courts — no doubt correctly — find it difficult or impossible to reach a decision on the basis of evidence in court as to whom is to blame for the breakdown of the marriage.

The two predominant grounds for divorce are adultery and a preceding legal separation which, without a resumption of the cohabitation, has lasted for at least one year (in Norway the time limit is one year when both spouses apply for the divorce, otherwise two years). The *Marriage Acts* provide for a number of other grounds for immediate divorce but most of these have no practical importance. However, divorce is sometimes granted on the basis of a *de facto* separation due to estrangement which has lasted for more than three years (in Finland, two years) and — but this is only a Finnish ground for divorce — that the other spouse is an alcoholic or a drug addict and the court finds that weighty reasons speak for the immediate divorce.

Sweden

The idea behind the new Swedish rules regarding divorce is that marriage is a form of voluntary cohabitation between independent persons. The consequence of this is that under no circumstances should a person be forced to continue in a marriage which he or she wants to escape. Accordingly, the new Act has abolished the separation institution and does not contain the traditional divorce grounds; it considers the question of fault or guilt as to the breakdown of the marriage as completely irrelevant both in relation to the divorce itself and to the ancillary questions such as maintenance and the custody of the children.

Spouses who agree that their marriage shall be dissolved have a right to an immediate divorce. If a spouse has the custody of his or her own child under sixteen years of age and permanently lives together with the child, the divorce must be preceded by a waiting period, or, as it is called in the Act, "a time of reflection," of six months. The waiting period is also required if only one of the spouses wants the divorce or if both spouses request the waiting period.

The reason for the waiting period is that the will of a spouse to have his marriage dissolved must be respected but only if that will is based on careful consideration. Too hasty divorces should as far as possible be prevented, especially in the interest of the children. The separation institution was, however, found to have certain drawbacks. Partly, the period of one year was considered too long, and partly, the rule that a separation ceased when the spouses resumed cohabitation counteracted attempts of reconciliation during the "trial period." Finally, the separation institution was found to have another drawback, of a more psychological nature, since it required a judicial decree to which a number of legal effects of an economic character were connected, which the spouses saw as a more or less definitive step towards the dissolution of their personal and economic interdependence.

The waiting period starts when the spouses jointly apply for the divorce or when the application of one of the spouses is announced to the other. After the six months each spouse may apply for the divorce but if no applications have been made within one year from the start of the waiting period, the application lapses.

As further grounds for divorce, the Act provides that if spouses have lived apart *de facto* for more than two years, either of them has a right to an immediate divorce without a waiting period. The same applies if the marriage was entered into between persons who are related to each other in the direct line of ascent or descent or who are brothers and sisters of the whole blood, or if the marriage is bigamous. In the last case the bigamist's spouse in the first marriage also has a right to an immediate divorce.

Divorce under these rules is now the only way to dissolve a marriage in Sweden as the new Act abolished the procedure of annulment of a marriage. Annulment could formerly be obtained when a marriage had been entered into contrary to certain more important marriage conditions but was found to be of no practical importance.[4]

Ancillary Questions

Since this chapter deals primarily with the procedural aspects of divorce or separation, ancillary questions, such as custody and maintenance, will be covered only in so far as necessary for better understanding of procedure.

As regards custody, all the countries agree that the welfare of the child is the dominating principle. In Sweden the court must decide this question in connection with the divorce. If the parents are in agreement, this must be accepted by the court unless it finds it clearly contrary to the child's welfare. A parent who later on finds that a joint custody arrangement is unworkable may ask the court to resolve the matter. The Danish and Finnish rules are similar except that it is not possible to agree on continued joint custody.[5]

In Norway the rules are the same as in Denmark and Finland but a private agreement between the parents is binding and need not be approved by the court. Furthermore, if the parents cannot agree on custody, they may leave this question to the decision of the County Governor instead of the court. The new Norwegian *Children's Act,* which came in force on January 1, 1982, has, however, introduced a new concept as it provides that married parents retain joint custody after a divorce or separation unless the parents cannot agree to this, in which case the court (or the governor) will take the decision, taking into account the welfare of the child.

The parent who does not get custody has in all the countries a right of access to the child. This is usually arranged by private agreement between the parents but if they cannot agree, the dispute is decided by the courts. In Denmark, however, the matter is completely outside the jurisdiction of the courts and is left to the County Governor's decision with appeal to the Ministry of Justice. Under Norwegian law, the parents may agree to place the question before the governor (with appeal to the ministry) instead of the court, but in practice this is never done.

As regards maintenance of the children or the other spouse, the Danish rules differ considerably from those in the other countries. A Danish court which pronounces a divorce or separation cannot decide the question of maintenance of the children as, under the *Children's Act* of 1960, this is a matter which, upon request, is decided administratively by the governor, with appeal to the ministry. In Norway, disputes regarding the maintenance of children are also a matter for the County Governor but may be decided by the court ancillary to the matrimonial cause. With respect to spousal support, a Danish court will decide whether there is a duty to pay maintenance and the duration of this duty, either for life or for a specified number of years, but the amount of the periodical payments is left to the decision of the governor with appeal to the ministry. In the other countries, the courts (or, in Norway, the governor if the spouses agree to leave the question to him) may also decide upon the amount payable but it should be mentioned that in Sweden an Act of 1978 provides as the principal rule that former spouses shall not pay maintenance to each other. A spouse may, however, be obliged to pay maintenance for a transitional period and if the marriage has been of a long duration and one of the spouses has difficulty in supporting him- or herself, the maintenance duty of the other spouse may be extended for a longer period.[6]

The legal matrimonial property system in all four countries is community of property. The division of this property is not linked to the divorce or separation but left to the private agreement of the spouses. If they cannot agree, the matter is handled in Denmark and Norway by a probate court and in Sweden and Finland by a liquidator appointed by the ordinary court. In all the countries except Finland it is possible for the court (in Denmark and Norway, the probate court) to decide that the property shall not be equally divided. In Denmark and Sweden this presupposes that the marriage has been of short duration. Conversely, in a case where the spouses have been married for many years but have separate property, so that no division should take place, a Danish court may, if it finds it reasonable, decide that the spouse whose separate property in value far exceeds the separate property of the other spouse, shall pay a lump sum to the other spouse. In this connection it may be mentioned that a Norwegian or Finnish court may decide that a spouse shall pay damages to the other when the divorce or separation is due to a gross violation of the other spouse, but in practice such damages are seldom given. Also, if the spouses have rented a flat, the court may, in the divorce or separation proceedings, decide which of them shall have the right to continue the lease. Finally, with the exception of Finland, the divorce court will also decide the question of the wife's right to a widow's pension when her former husband had died.

THE AUTHORITIES THAT HANDLE MATRIMONIAL CAUSES

As mentioned above, both Denmark and Norway have maintained a system comprising either judicial or administrative decrees, whereas decrees in Sweden and Finland are only granted judicially.

The Jurisdiction of the Administrative Authorities

Both in Denmark and in Norway the greatest number of divorces and separations by far are granted by the County Governor who is a local state authority (in Danish the *"statsamtmand,"* in Norwegian the *"fylkesmann"*). At present there are fifteen governors in Denmark and eighteen in Norway, each with a legally trained staff which deals with the cases. To obtain an administrative decree it is a condition that one of the statutory grounds for divorce or separation exist, but the other conditions for the jurisdiction of the governor differ considerably between the two countries.

In Norway all cases of immediate divorce without a preceding legal separation are handled by the courts except that a divorce based on a *de facto* separation for more than three years may be granted administratively if both spouses agree to this procedure. On the other hand, a divorce based on a preceding legal separation can only be granted by the governor and not by the courts. As for separation decrees, these are granted by the governor on the application of both spouses whereas cases of separation based on the breach of marital duties or on the breakdown of the marriage are usually handled by the courts but may be dealt with by the governor if both spouses prefer the administrative procedure. It is not a condition for the governor's jurisdiction that the spouses are in agreement as to the solution of the ancillary questions, as disputes may always be referred to the courts, but if a spouse demands a definite solution of one of these questions as a condition for the administrative separation, the governor cannot handle the case unless the other spouse agrees. In practice, the spouses will often have solved all the questions in a private agreement before they come to the governor. The decision of the governor may be appealed to the Ministry of Justice unless the spouses have renounced this right beforehand.

In Denmark the view has also been taken that the governor can only deal with noncontentious cases, but the method of achieving this is different from the Norwegian. According to Danish law, it is a condition for an administrative decree that both spouses want the divorce or the separation and choose the administrative procedure and, further that they agree on terms for the dissolution of the marriage (custody, spousal maintenance, widow's pension, the right to the lease of the matrimonial flat and, in cases of separate property, whether a lump sum shall be paid to the other spouse). Regarding the amount of the periodical maintenance to the other spouse it is, however, sufficient that the spouses agree to leave this question to the decision of the governor.

The governor may refuse to grant a decree if he finds it injudicious, for instance because he finds it doubtful whether there is a ground for divorce or finds that the spouses' agreement regarding custody is not consistent with the welfare of the children. Furthermore, as long as the decree has not been granted, either spouse may retreat from his or her agreement regarding the dissolution of the marriage and the ancillary questions. In all such cases the Danish governor will refer the spouses to the courts for the divorce or separation. It is, however, seldom that the governor finds it necessary to refuse the decree. As in Norway, the Danish governor's decision may be appealed to the Ministry of Justice.

The Judicial Authorities

In all four countries the competent courts of first instance are the ordinary lower courts. In Denmark a case is tried before a single judge. This is usually also the case in Norway although either of the parties may demand that the court be supplemented by two lay judges who are appointed by the court and must be of different sexes. In Finland the court consists in the cities of three professional judges and in the rural districts of a judge as chairman and some lay judges.

In Sweden the court of first instance consists of a judge and some lay judges but most divorce cases are handled in a simplified form before the single judge. The judge decides whether the divorce may be granted immediately or only after the waiting period and, if such period is prescribed, he makes the necessary interim orders regarding such matters as custody, and maintenance. In the final judgment of divorce, the single judge may also include the settlement of the ancillary questions if the spouses are in agreement as to these and he may also, on the application of the spouses, make decisions on contentious questions. However, if the spouses do not agree as to the custody of the children, this question is referred to the full court and the single judge pronounces only a partial judgment regarding the divorce. The decisions of the lower courts may be appealed to the High Courts.

THE PROCEDURE IN MATRIMONIAL CAUSES

Mediation

Obligatory mediation between the spouses was abolished in Sweden by the new *Marriage Act* but at the same time an Act regarding voluntary mediation between persons who are living together was passed. This Act will be discussed later in this chapter.

In the other three countries, mediation is still obligatory: in Denmark, in connection with all separations or divorces; in Norway, before all separation decrees and before a divorce based on adultery or *de facto* separation; and in Finland, in connection with a separation based on the mutual consent of the spouses. The mediation is either ecclesiastical or secular. In Norway and Finland it is left to the spouse who wants the divorce to decide which kind of mediation shall be used, whereas in Denmark the mediation is usually undertaken by a clergyman. However, if the spouses do not belong to the same religious community or if they both so prefer, the mediation is undertaken at the County Governor's office and in practice this is the most frequently used method. In Norway the mediation may, if both spouses agree, take the form of counselling by a recognized institution for family counselling.

In Denmark the spouses are compelled, under threat of a fine, to appear personally at the mediation. If a spouse fails to appear after having been summoned twice, mediation with the other spouse alone is sufficient. In Norway only the spouse who has applied for the mediation is obliged to appear and the question of the appearance is no problem in Finland as mediation is only used in connection with separation by mutual consent.

In all the countries the mediation usually takes places in the presence of both spouses but in Finland the mediator is also obliged to discuss the problems with each of the spouses alone. If the spouses are living too far from each other the mediation may in all the countries be undertaken separately with each spouse. The duties of the mediator are to try to uncover the reasons for their disagreements, to inform them of the consequences of a separation or divorce and to discuss with them the chances of continued cohabitation. If there are any children, the mediator must especially consider their welfare and emphasize this to the spouses.

The value of compulsory mediation is very doubtful. Although many clergymen no doubt try hard to accomplish a conciliation or at least a dissolution of the marriage in a friendly atmosphere, mediation, and especially the secular type, is considered by many to be an empty and delaying formality. It is significant that the present Danish Marriage Commission, which was set up in 1969, in a report in 1977 recommended that the obligatory mediation should be abolished and perhaps replaced by a system of organized family counselling on a voluntary basis, such as is found in Sweden today. A similar proposal was made by the Finnish Marriage Law Commission in 1972.

Procedure Before the Courts

Under the new Swedish divorce law, the court procedure will be very simple in the many cases where the spouses agree not only on the divorce but also on the ancillary questions, as in such cases the procedure is purely written and the spouses need not appear in person before the court. Only in respect to custody must the court sanction the agreement, but in most cases this is only a formality. If a waiting period has been prescribed, the spouses, or one of them, may within six months after the end of the waiting period, apply for the final decree of divorce. In such cases a single judge handles the case on the basis of the papers filed by the spouses.

If the spouses do not agree on the ancillary questions, the judge may choose to start the procedure with the filing of written statements or with a preliminary oral hearing. If there is a dispute on an ancillary question, an oral hearing is usual. The decision on the divorce itself may then be made by the single judge and the contentious questions referred to a hearing in the full court.

In Denmark, Finland and Norway the spouses do not have the right to dispose of a matrimonial cause by procedural agreements or admissions in the way that parties usually have in other civil proceedings. The reason for this is that the court has a duty to see that the compulsory rules regarding the grounds for divorce or separation are observed, just as a Danish or Finnish court must refuse to acknowledge an agreement regarding the custody if it is found inconsistent with the welfare of the child. On the other hand, as far as the economic consequences of the divorce or separation are concerned, the spouses may make agreements which the court must accept.

In these three countries the court has accordingly wider powers than in other civil proceedings and may call upon a spouse to produce evidence for his or her claim and subject a spouse to oral examination. In Finland and Norway the court may order that a spouse who has failed to appear shall be brought before the court; a similar power is given to a Danish court if it finds it necessary for its decision regarding custody. However, in practice, it is very seldom that the courts need to use these powers.

If the respondent appears without a lawyer or does not appear at all, a Danish court will assign a lawyer to him or her in accordance with the rules of free legal aid. Similarly, in Norway the court is entitled to assign a lawyer to a respondent who fails to appear but only with free legal aid if the respondent fulfills the economic conditions for this.

In all the countries, court sittings are usually public, but in Denmark and Norway this principle is broken in matrimonial proceedings as these are held *in camera*. Furthermore, the publication of the judgments in such cases may in Norway take place only with the permission of the court and in Denmark the name, occupation or address of any of the persons mentioned in the judgment may not be published. In Finland the court may conduct the case *in camera* if it finds it necessary on account of the particular nature of the case, and publication of information concerning individual divorce cases is prohibited by the provisions of the *Criminal Code*. In Sweden the court may also decide on application to conduct matrimonial proceedings *in camera*.

In all the countries, whenever there is a dispute regarding custody, the court has the power to procure expert evidence from child psychiatrists or clinical psychologists just as the court may ask the local social authorities to give evidence. A special problem is whether the child should be examined by the court as to its own opinion regarding custody. If an expert has been called, such examinations by the court will usually not take place, as the expert will be able to procure the necessary information. But in most cases expert assistance is not used and the problem is whether the court itself should examine the child and if so, what should be the form of such examination. This is a delicate matter. Accordingly, Danish courts have been reluctant to allow the examination of a child and it is usually refused if the child is under fifteen. In Norway a statutory rule provides that a child over twelve years should usually be heard before a decision is made regarding a question which concerns his person.[7] This rule is primarily directed to the parents but the courts have in practice found that it should be followed in custody cases. In Finland, children are at present hardly ever heard in person by the court but in the draft Government Bill mentioned above new fairly restrictive rules regarding examinations by the court and methods to be used have been proposed.

When an examination is allowed it will usually take place in the judge's chambers and not in the courtroom and the judge will usually perform the examination himself. In Denmark the lawyers of the parents but not the parents themselves have a right to be present during the judge's interview of the child. In Norway it seems that not even the lawyers are present.

Divorce and separation proceedings at first instance are in practice fairly expedient (from one to three months) in Sweden, Finland and Denmark unless there are complications, for instance concerning the custody of the children. In Norway the average time seems to be a little longer (four to five months).

In ordinary lawsuits the court will usually order that the losing party pay the costs of the other party but in matrimonial causes such orders are only made when the court finds special grounds for doing so. All the countries have a well-developed system of free legal aid which means that a lawyer is assigned to the petitioner or the respondent or both and the state pays the lawyer's fee and indemnifies the spouse for other expenses which he has justifiably defrayed in connection with the case at court. In Sweden the spouse must, however, contribute to the payment of the costs according to a gradually rising scale. The financial limits for obtaining free legal aid differ considerably from country to country. In Denmark about 75 percent of all applications for free legal aid in matrimonial causes are met.

Procedure in Administrative Cases in Denmark and Norway

An administrative divorce or separation may be initiated either by a personal or a written application to the County Governor's office. There are no formalities, but the spouses will often use the application forms which have been authorized by the Ministries of Justice in both countries.

In Denmark the spouses must agree not only on the divorce or separation but also on its terms (the ancillary questions). When the governor receives either a joint or a unilateral application his office summons the spouses to a meeting and in the summons it is stated that failure to attend without valid excuse will mean that the case cannot be handled administratively. However, if one of the spouses does not appear, a second summons will be issued before the case is dismissed. Usually the meeting is held with both spouses together but if they are living too far from each other it is possible, although rare, to hold separate meetings with each.

The main object of the meeting at the governor's office is the negotiation of the terms of the divorce or separation and, if a divorce is applied for, to establish that a ground for a divorce exists. If, for instance, adultery is alleged, it is necessary that the spouse and the third party personally appear and give evidence regarding the adultery and its date. The negotiation is conducted as an informal discussion between the legally trained officer from the governor's office and the spouses.

Very often the spouses will have submitted in advance a written agreement as to the solution of the ancillary questions. In such case it is the duty of the officer to go through the agreement and discuss it with the spouses to ensure that the agreement regarding the custody of the children is not inconsistent with their welfare and that the agreement regarding the other conditions is clear and not obviously unreasonable to one of the spouses. Although the spouses have a right to meet at the negotiations together with their lawyers it is in practice rather seldom that lawyers attend and, accordingly, the officer has a duty to advise the spouses so that they are aware of their legal position and realize what they may be foregoing in the agreement.

If the spouses have not made an agreement in advance the officer will discuss the problems with them and will often be able to reach an amicable settlement. In practice the officer will often carry out a conflict-solving function and may, if he finds it suitable, also try to reach an agreement between the spouses regarding the division of the community property, although such agreement is not a condition for the administrative divorce or separation. If the spouses cannot agree as to the community property the officer will inform them that they may ask the probate court to resolve this conflict. The officer will also inform them of the rather limited opportunities for changing the agreement subsequently.

The result of the meeting is entered into the County Governor's records book which must be signed by the spouses and the negotiating officer. The formal decree of divorce or separation is thereupon issued by the governor. According to the Danish *Marriage Act* (section 45) the terms stipulated in a judgment of separation are also binding after a divorce which is based on a separation. However, the court may decide that the question of the duty to pay maintenance and its duration may be reopened in connection with the later divorce. This means that if a spouse refuses to cooperate in an administrative divorce because he is dissatisfied with the terms of the separation judgment, the County Governor will inform him of the futility of his attitude, but if he still refuses, the decree cannot be granted by the governor. The other spouse is advised to go to the courts where the divorce will be granted notwithstanding the protest from the dissatisfied spouse. Although section 45 only applies to the terms of a judgment of separation, the same result will often be reached when the separation is granted administratively as it is usual that the spouses' agreement regarding the terms contains a clause according to which the terms also apply after a later divorce based on the separation.

As will be shown below, the Danish administration handles by far the greatest number of divorce and separation cases. This preference for the administrative procedure may seem odd as it forces the spouses to reach also agreement on most of the ancillary questions. As an explanation it has often been pointed out that the administrative procedure is inexpensive, fast and discreet, but this cannot be the real explanation. The judicial procedure is also rather inexpensive, at least when free legal aid has been granted which is done very liberally, and if the case is not complicated the judicial procedure is almost as fast as the administrative and just as discreet. Apart from tradition, the main reason why the administrative procedure is preferred is presumably psychological. Many people are scared by the thought of having to appear in a courtroom and publicly display their marital difficulties. The atmosphere in the court is alien to them and may often create an unnecessary feeling of conflict which is not conducive to an amicable settlement of a situation in itself often emotionally straining. Added to this psychological aspect is the fact that the rules of the administrative procedure are designed to ensure that the cases, although of a noncontentious nature, receive careful treatment by legally qualified administrative officers who usually have great experience in these matters.

In the last fifteen years the dual system has been subject to much debate in Denmark. A major reason for this was that the government considered the abolition of the office of the County Governor and the assignment of its many varied tasks, including the handling of the family law cases, to other authorities. In 1980 the government dropped this plan but this has only pushed the debate in another direction. Criticism of the present system is not levelled at the administrative decree as such but at the complicated structure of the system which often forces the spouses from one authority to another. A common example may show this. A wife applies to the governor for a separation. If the spouses cannot agree on the terms she will have to bring a legal action in court, perhaps after having applied to the governor for free legal aid. After the separation judgment, which has given her the custody of the children, she must again apply to the governor in order to obtain a decision regarding maintenance for herself and the children, and both spouses may appeal the governor's decisions on these questions to the Ministry of Justice. Similarly, the husband may ask the governor for a decision regarding his right of access to the children and this decision may also be appealed to the ministry. Finally, if the spouses cannot reach agreement as to the division of the community property, each of them may bring the matter before the probate court and its decision may again be appealed to the High Court and eventually, with permission from the ministry, to the Supreme Court.

There is no doubt that the treatment of the different aspects of what is in reality one social phenomenon, the breakdown of a marriage, by various authorities may be both time-consuming and confusing or irritating to the spouses who will often have to recite again and again the information regarding their personal and economic conditions which they have already given to other authorities. The Danish debate has, accordingly, been concerned with a simplification of the whole system and it has strongly been advocated that only one authority, a kind of family court, should be empowered to deal with all the personal and economic problems that may arise in connection with a divorce or separation. There is, however, no agreement as to the way in which this single authority might be organized and for the moment it is not possible to say what the outcome of the debate will be.

In Norway the administrative cases are handled on the basis of written statements only. The spouses need not agree on the ancillary questions as disputes on these points may be referred to the courts. The governor has, however, a duty to ascertain that a ground for divorce exists. If for instance a divorce is applied for on the ground of separation, the spouses must state in the application that the cohabitation has not been resumed during the separation and this statement must usually be corroborated by statements from two reliable persons who know the spouses well. If there is doubt whether the separation is still valid the governor may ask for further information and may ask for a hearing of evidence before the courts.

Furthermore, as the Norwegian governor may be obliged to grant decrees of divorce in cases where one of the spouses does not want the divorce, for instance when a separation has lasted for two years but only one of the spouses applies for the divorce, the governor must, besides the issue of the formal divorce decree, prepare a written decision in which he states the reason and the legal basis for his decision. The disappointed spouse may appeal this written decision within three weeks. The appeal (complaint) will be sent to the governor who, after having heard the other spouse, may cancel his own decree if he finds that the complaint is justified. Otherwise, he will forward the complaint to the Ministry of Justice together with the documents of the case.

Regarding the connection between a lawsuit and an administrative case the rule in both countries is that the governor cannot handle a case as long as a lawsuit is pending. In Denmark he may handle the case with the permission of the ministry but such permission will not usually be granted as long as the lawsuit has not been withdrawn. The reason for this rule is that the spouse who has brought the lawsuit should not be able to use the threat of continuing the possibly embarrassing lawsuit as a means of pressure against the other spouse during the administrative proceedings.

A minor disadvantage of the administrative divorce decrees is that some foreign states which will recognize a Danish or Norwegian judicial divorce may refuse to recognize an administrative divorce, presumably due to an unfamiliarity with the Danish or Norwegian systems. There will be no problem if the foreign state has ratified the Hague Convention of 1970 on the recognition of divorces and legal separations, as this convention also covers administrative decrees, but until now this convention has been ratified by a rather limited number of countries. Accordingly, the Danish Ministry of Justice has prescribed that before an administrative decree of separation or divorce is granted to persons who are foreign citizens or have their domicile in foreign countries (outside the other Scandinavian countries) such persons shall be notified that the decree cannot with certainty be expected to be recognized outside Denmark. If a person cannot get his Danish or Norwegian divorce decree recognized in another country he may bring a legal action in Denmark, or Norway, in which he asks for a declaratory judgment that his former marriage is legally dissolved by the administrative decree. Equipped with such a judgment it will usually be possible to have the dissolution of the marriage recognized in the foreign state in question.

STATISTICS

In all the countries the divorce rates have risen steeply during this century as will be seen from the two tables below which have been taken from the *Yearbook of Nordic Statistics 1980*.

TABLE 5.1   Divorces per 1,000 of the mean Population

Year	Denmark	Finland	Norway	Sweden
1921–30	0.56	0.21	0.26	0.30
1961–70	1.51	1.06	0.74	1.32
1971	2.70	1.56	0.96	1.67
1972	2.63	1.78	1.02	1.87
1973	2.52	1.89	1.18	1.97
1974	2.60	2.14	1.29	3.28
1975	2.62	1.99	1.39	3.10
1976	2.58	2.14	1.45	2.64
1977	2.63	2.13	1.51	2.47
1978	2.56	2.18	1.54	2.45
1979	2.55	2.14	1.62	2.45

TABLE 5.2   Divorces per 1,000 Married Women of the mean Population

Year	Denmark	Finland	Norway	Sweden
1921–30	2.90	1.31		1.72
1961–70	6.24	5.07	3.16	5.48
1971	11.11	7.02	4.03	7.04
1972	10.87	7.99	4.31	7.98
1973	10.50	8.47	4.96	8.46
1974	10.96	9.54	5.45	14.27
1975	11.11	8.87	5.88	13.63
1976	11.00	9.59	6.12	11.75
1977	11.32	9.57	6.40	11.11
1978	11.10	9.83	6.55	11.19
1979	11.15	9.67	6.94	11.28

It will be seen that the present rates in all the countries are very high but that there is a remarkable difference between the Danish and Swedish rates on the one hand and the Norwegian on the other hand. It may be thought that the sudden jump in the Swedish rates between 1973 and 1974 shows that the new Swedish *Marriage Act*, which came into force on January 1, 1974, has resulted in a steep rise in the number of divorces, but it has been suggested that the jump is more of a technical nature.[8] The new more liberal rules regarding immediate divorce have meant that divorces are granted earlier than before, and this explains why the rates in 1974 and 1975 went up so dramatically. No doubt this is correct as the divorce rates have gone down considerably in the years 1976–79 and seem to have found a more stable level; however, this level is somewhat higher than in the years before 1974.

The number of separations in Denmark, Finland and Norway differs considerably. For the last ten years the annual number of separations in Norway has exceeded the number of divorces by about 20 percent whereas the number of separations in Finland is only about 55 to 60 percent of the number of divorces. Unfortunately the annual number of separations in Denmark is not published in the official statistics but it may be assumed to be somewhat lower than the number of divorces. With respect to the relation between the administrative and the judicial handling of the cases in Denmark and Norway, it is assumed that the Danish governors handle between 85 and 90 percent of all divorces and separations, and that in Norway almost all separations and 85 percent of all divorces are handled administratively.

RECONCILIATION PROCEDURES AND FAMILY COUNSELLING

As mentioned earlier, obligatory mediation was abolished in Sweden in 1974. At the same time an Act regarding voluntary mediation between persons who are living together was passed. As its title shows the Act does not only concern married couples but also persons living together without marriage. In its report in 1972, the Swedish Family Law Committee states that family counselling is the most suitable means of avoiding premature divorces but as family counselling was far from developed in Sweden, the committee found it impossible to substitute such counselling for mediation and this was the basis of the Act regarding voluntary mediation.

The purpose of the mediation is to smooth out differences between couples living together. The mediator tries to help parties to solve their problems, whether this leads to a dissolution of their cohabitation or not. The task of the mediator is, however, not to try to reconcile the parties so that the cohabitation may be continued at any price. Under the Act, at least two mediators are appointed in each municipality. It has been found expedient to draw on the experience of vicars for this task although both mediators should not be clergymen. The mediator must act at the request of the man or woman if either of them is living in the community. He is subject to professional secrecy and is relieved of the duty to give evidence unless the party in whose favour the professional secrecy is prescribed consents. The cost of the mediation is paid by the municipality. A recent study has shown that it is rather seldom that married couples use voluntary mediation but, if they do, it often leads to what are called "happy divorces."

Apart from mediation, a number of family counselling offices have been established in Sweden by county, municipal or ecclesiastical bodies and from 1960 the state has contributed to these experimental schemes of family counselling. The first office of this kind was set up in Stockholm in 1951 and in the following twenty years the number has been gradually increased. According to a report (1974) by the Committee on Social Policy, thirty-six family counselling offices had been established by the counties and municipalities by 1971, and thirteen more offices were run by religious and ecumenical societies. Most of the offices were in the densely populated areas in southern and central Sweden with a concentration in the bigger cities, whereas four counties had no office. The offices had a total staff of about 100 persons. Each office had a psychiatrist and many also employed a gynecologist and a lawyer. About ten offices had child psychiatrists and other experts were found in varying degree. Since 1971 no substantial development of the family counselling has taken place.

In 1971 the offices handled about 7,000 cases. Typically, the couples had been married either for five to nine years or for more than twenty years. Most of the clients came on their own initiative after having heard about the office from friends, the media, medical practitioners, or social workers. The clients are not registered in official registers but only in the offices' own closed archives. Furthermore, a client may refuse to state his name, and this is done by a number of clients.

In Finland, dissatisfaction with obligatory mediation in cases of separation has in some municipalities resulted in a kind of informal divorce counselling. In these municipalities social workers acting as mediators or in connection with the preparation of social reports on children to the courts have formed informal pretrial working groups which may consist, according to the requirements of the case, of various specialists. These groups have further extended their services to pretrial divorce and separation cases and the basic working hypothesis of the groups is that the clients are presumed to have carefully considered their decision and that the divorce is in fact already a *"fait accompli."* The main task of this voluntary pretrial social work is to encourage peaceful settlement of all issues between the spouses and to provide for necessary help and advice by competent lawyers and other specialists in order to secure the best possible adjustment of the spouses and their children to life after the divorce.

In Norway there are a number of family counselling offices, especially in the bigger cities, but it is relatively seldom that they are used in connection with divorces or separations.

In Denmark a few family counselling groups have been established on private initiative but public family counselling in connection with the breakdown of marriages is very little developed. Certainly, according to the *Social Security Act* of 1974, one of the duties of the municipal Public Assistance Office is to give free guidance and advice to families who are in need thereof. However, if the problems consist of conflicts between the spouses the social officer must, according to a circular from the Ministry of Social Affairs, adopt a neutral attitude and only give factual information regarding the consequences of a divorce or separation and give guidance as to the proper authority (the court or governor) to which the spouses may apply.

JUDICIAL OR ADMINISTRATIVE DIVORCE PROCEDURE

It is well known that, with the exception of Denmark, Norway and Iceland, divorce and separation are granted by the courts in all countries. The present trend in most countries towards more liberal rules on divorce and separation, especially through the recognition of the principles of marriage breakdown and of divorce by mutual consent, has, however, had the effect that the function of the courts in many and perhaps in the majority of cases has been reduced to a kind of registration of the agreement between the spouses regarding the dissolution of a marriage which they find impossible to continue and regarding the terms for this dissolution. In all such noncontentious cases the judgment by the court is nothing but a rubber stamp on the agreement of the spouses and not the result of a usual judicial procedure solving a dispute between two private citizens.

The function of the courts in these noncontentious cases is accordingly similar to the function of the Danish-Norwegian County Governors. It seems to this author to be a matter of taste or tradition in the different countries whether the authority which handles such cases is a court or an administrative authority. The crucial problem is not the kind of authority which has jurisdiction but that the procedure before either kind of authority is made as rational, flexible and informal as possible.

Regarding contentious cases, however, I believe it is necessary that these are resolved by the courts under the usual judicial procedure with its built-in legal guarantees. However, this does not mean that it should be impossible to modernize the court procedure so that it is less rigid and accordingly less "frightening" to the parties. In this way, the chances of an amicable settlement of these unfortunate disputes are enhanced to the benefit not only of the spouses and their children but also of society as a whole.

NOTES

1. In Denmark and Norway new mixed ecclesiastical and secular courts were set up soon after the Reformation to handle matrimonial causes. These courts existed until 1797 when their jurisdiction was transferred to the ordinary courts.

2. Avioero (Divorce), Vammala 1980 (doctoral thesis, University of Helsinki).

3. Unlike the Danish Act, the Norwegian and Finnish Acts include drug addiction or depravity and the Finnish Act adds the contraction of venereal disease.

4. In the years 1959–70 a total of only twenty-nine marriages were annulled in Sweden.

5. In Finland a Government Bill was drafted in 1981 which would make a continued joint custody possible, and in Denmark a committee was appointed to consider the question.

6. In all the countries the spouses may settle the maintenance question both between themselves and towards the children by private agreement. In Finland, however, an agreement regarding maintenance of the children is enforceable only if approved by the social authorities or confirmed by a court. In all the countries it is possible to have maintenance agreements regarding children changed by the courts (in Denmark, by the County Governor) if they are found unreasonable or the circumstances have changed.

7. The Danish Commission on Marriage Law has in a report in 1974 suggested an age limit of twelve years for the hearing of children.

8. Ulla Bondeson: Lagens effekter och funktioner in Festskrift till Per Stjernquist, Lund 1978, 225, 238 ff.

Chapter Six

Mediation Conferences — The New Zealand Family Court's Alternative to Litigation*

J. M. Priestley

Barrister and Solicitor of the High Court of New Zealand

The function of a Court is to decide, according to law, the issue between the parties who stand before it. Legal proceedings stem from conflict. Resort to litigation will usually only arise when parties are unable to resolve a dispute themselves. Referral of a dispute to a Court need not result in a trial. Abandonment or settlement of the proceedings may result.

Assuming, however, that proceedings lead to a trial, in the common law system the function of the Judge is to decide the issue between the parties on the basis of the law and on the basis of the evidence which the parties choose to place before him. When he has reached a decision, the matter is then *res judicata* and subject only to such appeal rights as may exist.

Such is the tradition that most common law jurisdictions apply to the resolution of family conflict. In one area, the dissolution of marriages, the element of conflict has in recent years become scarce. A multiplicity of grounds for divorce exist throughout the various jurisdictions of the British Commonwealth and the United States but in all jurisdictions a contested divorce is an increasing rarity.[1] The requirement for judicial proceedings lingers on partly for historical reasons and partly, I suggest, because legislatures still require a significant degree of formality for the dissolution of a marriage.

The family conflicts most likely to come before a Court are those involving children and financial arrangements. The substantive criteria which the Court must apply will of course vary from jurisdiction to

---

* The author gratefully acknowledges the assistance given during the preparation of this chapter by their Honours, Judge P.J. Trapski, Principal Family Court Judge and Judge S.R. Cartwright.

jurisdiction. What all Courts share, however, is the duty to decide. At the end of a trial the Court will make its decision which will determine which parent is to have custody of which children, how much maintenance one spouse must pay another, what property is to be divided in what fashion, and frequency of contact between children and a noncustodial parent.

In the context of the common law judicial system this process is unremarkable. In the context of family disputes, however, it masks two features. First, the trial indicates that the couple have been unable to resolve between themselves the dispute which prompted litigation. Secondly, the decision of the Court will often leave one or both parties dissatisfied. Dissatisfaction can easily be a source of future disputes in the family context particularly where the parties must continue to have contact. Ultimately a decision of a Court is a decision that is imposed on the parties and can be enforced if need be. These features of a judicial decision can generate friction.

New Zealand's *Family Proceedings Act, 1980* has introduced into the New Zealand Family Law litigation process a new feature — the mediation conference. The *Family Proceedings Act* enacted wide-ranging substantive and procedural changes to New Zealand's family law which lie outside the scope of this chapter.[2] Amongst other changes was the introduction of a separate family court with specialist judges and professionally trained staff. For all intents and purposes the New Zealand Family Court exercises exclusive jurisdiction in matrimonial disputes.[3]

Procedurally, the mediation conference is the second tier of the New Zealand Family Court's three tier system. The first tier comprises the Court's counselling services, which are available at the request of the parties or their lawyers or which are mandatory before many applications to the Family Court can proceed.[4] The tier above the mediation conference is the trial itself before the Family Court Judge.

The underlying purpose of the mediation conference is to avoid unnecessary litigation. The procedural and substantive requirements of the Act are simple. A mediation conference is available in any case where a party has made an application to the Family Court for a separation order, maintenance order, custody order or access order.[5] Thus, litigation must have commenced. Any party may at any stage prior to the trial request the Registrar of the Court to convene a mediation conference.[6] Such a request by a party makes the calling of a mediation conference mandatory.[7] It is also possible for a Family Court Judge at any stage in the proceedings to arrange a mediation conference for the parties.[8] A date and venue (always in a Family Courthouse) is arranged and the parties are informed by mail. So too are their lawyers.

The objectives of the mediation conference are

1. to identify the matters in issue between the parties; and
2. to try to obtain agreement between the parties on the resolution of those matters.[9]

The mediation conference is chaired by a Family Court Judge.[10] However, the distinctive feature of the conference is that its Chairman is not acting in a judicial capacity and the conference itself is not a judicial proceeding. However, although in his capacity as chairman of the mediation conference the Judge is not sitting in his judicial capacity, the fact that he is a Judge endows the mediation conference with an authority and purpose which would be lacking from a counselling session. Undoubtedly the Chairman's judicial office, which is known to the parties, has some psychological effect. It also enables any agreements reached at the conference to be implemented without delay since the Chairman can revert to his role as a Judge to make consent orders. The parties are usually aware that the Chairman of their conference has the ability to make consent orders and in some cases this will act as an incentive to the parties to resolve their dispute, thus avoiding the more harrowing experience of a trial.

There is no prescribed format for a mediation conference, but the practice of the Family Court has been to stress informality. The conference rooms are simply but attractively furnished and decorated. The Judge in his capacity as Chairman sits at the same level as and close to the parties. Realistically perhaps the parties are not seated side by side but in close proximity, usually facing the Judge. Sometimes the lawyers in attendance will sit beside their clients. Sometimes they will sit apart from the parties.

The role of the lawyers at a mediation conference is extremely limited. There is no evidence or cross-examination. Intervention by a lawyer for a party is usually only appropriate if it helps to clarify an issue or make progress towards resolution of a dispute. Counsel appointed to act for children who are subject to custody and access disputes may play a more active role informing the Chairman and the parties of his investigations and recommendations. On occasion the parties' lawyers may not be present either by design or because the Chairman has, with the parties' consent, asked them to leave. The request of a party that his lawyer be present will always be respected. With the exception of counsel acting for the children, the Family Court Judges have made it clear that they expect the role of counsel at mediation conferences to be largely passive.[11]

The Judge in his capacity as Chairman will have read the file and will explore the issues with the parties. Often one party will have sought various orders that are not contested, and those matters that at a later stage can be dealt with by written agreement or consent orders, are identified. Once the parties are seated before him the Chairman will frequently invite one or both parties to explain the issues to him as they see them. This approach is valuable since it frequently leads directly to the heart of the dispute which divides the parties.

The mediation conference is, of course, held in private. Furthermore its proceedings are privileged. No information, statement or admission during the course of the mediation conference can be admissible in any subsequent proceedings.[12] The concept of privilege can create difficulties should a trial prove necessary. A trained lawyer will have little difficulty in setting aside those matters which were raised in a mediation conference as being unavailable to him for the purposes of evidence or cross-examination. Such a distinction, however, is not so easy to grasp by the litigant who will have to have it explained that the proceedings of the mediation conference cannot form part of his case in Court. The mediation conference provides the lawyer with a useful dimension not otherwise available to him. He is able to observe the other party and is further able to assess such matters as the credibility and demeanour of both parties — opportunities that a lawyer would seldom have in the pretrial phase.

If, as a result of a mediation conference it is apparent to the Chairman that certain orders which could be made by the Family Court can be made by consent, then the Chairman can revert to his judicial role and make such orders. If one or both of the parties at the conference are not represented by a lawyer, then it is usual to adjourn the conference to allow legal advice to be taken unless the unrepresented party expressly wishes a consent order to be made without benefit of legal advice. Any such orders made during the mediation conference are orders of the Family Court.[13]

Interestingly, the consent orders which can be made at a mediation conference may relate not only to the matters in respect of which a statutory right for mediation conference exists (separation, maintenance, custody and access) but can also be made in respect of property matters.[14]

It is obligatory for the Chairman to record in writing the issues at the conference showing separately those matters that are resolved by the parties and those matters that remain unresolved. Such a written record is attached to the Court file.[15]

Although the mediation conference procedure has at the time of this writing been in operation only for some five months in New Zealand, it is already having a dramatic effect on family litigation. Current indications suggest that the conferences are resolving approximately 60 percent of the disputes for which they are called. Indications in one large urban centre suggest that over 50 percent of mediation conferences have resulted in all issues being resolved and a further 20 percent have resulted in partial resolution of issues.[16] The procedure demands considerable effort and skill from the chairing Judge. The usual length of a mediation conference is approximately one and a half hours. From time to time, especially when the passions of the parties become inflamed, the Chairman may call a short adjournment. For the parties, however, the conference will, more frequently than not, result in a resolution of their disputes which they themselves have reached. Such a satisfactory result for the parties is achieved without formal evidence, cross-examination, omission of points of view or factors that the parties themselves think important, or an imposed decision.

Several features of mediation conferences, from a procedural point of view, merit mention. At a trial a Judge is seldom able to indicate before conclusion his likely decision. Such a course would immediately give rise to questions of bias. At a mediation conference, however, the Chairman, having examined the Court file, identified the issues, and discussed matters with the parties, will frequently give an indication of a likely result. The Chairman can give reasons and present a fair and impartial assessment in a friendly capacity, so that the Chairman's view often results in a party's accepting it as a suitable basis for a consent order.

There is no prohibition against a Family Court Judge who has chaired a mediation conference presiding at any subsequent proceedings between the parties.[17] In some cases the Judge who chaired the conference will also preside at the trial. Frequently, at the outset of the conference, the Chairman indicates to the parties that should a trial eventuate he will not be the Judge at it. Such a declaration undoubtedly assists the objectives of the mediation conference since the parties are likely to be less cautious and inhibited. In situations where the Chairman has indicated his own views of a likely result there could well be difficulties if that Judge were subsequently to preside at the trial since, in the eyes of one of the parties, there would be an element of bias. In the larger centres where there are a number of Family Court Judges it is most unusual for the Judge who acted as Chairman of the mediation conference to preside at the subsequent trial unless the parties specifically request it.

Another feature of mediation conferences is that frequently the parties will agree on some interim measure which will otherwise not be possible at a pretrial stage. In turn, that interim agreement can result in the dispute being more easily resolved or the resulting trial being less damaging. Two examples are illustrative of this process, both involving custody disputes.

In the first case, a *de facto* couple had two sons aged four and two. The couple had lived for some years in a house of which the mother was the tenant. The father had custody of a seven year old son of a former marriage. The couple were bitterly estranged partly because of the father's domineering temperament, partly because of the mother's lifestyle. At the time proceedings were issued, the father had been living in the mother's house with all three children while the mother lived elsewhere. The father had resigned from his manual job to care for all three children. Shortly after the issue of proceedings the mother, acting on legal advice, returned to her house and refused to leave. She took this step partly to protect her position as a tenant and partly to reestablish contact with the children. The atmosphere in the home became heated and the father's Social Welfare benefit was in jeopardy because he was "cohabiting" with another adult. To preserve his benefit entitlement, therefore, the father moved out of the house with the three children and installed the family in a tent on adjoining land! Both parties were in part motivated by financial considerations.

In the normal course of events the litigation process would have made a speedy resolution of this dispute very difficult. Counsel for the children had not yet been appointed. No reports from children's Counsel or Social Workers had been prepared. Affidavits dealing with the children's background environment and the suitability of the parents were not yet prepared and filed. The lawyer acting for the mother would clearly be reluctant to advise his client to leave the home. The lawyer acting for the father would equally be reluctant to advise the father to surrender custody of the children to the mother.

An urgent mediation conference was arranged with the Family Court. The Chairman listened to both parties and stressed quite bluntly that both parties were overlooking the interests of their children. The mother for her part was reluctant to let the father remain with the children because they were "hers." The father for his part was not prepared to return the children to their mother because of his objections to her lifestyle. The conference did not resolve the issue of custody but the parties accepted an interim solution in terms of which the children returned to the house and lived there with their father for five days of the week after which period the father left the house for two days while the children's mother came into occupation.

The second case involved a divorced couple with three children aged ten, eight and five who had had no contact with their father for some eighteen months. The father commenced access proceedings. The mother's position was that she was not prepared to let the father have access to the children because the elder two children had a deep-seated aversion to their father. This aversion stemmed in part from their dislike of the environment where their father lived — a commune with an underlying philosophy of uninhibited sexuality — and partly because the children recounted to their mother their distaste of certain sexual intimacies that the children said their father had conducted with them. The mother stated her position in these allegations in affidavit form. The father hotly denied those allegations.

Had such a matter gone to trial, a Judge would be faced with a difficult situation. Although he would have had the benefit of a report from Counsel for the children, he would nonetheless have had to resolve whether or not the children's allegations concerning their father's behaviour were correct. He would have had to resolve further the extent to which access against the inclination of the children would have been harmful to them.

At the mediation conference both parties stated their position. The Judge indicated that he considered the mother's denial of access was motivated by a very real concern for her children rather than by any animosity towards her former husband. He further indicated that the allegations made by the children raised important issues of principle which would have to be further investigated. As a result, the parties agreed that the Counsel appointed to act for the children should engage the services of a child psychologist to investigate the entire background; interview the parents; interview the children; arrange for initial access to the father if it seemed appropriate as a result of those investigations and monitor and supervise such access. Such a preliminary inquiry into a delicate area of great importance to the welfare of the children would not have been possible without the intervening mediation conference.

These examples perhaps serve to illustrate some of the advantages of the mediation conference procedure even though in both examples only a partial resolution was possible. The procedure enables the Chairman to direct the parties towards some form of interim or "trial" solution which may frequently satisfy the parties and form the basis of a final resolution of their dispute once the interim measure has been in operation for a period. In the litigation context such interim solutions are almost impossible since the Judge at a trial is required to decide. Frequently too, the mediation conference procedure enables the Chairman to place before the parties various forms of compromise that, by virtue of being so presented, will often result in a settlement. No such procedure is possible in the context of a trial. Finally, a full or partial resolution of the dispute at a mediation conference is one which leaves both parties satisfied to a large degree. Judges have observed that parties do not leave a mediation conference distressed, whereas distress is often evident when judgment is given at the end of a trial.

The New Zealand Family Courts mediation conference is an interesting procedural device standing midway between counselling and trial. Using a Family Court Judge as a Chairman of the conference is an innovative device which brings to the conference all the benefits of judicial experience without the necessity to adjudicate between the parties or to impose a decision. The objectives of the conference benefit both the parties and the Court. Nondisputed matters that are subject to the litigation can be dealt with and disposed of by consent orders. Frequently the entire mediation conference procedure results in the parties settling all their differences without the necessity of a trial. In those cases where a trial proves necessary the issues are frequently narrowed. The procedure lessens the likelihood of a trial. For the parties, a potential source of conflict is removed. For the Court there is a lessening of case load.

NOTES

1. In New Zealand there is now only one ground for dissolution of marriage — that the marriage has broken down irreconcilably. *Family Proceedings Act, 1980,* s. 39(1). Irreconcilable breakdown however, can only be established to the Court's satisfaction where the parties have lived apart for a period of two years: s. 39(2). A novel feature of the

New Zealand legislation is that an application for dissolution can be brought before the Court jointly by both parties to a marriage: s. 37(1)(b).
   2. See also the *Family Courts Act, 1980.*
   3. *Family Proceedings Act, 1980,* ss. 4, 8 to 11.
   4. *Family Proceedings Act, 1980,* ss. 9, 10, and 11. The Court's counsellors have a duty to arrange to meet both parties but the counsellor has a further duty to explore the possibility of reconciliation between the parties or to promote conciliation. The counsellor must further report to the Court as to whether the marriage can be saved or, if not, whether any understandings have been reached between the parties. s. 12.
   5. *Id.,* s. 13(1).
   6. *Family Proceedings Rules, 1981,* R. 29(1).
   7. *Family Proceedings Act, 1980,* s. 13(2).
   8. *Id.,* s. 13(1). This power of the Judge is in addition to the duty imposed on the Court by s. 19 to consider at all times the possibility of a reconciliation and, in appropriate cases, to adjourn proceedings to enable further counselling to take place.
   9. *Id.,* s. 13(2).
   10. *Id.,* s. 14(1).
   11. *Id.,* s. 14. The legislation gives to the lawyers of both the parties and the children a discretionary right to be present.
   12. *Id.,* s. 18(1)(b).
   13. *Id.,* s. 15.
   14. *Id.,* s. 15(1)(d).
   15. *Id.,* s. 14(7).
   16. These statistics are as yet unprocessed and result from approximately fifty mediation conferences held over the past five months in the Auckland Family Court.
   17. *Family Proceedings Act, 1980,* s. 16.

Chapter Seven

The Role of Mediation in Yugoslav Divorce: Court Versus Out-of-Court Mediation

Petar Šarčević

Rijenka University, Yugoslavia

INTRODUCTION

In the SFR of Yugoslavia, divorce is regarded as a remedy for dissolving marriages in which the marital relationships have broken down irretrievably. However, the remedy is not available immediately. Before a divorce can be granted, as a rule the spouses must first participate in so-called mediation hearings.

Under Yugoslav law, mediation in divorce proceedings is by no means a novelty but rather a tradition that has, however, been subject to reform. Forms of mediation include court-offered, court-ordered, and most recently out-of-court mediation. Regardless of who conducts the mediation hearings and how they are conducted, all forms of mediation have the same purpose, i.e., to give the spouses the opportunity to analyse their marital relationship and decide whether their marriage has lost its meaning for them and their children to the extent that divorce is the only acceptable solution.[1]

BRIEF HISTORICAL SURVEY OF THE IMMEDIATE POSTWAR PERIOD

After World War II, divorce in the SFR of Yugoslavia was regulated by the *Federal Basic Law on Marriage* which came into force on May 9, 1946.[2] According to Art. 80 of the said law, the president of the district court or a judge appointed by the former was to attempt to reconcile spouses who had filed for divorce.

This provision, which was regarded as a measure for discouraging hasty divorces, was later repealed by Art. 402–404 of the *Code of Civil Procedure* of 1956,[3] according to which the chairman of the board of judges handling the particular divorce suit was to preside over the mediation hearings. Mediation attempts were required even in cases in which the spouses had filed joint petition for divorce.[4] If the spouses failed to appear, the mediation hearing was considered unsuccessful and the judge continued with the divorce proceedings. If, on the other hand, the spouses did appear but were not reconciled, the presiding judge could either close the mediation hearings or, if he were of the opinion that there was a chance for success, set a new date for further mediation.

In general, it can be said that the mediation hearings were not very successful. As Prokop pointed out, the presiding judges were often young and inexperienced,[5] tended to schedule the hearings too soon after the divorce petition had been filed, and as a rule, were not duly informed about the living conditions of the parties and their families.[6] Consequently, mediation was often reduced to a mere formality and was thus criticized as being strictly a procedural institution.[7]

LEGAL REGULATIONS GOVERNING MEDIATION TODAY

With enactment of the *Federal Constitutional Amendments* No. XX–XLII of 1971[8] and the *Federal Constitution* of 1974,[9] legislation on subject matters related to marriage and the family, such as guardianship, parent–child relations, inheritance, divorce, etc., as well as the procedural aspects thereof, were placed under the exclusive jurisdiction of the socialist republics and autonomous provinces. The decentralization of jurisdiction led to a diversity of solutions in the various legislative regulations governing family relations, including those on mediation.

To date mediation is governed by the family laws of the respective republics and provinces[10] with the exception of the SR of Macedonia[11] where a special procedural law for family relations has been adopted. There are presently three different approaches to mediation. The laws in force in the SR of Montenegro (1973), the SAP of Kosovo (1974), the SAP of Vojvodina (1975), and the SR of Macedonia (1978) provide court mediation; those in the SR of Slovenia (1976), the SR of Croatia (1978) and the SR of Bosnia and Hercegovina (1979), out-of-court mediation; and those in the SR of Serbia (1980), a combination of court and out-of-court mediation.

It is evident that the earliest divorce laws continued the tradition of court mediation carried over from the former *Law on Marriage* of 1946 and the *Code of Civil Procedure* of 1956. Then, as a result of divorce reform during the second half of the seventies, court mediation was replaced by out-of-court mediation (with the exception of the SR of Macedonia).

Before we examine the existing legal regulations governing court and out-of-court mediation, it should be pointed out that as a rule, mediation is mandatory in Yugoslavia's republics and provinces.

Exceptions

Although the value of mandatory mediation has been questioned abroad,[12] Yugoslav legislators have nevertheless overwhelmingly chosen to make mediation compulsory, whether it be court or out-of-court. Thus, parties that have filed or intend to file for divorce must participate in mediation proceedings regardless of whether one of the parties has filed for divorce, whether both of the parties have filed a joint petition for divorce, or whether both of the parties have filed for divorce by mutual consent.

With the exception of the SAP of Vojvodina, the legislatures exempt parties from mediation in specific cases in which (1) one of the spouses is incapable of forming intent, (2) one or both of the spouses live abroad, or (3) the petitioner has filed for divorce on the grounds that the respondent has disappeared. These exceptions are subject to different restrictions depending on the legislation of the particular republic or provinces. In the SR of Croatia, for example, mediation can also be required in cases in which one or both of the spouses live abroad, if the spouses have an underaged child of their own or an adopted child, or are guardians to an underaged child (Art. 61 II).[13]

Unless otherwise stipulated by special provisions, the legislature of the SAP of Vojvodina has left it up to the court in each individual case to decide if mediation is required. Art. 77 of Vojvodina's *Law on Marriage* explicitly states that the court is not obliged to conduct mediation hearings if it is impossible for objective reasons or if it would produce exceptional difficulties for the parties. This provision should, however, by no means be regarded as a sign of leniency on the part of the legislature; on the contrary, statistics on court practice reveal that mediation is conducted in divorce suits in the SAP of Vojvodina just as often as in the other republics and provinces.

As an exception to the general rule that mediation is required in all cases, Art. 57 of the Croatian *Law on Marriage and Family Relations* provides that parties filing for divorce by mutual consent be exempted from mediation if they have no underaged child of their own, no adopted child, or are not guardians to an underaged child.

The legislatures of the other republics were not as lenient toward couples without children. In the SR of Serbia, for example, mediation is required in cases in which the spouses have no children, as well as in those in which the parties have children of full age; however, in these cases the court shall decide whether to conduct the mediation itself or to refer the parties to the guardianship authorities (Art. 353 II). If, on the other hand, the spouses have an underaged child or children, mediation falls under the exclusive jurisdiction of the guardianship authorities in the SR of Serbia, and no exceptions are permitted, not even in cases where the spouses have been separated for years. As Janković[14] points out, by ruling out exceptions, the legislature has provided a safeguard against the possibility that any such exceptions would have been interpreted too broadly in practice.

Court Mediation

In two of Yugoslavia's six republics and both of the provinces, mediation is still conducted before the court. As a judicial organ of the state, it is the duty of the court to uphold the Constitution and enforce the laws, including those extending special protection to the family and its nucleus — the institution of marriage. In a certain sense, this authorizes and obliges the court to emphasize the "uniting" rather than the "disuniting" elements of marital relationships.[15] Thus, the court is required to actively attempt to reconcile the spouses during the course of the entire divorce proceedings, especially in cases involving minors.[16]

In court mediation, the court sets a special hearing for mediation and summons both parties to appear without their attorneys. If the first mediation hearing brings no positive results, the presiding judge may schedule one or more further hearings and continue to do so as long as he believes that there is a chance for the spouses to be reconciled.[17] Nevertheless, in an analysis of fifty-one divorce suits in which mediation hearings were conducted before the court in Mostar, reconciliation was not attained in a single case.[18]

Perhaps the most important factor contributing to the poor results of court mediation in Mostar under the former *Law on Marriage* of the SR of Bosnia and Hercegovina[19] was the failure of the parties to appear at the hearings even though they had been properly summoned. In her analysis, Bubić points out that many of the scheduled mediation sessions could not be held due to the absence of the parties.[20] In cases where one or both of the spouses failed to appear, as a rule, the judge was free to review the circumstances and decide whether to set a new hearing for mediation or to conclude that mediation was unsuccessful and continue with the divorce proceedings. In general, failure to appear was interpreted as the parties' express wish to remain unreconciled, and accordingly the judge tended to discontinue mediation and schedule the divorce proceedings.

In addition to the above mentioned regulations which had been taken over from the *Code of Civil Procedure* of 1956, the legislators of those republics and provinces still providing court mediation have usually included special provisions aimed at forcing the parties — at least the plaintiff — to appear at the mediation hearing. Art. 80 of the *Law on Marriage* of the SAP of Vojvodina, for example, states that if a petitioner who has been properly summoned to appear at a mediation hearing fails to do so, his petition shall be considered to have been withdrawn. A similar provision has been adopted in the SAP of Kosovo when the parties file joint petition for divorce. If neither of the parties lives abroad and one or both of them fail to appear at the mediation hearing, their joint petition shall be considered to have been withdrawn (Art. 67 IV).

As for the role of the judge, Neuhaus[21] claims that the success of court mediation depends to a large extent on the personality of the judge and his ability to relate to the parties. To increase the judge's chances of winning the confidence of the parties, divorce legislation in the SR of Montenegro permits him to consult with each party separately if he feels that this could improve the chances for closing the hearings successfully (Art. 91 II).

On the other hand, as Neuhaus points out, judges are not qualified to take on the role of professional marriage counsellors: attempting to reconcile parties by consultation is something completely different from holding an inquiry to determine whether reconciliation can perhaps be attained.[22] Foreseeing this difficulty, the legislature of the SAP of Kosovo included a provision obliging the court to collaborate with specialized counselling services and other professional institutions dealing with marriage and family problems (Art. 68 II). To date, however, it is still not clear to what extent the courts have actually responded to this obligation and referred parties to professional counsellors.

Attempting to make divorce proceedings more humane, as Bakić puts it,[23] the Serbian law of 1974[24] had provided court-ordered counselling services. The presiding judge could either refer the parties to a professional counselling service or other institution for family affairs, or he could summon professional people from these institutions to participate in mediation hearings before the court. For the legislature it was important that the success of the hearing should not depend on the judge alone and that professional counselling be provided.

Out-of-Court Mediation

In view of the fact that court mediation, generally speaking, was not successful to a sufficient degree, reform was clearly indicated. The legislature of the SR of Slovenia took the initiative and eliminated court mediation, replacing it with a type of out-of-court mediation. According to the Slovenian divorce regulations of 1976, a divorce shall not be granted unless the parties have been counselled by the competent organ of the Municipal Department of Welfare. Upon receipt of a divorce petition, including those for divorce by mutual consent, the court forwards it to the Municipal Department of Welfare which then opens the mediation proceedings (Art. 68). Mediation is mandatory: in unilateral divorce suits, the proceedings shall be promptly suspended if the plaintiff fails to appear for mediation; or if the parties have filed joint petition for divorce, the proceedings shall be suspended unless both parties appear at the mediation hearing (Art. 71). A similar provision has been adopted in the SR of Croatia which has also introduced mandatory out-of-court mediation.

As was mentioned above, to date, out-of-court mediation is also mandatory in the SR of Bosnia and Hercegovina, while the SR of Serbia has settled for a combination of both types of mediation depending on whether the parties have underaged children.[25] The purpose of out-of-court mediation is to provide the parties with professional counselling. Under professional guidance the spouses analyse their marital relationship and decide whether the marriage has suffered an irretrievable breakdown. If reconciliation cannot be achieved, the counsellors shall help the parties prepare for the postmarital transition.

It is, therefore, of utmost importance that the authorities conducting the mediation sessions are staffed with personnel trained especially for this type of counselling. The problem of providing adequate counsellors has tended to discourage other countries from requiring out-of-court mediation in divorce proceedings. In the United States, for example, mediation or conciliation, as Krause refers to it,[26] has not been widely practiced due to the lack of trained personnel, the expense in view of the often limited chances for success, etc.

Contrary to the situation in the United States, where the constitutionality of required conciliation has been questioned,[27] in Yugoslavia the legality of mandatory mediation has never been questioned. Thus, the republics requiring out-of-court mediation have automatically assumed the responsibility for providing the necessary professional counselling services. In the SR of Croatia, for example, the guardianship authorities responsible for conducting mediation are staffed not only with social workers but also with lawyers, psychologists and psychiatrists qualified to counsel the spouses.

In the SR of Croatia, mediation constitutes a separate proceeding that must precede the divorce proceedings in court. The parties are required to contact the guardianship authorities in their area and request that a date be set for the opening mediation session. Failure to do so will result in the rejection of their petition for divorce (Art. 60).[28] During the mediation sessions the trained personnel of the guardianship authorities examine the causes of the spouses' marital discord and advise them how to resolve their differences.

In the SR of Serbia, the divorce petition filed at court is not handed over to the guardianship authorities. According to Jankovic,[29] this is a precautionary measure to conceal the contents of the petition from the respondent before mediation is conducted. In its report, the court is obliged to inform the guardianship authorities about the date the divorce petition was filed, the main grounds for divorce, the living conditions of any underaged children, etc. (Art. 353 II). Since no facts are to be included that could eventually offend the respondent, the grounds for divorce are stated in general terms, e.g., incompatibility, disagreement in matters concerning the upbringing of the children, and so on.

During mediation the parties are instructed about their rights and duties as spouses and parents, and in particular, about the effects of an eventual divorce on the upbringing of their children. If the parties cannot be reconciled, the counsellors attempt to help them reach an agreement regarding the care, upbringing and support of any underaged children, whether they be their own or adopted. If no agreement can be reached, the counsellors themselves propose solutions including regulating the parental rights, based on the specific circumstances of each case.

To insure the parties of prompt counselling services, out-of-court mediation proceedings in the SR of Serbia and the SR of Croatia are limited to a period of no longer than three months from the day the mediation proceedings are opened. The express consent of the parties is required in order to prolong the sessions. After mediation has been closed, the counsellors are obliged to send their report to the court without delay. If the sessions have been successful, the joint statement of the parties acknowledging their reconciliation shall be interpreted as the withdrawal of their petition for divorce.[30] If, on the other hand, the parties have not been reconciled and the counsellors hold the marriage breakdown to be irretrievable, their report must include the parents' proposal for regulating their parental rights and duties, or if none has been reached, the counsellor's proposal to this end. At their request, copies of the report are made available to the parties. All information contained therein as well as all information presented during the course of mediation is subject to official secrecy.[31]

Concluding Remarks

Current philosophy on divorce calls for a more humane treatment of the parties. At least in the preliminary stages of the divorce proceedings, the spouses need the help of professional counsellors who regard them as patients and provide therapy instead of citing paragraphs and imposing sentences. Whereas court mediation tends to be reduced to a mere procedural formality, in out-of-court mediation a team of experts advises the spouses and attempts to reconcile them or at least help them reach an agreement about the upbringing and support of any underaged children that is in the best interest of the children.

It is still too early to predict to what extent out-of-court mediation will affect the divorce rate; however, since the guardianship authorities have begun conducting mediation in the SR of Croatia, those institutions staffed with the necessary professional counsellors have already attained much better results than had been the case under former court mediation.[32] In view of the complexity of divorce cases today, the already overburdened judges have not been able to satisfactorily fulfil their obligation as mediators. Therefore, the legislatures of the most recent divorce laws in the Yugoslav republics have chosen to transfer the role of the mediator in divorce proceedings to social institutions experienced in dealing with marital problems.

NOTES

1. On this subject see Alinčić/Barkarić, *Porodično pravo (Family Law),* Zagreb 1980, 98; Bakić, *Porodično pravo (Family Law),* Belgrade 1980, 199; Mladenović, *Porodično pravo II (Family Law II),* Belgrade 1981, 698.

2. Published in the *Official Gazette of the Federal Peoples' Republic of Yugoslavia* No. 29/1946.

3. Published in the *Official Gazette of the Federal Peoples' Republic of Yugoslavia* No. 4/1957.

4. According to Art. 402 III mediation was not required (1) if one of the spouses were mentally ill or incapable of forming intent, (2) if one or both of the spouses lived abroad, or (3) if the petitioner had filed for divorce on the grounds that the respondent had disappeared.

5. Prokop, *Komentar osnovnom zakonu o braku II (Commentary on the Basic Law on Marriage II),* Zagreb 1960, 407, note 345.

6. *Ibid.,* 408.

7. *Ibid.,* Zuglia/Triva, *Komentar Zakona o parničnom postupku II (Commentary on the Law of Civil Procedure II),* Zagreb 1957, 358.

8. Published in the *Official Gazette of the Socialist Federal Republic of Yugoslavia* No. 29/1971.

9. Published in the *Official Gazette of the Socialist Federal Republic of Yugoslavia* No. 9/1974.

10. The *Law on Marriage,* published in the *Official Gazette of the SR of Montenegro* No. 17/1973; the *Law on Marriage,* published in the *Official Gazette of the SAP of Kosovo* No. 43/1974; the *Law on Marriage,* published in the *Official Gazette of the SAP of Vojvodina* No. 2/1975; the *Law on Marital and other Family Relations,* published in the *Official Gazette of the SR of Slovenia* No. 15/1976; the *Law on Marriage and Family Relations,* published in the *Official Gazette of the SR of Croatia* No. 11/1978; the *Law on Marriage and Family Relations,* published in the *Official Gazette of the SR of Bosnia and Hercegovina* No. 21/1979; the *Law on Marriage and Family Relations,* published in the *Official Gazette of the SR of Serbia* No. 22/1980.

11. The *Law of Special Procedure for Family Disputes*, published in the *Official Gazette of the SR of Macedonia* No. 13/1978.

12. See, e.g., Krause, *Family Law in a Nutshell*, St. Paul Minnesota (West Publishing Co.) 1977, 299; Neuhaus, *Ehe und Kindschaft in rechtsvergleichender Sicht*, Tübingen 1979, 198.

13. As for point 3, the following restrictions can be mentioned: In the SR of Bosnia and Hercegovina and the SR of Croatia, the residence of the respondent must have been unknown for at least six months; in the SAP of Kosovo for more than two years, while in the SR of Macedonia and the SR of Montenegro no time requirement was specified.

14. Janković, *Komentar Zakona o braku i porodičnim odnosima (Commentary on the Law on Marriage and Family Relations)*, Belgrade 1981, 273.

15. Triva, Pokušaj mirenja u bračnom sporu ("The Mediation Attempt in Marriage Disputes"), in *Anali Pravnog fakulteta u Beogradu* No. 2/1959, 178.

16. Bakić, *op. cit.*, 199.

17. Art. 68 I of the *Law on Marriage* of the SAP of Kosovo.

18. Bubić, Mirenje bračnih drugova ("The Mediation of Spouses") in *Zbornik Pravnog fakulteta u Mostaru* No. 1/1979, 226.

19. Published in the *Official Gazette of the SR of Bosnia and Hercegovina* No. 37/1971.

20. Bubić, *op. cit.*, 225.

21. Neuhaus, *op. cit.*, 199.

22. *Ibid.*

23. Bakić, *op cit.*, 199.

24. The *Law on Marriage*, published in the *Official Gazette of the SR of Serbia* No. 52/1974.

25. See page 109 of this article.

26. Krause, *op. cit.*, 301.

27. *Ibid.*

28. See the exception to this rule on page 109 of this article.

29. Janković, *op. cit.*, 274.

30. *Ibid.*, 276.

31. Art. 65 of the *Law on Marriage and Family Relations* of the SR of Croatia.

32. Alinčić/Bakarić, *op. cit.*, 99.

Chapter Eight

Procedural Aspects of Marriage Dissolution in Japan

Ichiro Shimazu

Hitotsubashi University, Tokyo

This chapter describes the divorce procedures in Japan, with special emphasis on divorce by conciliation: its structure, function, and procedure.

DIVORCE BY CONSENT

There are four types of divorce: divorce by consent, divorce by conciliation, divorce by Family Court determination, and divorce by Civil Court decision. These are explained in turn. The first type is the most common form of divorce, and constitutes as much as 89 percent of all divorces. Provision for divorce by consent was enacted in 1898. Two years earlier, a Drafters' Council meeting was held at which an overwhelming majority (sixteen members to one) agreed to adopt divorce by consent, rejecting unilateral divorce, which is divorce by the decision of one party, usually the husband. The Drafters' Council decided on this change chiefly to grant wives the right to consent and to participate in the divorce process, and in addition, to introduce the concept of "no-fault" divorce. They explained that if husband and wife find that they are incompatible and want to separate, the law should not force them to stay together.

In Japan today, the procedure for divorce by consent is extremely simple. It is accomplished by notifying the chief elected representative in the town of residence, corresponding approximately to the office of Mayor in the United States. Notification is usually made in written form; signatures are necessary for this, but they need not be those of the spouses themselves. The signature of a third person is acceptable. This means that sometimes notification is made without the consent of the spouse.

Divorce is effected by the acceptance of notification, and the chief representative proceeds to put the fact of acceptance into the Family Registration Book. There is no court involvement.

In some cases, perhaps only 2 or 3 percent of the total, notification is made by one spouse without the consent of the other. In these cases, there are two possible remedies: one that applies before notification has been made, and one that applies afterwards. If a spouse is considering notification *without the consent* of the other spouse, the other spouse may petition the chief representative *in advance* not to accept the notification. In this instance the chief representative returns the notification when it is made, and there is no divorce. Once notification has been made to the chief representative, the matter must go to a court to nullify the acceptance and delete it from the Family Registration Book. It will go first to the Family Court for conciliation, and if this is not achieved, the case must go to the Civil Court. Moreover, if divorce is agreed, but matters concerning child custody, child support, or division of property are contested, the spouse may apply to the Family Court for conciliation or determination.

In the period shortly after the Second World War, it was argued that, before the chief representative was notified, intention to divorce should be confirmed by the Family Court. This system was adopted in our neighbouring country, South Korea, in 1979, but Japan's Law Council decided in 1959 against enacting such an amendment. I believe that the present system should be maintained on the grounds that (1) the spouse knows best about his or her marriage partner, and the matter of divorce should remain a question for the family; (2) divorce by consent preserves family privacy with minimum state intervention; and (3) it serves to save government spending. The reordering of the broken family after a divorce is most smoothly accomplished when agreement is reached between the spouses with regard to child custody, child support, and division of property. Divorce by consent precisely embodies the spirit of "no-fault" divorce, by removing the "adversary" element.

DIVORCE BY CONCILIATION

Provision for conciliation of personal affairs in court was enacted in 1939. The provision institutionalized the old custom in which a leader of the village community used to settle disputes between community members. It was improved after the Second World War so that conciliation would be conducted on a more "scientific" basis.

In Japan, while divorce actions are dealt with by District or Civil Courts, conciliation in divorce cases is handled by Family Courts. By law, any person seeking divorce action must apply, in the first instance, to Family Courts for conciliation (Art. 18, *Law for Determination of*

Family Affairs). This is called the Principle of Preexistence of Conciliation Procedure. This means that conciliation is compulsory. Criticism of this procedure is growing, however, because conciliation is effective only when both parties are willing to undergo it voluntarily. In practice, therefore, the conciliation procedure fails when the other party does not wish to accept it.

The committee responsible for conciliation consists of a judge and two conciliators, usually a man and a woman. The judge does not usually attend each conciliation session. He hears reports from the conciliators and serves generally as an advisor or an overviewer. Conciliators are chosen among lay people. Those over forty years of age who have attended some lectures on family law at college or who have been trained as counsellors at vocational schools usually apply. They are selected by personal interview and on the basis of a test group discussion session.

The conciliation procedure starts with an attempt to create an atmosphere of trust among all members, with an understanding that all facts revealed during the sessions shall be confidential. The conciliators then try to ascertain the backgrounds of both parties. Sometimes they construct life histories going back to a person's infancy. In some cases, conciliators can find in the life history some important facts of which the parties concerned were not aware. This process helps the parties to gain objectivity, insight, and reason. The conciliators therefore aid the parties in thinking through their own problem and in reaching their own conclusion. Undeniably there are a few conciliators who fail, who try to press upon the parties their own value-judgments and who attempt to impose their own conclusions to save the marriage, rather than to serve individual needs. In these cases, conciliation procedures can not be said to be totally successful.

If and when it is decided that divorce is the right solution, conciliators encourage the parties to discuss custody, division of family property and compensation for mental distress. Custody of children in 80 percent of conciliation cases is granted to the mother, with no access for the father to see the children. Visiting rights, or joint custody, are rare because of the fact that, traditionally, the tasks of child-rearing remain almost entirely in the hands of women. When the father is granted custody, the father's mother, that is, the child's paternal grandmother, takes care of the child or children. When the mother is granted custody, the mother's mother takes care of the children because the mother must go to work for self-support. In Japan, more than 20 percent of all families are three-generation families; in this context, the older traditional family system of Japan survives. However, custody disputes between father and mother are now increasing. When custody is disputed, agreements concerning matters other than custody are sought under the conciliation procedure, and custody is determined by the Family Court (Art. 9, Para. 1, Group B, No. 4, *Law for Determination of Family Affairs).*

In the United States, the father may be awarded visiting rights or joint custody if he pays child support; but no such negotiation is possible in Japanese conciliation procedures. The father is obliged to pay child support simply because he is the father. If agreement is reached within the conciliation committee, this is entered in the protocol and is deemed final (Art. 21, *Law for Determination of Family Affairs*). The divorce is effective as of entry in the protocol. Divorce by conciliation constitutes about 10 percent of all divorce in Japan.

The most serious issue in divorce by conciliation arises if one of the spouses wants to divorce, but the other spouse wants to continue the marriage. In such cases, either agreement to divorce, or reconciliation, may be accomplished through detailed discussions between the parties. Here is an example to illustrate the way in which conciliation committees function. An application for divorce was filed into a Family Court by husband A. Wife B had left the household with daughter C after having had an argument with A's mother D who had been living with the family. A, though the owner of property worth $500,000, had gone heavily into debt because of gambling. B had tried to pay back A's debt amounting to $30,000 by borrowing from her own father. D had argued that A was involved in gambling because of his unhappy relationship with B. B left the house soon after this argument. The case was allocated to a conciliation committee. There were two possible analyses: first, that the discord was primarily one between the wife and mother-in-law, and second, that it was essentially between husband and wife. The first might lead to the conclusion that A and B should leave the mother, the second would point toward a divorce.

After a conciliation period of four months during which the committee counselled both A and B, the conclusion was reached that the difference between A and B was irreconcilable (i.e., the second analysis). The committee set up joint interview sessions so that A and B could come to such an understanding on their own. Since B wanted the marriage to continue, it was imperative that she should come to understand what A truly wanted. As B came to agree to the divorce, it was now necessary for the committee to facilitate the settlement. It was agreed (1) that A should divorce B, (2) that A should pay $50,000 in settlement ($30,000 for the debt, $20,000 for division of property and compensation), (3) that B should have custody of child C, and (4) that A should pay $150 a month for child support. That is a fairly typical case of divorce by conciliation in Japan. Conciliation is available not just for the divorce itself, but also for all matters related to divorce such as child custody, child support or division of property, and compensation.

There are four issues that need to be emphasized in considering the conciliation procedure in Japan. First, we must emphasize the fact that both informal conciliation and legal agreements are handled by the same committee within the same procedure. This is criticized severely by some scholars who point out that confidential background knowledge obtained in the process of conciliation can be used against one or other of the parties in making legal arrangements. However, the purpose of this committee is to bring about an agreement, whatever the outcome. Conciliators may utilize their knowledge about the background history or reports of investigation in their advice, but the advice is not binding. In this sense, divorce by conciliation is a variation of divorce by consent, but it is a form of divorce not to be found in any other country.

Secondly, we need to emphasize the fact that conciliation is structured to promote an amicable solution. For instance, if, upon receiving the first notice, the husband attempts to dispose of his property in order to avoid its division, the wife must safeguard her claims by applying to the civil court (not to the Family Court) for provisional injunction or provisional attachment. The Family Court judges who constitute the conciliation committee are not authorized to issue such coercive orders as provisional remedies, because they are in principle committed to encourage the parties to reach an amicable solution. They cannot operate a double standard. The Family Court judges may order a provisional injunction or attachment only after the divorce itself is already agreed by consent or conciliation. The division of property or child custody must be determined by the Family Court following the divorce (Art. 15-3, *Law for Determination of Family Affairs*).

Thirdly, we need to emphasize the fact that divorce is a formalized conciliation between husband and wife, directly expressed as the conciliation of husband–wife relationships. Application forms are easily obtainable from any Family Court. According to Judicial Statistics, divorce conciliation is concluded in about 40 percent of all applied cases, and about 44 percent of all applications are withdrawn. Including the conclusions after withdrawal of applications, 18 percent ended in reconciliation, and 40 percent ended in agreement to divorce. Relying upon these figures, we conclude that conciliation plays an important role in the stability of marriage and family in Japan.

Fourthly, we need to emphasize the role of investigative officers of the Family Courts. Their function lies mainly in investigation before the start of the conciliation procedure, definition of the problem, and clarification of the issue. Their function, however, is widened nowadays to include legal counselling during the procedure as well. They are fully trained graduates in psychology, sociology and pedagogy with practical experience and training at the Research and Training Institute for Family Courts Probation Officers. They are capable of handling abnormal emotional reactions, although in severe, longer-term cases, they enlist the assistance of psychiatrists of the Family Courts or, sometimes, independent practitioners.

DIVORCE BY FAMILY COURT DETERMINATION

The third type of divorce is one determined by Family Courts. This takes place, for example, in cases when divorce intentions are firm, but agreement with regard to settlements cannot be reached because, for example, of differences over maintenance. The Family court then determines the divorce as well as the appropriate settlements (Art. 24, *Law for Determination of Family Affairs*). Family Court determinations may be made without regard to the grounds for divorce provided for by the *Civil Code*, and without regard to the principle of recrimination under Supreme Court precedents.

Divorce determination by the Family Court has the character of a strong mediation at the last stage of the conciliation procedure. Thus, if objected to by either of the parties concerned, it loses effect (Art. 25, Para. 2, *Law for Determination of Family Affairs*). In view of this limitation, it is seldom used. Frequent points of disputes often determined by Family Courts are spousal support, property settlement upon divorce, and child custody (Art. 9, Para. 1, Group B, *Law for Determination of Family Affairs*). The determination of Family Courts is made without a formal procedure. Much is left to the discretion of individual judges. This leads to some problems. First, there is no guarantee of due process of law. In practice, direct and cross-examination is conducted in the closed court but there is no legal provision for it. Secondly, there is a problem concerning the treatment of investigation reports compiled by investigation officers (Art. 7-2, *Law for Determination of Family Affairs*. Also see *Bulletin of General Secretary, Supreme Court*, Sept. 20, 1974). Parties and their attorneys are often not permitted access to these reports (Art. 12, *Law for Determination of Family Affairs*). Nor can attorneys examine the officer in court. In Practice, the judge does exercise discretion to confirm some statements in the reports for the parties, if and when the investigated materials form part of his judgment. But this practice is far from sufficient to protect the fundamental rights of the parties. There may be facts which are better not revealed (e.g., a secret birth). On the other hand, due process of law is a fundamental necessity that must be provided by the Family Court procedures.

DIVORCE BY CIVIL DECISION

The fourth type of divorce is by the civil court, accounting for about one percent of all divorces. This is divorce by the adversary system. Trials take place in open court and decisions are declared publicly, according to the general rules of the civil procedure. Exceptions to general rules are that the judge may, on his motion, take evidence or consider facts not presented by the parties, and that the admission of a claim is not recognized (Art. 14, 10, *Law for Procedure of Personal Affairs*).

Divorce is granted if the civil court determines that there is a ground for divorce. Before the Second World War, the *Civil Code* adopted the "fault" principle for divorce, but it was amended in 1947 to a principle of "break-up with inquiry." This provides for the following grounds: adultery, desertion, absence for over three years, incurable mental illness and other grave reasons for which continuation of marriage is deemed difficult (Art. 770, Para. 1, *C.C.*). The court may dismiss the claim of divorce if it deems the marriage fit to continue in view of all circumstances, even where grounds for divorce exist (Art.770, Para. 2,*C.C.*).

Two points taken by the Supreme Court with regard to the above provisions should be mentioned. First, even though the *Civil Code* has since 1947 adopted the principle of break-up with inquiry, the Supreme Court still adheres to the rule of recrimination. It states that the action for divorce is not available for "the spouse who exclusively or mainly has caused the breakdown of the marriage" (Sup. Ct. Decision, Feb. 19, 1952 and others). As an example of the rule of recrimination, if a man who has a relationship with a woman other than his wife wants to divorce his wife and marry the other woman and his wife opposes the divorce, so that divorce by consent and conciliation is not possible, the action is not available to him as he is the "guilty party." In such a case, the husband would be obliged to go back to the conciliation process to try to settle the dispute; and usually the wife, knowing the strict stance of the Supreme Court, would claim a very large share of the property division, or settlement, which the husband would simply be obliged to accept. In such a settlement, we can feel the strong presence or shadow of the case law.

The second point concerns the application of Art. 770, Para. 2. In applying this provision, the Supreme Court used to dismiss a divorce action brought on the grounds of mental illness (Sup. Ct. Decision, July 25, 1958 and others). Thus, even if the wife suffers from severe mental illness, the husband cannot claim divorce, unless he can prove that he has "sought all possible measures for her medical treatment and future within his means." Since psychiatric treatment can be very expensive, the financial burden cannot be borne by the husband alone. There must be many cases in which the husband seeks divorce under the threat of bankruptcy. We can see a change in the stance of the Supreme Court in a recent decision (Sup. Ct. Decision, Nov. 11, 1970).

In conclusion, divorce by consent and divorce by conciliation are conducted on a "no-fault" principle; but divorce by law suit is conducted on the basis of guilt. Although many of the deficiencies of Japanese divorce suits are covered by divorce by consent and divorce by conciliation, there is clearly room for improvement in the area of divorce procedure where that outdated principle still operates.

Chapter Nine

The Role of the Expert in Judicial Divorce Procedures

Frank Bates

University of Tasmania, Australia

INTRODUCTION

Australian family law provides a useful paradigm for exemplary and comparative study:[1] although a federal system, marriage and matrimonial causes are within the province of the Commonwealth legislature[2] and the *Family Law Act* 1975 has created[3] a new and specialized court system.[4] There are specific legislative provisions which emphasize the interdisciplinary nature of the court. First, and probably most important, s. 22 (2)(b) of the Act specifies that a person shall not be appointed a judge of the Family Court of Australia unless "... by reason of training, experience and personality, he is a suitable person to deal with matters of family law."[5] Thus, the Australian *Family Law Act* has provided an opportunity for the expert to be heard in a sympathetic forum. Prior to 1975, Australian courts, with one graphic exception,[6] had not generally shown themselves sympathetic towards opinions expressed by psychiatrists,[7] although welfare officers tended to be regarded more receptively.[8]

The purpose of this article is to discuss developments which have taken place in Australia since the inception of the *Family Law Act* and to seek to extrapolate from them, in order to ascertain whether the novel Australian experience has any global application. At the outset, it is worth noting that the two fundamental principles of evidence law which prohibit the reception of hearsay and opinion evidence have not been subject to statutory modification as has occurred elsewhere.[9]

WELFARE OFFICERS

After the *Family Law Act* 1975, the courts appear to have taken the view that welfare reports are admissible, irrespective of whether they infringe the strict rules of evidence. In *In the Marriage of Hogue and Haines*,[10] Wood J. of the Family Court of Australia referred to s. 62 (4) of the Act, which empowers the court to obtain a report on "... such matters relevant to the proceedings as the court considers desirable." The judge noted that the court controlled the range of matters which were desirable to be investigated, but, "... in determining what matters are desirable to be reported on, the court should have regard to the fact that the ordinary rules of evidence will be applied at the trial, and the reporter should not be asked to go into fields of enquiry incompatible with those rules." Thus, Wood J. continued, if the court were to order a welfare report into matters which were essentially hearsay or opinion, then it might be that those matters were not matters which the court would properly consider desirable within the meaning of the Act. Once past that stage, however, when the report had been ordered, "... the discretion imposed in the court to admit the report into evidence is without limitation. I am of the view," the judge said,[11] "that such report can be admitted even though objected to on the grounds of hearsay or any other basis of admissibility. The question is not one of the admissibility of the report but the weight which is to be attached to the material which it contains." In addition, Wood J. stated[12] that he, personally, found that reports made by welfare officers, either those employed by the court or by accredited outside agencies, are very valuable since they were able to place before the court matters which it would otherwise be extremely difficult to introduce into evidence. "I hope," his Honour continued, "I am not being unduly optimistic in expressing the view that in due course the legal profession itself will come to realise the value of reports of this kind and be less prone to take exception to them on the basis that they contain inadmissible and arguable expressions of opinion."

Nevertheless, Wood J. emphasized[13] that, even though s. 64 (2) of the *Family Law Act* gave the court a wide discretion to receive this kind of evidence, there must be some limitation on the range of matters which the court should consider desirable to be canvassed in a welfare report and he noted that there would be no question regarding the admission of a report, in a custody case, upon the circumstances in which the child was living and the circumstances in which he would be living were a change of arrangements to be made. As has been already noted, the judge thought it a sound principle that, since the ordinary rules of evidence were to be applied at the trial, the reporter ought not to be asked to go into areas of inquiry that were incompatible with those rules. "This is not to say," said Wood J.,[14] "that the welfare officer is to anticipate objections to parts of the report and tailor it accordingly, nor is the welfare officer expected to be conversant with the basic rules of evidence in determining what matters to include in a welfare report. Indeed, it would be wrong for a welfare officer to proceed on this basis insofar as it may, on the one hand, inhibit the scope of his enquiry and, on the other, by reason of his lack of knowledge of the rules of evidence, result in his not reporting upon the matters which he would otherwise have included." Thus, although reception of welfare reports is not predicated upon the application of the strict rules of evidence, some caution is, at least, desirable in the preparation of the report. The broad view expressed by Wood J. in *Hogue and Haines*, was adopted, in very similar form, by the Full Court of the Family Court in *In the Marriage of Foster and Foster*.[15]

On the other hand, Broun and Fowler, in the leading Australian practitioners' text on family law, suggest[16] that the issue may not be as clear cut as the cases suggest. In *Hogue and Haines,* Wood J. referred to *Sing v. Muir, Priest* and the English case of *Official Solicitor v. K.*[17] in support of his view, but he also quoted a statement by Evatt C.J. of the Family Court of Australia in *In the Marriage of N. and N.*[18] In that case, the trial judge had excluded statements in the welfare officer's report that had purported to express the wishes of the children in question on the grounds that they were hearsay. Evatt C.J. made the following remark: "The only other matter I would like to mention is that I was rather surprised that various passages should have been excluded from the welfare report, particularly those passages in which the wishes of the children were set out — the wishes as conveyed by them to the welfare officer. This has been one of the recognised ways of obtaining information about the children's wishes and that process would, of course, be frustrated if that information were excluded from the welfare report on the ground that it was hearsay. In my opinion it was not strictly hearsay at all." In *Hogue and Haines*, Wood J. appeared to take this comment as meaning that the statements in the report would be admissible even if they were hearsay; in fact, Evatt C.J. said nothing of the kind, she was saying that the statements were direct, and not hearsay, evidence. Thus, suggest Broun and Fowler,[19] "To the extent that his Honour Mr. Justice Wood relies on an apparent misconception of the Chief Judge's statement and to the extent that the Full Court in *Foster* expressly adopts Mr. Justice Wood's reasons, in *Hogue*, the matter is not yet settled." Although there can be little doubt that Broun and Fowler are correct in their analysis, too much should not, it is submitted, be made of it; quite apart from *N. and N.* there exists, as has been observed,[20] considerable authority under the previous legislation that the strict rules of evidence are inapplicable. It would seem strange if the 1975 legislation, aimed as it is at informalizing court procedures,[21] were to require stricter standards in this area than were previously required.

The other objections raised[22] by Broun and Fowler appear to be rather more substantial. First, they suggest that, by admitting the whole of the report and regarding the contents as going simply to weight,[23] the parties and their legal representatives will be left in doubt as to what evidence they will need to adduce as they will not know beforehand the amount of weight which will be attached to particular items. Second, there is often no material in the report by means of which the weight to be attached to a hearsay statement can be judged, since the circumstances in which the report was made and the reliability of the maker may not be known. These problems may be further compounded if there is no opportunity to cross examine the welfare officer.[24] Finally, the authors suggest that the Full Court in *Foster and Foster*[25] seemed to be saying that a welfare report is acceptable evidence to be relied upon unless controverted by other evidence and, therefore, they say[26] that, "If there is sworn evidence controverting an allegation in a welfare report but that sworn evidence is rejected, it seems the contents of the welfare report would prevail even if the person who made the statement lacked credit." All these are valuable points which should be borne in mind by the courts and by legal practitioners who appear before them, but the present commentator would suggest that the points made by Broun and Fowler should operate as an injunction to parties and their representatives to prepare as much relevant evidence as possible in order to assist the court in coming to a proper conclusion. The problems raised by Broun and Fowler are inherent in discretionary areas such as child custody disputes, and one trusts that the specialist tribunal created in Australia by Part IV of the *Family Law Act* 1975 will be able to deal with them. The disadvantage of Broun and Fowler's approach is that, if the strict rules of evidence were to be applied, information of relevance and significance could well be excluded. This basic consideration, it is submitted, outweighs the more legalistic difficulties outlined by the authors and in a delegalized court, as Street C.J. referred to it in the important case of *Epperson v. Dampney*,[27] should clearly prevail.

    A further problem has arisen in relation to the role which the welfare officer is fulfilling when he makes his report. In the case of *In the Marriage of Sampson and Sampson*,[28] a custody matter which was particularly strongly contested by the parties, a preliminary issue arose as to the admissibility of evidence given by a social worker for the Catholic Family Welfare Bureau who had been seeing the mother regularly for several months. The question was whether consultation occurred in the social worker's capacity as a marriage counsellor, under Part III of the *Family Law Act*, or as a welfare officer supervising an order made under Part VIII of the Act. If the former, admission of the evidence was specifically prohibited by s. 18(2) of the legislation, but, if the latter, it might be admitted. Fogarty J. had handed down three rulings on the issue before proceeding to determine the dispute itself. In the end, he found that in the meetings with the social worker, the counselling content and the supervising function were so bound up with one another that they could not be disentangled. He, therefore, decided that all of the social worker's evidence as to the consultations was inadmissible under s. 18(2). Given the peculiar circumstances, it is hard to imagine what other course of action was open to Fogarty J., even though, from a policy point of view, his decision in that regard might have deprived him of valuable information for resolving the ultimate dispute.

The matter of cross-examination of welfare officers, referred to by Broun and Fowler, has also come before the courts and, indeed, reference to the court permitting "oral examination" of the officer making the report is made in r. 117(c) of the *Family Law Regulations.* But, in the case of *In the Marriage of McKee and McKee,*[29] Wood J. was of the opinion that, although parties were permitted to refute the welfare officers findings by calling their own evidence, they ought not to be allowed to cross examine the officer because to do so, "... would bring the welfare officers into a partisan situation where they are required to align themselves with the case of one party or the other ... and such would tend to destroy the reputation of impartiality and integrity in the counselling services of the court."[30] However, Fogarty J. in *In the Marriage of Harris and Harris,*[31] directly disagreed with the approach of Wood J. in the *McKee* case. On the facts involved in *Harris*, Fogarty J. was of the opinion that it would have been impossible to have determined a number of important issues without cross-examination. An additional difficulty which the judge faced was that, by reason of s. 37 of the *Family Law Act*, the welfare officers were designated as "officers of the court." His Honour was of the opinion that that did not confer any special or privileged position in the giving of evidence or in the ordinary judicial process. Indeed, the judge expressed[32] the emphatic opinion that it was inimical to the proper workings of the Family Court and, especially, to the proper organization of a welfare officer's functions that it be thought that welfare officers or their reports occupied, "... some special or privileged position before the court, unchallenged and unchallengeable, but yet perhaps decisive of the issue.... Where a welfare report is delivered which contains either factual matters or matters of opinion which a party desires to challenge but is not permitted to do so, that party may be pardoned for feeling that justice has not been seen to be done." *In the Marriage of Harris* is noteworthy also for a general statement of principle regarding welfare officers' reports. "Welfare officers attached to the court," Fogarty J. stated,[33] "because of their experience in these custodial fields are entitled to put forward views or opinions, and such views or opinions are admissible in the same way as are the views or opinions of any expert in his particular field or discipline and are to be accorded such weight as the circumstances justify. . . . The fact that the opinion emanates from a welfare officer or counsellor attached to the court does not give that opinion any greater validity or weight as such. Such opinions do not occupy any special or privileged position, other than arising from the obvious fact that the counsellors have great day to day experience and expertise in the jurisdiction together with their obviously neutral and unbiased position."

The view expressed by Fogarty J. in the *Harris* case regarding the possibility of dissatisfied litigants, were welfare officers not to be cross-examined, was adopted by Marshall J. in *In the Marriage of M. and M.*[34] In *M.*, the judge, during the course of the hearing and with the concurrence of counsel for both sides, allowed cross-examination of a welfare officer who had prepared a report. Marshall J. remarked[35] that that course of action was contrary to the view which had been expressed by Wood J.[36] and he agreed with some of Wood J.'s comments regarding the difficulties faced by welfare officers. Ultimately, however, Marshall J. shared the opinion of Fogarty J. in *Harris* and said[37] that, "If the contents of a welfare report are not open to challenge by cross examination, the court would leave itself open to the criticism of conducting a trial by report rather than on the whole of the evidence." The judge went on to say that he did not want to give the impression that he was advocating the cross-examination of welfare officers on their reports, but he noted that, in the instant case, the officer had suffered no embarrassment through the procedure.

It is suggested that the view expressed in *Harris* and *M.* is to be preferred; cross-examination is an established way of testing the reliability of evidence, whether presented in the form of a welfare officers's report or not. Indeed, cross-examination would seem to be all the more a necessary safeguard when some of the comments which have been advanced regarding welfare officers[38] are taken into account. The process of cross-examination is also likely to facilitate a proper understanding of the evidence; the comments which Diamond and Louisell make in relation to psychiatric evidence are just as applicable to welfare officers' reports. "[I]n all instances," they state,[39] "the psychiatric expert [should] be allowed to relate to the court exactly how he reached his opinion and what were the sources of his information. He should be required to describe in fairly precise terms his own process of revealing his source material: what information did he acccpt, and what did he reject; what sources did he place great weight upon, and what sources did he minimize; and why did he evaluate the clinical material in these ways." Finally, Broun and Fowler note[40] that many welfare officers personally welcome the opportunity to support and justify their opinions before the court because it is the only way in which their professional standing and expertise can ultimately be made apparent.

An allied issue was raised in the case of *In the Marriage of Triffitt and Triffitt and Triffitt (Interveners).*[41] There, the interveners sought a conference with a judge in chambers to raise certain complaints which they had concerning the contents of a welfare report relating to the custody of a four year old girl. They complained of remarks made to them by the welfare officer in the course of their interview, and sought the preparation of a fresh report. Wood S.J. was of the view[42] that the complaints which had been made regarding the conduct of the interview were unilateral and that the welfare officers had been given no opportunity to answer them. "It seems to me," his Honour said, "bad practice in any event, that a welfare officer should be invited to attend a chambers conference . . . where allegations are made, without notice, about lack of professionalism, especially when those allegations are not an affidavit and extend to allegedly improper remarks made to the applicant and the interveners in the course of interviewing them." The judge strongly emphasized that a welfare officer must be given the opportunity of answering any criticism of the way in which he had prepared his report and that the proper arena in which that challenge should be made was in the court at the trial. This view was admitted to be in accord with that which he had expressed in the *McKee* case,[43] but is more generally consonant with the broader body of case law and generally desirable principles. He concluded[44] by saying that, in this case, it was appropriate that the welfare officers attend for cross-examination. But if Wood S.J. is saying that the only truly desirable instance where cross-examination is appropriate is in situations such as that which occurred in *Triffitt*, it would seem to the present writer that, in view of the comments made by Fogarty J. in *Harris*,[45] any such restriction would seem an unnecessary limitation.

Another matter raised in the *Triffitt* case related to the duty of the welfare officer in conducting the interview. Wood S.J. did not consider that the welfare officer had totally discharged the duty which had been imposed on him and ordered[46] that a supplementary report be prepared aimed at assessing the child's relationship with specific members of her family. There had also been allegations that the applicant was living in a *de facto* relationship. Wood S.J. commented[47] that this, insofar as it affected the child, was a matter to be proved at the trial and was not properly the subject of investigation by a welfare officer at the request of a party. The judge then made the clear and strong statement of principle that, "The judge determines the scope of the report. The welfare officer is not an inquisitor. This court has no warrant or authority to send a welfare officer to persons outside the proceedings and demand that they supply information and be questioned about their private lives." The only situation where he would permit a person in these circumstances to be interviewed was where that person wished to volunteer information.

Throughout the case law on the position of welfare officers under the *Family Law Act*, the question of the weight to be attached to their reports has frequently been mentioned[48] and there are two major cases which deal directly with that point. First, in *In the Marriage of Hall and Hall*,[49] the Full Court of the Family Court of Australia had been faced with a report which they described[50] as "alarming," but which had subsequently proved to have been a false alarm. Had it, in fact, not been for that report, the judge at first instance would have made a different custody determination from that which he did. The court made[51] a number of observations regarding the weight to be attached to welfare reports: first, the court[52] reiterated the basic principle that, "There is no magic in a Family Report. A judge is not bound to accept it and there should be no suggestion that the counsellor is usurping the role of the court or that the judge is abdicating his responsibilities." Second, the court commented that reports were almost invariably valuable and relevant in assisting a judge to come to his ultimate conclusion but, they emphasized, when these views coincide with the court's judgment, it is not because they have been accepted automatically, but because the judge has found them to be consistent with the rest of the body of evidence before him. Third, their Honours thought that, while the counsellor's views will normally have weight with the court because of his experience and expertise, the counsellor will not normally have the same opportunity as a trial judge to weigh the evidence, observe the demeanour of the witnesses in court under examination and cross-examination and to make findings of fact based on evidence before the court which might not have been available to the counsellor. As a consequence, fourth, the counsellor's assessment of the parties may often be based on facts which the counsellor has accepted but which turn out to be wrong; or there may be favourable or unfavourable views formed by the counsellor from interviews with parties without the opportunity to test in depth the credit of people who may, in court, prove to be of different character from that which the counsellor has accepted. Fifth, sometimes of necessity, a report will be neutral in approach; although a positive recommendation will assist the court, their Honours made the point that, in many cases, a counsellor could quite properly conclude that the child's welfare would be equally well or ill served by custody being given to neither party. Sixth, a report will assist the court whether or not it contains a positive recommendation and, therefore, a counsellor ought not to be disturbed if a recommendation is not accepted by a court because the court has had the advantage of more material and more examination in depth than was available to the counsellor.[53] *Hall's* case, accordingly, represents a useful description of the relationship which the courts prefer to maintain with welfare officers who appear before them as expert witnesses.

A direct application of the observations made in *Hall*, may be found in the decision of Wood S.J. in the case of *In the Marriage of B.B.T. and J.M.T.*,[54] where problems arose regarding the qualifications of the counsellor. Although the counsellor in the case was a clinical psychologist rather than a welfare officer *per se,* the comments of the judge seem very pertinent to the present discussion. The father of the child involved in a custody dispute was very dissatisfied with the content of the report prepared by the officer in question. In the event, Wood S.J. had no difficulty in finding that the court counsellor was an expert[55] but, in reply to a contention by the father's counsel, he was of the view that neither the *Family Law Act* itself[56] nor the regulations made a welfare officer or court counsellor an expert *ipso facto*. The judge reaffirmed the statement which he had made earlier in *Hogue and Haines*[57] to the effect that any such report was admissible at the discretion of the judge, even over parties' objections. However, this was not to be taken as meaning that the expertise of the reporter could never be called into question and, indeed, in cases involving the evaluation of character and behaviour, the reporter's expertise was a matter of great importance. "According to the degree of expertise," he said, "so will a court attach weight to the opinions expressed as in the case of any other witnesses whom it regards qualified as an expert in the usual way." Further, Wood S.J. laid considerable emphasis[58] on the importance of the welfare officer's keeping contemporaneous notes of interviews.

Thus, it is clear that the Family Court of Australia is not unsympathetic to evidence given by welfare officers and does not seek to use the rules of evidence to circumscribe the way in which reports are presented. This is, from the point of view of the witness, important since it seems that it is the adjectival side (of which evidence is a part) of legal process which causes tension between practitioners in law and social work. Sloane, in particular, notes that the adversary system, "... with its right to confrontation and cross-examination of witnesses . . ."[59] is inimical to the methods used by welfare workers. In the more specific issue of attitudes towards evidence, another American writer, Tamilia, has written[60] that social workers are not infrequently impatient with legal requirements of proof, a fact which, in turn, results in the welfare officers' attitudes becoming polarized towards traditional legal process when tested by it. The Australian cases show, it is submitted, that it is possible to use the skills of welfare officers properly and, at the same time, to test effectively the application of those skills by appropriate legal technique and process.

PSYCHIATRISTS

The differences in judicial attitudes which may occur towards welfare officers and towards psychiatrists may be immediately observed from the decision of McCall J. in *Between Cartledge and Cartledge*.[61] In that case, the judge had admitted a welfare officer's report which contained statements made by the relevant children regarding their wishes as to custody; such a welfare report, said his Honour,[62] was, ". . . an accepted method of communicating the wishes of the children to the court."

However, McCall J. refused to apply that practice to other classes of people including, as in the instant case, a psychiatrist who had interviewed the children. The judge gave little in the way of policy reasons for this approach, although it seemed, from the facts of the case, that the psychiatrist had been engaged by the children's father, which might have cast doubts on the impartiality of his observations. Even so, McCall J. noted[63] that neither counsel had advanced authority supporting any contrary course of action — although he did not rule out the use of psychiatric testimony in appropriate cases.

There were two prior cases to which reference was made in *Cartledge* as to the kind of situation where use could be made of psychiatric evidence. Chronologically, the first was the well-known dictum of Lord Upjohn in *J. v. C.*[64] to the effect that medical evidence would weigh heavily with the court, ". . . where the infant is under some treatment or requires some treatment for some physical, neurological or psychological malady or condition." This statement had later been adopted by Street C.J. of the New South Wales Court of Appeal in the latter case of *Epperson v. Dampney*.[65] Although not directly concerned with divorce *per se*, there can be no question but that *Epperson v. Dampney* is the most important recent case to be hitherto decided on psychiatric evidence in family litigation in Australia.[66] Its crucial and global importance is that it graphically illustrates the dilemma faced by judges when deciding on the application of this kind of evidence. In *Epperson v. Dampney*, the Court of Appeal overturned an award of custody on the grounds that the trial judge[67] had given undue weight to expert evidence. In the Court of Appeal, in the majority, Street C.J. predicated[68] his judgment on the well-established idea that, ". . . our system of jurisprudence does not, generally speaking, remit the determination of disputes to experts." The Chief Justice went on to say that neither courts of law nor psychiatric consultation provided the ideal forum for resolving custody disputes. "Our society," he went on to say, "has selected a curial tribunal as that which in the greatest number of cases will come nearer to the best answer. Such a forum provides an opportunity for ascertainment of the facts and open deliberative discussion in which both parties participate. It is to be recognised that the clinical opinion of the scientist can properly and usefully be put before the judge for evaluation as part of the whole concatenation of elements to be weighed in reaching a conclusion. But the antiseptic philosophy of Huxley's *Brave New World* has not yet rendered absolute a human evaluation of the complex web of parental and filial emotions that entangle all the persons concerned in disputed custody cases. It is ultimately the conventional and human wisdom of the judge, experienced as he is in matters of this sort, that must be applied in resolution of the contest." Street C.J. then examined[69] the earlier case law — notably the House of Lords decision in *J. v. C.*[70] and the Australian cases of *Lynch v. Lynch* and *Neill v. Neill*[71] and turned his attention[72] to the facts of the instant case. It appeared that, in the space of five months, the two children had been subjected to five interviews with psychiatrists. "It is," said the Chief Justice,[73] "the recognition by judges of the undesirability of normal, healthy children being thus placed on the emotional dissecting table with all the attendant strains upon their love and loyalties for their respective parents, that leads judges to discourage the tendering of medical evidence where no question of ill health arises. If undue weight were given to medical evidence in contests of this nature, this could result in a child being dragged from consulting room to consulting room in search of psychiatric opinion capable of supporting the case of the particular parent happening to be the custodian at that particular time." By his mention of ill health, Street C.J. was adopting the same kind of approach as did Lord Upjohn in *J. v. C.*[74] where a distinction was drawn between cases where it had been suggested that a child was in need of some treatment, where medical evidence would have great weight, and other cases, where it would not. Although this view is likely to be attractive to the lawyer, because it is restricting the medical practititioner to those areas which are his immediate domain, it may, it is suggested, be too restrictive. This is certainly the case if one were to regard the views of Diamond and Louisell[75] as the most appropriate basis for the reception of this kind of evidence. The further point raised by Street C.J. regarding the possibility of the children's undergoing multiple sessions of psychiatric examination is one of very considerable importance; it is obviously undesirable that such a course of action should take place. However, it may be that the matter is more an administrative or procedural, rather than a substantive, issue. Some procedure could, surely, be devised whereby the nature and number of such visits could be supervised by the court, at least where proceedings are before it or pending. At the same time, however, the Chief Justice said[76] that he did not wish to be interpreted as underrating the value of expert evidence in appropriate cases and emphasized the importance of particular cases and facts and stated that, "The only generality I am prepared to accept is . . . that in a custody case the decision reached is to be widely based, with evaluation of family, personal, emotional, medical and all other relevant elements undertaken in order to reach a decision that will best serve the welfare of the child, the adjudicative process involving the recognition of basic human standards and expectations within our community." This last is not an easy passage to understand: it is well known that, in such disputes, the welfare of the child is to be the paramount consideration,[77] and various other criteria have, from time to time,[78] been utilized to facilitate the adjudication of these disputes. The problematical part of the passage, however, involves the requirement that the adjudicative process should involve, ". . . the recognition of basic human standards and expectations within the community." To what, one might ask, do these basic standards refer? If they refer to standards of conduct analogous to fault, then the Chief Justice's view would seem to be at odds with much of modern judicial and legislative thought. If they refer to some more amorphous standard, akin, say, to the "community standards" test used in obscenity cases in the United States[79] then the difficulties of its application are only too well known. As Douglas J., in a dissenting judgment, stated in *Miller v. California*,[80] "What shocks me may be sustenance for my neighbour. What causes one person to boil up in rage over one pamphlet or movie may reflect only his neurosis, not shared by others."

The strong dissenting judgment[81] of Hutley J.A. contains many interesting and important features. The first substantive legal issue that the judge dealt with[82] was the *dictum* of Lord Upjohn in *J. v. C.,* referred to earlier.[83] Hutley J.A. noted, immediately, that no other member of the House of Lords, in that seminal case, had concurred with Lord Upjohn in *J. v. C.,* and Hutley J.A. took further exception to what he described as an implicit limitation contained in Lord Upjohn's comment that, ". . . such evidence may be valuable if accepted but it can only be as an element to support the general knowledge and experience of the judge in infancy matters." Hutley J.A. noted[84] that a judge's experience might be very limited and, even if not limited, could be expanded with the assistance of expert evidence which, ". . . is itself a compendious way of expanding experience, theory being, if sound, the condensation and refinement of many minds." The judge then went on[85] to compare today's knowledge of child behaviour with earlier conceptions, and commented that the general knowledge and understanding of the judiciary had contributed to this development and that this example must lead to an appreciation that even specialized judges needed to be free to utilize the assistance of other disciplines. Probably the most globally far-sighted passage in this judgment follows straightway after: "It was said in argument," Hutley J.A. stated,[86] "that human nature does not change. Even if it were true, which it is not — it merely changes more slowly than those who want to change it would like — it is plainly false to suggest that the knowledge of human behaviour does not change. In the last three-quarters of a century it has grown enormously and is continuing to grow. It is principally through the evidence of the learned that judges acquire new knowledge. New theories, which can be fantastic, have to be tested against the judge's own knowledge, and as he has to make the decision, he may reject them. It is not a criticism of him that he accepts them." Hutley J.A. then referred to the cases of *Lynch* and *Neill*[87] and the judicial remarks therein, and commented that the fact that the expert only had access to the evidence of one party and, hence, might be working on false or one-sided evidence was a feature of all litigation and not peculiar to custody cases. From the point of view of the law of evidence, the next point made by Hutley J.A. is of particular importance: noting the comment by Begg J. in *Lynch v. Lynch*[88] that, "... the evidence of a psychiatrist usually has little place in a contested custody application," Hutley J.A. went on to say[89] that this comment, "... is only to be understood as an expression by his Honour of what he regarded as evidence likely to affect his own judgment. It does not render this type of evidence inadmissible and once evidence is admitted it is for the court to weigh that evidence with all other evidence. It may be that subjection to examination by psychiatrists and psychologists can be considered detrimental to the welfare of children but this is only given weight in deciding the fitness of parents to be awarded custody." This view, it is submitted, is entirely in accord with well established evidential principles and is the proper way to approach the issue. Hutley J.A. proceeded to act on the principles as he had stated them by examining[90] in detail, detail which is unnecessary in this article, the tests to which the children had been subjected, in particular the *Benet-Anthony Test*. The approach taken by Hutley J.A. is reminiscent of that of Lord Wilberforce in the Privy Council decision in the Criminal case of *Lowery v. R.*,[91] which was notable for his Lordship's express recognition of specific scientific processes and tests.[92] In Lord Wilberforce's words, the psychological evidence was admitted because it, "... was not related to crime or criminal tendencies: it was scientific evidence as to the respective personalities of the two accused as, and to the extent, revealed by certain well known tests." Although *Lowery* has not been generally adopted, especially not by Lawton L.J. in the later case of *R. v. Turner*,[93] it seems to the present writer to represent a realistic and humane attitude to the issue involved; a characteristic which it shares with the judgment of Hutley J.A. in *Epperson v. Dampney*.

This, then, is the dilemma; but how far has it been resolved in modern Australian law? The answer, regrettably, must be scarcely at all. The issue raised by Street C.J. in *Epperson v. Dampney*[94] regarding persistent psychiatric examinations was strongly taken up by Fogarty J. in *Harris*,[95] where it appeared that the relevant children had been seen by two psychiatrists, two psychologists and a social worker on, in his Honour's words, "... over 20 occasions per child, many of those occasions lasting for several hours ..." It also appeared that the tests done showed that the children were entirely normal, and further, that the children had protested at being subjected to the tests. Fogarty J. specifically approved their protests, noting that the major reason for the tests having been conducted was that the children had expressed the wish to be with their father and this seemingly aberrant view[96] ought to be clinically tested.[97] Despite the adoption[98] by Fogarty J. of the Lord Upjohn *dictum* in *J. v. C.*,[99] the practical policy enunciated in the *Harris* case seems, an earlier suggested,[100] entirely appropriate and capable of easy resolution.

The innately difficult issue of contradictory psychiatric evidence arose in *B.B.T. and J.M.T.*,[101] where the husband had called psychiatric evidence to the effect that it would be in the interests of the children were the father's claim to succeed. The evidence given by that psychiatrist seems not a little strange: despite his expression of opinion, he proceeded on the basis that the mother's relationship with the children was a good one, even though he had neither interviewed the mother nor observed the behaviour of the children with her.[102] Wood S.J. considered[103] that it was unnecessary for this evidence to have been called, but since it had been, it was both desirable and appropriate for the mother to call evidence in rebuttal which in fact she did. Wood S.J., assessing the totality of the evidence, found that the method used by the husband's expert witness was inadequate to enable him to arrive at the conclusions he reached regarding the placement of the children.

Therefore, it may be observed that the position of the psychiatrist-witness is altogether different from that of the welfare officer. At first sight, it is hard to tell why this should be, particularly when one takes the criticisms which have been made of welfare officers into account. As an aftermath of the *Maria Colwell* case, it had been claimed that social workers were preoccupied with maintaining family groups and were, hence, tending to use children as therapeutic agents for their parents.[104] Further, it had likewise been claimed that social workers were ignorant of recent legal developments and found it difficult to communicate effectively with many of their clients.[105] At the same time, the use of expert witnesses with psychological training has come under trenchant attack from Okpaku[106] and there is no doubt that, even within the discipline, there is dispute as to the role of the expert witness. The iconoclastic psychiatrist Szasz, for instance, has described[107] psychiatric expert testimony as, ". . . mendacity masquerading as medicine," whereas the views of Diamond and Louisell as to the function and utility of that kind of evidence have already been mentioned.[108] Nevertheless, hostility towards psychiatric evidence and suspicion of its relationship with traditional legal process does exist: even Diamond himself has gloomily commented[109] that, "All we psychiatrists can tell the law is that if you think you have trouble with our inconsistencies now, wait and see what the future holds." Again, the element of tension between the disciplines of law and psychiatry has been emphasized by Chambers J. of the United States Court of Appeals' Ninth Circuit in a dissenting judgment in *Wade v. U.S.*[110] when he stated that, "If we were going to see a psychiatrist, I am sure he would not let us bring our own couches along. When the psychiatrists came over to see us officially and testify, there is no valid reason I can see that they do not do business on our terms. . . ."

There are some clear explanations as to the suspicion in which psychiatrist-witnesses are held: in *Epperson v. Dampney*, for instance, Street C.J. was clearly concerned[111] at the risk of psychiatrists usurping the function of the court and deciding upon the ultimate issue. Again, the apparent divergence in the attitude of courts to psychiatrists and welfare officers may, and I must stress that this is an entirely impressionistic comment, be dictated by more or less inaccurate perceptions of the *personae* involved: thus, welfare officers are perceived as pleasant middle-aged ladies who discuss problems over cups of tea and are generally regarded as nice, whereas psychiatrists are perceived as remote and, indeed, frightening entities with an almost Frankensteinian aura.

CONCLUDING REFLECTIONS

In a sense, writing this article has been a rather dispiriting experience, in that it is quite clear that there is no coherent approach by Australian courts towards expert evidence in judicial divorce and ancillary proceedings, this being the case even where a new and specially constituted tribunal exists. Outside the major areas discussed earlier, there has been a very mixed and tepid juidical response to the counselling procedures contained in the *Family Law Act*.[112] It is certainly difficult to escape the conclusion that, even in a new tribunal, expert opinion is regarded as secondary to what Okpaku has described[113] as the ". . . experientially based discretion of trial judges."

Is there a rationally based solution? In the short term, there probably is not. Mutual suspicion will almost certainly continue to prevail between practitioners of the various disciplines involved in family litigation. At the same time, even a rather pious hope is preferable to inertia. First, it is apparent, I would venture, that the role of the expert needs to be clarified; it may be that the possibility of an *Evidence Code* as adverted to in Australia[114] and elsewhere[115] might go some way towards this goal. A simple statutory provision might, at least, assist: thus, in the United States *Federal Rules of Evidence* it is specified[116] that, "Testimony in the form of an opinion or inference otherwise admissible is not objectionable because it embraces an ultimate issue to be decided by the trier of fact." Specific provision is likewise made for cross-examination of the expert witness.[117]

At the same time,[118] far more, and on a greater variety of levels, needs to be done if the position of the expert is to be clarified and his expertise to be properly utilized. The practitioners from the various disciplines involved must be prepared, at the very least, to learn and appreciate each others' language and methodology. It may be that law schools must play a greater part in encouraging this development than they have done in the past.[119] In the words of McClean,[120] ". . . there are professional barriers to overcome, and disciplines have their own language and styles of debate which need much translation; but the rewards are considerable."

NOTES

1. See also F. Bates, "The Changing Nature of Marriage — The Relevance of the Australian Experience" in *Marriage and Cohabitation in Contemporary Societies: Areas of Legal, Social and Ethical Change* (1980, eds. Eekelaar and Katz) 104 at 104.

2. *Construction of Australia*, s. 51(xxi), (xxii). Advantage was not taken of this power until *Matrimonial Causes Act* 1959. For comment, see, for example, R.D. Lumb and K.W. Ryan, *Constitution of the Commonwealth of Australia Annotated* (3rd ed., 1981) at 160–64.

3. *Family Law Act* 1975, Part IV.

4. The State of Western Australia has taken advantage of s. 41 of the *Family Law Act* to create its own family court. It is, thus far, the only State to do so.

5. This is, of course, in addition to the more strictly procedural qualifications for appointment; see *Family Law Act* 1975, s. 22(2)(a).

6. *Barnett v. Barnett* [1973] 2 N.S.W.L.R. 403. For comment, see F. Bates, "Custody of Children: Towards a New Approach" (1975) 49 *Aust.L.J.* 129.

7. See, particularly, *Lynch v. Lynch* (1965) 8 F.L.R. 433 at 433 *per* Begg J., and *Neill v. Neill* (1966) 8 F.L.R. 461 at 462 *per* Selby J.

8. See *Priest v. Priest* (1965) 9 F.L.R. 384 at 409 *per* Gowans J.; *Sing v. Muir* (1969) 19 F.L.R. 212 at 216 *per* Burbury C.J.

9. See, for example, the English *Civil Evidence Act* 1968. Although, in the state of New South Wales, the Law Reform Commission has produced a substantial report on the Hearsay Rule, *Working Paper on the Rule Against Hearsay* (1976).

10. (1977) F.L.C. 90–259 at 76,385.

11. *Ibid.* at 76,386.

12. *Ibid.* at 76,388.

13. *Ibid.* at 76,386.

14. *Ibid.* at 76,386.

15. (1977) F.L.C. 90–281 at 76,514. The similarity in the forum is not surprising as Wood J. was a member of the court in *Foster* as well!

16. M.D. Broun and S. Fowler, *Australian Family Law and Practice* (1976) Vol. 1, para. 24–007.

17. [1965] A.C. 201.

18. (1977) F.L.C. 90–208 at 76,080.

19. *Supra,* n. 16.

20. *Supra,* text at n. 8.

21. See *Family Law Act* 1975, s. 97.

22. *Supra,* n. 16.

23. For further comment, see *infra,* text at n. 49.

24. For comment on this issue, see *infra,* text at n. 29 ff.

25. *Supra,* n. 15.

26. *Supra,* n. 16.

27. (1976) 10 A.L.R. 227 at 229. For more detailed comment on this case, see *infra,* text at n. 65 ff.

28. (1977) F.L.C. 90–253.

29. (1977) F.L.C. 90–258 at 76,383.

30. This view is by no means new; see, for instance, in Australia, *Reeves v. Reeves (No. 2)* (1961) 2 F.L.R. 280 at 284 *per* Barry J. and *Staats v. Staats* (1970) 16 F.L.R. 279 at

281 *per* Selby J. In England, see *In re K. (Infants)* [1963] Ch. 381 at 390 *per* Ungoed Thomas J., whose comment was approved in the Court of Appeal by Upjohn L.J., [1963] Ch. 381 at 405. See also *In re W.L.W.* [1972] Ch. 456.
31. (1977) F.L.C. 90–276 at 76,473.
32. *Ibid.* at 76,474.
33. *Ibid.* at 76,472–73.
34. (1978) F.L.C. 90–429.
35. *Ibid.* at 77,182.
36. *Supra*, text at n. 29.
37. (1978) F.L.C. 90–429 at 77,182.
38. See *infra*, text at n. 104 ff.
39. B.L. Diamond and D.W. Louisell, "The Psychiatrist as Expert Witness: Some Ruminations and Speculations" (1965) 63 *Michigan L.R.* 1,335 at 1,354.
40. *Supra*, n. 16 at para. 24–012. See also A. Marshall, "Social Workers and Psychologists as Family Court Counsellors Within the Family Court of Australia" (1977) 39(1) *Aust. Social Work* 9 at 11, and *In the Marriage of Hall and Hall* (1979) F.L.C. 90–713 at 78,819.
41. (1978) F.L.C. 90–489.
42. *Ibid.* at 77,532.
43. *Supra*, text at n. 29.
44. (1978) F.L.C. 90–489 at 77,533.
45. *Supra*, text at n. 31.
46. (1978) F.L.C. 90–489 at 77,533.
47. *Ibid.* at 77,533.
48. *Supra*, text at n. 23.
49. (1979) F.L.C. 90–713.
50. *Ibid.* at 78,826.
51. *Ibid.* at 78,819.
52. Consisting of Evatt C.J., Asche S.J. and Hogan J.
53. The court went on, (1979) F.L.C. 90–713 at 78,819–20, to mention the utility of cross-examination, see *supra*, text at n. 40 and its importance as a formal means of testing evidence. See *supra*, text at n. 31 ff. and the cases referred to therein.
54. (1980) F.L.C. 90–809.
55. *Ibid.* at 75,099. The witness was a qualified clinical psychologist of some thirty years experience.
56. Counsel contended that s. 64(5) of the *Family Law Act* 1975, which provides that custody and access orders shall, so far as practicable, be supervised by a court counsellor or welfare officer, had that effect.
57. *Supra*, n. 10.
58. (1980) F.L.C. 90–809 at 75,100.
59. H.W. Sloane, "Relationship of Law and Social Work" (1967) 12 *Social Work* 88 at 91.
60. P.R. Tamilia, "Neglect Proceedings and the Conflict Between Law and Social Work" (1971) 9 *Duquesne L.R.* 579 at 579.
61. (1977) F.L.C. 90–208.
62. *Ibid.* at 76,371. McCall J. was of the opinion that such a report was admissible whether it was regarded as an exception to the hearsay rule or as not infringing the rule. For a general commentary on the matter of children's wishes, see F. Bates, "The Relevance

of Children's Wishes In Contested Custody Cases: An Analysis of Recent Developments in Canada and Australia" (1979) 2 *Fam. L.R.* 83.

63. *Ibid.* at p. 76,371.
64. [1970] A.C. 688 at 726.
65. (1976) 10 A.L.R. 227 at 231.
66. For more detailed comment, see F. Bates, "New Trends and Expert Evidence in Child Custody Cases: Some New Developments and Further Thoughts from Australia" (1979) 12 *C.I.L.S.A.* 65.
67. Carmichael J. There was, apparently, little to choose between the parties and the facilities that they were able to offer the child, and, indeed, the trial judge would have made a different determination had it not been for the expert evidence.
68. (1976) 10 A.L.R. 227 at 228.
69. *Ibid.* at 229–30.
70. *Supra,* n. 64.
71. *Supra,* n. 7.
72. (1976) 10 A.L.R. 227 at 230–31.
73. *Ibid.* at 231.
74. *Supra,* text at n. 64.
75. *Supra,* n. 39.
76. (1976) 10 A.L.R. 227 at 231.
77. See, for example, *Family Law Act* 1975, s. 64(1). Also certain comments by Lord MacDermott in *J. v. C., supra,* n. 64 at 710, seem to suggest that the child's welfare is the *only* consideration. For a faintly critical comment, see M.D.A. Freeman, "Child Law At the Crossroads" (1974) 27 *C.L.P.* 164 at 184. *Cf.* F. Bates, "Redefining the Parent/Child Relationship: A Blueprint" (1976) 12 *U.W.A.L.R.* 518 at 520–23.
78. See, for example, S.M. Cretney, *Principles of Family Law* (3rd ed., 1979) at 494–98. For an attempt to institutionalize these criteria, see the Australian Government Report, *Family Law in Australia* (1980) at para. 4.49. For comment on the report as a whole, see F. Bates, "Family Law in Australia: A Long Engagement" (1980) 3 *Fam.L.R.* 15.
79. See *Miller v. California* 413 U.S. 15 (1974) at 24 *per* Berger C.J. and *Mishkin v. New York* 383 U.S. 502 (1967).
80. 413 U.S. 15 (1974) at 40.
81. The other judge in the majority, Glass J.A., (1976) 10 A.L.R. 227 at 241 ff., based his judgment on the view that the trial judge has failed to give sufficient weight to the notion that long-term welfare of the children required that they be in the care of their mother. This view is contradictory to that generally held in modern Australian law; see, particularly, *In the Marriage of Laidley* (1976) F.L.C. 90–120.
82. (1976) 10 A.L.R. 227 at 234.
83. *Supra,* text at n. 64.
84. (1976) 10 A.L.R. 227 at 233.
85. *Ibid.* at 234.
86. *Ibid.* at 234.
87. *Supra,* n. 7.
88. (1966) 8 F.L.R. 433 at 434.
89. (1976) 10 A.L.R. 227 at 234.
90. *Ibid.* at 234–37.
91. [1973] 2 All E.R. 662. For comment, see F. Bates, "Psychiatric Evidence of Character" (1976) 5 *Anglo-Am.L.R.* 99 at 102 ff.

92. In *Lowery*, the psychological tests involved were the *Rorschach* and *Thematic Apperception* tests.
93. [1975] 1 All. E.R. 70.
94. *Supra*, text at n. 73.
95. *Supra*, n. 31 at 76,474.
96. The children in question were aged six and eight years, *cf. In the Marriage of Laidley, supra*, n. 81.
97. It likewise appeared that the tests had been undertaken without the approval of the independent legal representative of the child as appointed under s. 65 of the *Family Law Act* 1975. For comment on the role of that *persona* in Australia, see D. Whelan, "The Wishes of Children and the Role of the Separate Representative" (1979) 5 *Monash U.L.R.* 287.
98. *Supra*, text at n. 31 at 76,475.
99. *Supra*, text at n. 64.
100. *Supra*, text at n. 75 ff.
101. *Supra*, n. 54.
102. See the comments of Wood S.J. *supra*, n. 54 at 75,103.
103. *Ibid.*
104. M.D.A. Freeman, *supra*, n. 77 at 179.
105. J. Renvoize, *Children in Danger* (1974) at 87.
106. S.R. Okpaku, "Psychology: Impediment or Aid in Child Custody Cases?" (1976) 29 *Rutgers L.R.* 1,117. For detailed comment on Okpaku's thesis, see F. Bates, *supra*, n. 66.
107. T. Szasz, *The Second Sin* (1973) at 40.
108. *Supra*, text at n. 39.
109. B.L. Diamond, "From *McNaghten* to *Currens* and Beyond" (1962) 50 *Cal.L.R.* 189 at 197.
110. 426 F. 2d 64 (1970) at 86.
111. *Supra*, text at n. 68.
112. See *Family Law Act* 1975, s. 14(6). For comment, see F. Bates, "Counselling and Reconciliation Provisions — An Exercise in Futility" (1978) 8 *Fam. L.R.* 248.
113. *Supra*, n. 106 at 1,153.
114. See F. Bates, *Principles of Evidence* (2nd ed., 1980) at 10.
115. See, for example, N. Brooks, "The Law Reform Commission of Canada's Evidence Code" (1978) 16 *Osgoode Hall L.J.* 241.
116. *Federal Rules of Evidence for United States Courts and Magistrates* 1975, n. 704.
117. *Ibid.* n. 705.
118. See, *supra*, n. 66, also F. Bates, "Expert Evidence in Cases Involving Children" in *The Child and the Law* (1976, ed. F. Bates) 229.
119. In Australia, the Faculty of Law in the University of Tasmania has introduced a Master of Legal Studies/Diploma in Welfare Law course with this aim in mind.
120. J.D. McClean, "The Battered Baby and the Limits of the Law" (1979) 5 *Monash U.L.R.* 1 at 16.

Chapter Ten

Divorce In South Africa — Principles and Practice

June Sinclair*

University of the Witwatersrand, Johannesburg, South Africa

South Africa is a country geographically isolated from jurisdictions where reform in family law is taking place. It is also shunned because of its politics.[1] We have much to learn both from improvements effected and errors made in countries where reform to overcome common problems has already occurred. Also needed is a rigorous examination of laws that govern (and frequently disrupt) the unit we perhaps too glibly refer to as the basis of our society: the family. In this chapter the two issues that will be canvassed are the granting of a decree of divorce and the award of custody of minor children.[2]

THE GROUNDS OF DIVORCE

Until 1979, when the *Divorce Act* was enacted,[3] there were four grounds of divorce in South Africa. Two of these, adultery and malicious desertion, derived from the Roman-Dutch law; and two came from a statutory source, the *Divorce Laws Amendment Act* of 1935.[4] The 1935 legislation was regarded as a concession towards the principle of marriage breakdown in that it permitted a divorce to be granted on the basis of the defendant's incurable insanity or his imprisonment as a habitual criminal. No more than a handful of divorces was based on these grounds.

The technical meaning of malicious desertion and adultery and the jurisprudential development of these grounds of divorce over a period of one hundred years have been described by South African authors.[5] It is

---

* I wish to thank my colleague Felicity Kaganas for checking the manuscript and to acknowledge her contribution of several of the footnotes. I wish also to acknowledge the financial assistance I received from the Human Sciences Research Council.

not proposed to elaborate on these issues, save to say that even before the replacement of fault by failure in 1979, the myth of one virtuous spouse deserving a compensatory remedy for the misdeeds of the other was exploded in South Africa as it was elsewhere.[6]

Undoubtedly the most significant feature of divorce proceedings prior to the recent reform was the attitude taken by our courts towards collusion. As in most other jurisdictions, the large majority of divorces were (and remain) undefended and, as has been observed, where there is no contest there is either agreement or acquiescence.[7] Judges, unable in a busy courtroom to investigate the facts of each case, had no real choice but to accept the ubiquitous, uncontroverted allegations of desertion and to grant decrees. Consensual divorce, dressed up as divorce for misconduct, became an established part of South African law.

Against this background the legislature, in 1979, replaced the former grounds of divorce with two new grounds:[8] the irretrievable breakdown of the marriage[9] and the mental illness or continuing unconsciousness of a party to the marriage.[10]

Irretrievable Breakdown

(1) A court may grant a decree of divorce on the ground of the irretrievable breakdown of a marriage if it is satisfied that the marriage relationship between the parties to the marriage has reached such a state of disintegration that there is no reasonable prospect of the restoration of a normal marriage relationship between them.

(2) Subject to the provisions of subsection (1), and without excluding any facts or circumstances which may be indicative of the irretrievable break-down of a marriage, the court may accept evidence —
   (a) that the parties have not lived together as husband and wife for a continuous period of at least one year immediately prior to the date of the institution of the divorce action;
   (b) that the defendant has committed adultery and that the plaintiff finds it irreconcilable with a continued marriage relationship; or
   (c) that the defendant has in terms of a sentence of a court been declared an habitual criminal and is undergoing imprisonment as a result of such sentence,

   as proof of the irretrievable break-down of a marriage.

(3) If it appears to the court that there is a reasonable possibility that the parties may become reconciled through marriage counsel, treatment or reflection, the court may postpone the proceedings in order that the parties may attempt a reconciliation.

Mental Illness or Continuous Unconsciousness

(1) A court may grant a decree of divorce on the ground of the mental illness of the defendant if it is satisfied —
   (a) that the defendant in terms of the Mental Health Act, 1973 (Act 18 of 1973) —

(i) has been admitted as a patient to an institution in terms of a reception order;
(ii) is being detained as a President's patient at an institution or other place specified by the Minister of Prisons; or
(iii) is being detained as a mentally-ill convicted prisoner at an institution or hospital prison for psychopaths, and that he has, for a continuous period of at least two years immediately prior to the institution of the divorce action, not been discharged unconditionally as such a patient, President's patient or mentally-ill prisoner; and

(b) after having heard the evidence of at least two psychiatrists, of whom one shall have been appointed by the court, that the defendant is mentally ill and that there is no reasonable prospect that he will be cured of his mental illness.

(2) A court may grant a decree of divorce on the ground that the defendant is by reason of a physical disorder in a state of continuous unconsciousness, if it is satisfied —

(a) that the defendant's unconsciousness has lasted for a continuous period of at least six months immediately prior to the institution of the divorce action; and
(b) after having heard the evidence of at least two medical practitioners, of whom one shall be a neurologist or a neurosurgeon appointed by the court, that there is no reasonable prospect that the defendant will regain consciousness.

These provisions apply to the dissolution of all civil marriages in South Africa, regardless of the race of the parties.[11] However, the various provincial and local divisions of the Supreme Court effectively hear only divorces of Whites, Coloureds and Asians. Although the Supreme Court has concurrent jurisdiction with the Divorce Court constituted in 1929[12] to dissolve the civil marriages of Blacks, very few Blacks can afford the cost of a divorce in the Supreme Court, where only an insignificant handful of White persons attempt to obtain *pro se* dissolution (which is often actively discouraged by judges) and where the attorney must employ counsel to represent his client.[13]

Commentaries analysing the wording of sections 3, 4 and 5 of the *Divorce Act* appeared soon after its enactment,[14] but only a handful of reported decisions elucidating the meaning of the new grounds of divorce make up our jurisprudence to date.[15] Factors explanatory of the paucity of judicial pronouncement on this aspect of our law may be that few divorces (among Whites) are contested;[16] that the "blanket" nature of section 4(1), the irretrievable breakdown provision, allows divorce where both parties proclaim their desire for it[17] and even in favour of a plaintiff guilty of misconduct, against a defendant who does not want the marriage to be dissolved.[18] Mental illness or continuous unconsciousness of a spouse, in the nature of things, cannot often be resorted to, yet there have been cases on the (unsatisfactory) relationship of section 5 (the mental-illness provision) to section 4 (the breakdown section).[19]

No reported decision exists concerning the interpretation of the guidelines listed in section 4(2) of the Act.[20] In one instance, reliance could have been placed by the court on a long period of separation, but the judge expressly chose to formulate his finding that the marriage had irretrievably broken down in terms of the general provision, section 4(1).[21] Regarded as ample proof that the relationship could not be restored was the plaintiff's "adamant determination not to resume life with the defendant."[22] In another case it was held that "breakdown is present when one of the spouses no longer wishes to maintain a marriage relationship with the other."[23]

On the whole, therefore, the legislation and the judicial decisions concerning its interpretation have confirmed that South Africa's conception of the enigmatic expression "irretrievable breakdown" seems to be more realistic than that adopted in England, for example. Fears expressed at the time the new law was enacted that the guidelines in section 4(2) would harden into three exclusive methods of establishing breakdown have proved unfounded. Breakdown, however caused, is what is looked for by the courts.

THE DIVORCE LAW IN PRACTICE

In undefended matters too (observed in the Witwatersrand Local Division of the Supreme Court),[24] where the procedure is by way of trial, plaintiffs appear to prefer the blanket provision for establishing breakdown. Counsel for the plaintiff merely states that the action is based on the irretrievable breakdown of the marriage and proceeds[25] to ask whether the parties are still living together. If he obtains a negative response to this question, he enquires when the plaintiff or defendant left the home. In several cases the answer to this question reveals a period of separation shorter than one year (the guideline contained in section 4(2)(*a*)), but only rarely does this fact prevent the granting of the decree.[26] Certain judges are known to refuse a divorce to a plaintiff living in the same house with the defendant, at times, regardless of counsel's attempt to lead evidence that no cohabitation as husband and wife exists between the parties.[27] In these matters, the reconciliation provision, section 4(3), is sometimes implemented and postponements of up to a year are ordered. According to some counsel, such judges are "avoided" by a request for a postponement of the hearing for one week, say, in the hope that the following Wednesday will produce a judge less demanding in this respect.

A notable feature of undefended matters in the Supreme Court is the added caution displayed by some judges in cases where there are minor children of the marriage. It can be said that stronger evidence of irretrievable breakdown is required in these cases and that some judges question the plaintiff about the problems that beset the relationship, the attitude of both parties to the marriage and the possibility of reconciliation. By contrast, where there are no children of the marriage, or the children are no longer minors, divorces are rapidly granted at the rate of approximately one every four to six minutes,[28] with very little enquiry from the bench. Towards the end of the roll, there are often repeated interruptions by the judge, who hurriedly declares that he is satisfied and asks counsel, "What do you want?" Before the advocate can complete his request for an order of divorce, the judge pronounces the marriage dissolved and the next matter is called. Plaintiffs quite often seem momentarily stunned, unable to appreciate that the "ordeal" is over, and they have to be asked to stand down.

The above description must be qualified. Some judges distinguish childless marriages of particularly short duration from those childless ones that have endured for, say, two or more years. In the former situation, postponements are sometimes ordered and the judge may remark that if the parties were sufficiently in love to marry only three or six or nine months before, it is not easy to conclude that their feelings should have changed so completely and so rapidly. Nevertheless, there are judges who do not make this distinction, and many marriages of young people which have lasted only a very short time are dissolved perfunctorily.[29] A number of the plaintiffs, moreover, seem not to be particularly upset and can be seen smilingly leaving the courtroom with friends, to discover the significance of their new status.

A very different picture is painted in the Black Divorce Court.[30] From the matters observed in the Central Black Divorce Court,[31] which has its headquarters in Johannesburg, and which handles a large proportion of all Black divorces in the country,[32] it is immediately apparent that the number of officially contested matters is much greater. Here it must be explained that divorces of Blacks are categorized by the registrar of the court into three types: contested matters, where the parties are quite often represented by attorneys (who have a right of audience in this court); uncontested matters, in which there may or may not be legal representation;[33] and "clerk-of-the-court matters," an expression signifying that the plaintiff has no representation and that the summons and particulars of claim were drafted gratuitously for the plaintiff by the clerk of the court.[34] These last-mentioned matters can be contested or uncontested, but are placed on a separate roll.[35] The distinction between uncontested and contested divorces is not as sharp as it is among Whites, Coloureds and Asians whose cases are heard in the Supreme Court. The reason is that procedural and technical rules are not as strictly observed in the Black Divorce Court.[36]

Great care, it was observed, is taken by the President and the two permanent members of the bench to question the plaintiff in cases where the defendant is in default.[37] Each case of this kind occupies the court for something like twelve to twenty minutes,[38] and a significant amount of this time is devoted to the investigation of irretrievable breakdown. Divorces are frequently refused where it is revealed that the parties are living in the same house,[39] even if it is alleged that they are not cohabiting as man and wife.[40]

The overall impression gained is that the informality of procedure and the lack of ceremony present in the Black Divorce Courts leads to a more relaxed atmosphere, but there is a genuine concern on the part of the presiding officer for the spouses (both of whom are usually in court), whose marriage is carefully investigated before it is dissolved.[41] While it can be said that a Black plaintiff whose innocent spouse opposes the divorce will have a little difficulty obtaining a decree, among Whites, Coloureds and Asians either spouse can obtain a divorce at will.

CUSTODY OF MINOR CHILDREN

An important provision in the *Divorce Act* is section 6, which compels the court granting a divorce to withhold the decree until it is satisfied that the best possible arrangements have been made for the welfare of the children of the marriage.[42] Of the matters observed in the Witwatersrand Local Division of the Supreme Court, in Johannesburg, about 60 per cent involved minor children.[43] Custody, an ancillary matter, is hardly ever contested. It is awarded not on the basis of the guilt or innocence of parents, but according to the universal standard of the best interests of the child.[44] Either the parties agree formally, in a written deed of settlement, which parent will have the care of the children, or the plaintiff claims custody and is granted it against a defendant who (it seems clear, acquiesces, because he/she) is typically in default regarding all matters pertaining to the divorce. In both types of case, counsel, or failing that the judge, will ask the plaintiff whether the party wanting custody can care adequately for the children. Not unexpectedly, the response is always positive. Arrangements for the children while the parent who is to be charged with their custody is at work are quickly explained to the judge and the award is then incorporated into the order of court. A predilection to grant custody of small children to their mother is apparent only from the mild surprise on the part of the judge or his more careful questioning of the plaintiff in cases where a father seeks custody or where a plaintiff-mother informs the court that she does not want the children to live with her. In several cases involving children under the age of ten years and in some where the children are babies aged less than two years, fathers are granted custody.[45]

The impression gained was that in this division of the Supreme Court, the so-called investigation into the welfare of the children is perfunctory and not worth very much, because a plaintiff claiming custody is not likely to admit that the children will not be properly cared for.

Intensive questioning takes place and more time is devoted to the issue of custody in each case in the Black Divorce Court, Johannesburg.[46] It was noted that parents are often exhorted to subordinate their own feelings and to reconcile rather than proceed with the divorce, in the interests of their children. Unopposed plaintiff-mothers who assert that the children are with them and are adequately cared for are nevertheless questioned about the size of the house they occupy, the number of occupants, the arrangements made for the care of the children while their mothers are out at work, the attitude of the other parent to the children, and whether the amount of maintenance claimed is adequate. It would, however, be wrong and facile to accuse judges in the Supreme Court of a dereliction of duty in respect of White, Coloured and Asian children.[47] A parent belonging to one of these race groups is nearly always represented, and it is probably significant that both the attorney and counsel will have had an opportunity to assess whether the plaintiff (or defendant) is fit to have custody and, more particularly, whether the maintenance claimed for the children is sufficient for their needs. Moreover, the critical housing shortage that causes great suffering to Black families does not afflict Whites as seriously, so that the concern of the court in this regard is not as urgently called for.[48]

Another reason (directly related to the housing shortage) why custody and maintenance are time-consuming issues in the Black courts is that custody is frequently contested. Defendants who do not oppose the action for dissolution of the marriage are often desperate to obtain custody. Evidence adduced usually reveals that both parents are fit and proper persons to have the care of the children and the expedient of granting custody of small children to their mothers is resorted to by the court to resolve a difficult issue. Further, unlike the attitude of the Supreme Court, which is to avoid splitting children, awards of custody causing Black brothers and sisters to be separated are not unusual. What is the explanation for this frenetic clamour of Black parents to retain or to obtain custody of their children? The devastating, tragic battle for accommodation is the answer.[49]

Entitlement to a residential permit in a Black township is governed by the regulations promulgated in terms of the *Black (Urban Areas) Consolidation Act*.[50] One of the conditions for the allocation of a dwelling is that the applicant has dependants who may lawfully reside with him in the prescribed area.[51] Cancellation of a permit can occur, *inter alia*, if the permit holder no longer occupies the dwelling with his/her dependants or if the permit holder is a male who divorces his wife or does not reside with that wife and dependants. In practice, it seems that these permits are retained by or transferred to the parent who is awarded custody of the children.[52] The parent who will not be caring for the children often becomes homeless and must rely on the goodwill and charity of neighbours or friends for a place to sleep. It cannot be firmly stated that this position prevails countrywide, but one might guess that the enormous housing backlogs in urban areas other than the Witwatersrand would produce similar consequences.

Finally, a man who obtains custody of his children will not have a maintenance order made against him and this factor also accounts, in some measure, for the number of contested custody cases. Suspicious that his wife will spend on herself the R25 to R30 per month usually ordered for the maintenance of each child,[53] a father will attempt to obtain custody of his children and then send them to his parental home, either in the urban area or, more frequently, in a Black homeland, where he is more sure that the money he sends for them will be used to cater for their needs, and where it will cost him much less to keep them.

CONCLUSIONS

First, this paper does not pretend to manifest the kind of empirical research from which firm conclusions can be reached. Much of what has been said in it is based on *a priori* assertions or intuitive assessment.[54] It is merely a modest beginning. A questionnaire circulated by the South African Law Commission[55] to gather information concerning the adequacy of the divorce law and the effects of its operation will, no doubt, be helpful to those officially burdened with the responsibility of recommending the direction reform should take. But it also is not enough. Careful and continued monitoring of divorce actions is required, and this cannot quickly or easily be undertaken by one or a few persons.[56]

Second, the ease and speed with which dissolution of marriage can be secured in South Africa led one writer to remark that "[a]n uninformed onlooker, seeing our divorce courts in action, will in all probability disbelieve any suggestion that the South African law ... [is] conservatively based on ... Biblical principles."[57] This observation was made in 1967, when divorce was still predicated upon matrimonial misconduct. The introduction in 1979 of irretrievable breakdown as the effective basis for the dissolution of marriage marked a final and complete departure from Roman-Dutch principle and, it is believed, an even greater facility in the matter of obtaining a decree of divorce.

We now have non-adversary law which requires the court to be satisfied of the existence of an objective, neutral situation — irretrievable breakdown. Non-adversary law does not accord well with adversary procedures.[58] What is anomalous is that in spite of the absence, in undefended divorces, of the elements of contest and risk, which typify adversarial litigation, the formal outcome of the process is still success for a plaintiff in a trial action prosecuted at considerable cost against a defendant who does not defend.[59] Responses to this paradox will vary. The element of contest can be reintroduced and some risk can be attached to the outcome of the litigation if the substantive law is changed to make divorce more difficult.[60] Also, procedural devices grafted onto the existing substantive law can make divorce more protracted[61] but, alas, also more expensive. Finally, procedures could be radically altered to bring the existing legal basis upon which divorce depends into conformity with the method of obtaining the decree. Which direction should the reform take? I intend to advance only the last of these possibilities but, before that, something ought to be said of the high incidence of divorce in South Africa.[62]

Fears that easy divorce breeds divorce are fairly widespread in South Africa and not easy to allay. A number of people believe that the dramatic increase in the number of divorces (among Whites) since 1979 is attributable to the fact that divorce was made easier in that year. Eloquently, and repeatedly, family lawyers have asserted that "as long as divorce can be obtained at all, at a cost which does not put it outside the reach of the ordinary man, the ease or difficulty with which it can be obtained plays a relatively minor part in the divorce rate."[63] While this view is unequivocally adopted by some and grudgingly accepted by others, the disquiet evoked by the statistics increases. The reality represented by the high incidence of divorce can perhaps be accommodated more easily if it is seen in perspective.

Divorce has always been easy in South Africa. An initial upswing in the number of divorces soon after the enactment of the 1979 legislation can be accounted for, at least in part, by the backlog of "guilty" persons desiring divorce but unable to obtain it under the fault-oriented system against an "innocent" defendant who wanted the marriage to continue.[64] Only to these persons did the change in the law represent a new opportunity to pursue freedom and individual happiness.

Far more important in the field of change is the now questionable assumption that marriage represents a lifelong commitment to one partner. Ideas about marriage are in flux. Demographic data and doctrinal writings to assist in the proof of this are easier to find in other jurisdictions than in South Africa.[65] However, there is no reason to believe that descriptions of changes that have occurred in the underlying assumptions of modern marriage law in Western industrialized societies (such as the United States, England, France and West Germany) have less than a striking part to play in the assessment of our situation. Notions once common to Western legal systems,[66] such as the terminability of marriage only by death or for serious cause; the allocation of the role of predominant decision maker and breadwinner to the husband-father and of homemaker to the wife-mother; the exclusive nature of sexual relations within marriage (at least for wives), have disappeared or are giving way to new assumptions.

The shift away from traditional perspectives of marriage is discernible among white South Africans from their acceptance of divorce on the ground of breakdown as a normal method of terminating a marriage; from their demands for spousal equality and increased sexual freedom; and from the emphasis being placed on individual happiness as a prerequisite for the maintenance of the marriage relationship. No less striking in this regard is their ever-increasing propensity to make use of the opportunity afforded them by the law to change their marriage partners. Among Asians and Blacks, religious sanction and customary regulation by the broader family, respectively, are probably still factors that help to contain the tide of divorce. However, for all race groups in the pluralistic South African society it can be said that the adoption of marriage breakdown as the principal ground for divorce effectively means that "either spouse can obtain a divorce at will. It is therefore accurate to say that today the concept of permanence has been eliminated from the legal definition of marriage."[67]

If the above description is accepted, attempts to curb the rate of divorce by making the law more restrictive or the procedure more complicated should be abandoned as futile. Whatever can be done to reduce the incidence of marriage breakdown must fall predominantly outside the realm of the divorce law.[68]

1979, the South African substantive law was brought into conformity with reality. Parties wanting a divorce have since then been permitted to reveal agreement to end their marriage, instead of being compelled to conceal the consensus and to ask for an unwanted court order threatening (the desired) divorce failing the defendant's compliance with a command to restore conjugal rights.[69] Corresponding changes in procedure to reflect reality are overdue. Only a very small proportion of divorces is contested. It must surely be inappropriate to apply a procedure, which may be suitable for these few matters, to the vast majority of cases that are undefended and involve no contest and no risk.[70] We must accept that the role of the courts "begins when the parties and their advisers . . . have failed to resolve the difficulties."[71] Seldom are the parties not *ad idem* in the decision to dissolve a marriage that has broken down, and the issues of custody and financial provision are resolved in a lawyer's office.[72]

In the light of these facts, the granting of decrees in undefended matters could be removed from the courtroom. Administrative divorce modelled upon the "special procedure" that has been applied in England in all undefended matters since 1977 is an obvious alternative that merits consideration.[73] One of its advantages is the saving in cost that would result to parties who litigate in the Supreme Court and use the services of an attorney and an advocate to procure the decree.[74] This saving, it is true, could also be achieved if more persons conducted their own divorces, but *pro se* litigation has its dangers.[75] Moreover, if the ritual involved in obtaining a divorce is unnecessary, it should be eliminated.

The disadvantages and inappropriateness of judicial hearings for undefended divorces have been copiously catalogued in the comparative literature. What has been said by Eekelaar[76] and Elston, Fuller and Murch,[77] and frequently elucidated by others to reveal similar deficiencies in systems outside of England,[78] applies with equal force to the South African procedure. Detailed recitation of the arguments supporting the removal of this particular issue from the courtroom is not called for.[79] Restatement of one of its important results is: valuable court time saved by simplifying an issue over which the law, in any event, has little control could be used by judges and lawyers in a non-adversary system to promote more equitable and harmonious resolution of problems related to custody and financial provision.[80] Even retention of the pronouncement of the decree by a judge may be seen as rubber-stamping.[81] But at least, if registrars in South Africa were permitted to perform the functions of their English counterparts, a significant step would have been taken towards creating uniformity between the substantive and procedural approaches to obtaining a divorce.[82]

Finally, my assessment of the procedure in the Central Black Divorce Court is that it is adversarial in theory but inquisitorial in practice.[83] The concern shown by the presiding officers for spouses and children is striking. Nevertheless, what does not seem justifiable is the separate judicial structure for the hearing of Black divorces. I strongly urge the bringing together of all courts handling civil-law divorce and the issues associated with it.[84] Whether the tribunals structured to undertake this task should be called family courts must not cloud the issue.[85] The South African Law Commission has not recommended them; the state will, no doubt, raise obstacles such as administrative burdens and expense.[86]

What is important is that all South Africans are subject to the same divorce legislation when their marriages[87] break down. Uniformity in the application of this legislation must be a priority. Its attainment will conduce to more justice and a better understanding of the deficiencies that require amelioration. These objectives will remain out of reach while people of different races must have recourse to different courts.

NOTES

1. These factors must account in some measure for the lack of impetus for reform in South Africa in the field of family law. Racial laws are certainly accountable for various injustices that will be described in this chapter.

2. Because of limited space, comment on the financial consequences of divorce and the extent of private ordering, which formed part of my original article has been omitted.

3. *Act 70* of 1979 came into operation on 1 July 1979. Its provisions are described below.

4. *Act 32* of 1935.

5. Professor H.R. Hahlo's work *The South African Law of Husband and Wife*, 4th ed. (1975) contains two lengthy chapters describing malicious desertion and adultery as grounds for divorce.

6. Several judgments contained reference to the fact that the public has no interest in maintaining a marriage that has irretrievably broken down. Many divorces were granted to the less morally blameworthy of two guilty spouses as a result of the use by the court of its discretion to condone the adultery of one of them in order to render that one a technically "innocent" party. By eschewing the consequences of the Roman-Dutch principle *culpa compensatio,* our judges afforded a number of people the opportunity to legalize their stable, "illicit" unions and to legitimate the children born of them.

7. Max Rheinstein, *Marriage Stability, Divorce and the Law* (1972) 247.

8. See s. 3 of the *Divorce Act 70* of 1979.

9. As specified in s. 4 of the Act.

10. As specified in s. 5 of the Act. It should not be overlooked that although s. 3 speaks of the mental illness, etc., *of a party* to the marriage, s. 5 refers only to the *defendant's* mental illness or continuous unconsciousness.

11. South Africa divides its population into four ethnic groups: Black, White, Asian and Coloured. Asians are usually Indians or of Indian descent; Coloured are descendants of Whites and either black Africans or Malays.

Blacks in South Africa can marry according to the civil law or what is known as their indigenous or customary law. The customary union is not recognized as a valid marriage because it is *de jure* polygynous. Consequently, a man, say, who has a customary-union wife may contract a civil marriage with another woman. The civil marriage automatically dissolves the customary union, but the woman of this union and her children enjoy some protection in terms of s. 22(7) of the *Black Administration Act 38* of 1927. This provision states that (upon the death of the man) the material rights of the woman and her issue are not in any way to be affected by the civil marriage and that the civil-law wife and her issue have no greater right to inherit from the man than they would have enjoyed had the civil marriage been a customary union. In addition, s. 22(6) of the Act lays down that community of property (the automatic proprietary system applicable to Whites, Coloureds and Asians who marry without entering into an antenuptial contract) will not apply to a marriage between Blacks, and that a man who has a customary wife is prohibited from marrying in community of property. The Appellate Division, in 1946, held that civil marriages of Blacks are automatically *out* of community of property and of profit and loss, but the husband has the marital power over his wife. (For other race groups it is only in marriages in community that the marital power applies.) The interrelationship between indigenous law and the South African civil law is complex and unsatisfactory. Criticisms of the present system and of the lack of research into the matter can be found in R. verLoren van Themaat "Die Verfyning van die Reg vir Swartes in Suid-Afrika" (1980) 43 *Tydskrif vir Hedendaagse Romeins-Hollandse Reg* 237.

12. By s. 10 of the *Black Administration Act 1927, Admendment Act 9* of 1929. For convenience, and in order to distinguish it from the Supreme Court, this court will in future be referred to as the "Black Divorce Court" although officially it is called the "Divorce Court."

13. The cost of an undefended divorce in Johannesburg is high. Fees of attorneys

(who pay the small disbursement of R85 to counsel) range from R500 to R750. Black divorces handled by the clerk of the court cost only the amount of the revenue stamp on the summons and the fee for serving the summons (a few rand). Legal representation for Blacks, whether in defended or undefended matters, costs about R200 to R250.

14. See, for example, A. H. Barnard *The New Divorce Law* (1979); H. R. Hahlo and June D. Sinclair *The Reform of the South African Law of Divorce* (1980).

15. See *Kruger v. Kruger* 1980 (3) SA 283 (0); *Swart v. Swart* 1980 (4) SA 364 (0); *Dickinson v. Dickinson* 1981 (3) SA 856 (W); *Krige v. Smit NO* 1981 (4) SA 409 (C): *Smit v. Smit* 1982 (1) SA 606 (0) and the appeal reversing this decision — *Smit v. Smit* 1982 (3) SA 34 (0); *Singh v. Singh* 1983 (1) SA 781 (C).

16. Uncontested matters would not be reported. Although more Black divorces are contested, judgments of the Black Divorce Court are not reported.

17. Arguably the best evidence of marriage breakdown.

18. See *Kruger v. Kruger* 1980 (3) SA 283 (0), which I ventured to describe in (1980) 97 *SALJ* 353 as a case of unilateral repudiation by the plaintiff of his wife. The plaintiff, aged seventy-six years, had been living in adultery for twenty-seven years and wanted his marriage of forty years' standing dissolved so that he could marry his mistress. His wife resisted the action for religious reasons and because she still loved her husband. The marriage was dissolved.

19. See *Dickinson v. Dickinson; Krige v. Smit; Smit v. Smit* (cited in note 15 above). The restrictive formulation of s. 5 encouraged reliance on the breakdown provision in these cases although the defendants were afflicted either by mental illness or physical disability. It seems that if breakdown can be established a divorce will be granted, regardless of causation.

20. For example, the meaning of "not living together as husband and wife," provided for in s 4(2)(*a*), could be controversial. Adultery which the plaintiff finds irreconcilable with the continuation of the marriage (s 4(2)(*b*)) has also not been judicially interpreted.

21. *Kruger v. Kruger* 1980 (3) SA 283 (0).

22. 1980 (3) SA 283 (0) at 286.

23. Per Flemming J. in *Swart v. Swart* 1980 (4) SA 364 (0) at 368 (my translation).

24. This court sits every Wednesday. No limitation is placed on the number of uncontested actions that may be set down for hearing on the next divorce day. Usually the roll consists of 100 to 150 matters.

25. After establishing the jurisdiction of the court and a valid subsisting marriage.

26. There is no real risk in this kind of litigation. Virtually every action on the roll which does not founder for some technical reason, succeeds.

27. Cessation of cohabitation was an essential element of an action for divorce based on malicious desertion prior to 1979. Nevertheless, it was accepted that "[i]t is possible for two persons to live in the same house . . . and yet be as far apart as the poles" (H. R. Hahlo, *The South African Law of Husband and Wife*, 4th ed. (1975) 392). Living under one roof, therefore, should not in itself constitute a bar to divorce. Other evidence may establish irretrievable breakdown.

28. In the Witwatersrand Local Division the weekly roll is often split so that two judges hear fifty to seventy-five cases each in one court day (four to five hours). This does not permit much more than five minutes per case.

29. Statistics reveal that in 1980, out of a total of 16,543 divorces of Whites, 782 marriages had lasted less than one year; 4,946 for more than one but less than five years; 4,249 for more than five but less than ten years; and 5,990 for more than ten years (576 unknown).

30. Established in 1929 to dissolve civil marriages of Blacks. This court has no

jurisdiction to dissolve a marriage if one party is Black and the other is classified Coloured. Whites are prohibited from marrying any person who is not White, but there is no prohibition on intermarriage between Coloureds (this group includes Asians) and Blacks.

31. There is also a Southern Black Divorce court with its headquarters in King Williamstown and a North-Eastern Black Divorce Court with headquarters in Pietermaritzburg.

32. Out of a total of 6,163 Black divorces in 1979, 3,333 were granted in the Central Black Divorce Court.

33. No definite figures could be established in this regard, but my guess is that plaintiffs are, more often than not, unrepresented.

34. In terms of the rules of the Black Divorce Court, the clerk of the Commissioner's Court has a duty to write out and prepare any process of court required by a party (Rule 14(6)). The R1 revenue stamp for the summons and the messenger's fee for service of process are the only expenses involved in a clerk-of-the-court divorce. Legal representation, whether in defended or undefended matters, costs on an average R200 to R250.

35. There are three courts in the Central Black Divorce Court, of which two at least usually sit every weekday except Wednesday. Approximately twelve contested matters are placed on the roll for any one court day and about thirty uncontested and thirty clerk-of-the-court divorces on two other rolls for any one court day. It is said to be very difficult to get a trial date, and the delay can be three or four months. *Cf.* the position in the Supreme Court, described in note 24 above.

36. H.P. Kloppers and T. F. Coertze, *Bantu Divorce Courts*, 2nd ed. (1976) 14, point out that the procedure in bringing divorce actions has "been simplified to enable litigants to obtain ready and inexpensive relief."

37. It appears that the reason for this added caution is that inaccurate returns of service in cases where the defendant has not received the summons have led to a number of applications for rescission of divorce decrees.

38. It is conceded that some of this time is taken up in interpreting the evidence of the plaintiff and the questions posed by the presiding officer.

39. Automatic refusal of a decree because the parties do not have separate residences attracts more criticism here than it does in relation to a similar and, it is submitted, incorrect attitude taken by some Supreme Court judges. The reason is that for Blacks to obtain alternative accommodation is virtually impossible. They must in many instances be compelled to remain under one roof in spite of the irretrievable breakdown of their marriages.

40. Postponements in terms of s. 4(3), to encourage reconciliation, are often ordered in these cases. Whereas, in the Supreme Court, counsel are apparently able to avoid judges who take the view that irretrievable breakdown cannot be present if the parties are living in the same house (by requesting a postponement so that the matter can be heard by a different judge), this kind of "forum-shopping" cannot take place in the Black Divorce Court. Once a matter is placed on the roll of "A" court or "B" court, etc., it stays there until heard again. Consequently, failing a change in the membership of the court, the same judicial officer will hear the case again.

41. *Pro se* divorce is common. Judicial officers are indulgent when technical imperfections in the pleadings are revealed and careful to elicit the necessary evidence by way of questioning. By contrast, judges in the Supreme Court do not lightly lead evidence for inefficient plaintiffs of other races. Unrepresented parties who make errors or do not adequately (and quickly) establish the necessary elements of a divorce action have been heard to be harshly criticized for failing to obtain expert (but costly) legal advice.

42. "Welfare" includes custody and maintenance. While some questioning always

takes place in connection with custody, it was noticed that in the Supreme court, whether the parties submit an agreement settling the amount of support for the children or the plaintiff merely claims a particular sum and the defendant does not object, attention is not given to the adequacy of the amount ordered. Perhaps this attitude is justified by the fact that plaintiffs are represented and the lawyers, it may be believed, would have seen to the sufficiency of the maintenance. Nevertheless, s. 6 is not being complied with. Judges have on rare occasions been heard to comment on the amount claimed and say that if inadequate it can be varied by a maintenance court. This, of course, is true, but it seems wrong for a judge to be forced by a lack of time and a long roll to make an order of court, the appropriateness of which he himself doubts.

43. Statistics show that of the 16,543 divorces of Whites in 1980, only 5,271 did not involve children.

44. Although the court is free, in terms of s. 6(3) of the *Divorce Act,* to make "any order which it may deem fit," joint custody orders do not seem to have caught on in South Africa. There are no reported decisions since 1979 revealing a request or an order for joint custody and, as far as I know, the Witwatersrand Local Division has not made such an order. Access for the noncustodian parent is usually included simply as "reasonable access." In the Witwatersrand Local Division judges display an antipathy to detailed access agreements, apparently because they are said to lead to disputes when not strictly complied with and because a rigid arrangement may interfere with the recreational activities pursued by the child. The invariable correctness of this reasoning could be debated, but is outside the scope of this chapter.

45. In one case, a (plaintiff) mother of two children aged three and five years displayed no interest in having them with her and stated that her husband (who worked all day) was better equipped to have them. Visibly distressed, the judge called for a social worker's report to be submitted to the court as soon as possible, but granted a divorce in spite of his misgivings. It is submitted that there was a failure to comply with s. 6 of the Act, but that the children would not have been better protected had the divorce been refused. In a busy courtroom, a searching enquiry into the welfare of children is impossible.

46. Whether the same can be said of the Black Divorce Courts in areas other than Johannesburg is unknown. Differences in tribal customs and in prevailing circumstances (such as the housing shortage in urban areas) may produce significant differences in decisions involving the custody of children.

47. See notes 42 and 45 above.

48. A description of the housing shortage, its causes and its consequences, is given in note 49 below. Coloureds and Asians, too, experience great hardship as a result of a chronic lack of accommodation in areas proclaimed "Coloured" in terms of the *Group Areas Act 36* of 1966. This legislation provides for specific areas in South Africa to be proclaimed "White," "Coloured" or "Black." It is an offence for a person to occupy premises in a place designated for a population group to which he does not belong. This is so even if there is no accommodation available for him and his family in the area in which he is required to live.

Photographs of Coloured or Asian parents and their children being evicted from their homes in "White" areas frequently appear in newspapers, and numerous people are criminally charged with and convicted of contravening the Act. A defence frequently raised in these cases is that of necessity in the light of there being absolutely no alternative housing. But this defence failed in the test cases of *S v. Adams* and *S v. Werner* 1981 (1) SA 187 (A).

49. The battle for lawful accommodation is preceded by the struggle for the right to remain in an urban area. Influx control legislation governs the movement of Blacks from one area to another.

Sheena Duncan, of the Black Sash, prepared for me a description of the impact of the pass laws and of influx control legislation on Black family life. (The Black Sash is a protest organization which aims to promote justice and to seek constitutional recognition and protection by law of human rights in South Africa.) Her statement follows:

Only those Black people who were born and have lived continuously in one town since birth, those who have worked continuously in one town in one job for ten years, or who have lived continuously and lawfully in one town for fifteen years, have a legal right to reside in an urban area. These "qualified" persons (in terms of s. 10(1) of the *Black (Urban Areas) Consolidation Act 25* of *1945*) are the only ones eligible for family accommodation in Black urban townships. For two decades, until an historic judgment of the Appellate Division in August 1980 (*Komani NO v. Black Affairs Administration Board, Peninsula Area* (1980 (4) SA 448 (A)), wives and children of this privileged group were denied the right to come to town to live with them. In effect, therefore, men have been spending their working lives separated from their families.

Restraint on the provision of family accommodation in urban areas has been one of the primary tools of influx control. Between 1968 and 1978 there was an almost total embargo on the building of family housing units for Black people in urban areas. The resulting critical housing shortage and overcrowding in existing houses has damaged the concept of family almost beyond repair. The stress and tension of living fifteen to thirty people in a house designed for six sets man against wife, father against son, brother against brother.

If proof is required that stable family units are the essential foundation of stable communities, it can be found in South Africa, where the breakdown of community in Black society is made manifest in suspicion and distrust between neighbours, the soaring crime rate in urban areas, increasing illegitimacy, rising numbers of abandoned children and old and disabled people, and widespread social disorganization. It is a terrifying picture and it remains to be seen whether the destruction wrought can ever be repaired.

50. *Act 25* of 1945.

51. Chapter II, Regulation 7(1)(*b*). How strange it must be for non–South Africans to be told that people here do not have an automatic right to live with their spouses and their children.

52. This information was obtained from attorneys who have large Black divorce practices. Although the residential permit usually follows the custodian parent, there is apparently a practice whereby the superintendent whose function it is to grant, transfer and cancel these permits delegates the duty to the various community councils in the Black townships. These councils, it is said, award permits to divorced persons on the basis of fault. The following story from the files of one attorney illustrates how pernicious the system can be: A husband in whose name a permit exists leaves the matrimonial home. His wife is threatened with eviction by the authorities because the permit can be cancelled if the holder no longer resides with his dependents in the dwelling allocated. The wife, specifically in order to qualify for a transfer of the permit, divorces him and obtains custody of the children. She applies for a transfer but the community council refuses it. The reason given for such refusal is that the husband has said his wife drove him away from the home. In any event the husband, she is told, is about to remarry and the existence of a new dependent — the second wife — will entitle him to retain the permit.

53. R100 and R150 per month is commonly ordered for White children.

54. The cogency is accepted of O. R. McGregor's warning (*Divorce in England* (1957)) that without empirical evidence "one cannot pass from the contemplation of unsupported conjecture to the study of reality" (quoted by Mervyn Murch, *Justice and Welfare in Divorce* (1980) 3–4). Murch's description of the lack in England ten years ago of information about consumer experience or opinion is suitable to South Africa today.

55. During February 1982. It seems to be directed mainly at the high incidence of divorce and it calls for suggestions to curb this. The questionnaire also represents the first official enquiry into the appropriateness of the divorce procedure.

56. Responses to questionnaires submitted by academics and practitioners are not sufficiently representative. Murch (*op. cit.*, note 54 above) has shown that consumer feedback is an important part of the investigation.

57. J. D. van der Vyver (1967) 84 *SALJ* 360.

58. Certain changes were made to the procedure in 1979. Section 14 of the *Divorce Act* abolished the requirement of the restitution order which preceded the final order of divorce in matters based on malicious desertion. Whereas two court appearances were required previously, only one is now necessary. The simplification was logical but cosmetic. Much deeper issues are involved.

59. Semantic changes in legal vocabulary cannot overcome this anomaly. Patricia L. Winks ("Divorce Mediation: A Nonadversary Procedure for the No-fault Divorce" (1980–81) 19 *Journal of Family Law* 615 at 620) refers to divorce becoming dissolution and plaintiff and defendant becoming petitioner and respondent. She points out that settlements are still won, child custody lost and spousal support awarded.

60. A little disquiet is evoked by some of the questions posed in the questionnaire disseminated by the South African Law Commission. Suggestions called for to restrict the increase in divorce; enquiries whether the elimination of fault contributed to the rise in the divorce rate and whether divorce is too easy; the possibility of introducing a prohibition on divorce within a certain period after marriage; compulsory counselling, all smack of increased state intervention. It is submitted that this is not the path to follow. Less control over the issue of granting a decree and more concern for financial provision and custody is the current trend.

61. See the previous note. A judge interviewed by me suggested the implementation of a compulsory waiting period between the institution of action and the granting of the decree, but only for spouses who have minor children. He considered that hasty, ill-considered divorce is prevalent and could be avoided if the process of dissolution were slowed down. The proposal is not, it is considered, without merit. If a waiting period were to be introduced, the suggestions which follow, to remove undefended divorce from the courtroom, would not be affected. Unlike a period of separation, this period is capable of precise computation and cannot be collusively concocted by the parties.

62. The total population of South Africa according to the 1980 census was 24,885,960 of which 4,528,100 were Whites; 2,612,780 were Coloureds; 821,320 were Asians; 16,923,760 were Blacks.

TABLE 10.1 Divorces*

	1970	1975	1978	1979	1980	1981
Whites	7,748	10,730	11,456	13,816	16,543	N/A
Coloureds	753	1,260	1,560	1,486	2,088	N/A
Asians	143	265	316	391	519	N/A
Total	8,644	12,255	13,332	15,693	19,150	21,875

* Figures compiled by Central Statistical Services.

Figures for Blacks are not included in the publications prepared by Central Statistical Services. They appear in the annual report of the Department of Co-operation and Development. There were 6,565 divorces in 1975, 5,560 in 1976, 6,131 in 1977, 7,632 in 1978 and 6,163 in 1979. The absence of any pattern showing a rise in these figures may be attributed in part to the exclusion of divorces in the Transkei and Bophuthatswana since 1976 and 1977 respectively, coinciding with the independence of these territories.

The total number of divorces granted by the Central Black Divorce Court was rising substantially: 2,764 in 1978, 3,333 in 1979 and 4,344 in 1980, but dropped to 3,685 in 1981.

63. H. R. Hahlo, "Fighting the Dragon Divorce" (1963) 80 *SALJ* 27 at 33, where the learned author relies for his conclusions on the studies of Rheinstein, Kahn-Freund and McGregor.

64. A comparison with the effect of the *English Divorce Reform Act* of 1969 supports this (see S. M. Cretney, *Principles of Family Law*, 3rd ed. (1979) 163). It is interesting to note that the number of divorces granted in the Witwatersrand Local Division during the first four months of 1983 was 1,657, compared with 1,946 for the same period in 1982 (figures supplied by the Registrar). The current economic decline may be influencing the decision to divorce.

65. There can be little doubt that white South Africans are becoming serial polygamists. In 1980, out of a total of 45,165 marriages of Whites, 9,326 of the husbands and 8,110 of the wives had been previously divorced. The incidence of remarriage after divorce among Coloureds and Asians is much lower. Out of a total of 20,966 marriages of Coloureds in 1980, only 968 husbands and 609 wives had been previously divorced. Out of 7,545 marriages of Asians in the same year, 204 husbands and 113 wives had been previously divorced.

Account should also be taken of the increasing number of persons who prefer cohabitation to marriage. The 1980 census showed a total of 702,460 South Africans living together without marriage (544,320 Blacks, 53,260 Whites, 98,940 Coloureds, 5,940 Asians).

66. Noted by Mary Ann Glendon, *State, Law and Family: Family Law in Transition in the United States and Western Europe* (1977); *The New Family and the New Property* (1981); "Modern Marriage Law and its Underlying Assumptions: The New Marriage and the New Property" (1980) 13 *Family L. Q.* 441.

67. Homer Clark Jr., "The New Marriage" (1975-6) 12 *Willamette L. J.* 441 at 444, quoted by Mary Ann Glendon *The New Family and the New Property* (1981) 4 n. 10.

68. It is possible that educating young people about the seriousness of marriage and the unhappiness occasioned by divorce may help. The remark is also opposite to relationships that are similar to, but do not culminate in, official marriage.

In 1948 it was suggested (in relation to the rising divorce rate among Whites) that "happy family life . . . can . . . be advanced, not by changes in our divorce laws, but by removing . . . avoidable causes of friction. One important cause is clearly the housing shortage and the resulting overcrowding of families in single rooms and small flats" (F.A.W. Lucas, K. C. (1948) *Commonwealth Law Reporter* 526 at 529). How strikingly appropriate this view is more than thirty years later in relation to South Africans who are not White!

69. Divorce on the ground of malicious desertion (used in over 90 percent of cases prior to 1979) was obtained in two stages. The final order of divorce was always preceded by an order for restitution of conjugal rights.

70. Although more Black divorces are contested and the procedure is in theory adversarial, the presiding officer frequently enters the arena to elicit evidence from a plaintiff (or defendant) who does not present his case adequately. It would be absurd to suggest that the person who, through lack of skill, fails to prove his case should have his action dismissed. Yet that is what a truly adversarial process implies. The discrepancy between theory and practice is undesirable.

71. The Right Honourable Sir Roger Ormrod, quoted by Mervyn Murch, *Justice and Welfare in Divorce* (1980) 221.

72. The view of the Lord Chancellor in England in 1976 was that the area of real contest concerns ancillary relief and not whether the petitioner should get a decree (quoted by Colin S. Gibson (1980) 43 *Modern L. R.* 609 at 610). In South Africa, the law governing the financial consequences of divorce is so rigid and certain that little room for contest or bargaining exists even in this area. It is to be hoped that more flexibility will be introduced when the impending matrimonial property legislation is enacted.

73. It is clearly not the only alternative and its detailed application would differ in South Africa. Simplification of the procedure would eradicate a cause for criticism of the law and its operation. The English procedure is described by Cretney, *op. cit.*, 159 ff. Curiously, Cretney (169) uses the present procedure in England to advance his argument for changing the grounds of divorce, while I am using the state of our substantive law as an argument for altering our procedure.

74. The attorney's fees are the main expense (see note 13 above). Allowing attorneys to appear in the Supreme Court would, therefore, not significantly reduce costs. Attorney's charges could be confined to consultation and negotiation in connection with ancillary matters. Obtaining the decree, if the matter is undefended, does not require their expertise — it is a clerk's job.

75. Especially if it implies that the services of an attorney/advocate are dispensed with altogether. I believe that spouses usually need some advice regarding financial provision and sometimes regarding custody. It should be remembered that the prevalence of *pro se* divorce among Blacks in South Africa is a result of poverty, not a matter of preference.

The availability of legal aid in England is, significantly, reserved for matters in which a hearing is required. Legal representation is accepted as being necessary in contested divorces and in disputes over ancillary matters involving financial provision and children (see Colin Gibson, "Divorce and the Recourse to Legal Aid" (1980) 43 *Modern L. R.* 609). For an emphasis of the dangers inherent in *pro se* litigation see C. I. McLachlan, "*Pro se* Marriage Dissolution in Connecticut — Some Considerations" (1977) 51 *Connecticut*

B. J. 15. It is surely in the public interest to reduce costs, but not at the price of proper advice. An instructive article on the position in the United States is Marilyn A. Meredith, "Divorce Kit Dilemma: Finding the Public Interest" (1980-81) 19 *Family L. J.* 729.

76. John Eekelaar, *Family Law and Social Policy* (1978) 143.

77. "Judicial Hearings of Undefended Divorce Petitions" (1975) 38 *Modern L. R.* 609.

78. See, for example, S. R. Feldman, "A Statutory Proposal to Remove Divorce from the Courtroom" (1977) 29 *Maine L. R.* 25.

79. Many South Africans may be unacquainted with these arguments but it would not be appropriate to detail them in this paper. Arguments sometimes advanced to justify the retention of judicial hearings in undefended divorces are convincingly dealt with by Murch et al. (1975) 38 *Modern L. R.* 638-39.

80. Judges interviewed by me indicated that it was the ancillary issues, particularly the welfare of children, that evoked their concern and that there was not much they could do regarding the granting of the decree. For this reason it seems pointless to retain the elaborate and costly machinery presently in operation merely to perpetuate perfunctory hearings that judges find burdensome and the public finds costly. These considerations provoked the adoption of the "special procedure" in England, described as judicial in form, administrative in substance (see Cretney, *op. cit.,* 159-60).

81. Cretney, *op. cit.,* 162 refers to a judge who granted twenty-nine decrees simultaneously "under considerable protest at being required to 'act as a rubber stamp'."

82. The adoption of English legal rules and procedures has been vehemently resisted by some South Africans while recognized as eminently sound by others. In family law the penchant to nurture Roman-Dutch principles is singularly inappropriate. Commendably, the South African Law Commission drew heavily upon research conducted in England regarding the grounds of divorce before recommending the reforms now contained in the *Divorce Act 70* of 1979. Religious opposition too was overcome then and acceptance encouraged of the ever-widening gap between church dogma and secular rules. We should continue in that tradition. A judicial hearing to obtain a divorce decree desired by both spouses is not a useful employment of our resources nor does it serve any ceremonial function to confirm that divorce is a matter seriously regarded by the state.

83. "Inquisitorial" is not used here in the derogatory sense of the average dictionary definition. On the contrary, it is meant to imply that the presiding officer does not act only as an umpire. By participating in the proceedings he seeks to discover the truth from the parties or their representatives in a less formal atmosphere than that which normally prevails in adversarial litigation.

84. I am not proposing that (contested) divorces of persons of all races should be heard in the Supreme Court, for the resulting increase in cost to Blacks would be most undesirable (unless greatly improved legal aid facilities are made available). A blueprint detailing the kind of tribunal that might be set up to resolve family disputes requiring adjudication cannot be set forth here. However, it is envisaged that stature equivalent to that of the Supreme Court would be essential; that a special (reduced) cost structure should apply to proceedings in this court; and that presiding officers should be judges aided, if necessary, by counsel eligible for appointment to the bench. Facilities to promote conciliation; to encourage settlement of disputes by mediation; and to ensure the protection of minor children should, I would suggest, be integrated into the restructuring of the divorce process.

85. A change of name does not necessarily signify a change of substance (see John

Wade, "The Family Court of Australia and Informality in Court Procedure" (1978) 21 *I & CLQ* 820 at 828).

86. Just as happened in England — see Murch, *Justice and Welfare in Divorce* 230 ff.

87. This excludes customary unions. Disputes involving customary unions are heard in the Commissioner's Court, not in the Black Divorce Court.

Chapter Eleven

Divorce Proceedings: Ends and Means

Henrik H.H. Andrup

Higher Official, Ribe Statsamt, Denmark

1. THE OBJECTIVES OF MATRIMONIAL PROCEDURES

It is clearly impossible to give an exhaustive account of all possible objectives of matrimonial procedures. We will therefore concentrate on the predominant aims and the typical means.

A. The Objective of Preserving Marriage

This objective appears in originally Christian societies as the historical background for the public dealings with matrimonial cases. In societies where opposition to divorce is so strong that divorces are simply forbidden, dealings with divorce cases do not occur. Rather concern is with separation, in cases where the parties have ceased living together, or are otherwise estranged. Where opposition to a divorce is prevalent, procedures are directed primarily at determining whether the lawful conditions for the dissolution of a marriage are fulfilled, thus preventing anyone from obtaining a divorce without a satisfactory reason. The nature of the grounds and the strength of the policy of upholding marriage are decisive factors relating to the course the proceedings have to take. There are often divergences between legislation and the practice of the authorities (Mnookin 1970). The standard that is actually to be maintained must be rationally enforced by the proceedings. The goal of preventing divorces requires that cases are conducted so as to strain, humiliate and stigmatize the divorcees, and therefore appear threatening (Dezalay 1976) or, to put it more mildly, the clientele's well-being is subordinate to that of the ideology of the authorities and the requirements of the law.

The intention to preserve marriage has, however, also had a milder consequence: it motivates the authorities to reconcile the married couple. This may, according to how strongly the intention is implemented, lead to rather heavy pressure by the authorities (Sweetman 1979) but also to intense efforts to make continued married life an attractive solution for both parties. These two methods require different techniques.

A notable decline in the goal of preserving marriage is observed in most of the industrialized world. The formal preservation of marriage is obviously not quite such an important matter as it was previously. This is due to competition between the policies to be mentioned below, and probably also to a feeling of futility in view of the prevailing tendency to abandon married cohabitation, and the pointlessness of enforcing the formal preservation of marriage when its substance is gone. (Molinski 1979; Rheinstein, Encl. 15).

B. The Moralizing Conflict-solving Objective

This objective, too, can have both mild and harsh manifestations. It offers help to the couple applying for a divorce, in so far as it settles their differences regarding the distribution of the burdens and advantages they have been sharing so far. In solving the conflict, the public authorities also protect the weaker party, or at least try to do so.

The less beneficent side of this policy becomes apparent when the authorities, in assisting the spouses, pay special regard to what they believe is in the interest of the community, sometimes to the disadvantage of both spouses. This objective builds on the assumption (which may not always be correct), that divorcing spouses are in dispute with each other. They are presumed to have conflicts, and these are placed on the same footing as all other disputes between citizens, and are dealt with accordingly, normally by the civil courts.

There are, however, some distinguishing characteristics. Normally, citizens who are in disagreement may decide for themselves whether they want a trial in court, or whether they themselves can come to an agreement. But if they choose to go to court, they run the risk of becoming the victims of an authority that is primarily concerned with society's interests, when deciding how "this sort of conflict" ought to be solved. The decision will then be used to "make an example." Thus their "private" dispute is raised from an "individual" to a community level, where it is used by the public authorities for their own purposes (Folberg 1974; Röhl n.d.; Dezalay 1976). By demonstrating what the state considers is most important, when its power apparatus is called upon to settle the citizen's disputes, the state motivates the citizens to behave in a way that is regarded as beneficial to the community, and of course also to avoid behaviour of which the community openly disapproves. The state may enhance this technique of influencing citizens' behaviour by withdrawing the right to settle their disputes among themselves. In this way, the state can enforce solutions it is most interested in, despite the fact that both parties might want a quite different outcome.

This moralizing technique of extended law enforcement has dominated matrimonial hearings, and is still used to a large extent, although to a varying degree in different countries. Private agreements about a divorce, distribution of the common assets and obligations, such as income, property and children, may still be overruled as being "against the limits set by law and decency" (O'Hoski 1981). A major feature of all this has been the possibility for society to "punish" (with the greatest possible moralizing effect) the spouse who is considered "guilty" of wrecking the marriage, and to reward the "innocent" one. The consequence which this technique seeks is to force certain patterns of behaviour on all spouses in their married life and to stabilize marriage on the whole.

As in the case of the first objective, the moralizing element in solving conflicts is also declining in most of the industrialized countries. The prohibition against the parties reaching agreement themselves, has to a great extent been modified. (Glendon 1977). Certain circumstances do however lead to the state being reluctant to withdraw its legal authority completely from agreements between spouses. In the first place, one often finds that the balance of power may be very distorted in a marriage, something which may easily lead to the stronger party exploiting the weaker. Secondly, and perhaps more important, a divorce has radical effects on the couple's surroundings, especially on their children, on the public social aid and tax systems, and on a variety of private economic connections. These interests should not be completely disregarded. This creates a need for public control over what spouses agree to on divorce, involving the right of veto concerning solutions that are either unreasonable for one of the parties, for the children, for the public or towards a third party.

While executing this controlling function, the authorities often mix the moralizing and the fiscal interests, in a way that is not so easy to perceive.

C. The Objective of Safeguarding the Best Interests of the Child

The traditional way of regarding the parents' divorce is that it, as such, raises doubts as to whether they will be able to continue to safeguard the children's interests. Procedures are intended to ensure that they are looked after satisfactorily. The intention is veiled by the love of children in general, but the object is just as much to ensure that children, the next generation, shall grow up under conditions that make them good, loyal citizens, which is in the interest of all communities. The purpose of the procedures is to find the best possible solution for the children: where they are to live, how they are to be brought up, and how to maintain contact with the noncustodial parent. This requires investigations and considerations of a type quite different from those required for objective B (to moralize), according to which the child was considered a part of the assets and obligations that were to be distributed to the parties as a reward for good behaviour or a penalty for blameworthy conduct, respectively.

Acting in the best interests of the child effectively demands that the official in charge is properly qualified to consider the future of the child. Furthermore, the objective also demands that disputes between the parents should be prevented. It is an acknowledged fact that disputes between the parents harm the children. Such conflicts are without doubt most harmful where they relate to the child itself, but principally any bitter dispute between the parents will place the children in a painful and distressing conflict of loyalties, which not only hampers their mental development, but often impairs it (Konig Encl. 65; Raschke 1979).

Consideration for the best interests of the child makes it essential to ensure that the dealings cause as little controversy as possible. This means that attempts must be made to solve the problems in a way that both parents are able to live with without feeling humiliated, injured or resentful, and if possible, with solutions they both can agree upon (Murch 1977, 1978; Giesen 1975). Thus this policy comes into direct conflict with the moralizing aim of objective B, which requires conversion of the problems into formal, acute conflicts, so as to present them in the most suitable form for the court's decision.

D. The Objective of Assisting Broken Families

The fourth and last objective to be mentioned here is aimed at helping and guiding divorcees through the difficulties which arise when their cohabitation is discontinued. As a policy, it is the most recent one, and therefore the most controversial.

This goal is clearly in conflict with objective A (to restrain divorce). But, as mentioned earlier, the desire to make couples maintain their marriage is on the decline, as is the desire to make a divorce even more difficult than it is in any case. But this does not lead to anything more than the removal of certain "artificial" obstacles that used to exist. However, to maintain that it is the duty of the authorities to *assist* the divorcees through their hardships, is to carry the idea much further, and this has not penetrated to the same extent in all countries.

It is worth pointing out that, as regards the confrontation between objectives A (to preserve marriage) and D (to assist divorcees), there is no "front-to-front clash between two opposite ideologies." Intention D has not emerged from a wish to accelerate the number of divorces. Its supporters admit, indirectly, that divorces are a deplorable phenomenon and argue, very convincingly, that in helping divorcees, you do not weaken the stability of family life (which is the real problem behind objective A) (Wright 1979; Konig, Encl.).

Objective D builds on the assumption that divorcees are the victims of cultural collisions, that they are unhappy people who need help, and who therefore plainly ought to get help. Nobody will deny that the disintegration of family life normally and typically puts the members of the family in a difficult position, confronting them with a swarm of problems and sufferings on several levels at one and the same time. Nor will anyone deny that the will to help them is in itself praiseworthy. But, it is argued, life does hold difficulties and sufferings for everyone, sometimes through their own fault and sometimes not. The state should be careful when interfering with such matters. Well-intentioned public activity on matters of "private life" is often open to criticism. Marriage causes suffering too, and it is a very old, established tradition that the state should keep out of domestic life.

Advocates of the claim for active assistance to divorcees do, however, base their claims on more than compassion and benevolence. They argue that the way the law has developed makes it unrealistic to refuse guidance just because the matter is "private." The difficulties of divorcees have increased enormously, because society has attached a massive legal apparatus on to the personal and private relationship of marriage. People who marry make a personal alliance to live together and believe themselves competent to evaluate its advantages and disadvantages. Society has gradually attached a multitude of legal consequences (often unknown to the spouses) to these "private cohabitation arrangements," which makes it impossible to foresee the implications of being given the special status of "wife" or "husband." Because of this, a divorce causes incomprehensible and unpredicted legal consequences, that suddenly place each of the parties in quite new legal situations, which they could not have foreseen. These new situations give rise to new relationships, not only between the spouses, but also regarding other citizens, and especially to the social aid and tax authorities, and to the children.

The conditions are so complicated that only an expert has a chance of estimating the consequences of the various options arising on divorce. Divorce, therefore, often raises a considerable risk for the parties, especially where no expert assistance was given before the spouses made their dispositions. Where legislation allows the spouses themselves to arrange under what conditions they wish to part, they are given the chance to take the legal effects into account in a sensible and considerable manner. But this is of no use when the legal consequences are not fully appreciated.

It is unjustifiable and unwise to let parties who cannot afford expert guidance, take these risks, while those who are better off can afford to be advised on how to avoid these dangers. Legislation has created such insecurity about possible consequences of divorce that people refrain from trying to arrange the future and well-being of the family, for fear of making unwise dispositions. They prefer to place the matter in the hands of the authorities to avoid personal responsibility (Mnookin 1979). This only makes matters worse for them, as the authorities do not pursue the interests of the family in trying to avoid as much harm as possible, but rather aim to administer their special set of rules as conscientiously as possible. All the officials involved only treat their individual concerns, not the relationship between them (Giesen 1975; Cavanagh 1976/77).

Finally, it is strongly emphasized that the community has a very great economic interest in reducing the damaging effects of divorce. It is mentioned under objective C (the best interests of the child), that it is in the interests of the state to protect the next generation from strains which might be damaging. It is very much a question of public economy. The conflicts between the parents prejudice them to some degree in the shorter or longer term. Quite considerable sums of money are paid from social aid accounts during and after these disputes. Society can hardly find a better way of investing its money than to transform the recipients of social aid into taxpayers. Positive help to get the members of the family back into productivity, in their new circumstances, is not only being "kind," it is simply silly not to do so when possible (Foster 1966). And very often it is possible. There is scarcely any other legal field where the will to come to an agreement is as strong as in divorce cases. It has been found that an agreement can be reached in 90 percent of cases, partly by giving expert assistance and partly by letting the couples decide for themselves (Rausch 1978; Glendon 1977). One can easily avoid most of the prolonged and traumatizing "traditional hearings." The objective leads to the following further claims.

It requires that proceedings are concentrated in time and that they are combined within a single, all-embracing institution. Only by doing this can the varying legal consequences be adapted in an expedient way to the advantage of all concerned. This, in turn, leads to the necessity of gathering the now separate specialities within one jurisdiction. This must be staffed either by different experts, or by some very highly trained specialists in "marriage dissolution," who should also have a very good knowledge of psychology (Murch 1980). By demanding this, the supporters of objective D come into direct conflict with traditional lawyers, who until now have been supreme in this field, and for whom consideration of psychology is alien to the principles of the administration of justice. Fear of the proceedings becoming therapeutic dominates a larger part of the opposition to the "Family Court Movement."

2. PROCEDURE AS A MEANS OF ACHIEVING THE OBJECTIVES

A. What Procedure Can Do

If we now turn to the question of realizing the different objectives in procedure, we find that it must consist, and in practice does consist, of a number of different functions such as reconciliation, investigation, advice, problem- or conflict-solution, enforcement, and so on. These different tasks are seldom solved by only one public institution and seldom at the same time. There are differences between countries as regards to which public authorities are given these tasks, and how they tackle them.

Here, reference is made only to publicly financed "proceedings." It is therefore obvious that the only alternatives are judicial or administrative "matrimonial proceedings." Public proceedings must be exercised as one of these. This distinction will be used in what follows, but first, some remarks are necessary.

The only possible way to define the two forms of proceedings clearly is by establishing a purely formal usage, namely by calling all proceedings in court, "judicial," and all "proceedings" carried out by the public administration, "administrative." But this will not be of much help. Some functions that in one country are exercised by a court, are exercised by public authorities in another, and vice versa. The specific character of matrimonial cases seems to lead the courts to treat them in an atypical, "administrative" manner, ("in chambers" for instance) and conversely, the administrative officials to take on tasks that traditionally would seem to belong more naturally in the courtrooms (as in Denmark).

When the word "judicial" is used in the following, it will be used in an "ideal" sense. Such proceedings contain a series of elements, that seem to recur, despite national differences, in all courtroom proceedings. These are, for example, legal representation, a requirement that every claim must be precisely formulated, formal restraints on the behaviour of the lawyers' witnesses and the parties during the proceedings, formal rules on how the evidence, the examination and cross-examination are to be handled, rules about the qualification of the judge and his impartial and unengaged attitude towards the parties and the evidence in the case. What is to be assessed in the first place is whether these typical judicial techniques are appropriate in an attempt to implement every one of the four objectives.

As "judicial procedure" is so restrictively defined, "administrative procedure" has consequently to be defined all the more broadly. All other public proceedings become simply "administrative." The only limit that reasonably might apply here is to assume that the administration cannot settle conflicts between private citizens, without exceeding its proper scope. This field has always been considered as belonging "naturally" to the courts of justice.

B. Traditional Court Proceedings

Traditional court proceedings are the most common way of conducting a divorce case, and the lively, current debate on legal policies is mainly concerned with finding alternatives to them.

Where the purpose of the proceedings is to settle whether the condition of fault is fulfilled (objective A), or to be able to place the fault on either of the spouses, and to draw legal moralizing conclusions from this (objective B), the traditional hearing appears as a rational divorce-restraining and morally conflict-solving instrument, because of its critical way of treating the evidence. If these tasks are to be effectively solved by means of judicial hearings, they must, however, be augmented with some special measures. The judge must be allotted nontraditional *ex-officio* activities. He/she must try a party's admission of guilt, and failure to appear in court cannot be considered as a confession. The problem may also be solved — as has actually been the case — by the state appointing a third barrister in the case, to defend "the marriage" and perhaps acting against both spouses.

If the question is whether there is sufficient evidence of the irrevocable breakdown of the marriage, the traditional court proceedings might seem less rational, as the evidence needed is not related to the past, but to the future. A well-founded presumption of this may seem to require thorough psychological investigation. The courts can only accept as evidence some typical indications that the spouses have not got on well together. Here, too, the court has to assume *ex-officio* activities to be able effectively to ensure that no one obtains a divorce without proper cause.

If guilt or the breakdown of the relationship is made the object of serious critical appraisals, the parties should be submitted to very painful and personal examination, which may very well be a deterrent in accordance with objective A (to sustain the marriage).

If practice or the law accepts simple confession of fault, or failure to appear in court, as a foundation for the court's rulings, in accordance with the plaintiff's assertions, or if the courts give up testing the evidence, the court's function is reduced to an "administrative" rubber-stamping of uncontrolled agreements. To use the expensive and complicated apparatus of law in this way, is indeed irrational. (Elston 1975). The law courts are obviously not well suited to be mediators. At the point where they judge meets the parties in court, they have long since assumed entrenched positions and fortified these with professional lawyers. Effective mediation demands insight and time. The judge has neither.

When evaluating the court's appropriateness as a means of effectuating objective B, ("moralizing and problem solving") we should draw attention to a contradiction between these two functions. On the one hand the courts are forced upon the citizens as an alternative to allowing them to settle the matter themselves. Society has forbidden them to take the law into their own hands. As a guideline for a solution, the interests of the society are set up, not only with respect to the solution of the conflict in question, but as to how this sort of conflict in general "ought" to be solved. But the state's concern in this regard is diminishing. This retreat has manifested itself by the introduction of rules that give the judges quite extraordinary authority to decide at their own discretion. This phenomenon really reflects the fact that the individual family's interest in obtaining the divorce as "amicably" as possible (compare objective D, to assist), is officially estimated as higher than the state's interest in moralizing. Consequently, the judicial rules are frequently interpreted as merely indicating solutions that can be resorted to in the absence of agreements — unless their application seems inappropriate to interests of the family group in the current case.

But the traditional court procedure is not very suitable where the point is to manage the process in the interests of the family. Making a rational plan for the settlement of the common cause demands an engaging, creative effort, which comes into conflict with the judge's prescribed professional role of being unengaged and impartial (Davis 1977). Furthermore, rational planning such as this demands professional psychological knowledge and command of a large part of the legal system, such as tax law and social security law, that normally lies outside the sphere of a traditional judge.

Objections very similar to these may be raised against traditional procedures as a rational means of safeguarding the best interests of the child. Court hearings are appropriate to the extent to which a child may be considered as part of the assets or burdens, to be distributed as reward for good or as punishment for blameworthy behaviour. The duty to see to the best interests of the child, may be a reminder to the judge to avoid decisions that will quite obviously harm the child, and be understood as a modification of the traditional approach. But if the intention is interpreted as giving the best interests of the child preference when disagreements between the parents are settled, the judicial machinery, which we are considering here, is evidently highly inappropriate. The problem is to choose, as between two possible dispositions, that which is most advantageous to the child's development. Instruction on such matters is not given at law school, nor does one learn much about them through judicial practice. It is not, however, primarily the fact that the task lies outside the qualified knowledge of the judge, that makes court proceedings irrational. The central flaw lies in the juridical mode of work itself.

In most cases about where the child is to be placed, the child's welfare would not seem to be threatened, even if it were to be placed with the party considered to be the second best one. No one has enough professional competence to predict how the child can be made most happy in the long run. A sober consideration of this will lead us to see that such decisions, in the absence of professional wisdom, must be made on the basis of pure common sense. And, although a judge as a person might seem to be able to make such decisions just as well as anybody else, the very way in which the courts work creates the worst imaginable conditions for the judge to apply common sense.

What is needed is simply an understanding of the people concerned, their character and psyche, their relationship with each other, and their potential of managing under changed circumstances. To attain this, one has to be in contact with them, to get to know them personally, so that one can get a reasonable idea about what they separately — and together — can offer the child.

The formalized, conventionalized technique of the proceedings in itself prevents the judge from obtaining a reliable impression of the parties in their everyday life. The judge does not speak naturally with them, or hear them talk together, still less with the child. The parents only make more or less instructed declarations, under conditions which seem quite distorted to them. They do not express themselves freely. What is to be explained is said on their behalf by their lawyers, whose statements can be far removed from the client's own comprehensions and concepts (Dezalay 1976).

The worst thing is that in court, the problem of the most sensible, and for the child the most advantageous, solution is often converted to a critical, verbal fight, with exaggerated accusations and the creation of mutual suspicions, whereby the parents — often reinforced by the lawyers — hurt each other and cause irreparable harm to the child, whose best interests the case was supposed to promote. The very procedure in court is normally in itself more opposed to the best interests of the child, than the "wrong" solution would be.

In the few instances where there is an obvious hazard connected with placing the child with the one party and not with the other, the choice is easy, no matter who has to make it. The occasions that give rise to a need for specialist assistance are the ones where there is uncertainty about whether there may be direct harm involved in the placing of the child. The judge is incompetent here, as expert knowledge can in fact be called upon. Experts on patterns of behaviour may often be able to see through circumstances which the layman and the judge cannot perceive. They can clarify whether the supposed or feared risks are real or merely imagined. When this problem is solved for the one who has to make the decision, it must again be plain common sense that takes over. Nothing more can be gained by calling in different psychologists after this stage. What they may say or write about the parties, in trying to motivate a choice between two parents, both reasonably well suited, merely serves the purpose of furnishing them with ammunition against each other, thus harming the children. Nor do the psychologists have sufficient scientific background to enable them to point out which solution will be best in the long run, if both of the parents seem suitable. Here they have to fall back on their own prejudices about upbringing, the importance of environment and such matters.

So much for the courts' suitability as an instrument to see to the best interests of the children. It only remains to be pointed out that the legal disputes between the parents *per se* — regardless of what they are about — are to the detriment of the child's interests, because they are apt to create and aggravate conflicts.

While considering the courts' aptitude in achieving objectives A, B and C, we have already seen that they are definitely irrational in realizing objective D, namely to assist the family. The courts were never meant to be an instrument of charity.

It is quite plain to see that in the cases where the courts do in fact afford assistance to the families it is a question of redirecting their functions, and that the ties to the traditional functions seldom permit the court's assistance to be really effective.

C. Administrative Matrimonial Procedures

To define this concept as has been done above — namely as all public proceedings other than the traditional court proceedings typified above — would make its scope enormous. It would be hopeless to try to examine all its possibilities within the scope of this chapter. What is of practical interest is to review the opportunities which arise through administrative procedures when seeking to achieve objectives C and D: to see to the best interests of the children and to give qualified assistance to the divorcees in accomplishing the rearrangement of their lives. This is illustrated by outlining a system of administrative proceedings, which is so constructed as to attain the above to the largest possible extent.

Hardly any country wishes to neglect objectives A and B (the marriage-sustaining and the morally conflict-solving intentions) to the extent expressed in the system outlined here. But the review will point out a series of elements, some of which may be introduced in some established system or other, either as an expansion of those of the courts or of the administering officials' methods. This could particularly be the case in countries where the weight is shifted from objectives A and B to objectives C and D. It is in these countries that criticism of the courts is harshest and the need for reform is strongest.

In the legal systems where the state has given up moralizing and putting the brakes on divorces, the basis of the procedures is that the spouses are assumed in principle to be competent to decide if they want a divorce, and how they are to share the burdens and assets which so far have been common. Where the families seem able to arrange matters themselves, the proceedings could be restricted to the necessary public recording of the divorces and the spouses' arrangements, mainly for the authorities' own reference. We know from experience, in Denmark and Norway, that the majority of couples are fully capable of making expedient, mutually reasonable agreements, which cause no harm to others, and it would be of no use to force a lengthy, elaborate, troublesome "public procedure" upon them.

However, in some instances the parties cannot, because of reasons mentioned above, foresee the consequences of the arrangements they propose to make, without assistance. They can only make justifiable dispositions when aware of the consequences. To avoid inflicting unintentional harm on the clientele or others, the public must make sure that they fully comprehend their situation before they commit themselves. They must therefore, first and foremost, be informed about their legal and factual situation — and receive instructions, advice and guidance.

The achievement of this is to be categorized as a natural administrative function, just as is the registration of the divorce. But this requires officials with extensive insight in the type of problems of a juridical and factual character that divorce generates. One might consider employing people who are thoroughly trained as specialists in family life, especially in "split-up" family groups, or a staff of specialists, each representing a narrower field (Dinkerspiel 1967). Knowledge about relevant current conditions in the community, such as the housing situation, the labour market, and insight in psychology, especially concerning children, is especially important.

All this expertise is to be applied rationally, first and foremost in order to reach an amicable settlement between the spouses, thereby constructing foundations for their future lives, which they can both accept. It may, of course, also inspire them to choose to live together instead of being divorced. The only decent way to mediate, is to point out the difficulties connected with divorce and life as a divorcee, so that they can compare these with the difficulties involved in continuing cohabitation, or reorganizing it so that it might be bearable.

The marked will of divorcee clients to come to amicable settlements, (Coulson 1969), guarantees the fact that the great majority of divorce cases could be effectuated on the basis of agreement. This would be a great advantage. Experience shows that duties imposed by common agreement are more willingly fulfilled than those forced upon us, and as far as the children are concerned, amicable settlements between parents are invaluable (Welzer 1969; Landsman 1978).

Even if the state has given up restraining divorces and moralizing, this is not to say that there are no limits to what the spouses may lawfully arrange. As mentioned above, the interests of the community requires control of the feasability and practicability of the arrangements, internally as well as externally. The official's approval must therefore be a condition for their registration and validity. It would seem natural to assign this controlling function to the advising, guiding and registering administrative authority. The result will then be the establishment of a public, administering institution to which the whole divorce clientele is directed and which deals with all the problems of divorce.

Under some circumstances only a short discussion between the officials and the couple will appear necessary. In other instances quite a comprehensive instruction, including perhaps renegotiation on a more realistic basis brought about by the officials, is called for. Qualified, legal formulation of the parties' settlements will most frequently be needed.

The Danish experience is that even "unprepared" spouses will, in most cases, be able to manage their own problems after a single talk alone with a qualified administrative lawyer. If the adviser succeeds in providing a complete settlement of which he can approve, he may draw up the required documents and make the required registrations, hereby concluding the proceedings without any court hearing at all. Ninety percent of all divorces are concluded in this administrative way in Denmark. With public administrative proceedings like this, the assistance of private lawyers or attorneys could also be dispensed with in the great majority of divorce cases. This would be of advantage to both the clients and to society. Assistance to the families will become more effective, and the "proceedings" will, as in the Danish experience, not take nearly as much time as court proceedings.

What normally is considered the main problem connected with administrative divorce procedure becomes evident in the minority of the cases, where either the administration cannot accept the parties' agreements — and therefore not register them — or where the parties cannot come to an agreement, in spite of the official's diligence. Different countries have different rules on whether a divorce may be granted, even if one or more practical questions still are unsolved. This problem cannot be dealt with here. It must, however, be reiterated that objective D (to assist) indicates that all questions are to be dealt with by one and the same institution. If the parties fail to reach agreement on one or more points, the public authorities must lend a hand and find solutions for them somehow in connection with the problems that they have solved themselves. If this situation is regarded as a "conflict between two private citizens," the administration will, under traditional analyses, be excluded from proceeding further if it is not to trespass on the sphere of the courts. It seems, however, to be questionable whether it is always correct to define such situations as conflicts, and to put them on the same footing as other types of conflicts between private citizens. Also when there are disagreements between the spouses about the placing of burdens and assets, and these definitely stand out as conflicts, it is doubtful if they are comparable with the disputes of citizens, who have not experienced the intimate contact of matrimonial cohabitation. Posing this question is especially justified where there are children in the marriage, and the disputes concern them.

If the task is really to decide what is in the best interests of the child, the conflict is not of a judicial nature. The decision must not, and cannot, form a precedent. It is an entirely individual decision, to be made completely dependent on the people concerned. The parents should also comprehend psychologically that the welfare of the children is not a question of being "right" or "wrong," but of finding out what is best for the child. If they have discussed their views with the expert advisers, it must from their point of view seem absurd to hand the case over to a judge who is less well informed and less of an expert on children. Also it must seem plain to them that the problem will not be better illuminated by court proceedings. In addition to this, there are the directly damaging effects the proceedings have on the children. This leads to the conclusion that the judge is less suited to make the decision as to where the child is to be placed than the administrative officials, who have negotiated with both spouses, and also — when necessary — spoken with the children. Exactly the same may be said about administrative procedures on the noncustodial parent's access to the child. And the same reflections may also apply to all the other questions that arise when parents decide to part.

When it is fully understood that parents who quarrel actually subject children to cruelty, there is a lot to be said for forbidding the parents to put on courtroom battles. The courts are very often misused by parents with children under age as a means of venting their malice. One could prevent this by subjecting parents to a sort of "compulsory administration," so constructed that the administration's advising and controlling executives simply could bring an end to the problem, by insisting on the solution that the advisers, during their work with the family, have found to be the one the parties ought to have been able to agree upon. That is to say, "conciliate them by force" to the *solution* that is estimated to be best suited for the welfare of the family group as a whole.

In cases where there are no children under age, there is less need for such a dramatic break with the traditional distinction between the judicial and the administrative sectors.

But if the state does place such an expert institution at the disposal of married parents, with the intention of helping them to come to adequate, law-abiding terms, and furthermore, in the minority of the cases where no solution can be agreed upon, authorizes this institution to lay down the final terms for the divorce, sparing the spouses the court trial it would be irrational to deny these facilities to childless spouses, if they want this help. To forbid them to cause each other harm in court disputes is not necessary — but might be reasonable as a means to keep up the dignity of marriage.

If one provides an administrative institution with authority to enforce solutions on the family, it must be recognized that one has created an administrative, powerful "authority," with the constitutional complications this might have.

REFERENCES

Cavanagh, Ralph C., and Rohde, Deborah L. "The Unauthorized Practice of Law and pro se Divorce — an Empirical Analysis." *Yale Law Journal*, vol. 86, 1976/77.

Coulson, Robert. "Family Arbitration — An Exercise in Sensitivity." *Family Law Quarterly*, vol. III nr. 1 March 1969.

Davis, Gwyn, and Murch, M., "The Implications of the Special Procedure in Divorce." *Family Law*, vol. 7, nr. 3, 1977.

Dezalay, Y. "The French Juridical Ideology in Working-class Divorce." *Sexual Divisions and Society: Process and Change*. London 1976.

Dinkerspiel, Richard C., and Gough, A.R. "The Case for a Family Court — a Summary of the Report of the California Governor's Commission on the Family." *Family Law Quarterly*, vol. I nr. 2, June 1967.

Elston, E., Fuller, J., and Murch, M. "Judicial Hearings of Undefended Divorce Petitions." *The Modern Law Review*, vol. 38, nov. 1975.

Folberg, J. "Facilitating Agreement — The Role of Counseling in the Courts." *Conciliation Courts Review*, vol. 12 nr. 2. Dec. 1974.

Foster, Henry H. "Conciliation and Counseling in the Courts." *New York University Law Review*, 1966.

Giesen, Dieter. "Zur Problematik der Einführung einer Familiengerichtsbarkeit in der Bundesrepublik Deutschland." Rechts und Staatswissenschaftliche Veröffentlichungen der Göres-Gesellschaft. Neue Folge, Heft. 17. udg.: Alexander Hallorbach, 1975.

Glendon, M. A. *State Law and Family*, Amsterdam, New York, Oxford: North Holland Publishing Co. 1977.

König, René in Chloros (ed.) *International Encyclopedia of Comparative Law IV.* Tubingen, n.d.

Landsman, Kim J. and Minow, M.L. "Lawyering for the Child: Principles of Representation in Custody and Visitation Disputes arising from Divorce." *Yale Law Journal*, vol. 87 nr. 6 May 1978.

Mnookin, R.H., and Kornhauser, L. "Bargaining in the Shadow of the Law." *Yale Law Journal*, vol. 88, nr. 5, April 1979.

Molinski, W. "Marriage — Freedom through Bondage." Paper presented to the International Society on Family Law, Uppsala 1979.

Murch, Mervyn. "The Role of Solicitors in Divorce Proceedings I." *The Modern Law Review*, vol. 40, Nov. 1977 and continued in vol. 41, Jan. 1978.

Murch, Mervyn. *Justice and Welfare in Divorce*. London: Sweet and Maxwell, 1980.

O'Hoski, John. "The Legal Recognition of Domestic Contracts. The Experience of Ontario, Canada," in John M. Eekelaar and Sanford N. Katz (eds.) *Marriage and Cohabitation in Contemprary Societies.* Toronto: Butterworths, 1980.

Raschke, H.J., and Raschke, V.J., "Family Conflict and Childrens Self-concepts." *Journal of Marriage and the Family*, 1979.

Rausch, K. and Zahlmann-Willenbacher, B. "Soziologische Betrachtung der Ehescheidungsreform." Bielefelt 1978. udg.: J. Folke.

Rheinstein, Max, in Cloros (ed.) *International Encyclopedia of Comparative Law IV".* Tubingen, n.d.

Röhl, K.I. "Der Vergleich im Zivilprocess — Eine Alternative sum Urteil." Alternative Rechtsformen und Alternativen zum Recht. Jahrbuch für Rechtssoziologie und Rechtstheorie Bd. 6. udg.: Westdeutschen Verlag.

Sweetman, R. *On our Backs, Sexual Attitudes in a Changing Ireland.* London and Sydney: Pan Books, 1979.

Walzer, S.B. "The Role of the Lawyer in Divorce." *Family Law Quarterly*, vol. III, 1969.

Wright, G.C. and Stitson D.M. "The Impact of No-fault Divorce. Law Reform on Divorce in American States." *Journal of Marriage and the Family*, 1979.

Chapter Twelve

The Completed Reform: The Family Office

Henrik H. H. Andrup* and Klaus A. Ziegert[†]

*Denmark †West Germany

FAMILY LAW IN DISARRAY

Introduction

Family law is in disarray in most industrial societies. The reason for this is the fact that family law is founded on the institution of *marriage* and not on the institution of the *family* (Andrup, Buchhofer and Ziegert 1980). Marriage, however, is under strong attack. The increase in divorce and the number of *de facto* marriages tends to make formal marriage meaningless. Also in substantive family law we find a continuing decline in the significance of marital duties. Consequently there are many who feel that it is necessary to buttress formal marriage so that it can better compete with other forms of living together. At the same time, however, there is uncertainty about how to deal with the consequences of such a family law concerning the problems resulting from the dissolution of marriages and the protection of family life in general.

In order to understand this better and to find, if possible, more adequate answers to the problems of family law today it is necessary first to analyse its deficiencies. We shall do that by putting family law in a wider context of societal reference and by looking at the solutions which reformers have achieved in practice. This will prepare the ground for a more comprehensive suggestion as to how malfunctions of the reformed family law could be explained and, possibly, be corrected.

Family Law and Family Functions

Two factors largely distinguish the living conditions of modern industrial societies from those in which the foundations for traditional family law were laid:

1. formerly efficient protection against the birth of unwanted children was lacking; and
2. single mothers were faced with extremely adverse conditions for bringing up their children to be healthy, self-sufficient and reliable members of society.

The absence of effective birth control meant that all sexual intercourse was identified with "procreation" and that society exercised strict social, and later state, control over the access to parenthood in order to achieve the vital goal of reproduction: strong, reliable and especially loyal children who could take over and keep the established social structure in good order.

It is clearly a central concern of society to ensure for its children the best possible conditions for their upbringing. This can be done by prohibiting — as efficiently as possible — all sexual activities of people who have *not,* by publicly respected and permitted marriage, accepted the responsibility *to that public,* i.e., society as a whole, for creating those conditions. In this way marriage and its monopoly on sexual activity had become, historically, a rational instrument for family and social policy.

The efficiency of this instrument, obviously, depends on its potential to control access to sexual activities outside marriage, and accordingly, state authorities have employed, and still to a certain extent continue to do so, their full authority to maintain the marriage monopoly by prohibiting, prosecuting and punishing all extramarital sexual relations. The maintenance of public "decency" and morality became an important function of ecclesiastical, criminal and civil courts and the police.

Nevertheless this was not a clear, conscious family policy which was imposed on individuals against their will. It worked on the understanding of the norm as a value in its own right: decency was something which was good for the individual him/herself and there was no need for further explanation. So it was as easy for the German moral philosophers of the eighteenth and early nineteenth centuries as it was for Søren Kierkegaard to hold that marriage had its meaning "in itself" — quite overlooking the fact that it was actually a complex normative structure organized by society.

However, if societal conditions change in such a way that sexual activities can no longer be identified with the procreation of children, there is no reason to be concerned about it. Furthermore there is no longer any reason to use the legal structure of marriage as an instrument against extramarital sexual activities, especially if extramarital children are no longer considered a threat to the social order. State authorities allow people to do as they please; there is no special public interest at all in how people arrange their mutual sexual relationships. Most importantly, however, the fact that the basis for a policy of morality has been undermined by social change does not mean that there has been a substantial change in the primary family function which is at the core of the public interest in the family: society remains interested, and always will be, in the procreation of healthy, self-sufficient and loyal children. The fact that the institution of marriage is crumbling has thrown up a number of problems regarding the important societal function of procreation and has "derailed" the social development of family law.

In the critical moment when parenthood, due to social change, emancipated itself from marriage, family law still centred on *marriage* — instead of following *parenthood*, which is of utmost public importance whether the parents are married or not. We hold this to be a serious mistake in family legal policy and we find that current reform of family law in many postindustrial societies frequently reflects a gradual attempt to change the orientation of family law by switching its focus from the regulation of the relations between the spouses to much more relevant issues concerning children. Therefore the reforms in family law which are taking place in many societies are, in our opinion, only the beginning of a long period of reform. This period will not come to a close before the incongruous and indiscriminate special treatment of married couples, barren or not, by family law disappears and the support of families with children, in any form, finds an adequate and socially acceptable legal solution.

READJUSTMENT: THE FAMILY COURT MOVEMENT

The consequences of this incongruity in serving the needs of societal family functions have been felt in all modern industrial and postindustrial societies. But consequent reforms were directed at the courts and *not*, structurally, at the functions of family law; in other words, obviously old-fashioned pieces of legal machinery were exchanged for more modern ones instead of looking for new legal structures. That this was not so clear for the reformers is demonstrated by the development of the so-called "Family Court Movement." That traditional family law was not working very well was obvious but there were few, if any, solid explanations as to why this was the case. So, for instance, the goals of the Australian *Family Law Act*, which was to become one of the most advanced of reform acts comprised the following:

1. that a good family law should buttress, rather than undermine the stability of marriage;
2. that where a marriage has irretrievably broken down, the legal shell should be destroyed with the maximum fairness and the minimum bitterness, distress and humiliation;

3. that the future of the children of a broken marriage needs to be considered by the best possible tribunal assisted by the skills of welfare officers and other counselling staff where needed;
4. that financial disputes between the spouses should be resolved as quickly and as finally as possible; and
5. that the whole process should be performed with dignity, relative privacy and as little expense as possible (*Report* 1980, 2).

We find here, in a nutshell, the experience of reformers with the traditional family law and their conclusions as to what had to be changed: new proceedings, or more generally, the divorce court and a new "family court," seemed to be the panacea (Finlay 1969) to overcome all the evils of traditional family law. But after its institution, did it really fulfil the expectation that a mere change of proceedings would solve the problems of family law?

The basic idea of the family court, even in its most "watered down" versions, is the reversal of the perspectives in which legal structures are employed: from the retrospective, punitive and normative perspective of the adversary procedure, attention is shifted to the prospective, preventive and instrumental perspective of administrative procedure. The basis for a decision of the court should not be so much whether people complied with legal and above all moral norms, but rather the answer to the question how the eventual situation could be turned into a prospective future for the family members concerned. The constructive element in the family court movement was the idea that law had to be lead back to its social purpose of helping people who are in "a fix" to make decisions. In the area of family law this meant that children should not suffer unnecessarily from the dilemma their parents were in.

Clearly this "welfare" idea of a "helping court" hints at an administrative function, and attempts to integrate it into a court structure take different forms. On the one end of the spectrum we find the Australian Family Court with a two-tier system of, on the one hand, a judicial department and, on the other, an extensive conciliation service department. At the other end, we have the West German inquisitorial judge who even arranges for the transfer of social security benefits shares (among other things) in consolidated divorce proceedings. Even further advanced (already outside the court system), we find the Danish and Norwegian solution within the framework of an administrative system, although with the (historical) short-coming of having two tiers of litigation as far as *contested* cases are concerned, which are dealt with by the ordinary courts (Andrup and Buchhofer 1981).

However the affiliation of the preventive, welfare dimension to court proceedings has consequences for the daily practice of these courts. For instance, the Australian Family Court solution does not mean in practice that the welfare problems in a divorce can be delegated to the conciliation service while the family judge can specialize in the legal aspects of the case, but, on the contrary, that the conciliation service is avoided as a waste of time (Singer 1979; Ziegert 1981) and the family judge has to apply rubber-stamp devices in order to cope with the case load (Ziegert 1981). Similarly, the management of the best interests of a child in a divorce and of superannuation and pension funds does not mean that the West German family judge has turned into a welfare officer, in spite of the renunciation of such judicial paraphernalia as a gown and a beret and the improvement of the "ecological components" (for example, the hearing is in the judge's office instead of the court room, etc.) (Freund 1979, 78). On the contrary what the family judge actually does is to try to deal with the future of the family, a task which is bound to fail as it takes place in the guise of traditional judicial decision making.

What we find, in short, is the fact that the incorporation of the prognostic perspective into a court structure has turned family courts which take this welfare dimension seriously into family administrations, run by (family) judges instead of administrators. This incongruous roleplay of the family judges in the family courts, however, is only one side to the family court coin. The other side is the truly legal aspect of divorce proceedings in family courts. As has been stated elsewhere (Rheinstein 1972, 13; Andrup and Buchhofer 1981; Ziegert 1981) it is only a minor fraction — about ten percent — of divorce proceedings which come before the family judge as contested cases. This indicates that in essence it is not the legal dispute between the parties, i.e., the spouses, which is at the very core of judicial divorce proceedings but *the public interest in the inspection of the results,* which the spouses reach by agreement or, if need be, by contested judgment. Even if family courts offer conciliatory devices for the execution of this autonomy of the spouses, as in the cases of the Australian and some United States family courts, or in essence, as in German family court proceedings which envisage the role of conciliator to be played by the family judge, it is highly doubtful whether the legal structure of adversarial proceedings, which are institutionalized in a court setting does not conflict with the principle of the autonomy of the spouses. Instead of avoiding the dispute in favour of consensual solutions, the family court in fact strengthens the adversarial structures by reintroducing the traditional element of legally "represented" parties. The West German family court proceedings make it compulsory for the parties to be represented by counsel. In the Australian family court, though optional, ninety percent of all spouses in divorce proceedings prefer to be represented by counsel (Ziegert 1981, 80). The strange contradiction of the desired effects and the actual judicial practice of the family courts is highlighted by the introduction of a special legal representative (counsel) for the child, if so ordered by the court or asked for by a third party in the Australian divorce proceedings (s. 65 *Family Law Act* 1975). This provision will more often than not fail to promote the advancement of the best interests of the child and rather aggravate the conflict between the members of the family, because a family problem is pressed into the Procrustean bed of the judicial solution.

In this way we find two functions of family law confused in the family court solution which can fulfil neither of them sufficiently well: while family judges in fact generally *manage* the consequences of family breakdowns, they are restrained from doing so properly by the adversarial procedures of a judicial legal structure; and as family judges *exercise the judicial control of family law principles* they are hampered in doing so by the bulk of their daily administrative work and its discretionary nature. To put it strongly, family courts are in fact administrative authorities without administrators and, largely, courts without judicial functions — or, as some Australian practitioners like to call them, the "funny courts."

THE COMPLETED REFORM

Judicial vs. Administrative Procedure

Obviously the main problem of family law reform on its way from marital conflict orientation to family support orientation is shifting from judicial procedural structures to administrative ones without losing their legitimizing effect. Before being able to make some suggestions on the amendment of the reform concepts of the family court we have to look deeper into the structural opposition of judicial and administrative legal procedure.

The most characteristic feature of *judicial decision making* seems to be that the solution for problems to be decided upon is prepared by norms which are given in advance for a class of situations. Whenever these norms are missing they are substituted by ideas as to how future situations "of this kind" should be classified in principle in order to bring about a systematic normative solution. The specific "judicial" element will in this way make the individual decision follow or set a precedent.

In contrast, the most characteristic feature of *administrative decision-making* seems to be that the decision reflects a choice of the most reasonable and fruitful solution in the circumstances of the specific case. Nevertheless administration is not taking place in a void but in the normative framework of legal rules and in fact the law is one of the most influential factors in "the given circumstances" under which decisions are made administratively.

Defining "judicial" and "administrative" in this way does not preclude the fact that in the daily practice of courts and administrations, judges in fact work administratively, as we have seen in the family court, and civil servants work judicially, as we have seen in the Danish and Norwegian administration of the dissolution of marriages. We have to concede that there always will be a considerable mix of these forms of decision making but at the same time it is obvious that there are distinct structural consequences between specialized organizations comprising different procedural elements.

There are clear conclusions to be drawn from the confusion of administrative and judicial functions in family courts and correspondingly, in reformed family law procedure:

1. There is no sound reason for the division, procedural and otherwise, of contested and uncontested marriage breakdowns, if the optimal goal of state involvement is *assistance* in finding the most reasonable legal solution for all family members involved and *not* state control.
2. There is no sound reason for mixing administrative and judicial functions in *one* agency ("family court"), if the special functions of administrative and judicial decision making can be procured better by *special agencies,* i.e., courts *and* administrations respectively.

Clearly the goal of assistance in finding the most reasonable solution for all family members involved in a marriage breakdown can be provided best by an agency which can incorporate the relevant specialists from various fields, i.e., legal experts, tax experts, social security experts, psychologists and especially pediatricians (in the wide sense), which corresponds to the basic idea of the Family Court Movement. However it would be inconsistent with the cooperative administrative functioning of such an agency to call the leading officials, who are responsible for the coordination of its activities, "judges."

The structural analysis of family law reform reveals that its aim is to manage the careers of families and to offer them help in making decisions. Therefore the proper name of an agency of this type should be the *family office* rather than the family court.

THE FAMILY OFFICE

The predominant feature of the family office as we conceive it, is consistent with the objectives of the Family Court Movement, *viz.* the consolidated administration of *all* family matters in one service-oriented state agency, which can coordinate several forms of special assistance and administrative decision making and which is headed by a qualified civil servant. In channelling all family matters to the family office, that office would be the first resort for all kinds of family troubles, handling not only broken marriages but other family crises and problems, and could at the same time provide families with advice about self-regulation *and* also take over from the courts the functions of legal decision making and registration.

In this way, most divorces would merely require registration of the agreement reached by the parties themselves. Perhaps there would be a routine inspection whether all necessary information on the consequences of the dissolution of the marriage had been provided or all alternative solutions explored. A few couples will need more comprehensive expertise to prevent uncertainty or ignorance from resulting in serious problems.

In spite of the primary goal of reaching consensual solutions, cases will always remain where such agreement cannot be achieved. But even here, a clear administrative procedure, which shifts the responsibility of decision making from the couple to the administrator will help to reduce the undignified spectacle of a court contest to that "minimum of bitterness" which the reformers envisaged.

Clearly, in line with the arguments put forward in this chapter, the central issue of the family office will be the children. The family office can discharge the main concern of a functional family law in protecting their interests and supporting their family ties better than a court can. In offering its service to parents with children, the family office could help reduce the strains of the dissolution of family relations by working for solutions which are least detrimental to the physical and emotional health and social welfare of children and can link these functionally to the general network of social security in a given society. The authority for this kind of interference in the internal relationships of families is derived from the autonomy of the family and under the terms provided by the family members themselves. The task of the administrator is to assist the family in its crisis and, above all, to look after the best interests of the children.

It is now necessary to consider the question of what would become of the special function provided by due process and judicial decision making, namely *security and reliability* as realized in a court. As we have seen in the functioning of the family courts, it is not the courts' proceedings *per se* that guarantee the security and reliability of the law, but a complex interplay of socially meaningful decision making *and* public control (legitimation). Also in this respect the disentanglement of administrative and judicial decision making and the organizational sharpening of their special features will help to clarify issues: the administrator does not move in a vacuum, but in the legal and constitutional confinement of the civil service. This means that his/her decisions and arrangements are subject to the direct control of the courts. If need be, these courts can alter, amend or abolish the arrangements made by the family office and they supervise its officials to ensure that they do not neglect their duties or exceed the normative framework of their discretion. Most important, however, the courts have to establish normative *limits* for this administrative discretion. It is only within such a framework of guidelines in the area of family law that the individual can understand the consequences of family roles and obligations and will be helped to make reasonable decisions regarding his or her family roles and relationships.

REFERENCES

Andrup, Henrik H.H. and Bernd Buchhofer. 1981. "The Social Function of Divorce Procedures: The Danish Administrative and the West German Family Court Solution," in *Conciliation Courts Review* 19, 2, 7-22.

Andrup, Henrik, H.H., Bernd Buchhofer and Klaus A. Ziegert. 1980. "Formal Marriage under the Crossfire of Social Change," in John M. Eekelaar/Sanford N. Katz, eds. *Marriage and Cohabitation in Contemporary Societies*, Toronto: Butterworths, 32-38.

Buchhofer, Bernd and Klaus A. Ziegert. 1981. "Family Dynamics and Legal Change: Empirical Sociology in Search of a General Theory on the Effects of Law on Family Life," in *Journal of Comparative Family Studies* 12, 4, 397-412.

Finlay, Henry. 1969. "Family Courts — Gimmick or Panacea?" in *Australian Law Journal*, 602 ff.

Freund, Herbert. 1979. "Der Versuch einer Theorie der Praxis" (The concept of a theory of practice: the example of the family judge), in *Deutsche Richterzeitung*, March, 72-78.

Müller-Freienfels, Wolfgang. 1979. "The Marriage Law Reform of 1976 in the Federal Republic of Germany," in *The International and Comparative Law Quarterly*, April, 184-210.

Neuhaus, Paul H. 1982. "Finis familiae?" in *Zeitschrift f. das gesamte Familienrecht* 29, 1, 1-6.

Report. 1980. "Family Law in Australia." A report of the Joint Select Committee on the *Family Law Act*, Canberra: Aust. Government Publ. Service.

Rheinstein, Max. 1972. *Marriage Stability, Divorce and the Law*, Chicago: University Press.

Singer, Michael. 1979. "Towards Mediation of Matrimonial Property Disputes," Canberra: ANU — Law Workshop III.

Ziegert, Klaus A. 1981. "Comparing Family Law: the Case of Australia," Sydney: unpublished research report.

Part Three

Mediation and Professional Roles

One of the characteristic features of the move away from court-centred resolution of family conflict has been the attempt to reach back in time so that mediation services might be made available to the parties in marital conflict at an earlier stage than court-based schemes could do. Such a development does, however, carry with it significant problems relating to the type of service that is provided and the status of those who provide it. How, for example, do these developments relate to the traditional marriage counselling agencies? Is a distinction to be made between marriage counselling and mediation, and, if so, is it to be made in terms of the function of the process or of the character of the professions performing it? It is common to distinguish the functions by ascribing to marital counselling the objective of restoring the marital relationship ("reconciliation"), and to mediation the task of achieving consensus on the terms of a separation ("conciliation"), but pressures from other professional groups may well impel marriage counsellors to broaden their role.

So, what is mediation and who should perform it? These may not, in fact, be two entirely separate questions.[1] In the opening chapter of this Part, (Chapter 13) Folberg, who is engaged in a comprehensive examination of mediation, offers an *a priori* definition of mediation. It is a "non-therapeutic process by which the parties together, with the assistance of a neutral resource person or persons, attempt to systematically isolate points of agreement and disagreement, explore alternatives and consider compromises for the purpose of reaching a consensual settlement of issues relating to their divorce or separation." Distinctions are made between this process and arbitration, negotiation and conciliation. Folberg sets out what may seem the ideal vision of mediation. There are surely good grounds for such optimism. But serious questions remain unresolved. Folberg recognizes the likelihood of interprofessional rivalry in the mediation market, and observes that mediation may be successfully undertaken by "therapists, counselors and other caring and sensitive people." He believes lawyers could make good mediators. This may be related to his concept of mediation as "non-therapeutic," but the concept itself may be challenged by mediators from a different professional base. In fact, Folberg himself envisages possible "inter-disciplinary co-mediation teams," which would have a therapeutic input. Apart from escalation in costs, it is clear that the mediation process may not turn out as simple as appears at first sight.

Folberg also presents a relatively straightforward ideological justification for mediation. It promotes, in his view, the policy of minimum state intervention in family life. This is a strong claim because it harnesses mediation to one of the dominant ideological movements in modern family law. But closer examination throws up a range of questions, to which no answers can yet be given. The legal system itself, as Folberg recognizes, overshadows the process in the form of its substantive legal provisions. But quite apart from that, the extent to which the outcome of mediation can be said to have been the result of individualized, "private," decisions of the parties, as in the paradigm of "private ordering," will depend on the impact of the mediator's role. Did he simply confine himself to providing legal information? If not (as is probable), did he appeal solely to the adults' interests or introduce normative standards of his own? Did he indulge special pleading on behalf of one or the other? Did he urge compromise on the basis of the children's interests, and, if so, by what values did he assess those interests? Until we know how mediators actually mediate, and what kinds of differences appear between different kinds of mediators (as distinct from how the books say mediators *should* act) we will be living with an idealized picture of mediation rather than the social reality.

Crouch's contribution (Chapter 14) takes up many of these problems in the context of the growth of mediation by lawyers in the United States. He points to the seeming unavoidability of the emergence of a conflict of interest between the two adult parties and considers various attempts to reconcile this with the professional ethical commitments of the lawyer-mediator. This is essentially captured in the opinion that "the lawyer who sees one party being disadvantaged cannot speak up and terminate the mediation without damaging the interests of the one who is prevailing." There is real danger of confusion of professional roles here, both in the mind of the lawyer and of the clients. Proposed safeguards, such as the submission of an agreement to independant lawyers, throw into doubt the claims of mediation as a cost-saving exercise. Crouch has advanced important and substantial arguments. For it appears incontestable that, unless reference is to be made to the interests of some third party (such as a child) the adults are indeed playing a zero-sum game. One of them may accept a compromise, and consequential diminution of rights, for apparent short-term personal gains. As Crouch puts it: "if one person wishes to be a doormat (perhaps for the sake of a quick exit from the marriage, or for less obvious reasons), is it proper for the mediator to let that person do it? Such a person's reasons might include a very real and deep distaste for even mediation-flavored divorce negotiation, which the other party and the mediator, by reason of their temperament, do not share or even understand. It must take the wisdom of Solomon to know what to do in most situations if the fairness one strives for is imperfectly defined."

It may be significant that Bissett-Johnson's (Chapter 15) discussion of mediation in the Canadian context concludes that mediation and arbitration are most likely to be used in areas involving "ongoing relationships, such as maintenance and custody." Where there are children involved, the mediator has a point of reference beyond that of the adults' sole interests by which to assess the value of compromise. The most developed, and publicized, mediation scheme in England has been practically confined to cases involving children.[2] Of course, as Bissett-Johnson emphasizes, this does not remove the importance of the mediator's normative or professional orientation. Perhaps, as he indicates, the adults should have a right to choose the mediator, a right conspicuously lacking in those systems which provide for the court appointment of a "welfare officer" who may make recommendations and even carry out some conciliation functions.[3]

This Part closes with two evaluations of experimental conciliation schemes. The first, by Pearson and Thoennes (Chapter 16) reports on a project designed to evaluate mediation in child custody and visitation disputes. The preliminary findings indicate the success of mediation in promoting the likelihood of nonlitigated agreements between spouses; greater satisfaction with the eventual outcome and (at least over an initial stretch of time) less likelihood to seek its modification; improved relationships between the adults and more frequent postdivorce contact between parents and children. Similar findings are reported by Irving and Benjamin (Chapter 17) as a result of a project conducted in the Toronto family court. These chapters must necessarily encourage the further development of such processes. However, this should not preclude the persistent asking of further questions. The mere fact of a high degree of settlement tells us little. Issues can be settled by authoritarian imposition or simple indifference. We need to know more about *what kinds of* settlements mediation brings about. It is, for example, very striking that Pearson reports that custody settlement following mediation is much more likely to establish joint custody than nonmediated settlement. This clearly reflects the esteem in which mediators hold joint custody — either as a good device to bring parties to agreement or as an arrangement genuinely believed to be in the children's interests. Perhaps we may think that this is what each party optimally desired and that mediation has simply lubricated a process of private ordering. But it is more plausible to conclude that the mediators are promoting (successfully) a particular view of the children's, perhaps the family's, interests. Mediation should not be condemned on that account. But we must be alive to these issues and to their implications.

NOTES

1. Gwynn Davis, "Conciliation and the Professions," 13 *Family Law* 6 (1983).
2. Lisa Parkinson, "Bristol Courts Family Conciliation Service," 12 *Family Law* 13 (1982).
3. John Eekelaar, "Children and Divorce: Some Further Data," *Oxford Journal of Legal Studies,* 2, 63 (1982).

Chapter Thirteen

Divorce Mediation — The Emerging American Model

H. Jay Folberg*

Lewis and Clark Law School; Portland, Oregon, U.S.A.

INTRODUCTION

The dramatic increase in the divorce rate during the past two decades has been accompanied by sweeping changes in the substantive law of divorce. The most significant of these substantive legal reforms has been the almost universal acceptance in the United States of some form of no-fault divorce. The decision to end a marriage, in most states, is now essentially a matter of private choice. There have, however, been few changes in the procedural law of divorce. Our judicial system, with its complement of lawyers, counsellors and experts continues to intervene in divorce with the same shell of procedural mechanisms that existed prior to the no-fault revolution. The increased number of divorce cases, coupled with the growing acceptance of divorce as a common life event, has raised serious questions about the appropriateness of judicial intervention and its accompanying adversarial process in all marital dissolution situations.

Divorce mediation, coupled with procedural reforms, has been proposed as an alternative to traditional judicial intervention and divorce litigation. It appears to be a rapidly developing trend as it is increasingly recognized that divorce does not necessarily end family relationships, but may require their restructuring in a way that better meets new needs while protecting the rights of family members. This chapter explores the alternative of divorce mediation and examines the promise it holds as well as the issues it poses.

---

* This chapter includes material in a book forthcoming from this author, who accordingly retains copyright in it.

WHAT IS DIVORCE MEDIATION?

The first question to be addressed in policy discussions about family mediation is: What is it? The practice of family mediation falls along a spectrum which defies a restricted definition. What family mediation is will be dependent in part on what is being mediated, who is doing the mediating and the setting in which the mediation is offered. This chapter focuses on divorce mediation — mediation of the incidents attached to the dissolution of a family relationship. The subjects of divorce mediation include, but are not limited to, those that would be resolved by a judge in court, except for the mediated settlement. It can thus be seen as an alternative or, at least, a complement to the court process. Divorce mediation is defined here as a nontherapeutic process by which the parties together, with the assistance of a neutral resource person or persons, attempt to systematically isolate points of agreement and disagreement, explore alternatives and consider compromises for the purpose of reaching a consensual settlement of issues relating to their divorce or separation. Mediation is a process of conflict resolution and management that gives back to the parties the responsibility for making their own decisions about their own lives. It is usually conducted in private without the presence of the parties' attorneys. It has identifiable stages and divisible tasks, but no universal pattern.

In order better to distinguish and isolate mediation from other interventions, we might look at what it is not. It is not, as defined above, a therapeutic process. Participation in mediation may or may not have a therapeutic effect on the parties, but it is not designed as a traditional therapeutic process. It is not focused on insight to personal conflict or in changing historically set personality patterns. It is much more an interactive process than an interpsychic one. Mediation is task-directed and goal-oriented. It looks at resolution and results between the parties rather than the internalized causes of conflict behaviour. It discourages dependence on the professional provider rather than promoting it. Though some approaches to therapy can make similar claims, therapy in any mode is a form of treatment, which mediation is not.

Mediation is not arbitration. In arbitration, the parties authorize a neutral third person or persons to *decide* upon a binding resolution of the issues. The process used in arbitration is adjudicatory, but is typically less formal than that utilized in court and is usually conducted in private. Other than its informality and privacy, arbitration is much like the judicial process, except the "judge" is chosen or agreed upon by the parties and derives his or her authority from the agreement to arbitrate. In mediation the parties may choose the mediator, but do not authorize the mediator to make the decisions for them. Arbitration may follow mediation, either as a separate proceeding or as part of the same "med-arb" process.

Mediation is not the same as traditional negotiation of divorce disputes. Negotiation is generally a "sounding out" process to aid dispute resolutions but is not accomplished through any established framework and may be pursued through representatives, most often attorneys. Negotiation does not normally utilize a neutral resource person and is premised on an adversary model. Private negotiation may, however, precede mediation, follow unsuccessful mediation, or in some settings go on simultaneously.

Mediation is not conciliation, though the two terms are often used interchangeably. The two can be distinguished by looking at their historical development and application to the field of family law. California first offered court connected conciliation services in 1939. The initial focus of these services was on providing marriage counselling aimed at effecting a reconciliation of spouses. With the adoption of no-fault divorce and the increase in the divorce rate, the focus of conciliation has shifted from marriage counselling aimed at reconciling parties to separation counselling and evaluation services for purposes of assisting the domestic-relations judges in making child custody and visitation orders. Indeed, in California, where mandatory custody mediation is usually performed by conciliation personnel, the distinction between conciliation and mediation has become somewhat obfuscated. Though private mediation may encompass financial and property issues, about which more is discussed later, court connected mediation rarely attempts directly to resolve money or property distribution matters. Conciliation is by practice and tradition limited to personal issues of custody and parental relationships among family members. That is not to say that conciliation staffs could not provide mediation services leading to a written resolution of all divorce issues.

THE RATIONALE OF DIVORCE MEDIATION

Divorce is both a legal event and part of a family process. It is a matter of the heart and of the law. The strong emotional forces accompanying the dissolution of an existing family relationship argue for more delicately wrought measures than could be provided in a court imposed solution. Mediation can educate the parties about each other's needs and provide a personalized model for dispute resolution, both now and in the future, should circumstances change or differences arise. It can help them learn to work together, isolate the issues to be decided and see that through cooperation all can make positive gains.

This advantage of mediation exists, in part, because mediation is less bound by rules of procedure and substantive law, as well as certain assumptions or norms, that dominate the adversary process. The ultimate authority in mediation belongs to the parties themselves and they may fashion a unique solution that will work for them without being strictly governed by precedent nor concerned with the precedent they may set for others. They may, with the help of the mediator, appropriately consider a comprehensive mix of their needs, interests and whatever else they deem relevant regardless of rules of evidence or strict adherence to substantive law. Unlike the adjudicatory process, the emphasis is not on who is right or who is wrong or who wins and who loses, but rather upon establishing a workable solution and resolution that best meets the family's own unique needs. Mediation is conducted in private, so that private matters may be discussed without becoming part of a public record.

Family mediation furthers the policy of minimum state intervention. The argument for minimum state intervention has been most eloquently made by Goldstein, Freud and Solnit relative to determinations of child care and custody in their book, *Before the Best Interests of the Child.*[1] Parents should be presumed to have the capacity, authority and responsibility to determine and do what is best for their children as well as what is best for their entire family constellation, regardless of how it may be rearranged following divorce. Psychological theory, as well as constitutional considerations, argue for parental autonomy and family privacy when there is no direct evidence that the interests of children are jeopardized in the process. Parents should have the first opportunity to meet the needs of their children and continue the maintenance of family ties without state interference.

A policy that provides parents with the option of mediation to facilitate their own decision making and encourages self-determination should enhance continuing family ties and reassert the dignity and importance of the family as a self-governing unit. One of the most noble functions of law is to serve as a model of what is expected. Family law and procedure, instead of providing a model, is too often used coercively to supplant family self-determination upon inadequate evidence that the personal and societal cost of such interventions are absolutely required.

The legal system is not well able to supervise or enforce the fragile and complex interpersonal relationships between family members that continue even after most divorces. Once the state intrudes into the decision-making role of parents, the family process is less likely to function independently in the future and continued state involvement and individual non-cooperation with imposed orders is likely. By definition, a consensual agreement, whether reached through mediation or direct negotiation, reflects the parties' own preferences and will be more acceptable over time than one imposed by a court. In the process of mediation, the parties formulate their own agreement and emotionally invest in its success so they are more likely to support its terms in the long run than one negotiated or ordered by others. The lack of self-determination in adversary proceedings is a suspect consideration accounting for never-ending divorce litigation surrounding family conflicts where postdivorce skirmishes in court may exceed the intensity of the initial divorce dispute. Not only do imposed judicial determinations of custody serve as the antithesis of the ancient concept of harmonious relationships, but judicial intervention also contradicts the current emphasis on individual freedom and minimum state coercion.

If the arguments are strong for minimal state intervention in the parent-child relationship upon divorce, they would appear even more persuasive as to allowing the parties to privately decide their own economic relationship upon the dissolution of the marriage. Divorcing parties should be free to contract between themselves and be encouraged to do so. The state should use its increasingly precious resources to intervene in economic relationships between adults only as a last alternative when all efforts for private ordering or settlement have failed.

Robert Mnookin and Lewis Kornhauser (1979)[2] have made a significant contribution to our thinking about private ordering. They identify the four distributional questions that must be decided in divorce cases: (1) marital property, (2) spousal support, (3) child support, and (4) child custody and visitation. They argue that divorce is now largely a matter of private concern and that divorcing parties, themselves, should negotiate a settlement of these questions with minimal state intrusion, but "against a backdrop of fair standards" determined by the state through its legislative and judicial processes. State statutes and appellate decisions now provide some guidelines or norms for divorce distributional questions, but they are seldom fashioned with "private ordering" as their goal and generally require legal help to interpret and apply them. Mediators can facilitate private ordering in divorce and other family disputes by providing common information to the parties on applicable legal norms and principles, as well as the probable outcome in court if the case is litigated.

Preliminary studies on the effects of mediation, while primarily limited to custody cases, indicate that the theoretical promises of mediation are indeed real and measurable.

Divorcing parents are likely to reach agreement concerning custody whether they choose mediation as an alternative to the adversarial process or are compelled to use it before being heard in court, and they are generally pleased with the process. The data is encouraging in substantiating that divorcing parties who mediate, rather than negotiate or litigate through the adversarial process, are far less likely to bring postdivorce disputes into the legal system. The cost and time studies have produced mixed results, but do generally indicate that mediation offers the promise of saving time and money for both the state and the parties.

ISSUES RELATING TO DIVORCE MEDIATION

The very elements that make divorce mediation so appealing and provide its advantage over the adversarial model also create its dangers and raise substantial issues not yet resolved. Because mediation distinguishes itself as an approach that recognizes divorce and family disputes as both matters of the heart and of the law, there exists an issue of how emotional feelings are to be weighed against and blended with legal rights and obligations and just what are appropriate subjects for mediation. Because mediation is conducted in private and is less hemmed-in by rules of procedure, substantive law, and precedent, there will remain the continuing question of whether the process is fair and the terms of a mediated agreement are just. This concern for a just and fair result has particular applicability to the provisions for custody and child support in recognition that the mediated bargaining occurs between parents and that children are rarely present during mediation nor independently represented.

Because mediation represents an "alternative" to the adversarial system, it lacks the precise and perfected checks and balances that are the principal benefit of the adversary process. The purposeful "a-legal" character of mediation creates a constant risk of overreaching and dominance by the more knowledgeable, powerful or less emotional party. Some argue that the "a-legal" character of divorce mediation requires all the more careful court scrutiny before mediated agreements are approved and incorporated into a decree. Others argue that if the parties have utilized mediation to reach agreement, there is no need for the expense, delay, and imposition of a judge's values, which are inherent features of the judicial review process.

Because family mediation is a new practice that crosses traditional professional boundaries and recognizes divorce as a family process within a legal context, there are likely to be questions about interdisciplinary cooperation and struggles for turf and assertions of professional dominance through claims of right, experience or unique expertise. Mental health professionals, attorneys and judges may not eagerly cooperate in creating joint roles nor in relinquishing their traditional roles during tight economic times in what is viewed as a growth industry. They may, however, become strange bedfellows in checking the emergence of a new "profession" of family mediators. Because family mediation does involve professionals in a new or hybrid role with few established rules and where fairness is a central concern, delicate issues of professional restraint and ethics will persist for some time without refined and tested answers.

Because there is wide public dissatisfaction with the present application of the adversary process to divorce cases and no clear direction from the legal profession for the improvement or replacement of that process, there will surely be exaggerated claims and expectations for mediation, which some will herald as a panacea rather than a promising and rational alternative with its own set of problems and no magic answers. Some will insist that it be mandated in all divorce cases, others will argue that it must always be voluntary. Naive, if not zealous, enthusiasm may create disappointment and frustration that could thwart long-term innovations and improvements. Only some of these issues can be discussed below; all are analysed in the more comprehensive writing from which this chapter is excerpted.

The Role of the Courts

The intriguing question has been raised of whether the courts should play any role when a mediated settlement is reached (or for that matter, when a nonmediated settlement is agreed upon). Our clogged family law dockets, as well as the expense and delay of judicial review when agreement exists, argue for some way to eliminate this judicial holdover from the era of fault-based divorce grounds. A stronger argument against this largely anachronistic judicial function is the preference for family self-determination and the reaffirmation of parental responsibility for the welfare of their children. The elimination of routine judicial review of divorce settlement agreements may exhance the ability of the courts to better fulfil their necessary role where unresolved controversy between divorcing spouses exists or when enforcement of settlement provisions is required.

Perhaps the current practice of court review of settlement agreements, particularly mediated agreements, is so cursory that there would be little factual difference between current realities and the reforms to be suggested here except for their underlying premises and the important role expectations they convey. Court review implies court power to change parental decisions and impose the decision of a judge in all cases. Mnookin and Kornhauser argue that divorce settlement agreements determining issues of money and children, within a broad range of acceptable norms, should not be reviewed by courts and need go through no judicial process. They do not, however, indicate a precise mechanism for determining which settlement agreements fall within acceptable norms in the absence of routine judicial review in all cases. They refer in a footnote to mediation as one alternative. The goal, which mediation may satisfy, is to weed out unconscionable agreements or those that fall outside of acceptable norms without requiring all divorcing couples to use the existing judicial process and unreasonably burdening the courts by maintaining a review task so large as to result in cursory or fictional scrutiny.

Arbitration decisions are now enforceable in many states without judicial review, pursuant to arbitration legislation. Legislation or court rules could encourage mediated settlements by exempting from court review divorce agreements reached through a *bona fide* mediation process or, at least, providing a judicial fast track for divorce agreements procedurally certified by a mediator. This approach, in distinguishing mediated divorce agreements from settlements reached by other than mediation, raises its own set of issues as to an acceptable definition of *bona fide* mediation, the qualifications of a mediator with certifying authority, and the justification for distinguishing mediated settlements from settlement agreements reached by the parties without a mediator, but space does not permit their discussion here.

Eliminating routine judicial review of mediated divorce settlement agreements would not entirely remove the courts from the divorce process. We know that some cases cannot be settled or mediated. There must be a fair and credible forum with procedural safeguards and rules to assure the peaceful resolution of disputes for the parties who are unwilling or unable to make cooperative decisions or recognize the benefits that may come from a less coercive process. The threat of court litigation, with all of the human and material expense that it requires, may be the very element that will help some parties cut through their egocentric nearsightedness to see that their self-interests, as well as the interest of the family, may be promoted through mediation rather than a court fight. If we can draw any parallel, the advent and legislative encouragement of collective bargaining in the labour management field did not eliminate the strike. Rather, the strike looms in the background of most collective bargaining as a guiding motivation to utilize the less coercive process as a way to achieve a more lasting and mutually beneficial resolution of very real differences.

The success of divorce mediation may be dependent upon the very existence of the courts and the potential for litigation. Mediation works best when guidelines exist as to how the law would be applied to resolve the dispute. Legislation is not precise enough to resolve the myriad of factual situations and differences that can exist when families attempt to disentangle their affairs. The courts, by creating precedents of how similar issues have been judicially resolved in the past, creates the framework by which mediators provide information about legal norms and offer remedies that have been adopted by courts following research and expert input that may not be readily available in mediated cases. As previously discussed, mediation is but another of the informal processes that might take place in "the shadow of the law."

Preliminary studies reveal that divorce mediation works most effectively when there is some time pressure on both parties to reach settlement. Because the parties to divorce are seldom in the same phase of adjustment and mutuality about the dissolution, one party may be less motivated than the other to bring the mediation to a conclusion. When the parties are referred to mediation by the court and must operate within the court's time frame or when the parties are in private mediation knowing that the filing of papers by either party may impose time limitations on the process, mediation can best achieve its task-oriented goal of bringing closure to a settlement of the issues. If the courts did not exist to set these time parameters and precedents, it is not clear that it could be done as effectively through any other mechanism.

Fairness

Suggesting the elimination of judicial review of mediated divorce agreements requires further inquiry about the issue of fairness. In considering whether mediated settlements will be fair and just, we must ask "compared to what?" We know that the great majority of divorce cases in the United States currently go by default in which one party fails to appear. The default may be a result of ignorance, guilt or a total sense of powerlessness. The default may also be a result of an agreement between the parties on the distributional questions eliminating the need for an appearance. The question persists in our present dispute-resolution system of whether such agreements are the result of unequal bargaining power due to different levels of experience, patterns of dominance, the greater emotional need of one divorcing party to get out of the marriage or a greater desire on the part of one of the parties to avoid the expense and uncertainty of litigation. The present "adversarial" approach does not require the adverse parties to be represented nor does it impose a mediator or "audience" to point out these imbalances and assure that they are recognized by the parties, as mediation should attempt to do. *Pro se* divorce is increasingly popular and sanctioned by our present system in which there need be no professional intervention prior to court review. Mediation, at least, provides a knowledgeable third party to help the couple evaluate their relative positions so that they may make reasoned decisions with minimal judicial intrusion.

The most common pattern of legal representation in divorce is for one party to retain an attorney for advice and preparation of the documents. The other party will often negotiate directly with the moving party's attorney or retain an attorney to do so without filing an appearance. If a second attorney has not been retained by the nonmoving party prior to preparation of the settlement agreement or proposed decree containing settlement terms, then the unrepresented party will often consult with an attorney to determine if the proposed settlement is "fair enough" not to contest and if all necessary items have been covered or discussed. Basically the reviewing attorney serves as a check to assure that all major items have been covered in the agreement or, at least, considered by the parties. Then the reviewing attorney informs the client of any other options to the suggested terms and whether the points of agreement fall within acceptable legal norms. These norms are often raised in the context of what would be the likely range of court outcome if agreement was not reached. The likelihood of a different court outcome than the proposed agreement is weighed against the financial, time and emotional expenses of further negotiation or litigation.

A similar pattern of independent legal consultation could, and should, be utilized for review of mediated agreements. Current mediation practice, influenced by ethical restraints, is to urge or require that each divorcing party seek independent legal counsel to review the proposed agreement before it is signed. Many mediators encourage the parties to consult independent legal counsel during the course of mediation. Though the criteria for independent attorney review of the proposed mediated agreement is not clear, the purpose of the review is no less clear than it is under the present "fair enough" practice. Given that the initial mediated agreement is formed with the assistance of a neutral person rather than someone ethically bound to advance the interest of one party, independent legal review by an attorney for one spouse pursuant to a "fair enough" standard should assure at least as great a fairness safeguard as the common reality of our present adversary system. When both parties to the mediation obtain independent legal review, as they are encouraged to do, then there is a double check of what is fair enough. In some complex cases, other professional review, such as that of a CPA, may be necessary for still another opinion and double check.

The mediator may have a professional responsibility to advise both parties as to whether the agreement reached is fair within the parameters of possible court resolutions. The responsibilities of a mediator on this point have not yet been resolved legally or ethically. In *Lange v. Marshall,* one of the first reported malpractice cases brought against a lawyer-mediator, the wife claimed that the mediated settlement was inadequate and that the attorney-mediator failed to protect her interest adequately in obtaining a better settlement from her husband. The lawyer conceded that he did not advise her regarding her rights and did not attempt to get the "best" settlement for her because these were not appropriate functions for a mediator. Although the Missouri Appellate Court did not reach the question of the appropriate responsibilities of a lawyer-mediator, in that it ruled the plaintiff suffered no damages, the case illustrates that a spouse may later question the fairness of a mediated settlement and seek redress against the mediator for a perceived bargaining disadvantage. Court review of mediated agreements as an incident to malpractice cases cannot be expected to refine standards of fairness in any systematic fashion that would serve as a helpful guide. Perhaps allowing direct attack to reform "unconscionable" or manifestly unjust divorce settlements would provide more of a case law standard, but this too has its problems and limits.

Another voiced concern about the fairness aspect of mediation is that mediation implies for some a process only of compromise, where each party is necessarily urged to move toward a centre position. It must be recognized that some demands and expectations that divide families are so insane or productive of harm or evil, whether by design or emotional blindness, that no compromise should be made toward their realization. The mediator should be prepared, if necessary, to facilitate the recognition of this possibility and not hide behind the easy rubric that all positions can be compromised. Though most positions are subject to reasonable compromise, some things cannot and should not be compromised. This potential problem might be minimized if mediation is recognized in its proper role as a process of conflict resolution and management, rather than a form of magic to make a conflict disappear never to be seen again. Mediation may produce better but not always happy results, and agreement will not be produced in every case.

Mediation, unlike litigation, may appropriately recognize the collision of legal norms with "person-oriented norms." These personal norms or standards, though not legally valid in court, may be important to the parties in reaching a fair settlement within the context of the emotional issues and characteristics involved in divorce disputes. The accommodation of these colliding norms may produce an agreement no less "principled" for the parties than a litigated result decided only on accepted legal norms or principles. For example, a personal norm that considers fault relevant to the financial outcome may be accommodated in mediation, even though this principal is no longer legally relevant in the courts of many states. If it is relevant in accommodating the parties' personal principles, knowing that fault would not be considered in court, can it be said that the resulting settlement is less "principled"? The accommodation of these nonlegal principles is one of the very advantages of private ordering facilitated by mediation that may make the settlement more acceptable and lasting for the divorcing parties. The contrast of mediation with litigation, in considering a larger universe of norms and principles and in being more open-ended than court proceedings, is not an indictment, but only a distinction.

Protection of Children

When the divorce does involve minor children, some would argue that the state has an interest beyond the efficient and speedy private settlement of the dispute between the parents. The state, however, under the well-developed doctrine of *parens patriae* has a responsibility for the welfare of children only when *parents cannot agree or cannot adequately provide for them.* Divorce mediation begins with the premise that parents love their children and are best able to decide how, within their resources, the children can best be cared for. The arguments for parental determination of a child's best interest have been concisely articulated by Mnookin and Kornhauser and by Goldstein, Freud and Solnit, who in their book, *Before the Best Interests of the Child,* assert that court review of parental agreements on child custody is not justified by our desire to protect children. They propose that the interests of children would be better served by allowing separating parents to choose to have their agreement "officially recorded to assure that it be recognized for tax or other non-custodial purposes."

Court review, as previously stated, implies court power to change parental decisions and impose the decision of a judge. When both parents love their children and are willing to utilize a process of mediation to agree on how to provide for them after divorce, it does appear presumptious and insulting to impose a third party, whether a judge or a child development expert, to determine if the parents' custody, support and care agreement is good enough for their own children. A mediated agreement of the parents about their childrens' custody, support and care is much more likely than a judicial decision to match the parents' capacity and desires with the child's needs. Whether the parents' decision is the result of reasoned analysis or is influenced by depression, guilt, spite or selfishness, it is preferable to an imposed decision that is more likely to impede cooperation and stability for the child. In any event, a resolution, negotiated by attorneys, reviewed by a court or litigated before a court, is no more likely than a mediated settlement to disclose which outcomes are the result of depression, spite, guilt or selfishness. Even if one were to assume that mediated settlements may produce some errors or mistakes relative to the child, there is no reason to think that the process of mediation would produce any more mistakes than the existing adversarial system. Indeed, a professionally directed process with the very goal of cooperative assessment of needs and abilities to reach a consensual and personalized parenting plan for the children would appear far less likely to produce error than an adversarial process that leaves one parent the winner and one the loser.

It is important not to lose sight of the increasingly evident truism that parents are primarily responsible for the day-to-day care of their children and that the state cannot provide the love, attention and care for a child that can be provided by even marginal parents. Nor can the state require parents to love their children. All the state is really capable of doing is supervising children of neglectful or abusive parents and, through its laws, policies and procedures, establishing a model of what is expected of parents. One of the primary expectations that we should have for all parents is that they be responsible for deciding upon the care of their children without relying on the state for their personalized decisions. Mediation is a process designed to enhance that parental responsibility.

The mediator should refrain from trying to second-guess parents or telling them what is "right." The principal protection that the mediator can offer the child is to see that the parents are considering all factors that can be developed between them relative to the child's needs and their abilities to meet those needs. The mediator should be prepared to ask probing and difficult questions and to help inform the parents of available alternatives. The mediator's ethical commitment, however, is to the process of parental self-determination and not to any given outcome. When asked who in the process is protecting the interest of the child, the answer must be the parents — as is their role. Mediation can assist the parents in carefully considering how that role can best be fulfilled.

Money vs. Children

If divorce mediation is a good idea whose time has come, its benefits may be needlessly restricted by focussing the mediation process, particularly in court settings, on only child custody issues and leaving resolution of the financial issues to a different process. Division between these aspects of divorce is only superficially separable because they are inextricably intertwined.

Issues of support, both spousal and child, cannot be decided in a vacuum. Financial issues are part and parcel of the decisions about who incurs the daily expenses for the child and who sets aside the time necessary to care for the child. It has been observed that each parent may, within a given range, "exchange custodial rights and obligations for income or wealth," and that support duties may be tied to custodial prerogatives as one way to enforce economic rights without going to court. As much as we would like to romanticize parenting and separate children's needs from the financial needs of parents, we know that custody and the attendant financial arrangements represent some trade-offs in the minds of divorcing parties that we can only pretend to keep separate.

Property Division

Mediation should, ideally, encompass division of property and conclude with a written settlement document. Dividing the property can serve as a vehicle through which the intense feelings associated with the marital breakdown can be played out. Parties may, in the process of dividing property, attempt to redress every imbalance believed to be perpetrated by the other. In the typical adversary process, the property settlement negotiation can be manipulated as a psychological defense against the deeper and more painful feelings associated with marital loss. To the extent that property settlement is viewed as a strictly legal and logical exercise, it supports manipulation and may retard opportunities for emotional resolution between the parties.

In mediation, whether by a counsellor or an attorney, the property settlement should be viewed as a vehicle for finishing and bringing closure to the relationship. It might be considered a ritual signifying the ending of a marriage: it is emotionally symbolic as well as legally and factually important. As each detail is negotiated, struggled over, or conceded, there is a simultaneous, if unconscious, emotional shifting regarding the approaching reality of the divorce.

The process by which the financial aspects of the marriage are brought to a close can be as important as the settlement document itself. Viewed in this way, the importance of the document is no more supreme than the cooperative process that produces it. Signing the property settlement agreement can become for the parties a mechanism for providing a ritualistic ending of the divorce that might otherwise be lacking in the mediation process, should there be no court hearing. It is not really surprising that the signing of the mediated settlement agreement is often accompanied by tears.

Who Should Serve as Mediators?

As with the exploration and establishment of any new territory, there are grave risks that there will be struggles for turf and assertions of professional dominance through claims of right, experience or unique expertise by both attorneys and mental health professionals. If mediation is viewed as a spectrum of services all aimed at returning decision making on family matters back to family members, including decisions about who can best assist them in the process, concerns about turf should be put in their proper perspective as products of professional selfishness, vanity and silliness, more than concern with the public good.

The problem, as stated earlier, is that divorce occurs both within the family system and within the legal system. Clinicians working in the area of divorce are concerned with family processes and decisions which move the parties through the emotional morass and adjustment to divorce and with the psychological barriers inhibiting their openness in communication. Lawyers working in the area of divorce must focus on the restructuring of the family's more visible or practical concerns: property division, support issues, and custody arrangements. Marital and divorce therapists are accustomed to working with multiple parties and looking at individuals in relation to each other as members of a family. A lawyer, on the other hand, by training and ethical constraints, is accustomed to responding to the legal needs of an individual and in championing the cause of an individual, rather than the well-being of the entire family constellation.

There are many types of professionals, and perhaps some nonprofessionals, who can legitimately offer family mediation services so that clients may have a choice of providers. Therapists, counsellors and other caring and sensitive people familiar with the divorce process can master the procedural and substantive legal knowledge necessary to help couples explore options and make choices that are then subject to review by the parties' attorneys, if they so choose, and possibly by the court.

Lawyers need not flatter themselves by thinking an intelligent counsellor dedicating his or her professional career to the subject cannot adequately master the basic legal principles necessary to mediate family disputes, again subject to review and formal memorialization by the attorneys for each party. There may be cases in which the tax, real estate or business planning aspects are complex enough to require consultation with or referral to an expert, but this is no different than dozens of other similar situations faced by counsellors — as well as general practice attorneys. In any event, those who choose divorce mediation should be encouraged to have any settlement agreement reviewed by legal counsel.

Mental health professionals are no less possessive in guarding their turf than are attorneys. Clinicians see themselves as uniquely qualified to move the parties through the psychological barriers inhibiting their openness and communication toward reaching agreement. Many therapists believe that only they can help the parties understand the underlying and even unconscious reasons for the marital breakdown adequately to deal with the issues surrounding divorce; that they alone can help deal with the ambivalence or nonmutuality around the decision to part. Some will claim that a clinician is necessary to help resolve the feelings of personal loss and grief as parties resolve the feelings of emotional attachment to one another. Attorneys, it is claimed, are self-selected by aptitude and training to deal with cold hard facts and logic rather than feelings, which are a necessary part of every divorce dispute.

It is submitted that lawyers can and should be offering their services as divorce mediators. Lawyers, by aptitude and training, are problem solvers who deal daily in their practices with the creative exploration of compromise alternatives. They are skilled at sorting through issues to isolate points of agreement from disagreement for purposes of suggesting settlement solutions. Attorneys, in the course of their practices, regularly help clients predict the consequences of various choices as well as interpret legal guidelines derived from cases and statutes so that clients can make knowing and intelligent decisions. One of the principal roles of a mediator is to help balance power by equalizing information concerning the law and financial issues. Lawyers are in a unique position to equalize bargaining positions, since the less informed spouse is more vulnerable to intimidation, or perceives him or herself to be disadvantaged.

A lawyer, as mediator, can review the issues to be addressed, the range of resolution that might be imposed in a court setting, and the options available for a negotiated settlement. The lawyer as mediator would serve as neither party's advocate. Rather, both parties could rely on the lawyer's legal expertise and experience with the understanding that full disclosure and a review of all the issues and options will lead to more informed and, presumably, more satisfactory choices. Attorneys are particularly accustomed to negotiation and should be able to help facilitate assessment and negotiation by divorcing parties.

Mediation is a task-oriented process — the product of that task being a settlement agreement. Attorneys are in the business of drafting settlement agreements and explaining their terms.

The argument that attorneys lack listening skills necessary for mediation, or that they are not adept at providing empathetic responses to facilitate discussion, also falls short of the truth. Any attorney who has successfully tried a jury case must be skilled at listening as well as talking and at picking up nonverbal clues as well as spoken ones. An attorney's first task in any case is to effectively interview clients for the purpose of establishing trust and rapport in order to obtain all the facts and learn of the client's feelings and wishes.

Just as counsellors are trainable in basic matters of the law and procedure, so attorneys are trainable in the common emotional aspects of divorce as well as educable about the phases of child development. Some cases will be psychologically complex and beyond the competence of an attorney. The attorney must know his or her limits and when to refer particularly difficult matters to others with special training, but this is no different from other similar situations faced by professionals whose clients' problems defy categorization. Divorce mediation may represent a new role for attorneys, requiring qualities of sensitivity and skills of facilitation which they can, with some effort, master.

Interdisciplinary Comediation Teams

Interdisciplinary comediation teams present the most flexible approach in relation to a theory of divorce mediation which stresses the interplay of emotional resolution with the comprehensive legal settlement task. Both team mediators must adapt to a role different from traditional lawyering and different from the practice of psychotherapy. While the lawyer's intervention focuses on the factual aspect of the settlement issues, the therapist focuses on the interpersonal and emotional aspects. The therapist manages the therapeutic milieu and in that regard is attentive to issues of trust, fear and safety. The lawyer provides information about the legal system and establishes legal parameters and guidelines for the mediation.

The comediation team provides a number of important benefits. First, the interdisciplinary presence makes an important statement to the couple that recognizes the complex fusion of legal, emotional and economic issues and together provides competency to help explore and untangle the issues. The comediation aspect of the team permits a great deal of flexibility in responding to the complex interfacing of emotional and legal issues that permit the continuous choice of psychological or legal task-oriented interventions. The interdisciplinary presence also provides a sense of safety to a party who might be fearful of an emotional disadvantage or to a party who is fearful of a disadvantage due to a lack of information about finances or the law.

Second, a male/female team can provide a model of autonomous and independent behaviour as an example of how a couple can work together with mutual respect. Balancing the male/female members provides an opportunity to be understood, validated or challenged by persons of both sexes, thereby minimizing sexual stereotyping and triangling. Transference issues are less likely to be played out in a way that creates difficulties in the relationship with one mediator when the other is free to comment and keep the process moving. Neither of the parties can project onto a single mediator behaviour reflective of the psychological issues alive for them as part of the marital breakdown. Trust, power, fairness and the behaviour of the opposite sex are, as we know, very sensitive issues for the parties during adjustment to divorce.

Finally, flexibility is greatly enhanced with two mediators. It is possible for one mediator to be more actively confrontive or supportive with a comediator capable of intervening and responding on the other side of the issue. It is difficult to always be "up" as a mediator, a lawyer or a therapist. Comediation allows for division of labour as well as collegial support, perception checks, continual cross-training, and the benefits of cross-disciplinary expertise. The skills of therapists in facilitating communication and unblocking emotional obstacles, when coupled with the assessment skills and informational resources of the lawyer, enhance the likelihood of a comprehensive negotiated settlement.

CONCLUSION

Divorce mediation has been touted as a replacement for the adversary system and a way of making divorce less painful. Though it may serve as an alternative for those who choose to use it, it is neither a panacea that will create love where there is hate, nor will it totally eliminate the role of the adversary system in divorce. It may, however, reduce acrimony by promoting cooperation and it may lessen the burden of the courts in deciding many cases that can be diverted to less hostile and costly procedures. Divorce mediation does appear to be a rational alternative attracting considerable interest. It is still in its infancy in the United States and, therefore, along with its promises, it has raised substantial issues. The resolution of these issues will require additional empirical research, experience and dialogue. This chapter has been offered to help explore the promise of family mediation, frame the initial issues and stimulate the dialogue.

NOTES

1. Goldstein, Freud and Solnit. *Before the Best Interests of the Child* (New York: The Free Press, 1979).

2. Mnookin and Kornhauser. "Bargaining in the Shadow of the Law: The Case of Divorce," 88 *Yale L.J.* 950 (1979).

Chapter Fourteen

*Divorce Mediation, Private Legal Practice and Legal Ethics in the U.S.A.**

Richard E. Crouch

Attorney at Law
Arlington, Virginia, U.S.A.

There is no denying that divorce mediation just now has enormous fad appeal. The public is being continually assaulted by articles at varying levels of sophistication extolling mediation as a remedy for the undeniable ills of divorce practice. The number of attorneys entering this lucrative field, and those waiting to enter it, is large. There are no major restrictions to keep large numbers from entering. However profitable for the practitioners, it has the appeal of humanitarianism. Repeating the cliches of the alternative dispute-resolution movement makes all of us feel good.

In reviewing the ethical significance of various aspects of mediation, we should make a careful distinction between court-run mediation or conciliation programs and private profit-making ones. Obviously many of the objections to unconscionable profiteering and financial exploitation of clients would not apply to the public-sector schemes, and these substantially fall outside the scope of this chapter. Also, a distinction must be drawn between the various mediation alternatives offered in the sphere of private legal practice, especially in their varying types of attorney involvement. Some are hardly as susceptible to conflict-of-interest objections if they assume the use of two and three attorneys, for instance. Some schemes contemplate one lawyer representing the "settled" parties to the court in obtaining the divorce, while others use the single lawyer only as a mediator, or only for postmediation legal advice. Another

---

* An article based on this chapter appears in *Family Law Quarterly*, vol. 16, 219–50 (1982).

useful distinction is between those schemes that actually contemplate dual representation in the procurement of the divorce, and those that assume the consented nonrepresentation of one party.

THE ATTRACTIVENESS OF MEDIATION

Obviously, there are reasons for a desperate search for alternatives to the old system, and some of the right ones are as follows:

1. Avoidance of unnecessary hostility and artificial antagonism that can destroy all chances of cooperation in constructing a settlement.
2. A measure of client autonomy in constructing the solutions — which is generally agreed to increase the chances of voluntary adherence to the agreement in future years.
3. Avoiding the traditional two-attorney fight in the settlement process (to say nothing of litigation) — which holds out much promise of reducing costs.

To clients, the appealing features include: (*a*) some consciousness of the reasons given above, (*b*) the prospect of saving money, (*c*) the appeal of preserving client dignity by self-determination ("private ordering"), (*d*) attorney-avoidance and conflict-avoidance (there is obviously much appeal to laying the pertinent matters before a supposedly neutral third party immediately present with the two opponent parties, rather than filtering one's desires through a lawyer who must wrangle with another lawyer over the probabilities of decision by a distant judge who can ultimately, in theory, be appealed to), and (*e*) avoiding the terrors of the courtroom.

Attractiveness to attorneys is reflected in the following considerations:

(*a*) First, there is money in it. Mediation, particularly in a city where there is already a raised mediation consciousness, or high susceptibility to fad appeal generally, is a potential gold mine for lawyers, and especially appealing as the salvation of a flagging, or young and struggling, law practice. If mediation is what the public wants, there are many lawyers who would rather give it to them than send the potential clients on to nonlawyers or — worse yet — the rival lawyer next door. Also, mediation practice feeds on itself geometrically. A mediation is likely to produce a measure of free advertising spread by two satisfied clients, whereas the lawyer who "successfully" litigates a divorce is very lucky if his one client goes away satisfied.

(*b*) Lawyers too are susceptible to fad appeal, and those of a reforming temperament can flatter themselves that they are participating in a proclient and antilawyer movement. If this selfless nobility can be pursued while making good money, the lawyer can flatter himself for being shrewd as well. Certainly the planned cheapening of divorce that reformers contemplate depends on the elimination of at least one lawyer from the business. Boarding the mediation bandwagon provides a hedge against first-purge elimination.

(*c*) The lack of restrictive rules in the mediation business reduces the dangers of transgression — making it a safer business while increasing opportunities.

(*d*) Mediation is easy money. For the family lawyer it spells an end to the rigors of trial practice: there is no uncertainty, no trial preparation, and no chance of losing fights. The tense atmosphere of the courtroom and the unpleasantness of facing an equally skilled professional across the negotiating table are both avoided.

(*e*) There is also the promise of court relief, which indirectly but substantially benefits the attorney. The severe overcrowding of dockets and courtrooms makes any alternative to litigation look inviting. Judges desperate for relief will encourage almost any device that keeps divorce cases out of the courtroom.

There is no question as to the need for a new rule, because the rationalizations of dual representation of divorcing parties that now exist are quite ineffective. That is, they do not honestly and rationally answer the ethical objections posed by existing codes or the general principles of the Kutak code.[1] The business, if legitimate, should proceed under a rule addressing it, and not on the fringes of legality as it does now. However, there is little doubt that any new rule characterized by an appreciable measure of ambiguity will be seized upon and exploited beyond its original intent by partisans interpreting it in less than rigorous good faith. This has been the context of the debate so far, and there is no reason to expect that it will change.

Since its historical preoccupation with precise analysis of moral questions has given the bar a facility for self-criticism, the bar must take especially seriously any challenges to its integrity from outside. The idea persists that it cannot, ethically and in good conscience, oppose any idea that is said to reduce lawyers' income, since opposing it would be economically self-serving. In this sense, the bar is the only group that cannot defend itself.

For similar reasons, skeptical lay reformers are not likely to be persuaded by bar arguments that do in fact happen to operate in a self-serving way. A consumer movement founded on ideas of economic determinism will see institutional greed in any attempt by the bar to question the propriety of various mediation schemes.

Yet there are real dangers which mediation poses to the client population. Dual representation by either lay or legally trained mediators is an invitation to one party's overreaching, and judges and lawyers will have to straighten out the results of mediated agreements that one party discovers cannot be lived with. Bar caution in approval of mediation also warns of the possible economic wastefulness of the process, although this may not be readily apparent to the consumer/client population.

ETHICAL ISSUES RAISED BY MEDIATION SCHEMES

Conflict of Interest in Single-Lawyer "Service" to a Divorcing Couple

Whether any "Representation" is Involved

Obviously the rules concerning representation are not applicable in this context if there is no representation, and no one thinks there is any. Canon 5 of the present code prohibits representing persons with conflicting or potentially differing interests. And though it includes an exception for mediating a dispute, that exception specifically prohibits later court representation by the mediator. Thus the Minnesota Bar Association rejected one mediation scheme which contemplated "impartial advisory attorneys."[2]

Dual Representation, Common Representation, and Mediation

Confusion of terminology has complicated the issue. Obviously there is much difference between mediation as traditionally conceived, service as an intermediary, common representation of coparty litigants, and "dual representation" in divorce. The Kutak Commission Final Draft of a new ethics code confounded all these. Their ideas as to service "as an *intermediary*" are plainly inapplicable to divorce practice, as is the previous law and learning on the subject of intermediary service and coplaintiff or codefendant representation. *Dual representation* contemplates, in its most innocent form, representation by one lawyer to the court of the one desire that warring parties can unite in: their desire for a divorce that incorporates the written agreement they have reached. *Mediation*, as in labour–management conflicts, contemplates each side's presenting their arguments to the other in the presence of a neutral third party who aims at a resolution of the issues that will represent the least detriment to each party.

The present Code of Professional Responsibility (EC 5–20) recognizes that lawyers can serve as "impartial arbitrators or mediators," but does not define these. When the New York City Bar Association stated a very cautious and tentative approval of divorce mediation (Opinion 80-23), it declared that application of labels such as "mediation" and "impartial advice" is dangerous to parties and inconsistent with the current code.

Representing Both or Neither?

Thus the New York City opinion (which does not address the issue of the nature of common representation to the court for uncontested divorce purposes after agreement) held that no representation is involved in mediation and the lawyer must so declare. So did the Boston opinion.[3] Various lawyers and groups engaged in dual representation and mediation rationalize the apparent conflict of their activities with the prohibition of representing opposing parties by saying that both are represented, or that neither is represented. There are instances of separation agreements produced by mediation which recite that each has had independent legal counsel and representation — which turned out to mean that the mediator "was the independent legal counsel and representation for both of us." Oddly, the Kutak Commission draft seemed to say that the mediator represents both parties, but then went on to speak of a situation in which they are not represented to a third entity such as a court, but have their views professionally represented to each other by the "intermediary."

The Boston Bar (Opinion 78-1), and the Oregon State Bar (Opinion 79-46) concluded that mediation activities were proper because neither client is represented. The New York City Bar opinion agrees. Silberman argues that the difference between these and the Kutak conception is "only a semantic one." In that evaluation either the "semantic" or the "only" must be questioned. The difference is a loaded and dangerous one.

The Maryland State Bar opinion (Opinions 80-55A, 78-25), pointed up the real difference between representation and mediation, where in the latter, "the attorney-client relationship does not necessarily exist and, while honesty would remain a fundamental duty . . . , loyalty would not. The attorney mediator, like the lay mediator, . . . has no particular . . . duty to give legal advice." It should be noted that the Coogler system,[4] and the Ohio and Virginia Bar rulings, contemplate only one party's being represented in the divorce proceedings that follow mediation, with the other party consenting to being unrepresented.

What Exactly Would "Representation" Be?

Does it include advice that benefits one party to the detriment of the other? Presumably so. The question that naturally arises is, what happens when the attorney-mediator sees one party being "disadvantaged" in negotiations? If the mediator cannot advise one party to break off mediation without hurting the interests of the one who is gaining by mediation, then a real conflict-of-interests problem seems to arise. Obviously the definitions of benefit and detriment in this context are infinitely debatable and presumably framed by the preliminary assumption that a fair, compromised and conflict-avoiding settlement is the desire of both.

Perhaps the similar question of what the mediator does when he perceives what is, by his definition at least, actual exploitation, is an easier one, but it still poses these difficulties. Mediation is a device which can facilitate exploitation by a shrewder or otherwise dominant party, and the underlying ideological premise that all issues are subject to compromise can, in rare cases, require an irrational compromise with something quite close to unmitigated evil and quite far from justice as the majority of reasonable people would define it.

The Maryland Bar opinion found as to the representation of both opponents to the court in preparing and presenting a postmediation written separation agreement that "such a preparation is likely to place the attorney in a position where he senses a conflict of interest." Silberman comments that since characterization of the lawyer who does post-mediation advice and drafting as providing representation "seems to pose Canon 5 difficulties, it might be more helpful" to say that he or she represents neither. She also notes that both the Boston and the Portland opinions found legal advice an important part of mediation.

The Role of Disavowals

Though the idea of representation by mediation persists, what consensus there seems to be among existing ethics opinions calls for express advice to the parties that representation is not taking place. The New York City opinion so requires, as do the Boston and Portland opinions.

However, the efficacy of disavowals like this is always questionable. The Maryland authorities warned that they would not consider proper the actions of an attorney who takes referrals automatically from lay mediators, fails to determine independently the interests of the parties, and "mechanically recites a litany of legal rights and obligations of the parties topped off with a written separation agreement." However, it is highly likely that this is an accurate characterization of exactly what will happen.

Abstract Representation Rationalizations

For as long as dual representation has been around, long antedating the mediation fad, some lawyers have rationalized the compromising of adversary loyalty by saying that they "represent the whole family" when doing this. That rationalization has been rejected as untenable since the family is an abstraction incapable of being a client. (Perhaps a better articulation would be in terms of its being a number of individuals whose interests might at any point diverge.) An excellent *reductio ad absurdum* is provided in the Maryland Bar opinion passing on the ethics of the "structured mediation" system.

Often lawyers involved in a custody dispute try to say that they "represent the child." But obviously the child is not paying any lawyer's fee, and at least some residual loyalty to the client who actually is paying the fee would necessarily compromise that supposed child-centred representation, should interests begin to diverge. At least, an adult paying client whose lawyer is, instead, representing the child would be no match for an opponent whose lawyer is wholeheartedly representing that opponent. Thus the child-representation rationale appears more or less untenable.[5]

Perhaps the most offensive formulation is that of the Kutak Commission's Professor Hazard — and doubtless others — who have suggested that a lawyer can be paid by the parties to "represent the situation."[6] In fact, this concept did not originate with Professor Hazard, or even with some mid-twentieth century theorist enamored of the term "situation eithics." It dates back at least to the turn of the century. When Supreme Court Justice Louis D. Brandeis twice found himself in legal difficulties as a result of having represented opposing parties, he invoked the concept in self-defense, but Frank,[7] opines that "counsel for the situation" was "one of the most unfortunate phrases he ever casually uttered." In fact, Frank adds that "if I may share a purely personal lesson, the greatest caution to be gained from study of the Brandeis record is, never be 'counsel for a situation'. A lawyer is constantly confronted with conflict which he is frequently urged to somehow try to work out. I have never attempted this without wishing I had not, and I have given up attempting it." Those practitioners who have had experience with the dishonesty into which real estate conveyancing work inspired by this concept is under constant pressure to descend, will understand this well.

It might be useful if authorities expressly rejected the "situational" terminology. This could be done without rejecting any other aspect of the mediation proposals.

The Coogler "independent advisory attorney" scheme[8] that was more or less rejected by the Minnesota and the Maryland authorities does partake of this idea to some extent. The "independent advisory attorney" is also a person whose continued membership in the potentially lucrative mediation referral panel may depend on his not throwing roadblocks in the way of the flow of settlements.

The "Mere Scrivener" Theory

A comfortable way to view dual representation of the opposing parties in a divorce is to say that the lawyer only serves as an amanuensis, or notary in the European sense, who is educated enough to "put into legal language" the parties' common intentions once their thoughts have been straightened out and agreement reached in mutual discussion. There are difficulties with this rationalization, however, as the Maryland opinion pointed out. It said that "if the preparation of a property settlement agreement in mediation can be equated to filling in blanks on forms, then the services of an attorney are probably not necessary," but that if it requires "a professional choice of what language best expresses intent and any expression of opinion on what promotes the best interests of the clients and is not unjust to one or the other," then the preparation is likely to create conflict of interest.

Obviously there are more difficulties if the mere scrivener is also the mediator. Avoiding these difficulties by sending the parties to two professionals in succession is a remedy, but one that adds to the expense, thus making the idea of mediation as a cost-saving alternative something of an illusion, if not something of a fraud.

As long as the "service" in question is called representation of both, the New York City Bar opinion considers it improper for a lawyer to act as the mere scrivener, regardless of consent. The rule the opinion sets forth declares that "lawyers may provide impartial legal advice and assist in reducing parties' agreement to writing only where the lawyer fully explains all pertinent considerations and alternatives and the consequences to each party of choosing the resolution agreed upon." The Maryland opinion explains how impossible it is for lawyers to "draft neutrally," that a lawyer-draftsman contributes nothing but the advancement of an individual interest, and that parties who want neutral drafting can do it themselves. Thus the idea persists that it is impossible for a lawyer ethically to act as less than a lawyer by providing these "scrivener" services without legal advice.

Thus the Boston Bar opinion also contemplates the attorney-mediator drawing the separation agreement but doing much more. This lawyer also is barred from providing representation of either party in later judicial proceedings. The Oregon lawyer who drafts the agreement is required to advise both parties to get independent counsel to review it.

What the Ohio and Virginia opinions seem to permit is the lawyer's allowing the parties to reach agreement, serving as a scrivener to formalize the understanding, and then representing *one party* while the other consents to being unrepresented. Thus the "mere scrivener" concept itself differs considerably according to whom one asks. The Coogler concept has the "impartial advisory attorney" serving as more than a scrivener, but hardly escaping ethical problems inherent in advising two antagonists. Thus the Maryland Bar Association refused to approve the concept.

Awkwardness of Postagreement Advice or Representation

Assuming the attorney sought out for advice after mediation was not himself the mediator, there still are problems. As Silberman notes, what clients are primarily seeking when they consult a lawyer after mediation is advice on whether the compromises each made were "intelligent and proper," or whether the settlement was reasonable as to each. It should be noted that these are not the same concerns each party brings to mediation itself.

Advice

Thus the Maryland opinion found the postmediation "impartial advisory attorney" concept embodied in the "structured mediation" theory dangerously unworkable, while the Minnesota opinion rejected it altogether. The Virginia opinion imposes limits on the concept as noted above. The Maryland warning about "mechanical recitation," noted above, is probably an accurate characterization of what will happen most of the time.

Representation

The authorities are radically divided on whether postagreement common representation should be permissible. Without it, of course, mediation is less likely to represent a major reduction in the cost of a divorce. The existing Code of Professional Responsibility (EC 5-20) bars it. The Boston Bar opinion contemplates an attorney-mediator drawing the separation agreement but not being allowed to represent either party in court, and the Oregon and New York opinions forbid the involved lawyers representing either party. As conceived by the Virginia and Ohio opinions, the common attorney represents one party in presenting the agreement and divorce pleadings to the court while the other goes unrepresented. The California case, *Klemm v. Superior Court*,[9] hints at a permissible dual representation in the divorce court for those who have worked out an agreement with the common attorney's help.

Representation if the Mediating Effort Fails — Disqualification

There seems to be little disagreement among the authorities that a lawyer who has participated in the mediation effort, or postmediation advice, should not represent one party if negotiations break down. This problem was treated in *Comden v. Superior Court*.[10] The Coogler system accepts this limitation, as shown in the form waiver/agreement with an "impartial advisory attorney."[11] This problem is of course avoided by an ethical rule that bars any postmediation representation by the involved lawyer even if settlement survives. This includes the New York and Oregon rulings.

However, the theories that contemplate the lawyer-mediator, common legal advisor/draftsman, and postmediation legal representative being two or even three different attorneys will be met with the objection that this is hardly a scheme designed to save clients money: ethical caution that is misunderstood by a public unschooled in the philosophical subtleties underlying legal ethics, and by those lawyers who themselves do not accept or understand them, is likely to raise the objection that such quibbling scruples are lawyer featherbedding in disguise.

The question is whether the bar should insist on no representation even absent breakdown. The ban on representation in agreed cases does not serve the same end as the ban on post-breakdown representation. However, it does serve at least two purposes: First, it precludes confusion of attorney and mediator roles, and can help assure that when an attorney is a mediator, he behaves like one; also, it serves to present an unprecedented increase in attorney power. Absent such a restriction, the lawyer will be the sole architect of the divorcing parties' entire settlement. In that position he will be tempted to ignore or minimize whatever difficulties arise because he has so much at stake. The difficulties of postagreement common representation are one more reason why there should be a warning to clients that this, like mediation and like common advice, is not what you traditionally pay an attorney for: it is a new kind of service designed to save the client money. In my opinion, exactly these words should be required.

The question whether prohibiting the dual representation that mediation and similar reform schemes contemplate amounts to institutional overreaching is a very real one. Not only the mediation-movement propaganda, but the resulting bar opinions, have wrestled with it. Hardly any popular or lawyer-audience article about mediation appears that does not mention clients' desperate need for an alternative. Thus, such opinions as the New York and the Ohio Bar rulings end up stating all the reasons why various elements of the mediation schemes present severe ethical dangers, and then say that it is nevertheless hard to believe that such a popular and needed alternative could be ethically barred.

Division II of the New York opinion[12] says that "ethical aspirations which recognize a lawyer's duty to assist the public . . . make it inconceivable to us that the code would deny the public the availability of nonadversary legal assistance in the resolution of divorce disputes."

In Ohio, which has a "dissolution of marriage" procedure allowing joint petitions, the state bar ethics committee's Informal Opinion No. 30[13] sets forth a very subtle and cogent analysis of why a lawyer attempting dual representation in dissolution of marriage must encounter irreconcilable conflict of interest, and declares that a lawyer cannot represent both spouses without violating the existing Code of Professional Responsibility. It nevertheless concludes by conceding that since the new dissolution process was designed "to avoid some of the usual adversary relationships in an action for divorce" and since most parties "may not choose to be represented by individual lawyers," a lawyer can represent one party and prepare the separation agreement with full waiver by the other side.

There is little question that lawyer scruples appear hypocritical to the public since the mystique of the profession has been demolished in recent decades. A public encouraged by many lawyer-reformers to think of themselves as "consumers" of "services" rather than clients of an advisor-advocate tends to look at all lawyer rationalizations of professional caution with a suspicious eye. Clients seldom appreciate a lawyer's scruples in forgoing any kind of representation (and its financial rewards) for conflict-of-interest reasons — especially if the whole fee from Day One is not to be refunded. It sounds like bad faith, a glaring example of economic determinism, and an indefensible featherbedding rule upheld by the chummy bonds of the bar's old-boy network when a couple are told that they must get two or three lawyers to do what appears to them to be a single job.

Obviously if present practices are to be defended, a vigorous public education effort is needed. An article in the Harvard Law Review[14] notes that "in cases in which the need for separate counsel is not readily apparent, public confidence can be diminished by an insistence upon additional attorneys; such insistence may serve only to generate public suspicion that the real motivation is the legal profession's self interest." Probably one of the last defenses of the other view was *Florida Bar v. Teitelman*,[15] concerning real estate conveyancing, which declared that "the profession's image and standing are more important than the expediency which supposedly demands mass production procedures."

Three-Attorney Requirement?

Aside from the question whether the lawyer inside the mediation system can juggle the four roles of mediator, advisor, draftsman and litigation representative without splitting into two or more persons, there is the question whether the work of the "inside" lawyer or lawyers must be supplemented by that of two outside lawyers — the real advisor-advocates for each individual party. Of course, requiring three lawyers not only means more expense, but may well undermine agreements already reached so as to cause expensive wasted effort, as the Boston Bar opinion and the Silberman article observed. Thus Silberman does not consider this method, which remains adversarial, "a real alternative" to present practices.[16] Mediation experiments with lowered expectations avoid some of the obvious difficulties in this way, however. Virtually all of the ethics rulings require the participating lawyer to advise both parties of the advantages of seeking independent legal counsel. This offers room for some form of mediation without raising most of the above-noted ethical difficulties. The introduction of a supposedly skilled and supposedly objective third party who gets to see both individuals before the judge does and without their counsel might still serve to accelerate settlement in some cases, but obviously this tends to limit mediation not under court auspices to those wealthier couples who can afford to pay several professionals.

Whether There is Always, Necessarily, an Unacceptably High Level of Conflict in the Divorce Situation

According to many authorities, the traditional view has been that representing both spouses is entirely prohibited because of the inextricable adversariness inherent in the situation. The Maryland State Bar Association expressed this view at one time, although it qualified it in its 1980 opinion.[17] It has been considered to lie outside the exceptions that the existing Code of Professional Responsibility provides for mediation or common representation with informed consent. An additional problem is the willingness of some writers to confuse such common representation of coparties having potentially conflicting interests with dual representation of opponents.

Legal scholars tend to make a distinction between "actual and potential" conflict of interest.[18] Is this an irrelevant distinction here, or, indeed, is it a very apt one, requiring us to face the fact that divorcing spouses are opponents, with the advancement of one's interests necessarily diminishing those of the other?[19] Though their desires may coincide on the sole issue of divorce itself, mediation necessarily involves many more issues. For the view that the divorce situation, however amicable the parties, necessarily presents too much conflict of interest for simultaneous representation, see Florida, Maryland, Massachusetts, New York and Ohio opinions.[20] The Ohio ethics opinion[21] declares the same view, but then adds that since no-fault reform statutes aim at dissolution of a marriage without "some of the usual adversary relationships," the lawyer can properly represent one party while the other waives representation. The problem, as described in the Maryland opinion is that the lawyer who sees one party being disadvantaged cannot speak up and terminate the mediation without damaging the interests of the one who is prevailing.

Attorney as Judge of his own Cause

The New York opinion's solution to all this is to say that the attorney must keep especially alert and be especially sensitive to evidence that one party is being disadvantaged — particularly by unfair exploitation on the other's part. This not only assumes a great deal about the lawyer's sensitivity to these concerns, and places great moral responsibility on his or her conscience, but also assumes scrupulous and rigorous honesty on the part of all mediating lawyers. However, assuming even a bit less of this last quality, one must worry about the desire of the lawyer and the mediation shop which referred the couple to him to see the mediation go through at all costs. In this sense, making the lawyer a judge of his own cause — although arguably lawyers' eithics codes do so, and have to do so, in many instances — is ill-advised. The New York opinion says in its introduction that although it concludes that "there are some situations... where ... dangers ... to the interests of the parties are so great that it is entirely inappropriate for a lawyer to participate in mediation or to attempt to give impartial legal advice," a lawyer who recognizes such a case in progress will realize that his participation may be prejudicial to the administration of justice. The rules the New York opinion sets forth are supposed to help him make that determination.

Also, the assumption that the lawyer can always solve problems by bowing out is perhaps a naive one. The parties who invest their time and money, emotions and energies in a mediation lose something when forced to begin over again with another lawyer even if (as we assume they will understand) they avoid something worse. The "investment" factor operates much the same as it does in real estate conveyancing. (That is, a purchaser-couple who have invested time, worry and money in getting close to settlement on a real estate purchase will do almost anything to avoid forfeiting it. This fear of "losing the house" is shamefully exploited.) The ethically scrupulous lawyer will be aware of the existing investment in a divorce mediation. Thus the Ohio opinion notes that "the lawyer ... would be materially shackled in any effort to obtain the information essential to a truly professional performance" from the parties.

WAIVER AND ITS DIFFICULTIES

Consent of the parties has always been assumed to be the answer to the ethical difficulties posed by attempting to serve both sides of a marital dispute. However, it has long been held by a number of authorities that because there is severe "actual conflict" of interests, rather than just "potential conflict," consents in the divorce area are not valid, or are perpetually retractable after the fact.[22]

Principally, the problem seems to be that of obtaining a consent that is sufficiently informed. For an informed consent, the attorney has to have made full disclosure of the important facts and considerations, and the person waiving the right of independent representation has to understand all of these. It has been observed that a valid consent could only be procured after the advice of an *additional* lawyer *who does not* have any conflict of interest.

As for the adequacy of explanation, it is hard to see how the client can fully, or even adequately, understand the subtle forces involved in this conflict of interest without at least having had three years of law school, if not several years of law practice.

Especially in a climate of defensive practice, it would seem that a prudent attorney has to adopt an attitude requiring so full an explanation and so severe a warning that reconsideration and withdrawal of the request really is likely to follow. In other words, a warning so honestly and conscientiously given that it will be effective, and achieve its ostensible purpose, overcoming any subtextual promediation message. The client can hardly be said to have waived exposure to dangers of which he or she is ignorant. Assuming such waivers can be effective, they would seem to have to take the form of agreements at the very outset between the lawyer and each party so that if the lawyer sees something unfair, the lawyer is not going to blow the whistle. However, the theory with which most clients go into this would seem to be a very different one: that one of the mediator's main purposes is to referee or police the negotiations to see that fair play is observed.

Expressing these fears is somewhat akin to admitting the suspicion that there will be no such thing as "simple uncontested divorce" if a party's attorney does a thorough and conscientious job. Of course that brings one immediately back to the often-expressed view that amicable divorces can "go along smoothly enough until the lawyers get involved." It cannot be denied that when the profession is at its most scrupulously ethical it sacrifices some public confidence in seeming to require a procedure that exacerbates adversary bitterness while lining lawyers' pockets. The lawyer operating in the defensive practice context will always try to secure an ironclad waiver and "get it in writing," but at least the Maryland Bar opinion has said that this is a conflict of interest that written waiver cannot eliminate.

At least one question we should answer is whether, in order for there to have been a valid waiver, the lawyer must have informed each client individually what is the best financial result he or she could expect from a court fight and the best result to be expected from a prelitigation settlement with full discovery, certain pressure tactics, and at least some wrangling.

MILITANT CONSUMERISM AS A FACTOR IN THE DEBATE

The desire to use mediation as a means of saving divorce litigants from unnecessary expense as well as unnecessary acrimony has long been a factor in mediationist rhetoric.

Suddenly, mediation is hotly desired by the prudent consumer of legal "services" approaching divorce — notwithstanding that much mediation as now practiced appears to be every bit as expensive as legal services in the same case, in a competent divorce lawyer's hands, would be. Advertisements and propaganda assume mediation to be ideal for at least 99 percent of the divorce cases. A lawyer — or the entire profession — may be accused of dishonest fee-milking tactics for counselling against mediation. (And yet the same lawyer might be accused of bad-faith profiteering when participating in a mediation scheme that drags discussions out beyond the time and dollar cost of swift and efficient divorce work in a relatively amicable case.)

It is certain that consumerist rhetoric depends on the existence of entirely "simple, uncontested" divorces, and that there is a danger (noted above) of such simplicity falling apart when either lawyer does a scrupulous, honest and professional job. Most "consumers" are surprised to find that the simple uncontested divorce does not include one involving property or children, and they regard this revelation as part of a bait-and-switch advertising scheme.

The lawyer's actions in mediation, dual representation, and other cost-saving schemes stand a good chance of later being labeled a sell-out by dissatisfied "customers." This is because the "customer" hardly ever fully appreciates how much he is being asked to waive. The supposed "consumer" of "services" really wants the traditional loyalty and adversary advocacy that lawyering has always imported in the public's mind. He wants to get a good deal on "services" as a consumer, but also wants the almost-mystical formation of a patron-client relationship. The important questions are whether the adversary system can ever be abolished, or even diminished, and lawyers still stay involved — and then whether that can be done in a climate of "defensive practice."

Possible Misuse of the Process; Financial Exploitation of Clients

Unwarranted Prolongation — Adding Unnecessary Layers

There is certainly some question whether mediation in many cases is indeed swifter or cheaper than either litigation, or traditional separation-agreement negotiation in the shadow of litigation. A partial answer of course is that some mediation clients know this and do not want swifter or cheaper processing. Another is that even if the process takes longer, the courts get more agreed cases not needing to go to trial. Sometimes it does mean sending battered parties back into the ring for another dull, grim round of stressful combat that is, if success is the avoidance of eventual litigation, doomed to failure with these particular parties. There may be cases where the traditional mechanism would be not only quicker and cheaper, but less stressful. One factual question is the extent to which it is just those cases that mediation tends to get.

A policy question is whether, and to what extent, attorneys offering or advising mediation should be required to evaluate these factors and warn parties about them.

Facilitating Exploitation of One Party

The fear is sometimes expressed that imperfect human mediators, stepping into a godlike role in the process, are deceived into allowing, and even contributing to, the unconscionable exploitation of the weaker by the dominant party. (In the unfathomable subtleties of long-standing marital relationships, this dominant party can even be the one who appears the weaker party, and even trained observers can be fooled for at least an appreciable length of time.) Also, an attorney or attorney-mediator can go to unwarranted lengths to preserve the "simple uncontested divorce" from breaking down, and this movement can be in the direction of allowing exploitation.

From a lawyer's viewpoint it seems likely that ignorance of what a court would do nearly always operates to one party's benefit and the other's detriment. This is still true, even if it is both who are ignorant.

What the attorney does in the face of overreaching, too-aggressive bargaining, deceit or coercion is not as simple a question as it might appear. Supposedly, he or she sounds the alarm and alerts the victim and curbs the transgressor. However, what is overreaching may be such a subjective question that the lawyer has, or should have, real doubts about curbing that which in fairness should not be curbed. These might be tactics which are only the full and free expression of deep feelings that mediation supposedly allows, or the advancement of substantively "unfair" proposals — all of which needs to be seen in the light of what a court would do. What is "unfair" in a property-dividing state might not be so unfair in a non-property-dividing state, for instance.

The mediator also has to ask just what is client self-determination and autonomy in the spirit of what has been called "private ordering." If one person wishes to be a doormat (perhaps for the sake of a quick exit from the marriage, or for less obvious reasons), is it proper for the mediator to let that person do it? Such a person's reasons might include a very real and deep distaste for even mediation-flavored divorce negotiation, which the other party and the mediator, by reason of their temperament, do not share — or even understand.

It must take the wisdom of Solomon to know what to do in most situations if the fairness one strives for is imperfectly defined. The mediator who knows exactly when to bow out and call a halt to the cooperative effort is still disadvantaging in that way the one party who was profiting the most by letting mediation go on. It is sometimes a very subtle judgment on the mediator's part to say whether, and when, mediation has "broken down."

There is also the tainted objectivity of the mediator-umpire whose stake in "successful" mediations would make him very reluctant to cut off the process too early. One of the great advantages to lawyers is the doubled "living advertisement" factor. Someone may be influenced to produce a compromise against justice and against reason because he is reluctant to jeopardize mediation by telling one party "you are just selfish and there is nothing more to this case." Nor is panel membership likely to last long for a lawyer who finds mediation unsuitable in over half of his cases.

Obviously if the attorney, either as mediator or as postmediation advisor, will be advising the couple what would happen in court or in non-face-to-face negotiations without mediation, there is a real danger of misrepresenting these potentials to one side unless the attorney is exhaustively thorough. It is also arguable that an adequate explanation is not possible unless the attorney sees each person separately for this purpose.

One wonders what happens when the attorney, in giving his initial advice, perceives that, as will frequently be the case, mediation is a much better alternative for one party than the other. Is he obliged to say that, or to keep it a secret? Will the comparative picture somehow always show mediation to be best for the couple?

The Maryland Bar opinion puts it quite simply: "if it appears to the attorney involved in mediation that one client is benefiting from the mediation while the other is being prejudiced, the attorney is placed in an untenable situation." The opinion points out that he cannot advise one client to terminate mediation "without adversely affecting the interests of the other," and that "despite this conflict, the attorney cannot keep silent without violating his obligation of loyalty." The Boston Bar opinion mentioned the problem of commitments having been made without the benefit of legal advice which then perpetuate a situation of unequal bargaining power.

The Mediation Shop as a Source of Ordinary Divorce Business

Though attorneys' solicitation of paying business can no longer be regulated the way it once was, some controls presumably remain. There is no question that many lawyers' motivation for getting into mediation or forming links with mediation operations is the potential for increasing business-as-usual in divorce work.

The New York opinion ended by warning that attorney participation must conform to DR 2-103(D)(4), which was drafted mainly to regulate closed-panel prepaid legal insurance plans. It opined that mediation businesses would not run afoul of those provisions particularly directed to the insurance plans and inapplicable to mediation. However, the first section of the DR — requiring that the organization involved derive no profits from the rendition of legal services — is worth noting. The New York opinion also says that to conform to the Disciplinary Rule, the lawyer "must not initiate or promote the divorce mediation program for the primary purpose of providing financial or other benefit to the lawyer" and "the purpose of the program must not be to procure legal work or financial benefit for lawyers — outside of the legal services program of the organization." Also, the clients must be free to select counsel other than those furnished or selected by the program. The last condition may pose some difficulty for mediation programs of the "structured" sort, which in some cases can apparently leave clients with no choice of lawyer. At the very least, the "structured mediation" programs draw from a very restricted panel because of the substantial amount of extra service and extra training required of the participating lawyers.

Among the constitutional limitations on bar regulation of solicitation practices are the rules of U.S. Supreme Court cases such as *United Mine Workers v. Illinois State Bar Association*,[23] *Brotherhood of Railroad Trainmen v. Virginia*,[24] and *NAACP v. Button*.[25] These cases are being invoked by mediation proponents, but even they are careful not to exempt "nonprofit" lay organizations founded by the lawyer only as a means of increasing his private business. Actually, it is likely that this is exactly what will happen with many mediation operations, and that a number of eager lawyers will disregard this detail, and find themselves in bar disciplinary proceedings.

As for the existing DR 2-103(D), Silberman suggests[26] that it "should not even be applicable to mediation programs" because it "clearly was not designed with divorce mediation in mind." The Virginia Bar ruled, in fact,[27] that a mediation centre does not fall within any of the above freedom-of-association exceptions to DR 2-103(D). Silberman calls for geographical bar/bar association sponsorship of all mediation shops as a resolution. This obviously is not what exists today.

The Maryland opinion raised the danger of a lawyer being influenced by the desire of the mediation centre "to see that the mediation process is prosecuted to fulfillment if he believes that the mediation process is working against the interests of one, or both of the clients." Acknowledging the problems of complying with DR 2-103(D) and DR 5-107(B), Silberman's answer is that "lawyers participating in mediation projects must be conscious of the sensitive nature of their role, but legal ethics committees must recognize their responsibilities in permitting experimentation within reasonable limits and with appropriate safeguards."

All of this suggests that any new rule which would allow mediation participation by lawyers should include firm warnings against this danger. Such a rule should not hesitate to make plain that it is unconscionable profiteering from mediation, compromising the independence and integrity of the lawyer with results detrimental to the client victims, that the organized bar is worried about. We may not be able to provide the desirable bright-line test, but there can still be a standard that a flagrant profiteer could be accused of violating.

Over/Under-Advocacy Evaluated by Hindsight: Defensive Practice

The effect of defensive practice pressures on the search for alternative dispute resolution strategies has yet to be very helpfully measured. The phrase "defensive practice" contemplates not so much a scrupulous caution in compliance with the bar's ethical rules as a pursuit of every phase of a case's prosecution with a wary eye to the possibilities of client second-guessing in a malpractice litigation context. The deepest difficulty presented is that defensive practice, as it has evolved in the light of some of the more notorious malpractice judgments in recent years[28] rests on the assumption of complete financial greed, undiluted by any moral, emotional or public-policy factors, on the part of each individual spouse. Mediation theory and practice, on the hand, seem to rest heavily on the assumption of just such a dilution. Mediation theory is actually closer to the long-standing traditions of domestic relations practice in this respect, since they were based to a considerable degree on the assumption of a decidedly different character of divorce-related advocacy. Defensive practice is also inconsistent with the swift and efficient production of divorces to minimize client expense and emotional strain.

Thus it is interesting that the New York Bar opinion in its review of the previous Oregon and Boston opinions characterizes them as recognizing "inequalities in bargaining power," along with "the potential for misunderstandings and later recrimination against the lawyer," and as concluding "nevertheless" and "with considerable reluctance" that a lawyer may undertake divorce mediation and the provision of impartial legal assistance after disavowing representation and obtaining consent.[29]

The entire passage is phrased like a very reluctant conclusion against one's better judgment.

If bar groups feel that, in endorsing experimentation with mediation at all, they are necessarily rejecting the defensive-practice assumption noted above, then they could do great service to the bar and public by saying so.

Mediation-Panel Membership and Lay-Control Rule

The New York opinion and Silberman's article posed a number of questions in this category and then failed to answer all of them. The lay-control questions are similar to and intertwined with the private-business-funnel, or profiteering, questions, and arise from the fact that First-Amendment organizations' exception from the prohibitions of the disciplinary rules are conditioned on nonprofit status, innocence of foundation motive, not functioning as a source of billable lawyer work, independence of the lawyer-client relationship from the organization, and complete freedom of the client to choose lawyers.

However, the gravamen of the rule against lay control of the laywer-client relationship is prevention of the compromise of essential loyalty — the danger that the independence of the lawyer's professional judgment on behalf of and advice to the client will be tainted by motives of loyalty to the organization. And the indications are that that is exactly what will happen. The dynamics of the mediation-panel relationship would seem to constitute the very evil that the rule against lay control was invented for, so that the current mediation-shop arrangements come squarely within the prohibitions of the rule. Lawyers will tend to approve of and defend mediation because they do not want to lose this source of business, but to date it would seem that the rationalizations have been imperfect. It should be noted that the Virginia ethics opinion concluded that a Coogler-inspired mediation centre could not bring its attorney-panel scheme within any of the exceptions to the DR 2-103(D) prohibition.

Then too, the Coogler plan's provision for involuntary selection of an attorney if there is no agreement on the attorney would seem to be an obvious violation of that rule.[30] The Maryland Bar rejected the Coogler method's provision for involuntary selection of a lawyer absent agreement.

Silberman recognizes the problems and finally ends up simply by recommending that some safeguards should be devised and that problems might be eliminated if panel referral is entirely under the auspices of local bar associations. This is hardly an answer; the mediation industry will not accept it and the geographical bar associations, with some exceptions, are not eager to set up mediation programs.

Closed-panel plans are something the mediation industry will not be at all happy to give up. They are important to the basic goals of the movement, because they contemplate assurance that the lawyer participating in or coming close to mediation has interdisciplinary training and is indeed something more than just a lawyer.

There may be no easy solution to these problems, but we should not let it appear that we have ignored them.

NOTES

1. This refers to the proposed Model Rules of Professional Conduct, June 30, 1982, considered for adoption by the voluntary but influential American Bar Association at its 1982 Annual Meeting and again at its 1983 Midyear Meeting. They were drafted by a special commission chaired by Robert Kutak, and are designed for eventual adoption by the supreme bar-disciplinary authorities of the various American states, which have final authority over American law practice. The existing codes include the last such ethics code adopted by the ABA in hopes of state emulation, the Code of Professional Responsibility, which was adopted by all the states within a few years of ABA promulgation, and the many variants which have been produced by years of individual state amendment of that code. Some states have recently undertaken such sweeping revisions of the local amended CPR that they have declared an intent to ignore utterly the ABA reform effort this time.
2. See Silberman, "Professional Responsibility Problems of Divorce Mediation," 7 Fam. Law Rep. 4,001, 4,007. (See same for further references to Silberman in this chapter.)
3. See 5 Fam. Law Rep. 2,606.
4. See Coogler, O.J., *Structured Mediation in Divorce Settlements*. Lexington: D.C. Heath and Co., 1978.
5. See its rejection in *Pelham v. Greisheimer,* 417 N.E. 2d 882, 7 Fam. Law Rep. 2,403.
6. Hazard, G., *Ethics and the Practice of Law.* New Haven: Yale University Press, 1978; see also Hagy, "Simultaneous Representation: Transaction Resolution in the Adversary System," 28 *Case W. Res L.R.* 86 (1977).
7. Frank, "The Legal Ethics of Louis D. Brandeis," 17 *Stan. L.R.* 683, 702, 708 (1965).
8. The "impartial advisory attorney" is a key person in the rigidly prescribed scheme of divorce mediation conceived by American lawyer O.J. Coogler and set forth in his book *Structured Mediation in Divorce Settlement* (1978), at 25, 27, and 85–92. The parties must agree to employ this lawyer together, and to consult no other lawyer while the mediation is going on.
9. 7 Cal. App. 3d 893, 142 Cal. Rptr. 509 (1977), 4 Fam. Law Rep. 2,185, 2,245.
10. 20 Cal. 3d 906, 145 Cal. Rptrs. 5, 576 P. 2d 971 (1978).
11. Coogler, *op. cit.* 192.
12. 7 Fam. Law Rep. 3,097, 3,099.
13. 1 Fam. Law Rep. 3,109.
14. "Developments in the Law — Conflicts of Interest in the Legal Profession," 94 *Harv. L.R.* 1,244, 1,310.

15. 261 So. 2d 140, 142–3 (Fla. 1972).
16. 7 Fam. Law Rep. 4,003.
17. See also the California, West Virginia, Florida and Ohio ethics opinions cited in Hagy, note 6 above, at 95.
18. See 94 *Harv. L.R.* 1,310–1; *Klemm v. Superior Court,* 75 C.A. 3d 897, 142 Cal. Rptrs. 509, 4 Fam. Law Rep. 2,185.
19. See Donald J. MacDougall, Chapter 2 of this volume.
20. Cited in 94 *Harv. L.R.* 1,311, note 132, and see additional opinions cited by Silberman, (note 2 above) at 12.
21. 1 Fam. Law Rep. 3,109.
22. See 94 *Harv. L.R.* 1,244, 1,310 ("Client consent will not legitimize such blatantly conflict-ridden representation").
23. 389 U.S. 217 (1967).
24. 377 U.S. 1 (1964).
25. 371 U.S. 415 (1963).
26. 7 Fam. Law Rep. at 4,008.
27. Opinion of 10 June, 1980; 7 Fam. Law Rep. 2,188.
28. See, e.g., *Smith v. Lewis,* 530 P.2d 589, 1 Fam. Law Rep. 2,265 (Calif. 1975) and *McCarty v. McCarty,* 7 Fam. Law Rep. 3,079 (1981).
29. 7 Fam. Law Rep. 3,097, 3,098.
30. Coogler, *op. cit.* 119.

Chapter Fifteen

Arbitration and Mediation of Disputes Involving Children and Matrimonial Property in Canada

Alastair Bissett-Johnson

Dalhousie University, Halifax, Canada

INTRODUCTION

On breakdown of marriage, a number of issues typically arise. These include the need for (i) a decree of dissolution, (ii) some division of matrimonial assets, (iii) a solution to questions of custody of and access to children, (iv) orders for spousal or child support, and (v) the proper interpretation of written separation agreements[1] or marriage contracts.[2]

It has been the almost universal experience that "adversarial court proceedings," even when tempered with "inquisitorial overtones," do not provide an ideal forum for the resolution of these issues. As Henry Finlay remarked of the schizophrenia of the traditional court model:

> It presupposes a conflict and implies a contest between the parties. Nevertheless, it was always recognized that other interests were also at stake, *viz*. The interests of the children of a marriage and, in a general sense, of society as a whole, since its framework was said to rest upon the family. These latter considerations forced upon the courts a vigilant function, to discharge which the framework of the *lis inter partes* was maintained, even where the parties might have been entirely *ad idem* and might have preferred to proceed by consent and even to have the matter out of the hands of the courts altogether.[3]

Legislators and lawyers alike have cast around for alternatives to the traditional court process. This article examines the sort of alternatives to the court process that have been provided for, and considers whether Canadian lawyers are likely to find them attractive for their clients and whether they are more suited to some rather than others of the four traditional aspects of breakdown of marriage.

The types of procedure for extrajudicial dispute resolution vary.

Conciliation and Mediation

Here, in its purest form, the mediator essentially attempts to bring the parties together to arrive at their own decision. The mediator does not make a binding judgment and court proceedings, as a possibility at a later stage, still exist. In its pure form the hope is that by being "off the record," a more flexible nonconfrontational approach may be adopted by the parties to the mediation. One might term this conciliation. The prime role of the conciliation is to help the parties to find areas in which they are prepared to compromise. In a variation of the pure form the mediator may make a report which the parties are free to make use of in subsequent legal proceedings though the report is not legally binding. If the report is by a distinguished behavioural scientist, it may be of considerable value to the party in whose favour it lies, and since the party against whom it lies agreed to the choice of mediator, it may be difficult for him subsequently to argue against the mediator's recommendation. If the mediator is professionally qualified in one of the medical or medical-related sciences, it may be possible to relate his intervention to the mental health of the parties and their children in such a way as to qualify for the cost of his or her services being borne by a medical insurance fund.

One advantage of mediation is that the emotional warfare exacerbated by the involvement of lawyers[4] may be avoided and the parties may feel, if not happy, at least that they have done the fair thing and can live with the result.[5]

Arbitration

Here the aim is for a decision as in a court of law, though the fount of authority in mediation and arbitration is the voluntary consensual agreement of the parties, supplemented by any applicable provisions of the *Arbitration Act*. The authority of the mediator/arbitrator is restricted to matters in which authority has been conferred on him or her by the parties, and rulings on other matters would be *"ultra vires."* The arbitration can be "open," i.e., very much like a court case, or "closed," in which the arbitrator makes his own enquiries and sees whoever he or she thinks can throw light on the enquiry. This latter approach requires careful drafting of the arbitration agreement to avoid the risk of subsequent allegations of the arbitrator's denial of natural justice by denying one of the parties the right to cross-examine witnesses or to know all the information on which the arbitrator is relying.[6] It may also be necessary to limit the area of referral to that of the arbitrator or mediator's expertise.[7] The "open" arbitration may be just as costly as a court case, or even more costly, if the arbitrator, freed of the judicial pressure to get through the docket, does not prevent counsel or the parties from going off on irrelevant, costly, and time-consuming tangents.

On the other hand the advantages may include (i) a choice of expert in whom both parties[8] repose confidence free of the vagaries of the choice of judge inherent in the docket system; (ii) the greater privacy inherent in such private proceedings, and possibly (iii) greater speed. Moreover, since family matters are particularly emotional and sensitive especially where children are concerned, recourse to the courts might properly be regarded as successive stages in a conflict resolution process outside the traditional court process.

TYPES OF DISPUTES AND ATTITUDE OF THE COURTS ON JUDICIAL REVIEW

Clearly the type of dispute will determine the nature of the expertise sought in the arbitrator or mediator, the time required and even the attitude of the Courts. The initial,[9] and recurring[10] reluctance of American courts to relinquish their power of supervision over the *parens patriae* power has been criticized, but seems to reflect an intuitive feeling by the courts, that since the terms of an arbitration agreement reflect the priorities of the parties they may not necessarily reflect those of the child. At the same time there may be an element of reserve about the criteria on which some behavioural scientist adjudicators[11] may base themselves, and which has not, at least in the eyes of the Court, been accepted as the received wisdom in the area under discussion. An example might be that of Goldstein, Solnit and Freud on visitation rights of noncustodial parents.[12] However, the number of cases in which the parties, or the courts, will want to probe the decision of an arbitrator may well be limited, and the criticisms of the courts' attitude should not be overstated. The courts in Canada have kept a similar residual discretion to go behind maintenance agreements without intervening so frequently as to undermine the incentive on the parties to reach a consensual agreement.[13]

CHOICE OF ARBITRATOR/MEDIATOR

This is a critical matter since one of the great appeals of mediation or arbitration is that the parties can choose an individual in whom they repose confidence.[14] In the United States, where expert resources may be more plentiful than in Canada, the American Arbitration Association has a procedure for supplying a list of arbitrators from its domestic relations panel, with a brief description of the panel members' education and experience. Each party can reject "unsatisfactory names" from the list and then list the remaining members in order of preference. The arbitrator with the lowest combined score is selected. Spencer and Zammit suggest that "nobody has ever requested or been given information of a more personal nature regarding the arbitrators' values or religious or other beliefs."[15] While this is perhaps understandable for lawyer mediators, or in cases not involving children, again one might question whether further scrutiny akin to a *voir dire* might be desirable to ascertain the attitudes of arbitrators, especially in child dispute cases. It is one thing to say in theory that an experienced lawyer, social worker, or child psychologist or psychiatrist will do an excellent job as arbitrator or mediator but it may be quite another in practice for a lawyer to find somebody pragmatic and relatively bias free. The appointment of a devotee of the Solnit, Goldstein and Freud[16] or Bowlby[17] schools is hardly going to commend itself to a noncustodial father fighting over access,[18] and the Wallenstein[19] or Grief[20] approach to custody may not commend itself to a custodial mother and her advisers. There is no substitute for knowing the bias of would-be arbitrators or mediators and finding relatively bias-free arbitrators may be exceedingly difficult especially in areas like Canada, where the American abundance of resources is missing. It is also important to know which clinics or assessment centres may be resorted to by the arbitrator/mediator to assist him or her in arriving at a resolution of the problem.[21] Clinics or consultants may have distinct approaches to problems. Obviously in rural regions where the resources are less plentiful, finding a suitable arbitrator or mediator is even more difficult.

FOLLOW UP

A further advantage of mediation or arbitration, assuming a suitable appointee can be found, is that procedures may be established for solving recurrent problems over parenting, schooling, visiting, and the like. This has an instant appeal to lawyers, who are only too familiar with such recurrent problems which not infrequently generate large numbers of out-of-hours phone calls. The attraction of getting cases out of the "in" tray into the "out" tray can hardly be overstated. Moreover these aspects of marital breakdown are the most emotional and painful for the parties and the ones where societal pressures, e.g., for the wife to seek custody, are most marked.[22]

QUESTIONS OF COST AND SPEED

In commercial and labour matters binding arbitration or concialiation has become a popular way of resolving disputes. At one time such procedures were both quicker and less expensive than going to trial. However, the advantages of speed and cost may well have been eroded for the more sought-after arbitrators, and the cost of providing such overheads as rooms for an arbitration (which are provided free to those involved in court proceedings) must also be calculated. Whereas, in construction or labour disputes where the benefits arising from the speed or expertise of the mediator or arbitrator may not pose problems of cost for corporate clients, the question of cost may be critical in family cases where resources are less abundant. As will be seen later the cost of mediation may involve ten to fifteen hours of the mediator's time; in the case of a challenge to an arbitral award in the courts, the duplication and additional costs may be considerable. The most sought after mediators or arbitrators may be those whose qualifications entitle them to set their expenses against medical or some other form of insurance.

In family matters the desirability of having an arbitrator trained in the behavioural sciences seems obvious. These are, however, far from the only skills that might be in demand. For example, in matters of division of family property or child or spousal support, there may be complicated questions of valuation of assets or tax liability which would place a premium on finding an arbitrator with a knowledge of revenue law. Even in jurisdictions that have placed an express statutory duty in the court to consider the tax consequences of its proposed division, the court may fail in its duty, if only because counsel did not lead sufficient evidence on this matter.[23] The ability to seek arbitration on such matters has in some cases been conferred by statute and one might have thought that this recourse would be sought. Yet the mere conferring of statutory authority to use an alternative to court proceedings does not ensure that such procedures will be used.[24] In Canada the typical approach is to try to resolve all matters at the time of divorce, although support, custody and access can resurface by way of variation and amendment. If the parties need a decree of divorce from a court, their advisers[25] will also be tempted to resolve the other "once and for all time" matter, e.g., division of matrimonial property, at the same time. To go to arbitration on questions other than the divorce decree appears to simply add to the legal costs. Moreover, there is probably a feeling by lawyers that they have a greater ability to keep in touch with reported court cases than with arbitrator's awards. Perhaps this, as much as lawyers' natural conservatism to new provisions or new procedures, explains why the provisions providing for arbitration of matrimonial property disputes have never been used in Nova Scotia in the first eighteen months since the Act was passed.

In light of the above, it is probably true that the breakthrough in utilization of alternatives to court proceedings was most likely to surface in those areas of support and custody and access which have a long continuum.

TIME SPENT BY THE MEDIATOR OR ARBITRATOR IN DEALING WITH CASES INVOLVING CHILDREN

The old adage of "beware the glib answer" is particularly true here. As with home-study reports, the time spent by the arbitrator-mediator on getting to know the parties involved in custody and access cases in the case is critical. An hour or so spent with the warring spouses and their children is hardly likely to be adequate. Several hours watching children interact with each member of their families in normal surroundings — meal times and playtimes can be particularly revealing — are a bare minimum in custody and access cases even if they add to the costs. In the Specimen Referral Letter contained in the Appendix to this chapter, reference is made to the fact that the Custody Project of the Clark Institute of Psychiatry in Toronto, probably Canada's premier centre, indicates that mediation and assessment rarely exceeds ten to fifteen hours. The Family Mediation Center in Atlanta requires a deposit to cover ten hours of the mediator's time. Unless such fees are provided by some external source such as medical insurance, the cost of the mediator's time including travelling time and transportation is considerable. The lawyer will need to be satisfied that the extra cost is justified, perhaps on the basis that the parties are more likely to hold to a mediated bargain. Nonpersonal issues such as division or property may be less time-consuming, though even here tax considerations may require time-consuming scrutiny.

PROBLEMS OF ARBITRATION OTHER THAN COST

The traditional role of the lawyer is as partisan to further his client's own interests,[25a] and any attempt to collaborate with the opposite side against his client's interests are caught by the canons of professional ethics;[26] he may even fear not so much the cost to his client as the loss of his own professional fees if he invokes mediation — "reconciliation can be a costly affair for the attorney."[27] Moreover, because emotions run so high in family disputes this may inhibit the ability of the parties to negotiate constructively.[28]

To counter this there has been some recognition by the legal profession of the many hats that lawyers wear. The American Bar Association has a discussion draft of New Rules of Professional Conduct which recognize the lawyer's role as negotiator and intermediary.[29] This perhaps follows from the *Klemm decision*,[30] in which a California Appellate Court recognized that the fact of a lawyer acting for both parties was consistent with the philosophy of the *Family Law Act* of 1970 which was to minimize both fault and the adverserial nature of such proceedings. Nevertheless, the Court was concerned to see that full consent and disclosure had been obtained against a background in which AFDC appeared to be underwriting a child support order which might properly have fallen on the father's shoulders.

THE PROCESS OF MEDIATION[31]

Unlike arbitration, which has a fairly well-defined framework, mediation has a certain flexibility according to the preferences of the parties and the mediator. A joint interview with the parties is necessary to put the negotiator "in the picture." Neutral open-ended questions enable the mediator to get some feel for the dynamics of the relationship. Further separate interviews may be necessary to get one spouse to "open up" or where there is hostility between the spouses. However, separate interviews may lead one or the other spouse, or both, to believe that they have missed something. The spouses may try to win over the mediator to their side. Another risk is that of transference and counter transference.[32] Some mediators try to be accompanied by a second mediator of the opposite sex to try to minimize this risk as well as to enable the mediators to cross-check their reaction with one another. Mediation in cases involving children will usually require the mediators to spend several hours seeing each parent with the children in ordinary surroundings. Once custody and access are solved, other questions such as support and property arrangements may tend to slide into place. Agreement on child support is facilitated if the parents are able to agree on matters such as whether the children are expected to go to university or to become self-sufficient.[33]

CONCLUSIONS

Although mediation and arbitration of family disputes has not become as popular in Canada as in the U.S.A., this may be due in part to the lack of specialist resources outside Toronto and one or two other urban centres. The conservatism of some Canadian lawyers may slow greater use of arbitration and mediation, but eventually an awareness of the recurrent nature of certain problems will force lawyers to use mediation and arbitration. The areas where this is most likely to come are those involving ongoing relationships such as maintenance and custody. However, the choice of relatively neutral arbitrators (in terms of values) will be essential.

APPENDIX

May 27th, 198–

Mr. Gordon Jones,
Marital and Family Mediator,
102 South Avenue,
Toronto, Ontario

Dear Mr. Jones:

Mr. and Mrs. Smith, by their Counsel, hereby refer to you for mediation questions relating to the custody of their children.

It is understood that you consent to act as mediator and this letter will set out the terms upon which the mediation is to proceed. They are:

1. As mediator, you will attempt to bring about an agreement between the father and the mother as to the determination of the following questions:
   (a) How much time should each child spend with each parent during the forthcoming school summer vacation; and
   (b) Should custody of the children, or any of them, be changed from the mother to the father?

2. In considering these questions, the parents and the mediator shall give primary importance to the needs of the children and how these needs, in the circumstances, can best be met.

3. In working out the custody and access arrangement which best meets the needs of the children, the parent may agree that:
   (a) One or the other of them shall have temporary custody of the children or one or two of them for a trial period; or
   (b) Both of them shall have custody of the children as joint custodians and the children, or one or two of them, shall live with one or the other parent, or first one parent then the other, during periods that are specified and set out in the agreement; or
   (c) Neither of the parents shall have custody of the children, but the periods of time (which) each child is to be with each parent (are) to be specified and set out in the agreement.

These alternatives are mentioned for the purpose of emphasizing that the parties are to make whatever arrangement is in the best interests of the children. Their choice may be one of these alternatives, or any better alternative that might emerge from the mediation meetings.

4. The separation agreement entered into under date of the 23rd day of September, 198–, shall not be binding on the parties in so far as the questions of custody and access are concerned.

5. The question of the children's maintenance or financial support is excluded from mediation and, if it arises, shall be referred back to Counsel for determination.

6. In attempting to bring about an agreement, the mediator may meet with and speak to the father, the mother and the child separately or jointly, and may consult such other persons and inspect such reports, records or documents as he deems necessary.

7. Any agreement reached shall constitute a settlement of the subject matter of the agreement and be produced for the information of the court in the legal proceedings pending between the father and the mother in the Supreme Court of Ontario or in any other relevant proceedings.

8. In the event that no agreement is reached within the period established for mediation, both parties shall have the right to pursue their legal remedies in the action pending between them in the Supreme Court of Ontario or in such other action or proceeding as they or either of them may be advised to take.

9. The period of time allowed for the mediation shall be established by the mediator in consultation with both Counsel after the mediator has interviewed both parents, but in no event shall be for more than six weeks from the date of this letter.

10. Evidence of anything said or of any admission or communication made in the course of the mediation is not admissible in the pending or any other legal proceeding.

11. The mediator will not be called as a witness by or on behalf of either parent in the pending or any other legal proceeding and the mediator shall not be required or permitted in the pending or any other legal proceeding to give any opinion or to disclose any admission or communication made to him in the course of the mediation.

12. Except to inform Counsel that:
    (a) No agreement has been reached; or
    (b) What the terms of the agreement are, there shall be no report made by the mediator of the mediation.

13. Your fee for the mediation shall be borne by the parents in equal shares and payable on such terms as are determined by you.

The mediation is agreed to by both parents in the confident expectation that, with your assistance, they can determine the questions above in a way that will be more satisfactory than any settlement imposed by a court or other process.

Please feel free to telephone either Counsel at any time for whatever information or assistance (which) they might be in a position to give. Counsel will refrain from initiating any contact with you in order to give you full freedom to act without interference.

We thank you for consenting to this referral and for acting as the mediator.

Yours very truly,

"L.M. Brown"

Solicitor for Robert G. Smith

"Mary McDonald"

Solicitor for Susan J. Smith

The following annotations elaborate further upon some of the points in the above referral.

Paragraph 1: "... *the following questions* ...": The first question relates to access as it has come to be considered by lawyers (as opposed to custody). Access, as defined by present-day practice, can be exercised outside the custodial home and is often spelled out in separation agreements and in court orders to include holiday periods of a specific duration (e.g., "the month of July or August each summer"). The second question is directed to a consideration of a possible change in permanent custody from the mother to the father.

Paragraph 2: "... *primary importance to the needs of the children*": This provision is intended to emphasize to the parties and the mediator that, in settling questions of custody and access, they are governed by the best interests or welfare of the children. In applying this principle, the guidelines discussed by Goldstein, Freud and Solnit in *Beyond the Best*

Interests of the Child (1973) would hopefully be accepted. These authors argue that it is misleading to speak of what is "best" for the child, because of the tendency to address the problem in terms of an ideal home and not in terms of what is available. One should not search for the "best" arrangement, but for the one which is, for the child, the least detrimental alternative to safeguarding the child's growth and development. In its report, the Justice Society of England (1975, 28) adopted this principle in formulating the general rule that:

> The welfare of any child, (who is) the subject of a custody suit, . . . is best served by whatever decision will minimize the risk of his suffering (or suffering further) injury, whether emotional, psychological or physical.

Paragraph 3: ". . . the parents may agree . . . (to) temporary custody, . . . (or to) custody . . . as joint custodians . . . (or to a timetable for the children with custody to neither parent)": This provision is intended to guard against the possibility that the discussion might be trapped into irrelevancies of who should have custody of the children rather than in concentrating on how the parents, in their homes and lives, can best cooperate to contribute to the successful growth and development of their children. A better elaboration of this provision might be something like the following:

> Both parents acknowledge that they require the assistance of an objective third party professional to help them to assess the impact of the separation upon the children, to identify problems raised by the separation, and to attempt to resolve these problems through discussion. They also acknowledge that, in developing solutions to child–parent problems, their own roles as parents must be explored. The parental role, of course, must be seen, not only in terms of the relationship between parent and child, but also in terms of the relationship of the parents to each other. It is expected that, in particular instances, the parents may disagree how to handle a problem centring on the child; accordingly, in the discussion with the mediator, the parents should devise a procedure of consultation with each other or some other means of resolving these conflicts.

> It is also acknowledged that preconceived notions of "custody" and "access" can impede the search for a plan which will enable the parents to provide for the best interests of the children. What is important is the recognition that both parents must be involved in their lives. In attempts to work out a process of collaboration which this entails, the legal labels of "custody" and "access" might be ignored, at least until the conclusion of this referral. In the meantime, consideration might be given to the concept of joint parenting with the children living in the home of one parent as their primary residence, and having frequent contact in the home of their other parent which would be known as their secondary residence.

Paragraph 5: ". . . the question of . . . financial support . . . is excluded": This exclusion from the mediation was inserted because it involves legal opinions beyond the training of the mediator. Similar questions relating to entitlement to property (both ownership and possessory rights), to interspousal maintenance and to the grounds for divorce are outside the scope of the referral. These questions should be sent back to the lawyers. It is important that the mediator and the lawyers work within their own limits and avoid overlapping and acting at cross-purposes. Frequent communication between mediator and lawyers is necessary with respect to role definition and to respective responsibilities.

Paragraph 6: "... may consult ... other persons": Under this term, the mediator has the right to interview other persons who have assumed a parenting role or who have had contact with the children, such as grandparents, housekeepers, teachers, and doctors.

Paragraph 6: "... reports, records or documents ...": These references would allow the mediator to examine material such as medical and school reports and other assessments of the family.

Paragraph 10: "communication ... not admissible in ... legal proceedings": This prohibition insures a closed mediation. Communications are to be kept confidential and protected from disclosure in any legal proceedings.

Paragraph 9: "The period of time allowed for the mediation...": The Custody Project of the Clark Institute of Psychiatry in Toronto, which provides mediation as part of its assessment process, advises that it is unusual for the total duration of mediation and assessment to exceed ten to fifteen hours (Form letter, June, 1976). The mediation rules of the Family Mediation Center in Atlanta (1977) require a deposit to cover ten hours of the mediator's time.

Paragraph 13: "... fee for the mediation ...": This stipulation requires the mediator to be involved to some extent in the arrangement of his fee. Some mediators prefer not to accept this responsibility and instead require payment from the lawyers who, of course, look at their clients. Regardless of how this is done, there should be a definite understanding from the outset about the clients' obligation and an express understanding about who has the responsibility for collection of the fee.

NOTES

1. In Canada these, or a court order, are a necessity if the spouse with a maintenance abrogation is to secure the benefit of tax deductibility under the *Income Tax Act*, S.C. 1970–71, c. 63 as amended ss. 56 & 60. See further Edwin C. Harris *Canadian Income Taxation,* 2nd edition, Butterworths Canada, 1981. Broad language in separation agreements such as reasonable access at reasonable hours on reasonable notice, or guaranteeing payment of reasonable dental expenses, all too frequently led to disputes about what are reasonable visiting rights in the one case and whether orthodontic

treatment is covered in the latter case. See J.M. Spencer and J.P. Zammit, "Mediation-Arbitration: A Proposal for Private Resolution of Disputes between Divorced or Separated Parents "(1976) *Duke L.J.* 911 at 914/15 for similar problems in the United States Court Orders. They also frequently suffer from the same problems of broad language; the writer has commented elsewhere on an undue willingness of Courts to make orders for reasonable access when the unreasonableness on the parties is self-evident. A. Bissett-Johnson, "Children in Subsequent Marriages — Questions of Access, Change of Name and Step-Parent Adoption," (1980) 11 *R.F.L.* (2d.) 289.

2. Marriage contracts have become more popular, though not to the extent that might have been predicted, as a result of the recent matrimonial property reforms in all the Canadian provinces. See further *Matrimonial Property Law in Canada,* eds. A. Bissett-Johnson and W. Holland, Carswell, Toronto, 1980.

3. H.A. Finlay, "Commonwealth Family Courts: Some Legal and Constitutional Implications," 4 *Federal Law Rev.* 287 at 290.

4. How many family lawyers have made their reputations by acting for a wife on "taking her husband to the cleaners," or by acting for the husband on leaving a wife destitute? These short-term victories are usually pyrrhic.

5. Interview with Henry Wilson quoted by Patricia Winks, "Divorce Mediation a Non Adversary Procedure for the No Fault Divorce," (1980/81) 19 *Jo. of Fam. Law* 615 at 653.

6. See the specimen referral letter in the appendix.

7. See the exclusion of maintenance in the referral letter, *ibid.* This ignores, of course, the involvement of the children and whether, if separate representation for them is desirable, they or their representative should have some say in the choice of arbitrator. The present climate seems to favour allowing the parents autonomy in decision making concerning their children except in exceptional circumstances. Solnit, Goldstein and Freud, *Beyond the Best Interests of the Child,* Free Press Paperback, 1973 and the same authors *Before the Best Interests of the Child,* Free Press, 1979.

8. See Spencer and Zammit, fn. 1 *ante.*

9. *Hill v. Hill,* 199 Misc. 1,035 (Sup. Ct. 1951) *Michelman v. Michelman,* 5 Misc. 2d. 570 (Supt. Ct. 1954).

10. *Agur v. Agur,* 32 App. Div. 2d. 16.

11. It should not be assumed that lawyers are free from such bias, Goldstein himself is a distinguished lawyer; see also Berger J.'s reference to *Beyond the Best Interests of the Child,* in *Re Squire* (1974) 16 R F.L. 266 (B.C.S.C.). It is not clear whether reference to the book was made in evidence or whether the judge took judicial notice of it.

12. See fn. 7 *ante.*

13. *Hyman v. Hyman* [1927] A.C. 601 (H.L.) this represents an unwillingness on the part of the courts to allow a husband to transfer to the taxpayer via the social security system an obligation of support that is properly his. The willingness of some wives to secure an agreement on questions of custody of their children by trading off support payments is well known. Compare with *Klemm v. Superior Court* (1977) 12 Cal. Rptr. 507.

14. Spencer and Zammit, *op. cit.* at p. 938, fn. 113.

15. *Op. cit.* 923, fn. 42.

16. A. Solnit, J. Goldstein, A. Freud, *Beyond the Best Interests of the Child,* Free Press Paperback, 1973 and the same authors *Before the Best Interests of the Child,* Free Press Paperback, 1979.

17. J. Bowlby, "Maternal Care and Mental Health," Geneva World Health Organization, 1952.

18. See the annotation to para. 2 of the Specimen referral letter in the appendix, which refers to the words "primary importance to the needs of the children" being understood in the sense used by Goldstein, Solnit and Freud. No doubt counsel for a noncustodial counsel would wish the words to be understood in the light of Grief's work.

19. J. Wallerstein and Berlin Kelly, *Surviving the Breakup — How Parents and Children Cope with Divorce*, London, Grant McIntyre, 1980.

20. J. Grief, "Access: Legal Right or Privilege at the Custodial Parents Discretion," 3 *Can. J. Fam. L.* 43.

21. See *Smallenberg v. Smallenberg* (1978), 5 R.F.L. (2d) 315 at 322 (B.C.S.C.), where the Superintendent of Child Welfare supported the step-parent adoption application which aimed at snuffing out access by the noncustodial parent "as it presents the least detrimental alternative." This is the precise language of Goldstein, Freud and Solnit. Earlier examples of expert witnesses espousing (or misunderstanding) the latest psychiatric, psychological or social work theories can be found, for example, in *Ader v. McLaughlin* [1964] 2 O.R. 457, 46 D.L.R. (2d) 12, the Ontario High Court allowed access for a mother who had deserted her children and had not seen them for five years between Christmas 1958, when they were seven and five, and 1963. Since the daughter had no recollection of her mother it was perhaps surprising that a psychologist who had not seen the children was prepared on the basis of Bowlby's work to recommend not merely that the mother should have access to the children but that she should be given custody! Other examples can be found of expert witnesses recommending that black African children who had spent virtually all their lives with white English foster parents be returned to their birth-parents. See also the decision in *Re O*. The *Times*, 5 December 1972, affirmed The *Times*, 27 February 1973 (C.A.), which is discussed by M.D.A. Freeman in his article, "Child Law at the Crossroads" (1974), 27 *Current Legal Problems* 165 at 184.

22. H.A. Freeman and H. Weihofen, "Client Counselling in Negotiating the Terms of Divorce," 18 *The Practical Lawyer* 41 at 49.

23. See for example the Nova Scotia Appeal Division's decision in *Lawrence v. Lawrence,* 47 N.S.R. (2d) 100 (N.S.C.A.) in which pension funds of $38,000 which could not be transferred by a husband from his old to his new employer, were treated as matrimonial assets worth $38,000 and equally divided between husband and wife notwithstanding that the effect of the rest of the order under the Nova Scotia *Matrimonial Property Act* S.N.S. 1980 c. 9 and the *Divorce Act,* R S.C. 1970 c. D-8 was probably to force the husband to "cash in" the pension — in which case at least half the pension monies would have been taken as tax. S. 13(m) of the Nova Scotia Act requires the court to consider, in deciding whether an unequal division of matrimonial assets is appropriate or whether to have recourse to other assets, "all taxation consequences of the division of matrimonial assets."

24. Nova Scotia *Matrimonial Property Act* S.N.S. 1980 c. 9.

ARBITRATION

30. (1) Parties to a marriage contract or separation agreement may, where both persons consent, refer any question as to their rights under this Act or the contract or agreement for determination by arbitration, and the provisions of the Arbitration Act shall then apply.

ARBITRATION AWARD

(2) A copy of an arbitration award made pursuant to this Section, certified by the arbitrator to be a true copy, may be made an order of the court by filing it with the prothonotary of the court who shall enter the same as a record and it shall thereupon become and be an order of the court and be enforceable as such (1980, c. 9, s. 30).

25. Do-it-yourself divorces are less common in Canada than in the United States.

25[a]. In the days of fault-based divorce, this was taken to its ultimate extent in *In Re Gale* 75 N.U. 526 (1879) in which the husband's attorney took on himself the role of correspondent — only to be disbarred. See further, Patricia Winks, "Divorce Mediation: A Non Adversary Procedure for the No-Fault Divorce." 19 *Jo. Fam. Law* 615.

26. Law Society of Upper Canada (1975, 11) provides that a lawyer cannot act for two or more clients where the interests are in conflict.

27. P. L. Conway, "To Insure Domestic Tranquility — Reconcilation Services as an Alternative to the Divorce Attorney," 9 *Jo. of Fam. Law* 408 at 416.

28. See K. Kressel et al., "Mediated Negotiation in Divorce and Labour Disputes — A Comparison. 15 *Concilation Courts Review* (1977) 9-12. Kressel identifies four factors as inhibiting successful negotiation. Although these were identified in a labour setting, they seem equally applicable to family disputes: (i) high levels of internal conflict in one or both parties, (ii) scarcity of divisible resources, (iii) inexperience of the parties with negotiations and with mediated negotiations in particular; and (iv) a wide discrepancy in the parties' relative power.

29. See Winks, *ibid.,* 633.

30. (1977) 75 Cal. App. 3d. 893.

31. See further Winks, 636, 637.

32. See further A. Watson, *The Lawyer in the Interviewing and Counselling Process* (1976) 23-25 and 75-93.

33. See Spencer and Zammit, *ibid.,* 931.

Chapter Sixteen

Custody Mediation in Denver: Short and Longer Term Effects*

Jessica Pearson, Ph.D.
Nancy Thoennes, Ph.D.

The Center for Policy Research†
Denver, Colorado, U.S.A.

TRENDS IN FAMILY LITIGATION

In the past decade, the incidence of marital separation and divorce has increased dramatically. For example, in the single year of 1979 there were nearly 1.2 million divorces affecting over two million adults and nearly 1.5 million children (Glick 1979; National Center for Health Statistics 1980). Nor is there reason to expect a decline. Demographers project that over 40 percent of current marriages will end in divorce (Preston 1975).

One result of the upsurge in divorce is that the court is overwhelmed by the demands being made upon it. Over half of the cases filed in all trial courts of original jurisdictions are concerned with matrimonial actions. Family disputes comprise the largest category of civil matters (Corey and Teachout 1979; Cotchett 1978; Feldman 1977). Many court systems are so overbooked that waits of nine to ten months are common for no-fault divorces, and contested divorces often have to wait for a year or two to be scheduled (Mnookin and Kornhauser 1979). Approximately 10 percent

---

* This is an earlier version of a paper which has subsequently appeared in *Family Law Quarterly*, Vol. 17, No. 4, Winter 1984 under the title "Mediating and Litigating Custody Disputes: A Longitudinal Evaluation".

† This research has been supported by a grant from the Piton Foundation of Colorado. We would like to thank Lois Vander Kooi for coordinating the operation of the mediation service and the collection of the research information. Thanks also to Julie Moulton, Sharon House, Becky Huper and Ruth Vander Kooi for conducting interviews and computer coding the interview data.

of divorce cases go on to full-scale legal battles over custody (Foster and Freed 1980).

In addition to the congestion of the courts, are charges that the adversarial system is simply inappropriate when applied to the resolution of many marital disputes. According to one writer, the adversarial model increases trauma and escalates conflict (Bohannon 1970). Irving and Irving (1974) argue that the adversarial system has the practical consequences of "pitting the marital couple against each other in mortal combat ... exacerbating the emotional trauma that already exists and rendering attempts at constructive communication even more difficult." Another writer argues that the adversarial system encourages "dog and cat fights" that run counter to the best interests of the child (Buttenwieser et al. 1966). The judicial process, it is said, fails to take into account the child's notion of time and often undermines the continuity the child needs in his or her relationship to a primary caretaker (Goldstein et al. 1973). Lawyers are accused of being poorly trained to deal with the psychological aspects of divorce (Kallner 1977) and encouraging their clients to take extreme positions that are unnecessarily divisive (Cavenaugh and Rhode 1976). Judicial proceedings are criticized for failing to address unresolved feelings about the marriage and separation that often precipitate custody conflicts in the first place (Milne 1979). Still others see the formalities and procedures of the adversary system as inappropriate for the negotiating and counselling needs of most divorcing couples. Because negotiating responsibilities are delegated to attorneys who perceive themselves as adversaries with specific legal goals, adversarial interventions foster low commitment to the eventual agreement (Macaulay and Walster 1977). They also fail to enhance the cooperative, communication and problem-solving skills of the parties (Herman, McHenry and Weber 1979). Some writers view adversarial procedures as obstructive to the process of truth-finding (Mund 1976). Still others fault the coercive nature of adjudication (Felstiner 1974) as well as the "twin dragons" of cost and delay (Kaufman 1976).

THE MEDIATION ALTERNATIVE

Increasingly, mediation is being regarded as a more favorable method of resolving family disputes. It is an alternative to formal litigation which, in cases of custody, often includes comprehensive mental health evaluations of all family members and culminates in a court imposed solution.

Mediation is a participatory and consensual process in which a third party — the mediator — encourages the disputants to find a mutually agreeable settlement by helping them to identify the issues, reduce misunderstandings, vent emotions, clarify priorities, find points of agreement, explore new areas of compromise, and ultimately negotiate an agreement. Rooted in African moots, socialist comrades' courts, psychotherapy and labour mediation rather than Anglo-American jurisprudence, mediation stresses informality, open and direct communication, reinforcement of positive bonds and avoidance of blame (Gulliver 1979). A cooperative dispute resolution process (Rubin and Brown 1975; Deutsch 1973), its central purpose is to

> reorient the parties toward each other not by imposing rules on them, but by helping them to achieve a new and shared perception of their relationship, a perception that will direct their attention toward one another (Fuller 1971, 305).

The benefits attributed to mediation are far-reaching. When compared to the adversarial system, it is believed to be more expeditious, inexpensive, private, procedurally reasonable and amenable to truth-finding and the complete airing of grievances. Supposedly, it is able to deal with the causes of problems, reduce the alienation of the litigant, and lead to the development of noncoercive, practical and satisfying agreements that are consistent with the preferences of the disputing parties, and perceived as fair and acceptable over time. Further, unlike adjudication, mediation presumably aids disputing parties in resuming workable relationships with one another (Buttenwieser et al. 1966; Cavenaugh and Rhode 1976; Danzig and Lowy 1975; Goldbeck 1975; Mund 1976; Spencer and Zammit, 1976; Mnookin and Kornhauser 1979; Witty 1980; Felstiner and Williams 1980).

Supporters contend that the process will also enhance the adjustment of children following separation and divorce. For example, Wallerstein and Kelly (1980) found that while 37 percent of the children in their study were "moderately to severely depressed" five years following the separation, the children who were doing best enjoyed easy access to the noncustodial parent and a postdivorce relationship that was relatively conflict free. To the extent that mediation promotes communication, compromise and participation in parent–child relationships following divorce, it would reinforce parent–child ties, reduce the incidence of bitter modification proceedings and enhance the psychosocial development of children.

Finally, mediation proponents contend that the process will improve the dismal child support payment performance of fathers following divorce. Numerous accounts indicate that noncompliance with child support orders is at epidemic proportions (Espenshade 1979; Cassetty 1978; Weitzman 1977; Carrad 1979). Not surprisingly, most separated mothers and their children live in poverty (Bradbury et al. 1979).

Mediation promises to improve the situation, by reducing the anger, feelings of loss, sense of injustice and separation from their children that many divorcing fathers experience. In the words of researchers who have compared the adjudication and mediation of numerous small claims matters, including unpaid bills:

> People are more likely to feel bound by an obligation they have undertaken voluntarily and more or less publicly than one imposed upon them in a court of

law ... Perhaps merely facing one's opponent for a time, having the opportunity to speak with, and to hear him or her humanizes and personalizes the process enough to affect the defendant's attitude toward payment (McEwen and Maiman 1981, 264).

The end result of such arguments is a tremendous growth in the popularity of nonadversarial approaches to marital dispute resolution. Various writers have urged Family Courts or social service agencies to establish mediation or conciliation counselling services (Weiss 1975; Weiss and Collada 1977), and courts in thirteen states have followed suit. Private mediation services have sprung up around the country and a number of practitioners have developed and published model approaches to divorce mediation (Coogler 1978; Haynes 1981; Milne 1978; Irving 1980). Finally, judges, lawyers and mental health professionals have become increasingly interested in this new area of practice.

Despite its growing popularity and use, mediation remains a little known process. Many theoretical and practical issues have yet to be addressed. The following is a systematic exploration of the long- and short-term consequences of resolving custody and visitation disputes using traditional adversarial approaches and mediation. The analysis attempts to provide answers to the practical questions of whether mediation works and how it compares with adjudication.

RESEARCH FORMAT

The information presented here was collected as part of the Denver Custody Mediation Project. Begun in March, 1979, and sponsored by the Piton Foundation of Colorado and the Colorado Bar Association, the Project involves the organization and administration of cost-free mediation services to divorcing couples in the Denver metropolitan area and the evaluation of the mediation process and its outcomes. The Project employs a rigorous, quasi-experimental design. As a result, it provides an excellent opportunity to examine the consequences of mediating child custody and visitation disputes, and to compare this process to the traditional adversarial system. In order to generate a sample of contested custody, child custody and visitation cases, setting clerks, referees, judges, investigators and attorneys in two metropolitan judicial districts identify and refer to the Project all suspected cases of contested custody or visitation. Once referred, cases are randomly assigned to mediation or control groups.

Consenting individuals in our control group are interviewed at three points in time: as soon as they file court documents indicating they disagree about custody and visitation matters; soon after the court promulgates final orders regarding custody or visitation; and again, six to twelve months later. All interviews are conducted over the telephone. Each one takes approximately twenty to forty minutes to complete.

Individuals in our experimental group are offered free mediation services. We explain that this is a method of resolving disputes that emphasizes communication and that in mediation, couples have an opportunity to try to work out their disagreements in an informal setting with the help of a neutral third party. Couples who want to try are typically assigned to male–female teams comprised of lawyers and mental health professionals who have been trained in mediation techniques. They are interviewed four times: prior to the commencement of mediation; immediately after the conclusion of mediation; soon after the court promulgates final orders regarding custody or visitation; and again, six to twelve months later.

About half the disputants offered free mediation services reject the offer. Although initially we were surprised to encounter such resistance, we have since discovered that refusals are common in all mediation programs. For example, Davis (1980) reported that 32 percent of those referred to the Brooklyn Dispute Resolution Center failed to appear and another 12 percent refused mediation outright. The Neighborhood Justice Centers report attrition rates to as high as 60 percent (Cook et al. 1980). Such disinterest may be due to the unfamiliarity of the general public with the mediation concept and/or the antipathy many disputants feel toward the prospect of cooperating with their adversaries.

Rather than merely dispensing with uninterested individuals, we chose to include them in the study as a "rejecting group." They were interviewed on three occasions: as soon as they rejected the offer to mediate; soon after the court promulgated final orders regarding custody/visitation; and again six to twelve months later.

The present article considers some of the effects of mediation and adversarial interventions on individuals with similar disputes. Not all follow-up interviews have been completed to date. Thus, the analysis of short-term effects is based on reports at the time of the first follow-up interview of 125 mediation clients, 63 individuals in the adversarial control group and 95 individuals who rejected mediation and also used the adversarial process. Longer-term effects are based on reports from mediation clients (N=92), the control groups (N=50), and the rejecting group (N=74) approximately six months after they received final orders regarding custody and visitation.

SHORT-TERM EFFECTS

Our analysis focuses on the effects of mediation and adjudication on five types of attitudes or behaviours at two points in time. The first time point occurs two or three months after the promulgation of court orders. The attitudes and behaviours we consider are (1) agreement-making skills; (2) satisfaction with the final decree; (3) compliance and relitigation; (4) quality of the relationship with former spouse; and (5) effects on parent–child interactions. These are, of course, by no means the only outcome variables upon which mediation and adversarial groups could reasonably be compared. However, these do touch on the major themes found in the current theoretical and empirical literature on mediation.

Agreement-making Skills

An initial benefit of mediation appears to be its ability to encourage stipulations. The Custody Mediation Project agreement rate currently stands at 58 percent. However, a majority (65 percent) of the Project's clients who *fail* to produce an agreement *in mediation* go on to generate stipulations prior to their court hearings. By contrast, half of the individuals in the adversarial samples who were never exposed to the mediation process stipulate before reaching court, and half rely upon a judicial determination.

Viewed from another angle, 80 percent of those exposed to mediation produce their own custody and visitation agreement, either during or after the process. Only 20 percent turn to the court for a solution. However, 50 percent of those never exposed to mediation rely on the court for a decision.

Further, even where postdecree problems have arisen and a modification seems likely, successful mediation clients are most likely to feel they can, once again, resolve their problems without resorting to court. Forty percent thought they could work out agreements with their spouses. Only 22 percent expected to resort to attorneys and the courts. By contrast, less than 20 percent of the control group and unsuccessful mediation clients, and less than 30 percent of those who refused the mediation offer said they would make needed changes informally. Approximately 70 percent expected to go back to court.

Satisfaction with the Agreement

The individuals most satisfied with their final decrees are those who were exposed to mediation. Regardless of the mediation's outcome, about 70 percent of those who tried the process report that they are satisfied with the agreements they finally obtained. The majority of those never exposed to mediation are also satisfied with their decrees, but at lower levels. Thus, about 56 percent of individuals in the reject and control groups are happy with the terms of their final orders.

The greater level of satisfaction associated with mediated agreements seems to be due to the mediation process itself. Individuals who successfully mediated are most likely to report the decision-making process as fair, most apt to see both parties as equally influential in determining the outcome, and most likely to perceive their decrees as complete and thorough. Indeed, even unsuccessful mediation clients like the process and see value in it. However, it is not clear why unsuccessful mediation clients, compared to the remainder of the adversarial sample, should be more pleased with their actual agreements in the long run, or the manner in which such agreements were finally made. Indeed, as we will see, the effect is not lasting for mediation clients who are not successful in reaching an agreement.

Improved Compliance and Reduced Litigation

Satisfaction without compliance would be a hollow victory for mediation. Fortunately, such does not appear to be the case. At the time of the first follow-up contact, no successful mediation clients had filed a motion for modification, and reports of temporary restraining orders in effect were also less frequent (15 percent versus 30 percent).

Not surprisingly, nearly everyone we interviewed claimed that he or she was in complete compliance with the decree. It was much less common for respondents to report that a former mate was in compliance. Among successful mediation clients, however, spousal cooperation was common. Fully 66 percent of the successful mediation clients reported that their spouse was in compliance. The rest of the groups reported compliance at about half that rate; i.e., in about 30 to 45 percent of the cases.

Finally, with the exception of the successful mediation clients, at the first follow-up interview between 30 and 40 percent of all respondents reported that serious disagreements had already arisen with the decree. Among those who successfully mediated, only 13 percent reported such problems.

Improved Spousal Relations

Whether or not it results in an agreement, individuals typically report that mediation helped them to better understand and communicate with an ex-spouse. For example, in the first follow-up interview, 69 percent of those who produced agreements in mediation and 31 percent of those who tried but failed, felt that mediation had helped them to better communicate with an ex-spouse. Not surprisingly, few (14 percent) of those respondents exposed only to the court system reported improved communications as a result of the adversarial process.

Similarly, 75 and 27 percent of successful and unsuccessful mediation clients reported that the process helped them to better understand an ex-spouse. This was reported by only 18 percent of those relying entirely on the courts. As one respondent noted, "You can't go to court and be civil, whether it's your nature or not."

Overall, when asked to describe their current relationship with an ex-spouse, about 80 percent of the successful clients described their relationships as no worse than "strained." Such responses were given by 50 percent of the unsuccessful clients and about 43 percent of those never exposed to mediation. There are several reasons why mediation clients perceive their relationship with an ex-spouse to be improved. The process encourages communication. In addition, it avoids competitive strategies and polarized outcomes. As one mediation client observed about the process: "There were no winners or losers, good guys or bad guys — we could do what was best for everybody."

Consequences for Parents and Children

There is a definite difference in the types of custody and visitation arrangements produced in mediation and the adversary system. Fully 70 percent of those who produced agreements in mediation opted for joint legal custody. Only 20 percent called for traditional, mother-only custody awards. Joint custody characterized less than 15 percent of nonmediated agreements.

It is worth noting that many joint custody arrangements in the Project are more conventional than the label implies. Only 27 percent of the agreements in the Project call for the regular alternation of the child between parents. More typically, our joint custody agreements recognize that both parents are fit and have legal responsibility for the care and upbringing of the children while delegating day-to-day care of the children to the mother. The joint custody designation, however, is very important to parents. For example, one father felt that "Without joint custody I never would have been able to enjoy parenting. It's striking how nurturing I can be as a man." And even where children reside primarily with the mother, fathers typically receive liberal and generous visitation. On the average, children whose parents work out visitation plans in mediation see their noncustodial parents eight days per month. Where parents do not resolve these issues in mediation, children see the noncustodian for an average of five days per month.

Summary of Short-Term Effects

Our analysis of the first follow-up interview indicates that regardless of the outcome, mediation promotes agreement making and improves communication and understanding between former spouses. We also find that individuals who produce agreements in mediation are more satisfied and are in greater compliance with their agreements than their unsuccessful mediation counterparts as well as those who exclusively rely on the adversarial system. Finally, successful mediation clients enjoy the most contact with their children including joint custody arrangements and generous visitation terms. (See Table 16.1 for a statistical outline of the results discussed in this section.)

TABLE 16.1   Follow Up 1 — Mediation Group

	Successful	Unsuccessful	Control	"Rejecting"
Agreement Making				
(a) Stipulated prior to final hearing	100%	65%	48%	53%
(b) Those interested in modifying who anticipate reaching decision on their own	40%	18%	16%	29%
Satisfaction & Compliance				
(a) Satisfied with decree	71%	67%	58%	54%
(b) Have filed motion to modify	0%	12%	20%	14%
(c) Report serious disagreements have arisen over settlement	13%	36%	40%	32%
(d) Report spouse to be in compliance	66%	30%	34%	46%
Relationship with Former Spouse				
(a) Relationship is "friendly" or "strained"	81%	50%	41%	45%
(b) Decision-making process improved:				
Communications	69%	31%	17%	10%
Anger	47%	23%	11%	10%
Cooperation	62%	19%	15%	12%
Understanding	75%	27%	24%	18%
Relationship with Children				
(a) Custody arrangement:				
Joint	69%	14%	7%	6%
Mother, sole custodian	20%	62%	72%	62%
(b) Average number of days per month the non-custodian sees the children	7.7	5.5	4.9	4.9
Sample Size	62	63	63	95

LONG-TERM EFFECTS

To what extent are the above cited effects temporary responses to adversarial and mediation experiences? To what extent are they more durable consequences of each method of dispute resolution? To answer these questions, we recontacted respondents in each of our samples approximately six months after the promulgation of final court orders. In our interviews, we were able to explore each of the outcome indicators discussed thus far. Obviously, further longitudinal work with these individuals would be helpful; however, at this second point of intervention we can already note some changes and emerging patterns.

Agreement-making Skills

Parties with mediated agreements remain the most confident about their abilities to work out problems and generate modifications with their ex-spouses and avoid returning to court. Respondents with nonmediated agreements are more likely to believe that a modification will necessitate litigation. Thus, one stable characteristic of the successful mediation client is his or her orientation to the autonomous resolution of future custody and visitation problems.

Satisfaction with the Agreement

Individuals with mediated agreements continue to express the greatest satisfaction with their divorce decrees and final orders. This is consistent with our findings at the first follow-up. Nevertheless, it is important to note that the amount of satisfaction has declined among successful mediation clients and that the samples are more similar in this respect. More strikingly, there is a very substantial decline in satisfaction reported by unsuccessful mediation clients, leaving them no more satisfied with their final court order than those parties relying solely on the adversarial system. Thus, it appears that for unsuccessful mediation clients, the process may have a halo effect that is short-lived and that the short-term satisfactions expressed by such clients may quickly fade. For successful mediation clients, however, the greater initial satisfaction they express seems to persist.

Compliance and Relitigation

Successful mediation clients continue to report the fewest number of serious disagreements over their settlements (although disagreements have not increased among any of the groups and slight declines are sometimes noticeable). Most of our groups also report better spousal compliance with the decree than at the time of the first follow-up interview. While successful mediation clients report the highest rates of spousal compliance (66 percent) only the unsuccessful mediation clients failed to experience substantial positive gains.

Relitigation patterns, however, are less clear cut. Although successful mediation clients are only half as likely to have filed for modification, compared to all other groups, filings for these clients increased by about 10 percent between the first and second follow-up interviews. This was comparable to the rates of increase observed in the other samples during the same time period. It may well be the case that successful mediation clients were slower to begin filing and may ultimately modify at comparable rates. At the time of the second follow-up interview, 20 percent of the control group had initiated legal modification proceedings.

Thus, while problems are not on the increase, filings for modifications have become more common for virtually all the groups. It is important to stress, however, that filing for modification is a relatively rare occurrence and that it is by no means the mode for any group.

Improved Spousal Relations

Compared to their adversarial and unsuccessful mediation counterparts, respondents who successfully mediated continue to report better communications with and understanding of their ex-spouses. These individuals are almost 40 percent more likely to describe their relationships as "easy" or "strained" rather than "just about impossible" or "impossible." Thus, successful mediation clients maintain their initially high levels of cooperation.

The picture is very different for unsuccessful mediation clients. Six to twelve months down the line, they are virtually indistinguishable in their relations with former spouses from those who never attempted mediation. The improvements they reported in the first interview were clearly transitory. Thus, improved spousal relations are characteristic only of successful mediation clients rather than all who try the process.

Consequences for Children and Parents

Between the first and final follow-up interview, the frequency of contact with children has increased in each of our groups but access is greatest among those who successfully mediate. Specifically, we find that successful mediation clients now see their children an average of nine days per month, while the other groups average between five and seven days.

Summary of Long-term Consequences

What can be said about our five general outcome factors over the long run? On the positive side, individuals who successfully mediate continue to report a number of very desirable behaviours and attitudes. Compared to the adversarial and unsuccessful counterparts, they are: more optimistic about resolving future problems with their spouses and avoiding court; most satisfied with their decrees and court orders; less likely to report serious problems with their orders; more likely to report that their ex-spouse is complying with child and financial terms of their orders; more likely to report good relationships with former spouses, including improved communication and understanding, and more likely to enjoy joint custody arrangements along with more visitation with their children.

Relitigation patterns for successful mediation clients as opposed to the other Project samples are less clear cut. Although successful mediation clients report greater compliance and fewer problems with their agreement, a rising proportion (9 percent) had initiated modification proceedings at the time of the second follow-up interview. Although this is only half the modification rate observed in the adversarial samples, it is not yet clear whether the lower rate indicates greater satisfaction with the decree or merely a delay in the initiation of modification proceedings.

Finally, our data indicate that over the long run, unsuccessful mediation clients do not greatly benefit from their exposure to the process. Their initial satisfaction with their agreements and reports of improved relationships with an ex-spouse soon evaporate. In these respects, unsuccessful mediation clients ultimately resemble those in the adversarial samples who were never exposed to mediation. The only real long-term differences between unsuccessful mediation clients and individuals who never used the process lie in the greater proportion of the former who have joint custody arrangements (14 percent versus 6 percent) and the greater average number of days per month noncustodians spend with their children (seven days versus five days). Thus, we may safely conclude that whether or not it results in an agreement, mediation inspires more co-parenting and visitation than adversarial interventions. (See Table 16.2 for an outline of long-term results.)

TABLE 16.2 Follow Up II — Mediation Group

	Successful	Unsuccessful	Control	"Rejecting"
Agreement Making				
(a) Those interested in modifying who anticipate reaching decision on their own	41%	16%	26%	14%
Satisfaction & Compliance				
(a) Satisfied with decree	63%	45%	54%	51%
(b) Have filed motion to modify	9%	22%	20%	20%
(c) Report serious disagreements have arisen over settlement	9%	36%	36%	20%
(d) Report spouse to be in compliance	59%	30%	30%	37%
Relationship with Former Spouse				
(a) Relationship is "friendly" or "strained"	81%	39%	54%	42%
(b) Decision-making process improved:				
Communications	50%	19%	34%	24%
Anger	46%	17%	32%	31%
Cooperation	43%	19%	30%	16%
Understanding	32%	11%	26%	13%
Relationship with Children				
(a) Average number of days per month the non-custodian sees the children	9.0	7.1	5.1	5.4
Sample Size	61	64	50	70

RIVAL HYPOTHESES

How reliable are our findings of benefits for successful mediation clients? Are the outcome measures we are employing — agreement making, satisfaction with the divorce decree, compliance and relitigation, relationship with one's former spouse, and relationships with children — truly related to the mediation experience, or more specifically, the experience of succeeding in mediation? Or are our outcomes, along with the initial agreement to mediate, and the ability to generate an agreement in mediation, actually determined by factors present before the mediation process begins?

To answer this question, we explored four plausible rival hypotheses to our contention that mediation produces positive outcomes. While these are not the only rival explanations possible, they represent the most obvious ways in which extraneous factors could produce spurious relationships between successful mediation and our outcome measures.

Cooperation

Are individuals who succeed in mediation intrinsically cooperative? Would they tend to report good relationships with their spouses, high levels of compliance and positive adjustments regardless of the dispute resolution process to which they were exposed?

Our data indicates that this is not the case. When cooperation level prior to mediation, as measured during our intake interview, is statistically controlled, the outcome measures continue to show associations with successful mediation.

It is true, however, that among originally "uncooperative" individuals the effects of successful mediation begin to wear thin by the time of the second follow-up interview — especially with respect to satisfaction with the decree. Among originally cooperative individuals, the successful mediation clients continue to hold their lead in this and other outcomes measures.

Winning and Losing

Another possibility is that the outcome measures largely reflect whether or not the respondent has custody. Thus, because a great many successful mediation cases result in shared custody — with neither party clearly losing — the successful mediation clients may appear to be better satisfied and more cooperative. If this is true, we could not claim that the mediation process had an impact, merely that joint custody has potential for reducing problems.

However, statistically controlling for whether or not the respondent has sole or joint custody, versus no custody, reveals that the relationships between successful mediation and our outcome measures is not merely a function of having custody.

Economic Strain

It might be argued that clients who succeed in mediation are those with fewer economic problems, and, in turn, economic stability produces positive outcome measures. However, even after controlling for self-reported financial strain, successful mediation clients continue to appear more positively on the outcome measures.

The Dispute

Finally, it does not appear that our outcome measures reflect a spurious correlation due to uncomplicated cases opting for, and succeeding in mediation, while also rating higher on outcome indicators.

When we statistically control for (1) the reported magnitude of the custody and visitation disputes and (2) the presence of serious economic disagreements, we find that successful mediation clients continue to score more positively on our follow-up measures. We can, however, note that modifications at the time of the second follow-up are more common among cases with severe disputes.

Summary of Rival Hypotheses

Although factors pertaining to the cooperative nature of the parties and the scale of their dispute help to explain some of the patterns we find in our outcome measures, they do not alter our basic conclusions. We accept the hypothesis that mediation and success in mediation produce lasting differences among disputants and that these differences cannot readily be attributed to factors that are extraneous to the mediation experience.

CONCLUSIONS

The Custody Mediation Project affords an opportunity to examine the consequences of mediation, especially as they compare to adjudication. When examined in light of previous research in the field of mediation, the findings presented in this article greatly enhance our understanding of the benefits and limitations of the process. In particular, we can speak with greater confidence about the decision to mediate, the proportion of mediation cases that result in an agreement, satisfaction with the process and the agreements generated in mediation and adjudication, perceptions of fairness, compliance patterns and relitigation behaviours.

As to the decision to mediate, we find that approximately half the disputants offered free mediation services reject them. This is consistent with the findings of other researchers. Due to refusals to mediate and to "no-shows," approximately 60 percent of the referred cases are never heard (Cook 1980). It is worth noting that at least part of the rationale for California's recently enacted mandatory mediation law is a desire to overcome the substantial attrition rate that most voluntary programs experience.

Similarly, our agreement rate of 58 percent falls squarely in the range reported in the literature on mediation. In Los Angeles, for example, the Conciliation Court reports an agreement rate of 54.5 percent. In McEwen and Maiman's sample of small claims cases, 66.1 percent of the mediation cases ended with an agreement (McEwen and Maiman 1981). Irving (1980) finds an agreement rate of 70 percent in the Conciliation Service of Toronto's Provincial Court. Of course, agreement rates have to be viewed with some caution given the variety of disputes handled in each of these mediation programs and the different types of agreements that may be counted as successes (e.g., agreements to seek further counselling, or temporary agreements pending later court action).

Not surprisingly, mediation leads to compromise. In the Denver Project, most couples who reach mediation agreements opt for joint legal custody, an arrangement rarely selected by those who are exposed only to the adversarial process. Among mediation couples who select sole custody, noncustodians receive more visitation than is commonly found in nonmediated agreements. There is clearly more give and take in custody mediation than custody adjudication. According to McEwen and Maiman mediated agreements in Maine's small claims program reflect greater compromise than adjudicated ones. While in nearly half of the adjudicated cases the plaintiff was awarded all or nearly all of the claim, this occurred in only 16.9 percent of the mediated cases. Additionally, the plaintiff was more likely to win something in mediation than in adjudication.

Time and again, we find that individuals who mediate are extremely pleased with the process whether or not they are able to generate a mediation agreement. In the Denver Project, for example, 77 percent of all those who tried mediation said they were satisfied with the process in the second follow-up interview. By way of contrast, no more than 42 percent of respondents in any of our samples (mediation or adversarial) reported being satisfied with the court process. In a similar vein, Felstiner and Williams (1980) reports that eight to fourteen months after mediating issues of assault, battery and harrassment in the Community Mediation Program in Dorchester, Massachusetts, most people are glad that they tried mediation (78 percent), think it helped their situation (50 percent), and feel that they had an opportunity to air their complaints (70 percent).

A fourth feature of mediation is the extent to which it is perceived as a fair process. In the Denver Project, clients who reached a mediation agreement were pleased with the agreement and impressed with its fairness. Similarly, compared to adjudicating litigants, parties who used Maine's small claims mediation service more frequently deemed their settlements fair (67.1 percent versus 59.0 percent), and were almost twice as likely to share their opponent's view of the outcome (McEwen and Maiman 1981). Not surprisingly, the give-and-take of negotiation has the effect of reducing polarization between parties to a dispute.

A related finding in the mediation literature is improvement in the relationship between disputants. In the Denver Project, all disputants who mediated experienced immediate improvements in their relationships, although lasting improvements were only noted for those who reached mediation agreements. These conclusions are echoed in Parker's (1980) research on divorce mediation in Atlanta. In his research on the mediation of felony offenses between acquaintances, Davis (1980) finds that adversaries who mediate are better able to understand one another. Indeed, plaintiffs who mediate are ultimately less angry at and fearful of "defendants" than those who adjudicate. And in Maine's small claims mediation program, McEwen and Maiman (1981) reach similar conclusions.

Along with other researchers, we find that mediated agreements result in better compliance. In the Denver Project, successful mediation clients report the highest levels of personal and spousal compliance and the lowest incidences of serious problems. McEwen and Maiman find that mediation clients perceive themselves to be legally obligated to comply, a sentiment lacking among adversarial disputants. Indeed, while 70.6 percent of the mediation agreements with a monetary settlement were reported to be paid in full, this was reported by only 33.8 percent of the adjudicated cases. Finally, Felstiner notes that mediation clients report that the other party complies in 68 percent of the felony cases he studied. Clearly mediation has a greater capacity than adjudication to secure compliance with the terms of settlement.

Compliance, however, does not necessarily eliminate the need for modification and/or relitigation. While several studies find that relitigation among mediation clients is rare (e.g., Irving concludes that only 10 percent of the mediated cases return to court by the end of one year and Cook (1980) reports no further problems in 70 to 80 percent of the cases mediated in the Neighborhood Justice Centers), those who compare mediating individuals with their adjudicating counterparts often reach different conclusions. For example, Felstiner notes no difference between adversarial and mediating parties in their relitigation patterns. Parker's work with divorcing couples finds no differences between the two groups in the number of contacts with third parties following the promulgation of a final decree. And Davis concludes that "there is little evidence that mediation was more effective than court adjudication in preventing recidivism during the follow up."

The findings of the Denver Custody Mediation Project are consistent with these patterns. Although relitigation is rare among those who successfully mediate and only 9 percent had initiated motions to modify at the time of the second follow-up interview (half the proportion relitigating in the adversarial samples), the rate of modification for this group was identical to the rate observed in adversarial samples. It remains to be seen whether successful mediation clients continue this level of modification activity. According to research comparing mediation and adversarial clients in Hennepin County, Minnesota, relitigation for mediation clients is ultimately lower (Doyle and Caron 1979).

As research in civil and criminal mediation continues, we will be able to speak with increasing assurance about many issues touched upon in this article — the kinds of cases suitable for mediation, the causes and cures for the pervasive underutilization of mediation services by the general public, the determining factors in the outcome of the process and the long- as well as short-range benefits and costs. Here we have shown that mediation results in substantial differences in behaviour and attitude among those who contest child custody and visitation matters.

The patterns are encouraging, but far from definitive. Indeed, many of our ultimate conclusions about the efficacy of custody mediation will be tied to the analysis of joint custody arrangements and their long-term ramifications for child development and the restructuring of the divorcing family.

REFERENCES

Bohannon, P. 1970. *Divorce and After.* Garden City, New Jersey: Doubleday, Inc.
Bradbury, K., S. Dansigner, E. Smolensky and P. Smolensky. 1979. "Public Assistance, Female Headship and Economic Well-Being," *Journal of Marriage and the Family,* 41:519-35.
Buttenwieser, Helen M., et al. 1966. "Arbitration and Protection of the Law," *Arbitration Journal,* 21:215.
Carrad, D. C. 1979. "A Modest Proposal to End Our National Disgrace," *Family Advocate,* 2(2):30-33.
Cassetty, J. 1978. *Child Support and Public Policy: Securing Support From Absent Fathers.* Lexington, Massachusetts: Lexington Books.
Cavenaugh, Ralph and Deborah Rhode. 1976. "The Unauthorized Practice of Law and Pro Se Divorce," *Yale Law Journal,* 86:104.
Coogler, O. J. 1978. *Structured Mediation in Divorce Settlements.* Lexington, Massachusetts: D. C. Heath and Company.
Cook, Roger F. 1980. "Neighborhood Justice Centers: What Types of Disputes Are Appropriate?" Presented at Annual Meeting of Law and Society Association.
Cook, Roger F., Janice Roehl, David Sheppard. 1980. "Neighborhood Justice Centers Field Test: Final Evaluation Report." Unpublished.
Corey, W. E. and R. S. Teachout. 1979. "Mediation in the Courts of Maine," *Maine Bar Bulletin,* 13, 33:54-56.
Cotchett, J. W. 1978. "Community Courts: A Viable Concept," *Trial,* 14:45-47.
Danzig, Richard and Michael Lowy. 1975. "Everyday Disputes and Mediation in the United States: A Reply to Professor Felstiner," *Law and Society Review,* 9:675.
Davidson, R. 1975. *Marriage and Family Law in Ontario, Vancouver and Toronto.* International Self-Counsel Press, Ltd.
Davis, Robert C., Martha Tichane, Deborah Grayson. 1980. The Effects of Alternative Forms of Dispute Resolution on Recidivism in Felony Offenses Between Acquaintances. Unpublished.
Deutsch, Morton. 1973. *The Resolution of Conflict.* New Haven: Yale University Press.
Doyle, Patrick and Wayne Caron. 1979. "Contested Custody Interventions. An Empirical Assessment," In Olsen, et al., "Child Custody," Unpublished Monograph, Minneapolis, Minnesota.
Epenshade, T. J. 1979. "The Economic Consequences of Divorce," *Journal of Marriage and the Family,* 41:615-25.

Feldman, S. R. 1977. "A Statutory Proposal to Remove Divorce from the Courtroom," *Maine Law Review,* 29:25-46.

Felstiner, William. 1974. "Influences of Social Organization on Dispute Processing," *Social Review,* 63.

Felstiner, William and Lynn Williams. 1980. *Community Mediation in Dorchester, Massachusetts Final Report.* Los Angeles: Social Science Research Institute, University of Southern California.

Foster, Henry and Doris Freed. 1980. "Divorce in the Fifty States: An Overview," *Family Law Quarterly,* 14,4:229.

Fuller, Lon. 1971. "Mediation — Its Forms and Functions," *Southern California Law Review,* 44:305.

Glick, P.C. 1979. "Children of Divorced Parents in Demographic Perspective," *Journal of Social Issues,* 4:170-82.

Goldbeck, Willis B. 1975. "Mediation. An Instrument of Citizen Involvement," 30, *Arbitration Journal,* 241.

Goldstein, Joseph, Anna Freud and Albert Solnit. 1973. *Beyond the Best Interests of the Child.* New York: The Free Press.

Gulliver, P. H. 1979. *Disputes and Negotiations: A Cross Cultural Perspective.* New York: Academic Press.

Haynes, John. 1981. *Divorce Mediation.* New York, Springer Publishing Company.

Herman, McHenry and Weber. 1979. "Mediation and Arbitration Applied to Family Conflict Resolution: The Divorce Settlement," *Arbitration Journal,* 34:17-21.

Irving, H. H. and B. G. Irving. 1974. "Conciliation Counseling Divorce Litigation, "*Reports of Family Law,* Vol. 16, 257-66.

Irving, Howard. 1980. *Divorce Mediation: The Rational Alternative.* Toronto, Canada: Personal Library Publishers.

Irving, Howard, et al. 1981. Final Research Report of the Conciliation Project: Provincial Court (Family Division), Toronto.

Callner, Bruce, W. 1977. "Boundaries of the Divorce Lawyer's Role," *Family Law Quarterly,* 10:289-398.

Kaufman, I. R. 1976. "Judicial Reform in the Next Century," *Stanford Law Review,* 29:1-26.

Maccaulay and Walster. 1977. "Legal Structures and Restoring Equity," in Tapp and Levine (eds.) *Law, Justice and the Individual in Society.* New York: Holt, Rinehart and Winston.

McEwen, Craig and Richard Maiman. 1981. "Small Claims Mediation in Maine: An Empirical Assessment," *Maine Law Review,* 33:237.

Milne, Ann. 1979. "Custody of Children in a Divorce Process: A Family Self-Determination Model," *Conciliation Courts Review,* 16:2-12.

Mnookin, Robert and Lewis Kornhauser. 1979. "Bargaining in the Shadow of the Law: The Case of Divorce," 88 *Yale Law Journal* 950.

Mund, Geraldine. 1976. "The Need for Community Arbitration," *Arbitration Journal,* 31:109-15.

National Center for Health Statistics. 1980. "Births, Marriages, Divorces and Deaths for 1979," *Monthly Vital Statistics Report.* Hyattsville, Maryland: U.S. Dept. HEW, 80-1120, 28, 12.

Parker, Arthur. 1980. Mediation Theory and Practice. Unpublished Dissertation.

Preston, S. H. 1975. "Estimating the Proportion of American Marriages That End in Divorce," *Sociological Methods and Research,* 3:435-60.

Rubin, J. Z. and B. R. Brown. 1975. *The Social Psychology of Bargaining and Negotiation.* New York: Academic Press.

Spencer, Janet and Joseph Zammit. 1976. "Mediation-Arbitration: A Proposal for Private Resolution of Disputes Between Divorced or Separated Parents," *Duke Law Journal:* 911–39.

Wallerstein, Judith and Joan Kelly. 1980. *Surviving the Breakup,* New York: Basic Books, Inc.

Weiss, R. S. 1975. *Marital Separation.* New York: Basic Books, Inc.

Weiss, W. W. and H. B. Collada. 1977. "Conciliation Counseling: The Courts Effective Mechanism for Resolving Visitation and Custody Disputes," *Family Coordinator,* 26(4): 444–47.

Weitzman, L. J. 1977. "Divorce and the Marital Partnership: The Problem of Legal Recognition of the Wife's Contribution," in B. A. Chadwick (ed.) *Government Impact on Family Life.* Provo, Utah: Brigham Young University Press.

Witty, Cathie. 1980. *Mediation and Society: Conflict Management in Lebanon.* New York: Academic Press.

Chapter Seventeen

A Study of Conciliation Counselling in the Family Court of Toronto: Implications for Socio-Legal Practice*

**Howard H. Irving Ph.D., Faculty of Social Work
and Michael Benjamin M.A., Family Researcher**

University of Toronto, Canada

Over the past twenty years, the rates of marital separation and divorce have slowly but inexorably risen in both Canada (Statistics Canada 1978) and the U.S. (Norton and Glick 1979). One consequence of this change has been an enormous increase in the population of troubled and unhappy people seeking help; another has been increasingly urgent concern over the means by which social service systems may be designed to provide the services required by these clients.

A case in point concerns the Family Court which plays a major role in the initiation and enforcement of various forms of family litigation associated with separation and divorce. While the demand on the Court was manageable, the Court's procedural system functioned well. More recently, however, a tremendous increase in service demand has created a serious backlog of cases, the delay between the initiation of litigation and court appearance has risen rapidly and, in general, strained the civil court system (Elkin 1973; Cochett 1978).

These problems have been accompanied by a growing concern within the legal and social service communities that the adversary system

---

* A fuller version of the material in this chapter appears in Howard H. Irving (ed.) *Family Law: An Interdisciplinary Perspective* (Toronto, Carswell, 1981).

† A dagger indicates a reference cited in Bahr (1980).

is neither appropriate nor helpful for many couples seeking judicial solutions to their marital difficulties (Kronby 1972, 123; Wheeler 1974, 12). The main basis for dissatisfaction is that the adversary system escalates conflict between couples (Coogler 1977)† while exacerbating the emotional trauma already associated with separation or divorce (Irving and Irving 1974; Weiss 1975).

Nor should this be surprising. Legal ethics require that lawyers represent their clients with vigor and determination. This recommends that lawyers often take extreme and unnecessarily divisive positions (Coogler 1977; Weiss 1975, 265); frequently this involves their advising their clients to engage in conflict-escalating behaviour.† Consequently, the process of marital dissolution continues to be structured as a contest between opponents.† Paradoxically, this serves to defeat the purpose for which the Family Court was created — the informal solution of marital and family problems — and suggests that adversarial court procedures may be contraindicated with respect to many family problems.

These remarks are not intended to imply that the Family Court no longer has an important and continuing role to play in family litigation. Rather, they suggest, first, that there are many families for whom adversarial court procedures are neither appropriate nor helpful; and, second, that alternative approaches to marital conflict and dissolution need to be found to complement the judicial process.

Conciliation counselling has been proposed as one such alternative. Essentially, this involves a neutral third party counselling persons whose marriage is in distress or has already broken down (i.e., separation, divorce). Accordingly, it may be defined as "a form of family intervention involving one or both spouses seen separately or together and designed to achieve one or more of the following outcomes: (1) reduce the level of real or perceived conflict between spouses; (2) facilitate communication between spouses, either in general terms or about specific issues problematic for them; (3) transform an amorphous problem into a resolvable issue; (4) suggest problem-solving strategies as a viable alternative to litigation; (5) provide the most efficient use of the legal system; and (6) optimally, help the spouses achieve a written agreement concerning one or more disputable issues or problems." (Irving et al. 1979, 14–15). Ideally, these outcomes are intended to soften the trauma traditionally associated with marital dissolution as well as reduce the private and public expense typically attendant on it.

Proponents of this approach assume that persons experiencing various family problems can benefit from third party intervention (Elkin 1973) and that even when reconciliation is impossible, conciliation counselling may minimize whatever emotional damage will be done (Lightman and Irving 1976). Further, assuming that this approach is superior to the traditional adversary system, they have argued for the widespread implementation of a conciliation counselling service (CCS)

(Weiss 1975, 112; Davidson 1975, 14; Irving and Gandy 1975; Sonne 1978; Haynes 1978).

The empirical bases of this argument are twofold. First, some support comes from the social psychology literature concerning bargaining and negotiation. In that context, several investigators report evidence that cooperative strategies work better than competitive ones in the prevention or the resolution of conflict (Rubin and Brown 1975, 263; Deutsch 1973, 252). Whereas the former promote trust and compromise, the latter engender suspicion and conflict. While persuasive and interesting, as laboratory effort, these data at best provide only indirect support for the conciliation approach.

A second source of support comes from a handful of clinical projects employing this approach. Thus, Elkin (1962, 1973) in Los Angeles (California), the Alberta Conciliation Service (1975) in Edmonton (Alberta), Weiss and Collada (1977) in San Jose (California) and the Frontenac Family Referral Service (1979) in Kingston (Ontario) all claim service effectiveness. While these studies have collectively made an important contribution, they remain problematic in so far as they are all primarily descriptive, fail to report operationally defined outcome measures, are noncomparative in design and/or suffer from sampling limitations.

While such efforts are, of course, encouraging, the fact remains that no research study currently exists which provides empirical support for the outcome effectiveness of conciliation counselling as an intervention strategy, either alone or in comparison to alternative (i.e., more traditional) intervention approaches. What appears to be needed is an exploratory study of conciliation counselling employing a comparative research design.

In response to this need, the Toronto Conciliation Project began operation in 1976. The Project was situated in the Provincial Court, Family Division, located in the Municipality of Toronto (Ontario) and was funded under the auspices of Health and Welfare Canada and the Ontario Ministry of the Attorney General. The Project initiated two interlocking studies. The results of the first study, Study 1, can be found in Irving et al. 1979. This chapter presents the findings of the second study, Study 2.

SAMPLE SELECTION AND EVALUATION SETTING

The findings of Study 1 (Irving et al. 1979) indicated that the outcome effectiveness of the CCS could be considerably enhanced by using a selected, as opposed to a random, sample. Accordingly, based on Study 1 data, four selection criteria were employed for sampling purposes:

1. Both spouses agree to participate in counselling. This means that the marital dyad was the primary unit of analysis.
2. Referral to the services must be made by either a judge or a lawyer. With respect to the latter, agreement to refer their client to the CCS must involve the lawyers of both spouses.
3. Both spouses must be able to speak and read English with some level of fluency.
4. Both spouses must agree to participate in the research project, at least during phases 1 and 3 (see below, p. 272).

Over a period of ten mouths (September, 1978 to June, 1979), a total of 193 out of 352 Court client couples (55 percent) met the above criteria and so were designated as the CCS study sample.[1]

All service delivery to and baseline evaluation of the study sample was conducted in the offices of the Provincial Court, Family Division, located in the Municipality of Toronto. The majority of follow-up interviews (see below, p. 277) were conducted in the homes of the respondents.

Service Characteristics

The CCS is best described in terms of the following four components. First, in accord with the aims of the service, conciliation counsellors sought to enhance cooperative behaviour between spouses in conflict and to help them use the resources of the legal and social service systems to their best advantage. Specifically, this involved (1) *focusing on objective issues* as one aspect of task-centred family intervention; (2) reducing *nonrationality* by helping to clarify purposes, intentions, gains and costs; (3) *exploring alternative solutions* to various marital problems; (4) *facilitating communication* between spouses in conflict, and (5) *identifying and promoting the use of additional resources* (other than the court). Second, all counsellors were holders of a Master of Social Work (M.S.W.) degree. Third, CCS workers had a relatively small case load (approximately five new cases per month per worker) and worked flexible hours, including one evening a week. Finally, all workers attended a special in-service training programme.

The programme consisted of twelve three-hour sessions given by experts in the fields of family law, family breakdown, family counselling and conflict resolution. It was primarily designed to orient the workers to the unique aspects of conciliation work and acquaint them with all relevant legislation.

272   Mediation and Professional Roles

Service Evaluation Procedure

Evaluation of CCS outcome effectiveness took place in four sequential phases, summarized in Figure 17.1.

Phase 1 involved the collection of baseline data. Upon arrival at the CCS office, client couples were met by the receptionist who was trained to explain the purpose and confidential nature of the study. She recorded the clients' file numbers and names on two separate copies of a forty-one-item Client Question Form and asked them to fill it out privately while in the waiting room. In order to minimize the possibility of bias, throughout

FIGURE 17.1   Flow Chart of Research Design

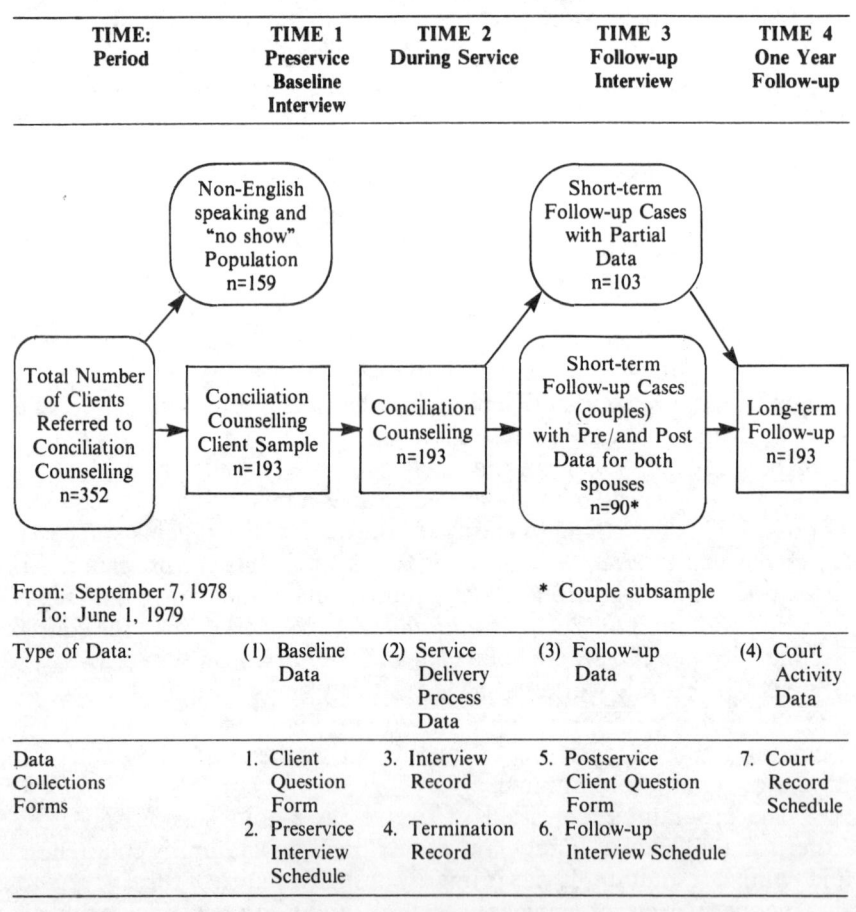

TIME: Period	TIME 1 Preservice Baseline Interview	TIME 2 During Service	TIME 3 Follow-up Interview	TIME 4 One Year Follow-up

Non-English speaking and "no show" Population n=159

Short-term Follow-up Cases with Partial Data n=103

Total Number of Clients Referred to Conciliation Counselling n=352 → Conciliation Counselling Client Sample n=193 → Conciliation Counselling n=193 → Short-term Follow-up Cases (couples) with Pre/and Post Data for both spouses n=90* → Long-term Follow-up n=193

From: September 7, 1978
To: June 1, 1979

* Couple subsample

Type of Data:	(1) Baseline Data	(2) Service Delivery Process Data	(3) Follow-up Data	(4) Court Activity Data
Data Collections Forms	1. Client Question Form 2. Preservice Interview Schedule	3. Interview Record 4. Termination Record	5. Postservice Client Question Form 6. Follow-up Interview Schedule	7. Court Record Schedule

* Ninety-five couples referred involved one (34 cases) or both (61 cases) spouses who did not wish to proceed with conciliation.

this and all subsequent phases of the study, data were collected from each spouse separately.

Apart from descriptive data, the form contained two specific research instruments designed and/or selected to provide a baseline for comparison with later follow-up measures, specifically, the Life Satisfaction Questionnaire (Part 8), modified from Campbell et al. (1976), and the Problem Severity Index (Part D). The former consisted of ten semantic differential items (Osgood et al. 1975) each of which consisted of a pair of polar adjectives (e.g., "boring" vs. "interesting"). Clients were asked to rate where they would place their present life circumstances on a six-point scale within the two extremes.

The eight items most highly intercorrelated (Campbell et al. 1976) were combined to provide a Life Satisfaction Index.

The latter instrument, the Problem Severity Index, was made up of problems common to people using the Family Court. This list of problems was compiled with the help of the staff of the CCS and the Traditional Intake Service. Clients were asked to rate each of the problems listed (eg., custody dispute) on a five-point Likert-type scale ranging from "Not a problem for me" to "A very serious problem for me."

Following completion of the Client Question Form, the client couples began their first counselling interview. At that time, the CCS worker reviewed the form for completeness (helping them to complete it if necessary) and subsequently administered a twenty-six-item Preservice Interview Schedule. The Schedule was primarily designed to collect sociodemographic data as well as to inquire, in further detail, into the clients' presenting problem(s). All workers were trained in the systematic use of this and all other research questionnaires. Furthermore, their work was routinely monitored and checked for accuracy, and periodic meetings were held to assure that uniform interviewing procedures were being employed.

Phase 2 concerned evaluation of the service delivery process. To this end, workers maintained a running record of each case by means of the repeated completion of a fourteen-item Interview Record Questionnaire and, upon termination of service, completion of a forty-item Termination Record Questionnaire.

The Interview Record Questionnaire recorded data pertaining to each interview (e.g., length of interview) with each client couple. The Termination Record Questionnaire provided summary information (e.g., who was involved) for each case as a whole.

Phase 3 concerned follow-up evaluation of client couples and was conducted six to twelve weeks after the termination of service. This involved administration of a thirty-eight-item Follow-up Interview Schedule and a seventy-two-item Postservice Client Question Form. The former schedule specifically focused on the clients' perception of the CCS as well as inquiring into the clients' perception of how such contact had affected their most important presenting problem. The latter form duplicated the items from the baseline Client Question Form (i.e., Parts A–E) but included, in an additional section (i.e., Part F), a further research instrument, the Court Service Satisfaction Questionnaire. This Questionnaire, as its name implies, examined the extent to which the clients perceived that contact with the CCS had altered their life circumstances. Both the aforementioned forms were administered in the clients' home by one of two specially trained research interviewers. Their work, like that of their counsellor counterparts, was periodically monitored for accuracy and uniformity of procedure.

Of the 386 individuals (i.e., 193 couples) constituting the study sample, 227 (58.8 percent) were successfully contacted and reinterviewed on follow-up. In terms of marital dyads, however, this return represented complete data on 90 client couples (46.6 percent); data were incomplete on the remainder (i.e., 103 couples; 53.4 percent). A file was judged "incomplete" if data were available with respect to only one spouse on follow-up or if one or both spouses failed to respond to 20 percent or more of follow-up interview items.

Finally, phase 4 concerned the use of the Court by the study sample within one year following the termination of service. This involved completion of a thirteen-item Court Record Schedule by an experienced court worker based on a thorough search of the Family Court records. The Schedule, developed with the assistance of a CCS worker, was designed to determine the frequency and type of litigation with which each of the study client couples were involved. In addition, at this time, all counsellors were interviewed by the senior investigator. These interviews were relatively informal and open-ended; they focused on the counsellors' general impressions of conciliation counselling, especially the most effective means of helping client couples reach agreement.

Data Analysis

As stated above, while data were available with respect to 193 couples, a complete data file existed for 90 of them. On the grounds that collapsing complete and incomplete files together would seriously compromise the validity of any pre–post comparisons, such comparisons were restricted to complete data files alone. In order to ensure that this procedure did not yield a sociodemographically biased subsample, partial and complete subgroups were compared statistically. Virtually no statistically significant differences were detected.

Available data were of two types, qualitative and quantitative. With respect to the latter, data were coded, punched on standard cards and "edited" for computer analysis using the Statistical Package for the Social

Sciences (Nie et al. 1975). Comparative analysis of data which achieved either a nominal (i.e., yes/no) or ordinal (i.e., less than/greater than) level of measurement (in form of a cross-tabulation table) involved the use of the Chi Square test (written x^2) of independence. Analysis of interval data (i.e., "mean" or average scores) involved use of the T-test for independent samples (Glass and Stanley 1970). For both tests, an alpha level of 0.05 was employed as the acceptable level of statistical significance.

With respect to qualitative data, these were initially examined by inspection. Wherever the data exhibited some clustering or redundancy, client responses were categorized, collapsed, quantified (in percentage terms) and subjected to statistical analysis using the same procedures as described above.

ONE YEAR FOLLOW-UP ON AGREEMENT CASES

In addition to court follow-up, the durability of agreements was also examined at one year follow-up. At that time, a 50 percent random sample was selected from among CCS client couples who reached agreement and for whom complete data were available (n=61). Of these (n=30), sixteen couples together with nine single clients agreed to participate.

Initial contact was made by letter. This advised them that they would soon be contacted by telephone for their assistance in completing a Telephone Follow-Up Questionnaire. This consisted of twenty items focusing on (1) their current marital status; (2) the current status of their conciliation agreement; and (3) their evaluation of and attitudes towards the CCS. All items were either of the Likert type or were of the multiple choice variety. The questionnaire was administered by a group of five graduate social work students as part of a research methods course under the supervision of the senior author.

Because of the small sample size, data analysis did not differentiate between single and couple clients; rather, analysis focused on the responses of the forty-one clients seen as single individuals.

LAWYERS' EVALUATION OF CCS

In order to determine lawyers' evaluation of the CCS, a list of seventy-five lawyers was first compiled, each of whom had referred at least one client to the CCS during the period 1978–79 inclusive. Following contact with these lawyers, fifty-two (69.3 percent) agreed to participate and provided usable data.

Each of the lawyers in question was mailed a copy of the Lawyer Questionnaire accompanied by a covering letter explaining the purpose of the study and asking for their assistance. This was followed two weeks later by a telephone call advising them when the questionnaire would be picked up.

The questionnaire consisted of thirteen items focusing on (1) the level of the respondents experience with the CCS; (2) their evaluation of that experience; and (3) their recommendations for the future of the CCS. All items were either of the Likert-type or the multiple-choice variety. The questionnaire was administered by a group of six graduate social work students as part of a research methods course under the supervision of the senior author.

RESULTS

The results of Study 2, Parts 1 to 3, are each presented below in summary form. For ease of presentation, the results of Part 1 are divided into four sections concerning client characteristics, service characteristics, outcome and follow-up, respectively. By convention, findings described as "significant" will have met or surpassed the alpha level of 0.05 while findings reported as "substantial" will be less than 0.10 but greater than 0.05.

Baseline Data

Baseline data provide the basis for constructing a capsule picture of the "typical" CCS client couple. Such couples were in their thirties (59 percent), had been married for more than five years (80 percent), had at least two children (66 percent) and reported that this was the first marriage for both spouses (87 percent). In response to longstanding problems (three to nine years: 81 percent), most spouses had been separated at least twice in the past (51 percent) and were currently separated (72 percent) and living part (85 percent), this arrangement having been in place for up to a year (67 percent). While most women worked on a full or part-time basis (55 percent) — typically at clerical (45 percent) or semi-skilled (19 percent) occupations — a large proportion (45 percent) stayed at home to care for the children and remained financially dependent upon their husbands. Most of the latter, like their wives, had a high school education (65 percent) and worked on a full-time basis (85 percent) at a skilled (23 percent) or semi-skilled (24 percent) occupation, with 52.3 percent of working women earning an average of $8,000 or more per year and 70.1 percent of working men earning an average of $12,000 or more per year.

Turning to their subjective state, couples reported a moderate level of life satisfaction (x=4.0) and a low level of marital satisfaction (20–75 percent depending on the specific issue). This was especially true of wives who consistently reported higher levels of marital conflict than their husbands. While spouses reported "serious" problems in all problem categories, most rated either custody (25 percent) or access (27 percent) as the single most important problem which brought them to court. While various categories of persons had been contacted about these difficulties, lawyers were seen by both spouses to have been the most helpful (37 percent) and it was their lawyer (44 percent) or the judge (47 percent) who referred them to the CCS.

Service Data

On arrival at the CCS, client couples typically had four to six counselling interviews (47 percent) in which they were seen separately as well as together (55 percent), with children included on at least one occasion (23 percent). Counselling tended to involve a combination of morning, afternoon and evening visits (41 percent) and cumulatively involved six or more hours (51 percent). The decision to terminate service was usually made by a joint decision of the client couple and the counsellor (78 percent).

In addition, there was general consensus among counsellors that especially aggressive outreach was required with respect to client couples in which one spouse felt correctly or incorrectly, that the other spouse would not be interested in attending counselling.

Outcome Data

The outcome of counselling was strongly positive in several respects. The majority of couples:

1. reached an agreement (70 percent), typically in written form (82 percent); of these, a small proportion also reconciled (12 percent).
2. reported that they had completely (54 percent) or partially (28 percent) accomplished what they sought to achieve in relation to their most important problem; for example, one wife noted that, as a result of counselling, the "door was open for discussion. It became clear that we (the kids and I) would have to move out. [It also] clarified the custody issue and allowed me to save some dignity."
3. agreed that in regard to the total situation, things had either gotten "better" or "much better" (76 percent) since counselling had begun; this

sentiment was aptly expressed by a wife who commented that, as a result of counselling, "I understand better the problems and questions that [may] arise and [can] cope with them to ensure that my son is not drastically affected." However, counselling also benefited individuals psychologically, as this wife states: "I have more time to myself and I am not as angry with my husband. [Also,] my daughter now sees her father, [something] I had refused before."

4. reported that, in comparison to baseline marital conflict over such things as bringing up the children, financial matters, life goals, in-laws, child support and access, conflict was considerably reduced; this was especially true of wives who, since they were initially most dissatisfied, showed the most dramatic pre-post decreases (e.g., wife: custody 67 percent to 35 percent; husband: custody 57 percent to 47 percent); the quality of such change is poignantly described by the following comment of a husband: "Up to conciliation, [my] wife and I had been unable to sit down and talk things [out] without arguing in front of the baby. [The] counsellor helped us to act more maturely." Similarly, a couple jointly commented, "[Counselling was] a great experience that brought us closer together."

5. exhibited a substantial decrease in the proportion of spouses who still reported a number of "serious" problems (e.g., wife: custody 75 percent to 39 percent; husband: custody 64 percent to 52 percent); in this context, for example, one husband reported that "at least now there is a chance my children will know I'm concerned enough about them that I will seek help [for my problem] in order to be able to see them regularly." Similarly, a wife noted that the CCS "was very good in that although [my husband and I] didn't accomplish as much as I had hoped, I think we can prevent going to court."

6. agreed that they had positive feelings about their contact with the CCS (75 percent) as one wife commented, "I feel more people should know about [the] service and be able to use it. It [was] an excellent opportunity to sit down with a third party and work things out. It would have been good to have come to conciliation before [going to] court."

7. agreed that they would return to the CCS if the need arose (80 percent); thus, as one wife commented, "if there are any problems I would rather go to conciliation than [the] court lawyers." Similarly, a husband stated that "if my wife was willing to go [back], I would."

8. agreed that conciliation was the main reason for any changes they had accomplished (59 percent) and suggested that its success was primarily attributable to improvements in communication, trust and understanding (35 percent), achievement of an agreement (12 percent) and/or reduced conflict and emotional tension (17 percent); thus, one husband noted that counselling "took [the] selfishness out of me [and] helped me [to] understand my wife." Another husband commented

that counselling was "an educational experience which generates trust." Similarly a third husband stated that "my wife and I are not trying to make life difficult for each other anymore. We spend our energy on mutual concern for each other and our child." Finally, a wife observed that, as a result of counselling, "[this is the] first time in five years my husband and I have not argued on [our] son's well-being." Another wife states that "my visits with the children are more relaxed [now]. I sense that reaching an agreement has lessened [the] tension [level] and [the] children are responding accordingly."

9. two additional findings are worthy of note based on counsellor interviews: *(a)* most counsellors felt that agreement was especially difficult, if not impossible, among client couples in which the spouses remained emotionally attached to each other; such couples were characterized by one spouse heavily invested in continuing the relationship while the other spouse was equally desperate to end the relationship; this combination almost invariably resulted in protracted arguing, intense emotionality and a high level of irrationality; conversely, client couples for whom separation or divorce was a mutual goal tended to reach agreement easily and with relatively little conflict; and *(b)* there was consensus among counsellors that reaching an agreement was made much easier if the lawyers in question were supportive of this end; in contrast, lawyers who were disinterested in the process or who persisted in adopting an adversarial approach substantially reduced the probability that an agreement would be reached.

INTERACTION EFFECTS

In addition, client variables and service variables were examined in terms of their interaction with outcome variables.

Client Variables

The findings were as follows:

1. agreement was significantly related to *(a)* rating custody as "mild problem for me"; *(b)* accomplishing what they set out to with respect to their most important problem; *(c)* stating that they found their lawyer or the Court most helpful with respect to their difficulties; *(d)* stating that the CCS influenced change for the "better"; and *(e)* feeling "better" about the problem(s) that brought them to the Court in the first place;

2. satisfaction with alimony, maintenance, access and custody, judgment that life circumstances had gotten "better" or "much better" following counselling and improvement in life satisfaction were all significantly associated with reporting that a range of issues, especially those pertaining to children, were rated as "mild" problems;
3. dissatisfaction with alimony and maintenance was significantly related with having been referred to the CCS by a judge as opposed to a lawyer;
4. judgment that life circumstances had gotten "better" was also significantly related to *(a)* having seen a lawyer within three months of referral to the CCS; *(b)* reporting that they felt "better" or "much better" about the problems that brought them to the Court; *(c)* having accomplished what they wanted to with respect to their most important problem; and *(d)* agreeing that the CCS was primarily responsible for any changes that occurred; and
5. improvement in life satisfaction was also significantly related to reporting that they found their lawyer "most helpful" in resolving their difficulties; client variables were more closely analyzed utilizing a conceptual framework and client typology derived from social psychology research literature.

Service Variables

1. Agreement was significantly related to *(a)* having included a child in counselling at least once, and *(b)* having attended four or more interview sessions for a total of between four and eight hours of cumulative interview time;
2. judgment that life circumstances had gotten "better" or "much better" was significantly related to *(a)* having attended three or more counselling sessions, and *(b)* that these sessions included morning, afternoon and evening visits; and
3. improvement in life satisfaction was significantly associated with attending three or more counselling sessions.

ONE YEAR COURT FOLLOW-UP

A final concern related to Court activity at one year follow-up. These data revealed that:

1. most client couples returned to Court (71 percent) one or more times during the year following counselling; and
2. much of this activity (80 percent) pertained to those issues which brought them to Court originally, so that one return to Court was

often "automatic"; more than one return to Court was indicative of unresolved disputes. Client couples usually return to Court under one of two conditions *(a)* if the presiding judge feels that the couple in question can benefit from conciliation counselling, he will adjourn the case for anywhere from one to three months and refer them to the CCS; if, at the end of that period, agreement has been reached, the parties return to Court at which time the judge issues a "consent order" which, in effect, spells out the terms of the agreement and gives Court assent to them; if, however, agreement cannot be reached, the case is returned to Court for trial; in either case, return to Court is automatic; *(b)* alternatively, if one or both parties fails to live up to the terms of their consent order or if one or both of them feel that the terms of the order are no longer satisfactory, then the case is returned to Court for further litigation; since this return to Court concerns the consent order itself, rather than the issues which originally brought them to Court, it is a return regarding a "new" or subsequent issue; of these two categories of Court return, most Court activity (80 percent) fell in category *"(a)"*: client couples returned to Court either for the issuance of a consent order or for trial regarding the issues which originally brought them to Court.
3. Further examination of these data revealed that: *(a)* return to Court with respect to issues which arose after counselling was terminated, was substantially related with having first seen a lawyer within four to six months of referral to the CCS; *(b)* return to Court two or more times with respect to the original issue was significantly associated with client's judgment that their life circumstances had gotten "worse"; reporting that contact with the CCS had made "no difference" to their problems; and, judging that financial support was a "moderate" to a "very serious" problem; *(c)* return to Court, irrespective of the issue in question, was significantly related to judging that life circumstances had gotten "worse" and having first seen a lawyer four to six months prior to referral to the CCS. In addition, while return to Court *per se* was statistically unrelated to agreement, inspection of these data showed that client couples who failed to reach agreement were twice as likely as those that did to return to Court four or more times (17 percent vs. 9 percent).

AGREEMENTS AT ONE YEAR FOLLOW-UP

Findings with respect to one year follow-up of clients who reached an agreement were as follows:

1. a minority of clients (22 percent) had reconciled, all within three to six months following the termination of counselling;

2. most clients (92 percent) felt they had a clear understanding of the terms of their agreement and, in addition, felt that this was also true of their spouse (76 percent);
3. although many clients reported having some problems with their agreement, only a handful (9.8 percent) returned to Court over the matter;
4. a substantial proportion of clients (40 percent) had made changes to the terms of their agreement, especially with respect to access; most of these (74 percent), however, had made these changes informally, that is, outside the Court system, and most (79 percent) were mutually acceptable;
5. all clients sought some help in keeping the terms of their agreement; however, this seldom involved formal agencies or organizations (e.g., police 1.9 percent; family or marriage counsellor 7.6 percent, clergyman 1.9 percent, psychiatrist 3.8 percent); rather, most clients relied on either their lawyer (25 percent), family or friends (19 percent) or their family doctor (13 percent), and most (75 percent) found such support helpful;
6. most clients reported that they were either "satisfied" or "very satisfied" with the terms of their agreement (e.g., custody 69 percent; access 69 percent);
7. most clients were either "somewhat satisfied," "satisfied" or "very satisfied" with their total agreement (81 percent);
8. the majority of clients (62 percent) did not feel pressured to reach an agreement; of those who did, most felt that they would have liked more time in counselling as well as follow-up contact (a service not now provided by the CCS); and
9. finally, a majority of clients (53 percent) stated that in the year following counselling, their overall family situation had "improved."

LAWYERS' EVALUATION

With respect to lawyer evaluation of the CCS, the findings were as follows:
1. a large proportion (49 percent) of the respondents had had a good deal of contact with the CCS, having referred anywhere from four to more than twenty-nine clients to the service during the period 1978–79 inclusive;
2. most referred cases primarily were concerned with either custody (85 percent) or access (89 percent);
3. most (82 percent) recommended that the CCS be continued on the grounds that it helped clarify issues (52 percent), narrow issues (56 percent) or facilitate dispute resolution (60 percent);

4. with respect to the issues of access and custody, most respondents reported that the CCS was either "very helpful" (70 percent) or "helpful" (62 percent); with respect to other issues, such as property disputes, the majority of respondents felt that it either had no effect (27 percent) or stated that they "didn't know" (62 percent);
5. most respondents recommended that the CCS be continued in its present form (78 percent) on the grounds that it "always" or "frequently" helped avoid unnecessary litigation (69 percent), better prepared the client to understand the issues (76 percent), allowed the client to use their services more appropriately (82 percent) and reduced the client's emotional turmoil (80 percent);
6. most respondents agreed that they would recommend the service to other lawyers (79 percent) and felt that it operated best as a court-based service, located either in the Family Court (46 percent) or in the Supreme Court (43 percent);
7. most felt that the CCS could be most helpful to their clients either on first contact with a lawyer (22 percent) or prior to making the decision to proceed with litigation (39 percent);
8. most felt that the goals and/or functions of the CCS were not in conflict with their role as a legal adviser (84 percent) insofar as dealing with legal problems was their area of expertise while dealing with the emotional aspects of divorce was better handled by the CCS;
9. in their qualitative responses, respondents noted that the service provides conciliation counselling for clients who would otherwise be unable to afford private counselling;
10. finally, with respect to the future, most respondents recommended that with respect to contested cases, clients be informed of the availability of the CCS either by the judge (59 percent) or by a court-initiated letter (47 percent).

IMPLICATIONS AND CONCLUSIONS

We began this study with three objectives:

1. to discover the effect(s) of applying conciliation to a selected as opposed to a random sample of client couples;
2. to inquire into the durability of conciliation counselling agreements at one year follow-up;
3. to examine the evaluation of the CCS by lawyers who have had experience with the service.

The answers to these questions provided by the findings discussed above are clear and unequivocal. Specifically, they suggest that the CCS provides at least seven major benefits, either to the client couples who use it or to the lawyers referring clients to it.

First, a substantial majority of client couples either achieved a written agreement or reconciled and resumed living together. These outcomes accounted for 70 percent of all client couples for whom a complete data set was available. Moreover, these agreements typically concerned custody, access or support, the very issues which the majority of couples regarded as their most important problem. These findings are strikingly at variance with those of Study 1 and strongly suggest that the outcome effectiveness of conciliation counselling is enhanced by the use of a selected sample.

Second, agreements achieved during the course of counselling tended to endure, at least as of our last follow-up at one year. Perhaps even more important, the maintenance and/or modification of these agreements was typically achieved informally, without recourse to the courts. It must be noted, of course, that these findings are in some doubt in the light of the small sample from which they were derived. However, the random nature of that sample provides at least some basis for accepting their validity. If so, they attest to the quality of CCS outcome effectiveness and suggest that the CCS not only benefits client couples who use it, but also the court system by helping to avoid unnecessary, wasteful and expensive litigation.

Third, in the same context, a group of respondents best qualified to judge the judicial benefits of the CCS, namely a group of lawyers (N=52) experienced with the operation of the service, unequivocally stated that not only did the CCS save the Court time and money by avoiding unnecessary litigation, but it also saved both lawyers' and clients' time by encouraging them to make better use of legal services. It is hardly surprising, therefore, that most lawyers strongly supported the continued operation of the CCS and noted that it did not conflict with their own legal functions.

Fourth, both clients and lawyers claimed benefit from the CCS in so far as it helped narrow and clarify issues in dispute between couples in conflict. It is not unreasonable to believe that the ambiguity surrounding many of the issues client couples bring to their lawyer derives from the intersection of the substantive and the emotional dimensions of conflict. In this context, the lawyers observation that the CCS was better suited than they in dealing with emotional tension helps to explain why issue clarification appears to be regularly associated with conciliation counselling. To the extent that a prerequisite for problem-solving is clear communication, it also helps to explain why the CCS appears to avoid many of the difficulties associated with the traditional adversary approach to divorce litigation.

Fifth, client couples consistently reported that counselling achieved its beneficial results by means of a twofold process: reducing conflict and emotional tension while simultaneously facilitating better communication and mutual understanding. While these data help explain the reduced judicial involvement of CCS clients, they also highlight the qualitative aspects of divorce litigation, namely, the intense and prolonged emotional turmoil typically associated with it. To the extent that such turmoil clouds judgment and intensifies hostility, it can often prolong conflict and worsen an already traumatic situation. In this context, reaching an agreement as a result of conciliation counselling is incidental; its primary benefit is subjective in the form of relief from emotional distress.

Sixth, by its combination of objective (i.e., agreement) outcome and subjective relief, conciliation counselling is strongly associated with significant improvements in life circumstances and/or marital satisfaction. This may have various meanings for the client couples in question, including improved mutual regard among married couples or assured child support and visitation for couples who are separated or divorced. Whatever the details, these data imply that such clients show an increased ability to cope with their life exigencies, the opportunity to get some satisfaction out of life and the possibility of achieving new or revised life goals, all novel achievements for many of these couples troubled for years prior to counselling.

Finally, reduced use of the court, better use of legal expertise, and so on, all imply that the CCS should be a cost effective method of handling pre- or postdivorce dispute resolution. Unfortunately, objective data in support of this expectation were beyond the scope of the present study. However, a Staff Report (1979) indicates that during the period of Study 1, the CCS was indeed effective in this way, yielding $155 in public saving per case. Insofar as the outcome effectiveness of that study was considerably lower than that of the present study, it is only reasonable that Study 2 can be expected to have improved in cost effectiveness over its predecessor. This reasoning finds further support from a recent study of Bahr (1980) who, among other things, examined the cost effectiveness of eight conciliation projects most of which were in the U.S. alone, and found that widespread implementation of conciliation counselling (which he called "divorce mediation") would yield $98 million annually in combined public and private savings. These data, taken together with our own, suggest that widespread implementation of conciliation counselling should yield a comparable level of savings in Canada.

All too frequently divorce litigation is seen as a matter pertaining exclusively to the marital dyad. Consequently, child involvement, when and if it does occur, is typically regarded as incidental to the main focus of counselling. This perspective, however, overlooks two insights long available to family counsellors, namely, that (1) an integral aspect of family life is the interdependence between and among constitutent members, and (2) all family members actively participate, either directly or indirectly, in the development and maintenance of family problems (e.g., Minuchin et al. 1978, ch. 2). It follows that the involvement of all family members must also relate to problem resolution preceding change. This suggests the need for a shift in the focus of conciliation from the marital to the family unit. This would recommend that, unless specifically contraindicated, counsellors encourage the involvement of all family members on the grounds that it may significantly contribute to increased outcome effectiveness.

In light of the foregoing discussion, we may conclude by suggesting that, while there is much yet to be done, the data we have examined in this study indicate that the CCS is a viable and useful adjunct or alternative to the adversary system in relation to problems of marital conflict and dissolution. We therefore recommend its widespread implementations and continued systematic evaluation in the strongest possible terms. The means by which this might be accomplished we considered in Irving (1980, 191-192).

APPENDIX

In the course of completing this research project, the authors formed certain opinions regarding the most advantageous means of establishing a conciliation counselling service. We offer them here as a matter of interest to the reader and with the hope that they will serve as a focus for creative discussion and critical debate. For a definition of any of the terms used below, the reader is referred to Irving (1980).

Recommendations For The Establishment Of Conciliation Court Services

1. It is helpful for such a service to be imbued with the legal status and authority of the court system.
2. The service should be located within the court, so that they may be closely connected and to give the service greater credibility. This is especially important for lawyers making referrals.
3. Ideally the service should be provided on a state or province-wide basis and be jointly funded by state or province and federal levels of government.
4. A conciliation counsellor should be available at all times to see an immediate referral following pretrial conferences or referrals from judges.
5. There should be an advisory board made up of representatives from the professional and client communities.
6. A director of conciliation counselling services should be appointed who is responsible to the chief judge or his designee.

7. Conciliation counselling should be made available to all who wish to make use of it, even before formal proceedings are instituted.
8. The service should perform both intake (initial screening) and dispute resolution functions in order to eliminate fragmentation and duplication of service.
9. There should be a conciliation team composed of social workers aided by consultation from lawyers, psychiatrists, and psychologists, as well as staff from the area's predominant social and ethnic groups.
10. The nature of the service should be short-term (approximately one to six interviews) and crisis-oriented, with dispute resolution as the mode of approach.
11. The service should be voluntary, but the court, through the use of its influence, should urge strongly that the service be used.
12. Conciliation counsellors should have professional backgrounds in the psychological and social sciences with experience in family counselling and negotiating skills.
13. An intensive in-service training program should be established to provide seminars in the socio-legal implications of family law.
14. Students from various disciplines should be affiliated with the service for part of their clinical training.
15. In order to allow clients to discuss their problems openly, conciliation counsellors should be granted privileged communication.
16. There should be opportunities for both mediation and arbitration depending upon the conciliator's assessment.
17. A research design should be developed prior to the establishment of a conciliation service, so that the service may be evaluated as it continues and so that further recommendations may be made.

NOTES

1. Ninety-five of the 159 cases excluded from the study sample were not offered conciliation counselling. Sixty-four could not speak English. Moreover, of those cases which met the selection criteria and were asked to participate in the study, only fourteen cases (4 percent) refused.

REFERENCES

Alberta Conciliation Services. *Demonstration Project*, #558-1-12. Ottawa: National Health and Welfare Canada, 1975.
Bahr, S.J. "Divorce Mediation: An Evaluation of an Alternative Divorce Policy." Provo, Utah: Brigham Young University, Unpub. MS, 1980.

Bohm, P. "Client Variables Associated with Outcomes of Conciliation Counselling." Toronto: Faculty of Social Work, University of Toronto, Unpub. D.S.W. thesis, 1980.

Campbell, A., Converse, P.E., Rogers, W.L. *The Quality of American Life.* N.Y.: Russel Sage Foundation, 1976.

Coogler, O.J. "Changing the Lawyer's Role in Matrimonial Practice." *Conciliation Courts Review* 1977, 15, 1-8.

Davidson, R. *Marriage and Family Law in Ontario.* Toronto: International Self-Counsel Press, 1975.

Deutsch, M. *The Resolution of Conflict.* New Haven: Yale University Press, 1973.

Elkin, M. "Short-contract Counselling in a Conciliation Court." *Social Casework* 1962, 43, 184-190.

Elkin, M. "Conciliation Courts: The Reintegration of Disintegrating Families." *Family Coordinator* 1973, 22, 63-72.

Frontenac Family Referral Service. *Couples in Crisis.* Kingston, Ont.: Frontenac Family Referral Service, 1979.

Glass, G.V. and Stanley, J.C. *Statistical Methods in Education and Psychology.* Englewood Cliffs, N.J.: Prentice-Hall, 1970.

Haynes, J.M. "Divorce Mediator: A New Role." *Social Work* 1978, 23, 5-9.

Irving, H.H. *Divorce Mediation: The Rational Alternative.* Toronto: Carswell, 1980.

Irving, H.H. and Gandy, J. "Family Court Conciliation Project: An Experiment in Support Services." *Reports of Family Law* 1977, 25, 47-53.

Irving, H.H. and Irving, B.G. "Conciliation Counselling in Divorce Litigation." *Reports of Family Law* 1974, 16, 257-66.

Irving, H.H., Bohm, P.E., Macdonald, G., Benjamin, M. *A Comparative Analysis of Two Family Court Services: An Exploratory Study of Conciliation Counselling.* Toronto: Welfare Grants Directorate, National Health and Welfare and the Ontario Ministry of the Attorney General, Demonstration Project No. 25555-1-65, 1979.

Kronby, M.C. *The Guide to Family Law.* Toronto: New Press, 1972.

Lightman, E.S. and Irving, H.H. "Conciliation and Arbitration in Family Disputes." *Conciliation Courts Review* 1976, 14, 12-21.

Minuchin, S., Rosman, B.L., Baker, L. *Psychosomatic Families: Anorexia Nervosa in Context.* Cambridge, Mass.: Harvard University Press, 1978.

Nie, N.H., Hull, C.H., Jenkins, J.G., Steinbrenner, K., Bent, D.H. *Statistical Package for the Social Sciences.* N.Y.: McGraw-Hill, 1975.

Norton, A.J. and Glick, P.C. "Marital and Instability in America: Past, Present and Future." In G. Levinger and O. Moles (eds.) *Divorce and Separation: Contexts, Causes, and Consequences.* N.Y.: Basic Books, 1979.

Osgood, C.E., Suci, G.J., Tannenbaum, P.H. *The Measurement of Meaning.* University of Illinois, 1957.

Rubin, J.Z. and Brown, B.R. *The Social Psychology of Bargaining and Negotiation.* N.Y: Academic Press, 1975.

Sonne, J.C. "On the Question of Compulsory Marriage Counselling as a Part of Divorce Proceedings. *Family Coordinator* 1974, 23, 303-305.

Staff Report Conciliation Project, Ministry of Attorney General, Ontario, August 1980

Statistics Canada — Population: Demographic Characteristics, Marital Status, 1976. Ottawa: Ministry of Industry, Trade and Commerce, Census of Canada, 1978: 1-17.

Stapleford, J.E.N. and Bell, N.W. *Marital Separation Counselling and the Uncoupling Process.* Toronto: Family Service Association of Metropolitan Toronto, 1980.

Weiss R.S. *Marital Separation.* N.Y.: Basic Books, 1975.
Weiss, W.W. and Collada, H.B. "Conciliation Counselling: The Court's Effective Mechanism for Resolving Visitation and Custody Disputes." *Family Coordinator* 1977, 26, 444–447.
Wheeler, M. *No-Fault Divorce.* Boston: Beacon Press, 1974.

Part Four

The Scope for Private Agreement

Part Three addressed the problem of the process by which agreements were reached; in particular, how far the presence of a third party might impinge upon the will and attitude of the parties in coming to a final agreement. This Part considers the extent to which the result of that process, the settlement, is and should be accepted as the conclusive basis for the parties' postdivorce lives. It is convenient to approach this question in two stages. The first looks at any requirements for external scrutiny of such agreements and the criteria that may be set for their acceptability. The second considers the circumstances, if any, in which either of the parties may properly depart from the settlement.

The opening chapter of this Part (Chapter 18) by Meulders-Klein reviews the policies on these issues adopted by a number of European countries and subsequent chapters examine in detail the position in four countries: Switzerland (Grossen, chapter 19); France (Peigné, chapter 20); Denmark (Munck, chapter 21); and Belgium (Pintens, chapter 22). They illustrate a wide range of responses to the first stage of the question described above. A simple policy is to require that all agreements relating to matters consequential to divorce or separation require judicial approval as a condition of validity. This is the Swiss solution. It should be noted, however, that such agreement and approval is not made a precondition of *divorce*. Indeed, if the agreement is reached only after the divorce is granted, its validity does not depend on judicial approval. Another approach is to require agreement to be reached before a divorce can be granted. Both France and Belgium do this, but only if the divorce is based on mutual consent. This is effectively the position in Denmark, too, where so-called "administrative" divorce can be granted by the County governor if both parties seek it and have agreed on certain matters. The rationale for such a requirement should not go unquestioned. It is presumably considered unacceptable to delay the granting of a divorce to a spouse who is "entitled" to it by reason of the *misbehaviour* of the other simply becaue they cannot reach agreement on financial and other matters, whereas a person relying on the other's *agreement* as the basis for the divorce can expect such agreement only if mutually acceptable terms have been arranged. In short, a party can set a price on giving his or her consent to divorce. This might be thought not only to perpetuate a questionable distinction between different types of divorce but to provide the parties to a consent divorce with a powerful, and not necessarily desirable, bargaining weapon.

A possible answer to this criticism would be to subject the settlement to judicial examination. On this matter the French and Belgian systems diverge widely. Meulders-Klein and Peigné describe the extensive powers of the French *Juge aux affaires matrimoniales* (Judge of Matrimonial Affairs), before whom the agreement is actually drafted, first as an interim document and then, at a second discussion (after time for further consideration) in its final form. The judge may refuse to confirm the agreement or grant the decree if he thinks it fails sufficiently to safeguard the interests of the children or of one of the adults. In Belgium, on the other hand, the judicial role is confined to ascertaining whether a valid agreement has in fact been reached. Apart from the limited opportunity given to the Public Prosecutor to institute proceedings before the juvenile court if the agreement raises serious misgivings concerning a child's welfare, the courts are only marginally concerned with the contents of such an agreement. The Danish approach is closer to the Belgian, preferring to deal with the problem of unsatisfactory agreements by means of subsequent invalidation rather than prior scrutiny. Grossen draws attention to significant difficulties in any system based on prior judicial scrutiny. Although a Swiss judge should only approve agreements that are fair, he has nevertheless only limited powers of investigation. In any judicial system, the constraints of time, personnel and space must restrict the adequacy of judicial vetting of divorce agreements. Furthermore, as Grossen remarks "the very notion of what is 'fair' in the case of a divorce agreement is by no means unproblematic." Is fairness to be measured by the degree to which the arrangement approximates the solutions laid down by law if there were no agreement?

The Anglo-American approach, which in this respect is similar to the Dutch, has been to eschew compulsory submission of agreements to courts for approval. Clive (Chapter 23) notes that the Scottish Law Commission recommended against the introduction of such a requirement on the ground that it would "err too much on the side of protection and would require a large number of acceptable agreements to be referred to the court in order to control a few unacceptable ones." On the other hand, certain provisions have *encouraged* parties to place their agreement before the court for incorporation in a "consent" order. There may be tax advantages in doing this and, in England, this is the only way to ensure that the agreement cannot be reopened at a later stage.[1] The process does give the parties a chance to reconsider their original agreement, but the court is unlikely to investigate it very closely and will even hold the parties to it despite the fact that it reflects an inequality of bargaining power between them, so long as this was not improperly exploited.[2] Here we touch the heart of the problem of self-regulated settlement of divorce disputes. Even if an agreement represents a true reflection of the parties' minds (itself a debatable proposition), it can only do this for a given moment in time. Minds can change; circumstances can alter. A contractually based solution must, however, as Meulders-Klein points out, ground its rights and obligations in the intentions as expressed at the moment of contracting. Yet even the strongest advocates of private ordering accept that a doctrine of immutability of agreements would be unacceptable. The extent to which, and the principles upon which, departure from agreed settlements might be permitted is addressed by Mnookin in Chapter 24.

Mnookin accepts that, in the aftermath of a marital breakdown, an individual may suffer "transactional incapacity" which could affect his or her judgment in crucial ways. This should be a ground for modification of the agreement, but only if exploited by the other. Exploitation would be found by evidence that the "terms of the agreement considered as a whole fall outside the range of what would have been acceptable to a competent person at the time of the settlement." He also suggests that either party should be free to rescind a settlement for a period of sixty or ninety days after its conclusion. A second range of circumstances where contracts might be modified is where, despite full competence of both parties, there has been an inequality of bargaining power between them due to such factors as the content of the applicable legal rules, the preferences of each party, their attitudes to the risks of litigation, their ability to withstand the emotional and economic costs of litigation and their employment of "strategic" behaviour. Mnookin believes that the doctrines of contract law are sufficient to deal with these issues, though the examples he himself poses illustrate the extreme difficulty which courts might face in their application. The Scottish Law Commission, too, felt it necessary to permit subsequent modification on the rather general ground that an agreement was not "fair and reasonable at the time it was made." In Switzerland there appears to be some doubt as to how far the principles of contract law apply to permit subsequent revision of an agreement, but the present position seems to be that only provisions as to maintenance are subject to subsequent modification. In Denmark, on the other hand, divorce agreements can be set aside or varied by reference to factors present when it was made, and this includes circumstances which would fall under Mnookin's concept of "transactional incapacity" although not, at least in the way it has been applied, necessarily covering inequalities in bargaining power.

Running through the various strategies which are described in this part is a further distinction which may be of profound significance. Mnookin recognizes a third set of grounds for subsequent modification of agreements, and this is where the settlement may affect interests other than those of the immediate parties. The most important of these are those of the children. Despite this recognition, Mnookin strongly supports a presumption that the arrangements made by parents for their children are in fact best for them. Yet the concession that there are interests at stake other than those of the parents is crucial. It is for this reason that settlements touching the children are characteristically treated in a special way by the systems discussed here. In Denmark, for example, the County authorities have wide discretion to modify agreements relating to child support and visitation (but not custody). In Belgium, it is on matters of child protection that the Public Prosecutor can intervene, and it is of interest to note that criticism has been expressed in that country that his jurisdiction in that regard is too narrow to adequately protect children's interests. In Switzerland, as far as it relates to the children, the spousal agreement is seen as no more than a "joint proposal" to the court, and the judge needs to inquire whether it in fact promotes the best interests of the child. In England and Scotland, the one matter on which judicial approval is required before a divorce can be granted are the arrangements proposed regarding the children. It may be that this is a more important distinction than the one between divorces by consent and divorces on other grounds. However, the scope of the concept of the children's interests may not be clearly perceived. As Grossen very rightly points out, "If the wife gets custody of her child, the way the problem of her own resources is solved (maintenance) is hardly less important to the child than the issue of child support." But these are probably the main types of cases where difficulties later arise. Munck notes that, in Denmark, there have been few attempts to modify agreements which affect the former spouses alone.

So what can be the conclusion about the scope of private agreements? Strong arguments are advanced in this Part in favor of allowing the adults to settle their divorce arrangements between themselves. But these are coupled with recognition that there needs to be some check on this process. To leave this *entirely* to *ex post* challenge of the settlement by one of the adults is probably less than satisfactory. Apart from the undermining effect this would have on the security of predivorce agreements, which Meulders-Klein observes, it would also seem inadequate if the weakness in the agreement is its failure to deal properly with the children's interests. Furthermore, if the flaw lies in the fact that one adult exploited the unwillingness (whether due to "risk aversion" or inability to withstand "transaction costs") of the other to resort to adjudication, it may not seem appropriate if the only avenue of challenge is for that party to take the matter up in court at a later stage. Does this mean that all agreements, or perhaps only agreements in cases involving children, should obtain judicial (or administrative) approval? The contributions here reveal the difficulties in a solution such as that. Some kind of compromise, taking into account the practical limitations of any judicial system, needs to be found. However, one concluding point should be made. Whether the agreement is left to the parties alone or is subjected to judicial approval, its content (and accordingly the scope for negotiation) will, as Clive points out, be heavily influenced by the norms of the applicable law. The more open-ended these are, the greater the scope for variations in bargaining outcome and the more difficult the question of its supervision. If, at least in cases where there are children, the community could define with reasonable clarity what it considered the respective obligations of the parents to be, the problems of resolving these conflicts, whether by adjudication or otherwise, would be considerably reduced. These questions are considered in Part Six. But before that, we turn to a special consideration of the problems posed for family conflict resolution in cases involving children.

NOTES

1. *Minton v. Minton* [1979] A.C. 593.
2. *Edgar v. Edgar* [1980] 1 W.L.R. 1,410.

Chapter Eighteen

Financial Agreements on Divorce and the Freedom of Contract in Continental Europe

Marie-Thérèse Meulders-Klein

Faculty of Law, University of Louvain, Belgium

The purpose of this comparative account of financial agreements on divorce in Continental Europe is to explore whether or not marriage is actually passing "from status to contract" according to the famous assessment of Sir Henry Maine about the movement of progressive societies,[1] and which kind of alternatives and problems may arise from that shift. Obviously this problem is not new. Nor is the contractual conception of marriage, as opposed to the institutional one, a recent construction. In Western countries, one can trace its origin, beyond the French Revolution and the Enlightenment, back to the early seventeenth century and the ideas of the Modern School of Natural Law,[2] and even, at least in part, to the Canon Law itself.[3] But notwithstanding the brief breakthrough of these ideas in the first Western codifications of the eighteenth century and the French Revolution,[4] the institutional aspect of marriage and divorce law has undoubtedly predominated up to a recent period which one can situate in the 1960s.[5] This institutional conception, expressed through the "public order" character of the rules pertaining to marriage and divorce (grounds, procedures and effects)[6] has largely impeded, in this area, the application of the liberal dogma of the autonomy of will, and has consequently limited the scope accorded to freedom of contract between spouses, whether it involves the arrangements of their marriage, their separation and, most of all, their divorce.[7]

According to this basic philosophical, social and legal concept, which was shared by Civil and Common Law jurisdictions, divorce by mutual consent was generally banned as such in the nineteenth and twentieth centuries, with some rare exceptions as in Belgium and Luxembourg, where the system of the *Napoleonic Code* remained in force.[8] For the same reason, agreements made in contemplation of separation or divorce were looked on with disfavour and, in some areas, like France and Belgium, regularly presumed void, whereas postdivorce contracts were free and binding, at least in financial matters.[9] The judicial rules followed the same pattern. Compulsory tentative conciliation was meant to uphold the marriage, not to negotiate the effects of its disruption. Neither mediation devices nor specialized courts were developed. Parties were obliged to adopt a litigious attitude in an adversarial procedure, even if they agreed to the divorce. The judge was limited by restrictive divorce grounds and had to render judgment on the basis of fault. However, as everybody knows, divorce by consent was practiced in all jurisdictions, under the veil of undefended proceedings, with the silent complicity of the judges.[10]

The recent reversal of this tendency in favour of a contractual conception of marriage, which coincides with a profound revolution in the very concept of the family (the "post-nuclear family"), in behaviour and in mores,[11] now finds expression, at various states of development, in all recent Western legislation, through a fundamental movement tending to leave to the spouses an ever greater liberty to "undo" their marriage, either by mutual consent, or by unilateral will, in the perspective of "no-fault divorce".[12] This movement, which manifested itself first with respect to the grounds for divorce (which became increasingly liberal) reveals itself also with regard to procedures and the arrangements concerning the effects of divorce, to the extent that the scope permitted for negotiation and amicable settlement between spouses expands, while the role left to judicial intervention seems to contract.

However, in comparing some recently modified European statutes on divorce, selected for their exemplary value, one may discern two distinct trends regarding the contractual freedom left to divorcing spouses in relation to their financial and other arrangements. I would like to explore these trends by examining three questions which are related mainly to divorce by mutual consent, since the question of reaching amicable settlement in contested divorces does not raise quite the same problems and is mainly a question of conciliation and mediation, whereas divorce by consent is entirely in the realm of the autonomy of will. The three questions are as follows:

1. In the case of joint petition to terminate the marriage, are the spouses compelled to settle between themselves the consequences of their divorce? If so, before the petition, or before the decree? Subsidiarily, in what form?
2. Are the spouses completely free to settle their arrangements as they like, or are these arrangements submitted to judicial or administrative review?
3. Are these agreements final or are they reviewable after divorce?

COMPULSORY OR FACULTATIVE AGREEMENTS?

The obligation to settle amicably the whole or a part of the consequences of divorce may appear either a wise and reasonable measure, or an excessive constraint on the acquisition of quick divorces.

The Belgian system, for example, which is still inspired by the *Napoleonic Code*, requires, as a mandatory precondition of divorce by consent,[13] that both spouses file with their application a notarial inventory and estimate of all their common or separate assets,[14] an agreement dividing these assets and dealing with all the other ancillary patrimonial questions (matrimonial advantages, gifts, surviving gains, and so on), and also an agreement about custody, access, maintenance for the children and (optionally) for the ex-spouse. These agreements cannot be modified during the subsequent proceedings, even by consent.[15] If one (or both) parties no longer agrees with the settlement, he (they) can only break off the proceedings.[16]

The French Divorce Statute[17] is more flexible, inasmuch as the agreement need not be final prior the petition.[18] Nevertheless, it is also restrictive despite the fact that divorce by consent was to be the favoured model in the new legislation.[19] The spouses have to submit to the Judge of Matrimonial Affairs (J.A.M.)[20] on their first appearance, together with their joint application, a temporary agreement for the duration of the proceedings, and a draft of the final agreement settling *all* the ancillary questions of the divorce. No less than three and no more than nine months after the first appearance, they have to appear for a second time before the J.A.M. with their final agreement. This must settle, among other things, the liquidation and division of the matrimonial property, the rights in the matrimonial home and the new "compensatory allocation" (*prestation compensatoire*), which is not designed to secure the maintenance of the economically dependent spouse, but rather to compensate once and for all for the economic disparity resulting from the termination of marriage by divorce.[21] The stated purpose is to avoid postlitigation conflicts. But it also puts a constraint on the parties. Furthermore, they have to appear personally and each has to be represented by counsel, unless they agree to use only one. If there are real assets to divide, the liquidation agreement has to be prepared by a notary.[22] All these requirements of course cost time and money.[23]

The new German *Statute on Marriage* (1976)[24] does not really recognize mutual consent but only irretrievable breakdown as a ground for divorce.[25] If both parties agree on divorce, they have to prove that they have lived separately one year before the application, and the judge has to scrutinize this as well as the reality of their consent.[26] If he is satisfied, an irrebuttable presumption of breakdown is inferred from the fact of the separation and of the mutual consent (§ 1566, al. 1, BGB).[27] As for the special formalities which are required in this case (§ 630 ZPO), the spouses have to file, together with the application,[28] a draft agreement on custody, financial support for the children and the other partner, rights over the matrimonial home and all the household effects (but not on the division of the matrimonial regime, the timing of which is left to their discretion, nor on the *Versorgungsausgleich* — division of pensions).[29] If they do not settle this most difficult point, the judge will have to do it *ex officio* (§ 1587b BGB), but if they cannot come to an agreement on the other points, divorce may not be granted on the basis of § 1566, al. 1, BGB. The parties must always appear personally (§ 613, al. 1, ZPO) and be assisted by counsel (§ 78 ZPO). The final financial agreement on maintenance rights, the matrimonial home and household furniture has to be settled in an enforceable act, generally drafted by a notary, before the divorce may be granted.[30] In practice, this regulation, obviously designed to inhibit overhasty and unfair divorces, places a burden on the parties. As a result of these requirements, including the one year separation delay, spouses may prefer the general clause of the statute with respect to marriage breakdown (§ 1565 BGB).[31]

In contrast, under the Dutch *Statute on Divorce* (1971),[32] which also recognizes only irretrievable breakdown as a ground for divorce (art. I.151 B.W.), parties who apply jointly (art. I.150 B.W.), need only propose, together with the petition, or later during the proceedings, a draft agreement on the child's custody and maintenance, and to tell the judge if, and if so how, they have settled their patrimonial interests (art. I.154–155 B.W.). They may of course make a complete agreement, and they often do so, since the *echtscheidingsconvenant* (divorce convention) was a long-tolerated practice in the Netherlands. But they may also decline to do this. It is noteworthy that the parties have to appear personally before the judge with their counsel (art. 827d, al. 1 and 827 c, al. 1 and 2 *Civ. Proc. C.*).[33]

Finally, in the Nordic countries, the administrative divorce procedure may be used in Denmark only if the parties agree on a number of precise questions: the right of the future ex-spouse to maintenance and its duration (but not the amount, which may be left to the discretion of the Governor), the right to continue the lease of the matrimonial home, the duty of one of the parties to pay a lump sum out of his or her separate property to the other to ensure that the latter does not suffer undue hardship after the divorce (or separation), and the right of the wife to a widow's pension. But the *formal* requirements are much easier and the agreement may be reached during the proceedings in the course of the negotiations with the County officer. Agreement on other ancillary matters such as the right of access to the child, the amount of the periodical maintenance to the spouse or to the child, and the financial adjustment regarding the division of estate, is *not* required as a precondition for divorce (or separation decree) from the County Governor.[34] In Norway, such agreements are not required at all in order to get an administrative decree of divorce.[35] But in both countries, it is necessary, whether the procedure is administrative or judicial, that one of the statutory grounds for divorce (or separation) exists and the parties have to appear personally.[36] In Sweden, where the divorce is always granted judicially, spouses who agree that their marriage shall be dissolved have a right to immediate divorce since the 1974 Act. If they also agree on the ancillary questions, the procedure will be purely written and the spouses need not appear before the Court.[37]

CONTROLLED OR UNCONTROLLED AGREEMENTS?

Freedom of contract implies that the parties are free to choose their own terms without any control or the requirement of ratification by a third party. How free are the spouses to make their own arrangements in contemplation of their divorce? And what is the role of the judge, or of the administrative officer in the case of administrative procedure?

A first paradoxical example is that of the Belgian system which seems at the same time to be both obsolete and progressive.[38] In this case, the preliminary agreements are completely free and in no case submitted to judicial control. In the logic of the *Napoleonic Code,* divorce by mutual consent was not supposed to be a frivolous divorce, but a divorce without an "alleged" cause, intended to protect the honour and dignity of the spouses.[39] Accordingly, agreement on the consequences is considered as the price of silence on the grounds, if not of the consent itself. That is why the judge is not allowed to control their content. He may refuse to grant the divorce only if the agreement is blatantly against public policy, for example if one parent renounces maintenance for the child, or his visitation rights.[40] Even in the child's interests, he has no right to control the adequacy of the spouses' agreement.[41] The counterpart to this complete "laissez-faire" is that it favours bargaining. Since, as we shall see later, the agreement follows the rules of contract and is not subsequently reviewable, except in the best interest of the children, this may raise problems.

On the opposite extreme is the French *Divorce Act* (1975), reintroducing divorce by consent in the French legal system, and giving the Judge of Matrimonial Affairs a considerable power of control over the proposed agreements, as well as the means to make a proper investigation in order to elicit whether the spouses' consent is free and whether the convenant adequately protects their and their children's interests (art. 232, 253, 278 Fr. *Civ. C.*). He may for instance, interview the parties and their counsel, as well as their notary, and have documents produced by third parties. He may suggest other terms, and may even refuse to ratify the agreement, and consequently to grant the divorce.[42] These provisions give the judge so much discretion that he can, in effect, through successive denials of approval, force the parties to adopt an agreement of which he is *indirectly* the author.[43] But it is also true that not all the French judges feel inclined to make a full investigation, and their task is indeed difficult in so far as they have to supervise the consent and the adequacy of the terms without being able to inquire into the deep reasons which have guided the spouses in their choice.[44] However, one has to state that in the French system of divorce by consent, private agreements are necessary but not sufficient. Therefore this system cannot be considered as a pure contractual divorce and it may be said that the new statute does not go nearly as far as the *French Revolutionary Law* of 20 September 1792.[45]

To a certain extent, although divorce by mutual consent does not exist as such in Switzerland,[46] where a reform is contemplated, a similar option seems to appear in article 158 of the Swiss *Civil Code*. According to this provision "agreements relating to the subsidiary effects of divorce or judicial separation prior to the decree require ... to be confirmed by the judge." In Chapter Nineteen of this book, Professor Grossen notes, however, that this control, which is intended to prevent exploitation of one spouse by the other during the proceedings,[47] is only a "summary examination," except when children are concerned, and that the judge has only to ensure that the consent is genuine and complete, not contrary to the law, and is fair. As to the last point he also underlines the distance between the end and the means, since the Swiss judge seems to be less well equipped than his French colleague with regard to investigation and the definition of what is "equitable" is very vague.

The German judge of the new *Familiengericht*[48] has more limited power of control and a distinction has to be made according to the subject matter of the agreements. The judge has a duty to control and fully investigate the adequacy of agreements with regard to the children's interests and also *Versorgungsausleichs* agreements in relation to the future economic security of the creditor. He may even modify them *ex officio* (§ 1671, al. 2 and 3; § 627 al. 1, ZPO; § 1587 o, al. 2, BGB). As for other agreements, especially financial agreements on division or reallocation of property and on maintenance between ex-spouses, the judge has no such powers since the law is silent about them.[49] It seems agreed that he may counsel the parties in order to avoid gross inequities, but that he cannot deny a divorce if he is satisfied that the spouses have lived separately for one year and have freely consented to the termination of their marriage. Yet he may refuse the divorce if he has doubts about the validity of the agreement or part of it.[50]

The Dutch judge has only the duty to oversee the child's interests and he may, accordingly, modify the proposed agreement *ex officio* (art. I.161 B.W.). As for other matters, the spouses are free to make their own arrangements as they think fit. Waivers of maintenance after divorce are admitted (art. I.158-149 B.W.), notwithstanding the general protection of art. I.400, 2., B.W. Theoretically the role of the judge is rather a passive one, even in family matters. In practice, however, he often uses the means of personal appearance by the parties (art. 19, 818, 825a, 827d, 1., *Civ. Proc. C.*) to collect information from them, to counsel them and to guide them to reasonable and fair agreements,[51] which he may incorporate in an enforceable protocol or in the decree itself, in whole or in part, if the parties so request (art. I.155, 2., B.W.). If he has doubts, he may refuse to do this, but cannot refuse the divorce nor modify the agreement.[52]

In the Nordic countries, the absence of *a priori* control on the proposed agreements seems to be a basic principle, with the exception of the terms concerning the children. The role of the judge, as well as of the County Officer in the Danish and Norwegian administrative procedure, is to make sure the consents are free, to inform the parties of their rights and to discuss with them a reasonable solution to their problems, before making the final order.[53] But this means that the parties appear personally. This is not the case in Sweden, where the procedure is entirely written and the spouses need not appear before the Court if they agree both on the divorce and on the ancillary questions.[54]

Thus we can discern both a liberal and a protective approach. But the choice between the two has relevance to a third question — the reviewability or otherwise of agreements.

REVIEWABLE OR UNREVIEWABLE AGREEMENTS?

In the law of contract, the terms of an agreement are binding. Any later modification may occur only by consent, or by invalidation for some initial irregularity. These questions are particularly crucial and controversial when applied to divorce agreements. If the parties do not agree to modify the terms, should such agreements be judicially reviewable in case of a later change of circumstances, or should the sanctity of contract prevail? If the agreements have been submitted to judicial control and ratification, would it be possible to get an invalidation on the basis of the general rules of contract? One of the main difficulties lies in the ambiguous legal nature of such agreements: are they judicial or contractual?[55] If incorporated in the divorce judgment, they may be considered as *res judicata* and attacked only in the same way as the judgment itself, whereas if considered as contractual they might be annulled. All the jurisdictions considered above struggle with these difficult questions and the answers reveal at the very least a lack of consensus and uniformity.

In the Belgian system of divorce by mutual consent, the agreement is not included in the decree nor is it ratified by the judge. It is a pure civil transaction (compromise),[56] which is considered as *res judicata* between the parties, and submitted to the very restrictive invalidation rules provided by article 2,052 and ff. of the *Civil Code,* which the courts have even strengthened.[57] They are considered the price of mutual consent. As a result, these agreements are not judicially reviewable, except with regard to the children,[58] unless they have been stipulated to be such; so that maintenance agreements for the ex-spouses, for example, cannot be modified or set aside, even in the case of a drastic and unforeseeable change in circumstances. For the same reason, the absence of terms concerning the ex-spouses' maintenance after divorce is considered a definitive waiver. The iron rule of contract is the price of the complete autonomy of will and the sanction of that kind of divorce. Counter offers made during the proceedings are void.[59]

In the new French system, where the matter is highly controversial, the reasons invoked by the majority of the Courts and of writers arguing that consensual divorce agreements are not liable to be invalidated are very different, but lead to the same result.[60] First, it is said that judicial control, with all the investigative powers of the judge, makes a flaw in the consent, such as error, duress, or even fraud, unthinkable, or at least very unlikely. Secondly, rescission in the case of unequal partition or undervaluation of assets, should not be admitted because the unequal partition may be explained by reasons which the parties are not obliged to disclose, or by the settlement regarding the "compensatory allocation," which is left to the discretion of the parties. Thirdly, the ratified agreements are part of the judgment. Consequently they are *res judicata,* and could not be annulled. The only case of revision of a judgment, which some authors would be prepared to admit in the matter of divorce, is in case of fraud under article 595 of the new *Civil Procedure Code.* And finally, since the agreement on the termination of marriage and the agreement on ancillary questions are so closely linked in fact and in the judgment itself, which pronounces the divorce at the same time as ratifying the agreement, the invalidation of the latter would bring the first into question.[61]

On the other hand, judicial modification of maintenance agreements on the basis of a change in circumstances is excluded, except with regard to the children, because of the invariability of the new *prestation compensatoire* (art. 273 French *Civil Code*), the purpose being to avoid postdivorce litigation. In the case of divorce by mutual consent however, the spouses are allowed to stipulate judicial reviewability in case of unforeseen changes in their respective income (art. 279, al. 3 French *Civil Code*) or to introduce automatic variation clauses such as indexation or revocation in case of remarriage. They may of course also revise their agreements by consent. But article 279, al. 2 of the *Civil Code* provides that this new agreement has to be ratified again by the judge. This is going much further than the ordinary law of contract does.[62]

In Switzerland, similar uncertainties exist concerning the legal nature of divorce agreements confirmed on the basis of article 158 of the Swiss *Civil Code* and about their variation or revision.[63] Once ratified, those agreements are considered an integral part of the divorce decree. Accordingly they can only be attacked in the same way and on the same grounds as the judgment itself. Revision grounds are very restrictive, and the question of whether a defect of consent would provide a ground for setting aside a confirmed agreement remains open. On the other hand, whereas it is admitted that maintenance agreements between ex-spouses can be modified by the judge on the basis of article 153, § 2, *Civil Code* when the parties cannot agree on a modification, this variation can only consist in a reduction or cancellation of the contribution, but not its increase. Other agreements, such as division and reallocation of property, cannot be modified by judgment.[64]

The legal answer is different in Germany where, besides the necessary agreements in case of divorce by consent (§ 630 ZPO), many settlements regarding the effects of divorce may be concluded during the proceedings.[65] All thes settlements are considered of a hybrid nature: civil contract and judicial compromise. Accordingly they have to satisfy both substantial and procedural rules of validity.[66] Since they are not incorporated in the divorce decree (with an exception for custody matters on which the judge has to decide himself and the parents may only propose an agreement (§ 1671 BGB))[67] they may be invalidated either before or after the divorce decree, under both kind of rules, especially the rules of contract such as if the terms are, in whole or in part, unlawful (§ 134 BGB) or against good morals (§ 138 BGB), if there is a defect of consent (§ 123, § 779 BGB), or for other special reasons (one of the spouses having obtained undue advantages on a price of his consent, the child having been the "object of bargaining," and so on).[68] The invalidation of the agreement or part of it does not involve the reopening of the divorce case even if consent to the termination of marriage has been given on the basis of the settlement.[69] As for variation in case of later change in circumstances, most of the terms may be modified either by consent or by judicial decision.[70] Accordingly, the way seems wide open for postdivorce litigation.

In the Netherlands the *echtscheidingsconvenant* keeps its contractual nature even if enacted in the divorce decree (art. I-155, 2. B.W.)[71] and may be annulled on the basis of general causes of invalidity or even of "abuse of circumstances," although this last point is controversial.[72] On the other hand, maintenance agreements may be varied in the case of a change in the situation (art. I-401 B.W.). Divorce does not put an end to the ex-spouses' reciprocal duty of maintenance in the Netherlands (art. I-157 B.W.) and conventional stipulations made before or after divorce (art. I-158 B.W.) are always reviewable in the case of new circumstances, even if these terms were closely linked with the property division and other benefits. The clause of renunciation of postdivorce maintenance (*Nihil beding*) itself may be set aside under the conditions of article I-401 B.W. and so also can a stipulation of non-reviewability (art. I-159 B.W.), in the event of exceptional hardship.[73] This makes the divorce convention rather insecure, especially if it has been made as part of a package deal.

Finally, it is striking to note that the far-reaching autonomy of the parties and, on a number of ancillary questions, the equally far-reaching informality of divorce agreements in the Nordic countries, has as a counterpart a wide scope for invalidation on the grounds of a broad set of rules of invalidity, as well as the possibility of having the provisions varied "if the concrete result of the agreement can be described as patently unreasonable" (section 58 of the Danish *Marriage Act*) as to the division of the estate, maintenance for the spouses and agreements on transfer of separate property.[74] There the price for the autonomy of will seems to be the fragility of the settlement.[75] To some extent, one could say that neither the sanctity of marriage, nor the sanctity of contract are safe under that compromise.

Summing up, although neat borderlines cannot be traced between the different systems, the two major trends which have been identified may be characterized (with the exception of the Belgian system, which is the only genuinely contractual system) as follows: (1) On the one hand, a growing propensity towards simplification, acceleration and autonomy in divorce, under the banner of liberty and privacy,[76] but with reduced security as to the settlement which has been the basis of the consent to the termination of marriage; (2) On the other hand, a protective approach not so much of marriage as an instituton but of personal freedom of consent and of private interests against unequal bargaining powers, with, as a counterpart, more delay and formality but also more security. These might be the alternatives between which we have to search for a reasonable middle ground.

If it is true that the legal admission of no-fault divorce and divorce by consent is deemed to allow a decent burial for a dead marriage, it might also be true that that burial has to be fair. To assume that complete freedom of contract and absence of formalities entails both decency and justice, as well as liberty, might be an oversimplification, as it has been observed in the field of labour contracts. Experience shows that even in divorce by consent, one party is generally less consenting or does not even consent at all, and that equality in the books does not mean equality in fact. Moreover, the ever growing complexity of property, tax and social law makes it risky to believe in the virtue of "do it yourself" divorces.[77] On the other hand, there is some inconsistency in seeking a "clean break" on divorce and at the same time opening the way to postdivorce litigation in order to modify, *a posteriori,* the spouses' negotiations. Although such litigation may be necessary to avoid hardship due to unfair bargaining, it may also encourage rash promises, soon withdrawn after the aim of divorce, has been achieved.

Consequently it might be concluded that predivorce safeguards should be preferred to postdivorce remedies. Availability of legal aid and counselling,[78] personal appearance and mediation, judicial safeguards and due process of law, concentration on a final, clear, precise and complete settlement at the time of the divorce decree may be considered as essential for this. After all, if divorce is to be a new start to new life, its conditions should be the fairest possible with regard to the past and to the future, and that remains, no doubt, a matter of social and legal policy.

NOTES

1. H.S. Maine, *Ancient Law*, Pollock's Ed., 1906, 170. But comp. R.H. Graveson, "The Movement from Status to Contract," 4 *Mod. Law Review*, 1941, 260–72.
2. See Dufour, "Autorité maritale et autorité paternelle dans l'Ecole de droit naturel moderne," in *Archives de Philosophie du Droit*, 1975, 89–124.
3. "On the Canonic Theory of Marriage as Contract and Sacrament," see F. Rigaux, *Les Personnes*, t. I, *Les relations familiales*, Bruxelles, Larcier, 1970, n. 561–72.
4. See M. Garaud and R. Szramkiewicz, *La révolution française et la famille*, Paris, P.U.F., 1978. See also V. Demars-Sion, "Libéralisation du divorce: l'apport véritable de la loi du 11 juillet 1975 à la lumière de celle du 20 septembre 1792," *Rev. trim. dr. civ.*, 1980, 231–65.
5. On the secular theory of marriage as an institution, s. esp. J. Bonnecase, *La Philosophie du Code Napoléon*, Paris, 1928, 143–273. S. also Marty and Raynaud, *Droit Civil*, t. I, vol. 2, Paris, Sirey, 1967, n. 61–67.
6. *Jurisclasseur Civil*, V° Ordre Public et Bonnes Moeurs, n. 116–17.
7. G. Cornu, "Le contrat entre époux," *Rev. trim. dr. civ.*, 1953, 461–93.
8. For a comparative review of divorce by mutual consent legislations, see generally D. Dumusc, *Le divorce par consentement mutuel dans les législations européennes*, Librairie Droz, 1980.
9. G. Cornu, *op. cit.*; P. Hebraud, "La pension de l'article 301 du Code civil et les conventions en vue du divorce," *Juriscl. Pér.*, 1952, I, 978; R. Savatier, Les conventions de séparation amiable entre époux, *Rev. trim. dr. civ.*, 1931, p. 335; J. Revel, Les conventions entre epoux désunis, *Juriscl. Pér.*, 1982, 3055, n. 40 et s.; H. De Page, *Traité élémentaire de droit civil belge*, t. I, Bruxelles, Bruylant, 1962, n. 699; Cass. belge, 22 juin 1967, *Rev. crit. jur. belge*, 1969, 126 and ff. note E. Vieujean; Cass. belge, 14 novembre 1974, *Pas.*, 1975, I, 304.
10. G. Chesne, "Le divorce par consentement mutuel," *Rec. Dalloz*, 1963, chron. XVI; H. Holzhauer, Le divorce et ses conséquences, in *Mariage et Famille en Question* — Allemagne, Ed. du C.N.R.S., Lyon, 1980, 119–53, sp. p. 121; D.C. Fokkema, "Evolution des structures juridiques de la famille aux Pays-Bas," in *Mariage et Famille en Question* — Suisse, Autriche, Belgique, Pays-Bas, Ed. du C.N.R.S., Lyon, 1980, sp. 136. See also gen. D. Dumusc, *op. cit.* (note 8).
11. M.T. Meulders-Klein, "La personne, la famille et la loi au sortir du XXe siècle,

Journ. Trib., 1982, 137-44; M.A. Glendon, *The New Family and the New Property*, Butterworths, Toronto, 1981.

12. M. Ancel, *Le divorce à l'étranger*, La Documentation française, Paris, 1975; A.G. Chloros, *The Reform of Family Law in Europe*, Kluwer, 1978; D. Dumusc, *op. cit.* (note 8).

13. Art.1287, 1288 of the *Judiciary Code* as modified by the law of 1 July 1972.

14. The purpose of the notarial inventory is to prevent any fraud on the part of one spouse "by concealing" assets from the other.

15. The formal reason is that the procedural rules of divorce are of "public order." The rule applies even to the terms concerning the children. See on that point F. Poelman, "Les conventions préalables au divorce par consentement mutuel, leur examen par le Ministère public et leur modification ultérieure éventuelle," *Rev. trim. dr. familial*, 1980, p. 171; F. Poelman, Pour une réforme urgente du divorce par consentement mutuel, *Journ. Trib.*, 1982, 369.

16. On divorce by consent in the Belgian system, see F. Rigaux and M.T. Meulders-Klein, *Les Personnes*, t. I, *Les relations familiales. Mise à jour*, Larcier, 1978, sp. n. 231-83.

17. L. n. 75-617, 11 July 1975.

18. On divorce by mutual consent, see art. 230-232 *Civ. C.* as introduced by the law n. 75-617 (1975) and art. 20-35 (Decr. n. 75-1124 5 Dec. 1975). On the procedure to follow for *divorce sur demande conjointe* see Ph. Bertin, "La procédure du divorce (Décret n° 75-1124 du 5 décembre 1975) à la lumière du Nouveau Code de Procédure civile," *Juriscl. Pér.*, 1976, I, 2,751, n. d-17 to d-43.

19. R. Lindon, "La nouvelle législation sur le divorce et le recouvrement public des pensions alimentaires," *Juriscl. Pér.*, 1975, I, 2,728, sp. n. 17.

20. On the role of the Judge for Matrimonial Affairs (J.A.M.) in divorce, see J.Cl. Grosliere, "Le juge aux affaires matrimoniales ou l'homme-orchestre du divorce, *Rec. Dalloz*, 1976, chron. XIV, and Chapter 20 of this volume.

21. As a matter of fact, the new "prestation compensatoire" available in case of fault-divorce or of divorce by consent is generally fixed under the form of a *periodical sum*, since most debtors cannot afford to pay a lump sum or to transfer a valuable asset sufficient to compensate the economic disparity resulting from divorce. The most interesting aspects of this new allowance are that it is *not variable* nor revocable — even in case of remarriage — except in very rare circumstances, or if it has been provided for in the case of divorce by consent, and that it must continue to be paid by the debtor's heirs after his death. See art. 270 to 280-1 Fr. *Civ. Code*. Thus the new French system is far more favourable for the ex-spouse than the former maintenance sytem. See R. Lindon, "La nouvelle législation sur le divorce, *Juriscl. Pér.*," 1975, I, 2728, sp. n. 173-198; J. de Poulpiquet, "La prestation compensatoire après divorce," *Juriscl. Pér.*, 1977, I, 2856; Y. Boyer, "La révision de la prestation compensatoire," *Rec. Dalloz*, 1980, chron. XXXVIII.

22. S.R. Vialatte, "Aspects nouveaux du rôle du notaire dans la procédure du divorce," *Juriscl. Pér.*, 1977, I, 2,846.

23. On the current practice on divorce by consent in France, See J. Massip, "Le divorce par consentement mutuel et la pratique des tribunaux," *Rec. Dalloz*, 1979, chron. XVIII.

24. Erstes Gesetz zur Reform des Ehe-und Familienrechts vom 14 Juni 1976. On the new German Divorce System, see G. Beitzke, *Familienrecht*, Beck, 1980, 131-54; D. Schwab, *Familienrect*, Beck, 1980, 127-72; G. Beitzke, "Les causes de divorce dans le nouveau droit allemand" et W. Muller-Freienfels, "Les effets du divorce dans le nouveau droit allemand," in *Le Nouveau Droit du divorce en Allemagne et en France*, Paris,

L.G.D.J., 1979, 33-45 et 69-101; H. Holzhauer, Le divorce et ses conséquences in *Mariage et Famille en question — Allemagne, précité* (note 10), pp. 120-57 and on the procedure of divorce, P. Schlosser, "La procédure relative aux affaires de mariage et de filiation," *op. cit.* 231-38; D. Dumusc, *op. cit.* (note 8).

25. H. Holzhauer, *op. cit.*, 123-24; P. Schlosser, *op. cit.*, 233; D. Dumusc, *op. cit.*, 169 ff.

26. Even in case of divorce by consent, the judge has to inquire, *ex officio*, in order to discover any objection to the dissolution, (§ 616, al. 1 & 2 ZPO); S. Schlosser, *op. cit.*, 233; Dumusc, *op. cit.*, 177.

27. Schlosser, *op. cit.*, 233.

28. The spouses are not allowed to file a joint petition. Each of them, duly represented by counsel, have to file a separate application, or the defendant may accept the petitioner's petition. However, absence of defence is not considered as consent. S. Schlosser, *op. cit.*, 232; 234; Dumusc, *op. cit.*, 169 and 173. In fact the required agreement may be elaborated or completed during the proceedings; s. Dumusc, *op. cit.*, 171.

29. Agreements on the *Versorgungsauslgeich* are allowed by § 1587 o, al. 1, BGB. Such agreements have to be drafted by a notary and approved by the judge (§ 1587 o, al. 2, BGB).

30. On all these formalities, see Schlosser, *op. cit.*, 237; Dumusc, *op. cit.*, 169 ff.; Beitzke, in *Le nouveau droit du divorce en Allemagne et en France, op. cit.*, pp. 38-40; Schwab, 140-42; Göppinger, *Vereinbarungemauslässlich Ehescheidung*, Beck, 1982, 27-30, n. 38-44, pp. 67-73, n. 122-36.

31. Dumusc, op. cit., 179-83.

32. Law of 6 May 1971, art. I. 150-167 of the new Dutch *Civil Code* (B.W.). See also art. I. 179 to 183. Divorce may not be granted less than one year after the marriage (art. I. 156 B.W.). On divorce by mutual consent in Netherlands, see Dumusc, *op. cit.*, 145-52; J.B.M. Roes in E.A.A. Luijten, *Het Personen en Familierecht in het nieuwe Burgerlijke Wetboek*, Tjeenk Willink, Zwolle, 1977, 181 ff.

33. M.J.A. Van Mourik, *Het Nederlands vermogensrecht bij echtscheiding*, Tjeenk Willink, Zwolle, 1978, 61 ff.; J.B.M. Roes, *op. cit.*, 199-200.

34. See Chapters 5 and 21 of this volume.

35. See Chapter 5.

36. See Chapter 5.

37. See Chapter 5 and Dumusc, *op. cit.*, 250-54.

38. S.F. Rigaux and M.T. Meulders-Klein, *op. cit.*, sp. n. 270. See also n. 259-60.

39. S.D. Roughol-Valdeyron, Le divorce par consentement mutuel et le Code Napoléon, *Rev. trim. dr. civ.*, 1975, 482-87.

40. Some lawyers even contest that point. See J.L. Renchon, L'obligation d'entretien des parents à l'égard de leurs enfants et la détermination des modalités de son exécution dans le contexte d'une procédure de divorce par consentement mutuel," *Rev. trim. dr. familial*, 1982, 163-206, sp. n. 27-31.

41. F. Poelman, "Une année de divorces par consentement mutuel à Bruxelles," *Journ. Trib.*, 1 and 81; Les conventions préalables au divorce par consentement mutuel, leur examen par le Ministère public et leur modification ultérieure éventuelle, *Rev. trim. dr. familial*, 1980, 1971; Pour une réforme urgente du divorce par consentement mutuel, *Journ. Trib.*, 1982, 369.

42. Art. 232, 253, 278 C. civ.; art. 24-33 Décr. 75-1124, 5 Dec. 1975; See Bertin, La procédure du divorce (note 18), n. d 28-d 41, d 101-d 102; J. Revel, Les conventions entre epoux désunis (note 9), sp. n. 29-30.

43. The French judge is never allowed to impose *directly* his own solution.
44. J. Revel, *op. cit.*, n. 30.
45. S. Demars-Sion, "Libéralisation du divorce: l'apport véritable de la loi du 11 juillet 1975 à la lumière de celle du 20 septembre 1792" (note 4).
46. However, here again undefended divorce, especially on the basis of art. 142 Civ. C. (irretrievable breakdown), plays the role of divorce by consent. See H. Deschenaux and P. Tercier, *Le mariage et le divorce,* Stämpfli, 1974, 101, n. 3.1.3.; M. Keller, Die Einverständliche Scheidung, *Rev. suisse jurispr.,* 66, 1970, 113 ff.; Nabholz-Haidegger, *Die Konventionalscheidung,* Thèse, Zürich, 1972.
47. After the decree, agreements between ex-spouses are free of judicial control.
48. The German Family Court has been created by the Law of 1976 on Marriage and the Family Law Reform (supra, note 24), but it is only a special section of the lowest Court, the Amtsgericht, and is composed of a single judge, without a specialized team or specialized formation. It does not exercise all the family jurisdiction. Its main jurisdiction is divorce (or separation) and ancillary questions. See "Bruggeman, Familiengerichtsbarkeit," *FamRZ,* 1977, 1 ff and 582 ff; Diederichsen, "Die Einführung der Familiengerichte," *Neue Jurist. Wochenschr.,* 1977, 601 ff; Walter, "Das neue Verfahren in Ehe und anderen Familiensachen," *FamRZ,* 1979, pp. 204, 259, 396, 663 ff.
49. Freedom of contract is the rule for division or reallocation of property (§ 1408 I BGB) and maintenance (§ 1585 c BGB). Waivers of maintenance after divorce are allowed, unless they are deemed to shift the maintenance burden on to Social Welfare or other relatives, instead of the debtor (such a waiver would be against good morals — § 138 BGB), since § 1614 BGB which prohibits such waivers during the marriage is not applicable after divorce. See Göppinger, *Vereinbarungen anlässlich der Ehescheidung,* Beck, 1982, 137– n. 308–318; Schwab, *Familienrecht,* 159; Beitzke, *Familienrecht,* p. 147; D. Langenfeld, Vereinbarungen uber den Nachehelichem Unterhalt in der Praxis, *Neue Jurist. Wochenschr.,* 1981; 2377–2381.
50. Göppinger, *Vereinbarungen anlasslich der Ehescheidung,* 44–47, n. 81–87; Dumusc, *op. cit.,* pp. 177–78; Beitzke, *Familienrecht,* 146–47.
51. It has been stated, in a inquiry made in Amsterdam (1976–1977), that in 734 adversarial divorce cases, the judge had finally led the parties to an agreement in 637 cases. S. R.C. Gisol and A.H.M. Santen, *Notaris, echtscheiding en echtelijke woning,* Kluwer, 1978, 17–18.
52. On all these points, see Dumusc, 148–52; J.B.M. Roes, *op. cit.* (note 32), 182–83, 188–89, 199–200.
53. See Chapters 5 and 21 of this Volume.
54. See Chapter 5.
55. On the hybrid nature of judicially ratified contracts and its legal consequences, s. I. Balensi, "L'homologation judiciaire des actes juridiques," *Rev. trim. dr. civ.,* 1978, 42–79, 233–56.
56. On the special contract of transaction (compromise) which is supposed to prevent or to put to an end once and for all litigation and the specific rules applying to that contract see art. 2044–2058 Belg. and French Civ. Code.
57. Even fraud is not admitted by the Courts, although art. 2053, al. 2, Civ. C. mentions it as a ground for invalidation.
58. However, judicial modifications are admitted by the Courts only in the interests of the child and not for the sake of the parents. Accordingly, reduction of the agreed child's maintenance is not allowed even in case of involuntary reduction of the debtor's income. See J.L. Renchon, *op. cit.* (note 40) and the quoted decisions.

59. On all these points, see especially M.T. Meulders-Klein, "Le principe de la convention-loi et les effets du divorce par consentement mutuel: Etendue et limites," *Rev. crit. jur. belge*, 1979, 468-500; F. Rigaux and M.T. Meulders-Klein, Les *Personnes*, t. I, *Mise à jour*, 1978, n. 270-82.

60. See R. Lindon and Ph. Bertin, "La convention dite définitive ou le talon d'Achille du divorce sur requête conjointe," *Juriscl. Pér.*, 1979, I, 2962; R. Guimbellot, "La convention définitive de divorce, en cas de divorce sur demande conjointe, peut-elle donner lieu à une action en rescision pour lésion?" *Répertoire Notarial Defrénois*, 1981, I, 32518 and *Rec. Dalloz*, 1981, 277; M. Lafond, "L'homologation par le juge aux affaires matrimoniales des conventions des époux en matière de divorce sur requête conjointe," *Juriscl. Pér.*, Ed. Notariale, 1977, I, 103; "Conventions de divorce et rescision pour lésion," *Juriscl. Pér.*, 1980, Ed. Notariale, 285; R. Lindon and Ph. Bertin, La convention définitive dans le divorce sur demande conjointe. "Nouvelle étude du problème," *Juriscl. Pér.*, 1981, I, 3021; M. Brazier, Note under Trib. gr. inst. Le Mans, *Gaz. Pal.*, 1979, 2, 549 and Caen, *Gaz. Pal.*, 1981, 1, 45; J. Massip, Notes under Trib. gr. inst. Nanterre, 17 octobre 1979, *Rec. Dalloz*, 1980, 297, Versailles, 19 novembre 1980, *Rec. Dalloz*, 1981, 460; G. Cornu, *Cours de doctorat*, 1977-1978, Les divorces gracieux, n. 447; Weill and Terre, "*Les Personnes, La Famille, Les Incapacités*," Précis Dalloz, 1983, n. 451; J. Revel, *op. cit.* (note 9), n. 33. Contra: A. Breton, "Divorce et partage," *Mélanges Hébraud*, 1981, 125 ff; I. Balensi, *op. cit.* (note 55) n. 47 ff.; R. Nerson and J. Rubellin-Devichi, *Rev. trim. dr. civ.*, 1980, 585 ff.

61. For instance, Fr. Cass., 28 mars 1979, *Répertoire Notariat Defrenois*, 1980, 32324, note Massip.

62. Y. Boyer, "La révision de la prestation compensatoire," *Rec. Dalloz*, 1980, Chr. XXXVIII, sp. n. 15-22.

63. J.M. Grossen, Chapter 19 of this book. J. Droin, La nature et le contenu des conventions relatives aux effets accessoires du divorce, in IXe *Journée Juridique*, Geneva, 1970, 53-77; A. Staehelin, "Rechtsnatur and Aufechtung der Scheidungskonvention," in *Familienrecht im Wandel, Festschrift fur Hans Hinderling*, Helbing and Liechtenhahn, 1976, 281-300.

64. Chapter 19.

65. Göppinger, *op. cit.* (note 49), pp. 3-4, n. 2-4.

66. Göppinger, *op. cit.*, pp. 43-44, n. 72-80.

67. Göppinger, *op. cit.*, pp. 314-325, n. 600-625.

68. Göppinger, *op. cit.*, 44-48, n. 81-90.

69. Göppinger, *op. cit.*, pp. 48-50, n. 93-99, sp. n. 95.

70. On maintenance agreements between ex-spouses, see Goppinger, *op. cit.*, 109-116, n. 219-38; Beitzke, *Familienrecht*, 146-47. Waivers of maintenance are not admitted with regard to the children (§ 1614, 1, BGB); Göppinger, *op. cit.*, 296-97, n. 579-82.

71. M.J.A. Van Mourik and A.K.P. Jongsma, *Het Nederlands Vermogensrecht bij echtscheiding*, Tjeenk Willink, Zwolle, 1978, 314.

72. Van Mourik and Jongsma, 74-79. Invalidation on the basis of "abuse of circumstances" may lead to another kind of abuse: insincere promises in order to buy a divorce quickly and renege afterwards.

73. Van Mourik and Jongsma, 303 ff.; J.B.M. Roes, in Luijten, *Het Personen en Familierecht* (note 32), 183 ff.

74. See Chapter 21.

75. Even if the action fails it will have caused a lot of troubles and costs. Third parties' interests might be at stake as well.

76. See also the English "special procedure" of "divorce by post" introduced in 1973 and extended in 1977 to all undefended divorce (sect. 41, M.C.A. 1973, M.C.R. 1977, r. 33 (3) 48. See S.M. Cretney, *Principles of Family Law,* 1979, 159–163.

77. M.A. Meredith, "Divorce Kit Dilemma: Finding the Public Interest," 19 *J. of Family Law* (1979), 729–43; H.U. Jessurum d'Oliveira, "Echscheiding uit de hobbyshop," *Nederlandse Juristenblad,* 1982, pp. 309–317.

78. Strikingly, legal aid has been suppressed in England for special procedure cases: S.M. Cretney, *op. cit.,* 160; M.D.A. Freeman, "Divorce Without Legal Aid," 6 *Family Law* (1976), 255.

Chapter Nineteen

Agreements Regarding the Financial Aspects of Divorce: How Free? How Binding?

J.M. Grossen

University of Neuchâtel, Switzerland

INTRODUCTION

In the words of section 158, para. 5 of the Swiss *Civil Code* "agreements relating to the subsidiary effects of the divorce or judicial separation require their validity to be confirmed by the judge."[1] This provision has now been in force for some time.[2] It is of the utmost practical importance.[3] There is an impressive amount of case-law and juristic opinion about its meaning[4] and, as a result, many a question has found a definitive answer.

This chapter deals with two issues which arise wherever the validity (or enforceability) of an agreement regarding the financial effects of a divorce is made dependent on its approval by a court. The first of these two issues is that of the role and power of the court. How free are the parties to reach the agreement which *they* find good? To what extent, and for what purposes, should the judge interfere? What sort of investigation is he expected to make? Under what conditions will it be right for him to refuse the approval which is applied for by the parties? The second issue to be considered is that of the ways and means of having a judicially confirmed agreement either varied or set aside. What is the legal nature of the agreement once it has been approved by the court? Whatever its legal nature may be, is there a way to depart from it if it no longer appears to be fair or practicable, or perhaps never was?

In the case of both issues it will be suggested that the present state of the law of Switzerland is not very satisfactory, but this is not the sole reason for the discussion that follows. Another reason is that the two issues are themselves part of much wider issues of the law of divorce, not to say of family law generally, such as the merits (or demerits) of a laissez-faire policy or the case for (or against) so-called "clean breaks."

THE ROLE OF THE COURT

Typically, section 158, para. 5 of the Swiss *Civil Code* applies to agreements made by the spouses in the course of the divorce proceedings (or at any rate while the suit is pending) and in contemplation of the dissolution of the marriage.[5] In addition, it has been held by several courts to be applicable, by way of analogy, to agreements relating to maintenance, child support, custody, etc., pending suit.[6] As yet the justices of the Federal Supreme Court have not had an opportunity to say whether they are of the same opinion or not. Assuming the stand taken by the lower courts to be good law, an agreement made during the time between the date of the presentation of the divorce petition and the date of the determination of the suit will only be valid if it is approved by the judge having jurisdiction to make an order for the same period.

By way of contrast, agreements reached after the divorce decree has become effective do not require confirmation by a court to be valid.[7] This is true, at least, if nothing is involved but the financial interests of the spouses. It is the unanimous view of both the courts and the legal writers that section 158, para. 5 of the Swiss *Civil Code* does not apply to such agreements.[8] The reason given for the distinction is that, once the divorce has been granted, there is no risk that one of the spouses might take an undue advantage from his or her position in the divorce procedure.[9]

Incidentally the theory allows us to catch a glimpse of what is expected of the court. The court should try to prevent a sort of exploitation of one spouse by the other. In practice, of course, an agreement between *ex*-spouses can entail just as much or as little risk of this as an agreement made prior to the divorce. It could even be argued that while the suit is pending, the spouses are more likely to meet lawyers, and get legal advice, than they would be at a later stage. As a general proposition and a basis for a legal distinction, the idea that ex-spouses are better equipped to look after their own interests than divorcing spouses is not beyond argument.

Where the court's approval is required, a further distinction has to be made between agreements pertaining to the financial interests of the spouses, on the one hand, and all other agreements, on the other.[10] In the latter case, such as child support, the agreement reached by the parents does not have greater effect than a joint proposal to the court. The judge has a duty to inquire whether the agreement is in the best interests of the child. If it is not, he must refuse his approval.[11] In the former case, with no interests at stake other than the financial position of the spouses, such as maintenance or the reallocation of property,[12] the will of the parties normally prevails. The intervention of the judge must not go beyond a "summary examination." As stated by the Supreme Court on a number of occasions, the judge should "only" [sic] make sure that the agreement is an expression of the free will of the parties and that it is clear, complete, not against the law and fair (or equitable, or appropriate under the circumstances.)[13]

There is, it must be conceded, much to be said for the distinction which has become well established practice. Clear-cut as it is, it cannot always convince. To give only one example: If the wife gets custody of her child, the way the problem of her own resources is solved (maintenance) is hardly less important to the child than the issue of child support. There is, therefore, no compelling reason why the judge should be more alert in one case than in the other. However, the main objection to the present system is that, in the cases of agreements relating to the financial interests of the spouses, there is an obvious contradiction between the means and the expectation, that is to say (1) the expectation that the court should only approve the agreement which is found to be clear, complete and fair, and (2) the means of a summary examination. The reality is that a summary examination (and in practice it can be brief indeed) necessarily entails the risk of inequitable agreements being approved.

In this context it should be added that the divorce court is not a criminal court. Some judges take more time than others to consider the agreements they are asked to approve. Whatever time they devote to the matter, their powers of investigation are limited. They are not supposed to inquire whether one of the spouses might perhaps have concealed property.[14] They have to make their decisions on the basis of the facts alleged and the evidence adduced by the parties.

To make it still more difficult, the very notion of what is "fair"[15] in the case of a divorce agreement is by no means unproblematic. For example, would an agreement be unfair if it took fault into account in a situation where the judge, had he to decide, could not take it into consideration?[16]

The generally accepted view is, of course, that an agreement regarding the financial consequences of the divorce may produce its own solutions, different from what the mere application of the Code would produce.[17] This is not disputed. Still one may wonder how far from the provisions of the law an agreement can go without becoming "unfair" for that very reason.

IMPUGNING AGREEMENTS

Before the agreement is confirmed by the court, the parties are nevertheless bound by it. Whatever suggestion to the contrary may derive from the letter of section 185, para. 5 of the Swiss *Civil Code*, the agreement is binding on the spouses, binding unless and until the court refuses to confirm it. Either spouse may, however, draw the attention of the judge to reasons, if any, which point against the court's approval.[18]

Once the agreement has been judicially approved, its clauses must be considered as integral parts of the divorce decree.[19] This is at least the prevailing view[20] and, in practical terms, it means that a confirmed agreement can only be attacked in the same way and on the same grounds as a judgment could be.

As far as variation is concerned, as noted above, ex-spouses may, in the name and within the limits of freedom of contract, make such agreements as they think fit. Agreements after the divorce decree has become effective do not require the approval of a court to be valid. By a new agreement, reached after their divorce has become effective, ex-spouses may, therefore, modify the judicially confirmed agreement they had made in the course of the divorce proceedings.[21] This is true, at least, in so far as the financial interests of the spouses are involved.[22]

If the ex-spouses cannot reach agreement, section 153, para. 2 of the Swiss *Civil Code* may be applicable:

> The party charged with an annuity by way of maintenance can demand its permanent suspension or reduction in amount, where the party entitled is no longer destitute or is in materially improved circumstances; and similarly where the annuity has ceased to be commensurate with the means of the party charged.[23]

According to this provision, the variation of the maintenance contribution can only consist in a suppression or a reduction of the same. The court cannot order an increase. This is a first and important limit, but its impact is weakened since the Supreme Court decided that it was permissible to insert a cost of living index clause into a maintenance agreement.[24]

Another limit is that section 153, para. 2 refers to maintenance only. Whether the amount of money concerned has been fixed by the judge himself or by a judicially confirmed agreement makes no difference. Nor does it matter whether the money is supposed to be wholly or partly by way of damages referred to in section 151, para. 1, or maintenance in the sense of section 152 of the Swiss *Civil Code*. But, in order to be subject to variation, the agreement must be about maintenance, not about other "financial aspects" of the divorce. In other words, section 153, para. 2 confers no power on the judge to vary an agreement concerning the reallocation of property or the determination of the matrimonial regime.

The result is that in some cases it will be easy to invoke section 153, para. 2 and force a judicial reconsideration of a well-balanced agreement (for example, an ex-husband who owes maintenance might start proceedings and simply allege that the amount which was agreed shortly before has ceased to be commensurate with his means; even if his petition for variation is eventually dismissed it will have caused a lot of inconvenience and expense).

By contrast, in other cases the procedure of section 153, para. 2 is not available, even though the agreement may have turned out grossly unfair (for example, if the matrimonial regime was liquidated in a particular way because one of the spouses was not sufficiently informed of the financial situation of the other). In such cases, if there is no variation procedure available, is there at least a way to have the agreement set aside? The answer is that a so-called "revision" may be available[25] though only in the rarest cases. The conditions for the revision of a judgment do not depend on federal law but on the cantonal codes of civil procedure. They vary from one canton to the other. If there is a common denominator, it is that they are usually very restrictive.[26]

Thus, under section 403 of the *Code of Civil Procedure* for the Canton of Neuchâtel, it will not be possible to have a judgment set aside unless evidence can be brought that the judgment could never have been obtained without fraud, false testimony, perjury and the like.[27] Surprisingly, an important issue remains controversial and, in a recent case, the question was left open by the Federal Supreme Court:[28] Would a defect of consent — in the sense of the law of contract — provide a ground for setting aside a judicially confirmed agreement?[29] The few authors who think that the court's approval does not change the nature of the agreement, that the agreement is basically and remains a contract, have no difficulty in answering the question in the affirmative.[30] Among the larger number of authors who regard the judicially approved agreement either as a part of the divorce decree or as a kind of compromise, the question whether the remedies of the law of contract are available or not is far from settled.[31] With respect, then, to the chances of having a judicially approved agreement varied or set aside, the overall conclusion must be that the present state of the law is neither quite clear nor very satisfactory. How could it be improved?

WHAT SHOULD BE DONE?

In spite of the reservations that have been made as to the operation of the present system there remains, it is suggested, a strong case for allowing spouses to enter into agreements about the financial consequences of the dissolution of their marriage. These agreements have in particular the advantage of making the divorce proceedings speedier, less expensive and, as a recent author writes, "less emotional."[32]

For this reason alone, the solution to any shortcomings cannot lie in a prohibition of the agreements referred to in section 158, para. 5 of the

Swiss *Civil Code*. In addition, no illusion should be entertained about the efficiency of such a prohibition. A party cannot be compelled to oppose a petition with which he or she is in agreement. Outside the criminal area, a court's decision will be based, of necessity, on the facts and evidence brought by the parties.

Assuming that agreements continue to be allowed, they will only have the advantage of making the divorce procedure speedier, less expensive and "less emotional" if the court is not expected to inquire into all the circumstances behind the agreement. If there were to be extensive investigations, one might as well allow the judge to decide on all the ancillary effects of the divorce. On the other hand, there seems little sense in requiring the courts to confirm agreements without adequate background information. The confirmation gives the agreement a formal authority which its substance may not merit.

As so often in the field of family law, there is probably no entirely satisfactory solution and the two following suggestions are formulated in full appreciation of the objections that can be raised against them. The first is that the validity of agreements relating to the financial interests of the (divorcing or divorced) spouses should depend only on the law of contracts. If necessary, the divorce court might be called on to take note that an agreement had been made, but not to approve or confirm it. The second is that agreements about maintenance should always be subject to judicial variation.

A waiver of maintenance or an agreement on a sum which is or becomes insufficient is in any case undesirable. In many cases they will involve not only the financial interests of the parties to the agreement, for the person concerned will have to be supported by someone else or by the state. This is why it is suggested that a maintenance agreement should always be subject to judicial variation, in other words, that it should always be deemed to include a *rebus sic stantibus* clause.[33]

For the rest, applying the law of contract and its remedies would have the advantage that, regardless as to the time of their conclusion, all agreements would be governed by the same rules. The parties and their advisers would have to take full responsibility for the agreement. They would have to bear in mind that they can rely on no more and no less than the application of the law of contract. The court would not be required to approve an instrument on which it can have only a very limited influence.

NOTES AND REFERENCES

1. The text as quoted is taken from the English translation of the Swiss *Civil Code* by Ivy Williams (Oxford 1925, reprinted Zurich 1976). The three official (German, French and Italian) versions read as follows:

> Vereinbarungen über die Nebenfolgen der Scheidung oder Trennung bedürfen zur Rechtsgültigkeit der Genehmigung durch den Richter.

Les conventions relatives aux effets accessoires du divorce ou de la séparation de corps ne sont valables qu'après leur ratification par le juge.

Le convenzioni sulle conseguenze accessorie del divorzio o della separazione richiedono per la loro validità l'approbazoine del giudice.

2. Together with the Swiss *Civil Code* as a whole it was enacted on 10 December 1907 and came into force on 1 January 1912. Prior to the latter date, legislation on the ancillary effects of divorce was a matter for the cantons, not for the Federal Parliament. This had not prevented the Federal Supreme Court from holding — as early as in 1884 and from the point of view of the law of contract — that an agreement made in contemplation of a divorce and with respect to the financial consequences of the dissolution of the marriage was not contrary to public policy, unless of course it tended to induce divorce, 10 *Recueil Officiel des Arrêts du Tribunal Fédéral* (hereafter: A.T.F.) 542. The inspiration for section 158, para. 5 came from the law and practice of the Town-Canton of Basle, see Eugen Huber, *System and Geschichte des schweizerischen Privatrechts*, I, Basle 1893, p. 219. In turn the provision of the Swiss *Civil Code* was to have an influence on para. 142 of the General *Civil Code* of Austria, as amended in 1914, as well as on the Scandinavian laws of divorce, see A. Egger, *Das Eherecht*, 2nd ed., Zurich 1936, 209.

3. The exact number of agreements is unknown. Well-informed lawyers do not hesitate to write, however, that an agreement is reached on all or part of the ancillary effects in a large majority of all the divorce cases. There is every reason to believe them. In 1979 out of 10,472 divorce petitions, only 54 were dismissed. The proportion of defended cases was very small (in Neuchâtel, for instance, less than one percent). It is a well known fact that divorce by mutual agreement, though not formally provided for by the Swiss *Civil Code*, is of frequent occurrence in Swiss practice. On this, see M. Keller, Die einverständliche Scheidung, 66 *Schweizerische Juristenzeitung* 113, 1970; L. Nabholz-Heidegger, *Die Konventionalscheidung,* Zurich 1972.

4. In addition to the standard works on the divorce law of Switzerland generally, such as W. Bühler and K. Spühler, Die Ehescheidung, Zurich 1980, 782–806 and H. Hinderling, *Das schweizerische Ehescheidungsrecht,* 3rd ed. Zurich 1967, 184–89 (with Supplement 1981, 132–37), reference should be made in particular to the monograph and articles by Emilie Hartmann, *Die Scheidungskonvention nach schweizerischem Privatrecht,* Berne 1954; J. Droin, "La Nature et le Contenu des Conventions Relatives aux Effets Accessoires du Divorce," in *Neuvième Journée Juridique*, Geneva 1970, 53–77; A. Staehelin, "Rechtsnatur und Anfechtung der Scheidungskonvention," in *Familienrecht im Wandel* (Festschrift für Hans Hinderling), Basle/Stuttgart 1976, 281–300.

5. As revealed by the text, section 158, para. 5 does not only apply in the case of a divorce but also in the case of a judicial separation (divorce *a mensa et thoro*). By the operation of section 134 of the Swiss *Civil Code* it would equally apply in the rather unlikely event of an agreement reached in the course of nullity proceedings and purporting to settle the consequences of the annulment of the marriage.

6. See the decisions referred to by Bühler and Spühler, *op.cit.,* 328, n. 426.

7. The ex-spouses may, therefore, agree (without judicial interference) to vary the financial effects which had been previously determined by the divorce decree or by a judicially approved agreement. This, however, does not apply to child support, 107 A.T.F. II 12 (1981).

8. See Bühler and Spühler, *op. cit* (*supra,* note 4), 791, n. 167 for a number of references.

9. Bühler and Spühler, *loc.cit.*

10. On this distinction see the already quoted writings of Hinderling (184), Droin (65)

and Staehelin (286). The Federal Supreme Court has had an occasion to say that the importance of the distinction should not be exaggerated: It is significant only with respect to the conditions of the court's approval, 93 A.T.F.II 156 (1967) at 158.

11. 94 A.T.F. II 1 (1968).

12. There had been some doubt in the lower courts as to the possibility to operate the division of matrimonial property through a divorce agreement (for references see Bühler and Spühler, *op.cit.*, 787, n. 156). Such doubt has since been removed, and so has been any doubt on the admissibility of an agreement on the litigation costs, including lawyers' fees (*ibid.*, n. 157).

13. See for instance *Wüest v. Wüest*, 102 A.T.F. II (1976) 65, at 68:

Zweck der Genehmigungspflicht ist es, dass die von den Parteien geschlossenen Vereinbarungen vom Richter auf ihre rechtliche Zulässigkeit, ihre Klarheit und ihre sachliche Angemessenheit geprüft werden... Die Prüfung der Angemessenheit einer Vereinbarung ist allerdings nur eine beschränkte, soweit lediglich die vermögensrechtlichen Beziehungen zwischen den Eheleuten selber in Frage stehen. (translation: The aim and purpose for requiring the court's approval is to make sure that a judge will examine whether the agreement reached by the parties is legally permissible, clear and appropriate to the circumstances . . . For what concerns the appropriateness of the agreement, however, the investigation must be a limited one in so far as only the property relationship between the spouses is involved.)

14. Bühler and Spühler, *op.cit.*, 798, n. 183 *in fine*.

15. Several legal writers point out that there must be an "important reason" to justify a court in refusing its approval on the ground that the agreement would not be fair enough, see for instance Bühler and Spühler, *op.cit.*, 798, n. 183; Hinderling, *op.cit.*, 185; U.P. Frey, "Die Abänderbarkeit von Scheidungskonventionen," 73 *Schweizerische Juristenzeitung* 188 (1977). This is indeed the opinion of the Federal Supreme Court as expressed in *Frei v. Frei*, 99 A.T.F. II 359 (1973) at 362 and in many other cases before.

16. There is a decision on the converse point in 104 A.T.F. II 237 (1978) at 244. The Federal Supreme Court found that there was no objection against an agreement providing for damages (in the sense of section 151, para. 1 of the Swiss *Civil Code*) in the absence of fault, whereas a judge could not allocate the same damages if there were no evidence of fault.

17. See for instance 81 A.T.F. II 587 (1955) at 591 and Bühler and Spühler, *op. cit.*, 799, n. 188, with further references. A closer examination of the cases decided in lower courts would tend to show that the judges will more readily approve an agreement by which one of the spouses undertakes more obligations than could be imposed upon him than waivers. In the case of waivers the judge will at least inquire about the reason for departing from the law.

18. See *Frei v. Frei* (*supra*, note 15) at 361, with reference to previous decisions. A good reason can, for instance, result from a change in the circumstances occurring in the time between the agreement and the confirmation procedure — as in *Basler Juristische Mitteilungen* 1972, 20 (since the agreement had been made, the husband had become blind).

19. See 105 A.T.F. II 166 (1979) at 169: "Es besteht rechtlich kein Unterschied zwischen einer vom Richter getroffenen Entscheidung über streitige Nebenfolgen der Scheidung und einer von den Parteien hierüber abgeschlossenen Vereinbarung, die richterlich genehmigt worden ist." (translation: There is no legal difference between a decision made by the judge on contentious ancillary effects of the divorce and an agreement reached on the same effects by the parties, with the court's approval.)

20. As just noted (*supra,* note 19) it is also the opinion of the Federal Supreme Court. Among writers "minority views" will be encountered to the effect that an agreement is a contract and remains a contract even after it has been approved by the court or to the effect that the agreement, once approved, must be equated with a compromise. Still another, and more sophisticated, view of the subject is proposed in the article by Staehelin (quoted *supra,* note 4). In Professor Staehelin's view (which is criticized by Hinderling, Supplement, 35) the judicially approved agreement is in the nature of a judgment in so far as the ancillary effects concerned are outside the scope of the spouses' freedom of contract, and, for the rest, it is in the nature of a compromise. The interest of the qualification is not only academic. The question whether and how the judicially confirmed agreement can be set aside or varied largely depends on it.

21. See note 7, *supra.*

22. Bühler and Spühler, *op. cit.* (*supra,* note 4), 790, n. 164 *in fine.*

23. Ivy Williams' translation (*supra,* note 1).

24. On this see Jean Guinand, "Le Problème de l'Indexation des Pensions Alimentaires," 111 *Revue de la Société des juristes bernois* 321 (1975).

25. See Bühler and Spühler, *op. cit.,* 805, n. 204, with references.

26. On "revision" generally *cf.* Walther J. Habscheid, *Droit Judiciaire Privé Suisse,* 2nd ed., Geneva 1981, 503–507.

27. In a recent case the High Court of Neuchâtel had to decide whether a petition for revision was admissible on the ground that, at the time of the agreement, the wife was of unsound mind. The Court came to the conclusion that no corresponding cause for revision was provided for in section 403 of the *Code of Civil Procedure* but thereafter proceeded to fill what it considered as a gap and finally found that the petition had to be admitted, 7 *Recueil de Jurisprudence Neuchâteloise* I 157 (1978). A more usual view of the subject is that an agreement made by a person of unsound mind is a nullity, and remains a nullity in spite of the court's approval, as stated in Bühler and Spühler, 787, n. 156.

28. *Frei v. Frei* (*supra,* note 15) at 361.

29. References in Bühler and Spühler, *op. cit.,* 805, n. 203.

30. See for instance A. Egger, *Das Eherecht,* 2nd ed. Zurich 1936, 210, n. 16 *in fine.*

31. See the variety of opinions given and by the authors quoted in note 4, *supra*: Bühler and Spühler, 805, n. 203; Hinderling, p. 187; Hartmann, 50, 62; Droin, p. 62; Staehelin, 291.

32. Frey (*supra,* note 15), 187.

33. This would not be a considerable change in the law since maintenance agreements are subject to variation by application of section 153, para. 2 of the Swiss *Civil Code* and courts show a marked reluctance to approve an agreement implying a waiver of maintenance.

Chapter Twenty

Financial Agreements on Divorce in France

J.P. Peigné

President of the Tribunal de Grande Instance, Creteil, France

---

THE HISTORY OF DIVORCE IN FRANCE

A liberal system of divorce was introduced in 1792, during the Revolution, and a stricter system continued in the *Napoleonic Code* of 1804. In 1816 divorce was abolished, and it was reintroduced in 1884. Recently, the law of 13 July 1965 permitted spouses a choice among a limited number of alternative matrimonial property régimes. The law of 11 July 1975 permits divorce *à la carte* on grounds of (1) fault; (2) irremediable breakdown and long separation; (3) mutual consent (for the first time since 1803); and (4) acceptance.

CHARACTERISTICS OF MATRIMONIAL PROPERTY IN THE CODE CIVIL

Modern legislation has introduced supervised liberty, in contrast to the wide powers granted to the husband by the Code of 1804, under the system of community of moveables and acquisitions. Traditionally no modification was permitted after the marriage, whether of the legal regime or of a duly notarized and authorized private agreement. This rule generated spurious divorces and remarriages simply to reorganize the matrimonial property regime. Amendments favouring the wife were made in 1938 and 1942 and in 1944 married women obtained the right to vote.

The more extensive amendments of 1965 gave the parties a choice among a limited number of options for community or separate property systems. Individual agreements might be judicially annulled. However, the *Primary Regime*, which was not variable by the parties, aimed at creating a conjugal association by controlling the parties' over-all rights and duties. Each space becomes personally liable and binds the other *vis-à-vis* third parties for expenditure and debts incurred for household maintenance and the education of children, unless this is clearly exaggerated having regard to their general standard of living. Each spouse is obliged to contribute to the household expenses according to his or her individual resources.

A quick and very cheap procedure was evolved for enforcing contributions to household expenses. The law governing the family residence was also intended to protect the other spouse and children in case of imprudent or spiteful acts by one spouse. Various provisions granted each spouse some independence of action, for example, the wife's right to a free choice of her profession and to open a personal bank account. Simple judicial procedures allowed one spouse to act as substitute for the other who was absent or prevented from exercising or improperly refusing to exercise his or her individual powers.

THE CHOICE OF MATRIMONIAL PROPERTY REGIME

The *Legal Regime* (community of acquisitions) is imposed if no alternative is chosen by notarial act before the marriage. Only moveable property acquired during marriage is community property, particularly that acquired from the income and earnings of the parties. Property owned before the marriage, and gifts and bequests received during it, remain the separate property of each spouse. On dissolution of the marriage it is necessary to determine what property adheres to each spouse and what is community, and to divide that community.

The spouses may, before marriage, choose one of the regimes offered by the law or, within certain limits and subject to judicial control, fashion their own system. French tradition greatly favours community systems, but separate property may be more appropriate for some people, such as tradesmen. Community may be thought to give greater security to those contracting with the married, and to protect in particular the wife.

After two years of marriage the parties may agree to modify their regime after application to the Superior Court (*Tribunal de Grande Instance*) justifying their actions and showing the changes intended. Precautions are taken to protect the children, particularly of a first marriage, and third parties. A "legitimate interest" must be shown and the court may refuse to allow the modification. The general evolution of the legislation has been towards greater liberalization, and the effect of the will of each has been strengthened.

CONSEQUENCES OF DIVORCE

Dissolution of marriage by death or divorce means dissolution of the matrimonial regime and division of the property. Even in a separate property regime, the spouses create community by purchases during the marriage. Dissolution and partition of the property also take place on judicial separation without divorce. The difficult questions involved in distribution are habitually entrusted to the notaries, who are independent but state-appointed, responsible but subject to some judicial control. Until recently, all agreements between the parties as to the division of their property on divorce or separation were considered void as conflicting with the immutability of matrimonial regimes unless they were duly executed and approved.

The new divorce law, evolving from the law of 1965, adopts a different attitude. It seeks to effect the quickest possible settlement of financial matters, if possible in one operation. This also favours the current search for amicable and agreed solutions between those who have been or are about to be divorced or separated. The law invites the judge to counsel the parties to this end. For example, *C.C. Art. 252*-2 provides that if the judge does not succeed, during the compulsory conciliation process, in dissuading the parties from divorce, he should try to guide them into amicably regulating its consequences, particularly as regards the children, by agreements of which the court may take account in rendering judgment. In the day-to-day practice of conciliation it is at this level that the intervention of a specialized judge may be effective. Reconciliation is rare and fragile, but faced with spouses determined to break with each other, the judge may make a preliminary study to see how their separate lives will work out as regards the children, and consider amicable partition of the common property, both sides making concessions. The judge may go beyond advice. By Art. 45 of the decree of 5 December 1975, even if the parties do not ask it, he may, in case of divorce for fault, require a notary or specialist to draw up a scheme regulating payments to be made after the divorce, and may ask a notary to draw up a scheme for the liquidation of the matrimonial regime. The law has sought to strengthen the powers of the judge and of the specialists he may appoint to prepare the dissolution of the regime. Thus *C.C. Art. 259*-3 provides: "The spouses shall communicate to each other and to the judge and any experts he designates all information and documents required to fix payments and allowances and liquidate the matrimonial regime. The judge may pursue any necessary inquiries with debtors or those holding valuables for account of the spouses and no professional privilege of confidentiality may be raised in opposition."

In this way the specialized judge may ascertain the exact situation of the spouses and may, for example, caution a spouse who, for a quick divorce, is prepared to grant excessive concessions to the other which he may not reasonably be able to fulfil in future.

THE SPECIALIZED JUDGE — THE J.A.M.

Juge aux affaires matrimoniales was created in 1975. He is the *Homme orchestre* (less respectfully the "One-man band") of divorce, particularly in respect of property and children. Knowing the techniques of communication and of matrimonial property law and with full information, he may help to dedramatize questions concerning the children and prepare amicable settlements of matrimonial property. He intervenes at all stages. He must see that the procedure functions smoothly (as *Juge de la Mise en Etat des Causes* — in charge of the Cause List) and must take all necessary urgent action (as *Juge des Référés*) He participates at the hearing *en banc* of matters he has supervised. For divorce by consent, in particular, he assumes the entire procedure. He hears the parties, first alone, and then with their advocates, at least twice, and he pronounces the final decision of which he is the sole judge. He may at any time amend measures already taken using quick and cost-free rules. His personal knowledge of the spouses permits him to adopt the role of arbitrator and conciliator. After the divorce has been pronounced, whether by mutual consent, for proved fault, or otherwise, he alone decides when in the future he should amend certain provisions of the judgment separating the spouses, especially as regards the children, whom he may choose to hear personally.

The problems of financial arrangements differ, depending on whether the divorce is by mutual consent or otherwise. In divorce for fault, or irremediable breakdown with separation, or by acceptance, the judge may take account of what the parties have agreed, but his intervention is not compulsory.

In divorce by mutual consent things are different. An agreement fixing the rights and obligations of the future divorced or separated parties, especially as regards heritable property, is in such a case strictly compulsory. The conclusion of such an agreement is imperative before the J.A.M. may, as sole judge, pronounce a divorce.

At their first discussion with the judge, the spouses must produce an interim agreement to regulate problems arising during the hearing, and a draft definitive agreement, which will govern all questions, especially maintenance payments and the sharing of the matrimonial assets and liabilities. The judge studies these documents: he may require some clauses to be modified or omitted if he finds them excessive or injurious.

In their second discussion, the spouses, heard first alone and then also with their advocates, will tell the judge how the interim agreement is working and produce a final agreement which may have been amended as a result of the first discussion. The judge will then verify if account has been taken of his comments. If so, he will pronounce the divorce and at the same time bring the final agreement into effect. On the other hand, under C.C. Art. 232, he may refuse confirmation and not pronounce the divorce if he considers that the agreement does not sufficiently safeguard the interests of the children or of one of the parties. The system should work satisfactorily.

In the old divorce procedure, to the payments due for the maintenance of the children was added a similar payment for the innocent spouse in need, usually the wife. Such a maintenance payment has been retained only in divorce for breakdown, for the benefit of the deserted spouse. In the three other types of divorce it has been replaced by a "compensation payment," the object of which is no longer maintenance of the innocent spouse but to ensure the continuance of the standard of living enjoyed during the marriage and so far as possible to compensate for changed living conditions. The spouse guilty of fault for which a divorce is granted is not entitled to any such payments, a link with the former maintenance payments. Under C.C. Art. 278, on divorce by mutual consent the spouses agree the amount and terms of the compensatory payments as part of the agreement they submit for approval by the judge, who may refuse approval (thus refusing a divorce) if the agreement provides inequitably for the rights and duties of the spouses.

For the legislator of 1975, anxious to see the process speedily completed and to settle quickly matters arising between the parties, compensatory payments may take the form of a capital payment or the transfer of an income-producing asset. In exceptional cases a periodic allowance may be paid. In practice, since most spouses live primarily on their earnings, the exception has become the general rule. Any such allowance must be index-linked to the cost of living, and in fixing its level the judge must take account both of the present needs of the disadvantaged spouse and of foreseeable variations in the situation of the parties. Uncertainties about the criteria applicable are further complicated by the fact that, as distinct from the maintenance payment that was always variable, the compensation payment is a form of forfeiture and cannot be varied unless some exceptional event occurs. The compensation allowance is in principle for life, but a judge dealing with young spouses may limit its duration in various ways. Spouses may escape the forfeiture aspect by inserting a provision for modification. Finally, the allowance may be payable by the successors in title, the children, if the paying party dies survived by the other.

The statute governing the compensation payment is at present the cause of many difficulties: the participation of judge, counsellors, advocates and notaries is essential to arrive at a solution as satisfactory as possible to all parties. To repeat: conclusion of an agreement is an essential condition for divorce by mutual consent.

CONCLUSIONS

Adopting an approach opposed to that of 1804, modern French legislation aims at recognizing the importance of agreements between spouses both as regards the regime of matrimonial property and in the liquidation of such regimes, especially on divorce or separation. It aims generally at conciliation, but in case of conflict leaves to the judge a large measure of control to safeguard the interests of an unprotected spouse, the children, and the household's creditors. In particular, for divorce by mutual consent, such conciliation is necessary and must be confirmed in writing if divorce is to be granted.

The new J.A.M. sometimes has a calming effect in situations of conflict. Not everything is yet settled, particularly the difficult question of the compensation payment. The present system requires the collaboration of the judge, advisers and notaries, all together striving to permit the least possible damage to parties liquidating their past so as to prepare a better future for each of them.

Chapter Twenty-one

Compromise as the Aim of Danish Divorce Procedures

Noe Munck

University of Aarhus, Denmark

PRINCIPLES — LIMITS OF AUTONOMY — FORMAL REQUIREMENTS

The compromise — the agreement between the parties as to the ancillary questions of the divorce and separation — holds a prominent position in Danish divorce procedure.[1] The way the arrangements function in practice seem to set as the goal the achievement of agreement between parties who are in a position to grasp the consequences of the overall result of the agreement. More specifically, Danish divorce procedures seem to rely on two basic principles:

(a) the spouses' agreement on the ancillary questions of the separation or the divorce is preferable to an authoritative official decision. The assistance from the authorities should therefore be designed primarily to provide the background of the parties' mutual agreement rather than establishing a basis for an authoritative decision, and
(b) the control of the contents and conclusion of the agreement necessary to protect the weaker of the spouses or to safeguard the interests of any extraneous third party (creditors, fiscal or social authorities) should be by subsequent invalidation of the agreement rather than its prior authoritative approval.

As described in more detail below, it is left initially to the parties to find on their own a solution to the ancillary questions of the separation or divorce. Sometimes the spouses are assisted by lawyers retained by each of them or jointly. If these attempts to reach an agreement fail, the authorities will try to assist the parties by advising them as to *locus standi* and by explaining the consequences of various solutions. But in practice the assistance of the authorities will go even further and take the form of an actual conciliatory function. Only where such efforts prove fruitless, or where the spouses have elected beforehand to abstain from such assistance, will an authoritative decision be made.

In the light of the basic principles referred to above, the spouses have been granted extensive autonomy. Subject to the possibility of subsequent refusal by creditors and certain authorities to recognize the agreement, the distribution of custody of the children is really the only matter over which unanimous parents do not have complete control. The welfare of the children is regarded as so significant that the safeguard of subsequent invalidation is not considered adequate. This point should also be seen in the light of the fact that the child is not a party to the case and therefore lacks personal representation. The authorities, however, make no assessment of the suitability of one parent against the other, the agreement of the spouses being regarded here as the best safeguard of a result satisfactory to the child. The main object of the control — according to the authorities' practice — is to avoid certain atypical arrangements regarded as contrary to the welfare of the child. This would apply to agreements providing for the child to alternate between the parents ("co-parenting") and agreements under which the custody is to pass from one parent to the other after a number of years. Nor is it possible to establish the arrangement now approved in Sweden, under which joint custody of the children continues also after a separation or divorce.

The formal requirements applying to agreements range from the very strict to the quite informal. Danish Law recognizes only the two extremes. The nature of the matter determines the formal requisite, the agreements governing the following five matters being subject to the strictest requirements:

1. The custody of the children.
2. The right of a spouse to maintenance and its duration (but not the amount of the maintenance, which may be deferred for subsequent determination).
3. The right to continue the lease of the dwelling occupied by the couple.
4. The duty of one of the parties to pay a lump sum of money out of his/her separate property to the other to ensure that the latter does not suffer undue hardship after the separation/divorce.
5. The right of the wife to widow's pension.

These terms have a special status in Denmark because agreement on those terms has been made a precondition for the competence of the County governors to grant separation or divorce. Where the parties fail to reach an agreement on one or more of these matters, the separation or divorce can be ordered only by a court of law, which will concurrently determine the matters at issue. If, on the other hand, an agreement is reached, such agreement will be entered in the County records, which are signed by both parties. Its legal basis, however, lies not in the agreement of the parties but in the decree drawn up by the County Governor based on the consent of the parties. Consequently, the parties are not bound by the concluded agreement until the County, perhaps a few days later, issues the decree of separation or divorce. Until then the parties may withdraw from the agreement.

On the other land, it is *not* a condition for obtaining separation that the parties agree on the other ancillary questions arising in connection with the divorce, such as:

6. The right of access to the child for the parent who is not granted custody.
7. The amount of the periodical maintenance to the spouse.
8. The amount of the periodical maintenance to the child.
9. The financial adjustment between the spouses relative to the division of the estate: (1) the amount of assets accruing to each of them (the *quantitative* division), and (2) the matter of which actual assets (house, motorcar, securities, furniture, etc.) shall accrue to each of them (the *qualitative* division).

The parties are at liberty to allow the terms indicated under (6) to (9) above to remain unsettled in connection with the separation or divorce, whether granted by the County or a court of law. The parties may be momentarily unable to find a solution, or it may be in their interest to defer their decision. Thus, the practice of the right of access frequently will not be arranged in detail but will be determined on a current basis by the needs and abilities of the parties. Also, in a transition period, the financial contributions to one of the spouses will sometimes be allowed to depend on the latter's needs to meet day-to-day expenses and the establishment of a new life. As regards the division of the estate, however, it is necessary, at the end of the calendar year, to determine — for taxation purposes — which assets belong to whom. If the parties wish to enter into an agreement as to the terms indicated in (6) to (9) above, this can be done quite informally; a verbal agreement, if it can be proved, will be completely valid. However, for reasons of evidence the agreement will often be drawn up in writing. This applies notably to agreements on division of the estate. Tax deduction rules may also make it a practical necessity to prepare written agreements on maintenance for spouses and children.

The far-reaching autonomy and on a number of ancillary questions, the equally extensive informality, is not entirely without risk. In some cases the spouses will be ill-suited to make decisions on a number of future matters at the time of the separation or divorce. The emotional stress of the dissolution of marital life and the uncertainty and confusion often resulting therefrom may constitute a poor basis for an arrangement founded so extensively on the autonomy of the parties. The system also entails a risk that a husband or a wife exploits his or her position of strength in their relationship or greater financial insight at the expense of the other. In order to prevent abuse it is necessary to provide reasonably wide access subsequently to set aside the agreement.

ASSISTANCE IN MAKING THE COMPROMISE (AGREEMENT)

In a substantial number of cases the parties manage to reach agreement on the matters referred to under (1) to (5) above without actual legal assistance. In many instances they have help from family and friends. The most difficult thing for the parties is probably to calculate maintenance for the other party, normally the wife. But the woman's income from gainful employment will often make it clear in advance that maintenance to her is out of the question.

Actual legal assistance is offered to the parties by social workers, family counselling centres, lawyers, the Counties and the law courts. It is not easy to describe in general terms the progress of the negotiation of terms in separation or divorce cases — particularly the efforts made by the two first mentioned categories. The comments below will therefore be limited to the contribution made by lawyers, the Counties and the law courts.

In cases where the parties are unable to reach an agreement between themselves, the "typical" sequence of the negotiation of terms will probably vary somewhat with the different social category of the spouses. In the case of separation or divorce in the higher social brackets, lawyers are likely to be implicated at a rather early stage. The continued negotiations then often take place through or assisted by the lawyers. If the negotiations are successful, they will in a number of cases result in "package solutions" that lay down the terms within several related areas. Thus the agreement on division of the estate may be linked with a specific solution of the matter of maintenance to the wife and possibly the question of transfer of separate property. The work of the Counties in connection with the fixing of the terms is then limited to a recording of part of the agreement arrived at through the lawyers.

At the middle or lower social levels the preceding negotiation will typically have occurred directly between the parties and they often turn up in the County office without having reached an agreement in advance. The conciliatory efforts of the deputy governor[2] become crucial here. Often the deputy governor will also try to contribute to a solution of issues other than the five that are a condition for obtaining an administrative decree — particularly the problem of division of the estate. In practice, the training of the deputy governor and especially the frequently tight time schedule for the meeting reduce the prospects of performing more extensive negotiations.

If the parties fail to reach an agreement on the matters referred to under (1) to (5) above, whether or not the negotiation of terms took place through lawyers or between the parties in the County office, the decision will be made by a court of law. Even during the proceedings, the judge will try to bring about a compromise. Most often, however, this will not occur until late in the trial when the matter has been sufficiently elucidated to optimize the prospects of compromise. As in the case of the procedure at the County, the judge performs a supervisory function in the matter of the parties' agreement on custody, but hardly in respect of the other questions.

Where the parties fail to reach an agreement on the amount of maintenance for the wife or the child or on the exercise of access to the child(ren), the decision will be made by the County on a purely written basis. Corresponding efforts to reconcile the parties will not be made by the County in those matters. The decision is arrived at by a somewhat awkward administrative practice. Thus the matter of access to the child is practically always given the same form: "right of access to the child one weekend per month, two weeks during the summer holidays, etc.". If the party who has been granted custody of the child refuses to comply with the County's decision in the matter of access, the other party is entitled to the assistance of the Bailiff's Court to enforce it. Even the Bailiff's Court will generally make an attempt to solve the problem by a compromise between the parties. Very substantial efforts are often displayed by the Bailiff's Courts to induce the parties to find a solution; the Courts normally seek to avoid enforced decisions on access because of the stress on the child.

As regards the *division of the estate*, the parties, as already mentioned, are free to enter into any informal arrangement upon which they can agree. As is mentioned later in this article, creditors and tax authorities will nevertheless have an opportunity to set aside the agreement in relation to themselves, so the parties should consider that fact when drawing up the agreement. If the parties fail to reach an agreement they will often each contact a lawyer. Normally, the initial result of such a contact is that the lawyer submits an application for free legal aid to the County, who will send it on to the Probate Court — officially with a view to obtaining an opinion from the Probate Court as to whether free legal aid should be granted. The Probate Court will then convene a meeting of the parties which is *de facto* a negotiation of terms by the Court. This generally results in an agreement on division of the estate, which causes the petition for free legal aid to lapse. If no agreement is reached, each of the parties (always provided that they meet the financial conditions) will normally have a counsel assigned to them.

If the continued negotiations between the lawyers also fail to produce a compromise, the matter will be brought before the Probate Court — officially in order to obtain a decision, but in fact often to seek the assistance of the Probate Court in the continued negotiations of terms. Sometimes the nature of these negotiations can be so heavy-handed that the agreement on the division of the estate assumes the character of an "enforced option." A suitable means of coercion is the fee and the costs payable to the Treasury if the Probate Court undertakes the administration and division of the estate with a view to pronouncing judgment on the disputed matters. By experience, the government taxes payable are a heavy burden for the parties, whose financial situation is already likely to be strained owing to the divorce.

In summary, it can be stated that because of the extensive conciliatory activity in connection with agreements on the division of the estate, probably more than 90 percent of the cases are settled without the intervention of the court. And out of the balance of less than 10 percent of "heavy" cases, the Probate Court is estimated to compromise about 90 percent, so that the conciliatory efforts can be said to fail in under 1 percent of all cases.

SUBSEQUENT INVALIDATION OF THE COMPROMISE (AGREEMENT)

This extensive autonomy, and in some matters, the absence of formality, enhances the problems of subsequent invalidation of agreements. The powers have been vested in the courts of law and the County Governors respectively, depending on the type of term involved in the agreement. Variation and invalidation of agreements relative to the matters set out in (1) to (5) above are the responsibility of the law courts whether the agreement was made before the County authorities or in connection with a lawsuit. Besides, the courts of law are entitled to set aside or vary agreements on the amount of maintenance for the wife (or husband) and on the division of the estate. The Counties are authorized to set aside agreements relating to the amount of maintenance for the child(ren) and the exercise of access to them.

This division of powers is not devoid of a certain inner logic, reflecting as it does an interaction between the substantive and procedural rules — between the nature of the issues, the contents of the rule of amendment, and the form of procedure. The Counties base their consideration of the variations purely on written statements, and the required information is obtained primarily from questions in writing to the parties. This form of procedure is reasonably well justified in cases where the criteria for invalidation are very wide and discretionary, which is exactly the case with agreements on maintenance for and access to the child(ren).

Variation of agreements by the courts of law, on the other hand, are subject to the customary judicial safeguards; it is therefore a more satisfactory form of procedure in cases where the legislation allows invalidation only in a few and especially qualified situations.

The courts' supervision of agreements between the parties is governed by what is broadly known as a set of "rules of invalidity," which reflect a general balancing of two opposing considerations: *(a)* on the one hand, the need for protection of a spouse against agreements with adverse effects due to that spouse's ignorance or lack of ability to grasp the scope of the agreement, mental instability or dependence on the other party, etc., and *(b)* on the other hand, regard for the other party under the rules of the law of contract, which imply that he cannot be arbitrarily deprived of the expectations he has entertained in reliance on the agreement. In Danish law the overall balancing has meant that agreements are largely confirmed. The reasoning is a different one where the children's situation is involved. Traditionally, the welfare of the children, at least in theory, is given greater weight than that of the parents. Agreements on maintenance for and access to the child(ren) are therefore subject to the County Governor's wider variation powers. A special position is held by agreements on the distribution of custody, which are governed by the more restricted variation powers of the courts of law, as described in more detail below.

The following is a discussion of (1) the possibility of contesting an agreement because of circumstances that were *present when the agreement was made,* and (2) the possibility of contesting the agreement due to *subsequent* factors. In essence, these rules are of a substantive content but it is difficult to describe the procedural systems without incorporating the substantive rules to a certain extent.

Under the *general rules on the validity of contracts* in Danish Law, an agreement between the parties may be *set aside in its entirety* if it was made under duress (sections 28 and 29 of the *Act of Contracts*) or by fraudulent representations or omissions (section 30 of the *Act of Contracts*), e.g., where one spouse induces the other to sign an agreement on the division of the estate by withholding relevant facts as to his or her financial situation. An agreement may also be set aside if one of the spouses takes advantage of the other's dependence or the other's ignorance or lack of knowledge of financial matters (section 31 of the *Act of Contracts*), or where one of them possesses such knowledge of relevant circumstances that it would be contrary to common honesty to uphold the agreement (section 33 of the *Act of Contracts*). Particular attention attaches to section 36 of the same Act — the so-called "omnibus clause" — according to which, generally speaking, an agreement may be set aside wholly or in part if it would be *unreasonable* or contrary to *proper conduct* to maintain it. It has been disputed whether this broadly formulated rule applies to agreements on terms between spouses, but it is reasonable to assume that it does. The problem has received substantial theoretical attention, but as the rule is rather new (it came into force on July 1, 1975) there are no published judgments to clarify the matter. This should probably also be seen in light of the fact that it is often a more obvious step to set aside the agreement in pursuance of the special rule in section 58 of the *Contraction and Dissolution of Marriage Act* (hereinafter referred to as the "Marriage Act"), which will be discussed below. Finally, a spouse is entitled to have an agreement on terms set aside if a material assumption of the agreement proves to be incorrect, but only if the court finds that it is reasonable to let the other party bear the risk of the failure of the assumption.

Due to the importance of stability in the sale and purchase of goods, etc., in normal contractual relationships, objections of invalidity cannot be set up against the contracting party who is not personally responsible for the reproachable circumstance and who is justly ignorant of it. Since the regard for business and trade does not apply to agreements between spouses, it is assumed that there is a more far-reaching possibility of holding the agreement invalid. Whereas the general grounds for invalidity are based primarily on the *circumstances* under which the agreement was made, the special rules in section 58 of the Marriage Act and section 17 of the *Legal Status of Children Act* (hereinafter referred to as "the Children Act") take their starting point in the *contents* of the agreement. Total or partial invalidation under these rules is possible only if the concrete result of the agreement can be described as "patently unreasonable."

The provisions of section 58 of the Marriage Act have great practical significance for the *invalidation and variation* of agreements on the division of estates, maintenance for the spouse, and agreements on transfer of separate property. According to its wording, however, the field of application of this rule is somewhat limited: only agreements made *with a view to* an impending and completed separation or divorce can be set aside — and only because of circumstances present already when the agreement was made. The evaluation of the contents implies a comparison of the concrete result of the agreement with the overall financial situation of the parties. This evaluation is made *partly* in the light of the alternative decision by the courts, and *partly* based on general considerations of equity, which also include a forecast of the developments in the parties' financial situations as they appeared when the agreement was made. In addition to those considerations, however, the courts have incorporated into the evaluation a number of factors relating to the circumstances under which the agreement was made — apparently inspired by the general grounds for invalidity previously referred to. An immediate application of the general rules of invalidity would often be difficult because of lack of evidence, but the considerations upon which the provisions are based may be included as supporting arguments for the application of section 58 of the Marriage Act. Judicial decisions of the past have thus stressed the following: What information was available to one or the other of the spouses when the agreement was made? Was there a prior discussion of the agreement before it was made? Was the spouse advised by a lawyer or a county deputy governor on that occasion? Did the spouse have sufficient insight to grasp the scope of the information produced, especially insight in financial matters? At the same time the law courts have considered which of the spouses actually determined the contents of the agreement, so that, generally, the agreement is upheld against the "aggrieved" party if the latter has offered the other party favorable terms in order to find an easy way out of the marriage. Finally, the courts have attached importance to the "aggrieved" party's state of mind when the agreement was made, including also whether the spouse was more nervous or unbalanced than would be normal in such situations.

The terms that have a bearing on the children are given special consideration. The above considerations of protection and of the validity of contracts, respectively, must yield in this context to the interests of the child. Due to the supervision of the content of agreements on custody performed by the County authorities and the law courts, there are no special provisions for setting aside agreements on custody due to circumstances present at the conclusion of the agreement. Another answer has been found to the question of varying agreements on access, because those agreements are not considered to have any legally binding effect and thus function solely by virtue of their morally binding nature. In consequence, it is difficult for the spouses to obtain a "package solution" which grants custody to one of the spouses in return for a favorable arrangement of access for the other party. Only the custody part of the Agreement would then have a legally binding effect.

As already mentioned, agreements on maintenance for the children may be set aside pursuant to section 17 of the Children Act if they can be described as patently unreasonable. Besides, the Children Act provides that the agreement may be set aside if it is contrary to the welfare of the child, a criterion that, as practised by the Counties, amounts to the setting aside of any agreement which deviates from the substance of the alternative administrative decision.

In particular cases the invalidation of agreements may be based on circumstances occurring after the agreement was concluded. The principal criterion is that the situation must have undergone "substantial change" and, in summary, the opportunity for variation must be described as extremely modest — apart from certain terms regarding the children. Here the principle of the validity of contracts is allowed to prevail. For most financial arrangements, there are no special provisions in the matrimonial legislation. Such arrangements can therefore only be set aside under the previously mentioned general rules of invalidity of the law of contract to the extent that those rules allow the incorporation of subsequent circumstances in the evaluation. That is true only for the omnibus clause in section 36 of the *Act of Contracts* and the maxim of failing implied assumptions. The latter therefore attracts special attention, but in the more recently published case law the matter of failing assumptions has only in one instance entailed the invalidation of the agreement. In section 52 there is a special clause concerning the duration and amount of the maintenance for the wife. The agreement can be set aside by the law courts if it would be patently unreasonable to uphold it due to materially changed circumstances. Judging from the sparse amount of reported cases, only few actions are instituted under this provision and these rarely result in invalidation.

Agreements between the parties relating to the children are partly subject to the courts' more restricted powers of variation, and partly the wider powers of the County governors. The greatest restriction is found in the variation of agreements on custody, probably reflecting the view that, generally speaking, children are best off remaining where they are, and that a legal action *per se* may have a harmful influence on the child. Under section 48 of the Marriage Act such agreements can be set aside only by the courts of law where, due to materially changed circumstances, it is deemed to be necessary out of regard for the welfare of the child. By contrast, under the County governors' practice, there is extensive power to set aside agreements concerning maintenance for the children, even though the conditions in section 17 of the Children's Act have been given a somewhat narrow formulation. The circumstances must have changed materially or the agreement must be contrary to the welfare of the child. The most far-reaching powers of variation apply to agreements on the exercise of the right of access, because the County is not bound by the parties' earlier agreement and thus has a free hand in its decision.

While the parties' opposing interests provide a certain amount of protection against agreements violating the interests of one of the parties, there is no such natural protection of third parties. The spouses will often share the same interest in favoring one or both of them at the expense of creditors and the fiscal and social authorities. The judicial system has therefore designed a certain protection of these interests, which entails at the same time an actual reduction of the spouses' autonomy.

The risk for the creditors may follow from a transfer by the insolvent spouse of his or her assets to the other spouse via an agreement on division of the estate, sometimes against exemption from payment of maintenance to the wife. Such transactions can be set aside in bankruptcy proceedings against the insolvent spouse and a subsequent invalidation of the transfer by the courts of law. More doubtful are the cases where in the agreement on division of the estate the insolvent spouse has waived his or her right to 50 percent of the other party's assets, which would otherwise accrue to him/her by virtue of the rules of community of property. It is a condition for the invalidation that the transfer has the nature of a gift within the meaning of the *Bankruptcy Act.* The problem is dubious and remains unclarified by case law.

The guiding principle of Danish tax legislation is that agreements on distribution of income and expenses have an influence only on the division of the estate, but no consequences as to taxation. No matter what the parties have agreed, the tax authorities regard the time of the separation or divorce as the deadline for taxability of income and deduction of expenses — or perhaps the end of the year where cohabitation ceased, whichever comes first. By contrast, transfers of assets after the deadline as an element of a division of the estate will generally have to be accepted by the tax authorities as regards property taxation and certain tax deductions. Normally, also, the tax authorities are compelled to accept an unequal division of the estate and cannot regard the excess as a taxable gift to the beneficiary.

The social welfare authorities face a particular risk in attempts by the spouses to shift the maintenance burden onto the social welfare schemes by their mutual agreement. In order to obviate such agreements, the authority that has disbursed social benefits to one of the spouses has been permitted to take the latter's place. The social authorities, on the spouse's behalf and against his/her wish, are thus entitled to require the County to impose maintenance contributions (for spouse as well as children) on the other spouse. Subject to the County's decision, such contributions are payable by the other spouse to the social authorities, to the extent that the authorities have disbursed social benefits to his/her spouse and the children. However, the social welfare authorities are entitled to set aside the agreement only to the extent that they can show that it was made with the object of shifting the maintenance burden onto the Treasury. In practice, however, it will be enough to demonstrate that, at the time of the agreement, the "needy" spouse had no realistic prospects of making ends meet without the maintenance contributions that were waived in the agreement.

FUTURE REFORMS

A proposal for further development of the tradition of compromise is contained in a recent memorandum for discussion ("Mother-Child-Father are getting divorced") published through the "Dansk Retspolitisk Forening" (the Society on Legal Policy) in 1980. The Working Party issuing the memorandum comprised professional people involved in matrimonial cases, county staff, judges, lawyers, psychologists, psychiatrists, and social workers. The impetus was a common feeling that the current divorce procedure functions inadequately in some respects and in itself can have the effect of creating and aggravating conflicts. The group has proposed amending the rules of competence and procedure with the object of establishing a new divorce procedure designed to avoid the drawbacks described below, particularly with regard to the children involved.

It is the group's opinion that the Danish divorce procedure functions reasonably well in less complicated cases, whereas the arrangement is less suited as an instrument for solution of "heavy" cases where the spouses find it difficult to agree upon anything at all. The following aspects are particularly important:

1. The various ancillary questions are governed by the competence of different authorities. First the spouses turn up at the County office and, failing agreement, they will usually be granted free legal aid to institute proceedings. Then they must enter an appearance in court where decision is made on the matters referred to under (1) to (5) above. But in order to have the maintenance for herself and the children fixed, the wife must now once again contact the County authorities. If the parties fail to agree, e.g., on the husband's right of access to the child, he must ask the County to determine the issue. If the wife fails to comply with this decision, the husband must now apply to the Bailiff's Court to have the decision enforced. The joint estate is divided by the Probate Court but, frequently, not until the parties have filed a prior petition for free legal aid for probate via the County. With each new authority, and sometimes with each new responsible person within the same authority, the parties must repeat part or all of the developments of the matter. This ritualistic description of the other party's faults and omissions during the marriage is time-consuming and often has a reinforcing effect on the underlying conflicts to the detriment of the parties' subsequent cooperation as regards the children. This scattered competence often makes it difficult to agree on package solutions of interrelated divorce terms.
2. The lawyers responsible for these matters in the Counties and the courts of law have no particular psychological insight, notably in child psychology, and therefore lack the background and tradition for problem solving in cooperation with the psychological experts. The group especially feels that serious objections can be raised against the existing arrangement where, when the parties fail to agree, it is left to the law courts to evaluate which of the parents would be able to give the children the best childhood, based on observations from the Bench of parents who are in the unaccustomed and stressful situation of being questioned in court.

The group has therefore suggested the following reforms to the Danish divorce procedure:

1. All negotiations for and determination of divorce terms should be gathered under a single authority. More time should be allotted to the cases so as to allow a more thorough negotiation of terms than now, including package solutions of interrelated divorce terms. It should still be possible to defer some divorce terms for subsequent determination. Where agreement cannot be reached, the authority in question will make the authoritative decision. The negotiation procedure should be arranged with a view to creating the optimum chances of reaching a compromise. If disagreement arises as to the children, a child expert attached to the authority should be summoned (a psychologist or a psychiatrist); the expert will then advise the spouses and the authority during the further negotiations.
2. Lawyers working for the relevant authority should be given supplementary education in psychology, especially child psychology. Likewise, via postgraduate education, an attempt should be made to make them better suited to solve the problems arising in connection with the division of the estate. Also, child experts should be attached to the authority.

NOTES

1. The expression "divorce procedure" is used to signify a broad spectrum of activities performed by the Danish authorities in connection with both separation and divorce.

2. These are described in Chapter 5 by T. Svenné Schmidt.

Chapter Twenty-two

Judicial Control of Divorce Settlements in Belgium

Walter L. Pintens

Institute of Family Law, Catholic University of Leuven, Belgium

INTRODUCTION

Belgian law knows two forms of divorce: divorce by mutual consent and divorce on specific grounds such as adultery, acts of violence, maltreatment, serious insults and ten years of factual separation.[1] The procedures regarding financial consequences depend on the form of divorce chosen.

With the first type of divorce (consent divorce), both parties not only have the opportunity to agree on all the consequences of the divorce, but are required to have done so (art 1287-1288, *Code Judiciaire*). This rule is in contrast with the situation in cases of divorce on specific grounds. With this type of divorce, there is no obligation to arrange the consequences of the divorce. It is, however, open for the spouses to make an agreement about the children's position (art. 1279, *C. Jud.*), but they rarely do this. This Chapter will deal only with settlements in cases of divorce by consent.

CONSENT DIVORCE SETTLEMENTS

Where divorce is by consent, the law requires the spouses to draft a notarial inventory, which lists all their movable and immovable assets. They also have to specify their mutual rights respecting those assets (art. 1287, *C. Jud.*). These rules imply the liquidation of the matrimonial property. Moreover, the parties are obliged on penalty of nullity of the procedure to agree on the following four items (art. 1288, *C. Jud.*):

1. The residence of each of them during the divorce proceedings;
2. The custody of their children and the right to visit them both during the divorce proceedings and afterwards;

3. The contributions for the maintenance and the education of the children;
4. The eventual amount of the alimony between the spouses during the divorce procedure and after the divorce.

This list is not limitative. Additional agreements are possible, for example, on the competent court or on the use of a spouses' name after the divorce.

A prior obligation to arrange all the consequences of the divorce has many advantages. First of all, the spouses are given the opportunity to arrange the consequences of the divorce themselves. They will thus know what will be the final outcome from the commencement of the lawsuit. The agreements constitute a tableau of the conditions of life after the divorce. There will be no surprises over the result of the proceedings. The system also puts an end to disputes between the parties. After they have brought the divorce proceedings to a conclusion, no other negotiations need to be conducted and no new proceedings initiated to arrange the division of their common properties.

The increasing popularity of consent divorce[2] is not only due to recent legal reforms which have made the procedures more flexible, but mainly to the opportunity of arranging the consequences of the divorce before the commencement of the proceedings. In consequence of this, this type of divorce presents some characteristics of a humane divorce law, whose aims are "to buttress, rather than undermine, the stability of marriage, and when a marriage has irretrievably broken down, to enable the empty legal shell to be destroyed with the maximum fairness and the minimum bitterness, distress and humiliation".[3]

Judicial control is exercised by two different authorities. First, settlements are verified by the Public Prosecutor, who must advise whether or not a divorce may be granted. Second, the court supervises the arrangement to some extent.

CONTROL BY THE PUBLIC PROSECUTOR

During the proceedings before the chairman of the court of first instance, the clerk sends a true copy of the agreement to the Public Prosecutor (art. 1292, second paragraph and 1296, *C. Jud.*). His control over the arrangements is limited. He checks whether the agreement covers all the items prescribed by law. He can also inquire whether the agreements might be tainted by nullity, because they are contrary to public policy or contravene proper morality (for example if the agreement contains a clause requiring celibacy or if one of the parents renounces his visiting rights over the children). However, the Public Prosecutor does have the power to institute proceedings before the juvenile court to take another decision concerning the children under the provisions of article 36,2° of the law of 8 April 1965, concerning youth protection. The measures taken are not related to the agreement between the parties. They do not change the agreement directly, nor can they commit the parties to its modification. The measures can, however, suspend the agreement indirectly, because the court is able to impose a decision that is contrary to the agreement.[4] The powers of the Public Prosecutor in this regard are of very limited scope. He can only bring proceedings if the health, safety or morality of the minor concerned is at risk, either because of the milieu in which he lives or because of his activities, or when the circumstances in which he is brought up are dangerous for the minor because of the attitudes of those who have custody of him (art. 36,2°). Thus, the Public Prosecutor will only be able to take action if the agreement violates the minor's interests very seriously. The fact that a better settlement concerning parental authority or alimony could perhaps be achieved is not in itself sufficient to involve the juvenile court.[5]

In 1977, the Public Prosecutor thought it preferable to change the agreements in the children's interest in only 34 of the 1,246 Brussels dossiers. However, only one of the 34 cases contained sufficient grounds to activate the jurisdiction of the juvenile court under art. 36,2° of the law on youth protection. In practice, some Public Prosecutors make use of the referral of the agreements to persuade the spouses to modify their settlement in the children's interest. In 1977, the office of the Brussels Public Prosecutor thought it necessary to interview the parents in the following cases:

1. no contribution to the maintenance of the children by the parent who has not obtained the custody (31 cases),
2. division of the children between the parents (27 cases);
3. custody of very young children to the father (27 cases);
4. no visiting rights (19 cases);
5. insufficient contribution to the maintenance of the children (8 cases);
6. change of custody arrangements during the proceedings (5 cases);
7. joint custody to both parents (1 case);
8. change of custody at a certain date (2 cases);
9. custody to one parent and factual custody to the other parent except over weekends (1 case).

Most of these cases require no modifications after a clarifying conversation. Thus it might turn out that there is no provision for visiting rights because the legal father was not the physical father. In 34 cases, a modification of the agreement seemed to be necessary. In 9 cases, the parents agreed with the modification.[6] If the Public Prosecutor does not succeed in getting the parents to modify their agreement and if he does not consider that any issue of public policy has arisen, he will not be able to hold up the divorce even if he himself considers a modification desirable. Art. 1279 C. Jud. defines the competence of the Public Prosecutor strictly: he can oppose the divorce only if the legal formalities are not performed.

SUPERVISION BY THE COURT

The Court's supervision over the agreement is very limited. The judge can only investigate whether the spouses have agreed on all the prescribed items and whether the agreement is not affected by nullity due to public policy or good morals. Other inquiries are not permitted. The court can only ascertain the existence of the agreements. The judge is not entitled to study the nature of the agreement or propose modifications. The court cannot investigate whether, at the time of the negotiations, pressure had been brought upon one of the partners or whether unduly onerous conditions were agreed to.[7] These rules apply for the agreements concerning both the children and the spouses.

APPRECIATION

In contrast with the French law (art. 232 C. Civ.), the Belgian judge's supervision over agreements is very limited. According to Belgian law, extensive supervision contradicts the essence of consent divorce, i.e., a divorce in which a real trial is avoided. Control over agreements means an interference in private matters of the partners. An agreement which turns out to the disadvantage of one of the partners may have its reason. If a judge's approval were required, there might need to be an explanation of these reasons. This is incompatible with a fundamental characteristic of the consent divorce settlement: the avoidance of investigation about the specific divorce ground.

The same rule, applied to the agreements concerning the children, can lead to situations in which the children's best interests are not fully taken into account. Parents often fail to make an agreement in which the children's interests are best promoted; children are divided between both the parents, intricate visiting arrangements put the children in a state of permanent flux, an award of the custody of the children becomes the prize of the divorce. Belgian *doctrine* regrets the fact that neither the Public Prosecutor nor the court has jurisdiction outside the exceptional circumstances of the law on youth protection to impose a modification of agreements if the children's interest requires it.[8] The Public Prosecutor of Brussels has therefore proposed subjecting these agreements to the sanction of the court on the analogy of divorce on specific grounds (art. 1279 C. Jud.).[9] In a discussion at the notarial congress at Mons in 1979, this proposal met with opposition. Several members of the committee mentioned that the intervention by the court was incompatible with the tradition of consent divorce. They held that this intervention could possibly disturb the laboriously concluded equilibrium of the arrangement. Moreover, these members thought that an agreement to which the partners could not be reconciled, even if it is objectively thought better, could never be applied in circumstances that are favorable to the child.[10]

These arguments point to the fact that a formula should be found that takes the wishes of the parents into account. To achieve this, it is recommended that the arrangements concerning the spouses and those concerning the children should be strictly separated. Following the German and the Dutch example, the arrangements concerning the children *de lege ferenda* should not have the nature of a settlement, but rather of a proposal originating with both the parents.[11] In this way, the child is the subject of negotiation, but to a lesser extent. The parents will know that if they make unsatisfactory arrangements, they incur the risk that the judge might reject their proposal and take the decision himself. It cannot be said that this result disturbs the equilibrium of the agreement, because the parents knew the risks. Moreover, the wishes of the parents are taken into account, because their mutual proposal will be the basis of the decision taken. Usually the parents are in the best position to work out the best solution for their children. Their mutual proposal will necessarily be an important element in the decision of the judge. He will only deviate from it if it is clear that the parents have not pursued their children's interests.

NOTES

1. For a general survey: Baeteman (Ed.), "Het echtscheidingsrecht in Belgie na de Hervorming 1974–75, Gent/Leuven, 1977; Van Houtte, "The Belgian Divorce Law," *NLJ*, 1977, 463.
2. In 1979, 36.4 percent of all divorce cases were divorces by mutual consent.
3. Law Commission, *Reform of the Grounds of Divorce: The Field of Choice*, 10; Cf. Bates, "Reforming Australian Divorce Law: Pragmatism or Conceptualism," *Family Law Quarterly* 1973, 404; Mikat, "Scheidungsrechtsreform in einer pluralistischen Gesellschaft," *FamRZ*, 1970, 337.
4. Gerlo, "De burgerrechtelijke bepalingen van de wet op de jeugdbescherming," *T.P.R.*, 1973, 150, no. 55, Janssens, "De rechtsbedeling bij gezinsmoeilijkheden," in *Recht in beweging*, blz. 604, nr. 44; Kebers," La protection des enfants du divorce," *J.T.*, 1964, 244, no. 59; "Protection de la jeunesse," in Nov., no. 104, p. 38; Poelman, "Une annee de divorces par consentement Mutuel a Bruxelles," *J.T.*, 1979, 5.

5. Poelman, *loco citato*.
6. Poelman, *loco citato*.
7. Baeteman, *opere citato*, no. 376, p. 257.
8. Poelman, *opere citato, J.T.*, 1979, 7.
9. Poelman, *loco citato*.
10. Koninklijke Federatie van Belgische notarissen, *Het juridisch statuut van het kind*, II–26.
11. Muller-Freienfels, *Ehe und Recht*, Tubingen, 1962, 223.

Chapter Twenty-three

The Legal Response to Private Financial Arrangements in Divorce

Eric Clive

Commissioner, Scottish Law Commission, Edinburgh, Scotland

HOW MUCH FREEDOM?

The first question that the law reformer has to ask about private financial arrangements between the parties to a divorce is whether they are a good thing, a bad thing or something in between. At one time the courts, at least in some countries, were extremely suspicious of private financial arrangements between the parties to a divorce. Such arrangements savored of collusion.[1] They might, moreover, involve attempts by the parties to transfer a burden of support on to public funds.[2] More recently, attitudes have changed. The idea of divorce by consent has ceased to horrify; collusion has been abolished in various jurisdictions, and is regarded as "a paper tiger" in others;[3] the idea that a person owes an obligation of support to a former spouse is no longer universally accepted;[4] and it is now generally seen to be a good thing if the parties settle the financial consequences of their divorce by private arrangement. A private settlement is likely to be less bitter and destructive, and certainly less expensive, than a court battle. On the other hand, there is a conflicting policy objective — the desire to protect the weaker party from exploitation. The law reformer who looks at this question today is, therefore, likely to see private financial arrangements on divorce as a good thing provided they are fair, or at least not manifestly unfair. And the law's basic response to private ordering in this sphere is likely to be not outright prohibition, nor the according of total freedom but rather the according of very considerable freedom subject to certain safeguards and controls. The area of debate is likely to be just how extensive, or how minimal, these safeguards and controls should be. The Scottish Law Commission (henceforth "the Commission") has recently considered this question and its approach may be of some interest.[5]

The present law on this point in Scotland is one, essentially, of nonintervention. Agreements on financial matters between divorcing spouses have never been regarded as amounting to collusion in Scots law, provided there is actually a good ground of divorce,[6] and there has never been any requirement to refer them to the court.[7] Such agreements are perfectly valid and binding. It seems to that the parties can validly renounce their rights to apply to the court for an order for financial provision.[8] I am referring here only to the spouses' own rights to financial provision after divorce: they could not renounce their children's rights to maintenance.[9] The courts have no power to vary financial agreements between the parties to a divorce. This noninterventionist approach is not the result of a conscious policy decision: it is just the way the law has developed and is the result of legislative inaction rather than legislative action. Although accurate information on the number of private financial arrangements on divorce entered into in Scotland is unavailable, there is reason to belive that the number is substantial.[10] The Commission considered, and invited the views of consultees on, various possible solutions to this problem.[11] One such solution would be to provide that an agreement on financial provision on divorce would not be enforceable unless approved by the court.[12] This, the Commission thought, would err too much on the side of protection and would require a large number of acceptable agreements to be referred to the court in order to control a few unacceptable ones. It would involve the court in a great deal of unnecessary work. Another solution would be to provide that the court could not grant a decree of divorce unless it was satisfied as to the fairness of any financial agreement.[13] This, too, the Commission thought would be overprotective. Both these solutions would also, although this was not a reason given by the Commission for rejecting them, make it more difficult to introduce simple administrative divorce. They presuppose judicial divorce. Another possible solution would be to give the court wide powers to vary agreements on financial provision at any time and to provide that any renunciation of the right to apply to the court would be void.[14] This, however, would remove much of the attraction of a settlement. As one English textbook puts it:

> One might cynically ask the riddle: "When is an agreement not worth the paper on which it is written?" and answer "When the court has an unrestricted power to vary it."[15]

It seemed to the Commission that what was needed was not a system which subjected all agreements to the court's approval or control but rather a system which assumed that agreements would be reasonable but gave some opportunity to aggrieved parties to challenge them if they were altogether unfair and unconscionable.[16]

The consultation carried out by the Commission revealed strong support for the propositions that it should be possible for the parties to enter into agreements on financial provision on divorce, and to renounce their rights to apply to the court for financial provision on divorce, without any requirement that agreements should be referred to the court for approval. There was more disagreement about the Commission's provisional proposal that the court should be given power to set aside agreements on financial provision on divorce which were altogether unfair and unconscionable. Some thought that there was no need to have any special rule to this effect and that the matter could be left to depend on the ordinary rules of law on setting aside agreements entered into under error, fraud, force or fear. The Commission gave careful consideration to this point of view but concluded that there was a need for some special provision.

> There may be cases where an agreement could not readily be challenged at common law but where it had been obtained by undue pressure or deliberate non-disclosure of material facts. The parties to a pending divorce action are not always on the same footing as two strangers negotiating freely from positions of strength. There are often opportunities for emotional blackmail, particularly if there are children, and it seems to us that on this ground, as well as on the ground of procedural convenience, it is desirable that the courts should have some power to control agreements on financial provision even if they are not challengeable at common law.[17]

Other commentators thought that the Commission's proposal was too narrow and that there should be power to set aside unreasonable agreements, particularly if the complaining spouse had not been legally represented. Others pointed out the desirability of having some time limit on the court's power to set aside agreements.

The Commission's approach to this problem was affected by its general approach to the whole question of financial provision on divorce (not favoring the idea of a continuing obligation of support after divorce: favoring finality whenever possible).[18] In the light of this policy, and the comments received, it recommended no change in the existing law on the parties' freedom to enter into agreements on financial provision on divorce, and to renounce their rights if they thought fit, without the need for court approval.[19] It recommended, however, that the court should have power, on the application of either party, to vary or set aside an agreement on financial provision on divorce if the agreement was not fair and reasonable at the time it was made.[20] In the interests of finality, this power would be available only at the time of granting the divorce or within such short time thereafter as the court might allow at the time of granting the divorce.[21] The Commission considered whether there should be any legislative list of factors which the courts should take into account in deciding whether an agreement was not fair and reasonable — for example, the strength of the bargaining position of the parties relative to each other, whether a party was induced to accept the agreement by any unfair means, whether material facts were withheld by one party from the other, and whether the parties were legally represented. It decided, however, that this matter could be left to the good sense of the courts and that it was not necessary to set out any legislative list of factors.

That, then, is the response which the Commission has given to the question of the basic attitude which the law should adopt in relation to private financial arrangements on divorce.[22] Essentially it is that the parties should enjoy complete freedom subject only to a right to challenge an unfair or unreasonable agreement at or shortly after the time of the divorce.

HOW CAN THE LAW HELP?

If it is assumed that fair private agreements on financial provision after divorce are to be encouraged, the next question is how can the law help in this direction? There is, of course, a limit to what the law can do but it can make things easier at the stages of reaching an agreement, enforcing it, and varying it (if the parties so desire).

Helping Parties to Reach Agreement: Conciliation

It is astonishing how in the last ten years or so the focus of attention has shifted from reconciliation to conciliation. The emphasis in the current statute law in the United Kingdom is entirely on reconciliation.[23] The Law Commission for England and Wales has, however, very firmly stressed the importance of conciliation in relation to the financial consequences of divorce. In its recent report to the Lord Chancellor on this topic, the Law Commission pointed out that reforms of the substative law could have only a limited effect in reducing feelings of bitterness and injustice and that procedural reforms were also important.

> We believe that everything possible should be done to ensure that only those cases which necessarily require adjudication come before the courts for trial of contested issues; and that the legal system should be so structured as to encourage the parties to reach an informed agreement about the financial and other consequences of the breakdown of their marriage, and to dispel the illusion that recourse to hostile litigation can produce magical solutions to intractable problems. In this connection, we would draw attention to the view of the Lay Observer[24] that in so many cases the

inevitable unhappiness associated with most matrimonial proceedings has apparently been considerably magnified by the adversarial nature of the court proceedings and of the preliminaries thereto. This view is widely held; and indeed might seem to be supported by the tenor of much of the response to the Discussion Paper from those who had themselves been involved in litigation.

14. You will be aware of the attempts made (often with encouraging results) by a number of precariously funded conciliation schemes (notably in Bristol) and of the research which has been carried out into their working. It may well be that further investigation of the potential for such procedures and of the proper relationship between conciliation and adjudication requires to be undertaken. It is also clearly the case that the extent to which such services should be provided by the state (as proposed by the Finer Committee) or by voluntary initiative (as with the schemes now in operation) is a matter for government decision, as is the question of how any such schemes might be funded. Nevertheless on the evidence available to us it seems that schemes of this kind have considerable potential, and we would urge that these matters be further investigated.[25]

The Scottish Law Commission did not deal directly with conciliation in its report, partly because the main problems seemed to be nonlegal and partly because any legal problems seemed to go beyond the question of financial provision on divorce. The Commission did, however, make one recommendation which could be of some relevance to conciliation — namely, that the court should have power to grant a divorce decree and continue the case for a specified time to enable the question of financial provision to be dealt with.[26] Under the present law, the court has to deal with applications for financial provision "on granting decree" of divorce.[27] Some judges in fact send the parties out of the court to see if they can come to an agreement, perhaps after the judge has indicated a view on certain matters, but this is an informal expedient. The Commission's recommendation would, in effect, enable the court to continue a case for conciliation.

That there are other legal problems in, and possible legal responses to, conciliation I do not doubt. This is a question, however, which goes beyond financial arrangements and is dealt with in other chapters in this volume.

Helping Parties to Reach Agreement: A Framework of Acceptable Principles

Although the emphasis in this volume is on procedures, there is an undeniable link between the substantive law and private ordering on divorce.[28] For one thing, the courts in deciding whether an agreement can be successfully challenged as unfair or unreasonable are likely to look, among other things, at how far it departs from the results which would have been reached by the courts under the general law. An agreement which is broadly in line with the general policy of the law is less likely to be challengeable than one which is out of line for no good reason.

More positively, and more generally, the law can help the process of settlement by providing a suitable backdrop to it. There are two extreme solutions, both of which have disadvantages. One is to have a system of fixed rules on the financial consequences of divorce. This provides certainty and should make it easier for parties to reach agreement.[29] The drawback is that fixed rules cannot in real life cater fairly to the many different situations that arise. They may make settlements easier to achieve, but they do not necessarily make *fair* settlements easier to achieve. Scots law had such a system before 1964 but it was widely, and rightly, regarded as primitive and unjust and was abandoned in favor of a more flexible system.[30] The other extreme solution is to give the divorce court an unfettered discretion as to the financial consequences of divorce. This is the present law in Scotland.[31] If different judges have different views (as is almost inevitable) and if the parties do not know until the day of the divorce which judge will hear their case (as is the situation in Scotland) the effect on the bargaining process is harmful. Although some spouses (risk avoiders)[32] may be so terrified of the possible results of litigation in these circumstances that they may be encouraged to reach a settlement, the settlement will not necessarily be regarded as even moderately fair. I was told, for example, of cases where the husband had inherited a large sum of money after the parties had separated and where he was advised by his lawyer that if he went to court, his wife might be awarded one-third to one-half of it. Even though husbands in this situation might feel that the wife had no claim to the money in question, they might feel obliged to settle for a large amount. I have heard of similar cases involving very short marriages where the wife claimed up to one-half of all the husband's property, even though most of it had been acquired before the marriage. Under this system, parties with no desire to risk a battle in the courts may agree to pay or accept sums which they regard as outrageous. The more usual consequence of the unfettered discretion rule, however, seems to be to exacerbate dispute.

> The system encourages a process of haggling in which one side makes an inflated claim and the other tries to beat it down. A battle of nerves ensues, sometimes right up to the morning of the proof. By that time it is known which judge will be dealing with the case, and this may become a factor affecting last-minute and hurried negotiations. Such a system does nothing to help the parties to arrange their affairs in a mature and amicable way. It is calculated to increase animosity and bitterness.[33]

The Commission has now recommended a new set of rules on the financial consequences of divorce. This is based on a framework of principles which, it is hoped, would be regarded as fair and acceptable by reasonable husbands and wives. It would, unlike the informal rules of thumb which have grown up among practitioners under the present system, be set out in a statute available to all. The Commission regarded this as important.

> It seems to us that any solicitor in any part of Scotland, even if not a divorce specialist, should be able to turn to a statute on financial provision on divorce and find some clear statement of the underlying principles on the basis of which he could advise his client and seek to negotiate a settlement. That is not possible under the present law.[34]

The actual content of the new law proposed by the Commission is not of direct relevance to the theme of this chapter, but as it may be of interest, clauses 8 to 11 of the draft Bill attached to the Commission's Report can be found appended to this chapter.[35]

Helping Parties to Reach Agreement: Financial Inducements

One potent inducement to agree is the thought that litigation will involve both parties in great expense. At present this inducement tends, in Scotland, to operate more directly on husbands than on wives, because the general rule is still that the husband is liable for his wife's expenses (costs) of divorce litigation, win or lose.[36] The rule is based on the theory that these expenses are necessaries for which the husband is liable. The Commission regarded this rule as an anachronism and has recommended its abolition. The result should be to increase the number of cases where the pressure to avoid unnecessary litigation expenses operates on both parties.

Another possible inducement to reach an agreement on the financial consequences of divorce could be provided by tax and social security laws. Two points should be made. First, the present United Kingdom law on the taxation of payments to children provides an actual *disincentive* to letting matters rest on a mere agreement. This is because periodical payments of income by a parent to his or her minor child under an agreement are treated as the income of the payer for tax purposes, whereas similar payments under a court decree will be the income of the child or the recipient parent depending on how the decree is worded.[37] This seems an unfortunate rule for which it is hard to see any sound justification. The second point is simply the obvious one that there is a question of public policy here. Even though it would be technically possible to provide tax or social security[38] incentives for certain types of agreements on financial provision on divorce or maintenance for children after divorce, there is the question whether it is right to favor this particular class of taxpayer or welfare recipient at the expense of the rest. There is already disquiet in the United Kingdom over the extent to which the tax laws enable a divorced or separated man to support his wife and children out of pretax income.[39] This would increase, justifiably in my view, if a particular class of divorced person were singled out for even more favorable treatment.

HELPING PARTIES TO ENFORCE THEIR AGREEMENTS

A court order will usually have advantages over an agreement between the parties when it comes to enforcement. The law can help in this respect by making it easier for the parties to get their agreement incorporated into a court order if they so wish.[40] If there is doubt about the court's power to do this, as there was, for example, in South Africa,[41] express power can be conferred by legislation.[42] It may be desirable to ensure that the court has a suitably wide range of powers to make orders for financial adjustment on divorce, so that the parties are not met by the argument that a useful provision in their agreement is beyond the court's powers and therefore incapable of being incorporated in the court order. This was a factor which the Scottish Law Commission had in mind when it recommended that the court's powers to make incidental orders in relation to financial provision on divorce should be widely expressed.

> One advantage of an open-ended range of incidental powers is that the court can give effect in its decree to an agreement between the parties, even if the agreement contains incidental provisions beyond the scope of the court's main powers.[43]

One price to be paid for having the terms of an agreement incorporated in a court order may, in many systems, be that the court has a discretion to modify the terms before incorporating them. This is the present position in Scotland[44] and the Commission has recommended no change. In this the Commission has been less adventurous than the Commissioners for Uniform State Laws here in the United States.[45] In practice, of course, courts very rarely refuse to give effect to an agreement which has been reached between the parties.

Another price which the parties may have to pay for having their agreement incorporated into a court order is that it may, contrary to their wish, be subject to variation by the court.[46] There is a very neat solution to this problem in the *Uniform Marriage and Divorce Act* which provides that terms of an agreement set forth in the court order are always variable if they relate to support, custody and visitation of children, but are not variable if they relate to other matters and if the parties have in the agreement expressly precluded variation.[47] The parties are therefore able to have a "once and for all" settlement incorporated in the court order if they so wish. The Scottish Law Commission did not deal expressly with this problem, on the assumption that under the law of Scotland the parties could already validly renounce their rights to apply to the court for financial provision or for a variation of an award.[48] On reflection, it might have been better to include an express provision to this effect in the draft Bill for the avoidance of doubt.[49]

Another difficulty which may arise if an agreement on financial arrangements after divorce is incorporated into a court order is that it may be doubtful whether the agreement is entirely superseded by the order or whether it continues to have contractual effect. The Commission invited views in its consultative memorandum on whether, for the avoidance of doubt, it should be provided that in so far as an order for financial provision was made, on the request of the parties, in terms of an agreement ("a joint minute"), the agreement should be regarded as superseded by the court order and should cease to have contractual effect.[50] The comments received were generally to the effect that this result followed in practice in any event, given the terms of joint minutes,[51] and that legislation was unnecessary. The Commission therefore made no recommendation on this point.

Lest it be thought that the Commission has not been very innovative in relation to the incorporation of agreements into court orders, it should perhaps be said that the present system seems to work well. Research done for the Commission showed that 35 percent of judgments on financial arrangements were in terms of an agreement ("joint minute") between the parties.[52] The general advice of consultees on this point was to leave well enough alone.

Helping Parties to Achieve Finality or Variability of their Option

I am concerned here with the situation where the parties have not had their agreement incorporated into a court order. The policy question is whether they should be able to achieve a final settlement of their financial affairs[53] if they so wish, or an agreement which is subject to variation by the court, if they so wish. The Commission thought that they should be able to do so.[54] The scheme recommended by the Commission is, therefore, that if an agreement on financial provision on divorce is not challenged at the time of the divorce it should thereafter be final — with this one exception, that a provision for a periodical allowance should be subject to variation by the court if the agreement expressly so provides.[55]

> This would merely extend a facility to the parties of which they could take advantage if they wished. It would do nothing to discourage agreements but, of offering a choice between finality and variability, might make them more attractive in some circumstances.[56]

It is implicit in this proposal (but should perhaps have been made explicit) that the parties may renounce any right to apply to the court for a financial provision after the divorce. An agreement would not achieve finality if one of the parties could apply to the court at a subsequent date for an order for financial provision.[57]

CONCLUSION

Family law practitioners have been aware for very many years of the importance of private financial arrangements on divorce. Such arrangements are very common. The question for the law reformer is how to react to them. The approach taken by the Scottish Law Commission has been to allow maximum freedom to the parties to make their own agreements, including final agreements, without any need for court approval, but with a limited right to challenge an unreasonable or unfair agreement at the time of the divorce. This, in fact, is slightly more protective than the present law in Scotland, which makes no special provision for challenge on the ground of unreasonableness or unfairness. It does involve treating both parties to a divorce as adults who are capable of deciding what is best for themselves. Is that a bad thing?

APPENDIX

EXCERPT FROM
FAMILY LAW (FINANCIAL PROVISION) (SCOTLAND) BILL
FINANCIAL PROVISION ON DIVORCE ETC.

Orders for financial provision

8. (1) In an action for divorce, either party to the marriage may apply to the court for any one or more of the following orders —
    (a) an order for the payment of a capital sum or the transfer of property to him by the other party to the marriage;
    (b) an order for the making of a periodical allowance to him by the other party to the marriage;
    (c) an incidental order.

(2) Subject to sections 10 to 15 below, where an application has been made under subsection (1) above for an order, the court shall make sure order, if any, as is —

(a) justified by the principles set out in section 9 below; and

(b) reasonable having regard to the resources of the parties.

An order made under this subsection is in this Act referred to as "an order for financial provision".

Principles to be applied

9. (1) The principles which the court shall apply in deciding what order for financial provision, if any, to make are —

(a) that the net value of the matrimonial property should be shared fairly between the parties to the marriage;

(b) that there should be due recognition of contributions made by either party for the economic benefit of the other party and of economic disadvantages sustained by either party in the interests of the other party or of the family;

(c) that the economic burden of caring after divorce for a child of the marriage should be shared fairly between the parties;

(d) that a party who has been financially dependent to a substantial extent on the other party should be awarded such financial provision as is reasonable in the circumstances to enable him the more easily to adjust over a period of not more than three years from the date of decree of divorce to the cessation on divorce of such dependence; and

(e) that a party who at the time of divorce seems likely to suffer grave financial hardship as a result of the divorce should be awarded such financial provision as is reasonable in the circumstances to relieve him over such period as is reasonable of such hardship.

(2) In subsection (1)(b) above, "contributions" means contributions made whether before or during the marriage and includes indirect and non-financial contributions and, in particular, any such contribution made by virtue of looking after the family home or caring for the family, and "disadvantages" means disadvantages sustained whether before or during the marriage; and in subsection (1)(c) above, "child of the marriage" means a child under the age of 16 years who is a child of the marriage or who is a child, other than a child boarded out by a public or local authority or a voluntary organization who has been accepted by both parties as a child of the family.

Sharing of value of matrimonial property

10. (1) In applying the principle set out in section 9(1)(a) above, the net value of the matrimonial property shall be taken to be shared fairly between the parties to the marriage when it is shared equally or in such other proportions as are justified by special circumstances.

(2) The net value of the matrimonial property shall be the value of the property at the date on which the parties ceased to cohabit or, where the parties have not ceased to cohabit at the date of service of the summons in the action for divorce, at the date, in either case after deduction of any debts incurred by the parties or either of them —
    (a) before the marriage so far as they relate to the matrimonial property, and
    (b) during the marriage,
which are outstanding at the date to which this subsection refers.

(3) Subject to the following provisions of this section, "the matrimonial property" shall mean all the property belonging to the parties or either of them at the date to which subsection (2) above refers which was acquired by them or him (otherwise than by way of gift or succession from a third party) —
    (a) before the marriage for use by them as a family home or as furniture or plenishings for such home; or
    (b) during the marriage but before the date to which subsection (2) above refers.

(4) The proportion of any rights of interests of either party under a life policy or occupational pension scheme or similar arrangement referable to the period to which subsection (3)(b) above refers shall be taken to form part of the matrimonial property.

(5) In subsection (1) above, "special circumstances" shall, if the court thinks fit, include
    (a) the terms of any agreement between the parties on the ownership or division of any of the matrimonial property;
    (b) the source of the funds or assets used to acquire any of the matrimonial property where those funds or assets were not derived from the income or efforts of the parties during the marriage;

The Legal Response to Private Financial Arrangements in Divorce 359

      (c) any destruction, dissipation or alienation of any of the matrimonial property by either party;
      (d) the nature of the property, the use made of it (including use for business purposes or as a matrimonial home) and the extent to which it is reasonable to expect it to be realised or divided or used as security;
      (e) the actual or prospective liability for any expenses of valuation or transfer of property in connection with the divorce.

    (6) For the purposes of subsection (2) above no account shall be taken of any cessation of cohabitation where the parties thereafter resumed cohabitation, except where the parties ceased to cohabit for a continuous period of 90 days or more before resuming cohabitation for a period or periods of less than 90 days in all.

Factors to be taken into account

11. (1) In applying the principles set out in section 9(1) above, the following provisions of this section shall have effect.

    (2) For the purposes of section 9(1)(b) above, the court shall have regard to the extent to which —
      (a) contributions by, or economic disadvantages sustained by, either party have been balanced by by contributions by, or economic disadvantages sustained by, the other party, and
      (b) any resulting imbalance has been or will be corrected by a sharing of the value of the matrimonial property or otherwise.

    (3) For the purposes of section 9(1)(c) above, the court shall have regard to —
      (a) any decree or arrangement for aliment for the child;
      (b) an expenditure or loss of earning capacity caused by the need to care for the child;
      (c) the need to provide suitable accommodation for the child;
      (d) the age and health of the child;
      (e) the educational, financial and other circumstances of the child;
      (f) the availability and cost of suitable child-care facilities or services;

(g) the needs and resources of the parties; and
(h) all the other circumstances of the case.

(4) For the purposes of section 9(1)(d) above, the court shall have regard to —
(a) the age, health and earning capacity of the party who is claiming the financial provision;
(b) the duration and extent of the dependence of that party prior to divorce;
(c) any intention of that party to undertake a course of education or training;
(d) the needs and resources of the parties; and
(e) all the other circumstances of the case.

(5) For the purposes of section 9(1)(e) above, the court shall have regard to —
(a) the age, health and earning capacity of the party who is claiming the financial provision;
(b) the duration of the marriage;
(c) the standard of living of the parties during the marriage;
(d) the needs and resources of the parties; and
(e) all the other circumstances of the case.

(6) In having regard under subsections (3) to (5) above to all the other circumstances of the case, the court may, if it thinks fit, take account of the responsibilities of the party who is to make the financial provision towards any dependent member of his household whether or not that member is a person to whom that party owes an obligation of aliment.

(7) The court shall not take account of the conduct of either party except where —
(a) that conduct has affected the economic basis of the claim for financial provision; or
(b) in relation to section 9(1)(d) or (e) above, it would be manifestly inequitable to leave that conduct out of account.

NOTES

1. See e.g., for English law, *Emanuel v. Emanuel* [1945] P. 115.
2. See *Hyman v. Hyman* [1929] A.C. 601.
3. Hahlo, *The South African Law of Husband and Wife* (4th edition, 1975) 364.

4. It is significant that for the purposes of supplementary benefit (the basic non-contributory state benefit in the United Kingdom for those whose resources are insufficient for their needs) a person is *not* liable to maintain his or her former spouse: *Supplementary Benefits Act 1976*, s. 17.

5. Scottish Law Commission, Report on *Aliment and Financial Provision* (Scot. Law Com. No. 67) Nov. 1981. "Aliment" is the Scottish term for maintenance or support as between husband and wife (during their marriage), parent and child and grandparent and grandchild. The word "maintenance" is also used in Scots law and, as it is probably more generally understood, I shall use it in this chapter.

6. *Walker v. Walker*, 1911 S.C. 163 at 168.

7. In cases where divorce is sought on the basis of two years' separation with consent, of five years' separation without consent, or where the defender is mentally disordered, the pursuer must include, in the summons, details of the financial position of both parties and the dependent children of the marriage and of the financial arrangements proposed or sought. The purpose, however, is to inform the other party rather than to seek the approach of the court, which is not necessary: Rules of Court of Session, rule 157(2).

8. *Dunbar v. Dunbar*, 1977 S.L.T. 169, not following *Hyman v. Hyman* [1929] A.C. 601; Clive, *Husband and Wife* (2nd edition, 1982) 514.

9. *Beaton v. Beaton's Trs.*, 1935 S.C. 87.

10. There is no claim for any financial provision in about two-thirds of divorce cases in Scotland. In the remaining third the claim is very often settled by agreement in the course of the action: See Scot. Law Com. No. 67, paras. 3.20 and 3.23.

11. In its consultative Memorandum, the Commission referred to the laws of Australia, England, France, West Germany, and the U.S.A. *(Uniform Marriage and Divorce Act).* See Scot. Law Com. Memorandum No. 22; *Aliment and Financial Provision* (1976) Vol. II paras. 3.106 to 3.110.

12. *Cf.* the *Australian Family Law Act* 1975, s. 87(2), which must be read with s. 86 allowing agreements to be registered and enforced without approval. Agreement in the latter category are however always variable by the court. See Finlay, *Family Law in Australia.* (2nd edition) 233–34.

13. The courts in Scotland and England already have to be satisfied as to the arrangements for children before granting a divorce: *Matrimonial Proceedings (Children) Act 1958*, s. 8; *Matrimonial Causes Act 1973*, s. 41.

14. *Cf.* the English *Matrimonial Causes Act 1973*, ss. 34 and 35.

15. Passingham, *Law and Practice in Matrimonial Causes* (3rd edition, 1979) 163.

16. See Memo. No. 22, para. 3.115.

17. Scot. Law Com. No. 67, para. 3.192.

18. More on this later.

19. Scot. Law Com. No. 67, para. 3.193.

20. *Ibid.,* para. 3.197.

21. *Ibid.*

22. The Commission's recommendations do not relate to child support. The parties cannot, by an agreement between themselves, contract out of their obligations towards their children: Scot. Law Com. No. 67, para. 3.196.

23. *Matrimonial Causes Act 1973*, s. 6; *Divorce (Scotland) Act 1976*, s. 2. For a review of recent developments in several countries see Eekelaar, *Family Law and Social Policy* (1978) 142–51.

24. Appointed under the provisions of the *Solicitors Act 1974*, s. 45. See his 5th Annual Report (1980) H.C. 507.

25. Law Commission; *Family Law: The Financial Consequences of Divorce* (Law Com. No. 112, 1981) paras. 13 and 14 (footnotes altered). With permission of the Controller of Her Majesty's Stationery Office.
26. Scot. Law Com. No. 67, paras. 3.116 and 3.124.
27. There is no decree *nisi* in Scots law.
28. See Mnookin and Kornhauser, "Bargaining in the Shadow of the Law: The Case of Divorce," 88 *Yale L.J.* 950.
29. *Ibid.*
30. See Clive, *Husband and Wife* (2nd edition, 1982) 509–510. Under the pre-1964 law, the innocent wife got the same share of her guilty husband's property as she would have got if he had died — i.e., a third of his movable property if there was a child and a half if there was not, plus a liferent of a third of his immoveable property.
31. *Divorce (Scotland) Act 1976,* s. 5.
32. See Mnookin and Kornhauser, *loc. cit.*
33. Scot. Law Com. No. 67, para. 3.37.
34. Scot. Law Com. No. 67, para. 3.37.
35. See Appendix to this chapter.
36. Clive, *op. cit.* 587–93. This rule has been weakened in recent years and is not now applied in cases based on five years' separation where the wife is legally aided: *Craigie v. Craigie,* 1979 S.L.T. (Notes) 60.
37. *Income and Corporation Taxes Act 1970,* Part XVI; *Yates v. Stanley* [1951] Ch. 465; *Shelley v. Shelley* [1952] P. 107.
38. At one time it was possible to maximize supplementary benefit by arranging for maintenance to be paid to, say, one of several children rather than to the spouse with custody. This has now been stopped: see *Supplementary Benefits Commission v. Jull* [1980] 3 All E.R. 65; *Social Security Act 1980,* Sch. 2, para. 30.
39. The Inland Revenue has even given its approval to a technique whereby a divorced or separated parent can pay a child's school fees out of pretax income: see [1980] 3 All E.R. 832.
40. The *Uniform Marriage and Divorce Act* obtains the best of both worlds by providing that if an agreement is set forth in a court order its terms are enforceable both as terms of a judgment and as contract terms: s. 306 as amended in 1973.
41. See Hahlo, *The South African Law of Husband and Wife* (1st. edition), 371–72;
42. As was done by the South African *Matrimonial Affairs Act No. 37* of 1953: see now the *Divorce Act 1979,* s. 7.
43. Scot. Law Com. No. 67, para. 3.141.
44. *Robson v. Robson,* 1973 S.L.T. (Notes) 4.
45. See s. 30 of the *Uniform Marriage and Divorce Act* (as amended in 1973) which, in effect, *obliges* the court to accept certain terms unless they are unconscionable.
46. *Cf. Jessel v. Jessel* [1979] 3 All E.R. 645.
47. S. 306. For another interesting model see the *Australian Family Law Act 1975,* s. 86.
48. *Dunbar v. Dunbar,* 1977 S.L.T. 169; *Thomson v. Thomson,* 1981 S.L.T. (Notes) 81; Scot. Law Com. No. 67, para. 3.193.
49. In case a Scottish court felt tempted to follow the reasoning of the English Court of Appeal in *Jessel v. Jessel* [1979] 3 All E.R. 645 notwithstanding the fact that the statutory background is different — most notably in that there is no statutory provision in Scotland making void a provision in a maintenance agreement purporting to restrict any right to apply to a court for an order containing financial arrangements.

50. Scot. Law Com. Memo. No. 22, para. 3.116.

51. This also appears to be the position in English law. See *de Lasala v. de Lasala* [1980] A.C. 546 per Lord Diplock at 560.

52. Where capital sums, as opposed to periodical allowances, were involved 63 percent of judgments were in terms of a joint minute.

53. I.e., as between themselves. Arrangements for children involve different considerations.

54. *Cf. Minton v. Minton* [1979] A.C. 593 per Lord Scarman at 608: "The law now encourages spouses to avoid bitterness after family break-down and to settle their money and property problems. An object of the modern law is to encourage each to put the past behind them and to begin a new life which is not overshadowed by the relationship which has broken down."

55. Scot. Law Com. No. 67, para. 3.194. This solution is similar to that of the *Uniform Marriage and Divorce Act,* s. 306.

56. Scot. Law Com. No. 67, para. 3.194.

57. The question whether the court should be able to make a "final" order, without the consent of the spouse affected, so as to cut off that spouse's right to apply for a periodical payment at a later date, is a different question from that considered in the text, but one which has given rise to much difficulty in England in recent years: see *Dipper v. Dipper* [1980] 2 All E.R. 722.

Chapter Twenty-four

Divorce Bargaining: The Limits on Private Ordering

Robert H. Mnookin

Stanford Law School
Stanford, California, U.S.A.

Three years ago, in an article published in the *Yale Law Journal,* I suggested an alternative perspective for family law scholars concerned with divorce.[1] It emphasized negotiation, not adjudication; private ordering, not regulation. This change in emphasis seemed timely, if not overdue. Available evidence has long shown that the overwhelming majority of divorcing couples resolve the distributional questions concerning marital property, alimony, child support, and custody without bringing any contested issue to court for adjudication. It therefore seemed clear to me that the primary impact of the legal system is not on the small number of court contested cases, but instead on the far greater number of divorcing couples outside the courtroom who bargain in the shadow of the law. Thus, my emphasis is on negotiation not adjudication.

Other evidence supported an emphasis on private ordering, not regulation. Since 1966, the American legal system has undergone a radical transformation that is still underway. Before the no-fault revolution, divorce law attempted to restrict private ordering severely: the state asserted broad authority to define when divorce was appropriate, to structure the economic relationship of the spouses, and to regulate their relationship to their children. The pretense of regulation has largely disappeared: American law now recognizes much more explicitly that a primary function of law at the time of divorce is to provide a framework within which divorcing couples are allowed great freedom to determine themselves their postdissolution rights and responsibilities. Divorce no longer requires a judicial determination of a "marital offense." With respect to spousal support and marital property, most states permit a couple to make binding and final agreements — i.e., not subject to later modification by a court. For those decisions that directly affect children — that is, child support, custody, and visitation — parents lack the formal power to make their own law. American courts are typically required to "review" the parental arrangement, which later can be modified in light of substantial changes in circumstances. But absent a dispute, divorcing parents actually have the power to make their own deals. Typically, separation agreements are rubber-stamped, even in cases involving children. Moreover, legislative changes approving joint custody and assorted appellate rulings increasingly acknowledge that the parties to a divorce should have a very broad latitude to decide for themselves by agreement the distributional questions posed by divorce. Indeed, the current interest in divorce mediation underlines the increasing emphasis on private ordering, for a mediator helps the parties reach a negotiated agreement but does not impose an outcome.

Regarding the original concept for this article I had been asked to defend the proposition that private ordering is a good thing — that the primary goal of the state at the time of a divorce should be to facilitate the process by which the parties themselves decide what the consequences of divorce should be. From the outset, it was clear to me that I was not prepared to defend the absurd proposition that the state should simply withdraw all resources from the dispute settlement process, and leave it to the divorcing spouses to work things out on their own, unassisted by any professional help or legal protection. To the contrary, my perspective, and its use of the term "private ordering" was never meant to imply either (1) that law and the legal system are unimportant; or (2) that there is an absence of important social interests in how the process works or in the fairness of its outcomes. Consequently, an adequate defense of private ordering required two prongs: first, a justification of why generally the legal system should permit (and indeed encourage) divorcing couples to work out their own arrangements; and second, a justification for imposing some limits on private ordering. When I began thinking about this article, I was confident that I could provide the first part — the general defense. But I was less confident that I could give reasons for limiting private ordering that would not in the process sabotage this defense.

Defining the limits of private ordering is of obvious relevance both to policy makers and those involved professionally in divorce bargaining on a day-to-day basis. The issue is posed in many different ways. Should mediators, for example, be concerned only with whether a deal is made? To what extent should lawyers representing individual clients be prepared to "sign off" with respect to an agreement that is substantially different from what a court would most likely impose? Should courts review divorce settlements, and if so, what principles should inform that review? Should divorcing couples be permitted to agree to an outcome that a court would not order? Under what circumstances should a party be able to object to the enforcement of an earlier agreement? When should persons not parties to the bargain (e.g., grandparents, children, the welfare department) be able to set aside an agreement, even if the parties to the bargain are not objecting?

This article does not attempt either to specify how these various policy questions should be resolved, or to detail the precise nature of various procedural and substantive safeguards that may be necessary. Instead it addresses what I see as the underlying question: should there be limits to private ordering at the time of divorce, and if so, why? I hope to answer this question in a way that provides a framework that will be helpful to those concerned with policy.

The article proceeds as follows. I first briefly present a general justification for private ordering. I then explore the reasons limits are necessary. I argue there are three justifications for limiting private ordering, each of which may justify procedural or substantive safeguards. The first concerns the issue of *capacity*. Are divorcing spouses able to make deliberate and informed judgments to decide whether it is in their interests to make a particular agreement? The second concerns *relative bargaining power*. I will show how, even against a backdrop of just substantive entitlements and fair procedures, bargaining inequalities can substantially affect outcomes. The third concerns *externalities,* the idea being that divorce bargains can often have important consequences for unrepresented third parties, most conspicuously the children. Using these three concepts — capacity, relative bargaining power, and externalities, I will provide a framework for understanding how one spouse can sometimes take advantage of the other and why there will be bargains reached that may not warrant enforcement. In short I hope to provide a theory that in essence justifies a presumption that favors private ordering, while also providing guidance about the reasons some safeguards are appropriate.

THE ADVANTAGES OF PRIVATE ORDERING

Let me begin with the arguments supporting the presumption in favor of private ordering. The core reason is rooted in notions of human liberty. Private ordering is supported by the liberal ideal that individuals have rights, and should largely be left free to make of their lives what they wish. In Charles Fried's words, a regime of law that "respects the dispositions individuals make of their rights, carries to its logical conclusion the liberal premise that individuals have rights."[2] Professor Fried has elegantly defended on a nonutilitarian basis the principle that "persons may impose on themselves [through contracts] obligations where none existed before."[3] He argues that "the capacity to form true and rational judgments and act on them is the heart of moral personality and the basis of a person's claim to respect as a moral being."[4] Thus, as a general proposition, enforcement of agreements made at the time of divorce can be justified as giving expression to a "free man's rational decision about how to dispose of what is his, how to bind himself."[5]

Private ordering can also be justified on grounds of efficiency.[6] Ordinarily, the parties themselves are in the best position to evaluate the comparative advantages of alternative arrangements. Each spouse, in the words of John Stuart Mill, "is the person most interested in his own well-being: . . . with respect to his own feelings and circumstances, the most ordinary man or woman has means of knowledge immeasurably surpassing those that can be possessed by anyone else."[7] Through negotiations, there are opportunities for making *both* parents better off than either would be if a court or some third party simply imposed a result. A consensual solution is, by definition, more likely to be consistent with the preferences of each spouse than would a result imposed by a court. Parental preferences often vary with regard to money and child-rearing responsibilities. Through negotiations, it is possible that the divorcing spouses can divide money and child-rearing responsibilities to reflect their own individual preferences.

Finally, there are obvious and substantial savings when a couple can resolve the distributional consequences of divorce without resort to formal adjudication. The financial cost of litigation, both private and public, is minimized. The pain of the formal adversarial proceedings is avoided. A negotiated settlement allows the parties to avoid the risks and uncertainties of litigation, which may involve all-or-nothing consequences. Given the substantial delays that often characterize contested judicial proceedings, agreement can often save time and allow each spouse to proceed with his or her life. In short, against a backdrop of fair standards in the shadow of which a couple bargains, divorcing couples should have very broad powers to make their own arrangements. Significant limitations are inconsistent with the premises of no-fault divorce. Parties should be encouraged to settle the distributional consequences of divorce for themselves, and the state should provide an efficient and fair mechanism for enforcing such agreements and for settling disputes when the parties are unable to agree.

CAPACITY

On an abstract level, I find the general defense of private ordering both appealing and persuasive. But it is premised on the notion that divorce bargaining involves rational, self-interested individuals — that the average adult has the intelligence and experience to make a well-informed judgment concerning the desirability of entering into a particular divorce settlement. Given the tasks facing an individual at the time of divorce, and the characteristics of the relationship between divorcing spouses, there are reasons to fear that this may not always be the case.

Informed bargaining requires a divorcing spouse to assess his or her own preferences concerning alternative arrangements. Radical changes in life circumstances complicate such assessments. Within a short period of time, separation and divorce often subject spouses to the stresses of many changes: "[S]pouses need to adjust to new living arrangements, new jobs, financial burdens, new patterns of parenting, and new conditions of social and sexual life."[8] It may be particularly difficult for a parent to assess custodial alternatives. The past will be a very incomplete guide to the future. Preferences may be based on past experiences in which child-rearing tasks were performed in an ongoing two-parent family, and dissolution or divorce inevitably alters this division of responsibilities. Child-rearing may now have new advantages or disadvantages for the parents' own needs. A parent interested in dating may find the child an intrusion in a way that the child never was during marriage. Because children and parents both change, and changes may be unpredictable, projecting parental preferences for custody into the future is a formidable task. Nevertheless, most parents have some self-awareness, however imperfect, and no third party (such as a judge) is likely to have better information about a parent's tastes, present or future.

Separation often brings in its wake psychological turmoil and substantial emotional distress that can make deliberative and well-informed judgments unlikely. It can arouse "feelings about the former spouse, such as love, hate, bitterness, guilt, anger, envy, concern, and attachment; feelings about the marriage, such as regret, disappointment, bitterness, sadness, and failure; and more general feelings such as failure, depression, euphoria, relief, guilt, lowered self-esteem, and lowered self-confidence."[9] Isolini Ricci has suggested that for many individuals "the emotions of ending a marriage" characteristically go through five stages during a two or three year period.[10] For the first three stages, if Ricci's characterizations are correct, an otherwise competent person may at times have seriously impaired judgment. She suggests that the pre-separation stage is often marked by "anxiety, depression, hostility, and recurring illness." The separation stage can bring with it three dangerous side effects: "poor judgment; accident and illness-proneness, poor reflex action; and depression." The third stage, which follows the separation, arouses strong emotions that are "both natural and nasty." "Emotional roller-coasters are common at this stage, causing many people to feel permanent emotional instability." According to Ricci, "this is the worst possible time to make any permanent decisions — especially legal ones. Thinking and believing the worst about each other is one of the chief hazards of this stage, and such thoughts, exaggerated and extended, can lead to serious complications."[11]

Such emotional turmoil may prevent for a time any negotiated settlement. Or it may lead to a settlement that a party later regrets.

> Frequently, the partner who wishes to end the marriage feels guilt at abandoning the spouse. Once the initiator finally broaches the topic of divorce, continued guilt, combined with the equally strong desire to leave, may produce a virulent form of the "settlement at any cost" mentality. At the same time, the spouse who wishes to keep the marriage may escalate demands, motivated by feelings of humiliation and anger, combined with prospects of a bleak and unchosen future. Unreasonable demands may also be a means to prolong the marriage and ultimately prevent the marital breakup.
>
> An opposite pattern was also noted by several of our respondents: guilt in the initiator may be expressed as anger directed at the non-initiator, in whom feelings of diminished self-worth may inhibit the ability to bargain constructively, or produce an abject acceptance of almost any terms. A settlement may thus be quickly arrived at whose inequitable and unworkable nature may not be apparent until several years and several court fights later.[12]

Some might think that the stresses and emotional turmoil of separation and divorce undermine the essential premise of private ordering — the idea that individuals are capable of deliberate judgments. I disagree. After all, for most persons the emotional upheaval is transitory, and the stresses are an inevitable consequence of having to make a new life. Temporary incapacity does not justify state paternalism for an extended period of time. Nonetheless, safeguards are necessary, and the wooden application of the traditional contract defense of "incompetence" may not provide sufficient protection.[13] More recent contract scholarship suggests a theory that respects the ideal of individual autonomy and the efficiency of private ordering, and avoids the unfairness of bargains that exploit a temporarily diminished capacity.

Professor Eisenberg recently suggested a concept of "transactional incapacity" to capture the notion that "an individual may be of average intelligence and yet may lack the aptitude, experience, or judgmental ability to make a deliberative and well-informed judgment concerning the desirability of entering into a given complex transaction."[14] Eisenberg's concern was with situations where one party exploits the other party's incapacity to deal with a complex transaction, "by inducing . . . a bargain that a person who had capacity to deal with the transaction probably would not make."[15] In such circumstances, Eisenberg suggests that neither fairness nor efficiency support application of the principle that a bargain should be enforced to is full extent. It is unfair because it violates conventional moral standards "to make a bargain on unfair terms by exploiting . . . incapacity." Moreover, "the maxim that a promisor is the best judge of his own utility can have little application: by hypothesis, the promisor is not able to make a well-informed judgment concerning the transaction."[16]

An analogous concept could be applied to divorce bargaining within a system that encourages private ordering at the time of divorce. When one spouse knows or has reason to know of the diminished capacity, and exploits this incapacity, a court should reopen the agreement. Proof of exploitation is essential, however. For this I would require a showing that the terms of the agreement considered as a whole fall outside the range of what would have been acceptable to a competent person at the time of the settlement.[17] By providing a remedy only if a party exploited the other side's incapacity by securing an unusually one-sided bargain, this test will not create uncertainty in most cases. Many divorced spouses may in retrospect think they were unwise in accepting some provision, and some might be able to show a lack of deliberative judgment, but few will be able to show that the settlement as a whole would have been unacceptable to a competent person. Any additional uncertainty created for parties making "out of the ordinary" deals may not be a bad thing.[18] Moreover, I would create a presumption against the application of this diminished capacity doctrine in any cases where the party making the claim was represented by counsel. Indeed, as Eisenberg suggests, "If a party who has been urged, fairly and in good faith, to seek advice, fails to do so, the doctrine of transactional incapacity would normally not apply, because the element of exploitation would be lacking" — at least where the party has sufficient capacity "to understand the importance of getting advice."[19]

A second prophylactic to guard against transitory diminished capacity would involve a "cooling-off" period, during which either party would be free to rescind a settlement agreement. In a commercial context, this period is often very short — typically three days. In the divorce context, I would make it considerably longer — perhaps sixty or ninety days. Like any safeguard, this one has costs. Some agreements may come apart even though they involve no exploitation whatsoever, simply because of ambivalence or a change of heart. Moreover, this cooling-off period might be used strategically by a party — a tentative agreement may be reached, only to be later rescinded, in order to wear an opponent down. Nonetheless, it would seem appropriate to have a fixed, reasonable "boundary line" as a rough estimate of the time within which the "transitory state of acquiescence" induced by guilt or anxiety might be expected to lapse. In cases where both parties have assigned counsel, it might be possible to have a shorter period.[20]

UNEQUAL BARGAINING POWER

Let me now turn to a second possible justification for imposing limits on private ordering — the basic idea is simple; in negotiations between two competent adults, if there are great disparities in bargaining power, some bargains may be reached that are unconscionably one-sided.[21]

The notion of bargaining power has intuitive appeal, but turns out to be very difficult to define. Without a complete theory of negotiations, it is hard to give precise substantive content to the notion of bargaining power, much less define precisely the idea of "relative bargaining power." Nonetheless, by briefly analyzing the five elements of the bargaining model I described in an earlier article, it is possible to suggest why some divorcing spouses may be seen as having unequal bargaining power.

First, there are the legal endowments. The legal rules governing marital property, alimony, child support, and custody give each spouse certain claims based on what each would get if the case goes to trial. In other words, the outcome the law will impose if no agreement is reached gives each parent certain bargaining chips — an endowment of sorts. These endowments themselves can create unequal bargaining power. For example, other things being equal, in a state where there is a tender years presumption in favor of maternal custody, a mother has considerably more bargaining power (at least if she wants custody) than the father. A new law creating a presumption against spousal support, on the other hand, would reduce the bargaining endowment of women as a class. To the extent that negotiated settlements simply reflect differences in bargaining power based on the legal rules themselves, this would not justify a claim of unfairness in an individual case. Instead, the legal endowments should be changed.

Second, a party's bargaining power is very much influenced by his or her preferences — i.e., how that party subjectively evaluates alternative outcomes. These preferences are not simply matters of taste — they can depend upon a party's economic resources and life circumstances. The parties' relative bargaining power depends on how they both subjectively evaluate the outcome a court would impose.[22]

A third element that effects bargaining power has to do with uncertainty, and the parties' attitudes towards risk. Often the outcome in court is far from certain, and the parties are negotiating against a backdrop clouded by substantial uncertainty. Because the parties may have different risk preferences, this uncertainty can differentially affect the bargaining power of the two spouses. If there is substantial variance among the possible court-imposed outcomes, the relatively more risk averse party is comparatively disadvantaged.

A fourth element that can create differences in bargaining power relates to the differential ability to withstand the transaction costs — both emotional and economic — involved in negotiations. A party who is in no hurry, enjoys negotiations, and has plenty of resources to pay a lawyer, has an obvious advantage over an opponent who is impatient, hates negotiations, and cannot afford to wait.

A fifth element concerns the bargaining process itself, and strategic behaviour. In divorce bargaining, the spouses may not know each other's true preferences. Negotiations often involve the attempts by each side to discern the other side's true preferences, while making credible claims about their own, and what they intend to do if a particular proposal is not accepted. "Bargainers bluff, argue for their positions, attempt to deceive or manipulate each other, and make power plays to gain an advantage."[23] Some people are more skilled negotiators than others. They are better at manipulating information and managing impressions. They have a more refined sense of tactical action. These differences can create inequalities in negotiations.

In short, the relative bargaining power of divorcing spouses depends upon how each evaluates the consequences of what will happen absent an agreement. This, in turn, depends not simply upon the legal endowments, but each party's subjective evaluation of the outcome absent a negotiated agreement, and the probable transaction costs of a court-imposed resolution. To the extent that a spouse sees himself as lacking alternatives, and is perceived as being dependent upon resources controlled by the other spouse, he lacks bargaining power. Bargaining power thus has both subjective and objective elements.[24]

The following examples illustrate these notions, and suggest why, even against a backdrop of "fair" legal endowments, some negotiated outcomes will seem very one-sided.

Case 1 — The Problem of Idiosyncratic Tastes

H and W, who are divorcing, have as their only assets $30,000 cash and an eighteenth-century French tapestry that cost $5,000 ten years ago and today could be sold to a dealer for $10,000. Under state community property law, a court is obliged to divide community property equally according to a fair market value. With a tangible asset that cannot be easily divided, such as a tapestry, the court has discretion to award it to either party, compensating the other with other assets, or to order it sold and the proceeds divided.

Suppose this particular tapestry has great sentimental value to H; he would, if necessary, pay $30,000 to keep it, even though he knows it has a fair market value of $10,000. If W knew this, then through hard bargaining she might end up with the $30,000 cash, while her husband received only the tapestry. In such circumstances H might be very resentful that he had to "pay" $15,000 (his half of the $30,000 community property) to buy W's half of the tapestry. Nonetheless, he might prefer this negotiated outcome to the risks of litigation if he thought there was a substantial chance that the court would award the tapestry to W and she would not resell it to him. This example is meant to demonstrate how private ordering can lead to "one-sided" outcomes because the parties' preferences differ, even though the legal rule (here community property) treats the parties as equals. In essence, because the husband has idiosyncratic tastes, and attaches a higher-than-market value to this particular tapestry, the parties are bargaining over how to divide this surplus.

This example illustrates a more general characteristic of divorce bargaining. In many respects it resembles a bilateral monopoly. In ordinary market transactions, one person doesn't have to do business with another — there are many alternative buyers or sellers. In divorce, the spouses must negotiate with one another, unless one or the other is prepared simply to accept the consequences — both legal and practical — of the non-cooperative solution where the court simply settles the dispute. Like a monopolist selling to a monopsonist, the two spouses (or their representatives) are locked in a dyadic relationship that cannot be easily avoided. One way or another, the distributional questions concerning marital property, spousal support, child support and custody must be resolved.

What are the consequences of this bilateral monopoly? First, there are often opportunities for *both* parties to gain through a negotiated resolution. Second, it will often be possible for one spouse to "take advantage" of the other spouse's preferences. Indeed, economic theory suggests that while the range of possible efficient exchanges can be specified, the actual bargain struck within the range is indeterminate because of possible strategic interaction. In this example, an efficient outcome requires that H get the tapestry, but the range of efficient outcomes might also give him anywhere from $0 to $10,000 in addition. The outcome can be affected not only by the preferences of each party, but by each party's knowledge of the others' preferences, and how the game is played.

This last point can be illustrated using the same tapestry example. Suppose a judge were to resolve the dispute by requiring one spouse to cut the cake (i.e., divide the property into two piles), and then having the other spouse choose the slice he or she prefers (i.e., picking a preferred pile).[25] Assume the husband values the tapestry at $30,000, and the wife values it at $10,000. If the parties know each other's preferences, and no recontracting between the spouses is allowed after the division, then the amount paid by H for the tapestry will depend upon who gets to slice the cake. The wife could presumably put the tapestry and $1 in one pile, and $29,999 in the other pile. She would know that the husband would choose the tapestry and $1, because by his preferences that pile is worth $30,001 while the other is worthy only $29,999. In essence, the wife could thus capture all the surplus. If the husband were dividing, on the other hand, he could create one pile with the tapestry and $9,999, and a second pile with $20,001 cash. He would be confident that the wife would choose the second pile, and as a consequence he would have "bought" the wife's half of the tapestry for only $1 more than its fair market value. Thus, he would have captured the surplus for himself.

Where each spouse is ignorant of the other's preferences, the situation becomes more complicated. Under these circumstances, it can be a disadvantage to be the one who cuts the cake. For example, if the wife is completely ignorant of her husband's preferences and assumes that his preferences may be just like hers, then the only way she can guarantee herself one-half the value of the property is by dividing the property into two parts that by her own preferences are of equal value. Presumably one pile would contain the tapestry and $10,000 while the other pile would contain $20,000. In this way, no matter which pile the husband chooses, she will guarantee herself the equivalent of $20,000. With any other division, she risks ending up with less than half the fair market value if it should turn out that the husband's preferences are the same as her own. For the husband, on the other hand, to guarantee himself the value of the property (by his own preferences), he would have to place the tapestry in one pile, and $30,000 in the other. Only with this division is he indifferent about which choice his wife makes. With any less extreme split, he risks ending up with less than half the value if it turns out that his wife's preferences are the same as his own.

Is it fair for W to be able to "exploit" H's idiosyncratic preferences by making him pay more than fair market value for her undivided interest in the tapestry? This normative issue does not seem clear. The husband might claim that ordinarily in a market economy a person is entitled to enjoy any consumer surplus generated by his own preferences. Accordingly, H might claim that if W attaches no special value to the tapestry, H should be entitled to the entire surplus. We, on the other hand, might claim that she owns one-half the tapestry, and as owner is entitled to sell it for whatever price she can get. Surely, if H and W were strangers, W would have the right to refuse to sell the tapestry at all unless H paid $30,000 for it.

Case 2 — Economic Inequalities and Urgent Need

Consider now a second example, which I find more troubling. H has substantial separate property and a high income. W has neither. Their only community asset is a house that H and W own outright. The housing market is presently depressed, and very few houses are selling. Realtors think that the house can be sold within six months for between $150,000 and $180,000, provided the sellers would carry back a $100,000 ten-year mortgage at 12 percent interest, which is below the present market rate of

12 percent. This mortgage could be resold for $65,000, making the net present value of the house between $115,000 and $145,000.

H knows that W is very short of funds, and eager to move to a new city where she wishes to buy a condominium and start over. Both H and W recognize that if there is no negotiated settlement it would be a year before a court would require the home to be put on the market. When W asks H to buy out her interest in the home, H offers W $40,000 on a take-it-or-leave-it basis, saying that he would just as soon continue to own the house with W. W reluctantly accepts, because she believes that if she does not sell to H now, it might well take two years before she can force the sale of the house, and get her equity out by reselling her share of any paper that is taken back. H and W both know that one-half of the present value of the expected sale price (taking account of the mortgage) is more than $40,000, but that there is no market for undivided one-half interests in residential real estate — if H doesn't buy her one-half interest, W must wait until a judge forces a sale of the house. Unlike the first case, where H decided to buy his wife's share of the tapestry at a price above the fair market value, in this case W has decided to sell for less than the fair market value in order to avoid the delays and inconvenience of an adjudicated result.

Should this case be characterized as one where W was forced to accept an "unfair price" because H exploited W's distress? Professor Eisenberg has suggested that in circumstances where one party "is in a state of necessity that effectively compels [her] to enter into a bargain with any terms [she] can get, . . . [n]either fairness nor efficiency, the two major props of the bargain principle," support enforcement of the deal."[25a] Eisenberg gives as an example an injured traveler stranded in the desert who must bargain with a geologist to save his life. In Eisenberg's example, the traveler is bargaining for his life; here W is bargaining for the opportunity to start a new life sooner.

What is the appropriate remedy in such a case? If there is a preliminary review of this agreement by a court, should it be rejected by the court? Even if the wife was not objecting? After H has paid W, should she later be able to rescind the agreement? Should W be able to argue that H received unjust enrichment, and that she was entitled to the difference between what she actually received, and what was reasonably and justly due?

In cases like this, the problem is not that W did not know what she was doing. To the contrary, her consent to this agreement is real. As Professor Dawson pointed out in his seminal article many years ago, "the more unpleasant the alternative, the more real the consent to a course which would avoid it."[26] The underlying issue concerns in part the question of what pressures can legitimately be brought to bear in bargaining, and how and whether it is possible to regulate the manner in which such pressures are exercised. This would be an easy case if W had shown that she accepted $40,000 because of physical threats by H. The doctrine of "duress" has traditionally permitted a defense to enforcement of a contract brought about by threats of illegal conduct. In this case, however, H's conduct is not illegal, but it is nonetheless plain that H is taking advantage of W's desire to sell quickly. One's appraisal of the morality of H's conduct might well be influenced by an evaluation of whether he was somehow responsible for W's urgent need. In the first case, W is not in any sense responsible for H's preference for French tapestry. In this case, however, we may well be prepared to treat H as responsible for W's distress.

While I am reluctant to allow a court to evaluate the fairness of the price in divorce bargains, I am deeply troubled by this second case. It seems clear that various doctrines of contract law are sufficient to permit intervention in egregious cases where it is thought that inequality in bargaining power has brought about unjust enrichment. The underlying philosophical and jurisprudential issues are difficult ones, but they do not, in my view, undermine the general reasons to favor private ordering, any more than the doctrines of duress or unconscionability undermine all of contract law. There are a variety of legal mechanisms to change the results. The bargaining endowments can be changed, and *ex post* review can be permitted to prevent unjust enrichment brought about by conduct that is viewed as morally unacceptable.

EXTERNALITIES — THIRD PARTY EFFECTS

Third party effects provide the last set of reasons that justify limiting private ordering. A legal system that gives divorcing couples freedom to determine for themselves their postdissolution rights and responsibilities may lead to settlements that reflect the spouses' interests. But negotiated agreements can also have important consequences for third parties, and affect social interests that are not adequately weighed in the private negotiations. The economists' idea of "externalities" — the notion that in some circumstances market prices that are affecting the behaviour of buyers and sellers will not adequately reflect the full range of social costs — has application here. In negotiating divorce settlements, the spouses may make decisions that have consequences for third parties, which, if taken into account, would suggest that some other settlement might be more socially desirable.

A divorce settlement may affect any number of interests not taken into account in the spouses' negotiations. The state's fiscal interests can be affected, for example. The economic terms of the bargain between the two spouses may substantially affect the odds that a custodial parent will later require public transfer payments.[27] The most important third party effects concern the children, although there can be externalities with respect to other family members as well.[28] At a conceptual level, it is easy to see how a negotiated settlement may reflect parental preferences but not the child's desires or needs. From the perspective of spouses who are negotiating their own settlements, marital property, alimony, and child support issues are all basically problems of money, and the distinctions among them become very blurred. Each can be translated into present dollar values.[29] Moreover, custodial arrangements can often be divided in a wide variety of ways. From a bargaining perspective, the money and custody issues are inextricably linked together.[30] Negotiated settlements will certainly reflect parental preferences with regard to these money and custody issues. These preferences, of course, will not generally be determined solely by self-interested judgments. One hopes that parental preferences reflect a desire for their children's happiness and well-being, quite apart from any parental advantage. Nevertheless, it is also certainly possible that some parents may engage in divorce bargaining on the basis of preferences that narrowly reflect their selfish interests, and ignore the children's needs. A father may threaten a custody fight over the child, not because he wants custody, but because he wants to push his wife into accepting less support, even though this will have a detrimental effect on the child. A custodial parent, eager to escape an unhappy marriage, may offer to settle for a small amount in order to sever relations soon. A custodial parent may negotiate to largely eliminate the child's contact with the other parent, not because of the child's wants or needs, but because he despises his *ex*-spouse and wants to have nothing more to do with her.

Concerns about the effects of the divorce on the children underlie many of the formal limitations on private ordering — e.g., the requirement of court review of private agreements relating to custody and child support; the legal rules prohibiting parents from making nonmodifiable and binding agreements concerning these elements. In addition, the potential conflict of interest between divorcing parents, on the one hand, and the children, on the other, have led many to advocate the appointment of counsel for children, so that the children's interests can be directly represented in the divorce proceedings.

Over the years, numerous commentators have expressed the fear that courts were rubber-stamping custodial arrangements in uncontested divorces, and that this was harmful for children.[31] In 1968, for example, Judge Justine Polier complained:

> In the vast proportion of cases where divorce is not contested, the question of the welfare of children, in terms of which parent has more to offer to their healthy development, is not considered by the court ... Divorce is granted, and the children automatically go to the plaintiff, as benefits or burdens go with the land that is sold.

The pre-divorce agreement between the parties may or may not reflect concern for the welfare of the children. The primary interest of one party in escaping the marriage, or financial considerations unrelated to the soundness of the custody or visitation agreements, control the disposition of the children. The mental health of the respective parents, past anti-social behavior, and their ability to be parents are not subjected to scrutiny.[32]

I have written elsewhere on these issues,[33] and I remain very skeptical about the wisdom of assigning counsel for children in uncontested divorces,[34] and the requirement of judicial review of negotiated settlements in all divorce cases involving children.[35] These issues involve more than an assessment of the practical usefulness of various safeguards. They are also related to a fundamental issue of principle: how should the power and responsibility to define what is in the interests of children be allocated at the time of divorce? Who gets to decide on behalf of the child? To what extent should the child's parents be given the freedom to decide between themselves how the responsibility for their children is to be allocated following divorce?

When a divorce affects minor children, the state obviously has interests broader than simply dispute settlement. The state also has responsibility for *child protection*.[36] To acknowledge this responsibility, however, is not to define its limits. Indeed, the critical questions concern the proper scope of the child-protection function at the time of divorce and the mechanisms that best perform this function.

I believe divorcing parents should be given considerable freedom to decide custody matters — subject only to the same minimum standards for protecting the child from neglect and abuse that the state imposes on *all* families. The actual determination of what is in fact in a child's best interests is ordinarily quite indeterminate.[37] It requires predictions beyond the capacity of the behavioural sciences and involves imposition of values about which there is little consensus in our society.[38] It is for this reason that I conclude that the basic question is who gets to decide on behalf of the child.

A negotiated resolution is desirable from the child's perspective for several reasons. First, a child's social and psychological relationships with both parents ordinarily continue after the divorce. A process that leads to agreement between the parents is preferable to one that necessarily has a winner and a loser. A child's future relationship with each of his parents is better ensured and his existing relationship less damaged by a negotiated settlement than by one imposed by a court after an adversary proceeding. Notions of child protection hardly justify general judicial suspicion of parental agreements; the state's interest in the child's well-being in fact implies a concomitant interest in facilitating parental agreement.

Second, the parents will know more about the child than will the judge, since they have better access to information about the child's circumstances and desires. Indeed, a custody decision privately negotiated by those who will be responsible for care after the divorce seems much more likely than a judicial decision to match the parents' capacities and desires with the child's needs.

If parents have the authority to decide custodial arrangements, there is no doubt that parents may make mistakes. But so may judges. More fundamentally, given the epistemological problems inherent in knowing what is best for a child, there is reason to doubt our capacity to know whether any given decision is a mistake. Therefore, the possibility that negotiated agreements may not be optimal for the child can hardly be a sufficient argument against a preference for private ordering. Moreover, because parents, not state officials, are primarily responsible for the day-to-day child-rearing decisions both before and after divorce, parents, not judges, should have primary authority to agree on custodial arrangements. This means that courts should not second-guess parental agreements unless judicial intervention is required by the narrow child-protection standard implicit in neglect laws. This is not to suggest that the state does not have an important responsibility to inform parents concerning the child's needs during and after divorce; nor does it mean that the state does not have an important interest in facilitating parental agreement. Nevertheless, the law in action, which acknowledges substantial parental power, seems preferable to existing doctrine, which imposes substantial restrictions on the parents' power to decide for themselves.

Because primary responsibility for child-rearing after divorce does and *should* remain with parents there should be a strong presumption in favor of the parental agreement and limits on the use of coercive state power by judges or other professionals to force parents to do what the professional thinks is best. On the other hand, I think the state has an important interest in encouraging parents to understand that the responsibility for their children extends beyond the divorce, that children are in many ways at risk during the divorcing process, and that in deciding about the child-rearing arrangements, the parents have an important obligation to meet their children's needs. Moreover, there is reason to think that by facilitating parental agreement, and helping the parents transform their old relationship into one in which they can now do business together with respect to the children's future needs, the interests of the children are being served.

CONCLUSION

From a legal perspective, separation and divorce pose four distributional issues, any of which may lead to a dispute between the spouses. These issues are: *(a)* How should the couples' property — the stock of existing wealth, separately or together — be divided? *(b)* What ongoing claim should each spouse have on the future earnings of the other? *(c)* What ongoing claims should a child have for his share of the earnings or wealth of each of his parents? *(d)* How should the responsibilities and opportunities of child-rearing be divided in the future? The legal system specifies both substantive rules (i.e., marital property law, alimony law, child support law, and custody and visitation law) and a set of procedures that is used to resolve these disputes.

I believe that the primary function of the legal system at the time of divorce is to faciliate private ordering — in other words, to provide a framework within which divorcing couples can themselves determine their postdissolution rights and responsibilities against a backdrop of fair rules and procedures. My general defense of private ordering is based on the ideal of individual autonomy and liberty, and arguments based on efficiency and cost. At the beginning of this article, I emphasized that my defense of private ordering was not premised on an absence of important social interests in how the process works or in the fairness of the outcomes. Important policy questions are ones of emphasis and degree: to what extent should the law permit and encourage divorcing couples to work out their own arrangements? Within what limits should parties be empowered to make their own law by private agreement?

While I have not attempted to answer these questions with any precision, or to define with exactitude the precise limits of private ordering, I have suggested three justifications for limitations: (1) problems of capacity, which go to the issue of whether in a particular case one party has exploited the other party's inability to make a deliberative judgment; (2) problems of inequality in bargaining power that may lead to unconscionable results, even if both parties are competent, and the legal endowments are generally considered fair; and (3) problems of externalities, where the concern is with the impact of the negotiated agreement on persons not represented in the divorce bargaining process.

My framework certainly does not make previously intractable family law problems disappear. But it does suggest an important intellectual agenda for those concerned with dispute settlement and divorce. How do the rules and procedures used in court for adjudicating disputes affect the bargaining process that occurs between divorcing couples *outside* the courtroom? How do various procedural requirements affect the parties' behaviour during the time they are resolving various distributional issues, and thereafter? What rules and procedures facilitate dispute settlement, and how do alternatives affect the future relationship of the former spouses to each other and to their children in subsequent years? In short, how do we best design rules and procedures that respect personal autonomy by facilitating private ordering, and ensure fairness by establishing appropriate safeguards against the risks that incapacity, or third party effects may lead to unjust results.

NOTES

1. Mnookin and Kornhauser, "Bargaining in the Shadow of the Law: The Case of Divorce," 88 *Yale L.J.,* 950 (1979).
2. C. Fried, *Contract as Promise,* at 2(1981).
3. *Id.* at 1.
4. *Id.* at 78.
5. *Id.*
6. I use efficiency here in the economic sense of Pareto efficiency. Such efficiency requires an outcome where neither party can be made better of without making the other contracting party worse off.
7. J.S. Mill, "On Liberty," in *On Liberty and Representative Government* 68 (R. McCallum, ed., 1947) (First edition, London, 1859).
8. Kressle, Lopez-Morillas, Weinglass, and Deutsch, "Professional Intervention in Divorce: The Views of Lawyers, Psychotherapists, and Clergy," in *Divorce and Separation: Context, Causes, and Consequences* (G. Levinger and O. Moles eds.,) (New York: Basic Books, 1979) at 256. Article originally in *The Journal of Divorce,* 2, 2(1978), at 119-55.
9. Graham B. Spanier and Robert F. Casto, "Adjustment to Separation and Divorce: A Qualitative Analysis," in *Divorce and Separation* (G. Levinger and O. Moles, eds.) at 213 (New York, 1979).
10. I. Ricci, *Mom's House/Dad's House* (1980) at 70. According to Ricci, these stages are: (1) The period just before the actual separation: the beginning of a crisis period; (2) The time of separation: a crisis period; (3) The eruption of strong emotions: a crisis period; (4) The adult adolescence of testing new roles, new identity; and (5) The more mature identity and new lifestyle.
11. The adversarial nature of our legal system can make matters worse by providing an outlet for these feelings. "Even the most conciliatory and mediative attorneys find it difficult to convince out-of-control clients that the legal process is not the appropriate arena for their intense feelings of fear, spite, or anger." [Ricci at 75].
12. Kressle, et al., *supra,* at 256.
13. Ordinary contract principles would require extreme impairment of cognitive capacity before allowing a defense of incompetence. Incompetence traditionally requires a showing that a party has childlike abilities, or is mentally disabled in a severe way. See 2 S. Williston, *A Treatise On Law of Contracts at 256.*
14. Eisenberg, "The Bargain Principle and Its Limits," 95 *Harvard Law Review,* 741, at 763 (1982).
15. *Id.* at 763-64.
16. *Id.* at 765.
17. This test would permit the reviewing court to take into account the possible transaction costs avoided by staying out of court. Because of transaction costs, a fully competent spouse might accept less than the expected value of an adjudicated judgment.
18. If independent counsel "signed off," a court should refrain from subsequent intervention to rescind. Perhaps the injured party should have a malpractice claim against the lawyer in an extreme case.
19. Eisenberg, *supra,* 95 *Harvard L. Rev.* at 770.
20. Eisenberg discusses the case of "unfair persuasion" which he defines to mean "the use of bargaining methods that seriously impair the free and competent exercise of judgment and produce a state of acquiescence that the promisee knows or should know is

likely to be highly transitory." Under traditional contract rules, "undue influence" was a ground of recision, but it required a pre-existing relationship between the parties where "one party is under the domination of another" or "by virtue of the relationship between them is justified in assuming that the other party will not act in a manner inconsistent with his welfare." (See Restatement [First] of Contracts section 497 (1932).) The commentary suggests that the relationship of husband and wife might ordinarily fall within this rule, but that it would depend on a question of fact whether "the relationship in a particular case is such to give one party dominance over the other, or put him in a position where words of persuasion have undue influence." Query whether the relationship between a divorcing husband and wife would often justify a party's belief that "the other will not act in a manner inconsistent with his welfare." See *Auclair v. Auclair,* 72 Cal. App. 2d, 165 p. 2d 527 (1946) (H and W have fiduciary obligations as a matter of law). In all events, Eisenberg suggests a doctrine of "unfair persuasion" that should be applied irrespective of the prior relationship between the parties, but "only where the promisee creates and exploits a state of acquiescence that he knows or should know is only transitory." He proposes a "cooling-off" period within which the "transitory state of acquiescence" can normally be expected to disappear.

21. Temporary incapacity is arguably a special case of unequal bargaining power. If one party is competent and the other is not, it would certainly seem they have unequal bargaining power. There are nonetheless distinct problems with this because it is certainly possible that the two parties might each be entirely competent and capable of exercising deliberative judgment, where one would nonetheless conclude that they had very disproportionate bargaining power.

22. Consider, for example, the differences between the following two cases, each in a state where custody law provides for joint custody. If both the mother and father are indifferent to whether they have primary custody or joint custody, the perceived endowments of the two parties are comparable. Now, consider a case where the father likes joint custody better than his having sole custody. The mother, on the other hand, has a strong preference for her own sole custody over joint custody. In such circumstances, if the father knows the mother's preferences, he would have greater bargaining power than the mother because he could force on the mother his preferred outcome (joint custody) and thus could require her to compensate him somehow if he is to accept some other arrangement.

23. S. Bacharach and E. Lawler, *Bargaining: Power Tactics and Outcomes* (1981) p. 42. Bacharach and Lawler suggest that "The task of a bargaining party is to convince its opponent that it controls resources, that the opponent needs the resources, and that it is willing to use power. These manipulative actions ultimately determine a party's bargaining power." *Id.* at 51. They believe "punitive tactics are central to bargaining as power itself... punitive tactics relate to the ability of one party to impose costs on the other party." Lon Fuller has suggested a distinction between bargaining to give the other side as little as possible, and bargaining to get as much as possible for oneself. A mediator, according to Fuller, can encourage people to avoid spite and to bargain for gains. The difficulty is that in the strategic game it is often possible to get more for oneself by making a credible threat to harm the other side. One reason I like mediation is because it tends to dampen strategic behaviour.

24. Bacharach and Lawler suggest that "analysis of bargaining power... requires a framework that (1) identifies the multiple dimensions constituting each party's potential bargaining power, (2) identifies the major types of bargaining tactics, (3) shows how the dimensions of bargaining power effect tactical action, (4) shows how tactical action can

alter bargaining power, (5) examines the conditions under which given tactics affect the bargaining outcomes, and (6) examines how outcomes at any given time affect potential power at later time." *Id.* at 47.

25. There is interesting literature about the problem of dividing an object (such as a cake) among a finite number of people so that each is satisfied that he has received a fair share, although each may have different opinions about which part of the cake is most valuable. See H. Steinhaus, "Sur la division pragmatique," *Econometrica* (supplement), vol. 17, 1949, pp. 315–19; Dubins and Spanier, "How to Cut a Cake Fairly," *American Mathematical Monthly,* Vol. 68, No. 1, January, 1961. For valuation disputes in divorce, one commentator has suggested a process in which one party proposes a value, and then allows the court to award the object to either party at the value placed on it. C. Markey, *California Family Law,* 24.45. See also King, "Guidelines for Domestic Relations Cases" (S. F. Sup. Ct., 1977), 10 (suggesting a modified bidding arrangement where divorcing parties cannot agree on value.)

25a. Eisenberg, *supra,* 95 *Harv. L. Rev.* at 754, 755.

26. Dawson, "Economic Duress — An Essay in Perspective" 45 *Michigan L. Rev.* 253 at 267 (1947).

27. For example, a mother might decide to forego all alimony and child support payments from the child's father in order to avoid any future relationship with him. If the father's resources were small, this decision might "cost" the mother and child very little or nothing, if public assistance payments make up the difference. Nonetheless, if the welfare system is premised on the private support obligation, the mother's decision (if it were binding on the state's power to claim reimbursement from the father) would have obvious effects on the public fisc. Indeed, in this example, a solution that largely respects the private agreement is possible. The economic agreement made by the spouses can be effective *inter se,* but can be treated as having no effect on the state's right to collect child support from the father.

28. For example, visitation and custody arrangements may reflect the parents' interests, but not those of grandparents and other family members.

29. See Mnookin and Kornhauser, *supra,* 88 *Yale L. J.,* 959–63. Although there are differences among the three elements with respect to termination and enforcement risks, the value of different bundles of the three elements can be compared. See *id.*

30. There are two reasons: first, because over some range of alternatives, each parent may be willing to exchange custodial rights and obligations for income or wealth; and second, parents may tie support duties to custodial prerogatives as a means of enforcing their rights without resort to court. See Mnookin and Kornhauser, *id.* at 963 through 966.

31. See Lynn Halem, *Divorce Reform: Changing Legal and Social Perspectives (1980) at 227.*

32. Justine Polier, *The Rule of Law and the Role of Psychiatry,* at 113 (1968).

33. See Mnookin, "Child-Custody Adjudication: Judicial Functions in the Face of Indeterminacy," 39 *Law and Contemporary Problems* (#3) 226 (Summer, 1975); Mnookin and Kornhauser, *supra,* 88 *Yale Journal* 950.

34. See "Bargaining in the Shadow of the Law," 88 *Yale Law Journal* at 988–90.

35. *Id.* at 994–96.

36. See "Child Custody Adjudication," *supra,* at 229, 232.

37. *Id.* at 255–62.

38. *Id.* at 258–61.

Part Five

The Special Position of Children

The Republic of Ireland is one of the few Western countries where full divorce is not available, and in general its family law offers only two alternatives to a marriage which is no longer viable — private ordering or the adversarial system. Where children are involved there is a strong bias for private arrangements, based on the belief that the family should ideally be inviolable and on an antipathy toward encroaching on its independence. Duncan (Chapter 25) discusses this conservatism and explains some of the constitutional factors which support it: the principle of family autonomy, the stress on procedural justice, and the emphasis on preventing intrusion into decision-making areas reserved to judges. Where forms of matrimonial relief such as divorce *a mensa et thoro* or annulment have been granted, the courts are not required to ensure that the arrangements for children are satisfactory, and become involved in cases of custody and access only when one of the parents initiates court proceedings. The *Guardianship of Infants Act* of 1964 gave the courts wide power for custody, access and maintenance orders. Court procedures are based on the adversarial model; a judge who presides in a custody dispute is neither specially appointed for the role nor specially trained. The parents, who are naturally partisan, are chiefly responsible for the introduction of evidence, which may include expert testimony — and may also include suppression by a parent of unfavorable professional opinion. Expert opinions, as we have found round the world, can be strikingly contradictory. And the child itself has no independent representation. Although judges customarily stress that custody is not to be granted as a reward to the "good" parent, and although the present President of the High Court has stated that a custody case is not a party dispute but a matter of the welfare of the child, such cases are indeed a contest between the parents. The fact remains that the court is limited in its choice to options presented by the parents. What is necessary in order to protect the child, Duncan believes, is a modification of the procedural framework which will recognize the interests at stake, the rights of both parents and the welfare of the child. Even with such changes, with a deeper probing by the judge, more is required before the rigidity of the system can be relaxed to take into realistic account the actual human beings involved. An increase of resources is a necessity to provide independent representation for the child or provision for expert services to the court.

In Chapter 26, Giller and Maidment investigate the benefits to children of their being separately represented in custody cases. Separate representation has joined mediation as a cure-all for the many problems in such cases. There is concern for the child in court that stems from the current children's rights movements, from the bureaucratic judicial monopoly, and from the fact that children may have interests that conflict with their parents'. In the United Kingdom, a major problem in separate representation is the confusion of what mode of representation should be adopted to prove effective. Three categories are available: the *amicus curiae,* which is merely informative and advisory to the court; the guardianship role, which interprets the information and presents a case in the child's best interests; and advocacy, which presents only the child's case to the court. Since there are no clear guidelines as to which form of representation is appropriate, different styles are used in a variety of cases and even in similar cases or at different stages of the same case. The resulting confusion may lead to negotiation or compromise on behalf of the child only within the limits of the system as understood by the court. The authors of this article believe that "The continued dominance of the 'best interests' doctrine, the attractions of the guardianship role . . ., and the belief in the inappropriateness of the adversarial model . . . all contribute to make representation at present a 'hollow right.' " Although they do not argue that the adversarial system is the most effective and suitable, they consider that the mere introduction of representation does not automatically improve the position of children in adjudicating conflict or provide "better" information which will lead to independent decisions. Clarification of the decision-making process in respect to children and of the role of the representative must precede any final conclusions. Until then more representation may mean "merely different or even a whole lot worse."

The next study (Chapter 27) again raises questions that must be answered in respect to the English laws and court procedures dealing with children. While Masson discusses a broad area, including juvenile justice, her conclusions are based mainly on the data of an examination of adoption by parent and step-parent from 1975 to 1978, in which more than 1,700 step-parent adoption applications were read and 90 guardians *ad litem* who had reported to the courts were interviewed. English law since 1926 provides that a guardian *ad litem* be appointed for the child in every adoption case, but even here, where the child is supposedly always represented, there are confusions and gaps through which the child may fall. The g.a.l. is appointed by the court and is usually either a social worker or a probation officer, and in spite of government reports and guidelines, almost a fifth of the g.a.l.s. interviewed had no social work training and more than a tenth no experience. Nevertheless the g.a.l.s. retain considerable discretion both over the investigation and the court report, and although the g.a.l. recommendations rarely offer the reasoning behind the recommendations, they are often followed by the court. Masson found, however, that there were marked differences between the practices and recommendations of the different g.a.l.s. and between the procedures and decisions of the courts. She describes the balance between the participants as changing along a continuum of three main models — the legal, where the judge exercises complete discretion; the social work, where the g.a.l. makes a strong recommendation and the judge simply adopts it; and the family, where the g.a.l. bases his recommendation entirely on what the family wants, and the judge accepts this — or where the judge rubber-stamps not the g.a.l.'s recommendation but the application itself. The author does not call for the end of the discretionary decision making or of the use of social workers in the court, but for consideration and evaluation of what decisions can actually be made, by whom, and how.

In the final chapter of this section (Chapter 28) James and Wilson treat a subject sparsely represented in the literature of divorce and custody — access to children by the noncustodial parent. The authors are probation officers, a class of persons often asked by English courts to prepare reports on custody and access, and their experiences have led them to believe that access arrangements might be as contentious as those for custody; that the principles on which courts base access decisions might be even more ambiguous than those used in custody; and that problems of access might cause even greater friction within the family. Because of the scarcity of studies and of consensus in the field, James and Wilson initiated a limited project in conjunction with a county probation service to obtain factual information which could lead to hypotheses on causes for the success or failure of access arrangements. Although this first breakthrough will, the authors hope, be followed by further study over a longer period, one tentative conclusion they reached was similar to those of other investigators: that the officers lacked sufficient training and experience — indeed, that there had been a decline in these areas over the last decade. Many of the officers, taking a negative view of a solicitor's ability to place enough importance on the interests of the children — a mistrust or outright hostility between disciplines noted in other chapters in this volume — would like an increase in their own training in this field, feeling that they were often the only impartial persons who could interview the children in divorce cases. Even so, and with varying practices by the members of the county probation service, a surprising number of parents expressed satisfaction with current access arrangements when court officers were involved, and in about half the cases it did not appear that under such arrangements the lives of the children had been seriously disrupted. These results do not seem to jibe with a study made by Wallerstein and Kelly in 1980 in the United States, where divorce counselling has become popular and may reflect a preponderance of families who recognized their need for help. One may wonder whether divorcing parents and their offspring in England are still keeping a stiffer upper lip than their counterparts in America.

Chapter Twenty-five

Decision Making Relating to Children in the Republic of Ireland — Restraints on Introducing New Models

William Duncan

Trinity College, Dublin, Ireland

For a country which struggled so hard for independence, the Republic of Ireland has shown what may appear as surprising conservatism in regard to the machinery of justice which it inherited from Britain. This is plainly to be seen in decision-making structures relating to children. Disputes concerning children, whether they focus on their rights, their welfare or their punishment are, in the main, set in the traditional adversarial framework of the common law, decided by judges, and with the emphasis on formality and procedural justice.

Proposals for reform tend not to be innovatory. In recent years, for example, the rapid increase in the number of custody disputes[1] heard in the High Court has led to a review of court jurisdiction.[2] The review was conducted solely in terms of improving the administrative efficiency and accessibility of the present system, and did not consider the possibility of any radical departures from existing decision-making models. The main proposal, which has now become law,[3] was to shift jurisdictions under the *Guardianship of Infants Act 1964* to lower courts.

It is the purpose of this article to identify and explain some of the factors which contribute to this conservative tradition. It would be tempting to rest responsibility on the legal profession, which exercises a disproportionate influence over the organs of law reform. But this is only part of the explanation. The conservative tradition is founded on certain social and legal values, reflected in and buttressed by some of the provisions of the 1937 Constitution of Ireland. The Constitution, which in many areas of substantive law has provided the launching pad for radical departures from common law tradition, has been an inhibiting factor (not invariably bad) in the development of new decision-making models in the area of family law. Three Constitutional values in particular have been influential — the principle of family autonomy, the emphasis on procedural justice (fair procedures), and the importance attached to preventing encroachments into those areas of decision making reserved to the judiciary.

The principle of family autonomy is supported by Articles 41 and 42 of the Constitution. The courts have developed a general principle of marital privacy requiring strong justification for state intrusion.[4] In the area of child law, parental rights are jealously protected in the sense that any attempt by the state to intervene in their exercise is subject to strict Constitutional control. The general principle is that interference with parental rights is justified only when a parent is unfit, unwilling or unable to discharge parental responsibilities.[5] Only recently have the courts begun to canvass the possibility that a child's interests may sometimes be given priority over the rights of a blameless and fit parent.[6] However, in the case of interparental custody disputes the Constitutional rights of parents cancel out and enable the courts to adopt as the sole criterion the child's welfare. In substantive law the principle of family autonomy has had mixed results; in the area of procedure it has had two influences. First, the principle of laissez-faire results in a wide area of decision making in relation to children which in some other countries might be made subject to judicial control or review, but which in the Republic of Ireland is left entirely to the parents. Thus the private ordering of custody and access arrangements, whether by formal or informal agreement or by default, is commonplace and is subject to control only in the event of disputes. Secondly, the Republic of Ireland has resisted any tendency towards excessive state "welfareism," in that compulsory intervention with the object of protecting or promoting the welfare of children (as, *e.g.,* in case and control proceedings) happens only on a small scale. In contrast, the principle of nonintervention is less influential in the criminal sphere where prosecutions against children are subject to few controls. The underlying assumption here is that the protection of the public offers a clearer justification for intervention than the often uncertain hope of bettering the child's welfare.

The importance attached to the concept of a fair hearing and fair procedures is now a hallmark of Constitutional justice in the Republic of Ireland, and one which, as will be shown, is deemed especially important in cases concerning children. This emphasis on procedural justice, though admirable in itself, has not been of unqualified benefit in children's cases. One perennial problem is that of reconciling the demands of due process with the welfare-orientated approach that is demanded, *e.g.,* in interparental custody disputes. Another is the difficulty of applying somewhat abstract principles of procedure to give practical as opposed to theoretical protection to the child's interests. This has been a particular problem within the juvenile justice process.

The third Constitutional value — that of preserving an exclusive area of decision making for the judiciary — has been a factor inhibiting experimentation in new decision-making models. The problem of defining the judiciary's preserve has been considerable, with the result, for example, that it is difficult to know whether the participation of nonjudges in various decision-making areas would be Constitutionally permissible.

As is apparent from these introductory remarks, the Constitutional principles referred to have an impact on decision-making procedures throughout the area of child law, and not only in the area of intrafamily disputes. To illustrate these principles further, one must look at decision-making structures which are strictly speaking beyond the writer's brief, in particular the adoption process and the juvenile justice system. The excuse for this departure is the pervasive nature of the influences displayed by these other structures; they must be studied in order to help determine the factors which limit or control any future development in the machinery for the resolution of disputes within the family.

ARRANGEMENTS FOR CHILDREN ON THE BREAKDOWN OF MARRIAGE

The courts in the Republic of Ireland exercise no control over the private ordering of custody and access arrangements by parents unless litigation is commenced by one of the parents or, as rarely happens, unless a third party intervenes in care and control or wardship proceedings to protect the child. Where a court is called upon to intervene, it is not bound by the terms of the parental agreement. "The court's duty in considering the interests of the children transcends the agreement of the parents..."[7] But agreements as to religious upbringing (*e.g.,* an antenuptial agreement made by partners in a mixed-religion marriage) are in general treated by the courts as binding.[8]

Full divorce is not available in the Republic of Ireland. In the granting of other forms of matrimonial relief (*e.g.,* divorces *a mensa et thoro* and annulments) the courts are under no obligation to ensure that satisfactory arrangements have been made in respect to children. Thus, in the great majority of cases the courts become involved in issues of custody and access only when there is a dispute between the parents and when one of them initiates court proceedings. The usual form of proceeding is an application under section 11 of the *Guardianship of Infants Act 1964,* which gives the court wide power to make custody, access and maintenance orders, and to give "its direction on any question affecting the welfare of the infant," and to "make such order as it thinks proper."[9] Indirectly, in the course of other proceedings, issues of custody and access may in effect be resolved, for instance, where a barring order is granted against a spouse under the *Family Law (Protection of Spouses and Children) Act 1981*.[10]

A judge hearing a custody dispute is not specially appointed for that function, nor does he or she receive any special training. Procedures are based on the adversarial model with its familiar drawbacks. The persons principally responsible for the introduction of evidence, including expert testimony, are the parents themselves, whose approach tends naturally to be partisan. It is possible at times that a parent may suppress an unfavorable but relevant professional opinion, and the system occasionally results in "a multiplicity of reports sometimes of a startlingly contradictory nature."[11] There is no system of independent representation for the child. The extent to which the child's own wishes will be consulted is at the discretion of the court.[12]

Some attempt has been made to mitigate the effects of the adversarial model. A judge will occasionally assume the mantle of a conciliator and jostle the parties in an argument. Judges have constantly stressed that custody is not awarded as a prize for good behaviour, in the hope (often vain) of deterring parents from using the courtroom as a battle ground.[13] Sometimes a court will take the initiative in appointing (with the consent of the parents) an expert such as a social worker or a psychiatrist to give independent advice to the court. The present President of the High Court, Finlay P., has indicated that he does not classify a custody case as a dispute *inter partes*, but rather as a matter *in re* the child, with the implication that the court is not bound to observe stringently the rules of natural justice as between the parents (*e.g.,* the principle of full disclosure in relation to expert testimony).

Despite all this, custody disputes retain their essential form of a contest between the parents. Indeed there is something unrealistic in not regarding a custody case as involving a dispute *inter partes*. It may be true that the court is not determining rights as between the parents and that in applying the welfare principle it focuses on the child's rights. But to suggest that the welfare of the child is the only matter in issue is to ignore the fact that the court is limited in the measures which it can take to those made available by the parents. The court is not simply taking a decision in the best interests of the child; it is choosing, albeit on a welfare basis, between options presented by the parents. The *rights* of the parents may not be in issue, but their *claims* most certainly are — for example, their mutual claims to provide the better alternative for the child. The court's decision represents an adjudication between competing claims, a matter which is of some relevance in relation to the Constitutional requirement of a fair hearing, which will be discussed later.

THE JUDGES AND THEIR RESERVED FUNCTIONS

The Irish Constitution rests on a "tripartite division of the powers of government — legislative, executive and judicial — as appears from an examination of Articles 6, 15, 28 and 34."[14] The most rigid dividing line is that which surrounds the judicial function. Professor Casey has observed that "The Irish Constitution goes beyond the approach traditionally found in the common law world. Not only does it provide the usual guarantees as to tenure and remuneration; it also maps out a sphere of operations for the judiciary and guards it against invasion by other branches of government."[15]

Justice in all criminal cases and in civil cases, except where they involve the exercise only of limited powers and functions, must be administered by judges appointed under the Constitution.[16] Moreover, the Constitution sees the adminstration of justice as being a specialist function by insisting that no judge may hold "any other office or position of emolument."[17] Ordinary legislation, by laying down judicial qualifications based on practice as a lawyer, has further confined this specialist activity to those with legal training and experience.[18]

These principles have important consequences for family law cases. First, the Constitution militates against the participation of lay persons in the administration of justice (save in the case of jury service). It does not forbid the appointment of nonlawyers as judges, but in effect it prevents the appointment as part-time judges of persons who are pursuing other professions. Secondly, ordinary legislation assumes that persons with a legal background are best equipped to decide justiciable family law issues. In addition, it may be said that the organisation and jurisdiction of the courts is based on the concept of a generalist judge. With only two exceptions, judges and justices are not appointed to specialize in family cases.[19] There is no system of family courts.

Some features of the present system are amenable to change by ordinary legislation. There is nothing in the Constitution to prevent the setting up of specialist family courts, and there has been much generalized talk about the idea, though few specific proposals.[20] However, any change which would involve an increase in lay participation in the decision-making process would have Constitutional implications.

There are two cases in which a person who is not a judge may decide a civil matter: (1) where the decision does not involve an administration of justice, and (2) where the decision, though constituting an administration of justice, involves the exercise of limited judicial powers or functions. The following characteristic features of an administration of justice were suggested by Kenny J. in the High Court (*McDonald v. Bord na gCon* (No. 2))[21] and provisionally accepted by the Supreme Court:

1. a dispute or controversy as to the existence of legal rights or a violation of the law;
2. the determination or ascertainment of the rights of parties or the imposition of liabilities or the infliction of a penalty;
3. the final determination (subject to appeal) of legal rights or liabilities or the imposition of penalties;
4. the enforcement of those rights or liabilities or the imposition of a penalty by the court or by the executive power of the state which is called in by the court to enforce its judgment;
5. the making of an order by the court which as a matter of history is an order characteristic of courts in this country.

It is probably correct to regard this list as laying down collectively sufficient rather than individually necessary conditions. The historical requirement is probably not an absolute one.[22] If civil judicial divorce were introduced it would probably constitute an administration of justice (depending perhaps on the grounds) even though as a matter of history the granting of full divorce *(a vinculo)* was at one time a function of Parliament rather than the courts.[23] On the other hand, the requirement of there being a dispute as to the existence of rights or the violation of the law appears to be more fundamental, so that if this element is lacking, a particular decision may not constitute an administration of justice even though it has traditionally been made by judges. As an example, Kenny J. in *McDonald's* case mentioned the jurisdiction which the High Court exercises over wards of court, which he described as the exercise of a semiparental jurisdiction.[24] The reasoning seems to be that where a court makes a decision solely on the principle of promoting the interests of a child, it is not deciding a disputed issue of rights.

If this last view is correct, it has implications for welfare decisions generally, *e.g.,* in custody and care and control cases. However, for reasons already expressed it may be wise to draw a distinction between decisions which do, and decisions which do not, involve an adjudication in relation to the claim of a parent. Thus, where ward of court proceedings are brought with the purpose of restricting the exercise of parental rights, the court's decision may perhaps involve an administration of justice.

The distinction between limited and unlimited judicial powers or functions depends on the nature and effect of such powers or functions rather than on their quantity.

> If the exercise of the assigned powers and functions is calculated ordinarily to affect in the most profound and far-reaching way the lives, liberties, fortunes or reputa-

tions of those against whom they are exercised, they cannot properly be described as limited.[25]

The application of this principle to specific functions has caused difficulty and led to apparent contradiction.[26] This, combined with the difficulty of defining an "administration of justice," has led to a situation in which it becomes difficult to draw with any real precision that line which defines the preserve in which judges have exclusive decision-making authority. The best illustration is provided by adoption procedures.

The function of making adoption orders was given in 1952 not to the courts but to an Adoption Board comprising a chairman and six ordinary members appointed by the Government.[27] The chairman must be a judge, a justice, or a barrister or solicitor of at least ten years' standing.[28] No qualifications are laid down for the six ordinary members, except where one is appointed deputy chairman, in which case he must be qualified to be chairman.[29] It has been the practice to appoint as chairman a District Justice, having no functions apart from adoption. The Adoption Board is the only example, within the area of family law, of a mainly lay tribunal constituted and geared to make welfare-orientated decisions relating to children. The advantages of the Board over an ordinary court are said to lie in its specialist qualities and in the uniformity which it brings to the adoption process.

It has never been doubted that the Board is bound to act judicially in the exercise of its functions. But doubts arose as to whether its powers and functions involved the administration of justice, were of an unlimited judicial nature, and thus could be exercised only by judges. On the one hand, the legislature had taken some care to avoid conferring on the Board the function of resolving disputes as to rights (one of the characteristics of an administration of justice). For example, when in 1974 a new and broad power of dispensing with consent to adoption was introduced, it was conferred not on the Board but on the High Court.[30] On the other hand, the Board does make decisions which have far-reaching effects on the lives and rights of children and their parents (suggesting an unlimited judicial function). Nor can it entirely avoid areas of dispute, and in the course of determining whether qualifications for adoption are satisfied, it may be called upon to decide matters which have traditionally been the preserve of the judiciary. For instance, in the case of an application by a married couple, it may be necessary to determine whether their marriage is valid — a particularly sensitive issue where the recognition of a foreign divorce is concerned.[31] Also the general requirement that a child may not be adopted unless illegitimate or an orphan[32] has forced the Board to consider issues of paternity. Such decisions are not *in rem* and therefore lack one important characteristic of an administration of justice — that of being a final determination of rights in a disputed matter. Nevertheless the adoption order itself which follows the resolution of such disputes does affect rights in a fundamental way and on a permanent basis.[33]

Matters eventually came to a head in 1976 in *M. v. An Bord Uchtala*,[34] a case involving a challenge to an adoption order of six years standing by natural parents who had married subsequent to the order. In the event the Supreme Court quashed the adoption order on the ground that the Adoption Board had not fulfilled its statutory duty to ensure that the mother's consent was properly informed and real and genuine. But in the High Court the whole system of adoption, and with it the validity of many thousands of adoption orders, was questioned when it was argued for the natural parents that the Adoption Board was unconstitutionally exercising civil powers and functions of an unlimited judicial nature. Butler J. rejected the argument on the ground principally that the Adoption Board is not involved in the resolution of disputed claims.

> The Board is not called upon to decide on or arbitrate between opposing interests nor to decide, as between competing situations, which is in the interests of the child. The mother . . . on the one side must consent; the adopting parents on the other must show their willingness by applying and fulfilling the conditions on their part.[35]

He then cited the characteristics of an administration of justice suggested by Kenny J. in *McDonald's* case and concluded that "the function of the Board in relation to the making of an adoption order possesses none of these characteristics."[36]

There the matter might have rested, for the issue was not discussed on appeal to the Supreme Court. But a view gained currency that, had the Supreme Court addressed the issue, it might well have reversed Butler J.'s ruling.[37] Such was the degree of uncertainty surrounding the Constitutionality of the adoption process following *M. v. An Bord Uchtala* that calls were made for a national referendum to amend the Constitution in order to make secure existing adoption orders. And, despite an *obiter dictum* of one Supreme Court Judge in a later case affirming Constitutionality,[38] a referendum was finally held in 1979, and a clause was added to Article 37, to the effect that an adoption order would not be invalid by reason only of its being made by a person or body that was not a Constitutionally appointed judge or court.[39]

This whole episode illustrates how precarious the Constitution makes it for the legislature to experiment in the area of child law with tribunals composed of persons other than judges. It has been suggested that the amendment of Article 37 was unfortunate in that it involved the implicit admission that the functions of the Adoption Board are not "limited," with the consequence that some other functions now in administrative hands may be deemed illicit.[40] Indeed it should have been possible to adopt an alternative formula in the amendment. The fact is that there now exists a formidable barrier to any movement towards extrajudicial modes of resolving disputes, not only in child law but in family law generally. If the Adoption Board which exercises a jurisdiction based on consent requires a Constitutional exemption clause, it becomes difficult to envisage the setting up of other similarly structured family tribunals with powers to make consent orders, even though their principal function may be to conciliate rather than to determine disputes.[41]

Proposals for the reform of the juvenile justice system have been subject to similar Constitutional hazards. The Republic of Ireland retains a system based on the criminal justice model inherited, under the *1908 Children Act,* from Britain. Lay magistrates have been replaced by professional District Justices. An Act of 1924[42] envisaged the setting up of full-time children's courts in the main centres of population (Dublin, Waterford, Cork, and Limerick), but only one such court was established, the Dublin Metropolitan Children's Court. Outside Dublin, cases involving children and young persons continue to be dealt with in the very busy District Courts, though at a different time or in a different place from normal sittings.[43]

A good deal of sympathetic consideration has been given to the introduction of a new juvenile justice model, in line with that operating in Scotland,[44] which would attempt to separate more clearly the criminal justice and welfare or treatment functions at present performed by the same court, and which would give the latter function to a tribunal (in Scotland a "hearing") comprising persons drawn from a panel of lay persons. But it is doubtful whether such a model would survive Constitutional scrutiny here.

One authority has suggested that a children's hearing on the Scots model, though not engaged in the prosecution of a juvenile, may nevertheless be administering justice in a "criminal matter" within the meaning of Article 37, a function which can only be performed by a judge.[45] The matter seems to depend on what is more central to the definition of a criminal matter — the nature of the conduct justifying intervention or the purpose of the ultimate decision or disposal. If it is the former, the fact that the commission of an offence can provide grounds for a hearing would seem to put it in the criminal realm. But if, as seems more likely, it is the latter, the fact that the hearing does not have a punitive objective puts it in the civil realm.[46]

Even if a hearing on the Scots model is not administering a criminal matter, the question remains whether it is administering justice in a civil matter, and if so whether its powers are of the limited kind which permit their exercise by nonjudges. The matter is not easy to decide. A parallel can be drawn with the Adoption Board; a hearing operates on a consent basis in so far as the grounds for referral must either have been accepted by the juvenile and his parents or established by a court.[47] On the other hand, the hearing has wide powers to make compulsory dispositions against the wishes of the child or his parents in a way which may well have that "profound and far-reaching effect upon the lives of those concerned" which is the hallmark of an "unlimited" function. But whatever the correct Constitutional position, the very uncertainty surrounding the interpretation of Articles 34 and 37 of the Constitution once again operates as a factor inhibiting the introduction of new structures except such as reserve the power to make decisions to a Constitutionally appointed judge. It is noteworthy that in the Final Report of the government-appointed Task Force on Child Care Services, Constitutional obstacles appear to have been avoided by a proposal that "a justice of the Children's Court may sit with not more than two assessors (drawn from a panel) in any case in which, in his opinion, such services may assist him."[48]

FAIR PROCEDURES

The Constitutional Requirements

The concept of a fair hearing transcends the boundary between civil and criminal cases. The Constitutional prescription that no person shall be tried on any criminal charge save "in due course of law"[49] has been held to "require fair and just treatment for the person so charged."[50] Some familiar principles are involved.

> Among the natural rights of an individual whose conduct is impugned and whose freedom is put in jeopardy are the rights to be adequately informed of the nature and substance of the accusation, to have the matter tried in his presence by an impartial and independent court or arbitrator, to hear and test by examination the evidence offered by or on behalf of his accuser, to be allowed to give or call evidence in his defence, and to be heard in argument or submission before judgment be given."[51]

The requirements of a fair trial are not indelibly fixed, but are subject to development by the courts,[52] and their strictness is proportionate to the seriousness of the offence charged and the potential consequences for the accused.[53] In *Healy's* case[54] this principle was applied in establishing a right to representation for a poorly educated youth of 18 years. The Supreme Court affirmed that such a right exists where a person's "liberty is at stake, or where he faces a very severe penalty which may affect his welfare or livelihood."[55] Also in such a case the state is Constitutionally obliged to provide legal aid to an indigent defendant, and he has a right to be informed of that right. *Healy's* case is also significant for its recognition that the youth or immaturity of an accused are factors influencing the degree of procedural protection required by the Constitution.[56]

In civil cases, the level of procedural protection is not so high. For example, no Constitutional right to representation has so far been recognized. On the other hand the closer the analogy between the civil proceedings and a criminal trial, particularly having regard to its potential consequences for the liberty or reputation of an individual, the stricter become the procedural requirements.[57]

The requirement of fair procedures is not limited to cases dealt with by judges. It straddles the dividing line between limited and unlimited judicial functions. There is no doubt that bodies, which are not courts but which perform limited judicial functions, are bound to act judicially.[58] But so too are some bodies which do not exercise strictly judicial functions within the meaning of Article 37. Thus, for example, the principles of natural justice must be observed by administrative authorities when their decisions impose liabilities or affect the lives of others.[59] While some of the terminology employed by the judges in setting out these principles has been confusing, the general principle operating seems, as in criminal cases, to be one of proportionality — i.e., the greater the potential impact of a decision on the individual concerned, the stricter are the procedural requirements.

Relevance to Cases Concerning Children

The Constitutional version of procedural justice has been developed mainly in the context of an adversary system. It assumes the basic model of a contest between opposing parties and seeks to ensure that the fight is a fair one. This emphasis, as already stated, is not necessarily appropriate to welfare-orientated decision making. This is not to say that the principles (*e.g.,* the rules of natural justice) are wholly inappropriate but rather that they require modification and supplementation.

The present approach to child custody disputes, as already described, illustrates the problem. The adversarial form of the proceedings, however much the judges may regret it, presents the case as a contest between parents. Yet paradoxically there is now doubt as to whether the parents are *parties* to a dispute — and hence doubt as to whether their contest is subject to the rules of fair play. On the other hand the child, who in theory is the focal point of the proceedings, in reality stands on the sidelines, usually too young to make his own case and without an independent representative to do it for him.

In fact, as argued above, it may be unrealistic to regard the welfare of the child as the sole consideration when the court is not considering the child's welfare in the abstract but in the context of the limited alternatives provided by two parents. For this reason what is needed is a modified procedural framework which recognizes the tripartite nature of custody cases: one which offers a fair hearing to each parent but at the same time affords the court a reasonable chance independently to judge the issue from the point of view of the child's welfare. It needs to be said that this last desideratum may not be achievable by procedural changes alone (*e.g.,* by a more inquisitorial approach by the judge); it requires also the injection of resources whether it be in securing independent representation for a child or ensuring the better availability to the court of expert services.

Within the juvenile justice process, the identification of due process with the adversary model is reflected in a philosophy that views the requirements of welfare and the requirements of justice as being mutually opposed. Hence the criminal justice model — the epitome of adversary justice — is seen as providing the juvenile and his family with the most effective protection against unwarranted state intervention — a danger which necessarily increases as the system moves further towards a welfare or treatment model. Such are the assumptions made in the long-awaited Final Report of the government-appointed Task Force on Child Care Services.[60] The treatment model, having regard in particular to the American experience, is seen as easily leading "to disregard of fundamental legal rights and ideas of justice and fair play in dealing with children."[61] This view appears to have influenced the Task Force's recommendations, which would not involve any significant movement away from the criminal justice model.

The truth is, however, that the building of the juvenile justice system into the criminal justice framework has not made it immune from procedural laxity, nor has it always ensured an effective protection for children's rights.[62] One authority has suggested that until recently the system has been characterized by its lack of system and formalism. "Within a generally understood legal framework there has been evidence of a casual approach, displays of judicial independence and a lack of guidance on important subsidiary matters."[63] Where there has been formalism, its effect has sometimes been to make proceedings incomprehensible to the child rather than safeguard his rights.[64] A recent report has described the procedures of the Dublin Metropolitan Children's Court as "formal, legalistic and bureaucratic, though interspersed with informal communication."[65]

In contrast, some juvenile justice systems based on the treatment model have managed to combine a high level of procedural protection with a strong element of informality.[66] The Scots system of children's hearings is an example, and although there may arise within it some tension between the requirements of welfare and the protection of rights, it is a system which is more comprehensible to the child and his parents, and which provides him with an opportunity to state his case. These are requirements of a fair hearing which are less easy to satisfy if the proceedings are, as in the Republic of Ireland, more formal.

The problem is not simply, as the Task Force appears to see it, that of ensuring the application to children's cases of the theoretical framework of Constitutional and other procedural safeguards worked out for criminal cases. The problem is rather that of determining, in the words of the U.S. Supreme Court, "what forms of procedural protection are necessary to guarantee the fundamental fairness of juvenile proceedings."[67]

CONCLUSION

This paper has deliberately avoided detailed exposition and criticism of existing procedures in the Republic of Ireland for resolving disputes concerning children within the family. The writer's views on these matters have been expressed elsewhere,[68] and many of the problems would at any rate be familiar especially to those coming from common law jurisdictions. Instead the attempt has been made to identify more basic influences which help to explain the retention of a somewhat old-fashioned system — influences which need to be identified and analyzed if changes are to come about.

The pressure of family breakdown is beginning to force attention on the defects in the conventional approach to dispute resolution — defects similar to those which have long been apparent in the juvenile justice system. More pragmatism is needed. The formal and rigid concept of procedural justice has proved ill suited to welfare-orientated decision making and has often failed to protect effectively the rights of children. A new concept of a fair hearing is needed, adapted to the special requirements of family disputes. Factors inhibiting the development of new decision-making models need to be reviewed. One particular requirement is a new and much clearer definition of the reserved functions of judges — one perhaps which confines those functions to those which a judge is, by virtue of his qualities and qualifications, exclusively fitted to perform.[69]

Only in recent years have the courts in the Republic of Ireland begun to deal with significant numbers of family disputes. It is not surprising therefore that little thought has so far been given to the construction of alternative mechanisms for resolving them. (The contrast with labour-relations law is obvious.) Irish family law is still in that era of legal development characterized by the two stark alternatives — the private ordering of disputes or their subjection to the rigors of the adversary system. The introduction of intermediate solutions, such as conciliation procedures, will require fresh attitudes, especially in the legal profession, and an acceptance of the need to divert some national resources into the building of new machinery.

NOTES

1. Twenty-eight special summonses were issued in 1973 under the *Guardianship of Infants Act 1964;* 285 in 1979.
2. See 20th Interim Report of the Committee on Court Practice and Procedure, *Increase of Jurisdiction of the District Court and the Circuit Court.*
3. *Courts Act 1981.* The main provisions took effect on 12 May 1982. See also Duncan, "Custody Disputes and the Courts Bill 1980," *FLAC File,* February/March 1981.
4. *McGee v. A.G.* [1974] I.R. 284.
5. Constitution of Ireland, Article 42.5. See especially *In re Doyle, An Infant* (21 December 1955), unreported, Supreme Court, and *In re J.* [1966] I.R. 295.
6. See *P.W. v. A.W., M.M. and A.G.* (21 April 1980), unreported, High Court.
7. *Per* O'Dalaigh C.J. in *Cullen v. Cullen* (May 1970), unreported, Supreme Court.
8. See *In re Tilson* [1951] I.R. 1; *In re May, Minors* (1957), 92 I.L.T.R. 1.
9. S. 11(1).
10. Or where a matrimonial injunction is granted, or even in criminal proceedings where, *e.g.,* a husband convicted of assault is bound over to keep the peace on condition that he remains apart from his wife and children.
11. Maureen Gaffney, "Child Custody Disputes. A Psychological Perspective," in *Children and the Courts: Custody Disputes,* CARE (1980).
12. See *Guardianship of Infants Act 1964*, s. 17(2).
13. See, *e.g.,* the slightly exasperated judgment of McWilliam J. in *E. v. E.* (February 1977), unreported, High Court.
14. *Per* O'Dalaigh C.J. in *Re Haughey* [1971] I.R. 217, 250.
15. "The Judicial Power under Irish Constitutional Law," 24 *Int. and Comp. L.Q.* (1975), 305, 306.
16. Constitution of Ireland, Articles 34.1 and 37.1
17. *Ibid.,* Article 35.3.
18. See *Courts (Supplemental Provisions) Act 1961.*
19. One District Justice is appointed to preside over the Dublin Metropolitan Children's Court, another to be chairman of the Adoption Board.
20. E.g., the Law Reform Commission's *First Programme* (1977) promised consideration of "the best type of judicial or court structure or structures appropriate to deal with different matters which fall under the general heading of family law," (p. 9). No proposals have yet emerged.
21. [1965] I.R. 217.
22. See Casey, *supra,* note 15, at 319.
23. See J. Roberts, *Divorce Bills in the Imperial Parliament* (Dublin, 1906).
24. *Op. cit.*
25. *Per* Kingsmill Moore J. in *In re Solicitors Act 1954* [1960] I.R. 239.
26. See J. Kelly, *The Irish Constitution,* (1980), 280–85.
27. *Adoption Act 1952,* s. 8(2)(3).
28. *Ibid.,* s. 8(4).
29. *Ibid.,* s. 8(4B), added by *Adoption Act 1974,* s. 7.
30. *Adoption Act 1974,* s. 3.
31. For the basic recognition principle see *In re Caffin* [1971] I.R. 123.
32. *Adoption Act 1952,* s. 10(c).

33. See *ibid.,* s. 24.
34. (October 1974), unreported, High Court; [1977] I.R. 287 (Supreme Court).
35. *Ibid.,* High Court, at p. 32.
36. *Ibid.*
37. An opinion to this effect was given to the Adoptive Parents' Association of Ireland by two distinguished Senior Counsel, D. Barrington and C. Condon. See also Duncan, "The Insecurity of Irish Adoption Orders. Why a Referendum is Needed Now," *Children First Newsletter,* No. 10 (Winter 1977-78), 21.
38. *Per* Walsh J. in *G. v. An Bord Uchtala* [1980] I.R. 32, 72. In the same case the question was expressly reserved by O'Higgins C.J. (at 60).
39. Inserted by the Sixth Amendment of the *Constitution (Adoption) Act 1979.*
40. J. Kelly, *The Irish Constitution,* at 285.
41. Such, *e.g.,* as those proposed by M. Murch in *Justice and Welfare in Divorce* (1980).
42. *Courts of Justice Act 1924,* s. 80.
43. *Children's Act 1908,* s. III(1).
44. See *Social Work (Scotland) Act 1968.*
45. Casey, *op. cit.,* at 314. The argument is that Scots law by reserving the possibility of prosecution in respect of conduct which would otherwise come within the jurisdiction of a hearing, treats such conduct as "criminal in the sense of attracting punishment rather than requiring treatment." And although a Scots hearing is not involved in determining questions of guilt or innocence, it does make "decisions as to the disposal of offenders" — an important element of the judicial power in criminal cases. However, it can be argued that a reference to a hearing implies a decision not to prosecute, and since it is not the function of a hearing to punish, it is not exercising a criminal jurisdiction.
46. For the emphasis placed on the punitive nature of the sanction see *Melling v. O'Mathghamhna* [1962] I.R. 1 and especially the judgment of Lavery J.
47. *Social Work (Scotland) Act 1968,* s. 42(6).
48. *Task Force on Child Care Services Final Report* (1980, published 1981), para. 18.4.6.
49. Article 38.1.
50. *Per* O'Higgins C.J. in *the Criminal Law (Jurisdiction) Bill 1975* reference [1977] I.R. 129.
51. *Per* Gannon J. (High Court) in *The State (Healy) v. Donoghue* [1976] I.R. 325, 335-56.
52. *Ibid. per* O'Higgins C.J. (Supreme Court), at 350.
53. *Ibid.*
54. [1976] I.R. 325.
55. *Ibid. per* O'Higgins C.J. at 350.
56. See *ibid. per* Henchy J. at 354, and O'Higgins C.J. at 350.
57. See *In re Haughey* [1971] I.R. 217.
58. See *McDonald v. Bord na gCon, op. cit.,* and Kelly, *op. cit.,* 181.
59. *Per* May C.J. in *R. (McEvoy) v. Corporation of Dublin* 2 L.R.Ir. 371.
60. *Op. cit.* see sections 17.4 and 17.7.
61. *Ibid.* para. 17.7.4.
62. See Duncan, "Juvenile Justice at the Crossroads," chapter 1 in *Juvenile Justice at the Crossroads* (eds. E. Cook and V. Richardson, 1971).
63. W.N. Osborough, "Irish Juvenile Justice: System and Formalism," *Administration,* vol. 27, No. 4, 494 at 497.

64. See the report of a Bar Council Committee, "The Inadequacy of Legal Representation in the Children's Court," *Irish Law Times and Solicitors' Journal* 2 and 9 February 1974.

65. *Youth and Justice. Young Offenders in Ireland* (eds. Burke, Carney and Cook, 1981), 72.

66. See J.P. Grant, "Children's Hearings: Some Legal and Practical Difficulties," chapter 3 in *Justice for Children* (CARE 1974), at 44–47.

67. *Re Gault,* 387 U.S. 1 (1967).

68. See note 3, *supra.*

69. See Casey, *op. cit.,* at 323.

Chapter Twenty-six

Representation of Children: Does More Mean Better?

Henri Giller and Susan Maidment

University of Keele, Staffordshire, England

The development of separate representation of children in legal proceedings has been a growing phenomenon in recent years. Calls for separate representation find their context and purpose in different though related ideologies. The first arises from the children's rights or juvenile justice movement. In the United States the critical questioning of the "lawlessness" of the juvenile court (exemplified in the decision of *In re Gault* (1967)) quickly spread to other therapeutic and welfare decision-making agencies in an attempt to limit the arbitrary nature of discretionary judgments against a background of the decline of the preventative and rehabilitative ethics. The discretionary practices of expanding social welfare bureaucracies and their manipulations of legal procedures became viewed with growing suspicion (Adler and Asquith 1981). Against such a background, concern with children's rights and attempts to introduce legality into the determination of children's issues has emerged (Freeman 1981). Like its American counterparts, therefore, Britain has begun to look to legality as an answer to some of the dilemmas posed in legitimating the role of the courts and the state welfare bureaucracies in children's disputes (see, for example, Morris et al. 1980).

The second ideology arises from the recognition that the *parens patriae* basis of the child care system is flawed, that judicial or social welfare decision makers do not have omnipotence or the monopoly of wisdom in issues concerning a child's best interests. King illustrates the contemporary climate of debate as follows:

> Child care statutes abound with phrases such as "proper development", "exposed to moral danger", "efficient full-time education", "in need of care and control", "unfit to have the care of the child", "the need to safeguard and promote the welfare of the child", "the welfare of the minor as the first and paramount consideration".

What is so striking about these phrases is that, while seeming to assume a consensus about child welfare, education and development, they leave so much to the discretion, prejudices and predilections of the particular judge or bench of magistrates hearing the case or to the individual social worker preparing a report for the courts. These vague phrases are interpreted by decision-makers and their advisers in whatever ways the facts of a particular case appear to suggest and are echoed by them as justifications for their decisions or assessments (1981, 129–30).

In a similar vein, Sutton comments on our ability to make "scientific" assessments of these issues:

Social workers and those that associate with them in offering expertise on matters of child care to the courts presently have little or no empirical data to support a professionalism that claims of [sic] knowledge of why a child acts as he does, what is likely to follow this or that intervention, etc. Neither at their present stage of development do their institutions hold forth the promise of the significant advances that would be required to establish such knowledge (1981, 94).

Separate representation is therefore seen as a way of attacking claims of the judiciary and welfare authorities to be the sole repositories of wisdom.

The third ideology behind separate representation is a concern that parental autonomy over children can hide the conflict of interest that may exist between them. The belief is that parents and children are autonomous legal persons with separate (and potentially conflicting) rights and interests. Separate representation of the child from his parents in children's proceedings thus ensures that all relevant parties in the proceedings are protected.

For different reasons, therefore, in both jurisdictions, the introduction of mechanisms for the separate representation of children has been a cornerstone of a legal renaissance. Separate representation has become a rallying call for those who seek to improve the method of adjudication in children's issues. More representation, be it legal, social work or psychomedical,[1] designed to promote and present the "best interests of the child," is taken to be axiomatic of a full adumbration of the issues in children's cases and, concomitantly, of better decisions in an area which has traditionally been seen as difficult. But can we take the case for increased representation at face value? Does more mean better? The precise purpose and functioning of representation has rarely been elucidated, the rhetoric of its advancement often subsuming any rational or empirical appraisal.

In this chapter, we wish to address two questions; first, will the introduction of separate representation in child care issues[2] meet the expectations of those who have called for it; and second, what does the instituting of separate representation for children tell us about the type of decision making that is intended to be produced?

Representation — The Procedural Context

Advocates of separate representation more frequently address the procedural arrangements whereby representation is to be provided rather than the substantive issue of what that representation should achieve. (The work of Goldstein, Freud and Solnit (1973, 1980) is one exception to this.) The blurring of these issues, however, frequently leads to confusion (Morris and Giller 1978). The assumption is often made that the institution of procedural formality will inevitably promote the best interests of the child. But is this necessarily so? There is a growing body of evidence which questions the assumption that the mere provision of separate representation for children will necessarily have an impact on the quality of the decisions being made.

The clearest indications of this come from those studies which have sought to assess the impact of the seminal decision of the United States Supreme Court *In re Gault* (1967, 387 U.S. 1). There, the majority judgment established that the juvenile had a right to counsel in delinquency proceedings in the juvenile court. In so doing, the Supreme Court reinstated the idea that "due process of law is the primary and indisputable foundation of individual freedom" and was not overreached by the *parens patriae* obligations of the juvenile court. Indeed, the Supreme Court went on to say that the imputation of a juvenile's right to counsel as the embodiment of the due process principle involved "no necessary interference with the special purposes of the juvenile court procedures; indeed it seems that counsel can play an important role in the process of rehabilitation." Without detailing the content of this integration, it seems that the Supreme Court may have been overoptimistic in its assumption.

Stapleton and Teitelbaum (1972), for example, in assessing the impact of the *Gault* decision in two juvenile courts (Gotham and Zenith) found inconsistent results. While increased legal representation in Gotham had little impact (other than to increase the chances of a child's incarceration), representation in Zenith resulted in more favorable dispositions. These differences in case outcomes could not be attributed to the nature of the judges, the experience or abilities of counsel, nor the personal or offence attributes of the children. What did account for the differential impact of the representation seemed to be something within the ethos of the courts themselves. In Gotham, the courts rejected attempts by the representatives to introduce adversarial elements in decision making designed to promote the social welfare interests of children. Consequently, lawyers were prevented from acting as advocates in the Gotham court and as a consequence exposed their clients to greater intervention. A recent replication of this study, in North Carolina, has further confirmed Stapleton and Teitelbaum's findings. As the authors conclude:

The assistance of an attorney was on the whole not helpful — and may have actually been detrimental — with respect to reducing the child's chance of being adjudicated delinquent and committed (Clarke and Koch 1980, 307).

Equally important to the implementation of due process requirements, therefore, may be the extent to which courts are willing to adapt themselves to the procedures required by those dictates.

In an English context, the available evidence certainly bears out the American experience in dealing with delinquency disputes. Studies by Priestly et al. (1977), Anderson (1978) and more recently Parker et al. (1981) all present evidence of a wide variety of styles adopted by juvenile courts in implementing the same legislation, the *Children and Young Persons Act 1969*. Depending on the area, intake and ideology of the bench, very different "productions of local juvenile justice" (Parker et al. 1981, 242 ff.) may arise, and with them dissimilar decisions for similar cases. The quality of legal representation (including both the role and the impact of the representative) depends much on the nature of the case, the style of the court and the extent to which the representative is aware of what tools are appropriate in the presentation of the case. Hence, the variable quality and impact of the representative may say as much about the forum within which he works as the quality of his professional skills. As Anderson notes, representation may well be seen as ineffective when the court sees the offence as only the *occasion* for intervention rather than its foundation.

> If the defendant's interests are not identified with the preservation of his personal liberty, the whole notion of legal representation as such is called into question. And this is so not only because such representation is less acceptable and therefore less efficacious, but also because it countermands the moral basis of action designed to help rather than restrain (1978, 54).

Such considerations, while more overt in the delinquency jurisdiction of the juvenile court, are not limited to that arena. More generally in disputed child care matters the courts' assumption of a benign interventionist stance, which seeks to protect and promote the "best interests of the child," may place the child's representative in an equally difficult position.

At one extreme, the court's belief in the integrity of the state's social welfare bureaucracies may make the child's representative a dummy player standing between those considered to be the "real" combatants in the proceedings — the parents and the state. Indeed, recent evidence suggests that that outcome is particularly likely in cases of alleged child abuse, and furthermore "that it is objectionable to set up the child's interests as if in opposition to the local authority's case" (Dingwall et al. 1981, 39).

At the other extreme, failure on the part of the representative to identify or produce distinctive interests of the child client may lead to allegation that the representative has overidentified himself with the wishes of the parents. As such, this may call into question the representative's ability to separate his client's interests and discredit his competence to promote and present to the court information which is unbiased by parental preference (see *Re DJMS* [1977] 3 All E.R. 582).

In an English context, these issues are complicated by the respective legal positions of the child and the parents in child care cases. Under the 1969 *Children and Young Persons Act,* for example, the child is the party to the proceedings and, as such, entitled alone to (legally aided) representation. Parents, not being parties in law, have no such right to representation and may only participate in the proceedings to rebut specific allegations made against them. In practice, however, the child's parents are often the ones who find a representative for the child, who apply for legal aid, and who may be asked to make a contribution to the cost of that representation. Moreover, in those cases where the child is too young to give instructions or be physically removed from the area, the parents will initially provide the representative with the facts of the case (and their interpretation of those facts). Unsurprisingly, in this context many solicitors acting in such circumstances express considerable confusion as to the appropriate role they should perform (Hilgendorf 1981, 140–41). Nevertheless, recent research does suggest that between these extremes:

> The role which solicitors adopt in a hearing can make a considerable impact on the case. In many cases it depends on whether the solicitor for the child takes an active part in testing the evidence put forward by the local authority and whether he calls his own witnesses as to how thoroughly the case is examined (Hilgendorf 1981, 138–39).

Such considerations bring us to the second area of uncertainty in relation to separate representation. For in addition to the variability in the response of the court to the presence of the representative, we must address the variable styles of the representatives themselves in seeking to develop their roles.

Representation — The Content

In discussing the roles that representatives are required to or may choose to take in children's matters, three broad approaches may be identified. These categories are not exhaustive but they do provide a useful starting point for analyzing some of the complexities of representation which hitherto have been largely ignored.

Amicus Curiae

In this role, the representative seeks to act as an intermediary between the various parties producing, presenting and clarifying information to the court for the judge to make the decision "in the best interests of the child." In theory, divorce court welfare officers are a pure example of this. This approach is seen by many as the hallmark of lawyers' contribution to the work of children's courts. As Hilgendorf comments:

> As part of his duty to the court the advocate must seek to put before the court all the matters relevant to its decision. This responsibility exists even if the material may be prejudicial to his client (1981, 49).

From the representative's viewpoint, the "client" here is primarily the court. As Goldstein, Freud and Solnit illustrate when arguing for this style of representation, counsel ". . . may look to the parents as sources of information but not for instructions" which come primarily from the court acting in its capacity as an "autonomous parent" (1980, 122). From the court's viewpoint, the traditional role of determining what is in the "best interests" of the child is least interrupted by this representational style. Fundamental dislocations of the traditional court procedure are least likely with this approach as the personal contribution of the representative is minimized. As Goldstein, Freud and Solnit put it:

> Counsel (may not) seek to have his personal child-rearing preferences impressed upon his "client" without regard to the state's notion of what is best for children (1980, 122).

Indicative of the marginal position of the representative is Goldstein, Freud and Solnit's recommendation that such representation is most appropriately employed *after* the adjudication of the grounds for modifying or terminating parental relationships with the child and *before* the dispositional decision is made.

> At that point, a child in most cases will require a legal representative who will assure that the process of disposition and the placement itself will make his interests paramount and provide him with the least detrimental alternative (1980, 114).

Guardianship

With this mode of representation, the representative seeks to make his own assessment of the perceived "best interests" of the child and adduce arguments and evidence to achieve an adjudication which serves that end. In Bersoff's language, by adopting this role the representative may be said to be acting "in behalf of" the child:

In this respect, representatives, while having a legal duty to oversee the welfare of the children in their charge, are under no duty to consult with them or, more importantly, act according to their wishes. Such a role is different from acting "on behalf of", which connotes that the representative is acting on the part of, in the name of another, or as the one represented might act (1976, 34).

In making such a judgment, a legal representative may be hampered by his lack of expertise in child care matters and may have difficulty in assessing the strengths and weaknesses of the professional judgments of others (Hilgendorf 1981, 50–54). Against this however:

Despite the difficulties of a solicitor for the child adopting a stance in relation to a case there are some advantages in him doing so. There is likely to be a greater coherence and point to his questioning of witnesses and his submissions to the court. Since he is also likely to take a greater part in the proceedings there will probably be a more thorough testing of the evidence and a greater chance that justice will be seen to be done (Hilgendorf 1981, 54).

To avoid the difficulties of the lack of technical knowledge the legal representative may employ the services of an independent social worker to compile a report on the merits of the opposition case. With such reports, however, there is no guarantee that they will support the legal representative's assessment. Kalogerahis (1975), extending the idea of the guardian expert, has outlined proposals for a "clinician-advocate" as a member of the court staff. The clinician-advocate would assess the child's assertions, evaluate conflicting wishes and weigh the implications of the available evidence for personality development (see Westman 1979, 285).

The Child's Advocate

In adopting this role, the representative acts in a fully adversarial capacity to protect the interests of the client as perceived by the client or as he would perceive it given the opportunity to do so. Here the representative seeks to represent his client "zealously within the bounds of the law" (ABA Code of Professional Responsibility), to exhibit "honest but firm concern for the protection of his client's rights," or more emotively "beat the rap." Here the representative has an active role at both adjudication and disposition to advance his client's view of the case and have the court accept it. Such a role promotes the adversarial interests of the parties, denies the appropriateness of inquisitorial investigations, and seeks to question the assumptions of those who wish to make "best interest" assessments which deny or distort the client's account. Such an approach is best suited to cases in which the client is capable of expressing an opinion, but even where this is not so there may exist legal presumptions which determine the boundaries of the court's decision. Bersoff, for example, argues for the representative in custody decisions to advocate the child's preference within a legislative framework allowing such preference to control the decision (Bersoff 1976, 48). Here also alternative social welfare reports may be obtained, but used tactically like expert testimony to advance a particular line of argument. As one independent social worker has recently written:

> If care proceedings are viewed as adversarial then the purpose of an independent social work opinion is to provide, for the assistance of the advocate and also to uphold the principle of justice, an alternative view, in direct contrast to that presented by the local authority (Rosser 1982).

This representational role provides the biggest challenge to existing child care legal structures, questioning as it does the judge's prerogative to make "best interest" determinations against the express wishes of the subject party. Such a role makes the representative directly accountable to the client and assesses his efficacy on the basis of achieving the client's wishes.

While these sketches of representational styles may oversimplify some of the varieties of representation actually used, they do delineate the broad terrain upon which the current system operates. At present, the state of the law and its procedures provide no firm guidelines as to which form of representation is appropriate. As a consequence, often the different styles of representation will be used in a variety of cases (e.g., advocacy is most likely in criminal cases, guardianship in care cases), and, more importantly, often the different styles of representation may be used in similar cases or at different stages in the same case (*e.g.*, at the adjudication or disposition stage). Given the lack of a clear mandate for determining which style of representation is appropriate, given the diversity of roles used by representatives, and given the different responses of courts to these various styles, there is good reason to argue that no coherent concept of the representation of children exists.

Illustrative of this proposition, firstly, is new evidence on the participation of lawyers representing children in care proceedings. According to Hilgendorf, both the solicitors and the social workers involved in care proceedings were confused and "vague about the nature of the benefits or the role of the representative" (1981, 58).

> There is a good deal of uncertainty and disagreement about how the role of the representative of a child should be defined and what might constitute effective role performance (1981, 48).

As a result, individual solicitors chose their own role and stance. Some described their role solely in terms of the presentation of information to the court (the *amicus curiae* role); others concerned themselves with the interpretation of the information and judgments about what to do in the best interests of the client (the guardianship role). Even where the child was old enough to give instructions, most solicitors were not willing to act purely as advocate (1981, 51).

The doubt and confusion resulted, according to Hilgendorf, in highlighting the complexity of the legal separate representative's role. Must he test the opposing case *on* behalf of the child, or should he involve himself in deciding what is best *in* behalf of the child? If his limited professional expertise makes him unable to confidently do the latter, then he may decide to restrict himself to an *amicus curiae* role. His problem is further confused where the child's parents are not themselves represented, as they currently cannot be in care proceedings. If he believes that the parents have a moral right to have their views represented, can he manifest sufficient intellectual detachment to present to the court the parents' *and* the child's point of view? Social workers observing the solicitors did not believe that such separation was possible (Hilgendorf 1981, 41).

Another recent example comes from a leading practitioner acting for a children's rights organization who describes how legal representatives should act in child care cases. He suggests that different styles of representation need to be adopted not according to the nature of the case, but according to the nature of the *client*.

> If the solicitor is satisfied that the child is capable of giving instructions then the solicitor should represent the child according to these instructions even if believing them to be contrary to the child's interests... The role of the solicitor who cannot obtain instructions is different. The crucial duty before the hearing is that of investigation. The solicitor should try and discuss the case with both the parents and the local authority clearly explaining to both of them his/her neutrality and shall go further and consider what other avenues should be explored (Warren 1981, 157).

For one class of client, therefore, the representative will act "on behalf of" the child, for the other he will act "in behalf of" or as neutral investigator. Little wonder then that representation often seems confused and confusing to observers and clients alike (see Catton and Erikson 1975). Similar evidence exists for the stances taken by solicitors in juvenile criminal proceedings (Anderson 1978).

A second illustration of the confusion in the concept of separate representation is the available evidence on the work of those statutory representatives which the law provides in certain child care cases. In adoption proceedings, for example, the court appoints a guardian *ad litem* (usually a social worker) who has the general duty of "safeguarding the interests of the child before the court." (*Adoption Act 1958* s. 9(7)). In practice the guardian *ad litem's* tasks straddle uneasily the *amicus curiae* and the guardianship approach. As Kent notes, the guardian *ad litem*

> ... is not simply the child's representative ... He is the court's representative whose primary function is to give an independent assessment of the application. In performing his task the guardian will certainly have regard to the child's welfare but it may be ancillary to his main duties (1979, 400).

A similar admixture of representative styles may be observed in the work of the Official Solicitor in wardship proceedings (Lowe and White 1979, 181–83), and the guardian *ad litem* under the *Children Act 1975*, in care proceedings. The guardian *ad litem* is intended to be a person of professional experience with children who will "safeguard the interests of the child" in care proceedings where it has been determined that the parents are unfit to represent the child because of a conflict of interest between them. Very few such guardians have as yet been appointed because the statutory provision is not yet fully in force, but it is quite clear that the confusion of roles manifested in both the adoption guardian *at litem's* position and the lawyer representing the child in care proceedings will arise here as well. The guardian *at litem*, therefore, uneasily straddles all three representational styles, leaving him free to select his own stance for reasons unrelated to the nature of the case or the client.

Recent evidence on the work of the divorce court welfare officers also shows an amalgam of all three styles of representation. Appointed in those cases where there is a dispute between the parties or concern about the parental arrangements over custody or access of children, the court welfare officer (usually a probation officer) is charged to provide as much relevant information as possible to enable the court to make the best decision (an *amicus curiae* role). As recent research shows, however, other more informal and less explicitly authorized tasks adopted by welfare officers fundamentally change the intended representational approach. Murch, for example, itemizes this hidden agenda as "cathartic listening, conciliation, child advocacy, family support and welfare rights advice" (1981, 156). Indeed, as a child advocate, the welfare officer is uniquely placed to represent the child's position, for as Murch notes:

> Apart from the court welfare officer and occasionally the judge, there is really no-one within the legal machinery of divorce with specific responsibility to listen to and understand the child's point of view (1981, 164).

However, when this informal role is placed alongside the others, it is clear that the welfare officer is primarily adopting a guardianship approach. As Eekelaar et al. concluded in their recent study of welfare officers:

> Although formally assigned an investigative role and even though they continue to categorize their role in that way, welfare officers also saw themselves as making a significant contribution to the resolution of the family conflict and thereby advancing the interests of the child (1982, 35).

Outside of statutory representation the evidence of confusion surrounding the representation role is even more overt. Various voluntary organizations in England have recently attempted to establish panels of social workers available to compile independent social inquiry reports for lawyers representing children clients in contested child care cases; such attempts have recurrently demonstrated a confusion in the representational role they wish to adopt. The following quotation from a handbook published by the Family Rights Group for the guidance of independent reporters refers to all three representational styles we have outlined:

> Independent reporters can help to provide better and fairer representation for families within the limitations of the present legal system. They may also reduce the need for some cases to go to court. Some reporters have been successful in negotiating alternative ways of dealing with the case, or have presented new informatic or new interpretations of events that have led the social worker or parents to change their views (Tunnard 1981, 4).

Against such a background, the formality of providing more opportunities for the representation of children may in no way ensure that their interests will be promoted or protected as many assume. The fulfilment of procedural safeguards through the provision of increased representation may merely mask the more fundamental question of the substantive right of the child to have his case promoted and heard, when no one is clear what the content of this substantive right really is. Evidence of this point emerges from recent work undertaken on the impact of independent social inquiry reports commissioned in contested child care cases (Giller and Morris 1982).

Independent Reports — a Case Study of Obfuscation

In 1978 as a result of growing number of petitions for advice made by parents resisting or challenging decisions of local authorities with respect to their children, the National Association for Mental Health (MIND) convened a panel of experienced social workers to provide, in appropriate cases, independent social inquiry reports to be used in court hearings. Lawyers acting for parents on behalf of the child who were challenging the decisions of local authorities could commission these reports for a fee. However, the MIND social workers used the concept of "independence" to mean that they would not inevitably support the party on whose behalf the report was commissioned. Rather than acting as partisan child advocates, the MIND social workers saw themselves working in a guardianship role pursuing the best interest of the child. Nevertheless, the expectation of both the lawyers and the MIND social workers was that a sceptical investigation of the decisions of the local authority would be made and that, in interpreting what was in the best interest of the child, emphasis would be given to the interests of the parents. As one MIND social worker put it:

> Primarily I am guided by the legislative framework to look for the best interest of the child as the first consideration. However, I think that legislation doesn't take account of reconciling one set of rights against the rights of other members of the family. I don't think you can find the child's best interest without looking at the parents' best interests. At most times they interlock (Giller and Morris 1982, 32).

Despite the thoroughgoing scepticism of the inquirer and the particular interpretation of the "best interests" ideology, in none of the cases investigated did the MIND social workers argue for total nonintervention in the lives of the children and families going through the courts. Rather they argued for *reduced* intervention (*e.g.,* for supervision orders where care orders were being sought) on the grounds that while some problems did exist within the home and the family they were not of sufficient severity to justify full intervention at this stage. Although the investigative stance made the inquirers sceptical towards the actions of local authority social services departments, they could not disregard the views the courts were likely to have of these departments or reject the values of an organization which dealt with "family problems." Accordingly they did not question the existence of "problems" but attempted to alter the classification under which the particular "problem" had been placed (and, therefore, its appropriate solution). In other words, "independence" in this situation took on a restricted meaning — describing the context in which the work took place, not the content of the investigation.

Such an approach had important implications for the MIND social worker's relationship with both the local authorities and the courts. A shared belief with local authority social workers that the court was an inappropriate forum for dealing with these types of dispute provided a basis for negotiation. Compromise was common. The legal outcome of the cases rarely resulted in a change of the order existing or desired by the local authority: a concession to the local authority social workers and their legal representatives. The practical outcome of the cases frequently resulted in change, such as increased access between parents and children, or a new placement: a concession to the MIND social worker and the parties' legal representative.

From the viewpoint of the courts, therefore, these alternative social inquiry reports are not necessarily *independent* reports. Undoubtedly, while such reports could unmask to the court certain interests, ideologies, and assumptions behind the "best interests" approach and highlight the subjectivity of the judgments made therein, this is not the inevitable outcome of receiving such representations. Because those representatives undertaking alternative social inquiries frequently acted as negotiators (*i.e.*, a guardianship role) rather than as challengers (*i.e.*, an advocate role), a thorough review of the grounds or form of the proposed intervention in court could be avoided. In other words, a service which *prima facie* is designed to protect the rights of children and families may, in fact, bargain those rights away.

REPRESENTING RIGHTS OR INTERESTS?

The evidence presented so far has aimed to show that the deceptively straightforward concept of representation contains within it complexities and contradictions which are frequently overlooked. The precise meaning of representation and the context within which it is performed need to be separately addressed as distinct realms of inquiry. As Bersoff has argued:

> To advocate representation without delineating the nature or mode of that representation may be to advocate a hollow right (1976, 34).

Yet consistently, it has been this unfocussed advancement of the representation equation — that more means better — which has dominated discussion in this area. What then does the rhetoric of increasing the availability of representation of children tell us about the nature of the decision making which tribunals and child welfare care bureaucracies wish to pursue?

Traditionally, as is well known, the rights of children, in the sense of those recognized by law, were few (Wringe 1981, Freeman 1981). Rather, the courts through the doctrine of *parens patriae* were willing to protect the *interests* of children, these interests being determined through the strategy of the "best interests" doctrine (Walton 1976). The legally recognized interests of children, since they were "interests" and not "rights," enabled children's claims to be negotiated, manipulated and where necessary subordinated to the wishes of adults. In essence, children were regulated through what Kamenka and Tay (1980) identify as the *Gemeinschaft* form of legal regulation — a particular rather than universal conception of justice which seeks to regulate the organic community (*i.e.*, the family) and in so doing "it elevates social harmony and subordinates conflict-resolution and resource allocation to a conception of the total social order" (1980, 16).

Dissatisfaction and disillusionment with the *Kadi* justice of *Gemeinschaft* legal regulation has led to calls for increased legality in both the form and content of such decision making. The introduction of due process requirements, including separate representation which is the subject matter of this chapter, and the proposals for legal presumptions to determine best interests (e.g., Goldstein, Freud and Solnit 1973, 1980;

Bersoff 1976) both illustrate the call for the development of *Gesellschaft* principles. That system, based on atomic individualism and private interest,

> emphasizes formal procedures, impartiality, adjudicative justice, precise legal provisions and definitions ... It is oriented to the precise definition of the rights and duties of the individuals through a sharpening of the point at issue and not to the day-to-day *ad hoc* maintenance of social harmony, community traditions and organic solidarity (Kamenka and Tay 1980, 18).

With specific reference to children, they write:

> The elevation of the — abstract — rights of children is an attempt to turn the family into a *Gesellschaft* and not a *Gemeinschaft* institution recognizing implicitly the bias of *Gesellschaft* law toward freedom and equality and against status dependence (1980, 22).

One should notice that Kamenka and Tay are at pains to say that the "abstract" concept of children's rights illustrates this development. But, as we have seen, the abstract concept can be diluted by the exigencies of practice. Why is this? Westman in a passage discussing the disadvantages of the adversarial model of adjudication (i.e., the *Gesellschaft* mode) in children's matters clearly illustrates the underlying issue:

> Employing the adversary system, a child with rights becomes a participant in a struggle for power. Because the adversary system depends upon pitting opposing forces against each other and awards children power, it is likely that a latent fear of the rebellion of children has been one of the deterrents to the full recognition of the rights of children in the past. Providing children with rights also provide them with influence and detracts from the power of the parents and the state (1979, 248).

Full recognition of the legal *(Gesellschaft)* rights of children would fundamentally dislocate the power arrangements within the existing decision-making framework for dealing with disputes concerning children. The attribution of power to children would not only weaken the power of the adults and the state in the dispute but would undermine the judicial supremacy to determine and apply the "best interests" doctrine. The *Gesellschaft* concept of representation, therefore, is manipulated to maintain the *status quo* of the adult-dominated *Gemeinschaft* form of child conflict resolution. The child remains the *object* of intervention, despite the fact that representation suggests that he or she is a fully participating *subject* of the dispute. The tension caused by the superimposition of the *Gesellschaft* concept of representation on what remains a *Gemeinschaft* type of decision creates and reflects the confusion of ideologies, purposes, and roles involved in the practice of separate representation. The continued dominance of the "best interests" doctrine, the attraction of the guardianship role of representation (legitimated by the assumed limited abilities of children to know their own best interests), and the beliefs in the inappropriateness of the adversarial model of adjudication in these disputes all contribute to make representation at present a "hollow right."

This is not to argue that the adversarial system with its logical concomitant of advocacy representation is the most appropriate for dealing with these types of disputes. What is being urged is that we delude ourselves if we believe the mere introduction of representation necessarily alters the fundamental position of children in adjudicating conflict or provides the decision making with "better" information upon which to reach an independent decision. Until we confront fully the nature of the decision-making process over children, more representation will not necessarily mean better. It may, in fact, mean merely different or even a whole lot worse.

NOTES

1. Throughout this chapter "representation" will be used in this generic form.
2. By child care issues we mean all of those matters in which a legal determination effects the arrangements for the upbringing and development of children including questions of custody, abuse, neglect and delinquency.

REFERENCES

Adler, M. and Asquith, S. (1981) "Discretion and Power," in Adler, M. and Asquith, S. (eds.) *Discretion and Welfare*. London, Heinemann Educational Books.

Anderson, R. (1978) *Representation in the Juvenile Court*. London, Routledge and Kegan Paul.

Bersoff, D. (1976) "Representation for Children in Custody Decisions: All That Glitters is not Gault," in *Journal of Family Law* 15, 27-49.

Catton, K. and Erickson, P. (1975) The Juvenile's Perception of the Role of Defense Counsel in Juvenile Court. Working Paper of the Centre of Criminology, University of Toronto.

Clarke, S. and Koch, G. (1980) "Juvenile Court: Therapy or crime control: Do Lawyers make a difference?" in *Law and Society Review* 14, 2630308.

Dingwall, R. Eekelaar, J. and Murray T. (1981) *Care or Control? Decision-Making in the Care of Children thought to have been Abused or Neglected*. A summary of the Final Report. Oxford, SSRC Centre for Socio-Legal Studies.

Eekelaar, J. (1982) *"Children in Divorce: Some Further Data." Oxford Journal of Legal Studies*. 63-85.

Freeman, J. (1981) "The Rights of Children when they do Wrong," in *British Journal of Criminology*, 21(3).

Giller, H. and Morris, A. (1982) "Independent Social Workers and the Courts: Advise, Resist and Defend," in *Journal of Social Welfare Law*, January, 29-41.

Goldstein, J. Freud, A. and Solnit, A. (1973) *Beyond the Best Interests of the Child.* New York, Free Press.
———. (1980) *Before the Best Interests of the Child.* London, Burnett Books.
Hilgendorf, L. (1981) *Social Workers and Solicitors in Child Car Cases.* London, Her Majesty's Stationery Office. With the permission of the Controller of H.M.S.O.
Kalogerakis, M. (1975) "Symposium: Children's Rights-Psychiatry and the Law," in *Journal of Psychiatry and Law,* 3:475-99.
Kamenka, E. and Tay, A. (1980) "Social traditions, legal traditions," in Kamenka, E. and Tay, A. (eds.) *Law and Social Control.* Ideas and Ideologies series. London, Edward Arnold.
Kent, P. (1979) "The Child's Representative — a Constructive Approach," in *Journal of Social Welfare Law,* 399-412.
King, M. (1981) "Welfare and Justice," in King, M. (ed.) *Childhood, Welfare and Justice.* London, Batsford.
Lowe, N. and White, R. (1979) *Wards of Court.* London, Butterworths.
Morris, A., Giller, H., Szwed E., Geach H. (1980) *Justice for Children.* London, Macmillan.
———. (1978) "Lawyers and the Juvenile Court," in *Legal Action Group Bulletin.* October, 227-79.
Murch, M. (1981) *Justice and Welfare in Divorce.* London, Sweet and Maxwell.
Parker, H., Casburn, M., Turnball, D. (1981) *Receiving Juvenile Justice.* Oxford, Blackwell.
Priestley, P., Fuller, R., and Fears, D. (1977) *Justice for Juveniles.* London: Routledge and Kegan Paul.
Rosser, P. (1982) "The Role of the Independent Social Worker," in Litigation (forthcoming).
Stapleton, W., and Teitelbaul, L. (1972) *In Defense of Youth.* New York, Russell Sage.
Sutton, A. (1981) "Science in Court," in King, M. (ed). *Childhood, Welfare and Justice.* London, Batsford.
Tunnard, J. (1981) "A Guide for Independent Reports," in Tunnard, J. (ed.) *Reports for the Courts.* London, Family Rights Group.
Walton, R. (1976) "The Best Interests of the Child" in *British Journal of Social Work,* 6(4), 307-13.
Warren, N. (1981) "Representing Children in Care Proceedings," in *Legal Action Group Bulletin,* July 155-58.
Westman, J.C. (1979) *New Professional Roles for Helping Families,* New York Free Press.
Wringe, C. (1981) *Children's Rights: A philosophical study.* London, Routledge and Kegan Paul.

Chapter Twenty-seven

Decision Making: The Roles of the Judge and the Guardian ad litem in England

Judith M. Masson

University of Leicester, England

The aim of this article is to contribute to the understanding of social work and judicial decision making through an examination of the decisions made in step-parent adoption cases. In particular, the relationship between the wishes of the parents, the recommendations made to the court by the guardian *ad litem* and the decisions made by the judge or magistrates will be analyzed in an attempt to show how those involved in the decision-making process influenced each other and the outcome of the cases.

The author undertook an empirical study of step-parent adoption[1] with Daphine Norbury, social work consultant, and Sandie Wall, research assistant, both of the British Agencies for Adoption and Fostering, for the DHSS monitor of the *Children Act 1975*.[2] The study included an analysis of the court records of all applications by parent and step-parent for adoption orders made in three local authority areas ("regions") between 1975 and 1978. A total of 1,733 applications from 1,255 families were included in the sample. In 1,629 of these cases, a guardian *ad litem* had prepared a report for the court. Interviews were held with all those who acted as guardians *ad litem* in these adoption proceedings in 1978 and were still in post in 1979. Ninety guardians *ad litem* were interviewed about the work they had done for their last g.a.l. investigation. Since this provided information which was bound to vary according to the circumstances of the cases the g.a.l.s. were additionally asked to complete a questionnaire based on a hypothetical case. Eighty-four (93 percent) agreed to do so. Data and information from all three sources are presented here.

WHAT IS STEP-PARENT ADOPTION?

If a parent marries someone who is not his child's other natural parent then at Common Law the spouse acquires neither rights nor duties in respect of the child. However, as soon as adoption was introduced into English Law in 1926, parents and step-parents began to seek adoption orders which could create a legal unit from their blended family.[3] Orders could be granted if either the other natural parent agreed to the adoption or, alternatively, his agreement could be dispensed with on a number of grounds *and* the adoption order was in the child's best interest. By 1975 two-thirds of all adoptions in England and Wales were step-parent adoptions. Following pressure from social work organizations and the recommendations of a Departmental Committee,[4] legislation was passed which included restrictions on step-parent adoption where the child had been a "child of the family" in divorce proceedings.[5] For these cases which the researchers termed *postdivorce*[6] cases, an alternative method of uniting step-parent and step-child was made available through a variation of the existing divorce court custody order. Judges hearing *postdivorce* step-parent adoption applications were then required to dismiss them if the matter could be better dealt with by a variation of the custody order. The Step-parent Adoption Study referred to above included a sample of 879 *postdivorce* applications made between 1975 and 1978; 566 were made before and 313 after the change in legislation.

A number of features which characterize step-parent adoption cases have contributed to the development of the current decision-making practices. The most important of these features are listed below. Although the points made in this article relate to the step-parent adoption process in England, similar developments may be seen elsewhere where some of these features exist, for example in other adoptions or in cases concerning custody and access where expert evaluations are used.

1. The welfare principle or "best interests" standard applies.
2. The order the applicants seek will not change where the child lives.
3. Disputed cases are rare.
4. The applicants expect to be successful.
5. A social work investigation and report are required.
6. The reporting worker is not required to have specialist training, qualifications or experience.
7. The worker's (g.a.l.'s) report is confidential to the court.
8. Representation by experienced lawyers is not usually available.
9. The hearings are informal and not open to the public.

ADOPTION LAW AND PRACTICE

Under English Law the High Court, country courts and magistrates' courts all have jurisdiction in adoption. In practice over 80 percent of cases are heard in the country court;[7] magistrates' courts avoid *post-divorce* step-parent adoption cases because they are unable to make the alternative joint custody order.[8] Proceedings are started by filing an application; the court then appoints a guardian *ad litem* to investigate the case and provide a report to the court. The Court Rules provide for a "preliminary examination of jurisdiction";[9] practices concerning this vary but it is generally accepted that cases should not be dismissed at this stage unless it is clear that the court lacks jurisdiction.[10] The main hearing date is fixed when the guardian *ad litem* is appointed but is postponed if the report is not ready. The hearing takes place in private, only the applicants, the respondent, the child, the g.a.l. and their legal representatives may attend. In step-parent adoption cases it is unusual for the child's non-custodial parent to be present; in fact, commonly only the applicants, the child and the g.a.l. are at the hearing. Hearings are often short and informal: the applicants give their names and state their wish to adopt, the judge may ask them a few questions and the order is then signed. When the research commenced, refusal of the applications was so rare in the courts in the study that court clerical staff prepared the orders for signing at the time the application fee was paid.

The following outcomes may be ordered by the court: *(a)* adoption order, *(b)* interim adoption order, *(c)* adjourment *sine die*, *(d)* refusal with consent to reapply,[11] or *(e)* refusal. The alternative of joint custody cannot be granted by the judge at the adoption hearing unless the court has jurisdiction over the original divorce custody case and the adoption applicants request joint custody.

THE GUARDIAN *AD LITEM*

The guardian *ad litem* procedure was introduced with the first *Adoption of Children Act* in 1926. Children involved in civil litigation had a "next friend" to conduct the proceedings. However, the g.a.l. was not only the guardian *ad litem* for the child[12] but also the "eyes and ears of the court." Adoption was such a serious step (it was then the only way the parent–child relationship could be broken permanently) that the court needed its own *independent* investigation of each case. Thus, from the beginning, the g.a.l. had to play two roles, the child's representative and the court's investigator.[13] What is required of the g.a.l. was succinctly stated in the Home Office *Guide to Adoption Practice,* published in 1970.

> Even where there is apparent agreement by all respondents, the guardian must be aware that he has the inescapable duty of satisfying himself and the court that there is no hidden conflict; this role is a positive one in that he must act in a frame of reference which has the law as the final arbiter acting in the best interests of the child, safeguarding parental rights, securing that a child is not unnecessarily

deprived of biological parents, kin and rights of inheritance, and that the adoption in the particular circumstances of each case can offer legal, emotional and physical security for the future.[14]

In the early years, adoption was not common and social work as it is practiced today was unknown; the courts therefore turned to respectable citizens, doctors, church ministers and their wives for g.a.l. services. In 1954, shortly after the establishment of the Children's Departments, the Hurst Committee recommended that only suitably qualified social work personnel be appointed.[15] Now the Court Rules provide for the appointment of a Director of Social Services, a probation officer or other suitably qualified person.[16] Allocation within social services departments is a matter for the department and varies widely. For example, in some places step-parent adoption cases are thought to require very skilled workers, whereas in others they are given to new recruits. In the Step-parent Adoption Study the magistrates' courts in region 1 employed a person who worked only as a g.a.l. but who did not have social work qualifications. One magistrates' court in region 2 and one-third of all the courts in region 3 appointed probation officers; all the other courts appointed their local Directors of Social Services who delegated the work to a member of their staff. Overall 82 percent of g.a.l.s had social work qualifications but over half were classified by the researchers as inexperienced in guardian *ad litem* work.

The guardian *ad litem* is appointed to safeguard the interests of the child in the proceedings, to carry out an investigation of the case, and to provide a report for the court. His duties are detailed in the Court Rules.[17] He must interview the applicants, obtain specific factual information about them, their home and their finances, and make qualitative assessments about the stability of their marriage and their capacity to parent the child. The g.a.l. must also ascertain the child's wishes and feelings about the adoption and must either personally or through an agent interview all the respondents. Further guidance is available to g.a.l.s in the *Home Office Guide to Adoption*,[18] DHSS circulars[19] and the writings of Jane Rowe and Alfred Leeding.[20] In addition, some courts and social services departments provide guidelines or even instructions as to how the work should be completed. With few exceptions[21] the instructions leave the g.a.l.s with considerable discretion over their investigations either because they are very general or because specific instructions are apparently not enforced.[22]

The descriptions given by the g.a.l.s of the work they did were generally similar despite the fact that they were employed by different agencies and were providing reports for different courts. Most visited the applicants before seeing others involved in the adoption. There they explained their role, usually in terms of ensuring the child's best interests and helping the judge to decide the case, and started to obtain the necessary information. Most said that they discussed the alternatives to adoption, but in some instances this was dealt with only very briefly. A few guardians stated that they used these discussions to encourage applicants to withdraw their cases. In region 3 the judges promoted this practice as a way of sifting out *postdivorce* applications at a stage before the final hearing.[23] Jane Rowe points out that the guardian *ad litem's* investigation may influence those involved unintentionally.

> Before he can give an opinion as to whether this adoption will be for the welfare of the child the guardian should acquire an intimate knowledge of the adopters, the child and the natural parent. In the course of obtaining this information he may very well find that the people concerned need help in coming to a decision. Sometimes it will be difficult to uncover attitudes without influencing them to some extent. The worker will have to use his own discretion in each case.[24]

It was not uncommon for the g.a.l.s to make no attempt to contact the father of an illegitimate child who had paid no maintenance.[25] Only a few g.a.l.s, mostly the very experienced or the completely inexperienced, made their own decisions to obtain further information about the child or his family by interviewing relatives or school teachers; some others did so because of agency or court requirements.

The guardians made their assessments through talking with the applicants, the child and other interested parties, listening to their replies and watching their responses. If respondents lived out of their district the g.a.l.s usually had to rely on the report of another social worker who acted as their agent and interviewed the person. On average the g.a.l.s spent five and one-half hours on each inquiry and made three visits (two to the applicants and one to the other natural parent). A third of the g.a.l.s saw the step-parent only with the parent; a third of the g.a.l.s did not see the child alone.

The reports written by the guardians *ad litem* for the court were highly stereotyped — in fact, they might remind a lawyer of conveyancing precedents. The fact that many reports were so similar is explained by the use of *pro forma*'s both for collecting the information and drafting the report. These acted as *aides memoires* for the g.a.l.s and also assisted the judges since they knew where to expect a particular piece of information in any report. Although there is no legal requirement on the guardian to make recommendation to the court, 80 percent did so. Including a recommendation was a long established practice arising out of requests made by the courts in earlier cases. Where local agency guidelines suggested including a recommendation they emphasized that reasons should be given. However, the reports frequently concluded with a bare statement such as:

> "it is recommended that the order be granted as being in the child's best interests."

The guardians who did not make specific recommendations fell into two groups — those like the court-employed guardian in region 1, who stated that it was improper for them to try to influence the judge in this way and those who were geniunely undecided what was the best course of action to suggest. The reports from the former group, while not recommending a specific outcome, rarely presented the cases for and against adoption in equal light; it was quite clear what the guardian thought was best. Nevertheless, these cases were coded as "no recommendation" in accordance with the practice of an earlier study.[26] The ambivalent tenor of the reports from the latter group may well have alerted the judge who expected a favorable recommendation. The extent to which the g.a.l. reports determined the outcome of the case by influencing the judge will be considered later. It was clear, however, that an unfavorable recommendation from the g.a.l.s led some families to withdraw their applications before the hearing. In a third of the cases that were withdrawn after the report had been completed, the guardian had recommended that an adoption order not be granted.

TABLE 27.1 Guardian *ad litem* Recommendation in Postdivorce Step-parent Adoption Cases after the Implementation of *Children Act 1975* subs. 10(3).

	Court Study %	G. a. l. Interviews %	Hypothetical Case %
No recommendation	12.7	16.0	4.0
Adoption order	78.0	79.0	18.04
Interim order	—	—	5.0
Joint custody	7.0	5.0	52.0
Refusal	1.0	—	16.0
Adjourned *sine die*	0.3	—	5.0
Total	100.0	100.0	100.0
N	(288)	(38)[1]	(81)

[1] The remaining 52 guardians had dealt with other types of step-parent adoption cases.

In the vast majority of the reports read for the court study the g.a.l. had recommended that the order be granted. This was also true of the guardians interviewed when they spoke of their last case, but not when they completed the hypothetical case questionnaire. Conversely, recommendations against adoption were rare in the actual cases.

What factors led the g.a.l.s to make the recommendations they did? Two-thirds of the guardians *ad litem* interviewed stated that they were in favor of the subs. 10(3) which restricted step-parent adoption but only 5 percent had made a recommendation against adoption. Their statements and answers on the hypothetical case[27] showed that they accepted the philosophy behind the new law, but their practice suggested otherwise. The guardians *ad litem* realized that the applicants would continue to care for the child whether the order was granted or not; Jane Rowe recognized that this and the limited time to complete the report might lead to superfical work:

> There is, inevitably, a strong temptation for the busy caseworker to feel that intensive casework is unnecessary since the situation will not be changed much whatever the outcome of the application may be . . . .[28]

It was thus more difficult for the g.a.l.s to discover factors which might indicate adoption was not in the child's best interest. The attitudes and actions of the applicants themselves also influenced the g.a.l.'s work. In particular they made it difficult for alternatives to adoption to be discussed. Many families had received no advice about the adoption proceedings before they made their application. The information they received when they filed their papers at the court was generally limited, although there were considerable variations between courts. Some applicants viewed the adoption process as akin to obtaining a T.V. license[29] and had no idea that there would be a social work investigation until the g.a.l. made an appointment or actually visited them. Responding to the g.a.l.'s inquiries, the applicants mostly remained adamant that they wanted the adoption, that they thought it was their right to do what they thought was best for the child. Similarly, many of the noncustodial parents who had agreed to or acquiesced in the adoption application were unwilling to discuss in detail other possible arrangements for their child. It was difficult for guardians faced with such views not to recommend adoption orders. Neither agency nor court requirements imposed on g.a.l.s removed their discretion over the recommendation. In fact, g.a.l.s in regions 2 and 3, where the judges were reluctant to make orders, continued to recommend adoption. However, the judge's practices could lead guardians *ad litem* who were aware of them to discount possible recommendations. For example, experienced workers in region 1 stated that there was little point in suggesting joint custody because the judge did not favor it.

The small number of cases with favorable recommendations did not produce sufficient information for the researchers about the features in the particular cases which led the g.a.l.s to their recommendations. The researchers therefore devised a hypothetical case which presented all the guardians interviewed with a series of different family circumstances[30] on which to make a recommendation. The results of this part of the research cannot be used to predict what any guardian would do, but they shed some light on the matters which g.a.l.s considered important.

Half the g.a.l.s gave the same recommendation whatever the facts were — for two-thirds of them this was joint custody, but 22 percent recommended refusal and 5 percent an adoption order (the remainder made no recommendation). The other guardians gave different recommendations as the circumstances changed. They showed considerable agreement about the seriousness with which they viewed different, favorable and adverse family situations. Thus, where the applicants' relationship was well established, more favored adoption and fewer refusal, but the converse was true where the noncustodial parent opposed the application or there was an older child in the family for whom no adoption application had been made.

For most of the guardians, completion of the report ended their active involvement in the case. Although they were required to attend the hearing, just a third of them were asked any questions by the judge; for the majority of these, this consisted only of inquiring whether they wished to add to their report. Almost all of the g.a.l.s thought that representing the child was an important part of their role, but it was not clear how they considered this could be achieved since only a third considered it an important part of their function to speak on behalf of the child at the hearing. In 1977 in *Re S,* the first reported Court of Appeal case on the provision restricting step-parent adoption, Ormrod L.J. said:

> It will also be necessary to examine carefully the motives of each of the adopters, and in this respect the court may require assistance from the guardian *ad litem* as the child's advocate in the form of cross examination.[31]

It is, however, difficult to see how the guardians *ad litem* could cross-examine the applicants. In the majority of cases the guardians whole-heartedly supported the application; there was no conflict between the guardian's view of the child's welfare and the order the applicants sought. Only in region 2 county courts did g.a.l.s ever play the part of advocate in court, and when they did so it was because of pressure put on them by the judge. This was resented by both the g.a.l.s and the social services department management staff, at least in part because they thought the judge was demanding more of scarce social work resources than these uncontested cases required. With some exceptions amongst those from regions 2 and 3, the g.a.l.s considered the hearings a mere formality — the important decisions had already been made.

THE JUDGES AND MAGISTRATES

The role of the judge is in theory much clearer than that of the guardian *ad litem*. In adoption, the judge is the decider of both issues of fact and of law. The judge is considered to need an informant — someone who can find out information which the applicants or the respondents might not put before the court. The recommendation by the Hurst Committee that only skilled social workers be appointed and the inclusion in the Court Rules of items requiring qualitative assessments suggest that the judge also needs an advisor. However, the question remains what the balance is between the judge and his advisor, the g.a.l. This is not easy to explore. It was not possible for the researchers to interview the judges about their views and practice as had been done with the g.a.l.s, nor was it possible to observe them conducting hearings.[32] The researchers were able to meet with some of the judges and discuss step-parent adoption with them; they also had information from interviews with g.a.l.s, court staff and applicants and, of course, the records of the sample cases. Table 27.2(a) shows the outcome of the cases in the Step-parent Adoption Study. By far the most common order made by the judges and magistrates was a full adoption order accounting for nearly 85 percent of all cases. Less than 5 percent of cases were refused. Table 27.2(b) provides the same information for *postdivorce* cases in the three regions. There was a significant difference between the regions, which was even more marked if only 1978 cases were considered.

TABLE 27.2   The Outcome of Step-Parent Adoption Cases (1975-1978)

(a) All Cases		(b) Postdivorce Cases by Region			
		Region 1	Region 2	Region 3	
Order	84.8	94.4	66.7	72.8	
Interview order	1.3	—	—	4.1	
Refused	2.7	1.7	6.0	7.7	
Adj. *sine die*	3.7	0.5	12.0	4.7	
Withdrawn	7.5	3.4	15.3	10.7	
	100.0	100.0	100.0	100.0	
N	(1,733)	(404)	(301)	(169)	(879)
		$x^2 = 134$ $p = 0.01\%$			

In their discussion with the researchers, the judges said nothing which suggested that they took a view of their role different from that laid down by the law. The guardians *ad litem* provided invaluable assistance when they did their work properly but were never considered to remove the judge's discretion. The views and experiences of the guardians *ad litem* and the applicants on this matter were somewhat different. Over 90 percent of the g.a.l.s thought that the judges gave either "a great deal" or "quite a lot" of weight to their report. Three-quarters of them had never had their recommendation disregarded and none stated that this had happened often. It was clear both from the few applicants interviewed and the g.a.l.s that the applicants considered it very important to obtain the support of the g.a.l. However, perhaps the most direct pointer to the influence of the g.a.l. was the information about the length of hearing (in very many cases the hearing lasted only a few minutes) and the data on recommendation and outcome.

THE DECISION-MAKING PROCESS

Table 27.3 shows that the judges agreed with the g.a.l.s in 94 percent of the cases where a full order was recommended but only 71 percent of cases where refusal was recommended. However, a further breakdown of the sample shows considerable differences in this pattern of decision making between the judges and magistrates, the types of step-parent adoption cases, and the regions in the study (see, below, Table 27.4).

TABLE 27.3 Recommendation and Outcome of the Step-parent Adoption Cases (1975–1978)

Outcome	No. rec. %	Order %	No order %	
Order	92.0	94.0	29.0	
No Order	8.0	6.0	71.0	
	100.0	100.0	100.0	
N	(401)	(1,140)	(55)	(1,596)[1]

[1] Excludes cases with an interim order or recommendation for an interim order.

The researchers hypothesized that the differences observed in the pattern of decision making related to differences in the balance of influence between the judge, the g.a.l. and the applicants. For example, the lay magistrates heard few cases and often had little experience of adoption so they might rely more heavily on the guardian *ad litem* than the county court judges did. Alternatively, the magistrates being "of the people" might sympathize with the wishes of the step-family more than would county court judges and make orders even when the g.a.l. recommended against it. The researchers constructed three models for the decision-making process, each identifying one possible set of the balance of influence. It was not thought that these models could account for every variation, rather that change occurred along a continuum on which the models marked three identifiable points.

1. The *legal model* The judge makes an individual exercise of discretion in each case using all the information including the guardian's report but coming to an independent decision on the merits of the case.
2. The *social work model* The guardian, through his recommendation

or the tenor of his report in the case, makes plain what decision he thinks would be in the best interests of the child. The judge merely adopts the guardian's decision when granting or refusing the order.
3. The *family model* The guardian does not assess each case individually but bases his recommendation or report entirely on what the family members want. Alternatively, the judge determines the case on the basis that the applicants and child want adoption and the other natural parent does not oppose it. He rubber-stamps not the guardian's recommendation but the application itself.

In the data, the *legal model* would be indicated where g.a.l.'s recommendations were more frequently ignored, the *social work model* where the court generally accepted the g.a.l.'s recommendation whatever it was, and the *family model* where the court accepted favorable but rejected unfavorable recommendations. Information about the way courts dealt with cases, particularly directions given by the judge, were used to assist the interpretation of the data.

Table 27.4 summarizes a series of tables which were originally produced for this analysis in the form of Table 27.3.

TABLE 27.4 Percentage of Cases in each Subsample where Outcome was the same as the g.a.l. Recommendation[1]

	Order %	No Order %
Court Type		
county court (all cases)	91.6	75.6
mags. court (all cases)	100.0	57.1
By Region		
county court region 1	98.2	50.0
county court region 2	82.0	100.0
county court region 3	94.9	68.0
mags. court region 1	100.0	100.0
mags. court region 2	100.0	50.0
mags. court region 3	100.0	57.1
Case Type[33]		
postdivorce	90.8	73.3
postdeath[2]	91.6	N/A
illegitimate	99.2	50.0
mixed	100.0	100.0
By Region		
postdivorce region 1	97.3	33.3
postdivorce region 2	80.4	81.2
postdivorce region 3	98.2	73.9

[1] Recommendation = outcome
[2] No recommendations were made in *postdeath* cases except for adoption orders.

This table shows the percentage of cases for each subsample where the outcome was the same as the g.a.l.'s recommendation. In general, where the g.a.l. recommended adoption more than 90 percent of cases resulted in an adoption order except in region 2. However, where the g.a.l. recommended refusal, the refusal rate varied between 33 percent and 100 percent. The figures in Table 27.4 suggest the *social work* model at least for the *mixed* cases and the magistrates' court cases in region 1. *Mixed* cases which involved the adoption of children from more than one different relationship included some of the most complex family circumstances. It is understandable that in these cases the court relied more heavily on the g.a.l. In region 1, most of the reports for the magistrates' court were prepared by a guardian who thought it was improper to give a specific recommendation; it is likely then that the magistrates would be more influenced by the few reports which included a recommendation. In the other magistrates' courts the pattern suggests that the *family model* applied. The magistrates always accepted recommendations for adoption but rejected about half those against it. The *family model* may well have been indicated elsewhere except in the county court cases (and *postdivorce* cases) in region 2 and possibly region 3. In region 2, where the county court judges held strong views against step-parent adoption, they directed the g.a.l.s to make wide-ranging inquiries with relatives and encouraged families to withdraw their applications and seek joint custody; in 1978 only 9 percent of *postdivorce* applications were successful in this court. These facts and the figures in Table 27.4 suggest the *legal model* operating almost as a reverse of the *family model*. The judges denied applications and this led to applicants being discouraged from applying by their legal advisors or information they obtained from the court or even the g.a.l. The process in region 3 was more complex, probably falling somewhere between the *social work model* and the *legal model*.

Variations in the operation of legal systems such as those described above are important if they produce injustice or if they indicate a flaw in the process itself. The research results, particularly the wide variation in the success rate of *postdivorce* step-parent adoptions, show that like cases were not treated alike. More importantly, the discussion above suggests that the process was not successful in distinguishing cases where adoption was not appropriate from other cases. This was due to a large number of factors. Lack of training, experience and time on the part of the g.a.l.s led to poor quality of work; lack of experience or even too much experience on the part of judges and magistrates led them often to accept the reports without question. The fact that the reports were confidential to the court meant that neither the applicants nor the respondents could query them, so they went unchallenged in the courts. The lack of standards for child welfare in these cases and of a clear, accepted rationale for the restriction of step-parent adoption made it difficult for both the g.a.l.s and the judges to handle cases consistently. For some, particularly, these lacks made it difficult to recommend against or to refuse unopposed applications. The fact that applications had traditionally been granted without difficulty made it even harder to refuse them.

REFORM

How then could the procedure for decision making be improved? First there must be more consideration of the roles of the judges and the social worker working for the court. If the judge needs an adviser, then the social worker's place should be firmly set on the bench as part of a court panel of decision makers. If not, clear rules must be set which ensure that the social worker's report truly presents both sides of the case and provides details of how much time was spent and what actions were taken to obtain the information so that others may make some assessments of the conclusions reached. The existence of a number of diverse aspects of the role of guardian *ad litem*-investigator for the court, advisor to the court, and child's representative perhaps suggests that more than one person is needed to perform these tasks if there is to be no internal conflict. Secondly, action needs to be taken to ensure that those involved in the process are accountable for their actions. This could include opening the reports to the parties to the case and ending closed hearings. There are some dangers in both of these which should not be minimized but must be balanced against the requirements of justice. Thirdly, both the social worker and the judges who handle cases concerning children should be specially trained and skilled in the issues involved. This may mean limiting the courts where cases can be heard and requiring direct appointment by the court of the social workers involved.[34]

It is not suggested that judicial discretion be replaced with rules. Rules are not appropriate for intimate, intricate and intractable family disputes although they may serve a purpose in assisting the family members to limit conflict. However, the degree of state involvement in family matters needs to be reviewed. State regulation of consensual divorce, custody agreement and uncontested step-parent adoption[35] has served to bring the state and the law into family life more deeply than into marriage or on the birth of a child. If there is no dispute, the state's interest is the protection of children, presumably from their parents' decisions. There are fundamental questions whether this itself can be justified, but leaving those aside the state should always be required to show accepted criteria for the decisions and a fair method of decision making before it may act. While the skilled social work and judicial resources are limited, it is wasteful to spend these on decisions which often only second guess the family. Efforts should be concentrated on cases where families or children need help because there are disputes, and on cases where there are decisions which can only be taken outside the family.

NOTES

1. The results of the research will appear in a book entitled, *Yours Mine or Ours,* to be published in England (forthcoming).
2. *Children Act 1975* s. 105 required that the legislation be monitored and reports presented to Parliament.
3. The first reports of step-parent adoption appear in (1927) 91 J. P. at 695.
4. The Association of Child Care Officers (ACCO) and the Standing Conference of Societies Registered for Adoption (SCSRA). Houghton Committee: *Report of the Departmental Committee on the Adoption of Children* (1972; Cmnd. 5107).
5. *Matrimonial Causes Act 1973* s. 52(1); *Children Act 1975* s. 10(3), "Where the [Adoption] application is made to a court in England or Wales and the married couple consist of a parent and step-parent of the child, the court shall dismiss the application if it considers the matter would be better dealt with under Section 42 (orders for custody, etc.) of the Matrimonial Causes Act 1973."
6. The other types of step-parent adoption were termed *postdeath*: parent applicant remarries after other parent has died; *illegitimate:* unmarried parent marries step-parent; *mixed:* children being adopted coming from different relationships, e.g.,parent has child, marries, has second child, divorces, remarries, parent and step-parent adopt both children.
7. OPCS, *Adoption Monitor, FM3* (published annually).
8. *Re B* [1975] 2 All E. R. 449, (1977) 141 J. P. 97–98, 561.
9. Adoption (County Court) Rules 1976 r. 9, a similar rule applies in magistrates' courts.
10. See Cox, "Step-parent Adoptions: Procedure in the Juvenile Court," (1978) 142 J. P. 56–57.
11. No reapplication may be made without the consent of the court, *Children Act 1975* s. 22(4).
12. Adoption (County Court) Rules 1976 r. 10.
13. In 1954, the Hurst Committee made it clear that the g.a.l.'s ultimate responsibility was to the court. Hurst Committee: *Report of the Departmental Committee on the Adoption of Children* (1954; Cmnd. 9248), Part II 3.74, 20.
14. Home Office, etc., *A Guide to Adoption Practice,* H.M.S.O. (1970), 106.
15. *Supra,* n. 13 at 3.76, 20.
16. Adoption (County Court) Rules r. 10(2).
17. Adoption (County Court) Rules, Sched. 2.
18. *Supra,* n. 14.
19. LAC 76 (22); (23).
20. J. Rowe, *Parents, Children and Adoption,* RKP (1966) A. Leeding, *The Guardian ad litem and Adoption,* ABAFA (1978).
21. In region 1, the report was checked by staff of the agency's central Adoption Unit. Some reports were rewritten and the researchers were told of one instance where the recommendation was changed.

22. For example, most region 1 and 2 g.a.l.s received agency directives requiring them to make both the case for and the case against adoption, but reports were routinely accepted which did not do this.

23. Applicants were spoken to by a member of the court clerical staff about the difficulties surrounding adoption when they went to apply; by the g.a.l., by the registrar at a preliminary hearing and by the judge. Orders were generally granted to the persistent, but a number of would-be applicants were dissuaded.

24. *Supra*, n. 20 at 265.

25. His agreement to the adoption is not required *Re M* [1955] 2 All E. R. 911 nor is he a respondent, Adoption (County Court) Rules 1976 r. 4(2).

26. E. Ctrey and R. Blunden, *A Survey of Adoption in Great Britain*, Home Office Research Study No. 10, H.M.S.O. (1971).

27. The hypothetical case was based on *Re S* [1977] 2 All E. R. 671, see *infra*, n. 30.

28. *Supra*, n. 14 at 280.

29. Platt, "The Guardian *ad litem* in Step-Parent Adoptions," (1979) 96 No. 2 *Adoption and Fostering*, 46. (There are no qualifications for a British T.V. licence, only payment!)

30. *Supra*, n. 27 The alternative factual circumstances presented included: (1) the applicants were expecting another child; (2) eighteen months cohabitation by applicants prior to their recent marriage; (3) opposition to the adoption from the natural father; (4) ... from the paternal relatives; (5) the female applicant had, as well as the child in respect of whom adoption was sought, a sixteen and a half year old daughter.

31. *Re S* [1977] 2 All E. R. 671 at 676c–d.

32. These limitations imposed on the public and on researchers are intended to protect the judiciary and the applicants.

33. *Supra*, n. 6.

34. There are plans to provide panels of social workers who will act as g.a.l.s D.H.S.S. Joint Working Parties on Costing, *The Cost of Implementing the Unimplemented Sections of the Children Act 1975*, DHSS (1980).

35. The author does not propose that the rights of noncustodial parents should be removed without a hearing, rather that step-parents should be able to acquire some legal recognition *without* court proceedings.

Chapter Twenty-eight

Towards a Natural History of Access Arrangements in Broken Marriages

Adrian L. James and Kate Wilson

Department of Social Administration, University of Hull
England

At first sight, the arrangements that are made following the breakdown of a marriage for the parent who does not retain custody of the children to maintain contact with them would appear a far less contentious issue than the actual decision as to which parent should have custody. However, our own experience as probation officers (who in this country may be asked by the court to prepare welfare reports on matters of custody and access, and whose advice may be sought independently by couples deciding to separate or divorce) led us to the view that this was not so. Indeed, it suggested that there might be greater ambiguity or at least uncertainty surrounding the principles on which the courts reach decisions about access, and greater friction caused within the family by the very nature of access arrangements, which require parties regularly to be involved in mutual decisions about their children. In addition, it was our impression that this is an area which receives little direct attention during training and that social workers, in undertaking this work, are thrown back on the trial and error of their own experience and the collective folk wisdom of the social work profession. The "collective folk wisdom," would seem on the whole to support the view that continued contact between separated parents and the children is not only the right of the noncustodial parent but, crucially, is in the best interests of the children. Such "wisdom" sometimes appears at variance, both with the beliefs and wishes of certain members of the families involved, and with the views expressed in some of the limited literature that touches on the subject. As probation officers, for example, we were frequently faced with the reluctance of the custodial parent to allow the noncustodial parent access to the children, on the grounds that the episodes were upsetting to, or not wanted by, the children; or, if access was to be permitted, an insistence on placing certain restrictions on it (such as location, who the child should be allowed to see, and so on). This view of the possible undesirability of access is given support in one of the few books which addresses itself to the topic and which has evidently been widely read by probation officers, *Beyond the Best Interests of the Child,* which recommends that "the non-custodial parent should have no legally enforceable right to visit and the custodial parent should have the right to decide whether it is desirable for the child to have such visits" (Goldstein, Freud and Solnit 1973).

The research we are currently undertaking with the probation service in a region in Northeast England represents an attempt to gain more information about this aspect of marital breakdown, and in this chapter we discuss some of the background problems and issues raised by it, and give a preliminary account of our findings as far as they are available.

In this country, an order concerning access has no legal standing on its own, but can only be made by a court as an addition to a custody order. The access may be left undefined under the broad provision for "reasonable access," or in situations where there appears to be greater conflict between the parties, conditions may be set concerning the detail of arrangements, such as location, duration and frequency of contact and whether it may or may not involve staying overnight. Furthermore, the court may require the probation service to supervise the arrangements for access, or may even make the child the subject of a supervision order where this appears to be in the interests of the child's welfare.

Recent decisions by the courts concerning the granting of access suggest that the uncertainties about the right to and the desirability of access which we discerned in our work are reflected in the attitudes of the courts. As Martin Wilkinson (1981) points out, while it might be expected that the courts would approach the question of access on the basis of the need to discover whether it is in the particular child's interest for it to be granted (given the requirement in section 1 of *Guardianship of Minors Act, 1971,* that "the court . . . shall regard the welfare of the minor as the first and paramount consideration"), in fact there is a powerful initial assumption that access should be granted, and compelling evidence is necessary if it is to be disallowed. Although, as Wilkinson (1981, 56–57) argues, the courts appear to have moved from the point (in *S v. S,* 1962) when access was seen as "in the ordinary way . . . the basic right of any parent" to the point (in *M v. M,* 1973) where it is seen as "a basic right in the child rather than a basic right in the parent," (nonetheless the granting of access is still seen as something which should be denied only in exceptional circumstances. Of course, as we discuss later in the chapter, the courts in the majority of cases tend to ratify existing arrangements (suggesting that these are not in dispute at the time of the court hearing), and it is arguable that because of the minimal conflict evident, there is little pressure on the courts to question their assumptions concerning its desirability.

Much useful background information to the legal context in which access is decided is contained in *Custody After Divorce* (Eekelaar and Clive 1977), which presents the findings of a study conducted by the Centre for Socio-Legal Studies of a total of 855 divorces in 1975 in England, Wales and Scotland. This study revealed that access was provided for in 55 percent of the sample but that conditions were placed on its exercise in only 4.5 percent of those instances (para 5.7). It also comments that one explanation for the remaining 45 percent of cases is that a court may prefer to make no order but leave it to the parties to make their own arrangements. Equally important to our study is the finding that access was specifically denied in only three cases out of the whole sample. The study also revealed a strong tendency on the part of the courts to preserve the *status quo* — i.e., to ratify the arrangements already made by the parties (para 13.14). It therefore becomes of central importance to explore the way in which such arrangements are negotiated, and in view of the fact that welfare reports were available in 8.2 percent of uncontested cases (para 4.6) and 53 percent of contested cases (tot. 11.3 percent of all cases) the view and perspectives of probation officers also appear an important area for investigation. Furthermore, the study shows a rapid fall-off in the exercise of access in the first twelve months of separation and an increased incidence of infrequent access, but the researchers are not in a position to offer an hypothesis as to the explanation for this.

That probation officers have an increasingly important role to play in decisions concerning the care of children following marriage breakdown is unarguable. Although matrimonial conciliation work undertaken by the probation service has decreased markedly in recent years, from 32,598 referrals in 1973 to 8,829 referrals in 1980, the number of children subject to supervision following matrimonial wardship, guardianship or divorce proceedings has increased steadily both absolutely (from 11,545 in 1973 to 16,003 in 1980) and proportionately (8 percent of total cases in 1973 to 9 percent in 1980). In addition, there has been a marked increase of nearly 40 percent in the number of inquiries concerning custody of and access to children, from 14,818 in 1973 to 20,475 in 1980 (Home Office 1981). In a medium-sized probation area such as ours in the Northeast, this is reflected by an increase in such reports from 244 in 1974 to 484 in 1978. This situation is a clear reflection of the generally rising divorce rate — it has been estimated that something like one million children are currently affected by divorcing parents with three out of every four divorces involving children.

While much research about divorce has been done, much of this is concerned primarily with overall rates and trends, with only passing attention being given to particular problems of access and custody. Also, while the presence of a broken marriage in a child's background has frequently been a variable in research into delinquent and neurotic behaviour, we have been able to identify little research which deals specifically with the impact of access on children's behaviour. Yet in the view of many of those personally involved, it is the continuation of contact with the parent who has left home, and in circumstances that are often coloured by uncertainty and discomfort, that gives rise to stress and unhappiness in the child. This belief is to some extent supported by the work done on the impact of separation upon children. Rutter (1972, 108) for example, in assessing the research on this suggests "that it may be the discord and disharmony preceding the break (rather than the break itself) which led to the children developing anti-social behaviour," concluding that "it is distortion of relationships rather than bond disruption as such which causes the damage." In an earlier study of children referred to psychiatric clinics, Rutter (1966, 81–82) similarly observes that broken marriages have been shown "to be associated with psychiatric disorder in the children (the association is probably related to conditions accompanying the 'break-up' rather than to the disruption itself)." More recently, Phillips (1979, 252) observed that "Many studies have shown that the parents' emotional state affects the child so that even a very young infant is sensitive to stress, anxiety, conflict, uncertainty, and a lack of affection from parents." Although, of course, these studies are concerned with the impact of separation on children, their findings would seem to support our contention that the question of permitting access is more problematic than it might first be held to be. With many separated couples the fact of access, with its reminders of the past, its underlining (where custody has been in dispute) of the actual situation, the need it imposes for two people who have probably been in considerable conflict to reach joint decisions about management, and its uncertainties, is a ripe source of potential conflict. If it is indeed the case that children are most vulnerable to stress in separation when that separation is marked by conflict and uncertainty; then even though we are no longer concerned with the separation itself, contact with the other parent might well be thought to perpetuate the conflicts surrounding the actual separation.

Further evidence of the complex emotions and decisions that are involved in the question of contact with the noncustodial parent lies in the fact that although, as was mentioned earlier, the courts tend to ratify existing arrangements for access, in a large number of cases the contact is not sustained and the arrangements subsequently break down. This raises a number of questions concerning the way in which the access arrangements are made, the kind of exploratory discussions and support that are available to both parents, and the effects on the children of a contact which gradually diminishes and then ceases altogether, presumably with little or no explanation. Our concern about the frequency with which this occurs is supported by some of the work of Wallerstein and Kelly (1980, 311) who comment that their findings "regarding the centrality of both parents to the psychological health of children and adolescents alike leads us to hold that, where possible, divorcing parents should be encouraged and helped to shape postdivorce arrangements which permit and foster continuity in the children's relations with both parents." Their conclusions, of course, are at variance with those of Goldstein, Freud and Solnit (1973) (whose work however is not a research-based study but a theoretical exercise based on premises which are far from universally accepted), and serve to highlight the lack of consensus about such issues and to underline the importance of understanding not only the impact of marital breakdown on families, but of those factors which contribute to the negotiation of successful access arrangements.

The only major piece of research to date in this country is that conducted by Murch (1980) who highlights the problems for professional workers in this area of practice which are "partly because there is, as yet, insufficient empirical evidence upon which to formulate reliable guidelines for practitioners" (67). This research found that there were many instances in which parents reported disturbances of one kind or another in their children's behaviour, although "More usually these referred to general disturbance caused by the parents' separation or even to the marital tensions that had preceded it. Only a few parents attributed disturbances specifically to access arrangements" (84). Murch concludes that access problems are often symptomatic of the fundamental problems facing divorcing parents of "how to disengage from the broken marriage while preserving a sense of being a parent with a part to play in the children's future" (93).

It seemed to us, therefore, that there were many issues surrounding the continued contact between separated parent and child that needed to be explored. The problems however in mounting such an investigation are considerable, involving as it does enquiry into matters that are highly sensitive and confidential, access to an appropriate sample, problems of comparability, or of comparability and availability over time, and so on. In addition, we felt so little was known about the actual process by which access arrangements were made, that until certain base information was available, it would be difficult to identify those crucial questions which demanded further exploration. We therefore decided to mount a limited project in conjunction with the probation service, which would obtain information of a factual nature about the early stages in which access arrangements are established — in a sense, the first moves in delineating a natural history of access. Through this, we aimed to throw more light on the ways in which these arrangements are made, and to see whether there were any common processes in the manner in which these decisions were reached or the arrangements sustained. We would then hope to be able to develop hypotheses about the processes which seemed to make it likely that access would be sustained or would break down, and to say something about the kinds of outside intervention that might contribute positively to their being satisfactorily worked out. We hope subsequently, in a second study involving a follow-up of couples over a period of time, to test out the hypotheses formulated from our current project.

We have asked all those probation officers in the region who prepare divorce court welfare reports during a given period, to complete a detailed questionnaire concerning the breakdown of the marriage, custody and access to the children, and a number of related topics which may prove of relevance to the ways in which access arrangements are negotiated and maintained. This process will continue until a sample of approximately 100 completed questionnaires has been obtained (a figure chosen as being large enough to allow us to carry out certain statistical tests and small enough for us to hope to complete the sample within a reasonable time scale). We chose this point in the decision-making process since the evidence suggests that the majority of court judgments merely ratify arrangements that have already been made (so that the actual court decision is not usually crucial to the process), and because it offered some means of ensuring that the couples involved were, in at least one sense, at a similar stage in the process of separation. There is of course wide variation in the point during the marriage breakdown at which people reach the divorce court, and in the timing of the welfare report. Again to try and ensure comparability, and that the events were reasonably fresh in respondents' minds, we stipulated that no more than a given time should have elapsed between the couple's physical separation and their application for divorce.

As a concomitant to this information, we felt that it was important to know something about those involved in preparing the reports, i.e., the probation officers, since they can be influential in the decision-making process and because they are acting as our agents in the principle area of our research. We were interested to discover the procedures they adopt in preparing reports on custody and access, their knowledge and value base concerning access and their training background, in order to see whether there is any link between these and the kinds of recommendations that they make. A questionnaire was therefore sent to each officer in the research region.

FINDINGS

At this stage in our research, our findings are only tentative and our comments relate to an initial analysis of sets of data which are at different stages of completeness. In the case of the probation officers' self-administered questionnaire, our returns are virtually complete. In the case of our main questionnaire, completed by probation officers preparing welfare reports on each family meeting our criteria, we have so far received less than a quarter of the number upon which we hope to base our final analysis. The sample is therefore comparatively small at this stage and any apparent trends must be treated with caution.

Probation Officer Sample

The figures presented below need to be treated with some caution as they are based on only fifty-five responses out of a possible establishment of eighty probation officers in the county service studied. We hope eventually to improve upon this figure slightly, but at this stage, small differences must be treated with caution and since we do not know how representative this service is of probation officers nationally (excepting with regard to length of service), any generalizations must be qualified and can only apply to the service concerned.

The main problem caused by the 69 percent response rate is knowing to what extent, if any, those who did not reply are different from those who did. One criterion by which it has been possible to test this is length of service, which we have been able to ascertain for the total establishment, and with the exception of the group with the shortest length of service (all of whom responded), the nonrespondents are distributed amongst all of the remaining groups. It is therefore unlikely that they have adversely influenced the results as far as length of service is concerned. They may of course be atypical in other respects, but we have no means of testing this. There appears to be some evidence however that length of service is an important variable and we can therefore have some confidence that, where we have examined other variables by length of service, it is reasonably safe to apply these results to the whole of area studied.

In order further to minimize any possible bias or distortion resulting from nonrespondents, we have regrouped the data into service of less than five years, five to ten years, and over ten years. More work is still to be done on the data and what follows are only our initial findings. Occasionally, the figures do not add up to the appropriate total — this is because some questions were not answered and this data is missing. The number of responses upon which the percentages are based will be shown throughout however.

The probation service in the area studied does not appear to be typical of the national picture in terms of the growth of the service. Nationally, based on growth figures for the probation service (Home Office 1976) from 3,426 in 1970, to 4,869 in 1975 and 5,304 in 1979 (full-time staff of all grades), there are 35 percent of officers with up to ten years of service and only 8 percent with less than five years. In the study area, however, 65 percent have up to ten years of service and some 40 percent have less than five years. It is quite clear, therefore, that the area has a comparatively large proportion of more recently trained officers, a fact which may present certain unique problems, particularly in terms of induction and in-service training needs. If length of service is tabulated with whether or not officers had any training specifically concerned with marital breakdown and its impact on children (Table 28.1) this view tends to be confirmed. This must clearly be of concern to those in social work education, but also to those responsible for this important area of work within the probation service. Moreover, in-service training does not appear to have been provided in a way which would meet this particular problem for less experienced officers, (Table 28.2), or in a way which takes into account whether or not an officer has already received training in this area of work.

TABLE 28.1   Length of Service by Training in Marital Breakdown

Service	Training	No Training	Total
<5 yrs	3(13)	20(87)	23(100)*
5–10 yrs	4(25)	12(75)	16(100)
>10 yrs	7(50)	7(50)	14(100)
	14(26)	39(74)	53(100)

*% figures in brackets throughout.

TABLE 28.2   Length of Service by In-Service Training

Service	Yes	No	Total
<5 yrs	6(26)	17(74)	23(100)
5–10yrs	7(44)	9(56)	16(100)
>10 yrs	4(29)	10(71)	14(100)
	17(32)	36(68)	53(100)

Probation officers were also asked about whether or not there was a need for more training (Table 28.3) and if so, what priority should be given to this (Table 28.4), 86 percent perceiving there to be a need for more training. The responses to this question are not related to length of service or whether or not an officer has already had training. There is however a clear trend (Table 28.4) for those with less service to accord a higher priority to the provision of additional training, although this also is not related to whether or not an officer has already had training. This may partly be explained by the trend for officers to be asked to undertake their first divorce court welfare report earlier during their service than used to be the case (Table 28.5) and by the fact that although none of the respondents regarded divorce court welfare reports as less difficult than criminal social enquiry reports, longer serving officers do regard them as less difficult than officers with less service (Table 28.6).

TABLE 28.3 Length of Service by Need for More Training

Service	Yes	No	Total
<5 yrs	21(95)	1(5)	22(100)
5–10 yrs	13(81)	3(19)	16(100)
>10 yrs	11(79)	3(21)	14(100)
	45(87)	7(13)	52(100)

TABLE 28.4 Length of Service by Priority to More Training

Service	High	Medium	Low	Total
<5 yrs	14(64)	6(27)	2(9)	22(100)
5–10 yrs	8(67)	3(25)	1(8)	12(100)
>10 yrs	3(27)	7(64)	1(9)	11(100)
	25(56)	16(36)	4(9)	45(100)

TABLE 28.5 Length of Service by Time before First Report

Service	<12 mnths	1–2 yrs	>2 yrs	Total
<5 yrs	13(68)	6(32)	0(0)	19(100)
–10 yrs	7(50)	5(36)	2(14)	14(100)
>10 yrs	3(27)	4(36)	4(36)	11(100)
	23(52)	15(34)	6(14)	44(100)

TABLE 28.6 Length of Service by Difficulty of Reports

Service	Much more	More	Same	Total
<5 yrs	11(52)	8(38)	2(10)	21(100)
5–10 yrs	9(60)	6(40)	0(0)	15(100)
>10 yrs	2(14)	9(64)	3(21)	14(100)
	22(44)	23(46)	5(10)	50(100)

Length of service therefore appears to be an important factor in determining some of the responses, but although it is clearly related to whether or not officers have had training specifically for work with marital breakdown, it is not related to their use of theory in practice. Table 28.7 however, shows that although the use of theory amongst those with training is not as high as might perhaps be expected, there is a trend for those who have had such training to be better able to identify specific areas of theory which they use in their practice, which might suggest that the conscious use of theory declines with length of service, resulting in the high proportion of officers seeing a need for extra training regardless of length of service (Table 27.3).

Towards a Natural History of Access Arrangements in Broken Marriages 445

TABLE 28.7 Training by Use of Theory

Training	Use of theory Yes	No	Total
Yes	8(53)	7(47)	15(100)
No	12(31)	27(69)	39(100)
	20(37)	34(63)	54(100)

But although over 80 percent of officers thought the probation service should be more actively involved in offering advice or counselling over access arrangements (Table 28.8), no clear relationship has emerged with length of service, although there is some evidence that those with less service are more likely to want increased involvement by the service. Of those with five to ten years however, 93 percent thought there should be increased involvement, a response which may be the result of other practice issues which have not been considered. Although much of the foregoing may appear peripheral to our previously stated concerns, it is of central importance in so far as it indicates by implication some important beliefs held by the probation officers acting as our agents in this research. They appear to feel undertrained for what they see as a challenging area of work in which the majority would like to be more extensively involved. It might perhaps therefore be inferred that they have an interest in and commitment to the research.

TABLE 28.8 Length of Service by Need for more Involvement

Service	Yes	No	Total
<5 yrs	19(86)	3(14)	22(100)
5–10 yrs	14(93)	1(7)	15(100)
>10 yrs	9(69)	4(31)	13(100)
	42(84)	8(16)	50(100)

The probation officers' views of and practice in relation to other involved professionals also produced some interesting responses. Over 77 percent of our respondents regarded it as their task to make recommendations to the court concerning both custody and access, regardless of length of service or whether they had training or not, and the remainder saw it as their task to present their reports in such a way as to indicate an opinion and suggest courses of action to the court. Our respondents viewed the courts' ability to give sufficient weight to the children's interests in divorce proceedings as quite high (Table 28.9), although longer serving officers appear to be less satisfied in this respect. Parents were seen as able to give sufficient weight to children's interests only sometimes by 84 percent of respondents, but 45 percent saw solicitors as never giving them sufficient weight (Table 28.10). The figures concerning parents tend to support a view of reduced parenting ability during divorce proceedings while the apparent view of solicitors suggests that they may be seen as being retained by and therefore representing only parental interests which it could be argued might, in the case of a dispute over custody or access, be contrary to the children's interests. When we examine these perspectives by whether or not officers have had training specifically in the area of marital breakdown (Tables 28.11 and 28.12) an interesting picture emerges regarding the probation officers' views of the welfare orientation of solicitors and courts. Those without such training appear to have a more negative view of solicitors and a more positive view of courts in this respect than do those who have had training. Taking length of service into account, this trend does not disappear and it is therefore related more to training than to length of service.

TABLE 28.9 Length of Service by Weight Given to Children's Interests by the Court

Service	Yes	Sometimes	No	Total
<5 yrs	15(71)	6(29)	0(0)	21(100)
5–10 yrs	8(50)	6(38)	2(12)	16(100)
>10 yrs	6(43)	8(57)	0(0)	14(100)
	29(57)	20(39)	2(4)	51(100)

TABLE 28.10 Sufficient Weight Given to Children's Interests

	Yes	Sometimes	No	Total
By parents	2(4)	43(84)	6(12)	51(100)
By solicitors	1(2)	27(53)	23(45)	51(100)

TABLE 28.11 Training by Weight Given to Children's Interests by Solicitor

Training	Yes	Sometimes	No	Total
Yes	0(0)	13(87)	2(13)	15(100)
No	1(3)	15(39)	22(58)	38(100)
	1(2)	28(53)	24(45)	53(100)

TABLE 28.12 Training by Weight Given to Children's Interests by Court

Training	Yes	Sometimes	No	Total
Yes	7(47)	8(53)	0(0)	15(100)
No	24(63)	12(32)	2(5)	38(100)
	31(58)	20(38)	2(4)	53(100)

We attempted to shed light upon whether there is any difference between probation officers' views of the weight which the court does give to the interests of parents and children, and the weight the court should give. Our respondents were all of the opinion that the custodial parent's interests were given sufficient weight and over half thought the interests of the noncustodial parent and the children, regardless of age, were also given sufficient weight by the court. Of those who thought the court should alter, the majority thought that more weight should be given to the interests of children, particularly in the six-to-twelve age group, and that some additional weight should be given to the interests of the non-custodial parent and children of other ages. In so far as courts tend to uphold the *status quo* in their decisions concerning custody and access, the parent with *de facto* custody is clearly in the stronger position and there is some feeling among our respondents that the balance should be adjusted to give greater weight to the interests of the noncustodial parent and the children.

Officers were also asked about their enquiry practice in relation to divorcing families. The responses to these questions were incomplete in too many cases for them to be conclusive and we are currently seeking further information about this important area of practice. The picture which is beginning to emerge, however, particularly in terms of the ages at which children are interviewed in the course of divorce court welfare enquiries and also in terms of other agencies contacted, is of considerable variation in practice between officers. What has also emerged, however, is that over 18 percent of officers always offer advice over access arrangements during the course of their enquiries, prior to any formal court decision, and that over 77 percent sometimes offer such advice, suggesting a substantial if unrecorded involvement of a counselling or conciliatory nature. As Table 28.8 showed, over 80 percent thought the probation service should increase its involvement in this area of activity, 41 percent giving this a high priority and 49 percent medium priority.

The above findings give some important background understanding of the training and attitudes of the probation officers in the area studied, which is of interest because they are providing data from their divorce court enquiries about families who are currently going through the divorce experience, through which we hope to increase our understanding of the dynamic human processes involved in such problems as negotiating access arrangements.

Divorcing Families Sample

Several important caveats must be made concerning the data we have received so far from probation officers about divorcing families. Completed questionnaires have so far been returned at a much slower rate than we had hoped and the discussion which follows is based on an initial analysis of twenty-five cases. The sample is highly selected, from cases proceeding to the divorce court, according to strict criteria — cases where the parties have been physically separated for longer than twenty-seven months, where the children were not all living with one parent, and where there has been no contact between the noncustodial parent and the children, have been excluded. These criteria were felt to be necessary in order to study the issues with which we are concerned, but have been partly responsible for the slow collection of data. It might also be argued that since difficult contested cases tend to be the subject of welfare reports, the cases being studied are biased in this respect also, and that there are a large number of cases in which welfare reports are not requested where one can therefore draw no conclusions at all.

In addition, it must be remembered that these data are not collected first hand but through probation officers whose attitudes may be important in interpreting some of the data. It must also be recognized that these are the results of *predivorce* enquiries, made of people who may be trying to influence the final outcome of the divorce process through the probation officer and the information and advice he offers to the court. It is impossible to determine the extent to which these factors have distorted the data, but in so far as the same data are used by the probation officer to construct his report and recommendations, they provide a valid and valuable base from which to proceed.

Of the twenty-five cases available for analysis so far, there are fourteen cases in which the custody of the children is contested. The age range of the parties is from twenty-three to fifty-three; in fifteen cases they are in their thirties. This is slightly older than the peak age for divorce nationally, which is twenty-five to twenty-nine (Office of Population Census and Surveys 1979). In sixteen cases, the marriage was ten to fifteen years old and in five cases more than fifteen years duration. In thirteen cases the husbands were unemployed. In eleven cases, the husband has stayed in the matrimonial home and in only eight has the wife remained there.

There are fifty-eight children (twenty-three boys, thirty-five girls) in the sample, the majority of whom are between the ages of six and twelve, (Table 28.13). The highest number of children in any family was four.

TABLE 28.13 Distribution of Children by Age

13–18	11
9–12	17
6– 8	18
2– 5	9
0– 2	3
N =	58

In nineteen cases the children live with the mother and in the other six with the father. In all of these six cases, however, custody is being contested by the mother. In only three cases had either party been married previously and in all but one case the children are of the marriage. Only seven cases reported there being previous separations and in four of these access had occurred. All twenty-five cases met the criterion of having been separated twenty-seven months or less when the probation officer made contact, and 50 percent had been separated for twelve months or less. The wives in the sample tended to report more preseparation discord in the marriage (fourteen cases) than the husbands (nine cases) and in no case did the husbands report more than the wife. Similarly, nine husbands but only one wife reported the breakdown of the marriage to be completely unexpected.

With regard to the decision regarding initial custody and where the children should live, in fifteen (60 percent) cases this was reached by mutual agreement, six (24 percent) being decided unilaterally. In sixteen (64 percent) cases, some or great difficulty was experienced in reaching this decision but in eight (32 percent) cases this process was seen as amicable. The children were not consulted at all in eleven (44 percent) cases, but in the remainder, one or both parents sought the views of the children, and in seven (50 percent) of these cases the children's views are reported as having influenced the decision greatly, and in a further six (43 percent) cases as having partially influenced the decision. In seventeen (68 percent) cases these arrangements had not altered since the couple separated.

The attitudes of the custodial and noncustodial parent to each other were rated on a five point scale ranging from warm to hostile. In thirteen (52 percent) cases, these were rated intermediately but in seven (28 percent) cases they were towards the hostile end of the scale. The attitude of the custodial parent towards the relationship between the noncustodial parent and the children was also rated on a five point scale, ranging from accepting to resentful, and seventeen (68 percent) cases were towards the accepting end of the scale, indicating a good level of acceptance of the relationship between the children and the absent parent. The attitude of the noncustodial parent was also positive in this respect in nineteen (76 percent) cases.

In eighteen (72 percent) cases, the custodial parent was recorded as being favorably disposed towards access, the remainder being at the midpoint on a five point scale or below. In slight contrast, all but two of the noncustodial parents are rated at the mid-point or above, with sixteen (64 percent) being reported as being strongly in favor.

Information has also been sought about the existence and possible influence of extramarital relationships on the breakdown of the marriages and subsequent attitudes towards access. In twelve (48 percent) cases the custodial parent currently has a relationship with another person, this being a factor in the breakdown of the marriage in seven (28 percent) cases. In thirteen (52 percent) cases the noncustodial parent also currently has such a relationship and in seven (28 percent) cases it was a factor in the breakdown of the marriage. In the majority of our twenty-five cases, however, this does not appear to have influenced the level of reporting of preseparation discord or subsequent attitudes to access. Also, in the majority (over 64 percent) of cases the third party is reported as being in favor of access.

In looking at probation officers' opinions about the general response of children to the separation of their parents (Table 28.14), nearly half of the children showed no clear reaction either for or against, with seventeen reacting negatively and only seven reacting positively. There are however some indications in this small number of cases that the nine-to-twelve age group may be overrepresented among those children who are seen as responding negatively.

TABLE 28.14 Response of Children to Parental Separation

			Positive 3	2	1	Negative
Child	oldest	A	5	13	6	
		B	1	8	9	
		C	2	4	3	
	youngest	D	–	1	–	
			8	26	18	

N = 52 (6 missing cases)

In assessing the response of children to the absence of the noncustodial parent, there appear to be very few extreme responses; but where unhappiness was reported, it affected the older children in each family.

Information was also sought on the incidence of specific behaviour disorders (bed-wetting, soiling, non-school attendance, school resistance, temper tantrums, thefts, eating difficulties, sleeping difficulties or other regressive behaviour) among the children — postseparation, during the twelve months prior to separation, or at any previous period (Table 28.15).

TABLE 28.15 Incidence of Behavioural/Emotional Disorders

None	7
Postseparation	10
Preseparation	2
Any pre- and postseparation	6

In only ten (40 percent) cases do such problems appear to be associated with the separation of the parents and in all of these cases school resistance was one of the reported problems. There appear to be very few extremes of attitude among any of the children towards the absence of the noncustodial parent; but where unhappiness was reported, it affected the older children in each family.

In fourteen (56 percent) cases, there had been some geographical disruption for the children as a result of their parents' separation, but in only three cases was it felt that the location of the new home was likely to create problems for the noncustodial parent in sustaining regular access. In ten (40 percent) cases, however, this had resulted in changes of schools, playmates, or play areas for the children, and in ten (40 percent) cases reduction or loss of contact with the extended family of the noncustodial parent had resulted. There were no cases reported of any of the fifty-eight children feeling stigmatized by the breakdown of their parents' marriage.

In only five cases had the question of access already been decided by a court. In fifteen (60 percent) of the cases, access had been negotiated solely between the parties and in three cases a probation officer was also involved. There was only one reported case of a solicitor being involved. The difficulty in reaching an agreement was rated on a five point scale, from no problem to very difficult. In eleven (44 percent) cases it was rated towards the no-problem end of the scale, suggesting that comparatively few problems had been reported in negotiating access arrangements. The children had been consulted in sixteen (64 percent) cases, compared with fourteen (56 percent) cases of consultation over the initial decision regarding custody, and in twelve (48 percent) cases the children's wishes are reported to have greatly influenced the decision. This tends to support the view of the majority of probation officers mentioned earlier, that parents are not necessarily incapable of giving sufficient weight to the interests of the children during the divorce process.

In fourteen (56 percent) cases, however, access arrangements were subsequently altered, suggesting that some difficulties had been experienced. In ten (40 percent) cases, no difficulties were reported. Among the fifteen (60 percent) cases where difficulties were reported, they remained unresolved in eight cases. In four of those seven where they had been resolved, this had been with the assistance of a probation officer. In general, however, the degree of satisfaction with access arrangements, on a five point scale, was quite high (Table 28.16), and in half of the cases no future difficulties in the access arrangements were expected by the parties. In the remaining cases where difficulties were anticipated, there were four where both parties expected problems, five being expected by the custodial parent and four by the noncustodial parent. In eighteen (72 percent) cases, the custodial parent is reported as neither facilitating nor obstructing access. In five (20 percent) cases, the custodial parent actually took positive steps to facilitate access and in only two cases was there active obstruction. In twenty (80 percent) cases, the probation officer would expect access to continue, which compares favorably with the numbers of parents who expressed average or better than average satisfaction with the access arrangements. There were no extreme reactions after access reported among the children, their general response tending to be slightly more positive. What is interesting about these figures is that they show an internal consistency of reporting and appraisal of situations by our respondents.

TABLE 28.16 Satisfaction with Access Arrangements

	Highly satisfactory 5	4	3	Highly unsatisfactory 2	1
Custodial parent	6	7	7	5	0
Noncustodial parent	5	8	6	4	2
	11	15	13	9	2

In twenty-two (88 percent) cases, the probation officer is not recommending any alteration of the *status quo,* which reflects the general trend in divorce court decisions. Out of the fourteen cases where custody is disputed, however, in one case an alteration in custody is recommended, and in two cases alteration of both custody and access arrangements are recommended. In seven (28 percent) cases the probation officer is recommending that the children should be made the subjects of supervision orders. In all seven of these cases, specific behavioural problems exist, although there were eleven other cases where such problems existed and no supervision has been recommended.

SUMMARY AND CONCLUSIONS

Since the research is still in progress, both in terms of collection and analysis of data, conclusions must be highly qualified. With regard to the training and attitudes of probation officers, however, a number of trends emerge from the data. It seems clear that length of service is an important variable in terms of training and other related issues. Our findings so far would suggest that the provision of training in this area has declined, and that in-service training has failed to recognize and meet the needs, both of more recently appointed officers who have not had such training, and of longer serving officers who are more likely to have had such training but who are no more likely to apply it in practice.

It also appears that training is an important variable in shaping attitudes to both courts and solicitors, the latter being viewed rather critically regarding their ability to give sufficient weight to the interests of the children. This particular view may be in part a reflection of the solicitor's role in the traditional adversarial model of justice discussed by Murch (1980, 32), which "tends to polarise and exacerbate family conflict and does not easily allow lawyers to act impartially for both parties or for the family as a whole, nor does it allow for the interests of children to be adequately represented." Despite this, 29.2 percent of parents in Murch's research perceived the main concern of the solicitor to be with custody and access to children, even though 70 percent to 80 percent of solicitors were reported as never having seen the children (26–27). In this research, however, at least 60 percent of parents were either satisfied or very satisfied with the services of their solicitor, although this may well reflect "the partisan role" of solicitors and the fact that "people are seeking champions to do battle on their behalf" (36). So far, our research tends to support this view both implicitly and explicitly, and there is no evidence so far of any extensive involvement of solicitors in the processes of negotiating custody or access arrangements.

In contrast, the probation officer in his role as divorce court welfare officer must strive to maintain neutrality, particularly with regard to assessing and offering advice to the court about what might be seen to be in the best interests of the children. Murch's research showed that "Another characteristic much favoured by parents was the neutral stance evidently adopted by many officers. This seemed to be a crucial aspect of the welfare officer's role" (52). It is perhaps this neutrality in contrast with the solicitor's partisanship which gives rise to the negative view which probation officers seem to have of the solicitor's ability to give sufficient weight to the children's interests.

Our results so far suggest that there are possibly important variations in the interviewing practice of probation officers, both in the interviewing of children and in the range of other agencies contacted. This also tends to confirm Murch's findings (51–66). Since the probation officer is often the only impartial person involved in the process who interviews or has the opportunity to interview the children, this also has clear implications for the training of probation officers for this work. Probation officers do, however, admit to a willingness to offer advice about access arrangements, for which our research shows some evidence in practice, and a widely felt desire to see an increase of the involvement of the service in this area.

The results we have reached so far in relation to events within families after the parents have separated, as reported by probation officers, do not appear to accord with the findings of Wallerstein and Kelly (1980). The caveats expressed at the beginning of the description of our initial findings must be borne in mind, as must the fact that many of their results were obtained during a substantial follow-up period, the benefit of which we do not have. The apparent divergence may be of particular importance, however, since, in the absence of a substantial body of comparable research in this country, their research is already being extensively referred to by both educators and practitioners. The picture which seems to be emerging is one of a lower level of discord between the parents and of fewer discernible behavioural or emotional problems among the children. This may reflect some underreporting by parents, although in his research Murch (1980, 67) found that "Most parents dealing with the divorce court welfare service found it helpful to talk about their own and their children's response to the marriage breakdown". There also seems to be a comparatively high level of the children's involvement in the decision-making process. Although it seems that many initial access arrangements need subsequent alteration and that there are some persistent difficulties, the general level of satisfaction with access arrangements is quite high for both custodial and noncustodial parents. This is consistent with Murch's finding that over 70 percent of his samples were satisfied with access arrangements (71), although there are some differences between his samples and rating scales, and those which we have used. Our finding of 60 percent of cases with access arranged by mutual agreement, however, differs from Murch's finding of 30 percent of such cases.

Some of these trends may well be a product of the fact that difficulties are being underreported by parents, possibly because of a desire to influence the ultimate decision of the court and the need to appear as a competent parent during the precourt stage. It is also possible that there may be cultural differences between the U.S.A. and the U.K. which might produce somewhat different responses and, since Wallerstein and Kelly's (1980) study was conducted within the context of a divorce counselling service, their results may reflect a preponderance of families who recognized their problems and their need to seek help. Even if such trends do not disappear as we gather more data, our findings will hopefully provide valuable background data for further research, particularly longitudinal studies where data is not being gathered through an intermediary. Such research is vital in terms of developing the ideas contained in this present research and identifying what, if any, factors in the predivorce negotiations of access influence their eventual outcome and what, if any, are the long-term implications for the children. Until such further evidence is available, much of what is recommended to and practiced by courts will remain guesswork.

REFERENCES

Eekelaar, J., Clive, K. et al. (1977). *Custody After Divorce,* Oxford, SSRC.
Goldstein, J., Freud, A. and Solnit, A.J. (1973). *Beyond the Best Interests of the Child,* New York, Free Press.
Home Office (1976). *Report of the Work of the Probation and After-Care Department, 1972 to 1975,* Cmnd. 6,590.

_____. (1981). *Probation and After-Care Statistics, England and Wales, 1980*, London, Home Office.

Murch, M. (1980). *Justice and Welfare in Divorce*, London, Sweet and Maxwell.

Office of Population Census and Surveys (1979). *Population Trends 18*, London, HMSO.

Philips, E.M. (1979). "Staying Together for the Sake of the Children," *Bulletin of the British Psychological Society*, 32, 252–54.

Rutter, M. (1966). *Children of Sick Parents: An Environmental and Psychiatric Study*, Oxford, University Press.

_____. (1972). *Maternal Deprivation Reassessed*, Harmondsworth, Penguin.

Wallerstein, J.S. and Kelly, J.B. (1980). *Surviving the Break-Up: How Children and Parents Cope with Divorce*, London, Grant McIntyre.

Wilkinson, M. (1981). *Children and Divorce*, Oxford, Basil Blackwell.

Part Six

The Financial Dilemma — The Search for a Solution

It is becoming increasingly realized that perhaps the most intractable problems which face divorced people arise from the fact that, although they themselves no longer share a legal (or personal) relationship, they nevertheless remain the common parents of their children. Legal systems seem to be moving away from the idea of the perpetual dependence of a former wife on her former husband, so that economic disputes between them, while they may be acute, nevertheless need not persist over time. But where the wife is also the mother, and where she continues to care for children, the dependent status of the children almost inevitably poses problems involving both parents during the course of their dependency. Furthermore, the freedom which divorce confers on the adults to remarry will frequently introduce a new set of dependent children into the picture. This Part is primarily concerned with the normative and practical issues which relate to the resolution of the conflict between the various interests, including those of the state.

Weitzman's (Chapter 29) report of her investigations in California and in England reveal how very differently two legal and social cultures can view the justice of postdivorce arrangements. The responses of the persons interviewed reflect legal ideology: the perception of lawyers as to how the law ideally resolves certain disputes. This ideology will, in turn, affect the expectations of the population and, in consequence, the agreements reached between divorcing parties. How far this ideology is translated into legal practice, especially in the light of the constraints imposed by limited finances and economic vulnerability, is of course another matter. But the interplay between legal ideology and social practice is a subtle process. Maclean and Eekelaar (Chapter 30) report on research into the actual economic circumstances of people with dependent children who divorced in England between 1971 and 1981. The research confirmed the existing evidence from a variety of sources and countries that after a divorce, a single-parent household with dependent children suffers severe economic adversity relative to other households with children. It proceeds to examine the possible sources of revenue for such a household and to compare its economic condition with that of the second parent and, where relevant, (his) new family. The findings raise broad questions about the just allocation of resources between different groups of children. A society needs to resolve these questions before a stable framework within which conflicts of the various interests involved can be successfully established.

The limitations of the present English machinery for resolving such conflicts and implementing their solution are described by Gibson in Chapter 31. Gibson stresses (as, indeed, do Maclean and Eekelaar) how limited are the resources usually available for the new and old families, at least until remarriage by both parents. This inevitably draws the state into the range of sources from which support may be drawn. But the principles on which the state should act and how they relate to private obligations are of great complexity. Very aware of these problems, Melli and Zink, in Chapter 32, set out a carefully considered proposal, under review in Wisconsin, as to how they may be approached. The proposal is that all eligible children living in a one-parent unit who have an absent liable relative will receive from the state a basic child support benefit, without regard to the income of the custodial parent. The sums will be calculated by reference to an assessment of the cost of raising a child. The state will have recourse against the absent parent by means of two taxes. The basic tax will be a child support tax, which will be calculated as a fixed percentage of the parent's income related to the number of children involved. If the resultant yield does not cover the amount paid out in child support benefit, the tax can be levied on the combined income of the absent parent *and his or her new spouse* (if any). If the absent parent in fact pays more than the child support benefit to his former family, that family can retain the excess. The taxes will be collected in the same way as standard income tax.

Although only a proposal in Wisconsin, a scheme similar to it has been introduced in New Zealand. This is described by Thomas in Chapter 33. For some years New Zealand has paid relatively generous benefits to single parent families. But the means of collection from the absent parent have been through the traditional mechanisms of private law. From 1981, however, those procedures have been abolished with respect to recipients of these state benefits. In their case, the contribution of the absent relative is fixed by a complex formula set out in the Twentieth Schedule to the applicable statute as described by Thomas. The collection process is administered by the Social Welfare Department. What is particularly important about the New Zealand scheme and the Wisconsin proposal is that the state has made a decision on how the resources available for the absent parent (and his new family, if any) and the former family are to be spread between them. Thomas concludes that New Zealand has opted for a distribution which gives the former family rather less than they would have achieved under the private law provisions, but is likely to achieve a greater level of compliance. Is this the best policy to follow?

Both the Wisconsin proposal and the New Zealand system rely on universal, and relatively generous, state provision to single parent families. The support obligation is no longer primarily placed on the absent parent, but is assumed by the state in the first instance, with a consequential right of recourse. But it cannot be taken for granted that states will make such provision. The United Kingdom government refused to do this when rejecting the proposals of the Finer Committee on One-Parent Families (1974), whose proposals the New Zealand scheme closely follows. Where policy options are governed by economic restraints of this kind, it is necessary to re-examine the potential of private law in correcting the imbalances between these families. In the final chapter in this Part, Krause (Chapter 34) describes recent developments in the United States designed to improve the efficiency of child support enforcement. The Federal involvement in this area has not been confined simply to interstate collection problems, but has extended to actively stimulating, overseeing and financing collection systems within states. These systems involve sophisticated "parent locator" procedures, rigorous pursuit of absent parents and strong enforcement measures. The service is available whether the former family is in receipt of welfare payments (when, however, it is particularly significant) or not. Krause shows that the consequence of these measures has been greatly to increase the sums recovered from absent parents, which has had the double effect both of reducing the burden that has been falling on the welfare authorities and adding to the income of many single parent families. In gross terms, then, the innovations appear successful. How far they have improved the lot of these single-parent families primarily reliant on state welfare provisions is unclear. It is also evident that improved tracing and enforcement procedures do not in themselves solve the problems of how the obligations between absent parents and their former families should be fixed. These issues, as Krause, echoing Melli and Zink, recognizes in the second part of Chapter 34, remain unsatisfactory and unresolved in the United States. They are indeed in a state of confusion in many countries. Perhaps it is the major issue of family policy which should be addressed in the immediate future.

Chapter Twenty-nine

Equity and Equality in Divorce Settlements: A Comparative Analysis of Property and Maintenance Awards in the United States and England

Lenore J. Weitzman*

Department of Sociology, Stanford University, California, U.S.A.

INTRODUCTION

This chapter compares the financial arrangements for divorce in California and England, focussing on property and maintenance awards. But the subject of the chapter is much broader, for the legal rules that govern divorce settlements reflect fundamental societal norms and values about marriage and family life. They tell us what type of behaviour is considered appropriate for men and women, husbands and wives, and parents and children. The perspective in this chapter assumes that when we change rules about divorce, as both societies have in the last decade, we also change the rules about marriage, and thus the norms about men and womens' roles in both the family and the larger society.[1]

As divorce slowly replaces death as the event that terminates most marital bonds, it also becomes a primary occasion for the allocation of

---

* I am indebted to Mavis MacLean, John Eekelaar, Ruth Deech, and William J. Goode for helpful comments on earlier drafts of this chapter and to Holly Wunder for research assistance. I also wish to thank the German Marshall Fund of the United States, Nuffield College, Oxford and The SSRC Centre for Socio-Legal Studies, at Wolfson College, Oxford for research support.

family wealth and property. For centuries family wealth and property have been transmitted on two occasions in Western nations: marriage and death. Rules governing these transfers — from bride price and dowry, to primogeniture and widow's dower — have long been recognized as essential features of the society's kinship and marriage system as well as the cornerstone of its body of family law. In recent years, however, there has been a fundamental shift in the life cycle of the family: a significant minority of families in Western societies terminate their marriage before the death of either spouse.[2] This has made necessary the allocation of family property at a third point in the family life cycle — upon divorce.

In contrast to the long established laws and customs that govern the transfer of property upon marriage and death, the rules for allocating and transferring property upon divorce (and the principles upon which they are based) are in a state of flux and uncertainty. On one hand, the instability is a result of the relative recency of a continuously high divorce rate in Western societies (i.e., in the past two decades), and thus of the relatively short time period that states have had to face the task of sorting out the financial affairs of so many families at divorce. On the other hand, the uncertainty and flux reflect a deeper uncertainty about the nature of marriage and marital property in the modern world. Throughout the Western world, law commissions and legislatures are struggling with the complex sociological implications of defining and allocating marital property.[3]

There are two sound reasons for examining family property in the context of divorce. First, it is clear that what is defined as marital property, as distinct from personal property, is increasingly being defined by the stipulations of divorce decrees in the Western world.[4] This is not to suggest that decisions about and transfers of family property are no longer made at marriage or death. It is evident that marriage is still an occasion for gifts and the acquisition of status-based rights to share and/or inherit a spouse's property and estate.

However, many couples are not aware of the legal rules that govern their marriage, and few elect to write explicit agreements or contracts to alter the *de facto* regime.[5] Thus it is common for couples first to confront the legal arrangements that society has made for their property when they face a divorce (or a spouse's death), rather than when they first enter marriage.

The second reason for focusing on property decisions at divorce lies in the increased prevalence of divorce in the Western world. A couple entering marriage in the U.S. today faces a 50 percent probability that their marriage will end in divorce.[6] In Britain the probability of divorce is closer to 33 percent. It is not important, however, whether the probability of a marriage ending in divorce eventually equals (or even *exceeds*) the probability of its ending in death. What is important is that *both* are now primary occasions for the allocation of family property, and that one occasion, death, has been extensively regulated (and studied) while the other, divorce, has not.[7]

This chapter is divided into four sections. The first section outlines the major legal differences between the two legal systems. The second section describes the research methodology. The body of the chapter is found in the third section which compares the outcome of two typical divorce cases in England and California. The final section summarizes the major findings and contrasts the concepts of "equity" and "justice" in the two systems.

BACKGROUND: TWO LEGAL SYSTEMS

While the legal systems in England and California differ in many respects, my aim in this section of the chapter is to provide a framework for the empirical results that follow by briefly comparing three fundamental elements in their divorce laws: the grounds for divorce, the rules for property ownership and division, and the standards for postdivorce maintenance.

Grounds for Divorce

California has a "pure" no-fault divorce law that embodies three basic principles: no-fault, no-consent, and no-waiting. The 1970 divorce law reforms completely abolished the need for any grounds or fault-based reasons to obtain a divorce. They also eliminated the need to obtain the consent of an unwilling spouse. Divorce is granted upon *one* party's assertion that "irreconcilable differences have caused the irremediable breakdown of the marriage." While there is a required six month lag between filing and the final decree, to allow the spouses to sort out their financial affairs, the law permits *one spouse* to obtain a divorce as quickly and as easily as possible.

The English law (The *Matrimonial Causes Act* of 1973) differs on each of these principles.[8] First, with regard to fault, it still permits a fault-based divorce if one party is guilty of marital misconduct. Second, with regard to consent, if a spouse is innocent of marital misconduct and does not consent to the divorce, he or she may deny the divorce until the parties have lived separately for five years.[9] Third, while the English law also recognizes "marital breakdown," or the parties' agreement to dissolve their marriage, as a sufficient justification for divorce, it requires two years of living separately as evidence of the breakdown.[10]

The English law thus establishes a three-tier system of divorce: on the first level is the quickest and most commonly used route to divorce: allegations of marital misconduct which, if proved, can result in an immediate divorce.[11] On the second level is a divorce by mutual consent based on two years of living apart.[12]

On the third level is a divorce that is the most difficult to obtain, a divorce to which an innocent spouse does not consent. This divorce requires a five year waiting period[13] and it may be denied if "the dissolution of the marriage will result in grave financial or other hardship."[14] The United Kingdom Parliament added this final provision in response to fears that a more liberal divorce law would give men a "Casanova's Charter" — a license to "dump" their dependent middle-aged wives. The five year waiting period and financial criteria were designed to protect dependent housewives from financial abandonment.

While there is some disagreement about the actual role that fault (and innocence) actually play in English divorce settlements, it is evident that the possibility of fault-based accusations and the three-tier system allow for something that the California law precludes: predivorce negotiations concerning the grounds and timing of a legal divorce. In this respect the English law gives the innocent and or unwilling spouse the power to delay or deny a divorce — and to use this power as a lever in negotiating property and maintenance awards. In California, in contrast, an unwilling spouse can in no way prevent or deny a divorce. She (or he), therefore, has no extra bargaining power in negotiating a property settlement or in securing postdivorce support.

Property Ownership

A second major difference between the two legal regimes is found in their rules governing the ownership and and division of property. California has a community property system in which all property acquired during marriage (i.e., all income and assets acquired by either spouse with the exception of gifts and inheritance) is considered community property, and it is owned jointly and *equally* by the husband and wife. This system reflects a partnership conception of marriage as each spouse owns — and is entitled to — one-half of all the community property. Upon divorce, the California courts *must* divide the community property *equally* between the two spouses.

England, in contrast, has a separate or common-law property regime in which each spouse owns the property he or she earns or acquires. In the past, the husband or wife who had title to property owned it exclusively. Since most income was (and still is) earned by husbands, the practical result of this rule was that the husband typically owned most of the property acquired during marriage. Before 1970 "the courts had virtually no power to readjust the entitlement of family members to capital assets" upon divorce.[15]

Under the English reforms of 1970 and 1973[16] the courts were empowered to make whatever property transfers or lump sum awards they deemed "reasonable." But the courts still begin with the assumption that they are dealing with "the husband's" property. They then consider how much of "his property" he should "give" his wife upon divorce.

The traditional rule of thumb has been to award a wife *one-third* of "the husband's assets" (in addition to maintenance) upon divorce. Although the English courts today have the authority to go beyond title, and to award property as "justice" requires, the one-third rule remains the starting point for their awards, and as such it provides a baseline norm for the average award.

Thus the two systems start with different premises about what is an equitable property award for a divorced wife: one-half of the marital assets in California, and one-third in England. Even though the English experts report that the "one-third rule" is no more than a rough starting point, a report that is substantiated by the discussion that follows, there is nevertheless a significant difference in the framework with which each society approaches the task of allocating property upon divorce.

Maintenance and Postdivorce Support

The third major difference between the two legal regimes lies in their statutory standards for maintenance or postdivorce support. While the courts in both societies are instructed to consider a number of factors in awarding postdivorce support, there is a basic divergence in the purpose of support in the two systems. One of the aims of maintenance under the English law is to *maintain the standard of living during the marriage* and, in so far as practicable, to place the parties in the financial position in which they would have been had their marriage not broken down.[17] This standard is based on a conception of *marriage as a life-long* bond with the husband having a life-long obligation to maintain "a comparable" standard of living for his former wife.

In California, in contrast, awards of postdivorce support are supposed to be based solely on economic factors such as the needs and resources of the spouses. As distinct from the English assumption that a divorced man has a continuing responsibility to support his former wife, the California standard assumes that the divorced man should be freed of this burden as soon as possible. And, distinct from the English assumption that a divorced woman (and her children) will remain financially dependent on her former husband, the California standard assumes that a divorced woman can be — and should be — financially *self-sufficient*. Thus the California standard seeks *to sever* the marital bond as soon as it is financially feasible, while the English standard acknowledges the existence of *continuing* financial obligations between formerly married spouses. In this respect the English standard tries to provide some protection and financial security for the divorced woman — and, in theory, promises to maintain the standard of living of her marriage in so far as possible.

Even this cursory summary of the two legal systems suggests two very different visions of marriage. The English law envisions marriage as a life-long commitment which is harder to break: it is more difficult to obtain a divorce in the first place, and it is more difficult to sever the financial obligations of matrimony in the second. In California, marriage is treated as a more voluntaristic and less permanent commitment. California therefore makes it easier for both spouses to extricate themselves from the marriage, and for the husband to extricate himself from his financial responsibility for his former wife.

We now turn to the question of how these legal systems differ in actual practice.

METHODOLOGY

In order to compare divorce outcomes in the two societies a sample of judges and attorneys (solicitors and barristers in England) were asked to predict the results of a series of hypothetical "divorce cases." These cases provided the focus for follow-up questions and in-depth interviews about legal norms and legal practices in each society.

The California interviews were obtained as part of a large scale research project on the social and economic effects of no-fault divorce in California.[18] This included interviews with 169 matrimonial attorneys (i.e., those who specialized in divorce and family law) and 44 family law judges (i.e., the judges and commissioners who regularly heard divorce cases) in San Francisco and Los Angeles in 1974 and 1975.[19] In addition, written responses to the hypothetical divorce cases were obtained from 29 family law judges who participated in a California judicial education program in 1981.

The English sample of legal experts is admittedly nonsystematic: it consists of a "convenience" sample of 26 solicitors, barristers, law professors, and judges who were obtained through a process of referrals from reputed experts. Every effort was made to interview persons who were identified as an expert by at least two other experts. The final sample consisted of 11 solicitors, 9 barristers, 4 law professors, 2 judges and 1 registrar. The subsample of solicitors was geographically diverse but the barristers, judges, and law professors were concentrated in London and Oxford.

The respondents were asked to predict the outcomes of five hypothetical divorce cases and to explain the rationale for their predictions. This chapter focuses on the experts' responses to two of the five cases: the Harris case, which involves a young couple with young children, and the Thompson case, which focuses on a long-married wealthy couple.

Structural Differences and Social Meaning

Before discussing the results of these interviews it is necessary to add a cautionary note about my methodology and the question of comparability. When I began this research I assumed that the same factual situation (i.e., the same case) would have the same "social meaning" in the two societies. Thus I translated the hypothetical divorce cases that I had used in California, with only minor changes, to English situations.[20] However, I soon discovered the following structural features of English society created a different set of options for English respondents dealing with the same "factual" case.

1. The English tax structure which, especially at the upper income levels, through deductions for alimony, etc., served to substantially "enlarge" the total amount of family income that was "available" to English families after divorce;
2. The more extensive system of social welfare benefits in England which included free medical and hospital care, mothers benefits for all mothers regardless of income, and virtually free education for all students through college. These benefits provided all divorced families, and especially those with lower incomes, with a better "minimal" standard of living after divorce;
3. The availability of council housing and other "entitlements" which the English courts could "award" as part of the divorce settlement. Although these entitlements were not treated as property with an established cash value, they nevertheless enlarged the pool of valuable family assets to be "awarded" upon divorce.
4. The lack — or the perceived lack — of employment opportunities for women with small children in England, especially in contrast to the perceived availability of jobs, including part-time jobs, and child care facilities for mothers of young children in California. (This is discussed further below.)

These unanticipated complications led me to be more cautious in reporting the quantitative results of this inquiry (i.e., the precise dollar awards and the percentage of family income awarded to each spouse) in the sections that follow. Instead, I have tried to adopt a more anthropological approach to the data on financial awards by reporting and analyzing the distinct cultural and legal contexts in which the two sets of experts approach these cases.

THE HARRIS FAMILY: A YOUNG COUPLE WITH CHILDREN

Let us now turn to two of the hypothetical cases that were presented to the legal experts in California and England. The first case involves a young couple with two young children.

Each of the experts was asked to predict the outcome of this case (or, in the case of judges, what they would award). They were told to assume that the parties had agreed that the mother would have custody of the children, a reasonable assumption in both societies.[21]

The following is the English version of the case:

CASE 1 — THE HARRIS FAMILY

Ronald and Margaret Harris met while both were university students. Ronald was studying accounting and Margaret was an English major. They got married after Ronald graduated from university. During their first year of marriage Margaret finished university while Ronald worked as an accountant. Their first child was born a year later.

After seven years of marriage they have decided to divorce.

Ronald has worked as an accountant for I.C.I for the past seven years. He has a gross income of £14,000 a year or £1,000 a month net (income after taxes) with some expectations of upward mobility.

At the time of the divorce Ronald is twenty-eight and Margaret is twenty-seven. They have two children — John, aged six, and Jean, aged four. Throughout the marriage Margaret has been a housewife and a mother. Since their son John was born soon after her graduation, she has never worked outside the home. Their daughter Jean is now four years old and has not yet started school.

Margaret does not want to take a job because she wants to be a full-time mother to her preschool daughter.

The Harris's have the following property:
(a) household furnishings worth about £3,000,
(b) a new sports car, and
(c) a family home.

The family home is worth £40,000 with an equity of £20,000. Title is held in Ronald Harris' name. Monthly payments on the home (including utilities) are £400 per month.[22]

Property: The Family Home

As might be expected, the two sets of respondents approached this case from different perspectives. In California, the experts' first concern was the required equal division of the community property. Since the major community asset was the family home, most of the California experts (close to two-thirds) said that the family home would "have to be sold" so that the proceeds could be divided equally between the two spouses.

The first priority for the English experts, in contrast, was the preservation of the family home for the children. Virtually all of them (87 percent) predicted that the wife and children would continue to live there with the husband's support. The English concern with preserving the matrimonial home[23] for the children is clearly articulated in the following quotations:

> (a barrister)
>
> First let's make sure the children are looked after... the children have always lived in that house... you want to finish a child's schooling.
>
> (a solicitor)
>
> The wife would get the house because she has to make a home for the children and the children come first — you don't want their home to be disrupted. You want to stabilize the situation for them.

It is important to note that the English experts did not predict that the mother would be awarded ownership of the home. Rather, they gave her and her children the *right to continue living in it*. Thus close to 70 percent of the English experts predicted that she would be entitled to occupy the home until her children were grown:

> (a law professor)
>
> The house will be held in trust for the children so they can live in it until the youngest finishes school or training — but only if she doesn't remarry or no other man is living in the house.

As this quotation suggests, two limitations were typically placed on the wife's (and children's) right to continue living in the family home. Two-thirds of those who said the wife would remain in the home said that she would have to sell it when her children were eighteen or finished their education, and a (somewhat overlapping) third said that the home would be sold before that if she remarried or cohabited with another man. Let us briefly consider the implications of each of these restrictions.

If the major rationale for maintaining the wife and children in the family home is to provide stability and security for the children, it would seem reasonable to plan to sell the house when the children are grown. These "Mesher orders"[24] for postponing the sale of the house were fairly common in the early 1970s, but recent years have brought an increased awareness of their long-term complications and the plight of the middle-aged housewife who, though no better off than she was at the time of the divorce, is suddenly forced to sell her home. In this regard, it is important to note that a significant minority of English experts, close to one-fifth, explicitly rejected the notion of a contingent home award. They predicted instead that the wife would be awarded the home (and its equity) outright.

The second restriction, requiring the sale of the family home if the wife cohabitats or remarries, may similarly appear reasonable at first —

if it is assumed that a male will immediately be able to (or willing to) provide a divorced woman and her children with alternative housing. However the "remarriage or cohabitation" standard is *not a means-related* standard — and it therefore suggests that "moral" rather than financial criteria are involved. The implication seems to be that as long as the wife remains "faithful to her former husband," she can retain her entitlement to the family home. It seems odd to expect a wife to remain faithful to her ex-husband — and especially odd to have the children's security in the family home be jeopardized by it.

An order that awards the house to the wife until the children are grown, typically specifies how the equity in the house will be divided when it is sold. The English experts predicted that Margaret Harris would, on average, receive one-third of the equity from the postponed sale. As noted above, this leaves the woman who has invested her life in raising children and maintaining her home with little equity (and no security) for her middle and older years.

The California solution for apportioning the equity in the family home avoids this problem by dividing the equity (and typically the home itself) at the time of the divorce. However, the advantage of having one's equity at the time of the divorce is achieved at the price of a forced sale of the family home and the accompanying disruption this typically causes for minor children.

The preferred solution for the Harris family in California was to order an immediate sale of the family home and to divide the equity between the husband and wife. A sizable majority of the California experts (close to two-thirds) predicted that the Harris family home would be sold. They offered two justifications for this solution: it permitted a "clean break" between the parties, and it did not unduly hamper the husband by tying up his equity in the house. The California judges and lawyers stressed the husband's "right" to "his half" of the family property. Since all of the family property in this case was, as it is in many divorce cases, in the home, a sale of the home was necessary to give the husband the money he would need to start a new life.

In contrast to the English interviews, the "rights" or "interests" of children were rarely mentioned in California: marital property was defined solely in terms of the relative rights and interests of the husband and wife, and it was divided between the two of them.

A minority of the California experts (slightly more than a third) predicted that the sale of the home would be postponed to allow the wife and the children to continue living in it (in contrast to 87 percent of the English respondents who predicted that the wife and children would remain in the family home). In some of these cases, as in England, the sale of the California house was postponed until the children reached majority.[25] However, a number of California experts predicted that the wife and children would have to leave the family home before the children reached eighteen; they would be allowed to live there for only three or four years, enough to provide "a cushion" during the transitional years.[26]

Even though recent developments in California law have given judges the discretion to delay the sale of the home when the pressing needs of minor children are at stake,[27] many of them appear reluctant to issue these orders. For example, in informal interviews with California judges about this case in 1983, several judges said that the children were so young that it would be unfair to "tie up" the husband's equity in the house for the fourteen years until his daughter reached eighteen. While a few, when pressed, said they might delay the sale for a year or two, they saw no ultimate advantages in that because the children would have to move eventually.

One very basic and important difference between the response of the experts in California and England is that the English awards show much more variation. Thus, while the California wife can be certain that she will receive half of the assets accumulated during the marriage, the English wife, who is subject to the registrar's or judge's concept of fairness, may receive anywhere from 0 to 100 percent. In the Harris case, for example, the English wife's share of the equity in the house varied from 0 to 50 percent of the proceeds, when the experts predicted a delayed sale of the house, and from 50 to 100 percent of the equity in the house, when the experts predicted she would be awarded it upon divorce.[28] The typical English wife, however, eventually got a third of the equity (after being allowed to live in the house with her minor children).

One may be tempted to conclude that English wives with minor children are better off after divorce than those in California — if they own or are purchasing a family home. Almost all of them are allowed to live in the family home while raising their children, and about a third of them are awarded the entire equity at the time of the divorce. Even those who are not awarded the home outright, but who are nevertheless allowed to live there with their children, have been awarded an "entitlement" of considerable financial value. These advantages however, are mitigated by the restrictions on the English wife's personal life (i.e., on her cohabitation and/or remarriage) and by her typically lower share of the equity when the house is sold.

Maintenance Awards

Let us consider next the maintenance awards in the Harris case. Because tax incentives in the two countries lead to the differential labelling of maintenance awards as "wife support," "child support," and "mortgage payments," I have added all maintenance awards together (including the amounts awarded to pay the home mortgage in England).

Overall, the total amount of maintenance awarded is greater in England. In the Harris case, the English wife and children would typically be awarded 51 percent of the husband's gross salary, in contrast to the typical 43 percent in California.

The difference can be explained in terms of the priorities in the two systems. In England the first priority is the children. As one English solicitor explained:

> There is so little to go around the emphasis of the court must be on the wife and children. Why should they be relegated to a lower standard of living than the husband?

In California, in contrast, greater concern is expressed for the husband. The California experts stressed the importance of maintaining *his* standard of living and *his* incentive to earn. As two California judges explained their awards in the Harris case:

> You have to have enough money for him to be satisfied, to give him an incentive to keep earning and improving in his profession.

> He can't live on less than $7,000 a year and exist. So I have to leave him with $7,000. That leaves $5,000 of his net income for her.

Thus the California husband with a dependent wife and two small children is typically allowed to retain more of his salary than his English counterpart. (The after tax differences between the two awards are, however, somewhat less pronounced.)

A second and perhaps more critical difference between the two societies lies in the assumed purpose of maintenance, and in its intended duration. The husband's *life-long* responsibility for his wife and children's support — and their dependence on him — are basic tenets of the English law (see, for example Hilary Land's excellent essay on taxation, social security, and housing policy).[29] It is therefore taken for granted that the husband's responsibility for support continues after divorce — as does his ex-wife's dependency on him.

In the U.S., in contrast, the husband's postdivorce responsibilities are more circumscribed — and so is the system's tolerance for a dependent wife. Thus maintenance after divorce is viewed as a *temporary* solution in California — a means of assisting the wife *until* she becomes self-sufficient.

In light of these contrasting views of maintenance, it is not surprising to find that none of the English respondents put a time limit on Margaret Harris' maintenance award. In California however, slightly more than half of the experts predicted that Margaret Harris's spousal support (i.e., wife support) award would be reviewed by the court and/or terminated in *an average of two years*. (Most California experts assumed that she could become self-sufficient in two to five years.)

The California assumption of *a transition to self-sufficiency*, as distinct from the English assumption of *continued dependency*, is most clearly reflected in the contrast between the experts' attitudes towards the possibility of Margaret's working in the paid labour force. Consider first the California enthusiasm for Margaret's becoming employed.

> She has to go to work... but she will need time — about 2 or 3 years — to get into the job market and earn decent wages.

> This wife is young and college trained. She will have to be retrained and enter the labour market. I would expect her to become self supporting in 5 years. So I would maintain jurisdiction for 5 years and terminate her support then unless she can demonstrate a continued need for support. I'd put the burden on her to show need at that time.

> You have to encourage her to work and use her education. I'd give her $3,000 the first year and reduce it to $2,000 the second year to give her an incentive to find a job *soon*.

In England, in contrast, no one said that Margaret Harris would *have* to work, although a number of the English respondents did discuss the possibility. However, the tone of their discussion underscores the different presumptions in the two societies. As one London solicitor summarized the English attitude toward this case:

> Now what on earth are we going to do for this poor woman? She doesn't want to work and why should she? She has two small children. Mind you, if she wants to work she'd be better off... (and I'd tell her that because she'd increase the family income. But you say she doesn't want to — so fair enough — she won't).
> Now, if we gave her one-third of the income that's £4,666 a year or £388 a month. But that isn't enough. So she's got to have more than one-third to provide a home for the children. It's hard cheese on the husband but she'll probably get about £6,000 a year for herself (and £1,250 a year for the two children). So he'll pay out about half of his income to her. But he'd get tax relief on it, so it won't be so bad.

While one can discern some seeds of change in the solicitor's remark that Margaret Harris "would be better off" if she got a job, it is nevertheless clear that most divorced mothers in England still have the option of choosing to work — while most divorced mothers in California do not.

The different assumptions in the two systems may be explained, in part, by three structural differences in the situation of single-parent families in the two societies:[30]

1. The much more limited employment options for English women in general, and in the recession and high unemployment crisis of the early 1980s in particular;
2. The lack of day care facilities and other supports for working mothers in England; and

3. The availability of a system of supplementary benefits in England that helps to "cushion" the economic hardships of divorce.

In fact, some English respondents suggested that even if a divorced mother with young children were fortunate enough to get a job, she might nevertheless be financially better off living on supplementary benefits after she paid for child care, transportation, etc. Thus the seeds of change in England may depend as much on changing the structural opportunities for divorced mothers as on changing ideologies of appropriate women's roles.

THE THOMPSON FAMILY: A LONG MARRIAGE, WEALTH, AND OLDER HOUSEWIFE

The differences between the ideologies of appropriate women's roles are equally pronounced for older housewives. Our second case involves a fifty-three year old housewife for whom the two societies have sharply different expectations. It reads as follows:

CASE 2 — THE THOMPSON FAMILY

Victor Thompson, age fifty-five, is a merchant banker with a gross income of £72,000 per year (or £6,000 per month).
His wife Ann has been a housewife and mother throughout their twenty-seven year marriage, raising three children (who are now full-time university students). She has never been employed outside of the home.
This was the first marriage for both the husband and wife. At the time of the divorce Ann is fifty-three; Victor is fifty-five.
This divorce action was brought by Ann Thompson, age fifty-three, on the ground of unreasonable behaviour. Victor Thompson was bored with the marriage, had fallen in love with a younger woman and was willing to be at fault in the divorce.
The couple has the following property:
(a) a home and furnishings with an equity value of £90,000,
(b) a car worth £5,000,
(c) a second car worth £2,000, and
(d) stocks and shares with a current value of £10,000.

Maintenance or Spousal Support Awards

Once again the framework with which the two sets of legal experts approached this case was radically different. While the English respondents talked of the wife's "entitlement" to maintain her standard of living and be supported by her husband, the American judges talked of helping the fifty-three year old housewife build a new life.

Consider first the English views of the wife's entitlement to a home, financial security, and life-long support. There is an unquestioned assumption that Ann Thompson "has earned" the right to life-long support and that she "deserves" to be taken care of in a comfortable standard of living:

(a law professor)

The emphasis in this case is providing a home for her and being sure she has security. The exact amount of money doesn't matter that much.

(a high court judge)

She's an older wife and that has to be considered. He has to protect her — he has to house her and give her a portion of his income and security for the future. She's entitled to the total assets a wife should get: she's been married 27 years and had three children. She's done everything a wife can do except keep him amused.

(a solicitor)

First thing the court would do is provide the wife with a house at their standard of living. After 27 years of marriage and bringing up three children with the husband entirely at fault, the court would be most sympathetic to the wife... She'd get 1/3 of his income and 1/2 of the house.

(a family court judge)

He will have to provide his wife with an income and a home. She is 53 years old and isn't earning so she cannot get a mortgage... So, he'll have to buy her a flat and provide her with an income. Or he can buy an annuity to assure her of an income of £15-20,000 a year for the rest of her life.

It is clear from these statements that none of the English respondents expect Ann Thompson to get a job or to consider supporting herself. The responsibility for her financial support lies squarely on her husband. As two solicitors explained:

She is comparatively late in life and she has not worked and is not used to working. She wouldn't (and shouldn't) have to work.

The court would not expect this wife to go out and work. She'd get the house outright and if I was advising her I'd be after a capital sum as well (and let her invest it).... I'd also advise her to hang on and not get divorced — after 5 years she'd show financial hardship. He'd have to buy some sort of insurance for her to get 1/2 of his pension after death.

When pressed about the possibility of work for the fifty-three year old Ann Thompson, most respondents said it *might* be considered in *unusual circumstances*. As one London registrar commented:

> I wouldn't expect the wife to work at this age, although if the issue was raised, I'd have to listen to it. Five years ago no one would even have raised the question of if she should work. To do it now is like changing the rules of the game in the middle of the game.

The California respondents were, in contrast, more divided about the appropriateness of "changing the rules in the middle of the game" for older women. The majority of the California experts, (about 63 percent), agreed with the English respondents and predicted that an older housewife like Ann Thompson would be supported — without question — for the rest of her life. But a significant minority, slightly more than a third, predicted that the courts would put some pressure on her to find work and share the responsibility for her support. As one judge remarked:

> The wife should be entitled to support for substantial time due to the lengthy marriage. On the other hand she should also *become prepared* to support herself.

Among the 37 percent minority who sought to "encourage" Ann Thompson to go back to school, get counselling and retrain to secure employment, were judges who spoke of "lecturing her on the importance of finding a job and starting a new life" and "explaining to her that *she* will benefit." Other judges said they would require that "she set herself a training schedule," while still others would require a progress report from her in a few years. For example:

> I'd set a hearing 2 to 3 years away to review wife's need and her progress towards self sufficiency.

> I'd set up a schedule for her training for employment. Depending on her education — I'd allow her maybe 1-2-3 or more years. Then I'd want to review the case for a stepdown (a decrease in maintenance) after she has a job. She should be able to have a job in a few years.

While all of the California respondents felt that the husband had a continuing responsibility to support his former wife after a marriage of twenty-seven years, those judges who encouraged Ann Thompson to work envisioned a better future for both of them if she created a "new life" for herself. They spoke of her "sharing" some of *his* responsibility by earning some income on her own. As one judge summarized this attitude:

> Ann's standard of living during the relationship should be recognized and maintained. But Ann should be encouraged to become self supporting to the maximum extent possible. They will both benefit.

It should be emphasized that none of the California respondents predicted that the court would *require* Ann Thompson to become self-sufficient. All of them predicted that she would be awarded spousal support (i.e., maintenance), and these awards averaged between $2,000 and $2,500 a month (or between $24,000 and $30,000 a year).

Comparing the maintenance awards in this case is complicated by the fact that the first ten English questionnaires omitted the word "net" before Victor Thompson's income. Since all ten respondents assumed this was a gross income figure, the word gross was inserted in the questionnaire. As a result the California judges based their awards on a net income figure, the English respondents on a gross income figure. When this difference is compounded by the differential impact of the two tax systems, a direct comparison between the two samples is *virtually impossible*. The median maintenance award for Ann Thompson among English respondents was £20,000 a year or 28 percent or Victor's *gross income of £72,000*. In California, as noted above, most of the awards were between $24,000 and $30,000 a year, or between 33 percent and 42 percent of Victor's *net* income of $72,000.

All of the English respondents assumed that Ann Thompson's maintenance would continue for the life of the parties. While this was also the model response in California, a minority of the Californians discussed the possibility of a reduced award if Ann Thompson entered the labour force — which this minority thought should be encouraged. In both societies, however, postdivorce maintenance would automatically terminate if Ann remarried.[31]

Property Awards

Turning next to the property division in the Thompson case, it is easier to compare the outcomes. Once again, there is a basic difference in orientation: the California judges approach the problem as a mathematical calculation: they add up the net value of the assets and divide the total into two equal shares. In contrast the English respondents begin by trying to provide the wife with an adequate home. For example:

(a family court judge)

He will have to provide his wife with an income and a home. She is 53 years old and isn't earning so she cannot get a mortgage ... So, she'll have to buy herself a flat and provide herself with an income ...

(a solicitor)

This is a wife who's got to have a decent home for the rest of her life. He'll have to buy her a home or a flat outright — she won't have to pay a mortgage. (How much would that cost?) Well it depends where she is living. But she could probably buy a nice flat or a smaller house for £45,000 or £50,000. Mind you she'd get £60,000 or so if that was what was needed ...

(But that is more than half. What about the one-third rule?) The one-third rule is only a starting point. First, he has to house her. If you only give her one-third of the home that isn't really fair. But there is too much equity in the house so they won't let her keep the whole thing.

(a law professor)

Husband will argue the house is too big for her, but she'd probably get at least 1/2 of the £100,000 in capital available. So she will have £50,000 for housing and can easily buy a smaller house for herself for that.

(a high court judge)

If she wants to stay in the house and he agrees — fine. If not, I'd sell the house and give her 1/2 to buy a new house. You can't expect her to live in anything of less value [than] £45,000 ... But she'd do all right for that and she'll own it free and clear (i.e. no mortgage).

As these statements suggest, there is much more variation in the English responses. While almost 60 percent of the English respondents would give the wife between £45,000 and £50,000 (roughly half of the equity in the current house, or half of the equity in the home and the stocks and shares), these awards seem to be based on a notion of equity in housing rather than a notion of an equal division. In addition almost one-third of the respondents (30 percent) gave the wife two-thirds of the equity in the house to buy a new house — awards which more clearly differ from the concept of an equal division. In California, in contrast, virtually *all* of the property awards involved a strictly equal division as required by law. (They varied from an award of 49 percent to 51 percent of the total property to the wife.)

A second major difference between the two countries stems from the English assumption that the husband has a responsibility to provide for his ex-wife for the rest of *her* life. To insure that this responsibility is met, the English courts have typically required an older (and well-to-do) husband to purchase an insurance policy or an annuity to compensate his wife for the widow's benefits she forfeits by getting divorced. As one solicitor explained:

He has an obligation to take out an annuity to provide her with the same benefit she would have received on his death. To calculate what her benefit would be you can either:

1. figure out what sum you'd need to produce the income she would have received and buy an annuity for that;
2. *or* make him undertake to make provision in his will for that amount.

She can also claim as one of his dependents under the *Inheritance Act*.

This type of provision, which provides the older housewife with the assurance of financial security, is virtually unheard of in California. However, California, like England, does recognize the divorced wife's entitlement to a share of her husband's pension (unlike many other states in the U.S. and Western Europe). In California this is typically valued and divided upon divorce. In England it is typically handled through a variation in the wife's maintenance award when the husband retires.

SUMMARY AND CONCLUSION

Before summarizing the major findings of this inquiry, a cautionary note about generalizations is in order. It is evident that the results of any particular divorce settlement will depend not only on the legal system, but also on the socioeconomic status and life circumstances of the divorcing parties. Thus the scope of any property settlement must be limited by the amount of family property that is available to the court, and the scope of any maintenance award must be limited by the available family income. While the courts have some power to enlarge the pool of available assets, (as, for example, they do by including the right to live in publicly owned council housing in England) and some power to enlarge the pool of available income (as they do when they require a housewife to enter the labour force after divorce) they are, on the whole, limited by the economic circumstances of the parties.

Thus, whatever the legal rules, men and women of the upper class will, on the average, be better off after divorce than working-class men and women. These class factors are as critical in determining divorce settlements and postdivorce consequences as the legal rules and, in any particular case, they set the parameters within which the legal system can act.

Consider, for example, the effects of the size of the family estate on the financial equality of the divorce settlement. In families with limited property in which the only asset is the family home, the English wife is likely to be better off than her former husband because the English courts, with their considerable discretion, give priority to maintaining a home for her and her dependent children. On the other hand, in families with larger estates — including, let us say, more than one home, substantial investments, and a family business — the English wife is likely to be awarded considerably less property than her former husband. In this case judicial discretion to make a "just" property award will probably result in the wife's getting about a third of the family property — to her husband's two-thirds.

Although the California wife will be awarded half of the family property in both cases, the practical consequences of the award for her children's and her own well-being after postdivorce will also depend, in large part, on *the amount* of family property the courts had to divide.

Social class influences divorce settlements in a second important respect. Since laws have always been written by people with property, the law is based on the assumption that there is enough family property (and/or income) to carry out the law's aims. Thus a divorce law that assures an older housewife an income for life may well serve to protect the wives of upper-class men. However the same law may be of little practical value to the wife of an unemployed labourer who neither owns a home nor has the income to buy an annuity for her old age.

Along the same lines, it could be argued that a woman's well-being after divorce is as much a result of her age (and her other social statuses) as it is a result of the legal rules that govern her divorce settlement. It is evident that twenty-seven year old Margaret Harris will have an easier time of adjusting to any divorce settlement when compared to the fifty-three year old Ann Thompson — if all other things are equal.

I do not mean to suggest that legal rules are of little consequence. Rather, this brief discussion is meant to underscore the importance of social class and social status — in addition to the legal factors that are the focus of this chapter.

Let me now turn to a summary of the fundamental differences between the legal system of divorce in England and California.

This chapter began with the thesis that rules that govern divorce reflect the society's norms and values for marriage and tell us what is considered appropriate behaviour for men and women, husbands and wives. The rules and legal practices that determine property and maintenance awards, and the empirical results of those rules, reviewed above, point to four basic differences in the assumptions about marriage and family roles in the two societies.

The first major difference between the two systems lies in their attitudes towards divorced women (and thus toward married women as well). A more protective and paternalistic attitude is discernible in England. The English respondents are more likely to describe divorced women as both *needing maintenance* (*i.e.*, as being financially dependent on their husbands for support) and as *deserving of maintenance* (*i.e.*, of having a moral entitlement to maintenance). They are also more likely to emphasize *the husband's responsibility* "to protect, support and look after" his former wife. In California, in contrast, there is a new norm of *self-sufficiency* for divorced wives. The husband's responsibility is defined in more limited terms, and, wherever possible, it is restricted to a *transitional* period to enable the divorced woman to become self-sufficient.

This difference is reflected in their contrasting attitudes towards working mothers. In England it is assumed that a divorced woman with young children should be supported so that she can provide them with the care and attention they need. In California, in contrast, it is assumed that the divorced mother should get a job and become self-sufficient — whether or not she has child-care responsibilities.

It is not clear whether the English wife is better off than her American counterpart. On the one hand, she obviously benefits from a greater maintenance award and from the English assumption that she has a right to stay at home to care for her children instead of being obligated to work for pay to support herself. However, the benefits she enjoys are not without their "costs." First, while the English ex-wife is "looked after" and taken care of by her former husband, she is, as we noted above, also expected to remain faithful to him, and her right to continue living in the family home with her children may be contingent on her not cohabiting or remarrying. Second, the English wife typically receives a smaller share of the family property than the California divorcee. While all California wives are guaranteed one-half of the family property, the English wife is typically awarded only one-third.

When we consider the situation of older women, especially those who have been housewives and mothers in marriages of long duration, there can be little doubt of the advantages of the English system. The older housewife in England is assured of her husband's continued responsibility for her support. And, if he can afford it, she is assured of being able to continue living comfortably, with dignity. In California, in contrast, the rules have been changed in the middle of the game for many older housewives. They are increasingly faced with pressures to retrain and become employed at fifty or fifty-five and sixty — an age when they are certain to encounter job discrimination in addition to problems created by their lack of work experience, self doubt and fears — and to start a new life. In contrast the English system provides the same woman with the security of a home, a reasonable maintenance award, and an annuity in the event of her husband's death.

The second fundamental difference between the two systems is the relative importance of children and a child's entitlement to share the family's wealth and property. While the two legal systems pay lip service to the life-long responsibility of parents for their children, this responsibility, like the responsibility for a wife, seems to be taken more seriously in England.[32] The English experts were more likely to emphasize the importance of children and their social and financial "rights" to both property and maintenance after divorce. Almost all of the English respondents emphasized the child's independent "right" to the matrimonial home and the child's interest in remaining in a stable home environment. In addition, the English were more likely to talk about the child's financial right to have his or her future standard of living maintained. In California, in contrast, both property and maintenance are perceived as issues for the two adults. Marital property is divided between the husband and wife. *Not one* California respondent mentioned the possibility of a child's entitlement to share the marital assets.[33]

A third important difference between the two systems lies in the amount of judicial discretion. This is most evident with respect to property awards. California judges have relatively little discretion in dividing property — they must divide the community property equally between the husband and the wife. English judges in contrast, are free to allocate property as "justice" requires. Their greater discretion results, as we have seen, in much more variation in English property awards.

One advantage of the greater discretion of English judges is that they can be more responsive to the unique circumstances of individual couples and can tailor their awards to their individual needs.

On the other hand, judicial discretion allows for variation among judges — as well as variation according to the circumstances of a particular case. Variation among judges may encourage "forum shopping" and outcomes that are determined by individual prejudices instead of legal principles. Thus, as we noted, when faced with the same case, English jurists show much more variation in what they would award than California judges do. For example, we found that the English predictions for Margaret Harris's property award ranged from 0 to 100 percent of the home equity. Even though most experts predicted that she would eventually get one-third of the equity, neither that percentage nor her right to live in her home with her children could be assured.

Judicial discretion and the resulting uncertainty about the outcome of a property award has two other disadvantages. One is that uncertainty typically encourages litigation, while knowing what one can expect to be awarded in court provides a clear-cut framework for private settlements. Thus when California adopted a strict equal division rule for the division of community property there was an increase in private settlements about property.[34]

A second disadvantage of uncertainty is that it generally serves the interests of the person with more power and/or resources. It may therefore disadvantage the weaker family partner in divorce negotiations. Thus, if the husband has more money or resources, or has access to better attorneys, he is likely to benefit from ambiguity in the system — and to use his advantages to obtain a more favorable settlement.

The fourth and last fundamental difference between the two legal systems involves their conceptions of the marital bond. In England, it is still assumed that marriage is a life-long bond (although the appropriateness of this assumption has recently been questioned).[35] This results in postdivorce continuation of more of the rights and obligations of marriage in England. For example, maintenance for the wife is awarded for a longer period of time (typically for life or remarriage), and there is more sharing in property arrangements (such as maintaining joint ownership of the matrimonial home). However, the English divorcee also faces more constraints on her postdivorce life as she too is expected to abide by some of her marital obligations — and to remain "faithful" to her ex-husband if she and her children continue to reside in the family home.

In California, in contrast, marriage is seen as a less permanent and more voluntaristic commitment. It lasts as long as it is "good" for both spouses. This has the advantage of allowing each spouse to obtain a divorce more easily, but it also allows a husband to free himself from his marital responsibility for the support of his former wife. It thus results in less postdivorce protection for a dependent homemaker and mother.

In summary, the two systems rely on different conceptions of justice and equity. In England, justice is typically assured by providing security (in the form of housing and maintenance) for a dependent housewife (and the minor children in her custody) after divorce. In apportioning the family's property, the English system places the welfare and security of the children first. It then tries to divide the remaining family resources to provide roughly equal standards of living for husbands and wives after divorce. Justice in this system means that the young mother with young children will typically remain in the family home, and the older woman who has been a housewife and mother will be taken care of, with housing and maintenance, for the rest of her life. Although the security and protection that a wife receives will always be dependent on her husband's resources, and will therefore be limited for many divorced wives, the English system's vision of justice is one that assures her that her husband will remain responsible, according to his means, for her welfare and support. Since he will be there to "provide for her" the law does not guarantee her any fixed share of the family property.

In California in contrast, justice is typically assured by awarding both the husband wife one-half of the family assets and the "freedom" to build a new life. The division of family property is exclusively between the husband and wife, with no mention of the potential interests of children (other than their right to be supported by their parents after divorce.) Justice in this system means that the family home will often be sold, so that the husband can be assured of his half of its equity. Equity in this system is the assurance that each spouse will leave the marriage with an equal amount of the proceeds with which to "start" over. Both the young mother and the older housewife are assured the same amount of property as their former husbands — and both are encouraged to build new lives.

While the California woman is assured a fixed share of one-half of the family property, more than her English counterpart would typically expect, she is also expected to bear the economic consequences of her equal treatment without help from her former husband. Thus the California vision of justice, which relies heavily on the assumption of a new equality between men and women, may be based on the erroneous assumption of economic equality between men and women in the larger society. Since it is women who have typically been economically disadvantaged by marriage in that they are more likely to have dropped out of the labour force (or worked part time) because of their family responsibilities, and since it is women who are typically going to continue to bear the lion's share of the family responsibilities after divorce if they have minor children, equal treatment for men and women in divorce means, in practice, that divorced women in California will be left alone to shoulder the economic disadvantages they face because of their experience in marriage.

NOTES

1. For further development of this perspective see Lenore J. Weitzman and Ruth B. Dixon "The Transformation of Legal Marriage Through No-Fault Divorce," in John M. Eekelaar and Sanford N. Katz, *Marriage and Cohabitation in Western Societies*. Butterworths, 1980.
2. For a review of the ten major sociological changes in family patterns, see Lenore J. Weitzman, "Changing Families, Changing Laws: Ten Major Trends That Have Altered the Lifestyles of Parents and Children," *Family Advocate*, Summer 1982.
3. As Kevin Gray observed, "The law regulating the spouses' property relations is fundamentally an index of social relations between the sexes. It affords a peculiar wealth of commentary on such matters as the prevailing ideology of marriage, the cultural definition of the marital roles, the social status of the married woman and the role of the state vis-à-vis the family." Gray, *Property Allocation Upon Divorce*, 1977, 1.
4. A further complication, not discussed here, is that posed by family trusts and marriage settlements. These however only affect a comparatively small number of upper income families.
5. Awareness of the implicit legal contract in marriage appears to be increasing, along with a rising interest in writing individual contracts. See generally, Lenore J. Weitzman, *The Marriage Contract: Spouses, Lovers and the Law*, 1981.
6. Kingsley Davis, "The Future of Marriage," *Bulletin of the American Academy of Arts and Sciences*, May 1983. Davis shows that the exploding divorce rate in the U.S. has been followed, with about a twenty year time lag, by the other eighteen industrialized countries.
7. The situation is similar to the institutionalized social role of the widow, in contrast to the divorcee, analyzed by William Goode in *Women in Divorce (1963)*. The social and legal differences between the two occasions are substantial. One difference between death and divorce is that the interests of the two spouses are likely to coincide at death, while they are more typically at odds at divorce. In addition, while only one spouse has to live with the consequences of testamentary allocations, both spouses must live with the financial arrangements made at divorce. Finally, one only dies once but one may face divorce and its financial consequences more than once.
8. For an excellent statement of the policy aims, the content and the results of the English law see, generally, Stephen Cretney, *Principles of Family Law*, 1979, 85–169.
9. In theory, the court may deny this divorce if it will cause grave financial hardship to a dependent spouse.
10. An additional waiting period is imposed by the ban on divorce within the first three years of marriage. In a 1980 working paper (No. 76) the Law Commission concluded that this should be modified as it served primarily to delay marriage — not to prevent divorce.

11. In 1977, 26 percent of the divorce petitions alleged adultery and 37 percent alleged unreasonable behaviour (Cretney, 1979, 166). Together these two fault-based grounds accounted for close to two-thirds of the divorces.

12. They comprised 22 percent of the divorce petitions in 1977, *Ibid.*

13. They comprised 9 percent of the divorce petitions in 1977, *Ibid.*

14. Section 5, *Matrimonial Causes Act* states "The respondent may oppose the grant of a decree on the ground that the dissolution of the marriage will result in grave financial or other hardship to him and that it would in all the circumstances be wrong to dissolve the marriage. The Act goes on to state "for the purposes of this section hardship shall include the loss of the chance of acquiring any benefit which the respondent might acquire if the marriage were not dissolved."

15. Cretney, 1979, 219.

16. The *Matrimonial Proceedings and Property Act* of 1970 has been incorporated into Part II of the *Matrimonial Causes Act* of 1973.

17. Section 25, *Matrimonial Causes Act*, 1973.

18. See generally, Lenore J. Weitzman, "The Economics of Divorce: Social and Economic Consequences of Property, Alimony, and Child Support Awards," *UCLA Law Review*, August 1981, Vol 28, No. 6, 1,181-1,268; Ruth B. Dixon and Lenore J. Weitzman, "Evaluating the Impact of No-Fault Divorce," *Family Relations*, January 1981; and Lenore J. Weitzman and Ruth B. Dixon, "Child Custody Awards: Legal Standards and Empirical Patterns for Child Custody, Support, and Visitation After Divorce," *U.C. Davis Law Review*, Vol. 12, Fall, 1979.

19. The selection and sampling procedures are described in more detail in Lenore J. Weitzman and Ruth B. Dixon, "The Alimony Myth: Does No Fault Divorce Make a Difference?" *Family Law Quarterly*, Fall, 1980.

20. For example, an accountant for IBM became an accountant for ICI in England, a California truck driver became a lorry driver, and a California husband who alternated between a wealthy surgeon and a bank vice president became a merchant banker in the English version.

21. A 1977 study of English registrars conducted by Eekelaar and Clive revealed that both women and men expect women to have custody and typically agree to this arrangement. Children were living with their mother after separation in 73 percent of the cases, and the court typically confirmed the *status quo*. John Eekelaar and Eric Clive with Karen Clarke and Susan Raikes, *Custody after Divorce: The Disposition of Custody in Divorce Cases in Great Britain*, Oxford: Centre for Socio-Legal Studies, Wolfson College, 1977.

Similarly, Susan Maidment's study of custody decisions in England revealed that in 81 percent of divorce court cases and 94 percent of magistrates' cases, custody was given to the mother. Where there was a contest by the father, however, the outcome was not as predictable. Susan Maidment, "A Study in Child Custody," (Parts I and II) *Family Law*, 1976, 195-241.

There is a remarkable similarity between these two studies and Weitzman and Dixon's research in California. Interviews with men and women reveal that both typically agree to mother custody after divorce, and custody was awarded to the mother in 89 percent of the divorce cases in 1977. However, the California research also found that fathers who want and contest custody are fairly successful. Lenore J. Weitzman and Ruth B. Dixon, "Child Custody Awards," *supra*, note 18.

22. Many of the facts in this case were varied in different California versions with no apparent effect. For example, the parties were given names in one version but not in

another. The ages of the children varied from three and four, to four and six (as in England), to five and eight, and the ages of the parents from twenty-three and twenty-seven, to twenty-seven and twenty-eight (as in England), to thirty-six and fourty-one. In one California version the husband worked as an accountant for IBM, in another he was a self-employed accountant. Finally, in several versions custody was at issue and the couple did not own their home.

23. In a nationwide study of English registrars it was reported that about one-half of the couples either owned or were purchasing the matrimonial home (Barrington Barker, 1977, 36). Similarly, in California 48 percent of the 1978 divorcing couples owned or were purchasing a family home (Weitzman, 1982).

24. Named after the case that established the practice.

25. Majority in California is fixed at age eighteen in contrast to the variable English standard that allows a full-time student to remain a minor while completing his or her education.

26. In either case, the California husband would receive a note for his half of the equity in the house at the time of the divorce, payable, with interest upon sale of the house. If the home increased in value while the wife was living in it (and maintaining it), the increment belonged to her.

27. See, for example, *In Marriage of Boseman,* 31 Cal. App. 3d 372, 107 Cal. Rptr. 232 (1973).

28. The 13 percent of the English respondents who predicted that the family home would be sold upon divorce typically gave the wife a much larger share of the equity (a median share of three-quarters of the home equity) to enable her to buy a smaller house for herself and her children.

29. Hilary Land documents the legal presumption of a married woman's financial dependency on her husband found in the English social security system, tax system, national insurance system and in housing policy. Hillary Land, "Women: Supporters of Supported," in Leonard and Allen (eds.) *Dependence and Exploitation in Work and Marriage,* 1976; and Hilary Land and Roy Parker, United Kingdom," in Sheila B. Kammerman and Alfred J. Kahn (eds.) *Family Policy: Government and Families in Fourteen Countries,* New York, Columbia University Press, 1978.

For example, only the husband can sign the couple's joint income tax return (unless the wife has opted for separate taxation). "Should too much tax be deducted from a woman's pay, the rebate may be sent to her husband because, legally, it belongs to him. Even if the marital home is jointly owned it is assumed that he will claim the tax relief on the interest element of the mortgage payments" (Land and Parker, 1978, 343).

Along the same lines, Katherine O'Donovon observes that even if a wife works, it is assumed that she is merely supplementing her husband's wages — and, of course, it is always assumed that she nevertheless retains her full responsibility to care for her children, husband, and sick or elderly relatives. Thus the English tax system allows married men with incapacitated wives an additional personal allowance. Katherine O'Donovan, "The Male Appendage — Legal Definitions of Women," in Burman, *Fit Work for Women* (1979), pp. 134–52.

30. In England, in 1979–81, one-parent families were 11.9 percent of all families with dependent children. Popay, Rimmer and Rossiter, *One Parent Families* (Study Commission on the Family, 1983) 10. In the U.S. single-parent households comprised 14 percent of all households in 1980.

31. In a follow-up version of this case, both sets of respondents were asked what would happen in subsequent years if *(a)* Victor remarried an employed woman with two sons, and *(b)* Ann began cohabiting with a free-lance writer. These results will be reported separately.

32. In fact, English sociologist Diana Leonard suggests that it is the English concern with maintaining the standard of living for the children (of men of breeding), that underlies the apparent concern for the women who are their caretakers. Personal conversation, June 1981.

33. For an evaluation of child support awards in terms of the children's needs, see Weitzman, "The Economics of Divorce" *supra,* note 18, 1,235-37.

34. Lenore J. Weitzman, "The Economics of Divorce" *supra,* note 18, p. 1,195 n. 42.

35. See, for example, The Law Commission, *The Financial Consequences of Divorce: The Basic Policy* 1980, and Campaign for Justice in Divorce, *An Even Better Way Out,* 1979, 4, n. 8.

Chapter Thirty

*The Economic Consequences of Divorce for Families with Children**

Mavis Maclean and John Eekelaar

Centre for Socio-Legal Studies, Wolfson College, Oxford, England

---

This chapter examines the actual economic situation in 1981 of a nationally representative sample of families with dependent children which had undergone divorce within the previous ten years in England. This time period was chosen because a reformed divorce law, allowing easier divorce and enhancing the courts' powers to make financial provision on divorce, came into effect on 1 January 1971. One of the purposes of the research project was to consider the effects *over time* of divorce settlements, whether informally arranged or imposed by court order. In the context of families with children, this examination entailed a consideration of the extent to which child support was in fact paid, its significance for the receiving family and its effects on the payer and (his) new family. In other words, how were family members actually resolving the questions of competing claims on their resources?

In making this investigation, it was impossible to avoid detailed consideration of the role of state provision. Indeed, decisions about whether to seek employment, to remarry, to seek maintenance or rely on state benefits are all interrelated in a complex way. We could not show precisely how such decisions were made, but we were able to produce information about how the results of such decisions affected family income. In order to assist the formulation of normative judgments, we also sought to make comparisons, both between the researched popu-

---

* This chapter is based on the authors' paper, *Children and Divorce: Economic Factors* (SSRC Centre for Socio-Legal Studies. Wolfson College, Oxford) where the supporting data is fully set out.

lation and the population at large and between subgroups of the researched population. We do not draw such judgments ourselves, but believe that we provide the basis upon which they may be made. We believe that important issues concerning justice between different groups of children are at the very heart of the major conflicts which arise on marriage breakdown and that a legal system needs to develop a policy towards them. This policy should provide a framework within which the conflicts should be resolved.

The first part of this chapter explains briefly the aims and methods of the research project. We then consider the evidence of the economic condition of divorced, non-remarried parents with dependent children in their household and the resources available to them. We proceed to consider these resources in turn: the assets of the former family; the earning capacity of the custodial parent; the earning capacity of the noncustodial parent and state provision. Finally, we consider the impact of remarriage on the family's economics.

AIMS AND METHODS OF THE SURVEY

For the divorcing population we have basic data on the numbers of petitions filed, divorces granted and ancillary orders made, and for various subgroups we have further information, for example, about single-parent families on supplementary benefit. But it is difficult to piece together from these different sources any clear idea of how divorce affects the financial position over time of those involved. The Centre for Socio-Legal Studies, with funding from the SSRC and Equal Opportunities Commission, has attempted to contribute towards filling this gap by undertaking a survey of the financial consequences of divorce. We wished to be able to compare the sources and levels of income of men and women who had formed new families with those who had not, to look closely at their household composition, their housing and employment position, and to examine income transfers between households in the form of maintenance. In addition, we wished to describe the process by which financial adjustments had been made at the end of the first marriage, to investigate our respondents' attitudes to the outcome in their own case and discover their views on the question of postdivorce support obligations.

With limited resources, and concern to produce data quickly as pressure for legal reform mounted, we decided that existing data sets were not suitable either for producing the information needed or even as sampling frames for locating the individuals we wished to interview. The existing data sets either covered only a subgroup of the divorced population, or would not enable us to trace people who had been divorced for any length of time. We wished to collect information from a nationally representative sample of men and women, petitioners and respondents, with and without children, with varying income levels, who had been divorced since the reformed divorce law came into effect in January, 1971. We therefore used an omnibus survey quota sample of 7,257 adults, controlled for sex, age and socioeconomic group, based on 180 sampling points, designed to represent the adult population of England and Wales. Screening interviews were carried out in May 1981, asking whether the respondent or any other household member had been divorced since 1971 and if so, permission was requested to call back and talk about the financial effects of divorce. A total of 154 male-reported and 206 female-reported divorced people formed our full recall sample at 314 addresses. Ten addresses were used in a pilot study, refining the questionnaire, and so the final recall sample consisted of 304 addresses. Of these, 23 were out of scope (ineligible, or vacant or derelict addresses). At the 271 in-scope addresses, a response of 85 percent (n. 229) was achieved, with information from 92 men and 184 women.

ECONOMIC CIRCUMSTANCES OF NON-REMARRIED DIVORCED PARENTS WITH DEPENDENT CHILDREN

The evidence describing the adverse economic circumstances of the remnant mother–child family after divorce is overwhelming. Chambers (1979, 48) calculated that, deprived of economies of scale, a mother with two children requires 75–80 percent of the former family's total income in order to retain, after divorce, the standard of living enjoyed before separation. Yet it is precisely this unit which has the least capacity for maintaining this level of income. The problems and costs of obtaining child care are compounded by the well known disparity between the earnings of men and women (see Law Commission 1980, 32–33; Glendon 1980, 130–31; Rimmer 1982). The result is the massive extent to which mother–child families are dependent on supplementary benefit (the basic subsistence allowance in the United Kingdom) for their main support. Three hundred and fifty thousand of the 650,000 such families in the United Kingdom in 1976 relied on state benefits for their main source of income (Study Commission on the Family 1981). In the United States, 42 percent of mother–child families were below the poverty level in 1978 (Glendon 1981, 134). In 1979, 62 percent of New York's mother–child families were in receipt of welfare benefits compared with 4.6 percent of two-parent families (*New York Times* Feb 14, 1982). The incidence in the United Kingdom of prebenefit poverty in single-parent families in 1974–76 was 50.8 percent, twice that of the national average, and the incidence after taking into account benefits was 12.3 percent compared with 9.6 percent of all nonpensioner households (Beckerman and Clark 1982, 39–43). Layard (1978) described a third (28 percent) of all families but nearly two-thirds (58 percent) of single-parent families as living close to poverty, defined as below 140 percent of their supplementary benefit entitlement. This is because the latter have lost the chief protective device against poverty — the possibility of a second earner in the household.

We suspect this represents a major movement into poverty by mothers and children formerly outside. Hoffman (1977), using data from the American Panel Study of Income Dynamics, showed that between 1967 and 1973 the real income of families unaffected by separation or divorce rose by 21.7 percent, whereas that of women who divorced or separated during that period fell by 29.3 percent. Relating income to needs (by relating the Department of Agriculture's Low Cost Food Budget to the size and age/sex composition of the family) the standard of living of the intact family rose by 20.8 percent and that of the divorced or separated woman fell by 6.7 percent. Since children are overwhelmingly likely to remain with the former wife after separation or divorce (in only 10 percent of a national sample of divorce cases in 1974 were the children left with the father only — see Eekelaar and Clive, 1977), economic decline almost invariably affects the children of divorce. Comparable British data from longitudinal studies is not available. However, of the 150 families in our sample with children under sixteen (or sixteen to eighteen in full time education) at the time of interview, 52 were single-parent families (in 5 of which the adult was the father) and 98 were families which had reformed a two-parent family either through remarriage or cohabitation (referred to as "reconstituted families"). We found a larger proportion of all families reporting welfare payments as their main source of income at the time of interview than at the time of their marriage and separation. But the increase was far greater for those who remained single parents (see Table 30.1).

Our data were able to provide still more detailed comparisons between the financial circumstances of the families of the divorced and other families and between divorced families. In order to do this, and to avoid the problems of inflation over time, we needed to relate total net disposable household income to a household equivalent scale, i.e., a scale indicating a relationship between needs and means. The scale most widely used and understood in this country is that used by the supplementary benefit authorities (see van Slooten and Coverdale 1978, 27–29). We therefore calculated the short term supplementary benefit allowance (excluding special needs but including the current housing allowance) for each household at the time of interview (November, 1981), and taking the mid point in the band reported for total net disposable household income, we were able to calculate the percentage of supplementary benefit income level received by each family. This enables us to compare our groups with the poverty literature which uses various cut off points such as 140 percent or 120 percent of supplementary benefit level (see, for example, Layard 1978; Townsend 1981).

TABLE 30.1 Divorced Parents Reporting Welfare Payments as their Main Source of Income over Time

Present status of respondent	At marriage	At separation	At divorce	November 1981
Single parents (n.52)	0	8 (15%)	24 (46%)	29 (56%)
Reconstituted parents with children from first marriage (n.36)	1	3	10	7
Reconstituted parents with children from first and second marriages (n.34)	0	0 } 8%	4 }17%	3 }15%
Reconstituted parents with children from second marriage (n.28)	0	5	3	4
Total	1	16 (11%)	41 (27%)	43 (29%)

We also wished to place our groups of parents in the context of some measure of average family income. This is a "common-sense" concept which is extremely difficult to approach with any precision. However, for our purposes it seemed reasonable to take the average income of a two adult, two child household as measured each year by the Family Expenditure Survey. In order to compare relative standards of living between our groups and the FES two adult, two child family, we converted the incomes of our sample and the FES family into a proportion of each family's supplementary benefit entitlement. For the FES two adult two child family (assuming one child to be under ten and one between ten and fifteen) the average income for such a family forms 200 percent of their supplementary benefit entitlement at November, 1981, rates.

In Table 30.2 we follow Layard (1978) and use 140 percent of Supplementary benefit entitlement as our "Poverty Line" and the FES average family income, i.e., 200 percent of supplementary benefit entitlement, as the "Happy Family Line." Using this measure of the income/needs ratio for each family, nearly two-thirds of the single parents were living close to or below the supplementary benefit level, and 4 out of 5 below our poverty line of 140 percent of supplementary benefit entitlement, compared with less than a fifth of reconstituted families at close to or below supplementary benefit level, and a third below 140 percent supplementary benefit. Fewer than one in ten of our single-parent families enjoyed what could be called an average family standard of living, compared with one in four of the reconstituted families. The noncustodial parents without children in their present household were less likely to appear in the just above poverty/just under average group than the reconstituted families, but more likely to appear at both extremes.

TABLE 30.2 Household Net Disposable Income as a Percentage of Supplementary Benefit Entitlement for Each Family for Single and Reconstituted Parents

Supp. Ben. %	Single (n.52) %	Reconstituted (n.98) %	Non custodial parent without ch. in present h/h (n.19) %
300+	4)	9)	20)
250–229	2) 8%	5) 26%	25) 45%
200–249	2)	12)	0)
	HAPPY FAMILY LINE		
180–199	0)	8)	10)
160–179	2) 12%	9) 37%	0) 15%
140–159	10)	20)	5)
	POVERTY LINE		
110–139	17)	13)	25)
90–109	31) 79%	11) 30%	5) 40%
below 90	31)	6)	10)
DK	2	5	0

To give a clearer picture of the spread of the income distributions of these households in relation to those of the average (Family Expenditure Survey) family, we divided our single and reconstituted parents into quantiles in order to compare our data with the Family Expenditure Survey for 1981, published in *FES 1982*. Table 30.3 makes it possible for us to see the size of the gap between the standard of living of single and reconstituted parents, but also the nature of the gap between the standard of living of reconstituted parents and the average two adult, two child household. Although the incomes of the top quantile of reconstituted parents is very close to the FES family, the median income and the lower quantile of the reconstituted family are clearly below that of the "average" family. We are unlikely to be able to solve the financial problems of the single parents by looking to the majority of reconstituted parents for increased resources to be transferred. Although their earning *capacity* is not affected by divorce and remarriage, yet their incomes reflect the larger numbers of divorce cases among lower income households (Dunnell 1980; Gibson 1974) and the larger family size which may result from a remarrying woman bringing with her children from a former marriage and going on to have more.

TABLE 30.3 Average Disposable Household Incomes of Parents in Quantiles Presented as a Percentage of Supplementary Benefit Entitlements

	Single Parent (n.52) %	Reconstituted households (n.98) %	2 adult, 2 child FES family* (n.1046) %
Top decile	268	327	328
Top quantile	185	279	254
Median	96	158	200
Lowest quantile	72	102	150
Lowest decile	67	84	112

* See *FES 1982*, Table 26, p. 72.

On divorce there are essentially four sources from which support might be found to arrest the decline in the economic circumstances of the former family. The first comprises the *resources of the former family* as they stood at the moment of the dissolution. However, as most studies have shown, these are generally meagre (Todd and Jones 1972; Manners and Rauta 1981). But where an independent household existed, a dwelling, either owner occupied or rented, is likely to be the most significant item. The second is *the earning capacity of the custodial parent* (which we assume for simplicity to be the mother). The third is *the earning capacity of the noncustodial parent* (the father). And the last resource is to be found in *state provisions*. Any close examination of the economic consequences of divorce must examine the interplay of each of these elements, not only on divorce (or when a court order is made) but also over time noting especially *the effects of remarriage,* for remarriage introduces a fifth and powerful economic resource for the remnant family. Only when this whole process is understood can a true appreciation be made of the economic effects of divorce and perhaps from that appreciation we may begin to estimate to what extent these events influence the life chances of the individuals concerned.

RESOURCES AVAILABLE FROM THE FIRST MARRIAGE

Property Owned at Separation

Fewer than one in five of our total sample (n.274) had savings of over £500 at the time of divorce. Clearly capital assets could not affect the income levels of most families after divorce. The main asset at the end of marriage for most couples is either a council (public authority) tenancy or the equity in a home being bought with a mortgage.

Housing

Of our fifty-two single parents, nineteen possessed a council tenancy at separation and all except one remained in local authority housing. Of the twelve in privately rented housing, five remained there; five were rehoused by the local authority and two went home to their parents. Twenty-one of our single parents (including one man) had been in owner-occupied housing at the point of separation. Of these, ten women and one man stayed in the matrimonial home, though only four women were able to take over responsibility for mortgage repayments. For three of these single mothers remaining in the matrimonial home, the former husband retained an interest, and two reported their husbands as taking responsibility for the mortgage in lieu of maintenance payments. The remaining house was owned by a friend. Of the ten women who left the owner-occupied matrimonial home, seven left with a share of the equity which enabled two to rent in the private sector; four were able to buy again, and one went home to her parents. Of the three who left without any share, two were rehoused by the local authority and one went home to her mother. Thus, almost all those in council housing remained there, and some former private tenants went over to council housing. Of those in owner-occupation, three out of four were able to remain in the private sector, though in several cases only with support from the former partner who was also quite likely to retain an interest in the property.

Of the ninety-eight parents who reformed a family, thirty-four were in local authority housing at the time of separation and the majority remained there, except for a group of eight women who moved into owner-occupied housing with their new partners. Twenty-three were renting in the private sector at the time of separation, of whom a small number (four) stayed; seven went into council housing and twelve (all women) moved into owner-occupation with the new partner. Of the forty-one in owner-occupied housing at separation, the men were more likely to remain in the matrimonial home than the women. Seven of the twelve men stayed (four of whom gave their wife a share of the equity) and five left (two of whom bought again, one went into local authority housing, one moved into a new partner's own home, and one into a new partner's council house). Of the twenty-nine women, only five stayed in the matrimonial home (of whom two held the house with their former partner on trust for sale; one had bought out her husband). It appears that a second husband only rarely moves into the former matrimonial home. If a new partner enters the former home, it is more likely to be the husband's new wife. Of the twenty-four women who left, fourteen took a share; nine moved into owner-occupied housing with the new partner and three into council housing; and two cohabitees went into privately rented housing. Of the ten reconstituted women who left without a share of the equity, two went into council housing, one into the private sector, and the other seven moved into owner-occupied housing with their new partners. The housing resources of the first family are not generally being used as the foundation for the mother's second family. On remarriage, her housing status will depend primarily on her second husband although in some cases she may be assisted by a small lump sum from the realization of the first house.

EARNED INCOME, MAINTENANCE AND SOCIAL SECURITY

In 1978 Layard reported that "the same fraction of single-parent mothers work as all mothers — but as mothers they have a relatively low earning capacity." Seventy percent of working mothers work part-time compared with only 26 percent of working women without dependent children (see Joshi and Owen 1981), and without male earnings coming in, "even the families of single-parent mothers who work tend to be below the average level of economic welfare."

Of our forty-seven single mothers, ten were working full-time and sixteen part-time, i.e., 55 percent were working, of whom one-third were working full-time. One was on a grant of £58 per week. But what is the significance of these earnings for the total household income of these women in view of the fact that they may also be receiving social security benefits and support from a former partner, and that entitlement to and receipt of such support is interrelated? Does this pattern of full and part-time employment mean that these women are maximizing their resources? For those working full-time (n.10) and thereby not entitled to supplementary benefit, we calculated the level of supplementary benefit to which they would have been entitled had they not been working, and also their levels of income if they had worked part-time and been "topped up" by supplementary benefit to an income level which would exceed basic supplementary benefit by £12, the earnings disregard level currently applied to single parents, in order to see what effect full-time employment was having on the households' net total income. It turned out that three women were working full-time for, in effect, under £5 and four more women for under £15 per week more than they could have received if they had worked part-time and relied on supplementary benefit as part of their income. Only two women earned more than £25 above what they would have received had they been relying on supplementary benefit as their sole source of income.

It appears that the receipt of maintenance by women working full-time helped to bring the total household income above the level which could have been achieved by working part-time, but only a little above. It seems that nonmonetary factors were probably involved in these women's decision to work full-time. On the one hand, many people prefer the independence of living on earned income together with the company of other people at work, which may be particularly important to single parents. But on the other, full-time working involves travel expenses, eating away from home and child minding, and precludes using supplementary benefit as a passport to other benefits in kind, such as cash and clothing grants and free school meals. In the case of the full-time earners, maintenance played only a marginal role *vis à vis* the household's income level, but in two cases it enabled the recipients to do a little better in full-time employment than if they had relied on supplementary benefit and part-time earnings.

Of the sixteen mothers working part-time, eight were not in receipt of supplementary benefit (the latter included one woman who had remarried, been widowed, and received the widowed mother's allowance, which is not related to earnings, and £12 maintenance). All eight who did not receive supplementary benefit (except the widow) were living at or below our estimate of their supplementary benefit level of household income. Three were receiving maintenance (weekly payments of £10, £8 and £25), which must have enabled these women to avoid drawing supplementary benefit. Of the eight women receiving supplementary benefit, five received maintenance (three had maintenance orders made over to the Department of Health and Social Security (DHSS), one received £6 directly, and one had it paid through the DHSS). Thus in almost all the instances where maintenance was an element of the income of a part-time worker, it in fact benefited (directly or indirectly) only the state. It did not increase the household income of the women and children for whom it was paid. In fact, in the three cases where the women lived on their earnings plus maintenance rather than supplementary benefit, they were worse off than they might have been if entirely reliant on the latter, so the maintenance element may well have had the result of effectively depressing their potential income.

We found a similar situation among the twenty women who were not working at all. Only three were not receiving a supplementary benefit; one had returned to her family of origin, while two lived on maintenance plus child benefit — both of them at a level below our estimate of their supplementary benefit entitlement. As in the cases of the three part-time workers, the payment of maintenance indirectly benefited the DHSS, but the result was that the actual income of these women was lower than it might otherwise have been. And for the other twelve women of the seventeen on supplementary benefit who were receiving maintenance, the benefit went directly to the DHSS.

In all, it appears that one woman in full-time work, three women in part-time work and two women not in employment were probably able to avoid claiming supplementary benefit as a result of receiving maintenance. In these cases, the actual household income remained close to the supplementary benefit level. And in seventeen cases where maintenance was received by women on supplementary benefit, the benefit went directly to the state. In only three cases did maintenance raise the household income level, in one case because another benefit was disregarded, and in two cases because full-time earnings plus maintenance brought the household above the maximum supplementary benefit level augmented by part-time earnings.

Layard (1978) reported that although wives work at all income levels, they are more likely to do so in families which would otherwise be below the poverty line, i.e., the best protection against poverty is the second earner. This option is clearly not open to the single-parent families. As the above analysis shows, the extent to which this shortcoming is reduced by drawing on the resources of an earning ex-member of the family seems to be limited. Indeed, in the case of part-time workers or nonearners, the availability of such resources was either of no real benefit to them and even an actual detriment when seen in relation to the actual or potential availability of social security benefits.

LEVELS OF MAINTENANCE PAYMENTS RECEIVED

An American study (Sorenson and MacDonald 1982), based on three survey sources, reports that child support payments are low and not received by very many households, but where they are received they do raise the remnant families above the poverty line. It is difficult to attempt this kind of assessment in the United Kingdom because of the relationship between earnings, maintenance transfers and supplementary benefit. However, we can attempt to discover the extent to which maintenance payments form part of the actual or notional income of the families of children affected by divorce; that is, how far their former major source of support continued as an element in their income resources.

Of our forty-seven single mothers, only nine had no maintenance agreement in their favor at time of divorce. The most frequent reason for this was the husband's unemployment. In one case, a custody dispute was mentioned. Six had agreements which were not complied with and two had a mortgage paid in lieu. If we include the men making mortgage payments, this means that some form of regular support payments were in fact received by two-thirds (68 percent) of the single mothers. Fewer of the sixty-four mothers with custody of a child from their first marriage who had reconstituted a family received maintenance, but nevertheless, the proportion reporting payments amounted to 47 percent. Hitherto, the significance of maintenance payments has been assessed on the basis of the amounts ordered to be paid and the degree of compliance with such orders. The Finer Committee in particular were very unimpressed with the sums ordered by magistrates, pointing out that they were much lower than the recipients' supplementary benefit entitlement and that the higher they were the quicker they fell into arrears (see Finer Report 1974, vol. 1, 101–104). Doig (1982, 28) found evidence that child support orders in Scotland were "likely" to be paid in one-quarter of cases, but observed that there was no indication one way or the other for nearly half of the orders. Although we are not able to take into account the effects of the passage of time over the long term, it does appear, looking at our data based on the reports of those entitled to payment, that the *degree* to which some resources move across families is not inconsiderable.

The *amounts* which are so transferred are, of course, another matter. They are often very small; half (n=14) below £10 per week; a quarter (n=7) between £10 and £20 and only a quarter (n=8) above £20. But in over half the cases these payments had been received for over five years, 15 percent for over ten and 42 percent for six to ten years, thus adding up, over time, to considerable sums. Indeed, these amounts can represent a significant part of the receiving household's income. For one in five of the single mothers, the payments represented less than 10 percent of their income, for three out of four, less than a third, for a quarter, more than one third, and for 7 percent, more than a half. But it must also be remembered that for seventeen of these cases the maintenance paid did not in fact affect the household's income at all, but benefited directly or indirectly the state. The amounts paid to reconstituted families were lower (70 percent were under £10 and 13 percent over £20) but, as these families were not on supplementary benefit, these payments were, ironically, more likely to have an actual impact on their household income. It also appears that the lower the family income level, the higher will be the proportion of that income represented by maintenance payments, although here again it is necessary to remember that for the poorest families the maintenance payment is of no direct benefit.

THE RESOURCES OF THE PAYERS

Twenty-nine men in our sample had children of their first marriage living in another household, of whom twelve currently had other children in their present household and seventeen had not. Of these twenty-nine, nine men were not paying maintenance regularly. Five of these men were unemployed, one of whom also described an access dispute. Two had stopped paying maintenance when their former wife had remarried, and in one case, maintenance was not paid because custody of the child was shared. It seems clear that unemployment is now a major cause of inability to pay maintenance. These figures refer to unemployment at the time of interview. It is important to remember in addition that one in four (12/47) of the husbands of our single mothers were unemployed at the time of the divorce. This association between marital breakdown and disruption of work performance has been recorded by the General Household Survey for some years and is discussed by Daniel (1981, Table II.30) in the context of entry into unemployment. Twenty fathers of children under sixteen were paying maintenance (nine of the twelve with other children in the household, and eleven of the seventeen without). The payments made are described as a percentage of household income for men with and without children in the present household.

The men without children in their present household were more likely to pay over 10 percent of their household income to their noncustodial children than the men with a second family. But the part such payments play in the household economy of the maintenance payer appears far less significant than in the receiver's household economy. For only just over a third of the men (35 percent) did the transfer represent over 10 percent of their household income, whereas maintenance constituted over 10 percent of the income of over half the women. If the women are divided into those who reconstituted and those who remained alone, the payments formed over 10 percent of the household income for one-third of the reconstituted women, and for 74 percent of the women alone (though not always directly affecting their actual income).

We wished to examine more closely the position of the men who paid maintenance, to see whether extra resources might be released for the remnant families. We looked to see whether the proportion of income transferred bore any relation to the income level (as expressed by supplementary benefit percentage entitlement) of those paying. We did so by comparing the household income level of men paying maintenance (payers) with all men who had at least one child (whether their own or step) in their current household. It was found that, while 55 percent of the payers had below average incomes (*i.e.*, under 200 percent supplementary benefit entitlement), 71 percent of all custodial men were in that position. But this is almost entirely due to the fact that men under supplementary benefit level do not pay maintenance. Nevertheless, 40 percent of payers had above average incomes compared to 28 percent of the others, so payment is being made by men who are slightly better off than custodial men generally are. But the *proportion* of income handed over varied very little despite variation in income level. Could the fathers with above average incomes (both those now paying maintenance and those not) transfer more to their noncustody children? We could calculate, for the ten fathers with above average incomes with children under sixteen in another household, how much surplus income was left after allowing them 200 percent of supplementary benefit entitlement, *i.e.,* an average income. Two of these men had children in their present household, as well as elsewhere. After paying their current maintenance, one had £2 surplus and the other £7. Clearly there were no untapped resources in this group. But of the eight with no children in their present household, all but two had over £10 surplus, sometimes considerably more, after paying existing maintenance. These figures represent surplus income at one point in time, and these men's incomes may vary over time. But it seems possible that for a small group, increased maintenance could be paid without depressing the payers below an average standard of living. We do not know the standard of living of the children outside the household of these particular men, but, if it were below the average standard, the discrepancy between them is hard to justify.

RECONSTITUTED FAMILIES: EARNED INCOME, WELFARE AND MAINTENANCE PAID AND RECEIVED

The children in our sample who had acquired a second parent through remarriage or reconstitution had spent varying periods of time in single-parent households: 36 percent, one to two years; 41 percent, three to five years; and 23 percent, over five years. We know that a number were dependent on welfare support at divorce (17 percent), and 15 percent remained in this position at the time of interview, *i.e.,* a proportion very close to that for all families with children (see Layard 1978). These children were far less likely to live at or below the poverty line than those in single-parent families. Of the reconstituted parents who are in financial difficulty, can we see why? Which of these resources which are acting to protect the majority of reconstituted families from poverty are not available to some of the reconstituted families?

It is clear that there were two main causes of difficulty for the twenty-nine reconstituted families below our poverty line of 140 percent supplementary benefit level; only 60 percent had a head of household in full-time work, compared with 94 percent of those above the poverty line. And in only 28 percent of these households was there a second earner, compared with 46 percent of those not in difficulty. Family size and transfers between households appear to play a relatively small part. Only 7 percent of reconstituted families received more than half of their income in the form of maintenance payments; it was under 10 percent for nearly two-thirds of them. Nor did maintenance payments-out affect the standard of living of reconstituted families very much. Indeed, as we have seen, there may be some scope for larger transfers in a small number of cases.

Although it is being increasingly suggested that reconstitution involving step parenting leads to many social and emotional difficulties for those involved (see Burgoyne and Clark 1983) it does at least reduce the likelihood of some children spending their childhood in poverty — though the reconstituted families do not appear to offer a large-scale untapped source of support for remnant families. Indeed, they appear slightly worse off than the population generally. This may be attributable to the higher incidence of divorce among manual workers, and their age distribution. The remarried are likely to be in their thirties, and an unskilled worker's earnings begin to tail off in his late twenties. They are also likely to have larger families, where remarried women have brought children into the family. Only where there were no children in the present household did the father appear to have any capacity for increased maintenance, and though this group contained some who had remarried, these men might not continue childless in their second marriage.

CONCLUSIONS

The data presented here illustrate the degree to which children living in single-parent families after divorce suffer economic deprivation relative both to the generality of the population and children of reconstituted families. The most effective way of recovering their position is by the remarriage of the single parent. Remarriage thus constitutes the major social mechanism for mitigating this particular form of adversity. If both parents remarry, some form of equilibrium is restored, although it will not be perfect because of the tendency of remarriage to generate families of larger size than first marriages. No other form of income transfer arrangement comes remotely near to remarriage in effectiveness in restoring equity between children of divorce and other children. Reliance on the labour market by the mother does little to alter substantially the position. This ought to be a major consideration when, whether through mediation or otherwise, the parties are attempting to plan ahead for their post-divorce lives.

The disparity in household income between the mother–child family and that of their former breadwinner, even taking into account transfers of income between them (whether ordered or agreed) and state benefits, poses a major challenge to policy. The disparity is accentuated when the man has not acquired new child dependents. Our data does not suggest that the calls made by a man's former family on his resources could operate as a deterrent against his remarriage. Once a man has acquired a new set of dependents, our data shows that a disparity between his former and his new family persists, but that little more could be taken from him to help the former family if the latter are not to fall below an *average* standard of living. But the former family will probably lie well below the average standard in any case. What is the fair way of achieving a balance between them? The situation is frequently significantly complicated by the relationship between private support payments and supplementary benefit. We have seen that, for a significant number of single-parent family recipients, the sums paid either accrued solely or partly to the state or did little (even when additional to earnings) to raise the standard of living much above poverty levels. One response to this situation is to enhance the state's primary obligation to these families, allowing it to recover what it can from the fathers and this, of course, was the solution opted for by the Finer Committee. But since this seems politically unattainable in the foreseeable future, we should perhaps look afresh at the relationship between state and private resources. It should be noted that, when having recourse against a liable relative (in this case, the father), the British practice is not to reduce him below an income representing his supplementary benefit entitlement (including household costs) plus one-quarter of his net disposable income (or £5), whichever is the greater (see Finer Report 1974, vol. 1, 137). The effect of this is that the state permits the payer and his new family (if he has remarried) to benefit to that extent by its subsidy of the former family. But why should the father or the second family alone benefit from such indulgence? The practice is the more questionable when it is recalled that the payments mean so much more to the former family. It might be argued that the benefit of this remission should be shared between the families by halving the margin of immunity of the payer and allowing the additional payments this would generate to be disregarded as against supplementary benefit entitlement of the receiver or (a more generous measure) by keeping the immunity margin but introducing a disregard (perhaps £12, as for part-time earnings) of the support payment. Would it be reasonable to suppose that a man would be more ready to make *voluntary* payments to his former family if he knew that they conferred tangible benefits on his children instead of being engulfed by the anonymity of the state? Furthermore, it would represent a partial move towards redressing the inequality between these children and their father's new family. The cost to the state would be marginal compared to the gain to these families, and considerably less than any guaranteed maintenance scheme. Our findings show a high degree of acceptance by men of *some* responsibility towards their children of an earlier union. We are not sure *how far* they, or society at large, understand this responsibility to extend. Conflict resolution will always remain problematic while such moral uncertainty persists.

REFERENCES

Beckerman, W. and Clark, S. (1982) *Poverty and Social Security in Britain Since 1961.* (Oxford: Oxford University Press).
Burgoyne, J. and Clark, D. *Making a Go of It: A Study of Step-Parents in Sheffield* (Routledge and Kegan Paul, forthcoming).

Chambers D.L. (1979) *Making Fathers Pay: The Enforcement of Child Support* (University of Chicago Press).
Daniel, W. (1980) *The Unemployed Flow*. London: Policy Studies Institute.
Douglas, J.W.B., Ross, J.M. and Simpson, H.R. (1968) *All Our Future* (Peter Davies, London).
Doig, B. (1982) *The Nature of Scale of Aliment and Financial Provision on Divorce* (Scotland, Central Research Unit Paper).
Dunnell, K. (1980) *Family Formation* (London, HMSO).
Eekelaar, J. and Clive, E., with Karen Clarke and Susan Raikes. (1977) *Custody after Divorce* (SSRC Centre for Socio-Legal Studies, Oxford).
Finer Report. (1974) *Report of the Committee on One-Parent Families,* vols. 1 and 2, (Cmnd. 5629) (HMSO) GHS (1980).
Gibson, C. (1974) "Divorce and Social Class in England and Wales," *British Journal of Sociology* vol. xxv, 79-83.
Glendon, M.A. (1981) *The New Family and the New Property* (Butterworths, Canada).
Hoffman, S. (1977) "Marital Instability and the Economic Status of Women," *Demography,* vol. 14, 67-76.
Joshi, H. and Owen, S. (1981) *Demographic Predictions of Women's Work Participation in Post War Britain* (London, Centre for Population Studies).
Law Commission (1980) *Family Law: The Financial Consequences of Divorce: The Basic Policy,* Law Commission, No. 103 (HMSO).
Layard, R. (1978) Background Paper no. 6, *The Causes of Poverty* RCDIW, (HMSO).
Manners, A.J. and Rauta, I. (1981) *Family Property in Scotland* (HMSO).
Rimmer, L. (1982) *Employment Trends and the Family* (London, Study Commission on the Family).
Sorenson, A. and MacDonald, M. (1982) "Does Child Support Support the Children?" *Children and Youth Services Review,* Vol. 4, 53-66.
Study Commission on the Family (1981) *Family Finances: An Interim Report from the Working Party on the Financial Circumstances of Families* (Study Commission on the Family).
Todd, J.E. and Jones, L.M. (1972) *Matrimonial Property* (London, HMSO).
Townsend, P. (1981) *Poverty in the United Kingdom* (Harmondsworth, Penguin Books).
van Slooten, R. and Coverdale, A.G. (1978), "The Characteristics of No-Income Households," *Social Trends* 8, 27-29 (London, HMSO).

Chapter Thirty-one

Maintenance and Family Support: The Social Reality in England and Wales

Colin S. Gibson

Bedford College, University of London, England

The year 1980 saw some 148,000 marriages dissolved by the divorce courts of England and Wales. All but a minority of petitions were processed by administrative action, under what is known as special procedure. As long as the respondent spouse does not dispute that the marriage has irretrievably broken down — as shown by the facts set out in the petition — then neither party will normally be expected to attend court to give evidence or be examined on the history of the marital breakdown. Conflict within the legal arena arises in the court's resolution of the so-called ancillary matters of financial support, property resolution and issues of child custody and access.

This chapter focuses upon some of the problems of financial support and how they are handled by the courts in England and Wales.

THE TWO-TIER COURT STRUCTURE

Wives seeking maintenance for themselves or their children have the choice of two courts. Those who seek a license to marry again turn to the divorce courts that are sited in the larger towns and cities. For others not seeking divorce or judicial separation, the 1,100 magistrates' courts have power to award maintenance and adjudicate on questions of custody and access. However, survey findings show that some 70 percent of these marriages will eventually end up in the divorce court. The last decade has seen the number of new maintenance orders made by magistrates decline sharply as wives show greater propensity to proceed directly to the divorce court.

Divorcing wives with already existing magistrates' courts maintenance orders will often let such orders continue unchanged at the time of the divorce hearing. This is partly because of the more practical enforcement procedure operating in the summary courts compared to that of the divorce courts. For this reason 1980 saw an additional 19,630 divorced wives have their divorce court maintenance orders transferred to the magistrates' courts. These trends have resulted in some two-thirds of all maintenance orders that are held in the magistrates' courts being for the benefit of divorced wives or their children rather than for separated wives. In other words the magistrates' courts still play an important part in the overall English court structure for handling maintenance matters.

COURT ATMOSPHERE

Inadequate court buildings and facilities are anathema to a sympathetic judicial resolution of matrimonial troubles. The Finer Committee observed that a family court should ideally be able to "organise its procedure, sittings and administrative services and arrangements with a view to gaining the confidence and maximising the convenience of the citizens who appear before it."[1] The two-tier structure of divorce and magistrates' courts reveal their respective historical pedigrees by their differing standards and approach. In the former, the waiting rooms are pleasantly painted and have chairs for all those attending. Appointments are issued for fixed times compared to the magistrates' courts where all those concerned in the separate hearings set down for that session will usually be told to report at the same time. Consequently, delays of several hours may well be experienced by people who are naturally nervous and upset over the proceedings.

Domestic hearings in the magistrates' courts still usually take place in the formal rigidity of a courtroom setting. Spouses and their lawyers (if any) sit in rows facing the bench of magistrates. A witness box for the presentation of evidence is sited to one side of the room. Administrative attitude of a particularly outdated form is shown in extracts from a recent letter of a justices' clerk who is responding to the plea for greater informality in the magistrates' domestic court.

> Marriage is undertaken either by solemn religious vows or by civil contract. It is surely not the job of the magistrates to try to attract to their courts those who are contemplating breaking those vows or that contract. Surely the courtroom should not be made like a committee room . . . The dignity and possible awesome atmosphere of a court may at last bring home to them the importance of the decision. . . . (The court) . . . is where the reality of personal responsibility has to be impressed on those attending it. Hard seats and a bleak atmosphere help to bring the parties up against the reality of the decisions which have to be made . . . It is the bucket of cold water which may, at last, bring the parties to their senses.[2]

Old habits and practices die slowly in some of our courts. But an unsympathetic court atmosphere will not ease the problems of marriage breakdown.

The magistrates' matrimonial jurisdiction still operates within a court that handles over 98 percent of all criminal trials in the country. These courts have recently seen the introduction of domestic court panels; they are intended to provide a better trained Bench, and a more sympathetic civil court approach. But the setting and atmosphere that still remains in many of these courts makes them far from ideal for the resolution of marital disharmony. Lack of government finance to rectify the outdated design of many of the older court buildings together with the very few modern-purpose built structures and the overcrowded list of criminal matters set down for hearing means that it is often not possible to separate the related assembly of accused, police, lawyers and witnesses from those who are attending domestic hearings. The public see their local magistrates' court as a criminal court. The reality of being a "Police Court" remains chiselled in stone lettering on the face of some of the older buildings.

All this compares to the setting in which a registrar of the divorce court hears maintenance matters. His office (or chambers) is housed in the county court, where only civil matters are dealt with. As a result, symbols of the criminal court such as docks and police officers are absent. The registrar normally sits at the top of a rectangular table with the parties sitting opposite each other. People speak remaining seated. All this goes to create a generally more agreeable and civilized atmosphere for the hearing of the case.

MAINTENANCE MATTERS AND OFFICIAL STATISTICS

Study of maintenance dispute resolution should ideally be underpinned by the availability of comprehensive annual statistics that focus on the legal and social aspects of marriage breakdown. The presentation for England and Wales is not entirely satisfactory, especially on matters of maintenance.

Official statistics on divorce are to be found mainly in two government publications. Demographic data about the couple's previous marital condition, ages at marriage and at divorce, length of marriage, and the number of children of the marriage and their age at divorce, are provided by the Office of Population Censuses and Surveys.[3] Legal information comes from the Lord Chancellor's Department; their statistics record the annual number of divorce petitions together with their allegations, whether they are by husband or wife, the facts proved, and the number of decrees granted.[4] Unfortunately, the latter source does not provide reliable information on the number of maintenance orders made by the divorce courts. The only statistic provided is the number of ancillary relief orders annually made, which in 1980 numbered 93,184.[5] These orders cannot be used as an indicator of propensity to seek maintenance for they do not directly relate to the current divorcing population. The minimal information necessary to allow a meaningful ongoing legal and social analysis of our maintenance laws and procedures would have to be far more relevant and reliable than the one figure currently provided. For instance, we need to know how many wives actually seek a divorce and maintenance order either for themselves alone, or only for their children, or for themselves and their children. This leads to further questions such as how many applications are successful, what amounts are ordered and to whom? How regularly are the orders paid and for how long do they continue? How many couples come to a private agreement, and what proportion do not resort to a court order? There are no satisfactory statistics concerning the resolution of matrimonial property or how such orders may be related to the court's decision on maintenance.

MAINTENANCE AND INCOME DISTRIBUTION

One of the purposes of a national survey of divorce petitions undertaken from the Centre for Socio-Legal Studies, Oxford, was to fill in some of the missing maintenance information. The study was based on a random sample of 1,146 petitions that were filed during the first six months of 1972. Analysis of the data showed that after divorce a maintenance order was made in 26 percent of all cases, while in a further 24 percent of all cases there was an existing magistrate's court maintenance order that continued unchanged at the time of divorce. Altogether, a maintenance order existed for the benefit of either wife or family in half (50 percent) of all divorces; this proportion increasing to almost three-quarters (72 percent) in those cases where there were dependent children.

The 1972 study followed on from a similar examination of 1961 divorces. A major finding that emerged from the 1961 study was that marriages in which the husband had a manual occupation formed almost two-thirds (64 percent) of all divorces. The greatest probability of divorce occurred within those marriages in which the husband was employed in an unskilled manual occupation (social class 5) such as a labourer. Marriages within this social group had over double (2.3 times) the chance of ending in divorce compared with those marriages where the husband had a professional or managerial post (social class 1).[6] The 1972 survey provided an almost similar finding of increased propensity to divorce in the lower social class grouping (social class 5) compared to social class 1 (rate of 2.4 to 1). By 1972 the proportion of divorcing husbands employed in manual occupations had risen to 68 percent, an increase of 4 percent on the 1961 survey result. I would expect similar results if the same exercise were to be undertaken now. These findings highlight one of the major realities within the current maintenance question; namely, that marriages in which husbands have the lowest incomes have the highest rate of marriage breakdown.

Government statistics reporting the gross weekly earnings of men aged twenty-one and over who were in full-time employment in Great Britain in 1972 show that those not manually employed earned a third (33 percent) more than those engaged in manual work.[7] Within the divorcing population, husbands in nonmanual employment had incomes averaging 62 percent above those employed in manual occupations. As would be expected, income distribution was directly associated with social class, with husbands in social class 1 earning over three times the income of those in social class 5. It is the top two classes that have incomes noticeably higher than the other four groupings. For instance, 58 percent of husbands in social classes 1 and 2 combined (professional, managerial and intermediate white-collar work) had annual incomes of over £2,000 compared with that found in social classes 3 nonmanual: clerks, white-collar workers (7 percent); social class 3 manual: skilled workers (9 percent); social class 4: semiskilled manual workers (6 percent); and social class 5 (0 percent).

The problem of income distribution and family support is further intensified as a consequence of divorcing wives from the lower income groups having larger families than their more wealthy counterparts. This demographic reality is reflected in the 1972 survey finding that those divorcing from social class 5 had three times the proportion of families with three or more children under the age of sixteen at divorce than was found in social classes 1 and 2. The inverse association between large family size and low income directs attention to one of the major problems the judiciary have to face when making maintenance decisions. This is that fathers of large families are generally those least able to provide a proper level of financial support.

REMARRIAGE

Some two-thirds of the 150,000 husbands annually passing through the English divorce courts will utilize their licence to marry again, and so take on a further obligation to support their new wives. In England and Wales in 1979 there were 79,812 bridegrooms who had been previously divorced. They formed a fifth (22 percent) of all new marriages in that year compared with 8 percent in 1969. Almost two-thirds (66 percent) of the previously divorced men marrying in 1979 had brides aged under thirty-five and who, as such, might well expect to bear children. At the same time the law expects the divorced wife and family to be maintained. Economic reality and legal expectation are incompatible.

One result of the tendency for divorced men to hopefully seek happiness in a new union is that an increasing proportion of divorcing husbands have been previously married. Such husbands formed 5 percent of all men divorcing in 1969, a decade later the proportion had risen to 9 percent. The evidence for 1979 suggests that these husbands experienced a divorce rate that was one and a half times (148 percent) above that calculated for divorcing bachelor bridegrooms (100 percent).[8] This pattern of serial monogamy causes many of the previously married men to have still existing maintenance commitments from their earlier divorce on top of their new family support obligations. The 1972 survey found that in over half (55 percent) of the failed marriages where the husband had been previously divorced there was at least one child aged under sixteen.

These are some of the demographic and social realities against which issues of maintenance resolution have to be set.

MAINTENANCE RESOLUTION AND JUDICIAL PRACTICE

It has been observed earlier that within the English divorce system it is the registrar who adjudicates upon the great majority of maintenance and property hearings after the divorce has been granted. Nothing was known about the way individual registrars exercised that largely discretionary jurisdiction until the Centre for Socio-Legal Studies mounted an enquiry. In particular, the hope was to throw light on the way maintenance decisions were reached. The enquiry involved interviewing over half (57 percent) of the 142 registrars existing in England and Wales in 1973. The findings were published in 1977.[9]

The registrars' approaches to maintenance resolution could be polarized into two contrasting types. The majority felt their role to be that of an adjudicator, as expressed by the comment "my job is to ensure the proper distribution of the available resources, both capital and income, according to the statutory provision."[10] Another felt "my role is judicial — it is wrong to play a social role. In an adversary game our role must be that of judge."[11] On the other hand about a third of the registrars felt it was their duty to encourage conciliation between the parties. As one registrar observed: "the parties have to accept that they have been through a very unfortunate experience and I try to readjust the position so that they can lead their lives in the future in the best possible way. I try to arrange matters so that they can put their problems behind them and try to create the best environment for them to do so."[12]

With the introduction of the new divorce law in 1971, the courts were given specific instructions for the first time as to those matters they should have special regard to when deciding financial matters. These guidelines are now set out in section 25 of the *Matrimonial Causes Act 1973*. Among the matters that courts must give regard to are: "the financial needs, obligations and responsibilities which each of the parties to the marriage has or is likely to have in the foreseeable future." The courts are finally given the duty to place the parties "in the financial position in which they would have been if the marriage had not broken down and each had properly discharged his or her financial obligations and responsibilities towards the other." Such prognosticative powers are claimed by few mortals.

The Oxford researchers have observed that "in drawing the adjudicator's mind to certain matters, the legislator hopes to 'structure' his choice within a framework of specific standards."[13] We were particularly interested to see what weight the registrars attached to the criteria laid down in the Act, especially the ultimate aim of the court as set out in the final subsection. Most of the registrars felt that the economic realities did not allow the couple's original financial position to be maintained after divorce. As one registrar emphatically observed "You cannot place them in the same position. One tries to give weight to all the matters but it is often a question of the cake not being big enough." The reality is that this legislation, in the critical words of the Finer Committee, "... has not made any contribution to the solution of the problem, in assessing maintenance as between people of small means, of how to effect an adequate distribution of inadequate resources."[14]

Wives in one-parent situations who have incomes below the subsistence living standards set by the government have the right to claim family support from the state for themselves and their children. This financial support is known as supplementary benefit, and is run on a nationwide basis by the Department of Health and Social Security. It has already been observed that survey results have shown that many divorcing wives have husbands whose income is insufficient to maintain two households. The question arises as to what extent the availability of welfare support funds should be taken into account when considering the wife's needs, and the reality that husbands will be less willing or able to pay if too heavy a liability is placed on them. It was against this background that registrars were asked to what extent the presence of supplementary benefit was taken into account when assessing the parties' financial resources. Over half (58 percent) of the registrars replied that they ignored the existence of supplementary benefit when making their decision. One held the view:

> I don't think it affects me. I am only concerned with what (the husband) can pay and if he does. I don't think that the taxpayer should pay. Regard should be had to social security only when an order would be financially disastrous for the husband.[15]

This observation underlines the belief of many registrars that the husband should, whenever possible, be expected to undertake the support of his wife and children. But there were other registrars who believed that the economic circumstances required them to consider the existence of social security. Two viewpoints expressed were:

> It is bound to affect the decision. I assume I am not the guardian of the public purse. If there was no such thing as social security you would have to take all you could (from the husband) down to the shirt on his back where the wife was in need, whereas, rightly or wrongly, you can give less where the wife is on social security.[16]

> I have been tempted in some cases to make an order leaving both sides on social security, but (the husband) won't pay. His bread is buttered on the side of the woman he is sleeping with.[17]

The truth is that in a large number of cases the financial cake is too small for the registrar to cut a sufficiently large slice to provide for the wife and children's needs. The inadequacies of the private law's obligation to maintain is made acceptable by the existence of the welfare law's safety net of financial support to all citizens unable to maintain themselves.

In those cases where the wife is already receiving supplementary benefit and the husband has a low income, the reality is that the registrar will usually be determining the amount that the husband should reimburse the state, thereby relieving taxpayers of some of the husband's maintenance obligations. In 1979, the Supplementary Benefits Commission paid out £367 million to divorced and separated wives but only received back from husbands some 8 percent of this sum (by way of the maintenance payments diversion procedure). It was the overwhelming evidence of this relationship between the private and public laws governing the obligation to maintain that led the Finer Committee on One-Parent Families to recommend a radical restructuring of the way maintenance was assessed and ordered. In brief, their Report proposed that in those cases where the wife was entitled to supplementary allowance the Supplementary Benefits Commission should calculate the amount the husband would pay the Commission and then make an administrative order.[18] In essence, much of the maintenance work would have been transferred from the courts to the Department of Health and Social Security. The proposal was no more than a reflection of the reality that the Department already supported a very large number of divorced and separated wives and their families. This recommendation has not been accepted by Parliament largely due to the apology of financial impoverishment. Implementation of the Finer Committee's proposal would have helped move maintenance resolution away from the adversarial procedure that the system still develops.

MODERN NEEDS AND OLD PRACTICES

Behind the increasing number of broken marriages resorting to the courts lies the harsh economic truth that few men have the means to properly support two households, let alone the first as well as the current family. In the majority of cases coming before the courts, the judges, registrars and magistrates face an impossible task of trying to extract a quart from a pint pot.

Regrettably, very little has been attempted by the court authorities to try to improve the maintenance system towards the needs of the consumers. Innovation has been conspicuously lacking. Yet the last decade has seen the most radical change in the handling of divorce since it was transferred to the civil courts in 1857. Divorce has been transformed from a judicial to an administrative process in which virtually all petitioners (99 percent) obtain a decree by what is known as special procedure. However, it has to be said that the conversion of special procedure to the now standard procedure was brought about by the need to save legal aid expenditure and not from a purposeful parliamentary rethinking of what the legislative, administrative and social needs of a modern divorce policy should be.[19] The result has been to make ancillary proceedings "the areas of real contest between the parties to divorce proceedings today, not the question whether the petitioner should get a decree."[20]

It is readily accepted that the family does not end with the marriage breakdown. The build-up of anger between the spouses may well solidify into long-lasting bitterness that augers ill for the resolution of financial support. Maintenance disputes can flow over and become part of the ill-will felt by both parents over the issues of custody and access. It is far better that those who experience disputed issues should try to resolve them before commencing contested court proceedings. A court hearing is all too likely to harden existing acrimonious attitudes into long-lasting resentment.

Conciliation as a method of approach has been defined as "the process of engendering common sense, reasonableness and agreement in dealing with the consequences of estrangement."[21] It is intended to provide an alternative approach to contested court proceedings, though not as a substitute for legal advice and assistance. However, official enthusiasm has been restrained and cursory. So far, the only city with a full-time conciliation agency has been Bristol.[22] It was about to close through lack of funds in April this year after operating for three years. Somewhat belatedly the Home Office has agreed to finance the agency for at least another year as a pilot project. The Bristol Courts Family Conciliation Service handles about 300 cases a year. Local solicitors back its operation with more than 100 firms cooperating with the conciliation service.

The past six months have seen reports from three separate bodies calling on the government to actively encourage such a service. The Law Commission, in its Report on *The Financial Consequences of Divorce*, argued that:

> everything possible should be done to ensure that only those cases which necessarily require adjudication come before the courts for trial of contested issues; and that the legal system should be so structured as to encourage the parties to reach an informed agreement about the financial and other consequences of the breakdown of their marriage, and to dispel the illusion that recourse to hostile litigation can produce magical solutions to intractable problems.[23]

The Law Society, in its annual report to the Lord Chancellor on the operation and financing of legal aid, observed that conciliation "has considerable potential for making divorce less adversarial — which is of great benefit to those directly involved."[24] The Lord Chancellor's Advisory Committee on Legal Aid enthusiastically subscribed to the view that conciliation services were "the most important development in the matrimonial field in recent years. We . . . consider a decision is long overdue on how such initiatives should be directed and funded."[25] But the history of the past suggests that official support is only likely to be forthcoming if it can be shown that the provision of such services does lead to a savings in court time and in the current annual legal aid expenditure of some £50 million.

It has been shown that the courts' clients are often the poorest and least educated of the population. We need to give them a proper choice of seeking either a negotiated settlement or trial of the dispute by the court. Ancillary services should be part of the overall structure for maintenance resolution. For instance, a court investigating and enforcement officer could help to make enquiries into the parties' financial affairs. It should not be too difficult to devise a clear and simple standard financial means questionnaire. Marriage breakdown requires more attention and thought than our system yet provides.

NOTES

1. *Report of the Committee on One-Parent Families*, Cmnd. 5,629, 1974, 174, par. 4.283.
2. H.E.G. Wells, *The Magistrate*, Vol. 38 (April 1982), 62. [This letter to the editor was with reference to Feb. 1982 issue, p. 28. See also two letters in June 1982 issue, p. 89.]
3. OPCS, *Marriage and Divorce Statistics for 1979*, Series FM2, no. 6, HMSO, London, 1981.
4. *Judicial Statistics* for 1980.
5. *Ibid.*, Table D. 8(e).

6. Colin Gibson, "The Association Between Divorce and Social Class in England and Wales," *British Journal of Sociology*, Vol. XXV, no. 1 (1974), 79–93.

7. *Social Trends*, No. 4 (1973), T.45, 103. (The calculation includes overtime, but excludes subsidiary earnings, income in kind and tips.)

8. The divorce rate for divorced bridegrooms in 1979 was 10.8 divorces for every 1,000 divorced men in ongoing marriages; single bridegrooms experienced 7.3 divorces per 1,000 related marriages. OPCS, *op. cit.*, 1979, T.4.6, 98.

9. W. Barrington Baker, John Eekelaar, Colin Gibson and Susan Raikes, *The Matrimonial Jurisdiction of Registrars*, Centre for Socio-Legal Studies, 1977.

10. *Ibid.*, 63.

11. *Ibid.*

12. *Ibid.*, 64.

13. *Ibid.*, 3.

14. *Report, op. cit.*, 87, para. 4.59.

15. W. Barrington Baker et al., *op. cit.* 12.

16. *Ibid.*, 13.

17. *Ibid.*

18. *Op. cit.*, Pt. 4, S.12, 152–70.

19. See Colin S. Gibson, "Divorce and the Recourse to Legal Aid," *The Modern Law Review*, Vol. 43 (1980), 609–25.

20. Lord Elwyn-Jones, The Lord Chancellor, *H.L.Deb.*, vol. 371, cols. 1,218–19.

21. Finer, *Report, op. cit.*, 183, para. 4.305.

22. Lisa Parkinson, "Bristol Courts Family Conciliation Service," *Family Law*, vol. 12 (1982), 13–16.

23. Law Commission Paper No. 112, HMSO, 6, para. 13.

24. 31st Legal Aid Annual *Reports* of the Law Society and of the Lord Chancellor's Advisory Committee (1980–81), HMSO, 1982, 18, para 60.

25. *Ibid.*, 90, para. 30.

Chapter Thirty-two

Alternatives to Judicial Child Support Enforcement: A Proposal for a Child Support Tax

Marygold Melli and Sherwood Zink

University of Wisconsin Law School
Madison, Wisconsin, U.S.A.

One of the major social problems of the 1980s is that of providing support for children who live with only one parent. The dimensions of the problem have been described many times. In a decade the number of children in single-parent households has grown dramatically. In 1970, census figures showed 8,265,500 children living with only one parent. In 1980 the number had grown to 12,163,600, an increase of nearly 50 percent.[1] An escalating divorce rate[2] and a great increase in the number of children born to unmarried parents[3] have resulted in current estimates that one of every two children born today will spend some time in a single-parent household before reaching the age of eighteen.[4]

Although these children live with only one parent, most of them have an absent parent who under the laws of all American jurisdictions is at least partially responsible to provide support for the child.[5] It is the inadequacy of this support system which is the cause of the public concern. Children in single-parent households are poor;[6] they do not receive support from their absent parent. The latest figures available show that, nationally, only 59 percent of women potentially eligible to receive support have child support awards. Of those awarded child support, only 49 percent received the full amount due them while 28 percent received nothing.[7]

This chapter outlines the problems with the present system and then describes a proposal to replace it with a child support tax which would be assessed and collected in a manner similar to income tax withholding.[8]

THE PRESENT SYSTEM

There is common agreement that the present child support system is deficient both (1) in the determination of the amount of the award and (2) in the collection of the support once an award is made.

Setting the Amount of the Award

At present, the amount of a child support award is set on a case-by-case basis by a judge in a judicial hearing at which both parents have the opportunity to present relevant evidence. The decisions are intended to be individualized, i.e., tailored to the needs of the particular child and the resources of its parents.

There are two problems with this approach to setting the amount of child support. In the first place it is very expensive, both in terms of time and cost to the parties as well as in the delays for the child needing support. In addition, it is expensive to the public in terms of the time of judges and other court personnel. As the number of child support determinations continue to increase, concern has been expressed as to whether these costs are justified.

Unfortunately, information is not available on the cost of the present individualized enforcement system. A detailed study of twenty-eight counties in Michigan by David Chambers found that, in the Michigan county where 60 percent of the supporters paid 80 percent or more of the child support due, they were each the object of an average of five enforcement efforts. Most of these efforts were by the staff of the Friend of the Court, the administrative office attached to the court and charged with the responsibility of enforcing the program, but one in eight supporters required a hearing by the judge.[9] In doing research for this chapter, we could find no estimates of the cost of these enforcement efforts.[10]

The second problem in the present individualized system for setting child support awards relates to the variations in the amounts awarded. Although there is a clearly discernible trend toward legislatively set guidelines for establishing the amount of a child support award, the courts still exercise enormous discretion in determining child support obligations.[11]

The present system was described recently as follows: "The amount of child support an absent parent pays depends not just on ability to pay, but on the varying attitudes of local judges, district attorneys and welfare officials, the beliefs and attitudes of both parents, the current relationship between the parents, and the skills of their respective lawyers. Nearly every absent parent can find someone earning more who pays less."[12]

In spite of the frequent concern about the variations in the amount set for child support, very little empirical information is available on it. In preparing this chapter, we reviewed three recent studies: a study of 432 cases of child support and spousal support in divorce actions in Orange county, Florida;[13] an analysis of 135 child support cases under the *Uniform Reciprocal Enforcement of Support Act* handled in the Denver, Colorado district court[14] and an examination of child support awards in 203 divorce cases in Dane county, Wisconsin.[15]

In the Florida study, the researchers identified nine variables which they considered covered all essential factors in determining the amount of a child support award. Analyzing the case load of each of the nine judges, it was discovered that although each judge was consistent among his cases as to his own model, the rank ordering of the factors was quite different for some judges. Three judges agreed on one variable as the most important, two others on a different one while the other four each had used another variable as the most significant.

The Colorado study of the Uniform Reciprocal Enforcement of Support actions found even greater variation. The author of that study concluded that not only was there no consistency between the judges who decided the cases but also the individual judges were erratic as to the amount of the award.

The conclusions of both the Florida and Colorado studies suggested that the present system of individualized determination of support is dysfunctional in that it results in great inequities, in just the kind of problems described in the quotation earlier in this section.

The results of the Wisconsin study raise a different issue. In the Wisconsin study data relating to fifteen variables judged to be involved in decisions as to the amount of a child support award were analyzed using regression analysis in an attempt to determine the predictive power of the variables in setting the amount of a child support award. The income of the noncustodial parent was by far the most important factor in explaining the amount of an award, explaining 49 percent of the variation in the amount. Furthermore, this importance remained constant across the four judges whose cases were involved in the study. In other words, the judges consistently placed greatest weight on the income of the noncustodial parent.

Because of the overwhelming role of the income of the parent, the Wisconsin results raise questions about the function of an individualized format where the constraints are so great that the results might not be much different from a predetermined percentage of income as child support.

Collection of Child Support

The second problem area in the present child support system is that of the collection of the money once the award is made. The standard procedure has been that the court orders the noncustodial parent to pay and the enforcement of that order is left to the beneficiary of the order, the custodial parent. This means that the custodial parent has to initiate legal proceedings to enforce the court's support order. The usual procedure for doing this is by citing the nonpaying parent for contempt. This legal proceeding is fraught with numerous difficulties. Frequently, it requires the custodial parent to employ legal counsel — a substantial burden for a parent already not receiving support; it often requires difficult fact determinations because of lack of adequate records of direct payments to the custodial parent. The sanction for wilful nonpayment is drastic: imprisonment in jail.[16]

This system is generally regarded as ineffective. There have been a number of studies of payment experience under child support orders. Although many of these have involved families in the aid to families with dependent children (AFDC) program where low compliance might be expected[17] studies of representative samples of parents with support orders have been almost as bleak.[18]

The most recent and the most detailed study of payment performance is that done by Chambers in Michigan of child support enforcement in twenty-eight Michigan counties in 1974–75. It found a great variation between the counties studied in the rate of performance from a less than 50 percent collection rate for two counties to two other counties which collected 81–90 percent of the support due.[19] Chambers looked not only at the record of performance but also at the determinants of payment performance. He found that the differences in collection rates between counties were not the result of differences in the population ordered to support but in the enforcement structure of the county. Michigan, unlike many other states, has a system of public monitoring of child support payments. Payments are made to an official agency, the friend of the court, and that agency is authorized by statute to take action in the event of nonpayment.

The study found three factors which seemed to be the most important in explaining differences in collection rates:

1. The aggressiveness of the friend of the court in enforcing the child support order. Counties where the friend of the court followed up nonpayment without waiting for complaint by the custodial parent, i.e., where the enforcement mechanism was self-starting, had the best payment record.
2. A high rate of jailing for noncompliance, but only if the county had a self-starting enforcement mechanism. Counties with a high rate of jailing but no self-starting enforcement mechanism collected no more than counties that jailed almost no one.

3. The population of the county — the larger the county, the lower the collection rate.

The Michigan study is very informative because it points to the importance of the enforcement structure in collecting support.[20]

Legislation to Improve Collection

The ineffectiveness of support enforcement has not gone without legislative notice. The states have enacted a multitude of statutes intended to improve the succes of support collection. Some examples are discussed in the following paragraphs.

Although general execution statutes apply to enforcement of past due child support, a large number of states have enacted specific child support provisions on attachment, garnishment, liens on property, etc.[21] Whether enforcement under these statutes is more effective than under general statutes is not known.

Partly as a result of the findings of studies like the Chambers one in Michigan, the states have also, often with federal government urging,[22] enacted legislation intended to improve the collection process and, thereby, to increase its effectiveness. Some states now require that child support payments be made through a public agency, such as the Michigan clerk of court, so there is an official record of payment and the possibility of monitoring default. Some states have provided the mechanism for early action on default thus providing the basis for the Michigan self-starting enforcement. Most states, in response to federal requirements,[23] have statutory provisions making public agency help available to custodial parents who are not receiving their child support payments — another lesson of the Michigan results. Requirements that supporting absent parents notify the court or some other public agency of changes of addresses and provisions for the location of absent parents, all intended to improve the collection mechanism, are also found in statutory schemes.[24]

Another direction taken by the states has been that of preventing nonpayment. Sometimes that result has been achieved by providing for payment in spite of default such as requiring a bond to be furnished in a certain amount to cover payment. The most favored approach, however, has been preventing default by means of mandatory wage assignments or provisions for employer withholding of support amounts from wages. Statutes of this last type have been enacted by a number of states and are the most frequently recommended improvement in child support enforcement because of the ease and certainty of collection.[25]

In spite of the current popularity of the wage withholding approach to child support collection, no studies are available as yet as to their effectiveness or cost. One problem area with most of the present statutes is that they do not authorize the use of a wage assignment or withholding until there has been a default in payment. Another problem is the cost to the employer of administering an employee specific deduction, i.e., one in which the amount to be deducted is determined by a court order in an individual case. Other important problems are difficulty in following a supporting parent who changes jobs and, therefore, must assign wages from another employer and the inability of the system to respond to changes in the income of the supporting parent with the result that the amount withheld may be disproportionately large when the paycheck is lower than it was at the time the order was made and vice versa.

Public Support in the Present System

No discussion of the present program for support by absent parents is complete without considering the program for public support of children with absent parents, the aid to families with dependent children (AFDC) program. Nearly half of all children living in female-headed households are in that program. The payment record of the fathers of these children is very poor. Currently, child support is collected from only 10 percent of them.[26]

The AFDC program was established in 1935 for quite different purposes than those it now serves. It was intended to provide support for the families of deceased fathers in a society in which it was considered undesirable for mothers with children to work. Today, the program is primarily for children who have a living absent parent legally liable for their support and a custodial parent who is expected to work.

The orientation of the original program has created two problems. In the first place, as a welfare program the benefits were reduced by income earned. It made sense in an income-tested welfare program intended to benefit stay-at-home mothers not to be concerned about a structure which discouraged mothers from working. This structure is clearly out of place today in a society which expects mothers to work and the AFDC program has been amended accordingly. Nevertheless, as an income-tested welfare program it is not properly geared to the role of a program to supplement the earnings of the custodial parent.

The second problem with the original AFDC program as originally conceived was that it paid little attention to the issue of child support payments.[27] Therefore, originally there was little concern about the ability to collect support let alone any thorough study of the issue of whether the adversarial structure of the existing system for deciding private disputes was suited to the task of apportioning the support of poor children among the custodial parent, the absent parent and the public.

The proposed program for a child support benefit and tax is conceived as a possible solution to these problems of AFDC.

Summary of the Present System

From the foregoing discussion several points emerge:

1. Judicially determined support orders are generally seen as inequitable.
2. The cost of setting the amount of support in individualized hearings and enforcing collection after default through individualized hearings is probably disproportionate to the amounts recovered for child support.
3. The most effective type of enforcement has proven to be withholding of amounts due before payment of wages.

PROPOSED CHILD SUPPORT BENEFIT AND TAX SYSTEM

It is clear that the major goals of any child support program for children with absent parents is two-fold: (1) to provide adequate support for children who do not live with both parents; and (2) to require that absent parents share in the cost of supporting their children.

A proposal now under consideration in Wisconsin is intended to alleviate many of the problems described in the present system and to promote both of the above goals.

The proposal would replace the present semiprivate child support system with a new one consisting of a child support benefit payable on behalf of all children with legally liable absent parents and a support collection system based on a child support tax payable by absent parents and collected under a procedure patterned after the income tax withholding system.[28]

Coverage of Program

The current child support system is a state one. Each state has a statutory structure which establishes the duty of a parent to provide support for out-of-custody children under which the duty of absent or noncustodial parents to pay money toward the support of their children is assessed and enforced. The proposal under discussion is, like the present system, a state scheme.

However, it is recognized that a nationwide program, regardless of its other features, would certainly be a step toward solving some of the problems of the current collection system: location of absent parents; obtaining and enforcing awards against out of state parents. It has been suggested that a nationwide system could be tied to the social security system or the income tax collection system. The proposed system is one which could very easily be made nationwide if sufficient support for it develops.

The Child Support Benefit

The plan establishes a basic child support benefit which is a set amount, based on the number of eligible children in the custodial unit. It is payable to the custodian of the children without regard to the income of the custodial unit. In other words, it is not income tested; all eligible children living with only one parent receive it. However, as will be discussed later in connection with the child support tax, in order to avoid public subsidies to families with no need, the custodial unit is subject to a special surtax in cases where the absent parent pays less in tax than the amount of the basic or minimum benefit.

All eligible children will receive the basic child support benefit regardless of the amount paid by their absent parent. When the absent parent cannot pay child support equal to the basic benefit, the difference between what the absent parent pays and the basic benefit will be provided out of general revenues. This, of course, is the source of current welfare payments. This approach is based on a two-fold judgment: (1) that for mother-headed households, now on welfare, it will be no more expensive to provide a nonincome tested minimum child support benefit than to make welfare payments and (2) that the preferred way to increase the well-being of these mother-headed families on welfare is to offer them an alternative opportunity for a nonwelfare benefit which, when combined with at least part-time work, will be superior to welfare.

Children whose absent parent pays more than the amount of the basic benefit in child support tax will receive the additional amounts paid by the absent parent. Therefore, all eligible children will receive either the child support paid by their absent parent or a basic child support benefit, publicly guaranteed, whichever is larger.

Payment of the child support benefit may begin either on the application of a custodian of an eligible child or on notification by a court in a divorce, separation or annulment proceeding, a paternity action, or a separate action for support. Under the present proposal, payment of the benefit will begin after support is collected, i.e., the second month after the notification to collect the child support tax is made in response to the application for the benefit or the judicial determination that child support is due. Hopefully, the lag between these two events — determination that support is due and payment of the benefit — can be reduced in operation.

Eligibility

To be eligible for a child support benefit, a child must satisfy several characteristics. First, because the program is limited to a single state, the child must be a resident of the state of Wisconsin. Second, the child must be one to whom a duty of support is owed. Under the laws of Wisconsin, therefore, the child must be under the age of eighteen, or if still attending high school or its equivalent, under the age of nineteen.[29] Third, the child must have a legally liable absent parent. This means that the child must have an absent parent who is a Wisconsin resident subject to the child support tax (to be discussed later) or, if a nonresident, has been, or can be, ordered to pay child support. Children with a deceased parent are not included; they are usually eligible for social security payments provided by the deceased parent's work related social security tax. Children of unmarried parents are also not eligible unless paternity has been established. If paternity is not established, they are eligible, as at present, for an income tested benefit under aid to families of dependent children.

Amount of the Child Support Award

What should the amount of the child support benefit be? One of the advantages of establishing a new universal public child support benefit program is that it provides the opportunity for addressing public policy to the issue of what the child support benefit "ought" to be, i.e., a normative standard of what a parent ought to provide for child support.

Ideally a standard for child support ought to relate closely to the cost of raising a child reduced by some percentage to reflect the contribution to be made by the custodial parent. Such an approach is a definite break with the present child support system which relies primarily on an assessment of the needs and ability to pay of the absent parent in setting the amount of support.[30] As part of the research for the Wisconsin proposal, Jacques van der Gaag, of the Institute for Research on Poverty at the University of Wisconsin-Madison reviewed some of the literature in the century-long development of economic studies on the cost of raising children as the first step toward setting a normative standard.[31] The results of this research are very informative even though there is a lack of hard data as well as agreement on exact figures. Although a variety of different approaches have been taken to the issue of how to determine the cost of raising a child, the one used by most researchers looks at how much

TABLE 32.1 Estimated Benefits and Costs of Child Support Reform For Fiscal Year 1980 ($ Millions)

Description of Plan			Amount Collected				% Who Pay Minimum	
		(1)	(2)	(3)	(4)	(5)	(6)	(7)
			Tax on	Tax on		Net		Absent Parent
			Absent	Custodial	AFDC	Savings	Absent	Plus Custodial
Benefit	Tax Rate %	Benefits	Parent	Parent	Savings	(2)+(3)+(4)−1)	Parent	Parent
			Collect Nothing from Poorest 20% of Absent Parents					
1st Child $3000	20	540	344	84	159	47	38	53
2nd Child 1500	10							
Maximum	40							

income a couple with a child needs to obtain the same level of economic well-being as a childless couple.

The amount of money which parents spend on raising their children varies with the income of the parents, i.e., parents with high incomes expect to spend more money on their children. However, equivalence of scale is virtually constant over a large income range (up to almost $50,000). This means that parents, regardless of income, tend to spend approximately the same percentage of their income on children. For the first child the Poverty Institute research estimated expenditures are almost 25 percent of the income of the couple. The cost of the second child is approximately half that of the first. This is true of the third child also. Thereafter, additional children cost one-half of the second child.

Using these figures the amount of the basic child support benefit for the cost estimate of the proposed program in Table 32.1 was set at $3,000 for one child, based on the cost of raising the first child in a family with an income of $12,000.

The Child Support Tax

The argument for a child support tax, i.e., a legislatively determined child support obligation based upon a simple normative formula dependent upon the income of the absent parent and the number of children for whom he or she is responsible rather than on judicial discretion is threefold:

1. It is the best method of achieving equitable parental financial responsibility.
2. It is more efficient and economical than the present system of individualized judicial determination.
3. The most effective way to collect the support obligation of the absent parent is to assess it as a tax and collect it through a wage withholding system.

In the proposed plan there are two types of taxes. The basic one, the child support tax, is assessed against absent parents who are residents of the state. The amount of the tax is a certain percentage of income, up to a legislatively determined maximum based on the number of children.

The estimates in Table 32.1 are based on a tax rate of 20 percent for the first child and 10 percent for the second child. The selection of this rate was based on several different pieces of data. First, the van der Gaag study of the cost of raising children found that a reasonable estimate of the additional income needed to maintain the living standard enjoyed without children was 20 to 30 percent of the prechild income.[32] Furthermore, the cost of the second child was half that of the first. This information suggested that a 20 percent rate for the first child and a 10 percent rate for the second child would reflect the lower end of an expenditure a parent would make in an intact household.

Second, the results of the present individualized support setting mechanism were examined to determine if any guidelines could be found. For this purpose, we examined three sources: (1) a survey of judges' attitudes toward support in Illinois,[33] (2) an analysis by Judith Cassetty in *Child Support and Public Policy*[34] from the Michigan Panel Study of Income Dynamics, and (3) the Wisconsin study of 203 cases of child support awards in divorce cases.[35]

The Illinois survey reported the views of 143 judges in that state on divorce matters, including support for children of the dissolved marriage. They said they increased the amount of support awarded as the number of children in the family increased but they did so on a declining basis. This meant that there were smaller individual allocations for children in larger families. On the question of the percent of the supporter's income which might be allocated to child support, the judges answers ranged from 20 to 50 percent. Only one judge reported ever awarding more than 50 percent of parental income.

The Cassetty study involved a sample of 578 cases from the Michigan Panel. In 193 cases sufficient information was available to figure the percentage of the absent father's income awarded in child support. The percentages varied from 10 to 33 percent with higher incomes having lower percentages in child support.[36]

The Wisconsin study of child support awards found that the percent of income awarded in child support ranged from 25 to 30 percent regardless of the amount of the absent parent's income.

The estimates in Table 32.1 are also based on the application of the tax rate to incomes up to $50,000. This maximum rate relates again to the cost of raising children information which shows that the percent of income spent on children remains quite constant over a broad range of salary up to $50,000.

Collection of the child support tax will be handled in a fashion similar to the collection of the income tax. Amounts will be withheld based on reporting by the absent parent. However, the system will be initiated by an official notice that the tax is to be collected either because an application has been filed for a child determined administratively to be eligible for a child support benefit, or a judicial determination has been made in a divorce, separation or annulment proceeding, a paternity action, or a separate action for support (including a URESA action) that the parent is liable for the child support tax.

The second tax is one which will be assessed against the income of the custodial unit, i.e., the income of the custodial parent and his or her spouse, if any, only in cases where the tax paid by the absent parent is insufficient to cover the amount of the basic child support benefit. This tax will be payable at the time of filing income tax returns because it will depend on a determination of the amount due at the end of the year.

The reason for taxing the custodial unit is to avoid a public subsidy for a family with no need.

Case Management

The collection system under the proposed child support reform will require a sophisticated computerized control registry which will track individual children so their benefits can be matched with the parental payments. It will also require that, at least, in those cases where absent parent's contributions are insufficient to meet the minimum child benefit, information on the income of the custodial parent be available. Close monitoring to be sure that the taxes are being withheld is also essential. The certainty of enforcement and quick reminders when compliance is not made are clearly important elements in a successful child support collection program.

Nonresident Payors and Children

As stated earlier, the plan is limited to residents of a single state. Therefore, a child who is a resident of Wisconsin will be eligible to receive the child support benefit even though the legally liable absent parent is a nonresident. In that case, the court ordered child support will be paid to the state to reimburse it for the benefit with any amounts above the basic benefit being paid to the child.

Enforcement of child support owed by a nonresident parent will be by the traditional routes with liability determined in a local proceeding if jurisdiction can be obtained[37] or through the *Uniform Reciprocal Enforcement of Support Act.* (URESA).[38]

If a resident absent parent who is subject to the tax has a nonresident child, the child support tax will be collected and that amount forwarded to the child. Child support liability for a nonresident child which is determined in a court of another jurisdiction can be fitted into the child support tax system via URESA which will result in a judicial notification that the child support tax is to be collected from the resident absent parent.

Cost Estimates

Obviously, a crucial issue in the viability of the proposal under discussion is the cost of such a program. Table 32.1 is an attempt to give some idea of the cost based on crude estimates. Several shortcomings of this information must be noted:

1. The best available information on the eligible population is from 1975.[39] The number of eligible children has increased substantially since 1975 because of increased divorce, separation and births to unmarried mothers.
2. The available data had no information on the income of absent parents so this was estimated using characteristics of custodial parents as the basis.
3. Obviously, the effectiveness of the new system is unknown and this must be estimated. Table 32.1 is based on not collecting anything from the poorest 20 percent of absent parents.

As pointed out earlier, Table 32.1 estimates are based upon a basic benefit of $3,000 for the first child and $1,500 for the second. The tax rate is set at 20 percent for the first child and 10 percent for the second. The custodial parent tax is figured at half that of the absent parent.

Interim Steps toward Reform: A Demonstration Project

As a first step in assessing the workability and impact of the proposed child support tax proposal, Wisconsin will conduct a pilot demonstration in five pairs of counties in 1982-83. The counties will be chosen to represent the kinds of situations in which the reform program will be expected to operate, e.g., urban-rural, high unemployment-low unemployment. The reason for a demonstration project is concern that a reform of less major proportions may be as effective as the proposal in improving the child support system.

The demonstration will pilot test the four major concepts of the proposed child support reform:

1. Automatic establishment of a normative support payment level based upon a percentage of an absent parents' gross income.
2. Use of a data processing system for case monitoring, distribution and delinquency control.
3. Collection of payments by a wage withholding system.
4. A guaranteed child support benefit to all eligible children.

In one pair of counties all of the key aspects of the program described above will be introduced.

In each of the other pairs of counties, only parts of the proposed support system will be implemented.

In a second pair of counties, the payment level based on a percentage of income and the data processing system will be introduced. The purpose here is to determine whether the use of two of the suggested improvements, the use of a normative standard for establishing the amount of the award and improved case management, will improve the child support process significantly without more major change in the present system.

In a third pair of counties, the automatic wage assignment will be implemented. In the fourth pair of counties, only the data processing improvements will be made, and in the fifth set, only the use of a payment level based on a percentage of income for the amount of the support will be implemented. The objective in these last three sets of counties is to determine the extent to which the individual improvements in the system are sufficient to lessen the need for more thorough change.

In practical terms, the project means: establishing support obligations as a "tax" rate, collecting the "tax" from income, and "auditing" the payers; comparing the results to child support ordered and collected in the traditional manner.

SUMMARY

The present support system for children with absent parents is sorely inadequate both in establishing the amount of the award and in enforcing it. This chapter has attempted to give a skeletal outline of a proposal for a major reform of the child support system which will radically change the way in which the amount of support is determined and will strengthen considerably the manner in which it is collected. Under the proposed reform, child support would be a legislatively determined percentage of the income of the absent parent collected through a withholding system similar to that used for the income tax.

The chapter has also described briefly an interim step in the process of reform — a demonstration project involving ten counties which will implement certain parts of the proposal.

NOTES

1. U.S. Bureau of the Census, *Characteristics of American Children and Youth: 1980*, Current Population Reports, Series P-23, No. 114 (1982).

2. Between 1960 and 1978 the divorce rate more than doubled. U.S. Bureau of the Census, *Divorce, Child Custody and Child Support*, Current Population Reports, Series P-23, No. 84 (1979).

3. Up from 78,500 in 1940 to 515,000 in 1977. *Hammond Almanac* 251 (1980). In 1979, an estimated 595,000 babies, one of every six children born, was illegitimate, up 50 percent since 1970. *Time* Magazine, p. 67 (Nov. 9, 1981).

4. *Divorce, Child Custody and Child Support, supra,* note 2.

5. It is estimated that one out of every five children in the United States is potentially eligible for child support. 1 Institute for Research on Poverty (University of Wisconsin-Madison) *Child Support: Weaknesses of the Old and Features of a Proposed New System* 1 (1982).

6. In 1975, 27 percent of the families headed by women (the overwhelming number of single-parent families are headed by women) were below the federal poverty line. *Divorce, Child Custody, and Child Support, supra,* note 2.

7. U.S. Bureau of the Census, *Child Support and Alimony: 1978 (Advance Report),* Current Population Reports, Series P-23, No. 106 (1980). Little is known about the support of children in paternal custody, i.e., the extent to which noncustodial mothers pay child support. A study of 203 cases in Dane county, Wisconsin, found that child support was not ordered in any case in which the father obtained custody. M. Melli, *Child Support Awards: An Empirical Study of One County* (unpublished).

8. The proposal to be discussed was developed by a research team of the Institute for Research on Poverty, University of Wisconsin-Madison, headed by Irwin Garfinkel, under a contract with the Division of Economic Assistance, Department of Health and Social Services, State of Wisconsin. The proposal is available in a three volume report. See *supra,* note 5.

9. D. Chambers, *Making Fathers Pay,* 155 (1979).

10. In Wisconsin, an effort has been made to calculate the hourly cost of a trial judge, which, including salary, fringes and support costs, was $150 per hour. Wisconsin Senate Bill 769 (1981–82 sess.) fiscal note. Administrative costs in the child support enforcement program are also available. U.S. Dept. of Health and Human Services, Office of Child Support Enforcement, *Child Support Enforcement,* Fifth Annual Report to Congress for the Period Ending Sept. 30, 1980 (Dec. 31, 1980). It shows, for example, that Wisconsin, which is ranked as the seventh most cost effective state in terms of child support enforcement, expended nearly $300 per paying case per year. See Tables 8A and 15.

11. Thirty-five states now have statutes that specify some factors to guide the court in setting support in dissolution of the marriage. A lesser, but still substantial number, twenty-three, provide them for paternity proceedings, M. Melli, *Child Support: A Survey of the Statutes* (Report of the ABA Section of Family Law, Comparative Family Support Law Committee, S. Zink, Chairperson).

12. Institute for Research on Poverty, *supra,* note 5 at vii.

13. K. White and R. Stone, Jr., "A Study of Alimony and Child Support Rulings with Some Recommendations," 10 *Fam. L. Q.* 83 (1976).

14. N. Yee, "What Really Happens in Child Support Cases: An Empirical Study of Establishment and Enforcement of Child Support Orders in the Denver District Court," 57 *Denver L.J.* 21 (1979).

15. M. Melli, *supra,* note 7.

16. An excellent discussion of enforcement of support under the present system can be found in H. Krause, *Child Support in America: The Legal Perspective* (1981) particularly pp. 81–94.

17. Surveys of AFDC clients are made periodically. The 1977 survey found that 38.6 percent of the mothers with child support awards received payments. A. Sorensen and M. MacDonald, *Child Support: Who Pays What to Whom?* in III Institute for Research on Poverty, *supra,* note 5 at 90.

Collections have improved as a result of the federal child support enforcement program 42 USCA §§651–62 (1975–1980) supp.) The 1973 AFDC survey found that only

21.8 percent of the families with awards received the full amount of the court ordered support. Staff of Senate Comm. on Finance, 94th Cong., 1st Sess., *Child Support Data and Materials,* 88-89 (Comm. Print 1975).

There are two reasons why child support payments for AFDC families might be less than the general population:

(1) Although there is evidence that there are many affluent absent parents of families on AFDC (M. Winston and T. Forsher, *Non-Support of Legitimate Children by Affluent Fathers as a Cause of Poverty and Welfare Dependence,* Rand Corp. 1971) quoted in S. Rep. No. 93-1356, 93rd Cong. 2d Sess. in 1974 U.S. Code Cong. and Ad. News 8133, 8146, the Program has a much higher percentage of poor absent parents than is found in the general population.

(2) Prior to the federal child support enforcement program which requires states to provide that child support payments for families on AFDC be paid directly to the state (42 U.S.C.A. §654, 1975-1980 supp.) underreporting of child support was assumed because AFDC payments are reduced by the amount of child support received. A. Sorensen and M. MacDonald, *supra,* at 86.

18. See *supra,* page 1 and note 7; also, A. Sorensen and M. MacDonald *supra,* note 17. An earlier study in the mid 1960s of 163 fathers ordered to pay support in divorce cases in Wisconsin in 1955 found that at the end of the first year, there was only 58 percent compliance and one-third of those complying did so only partially. By the tenth year only 21 percent of the fathers were making payments. K. Echhardt, "Deviance, Visibility and Legal Action: The Duty to Support," 15 *Soc. Prob.* 470 (1968). See also C. Jones, N. Gordon and I. Sawhill, *"Child Support Payments in the United States,"* Working Paper 992-03, The Urban Institute (1976); Note, Child Support Enforcement 52 *Wash. L. Rev.* 169 (1976).

19. D. Chambers, *supra,* note 9 at 82.

20. *Ibid.* at 90. The importance of the enforcement structure has been noted in other studies, C. Jones, N. Gordon and I. Sawhill, *supra,* note 18; A. Sorensen and M. MacDonald, *supra,* note 17.

21. M. Melli, *supra,* note 11.

22. In 1975 Congress enacted the child support enforcement program as Title IV-D of the *Social Security Act,* 42 U.S.C.A. §§651-662 (1975-1980 supp.) The primary focus of the program is to reduce public aid expenditures by requiring absent parents to contribute to the support of their children who receive AFDC, but the program is also available to non-AFDC parents. There is no doubt that the program has greatly improved child support collections. Staff of Senate Comm. on Finance, 96the Cong., 1st Sess., *Staff Data and Materials in Child Support* 2 (Comm. Print, 1979).

Regulations implementing the child support enforcement program are found in 45 C.F.R. §§232.1-232.49, 301.0-305.50 (Rev. Oct. 1, 1981).

In spite of the importance of the federal role, child support enforcement is still a matter of state implementation. There has been growing interest, fostered by the federal Office of Child Support Enforcement (OCSE), in improving state legislation. The National Conference of State Legislatures has published an excellent book outlining desirable changes in child support laws. C. Kastner and L. Young, *A Guide to State Child Support and Paternity Laws* (National Conference of State Legislatures, 1981). The Family Law Section of the American Bar Association has a Comparative Family Support Law Committee which has done a compilation of state child support and paternity laws as the basis for law reform. See *supra,* note 11.

23. The child support enforcement program requires each state to have a program of child support collection and paternity establishment for both AFDC and non-AFDC families. 42 U.S.C.A. §654(6) (1975-1980 supp.)

24. The federal child support enforcement legislation requires states to "establish a service to locate absent parents" 42 U.S.C.A. §654(8) (1975-1980 supp.)

25. C. Kastner and L. Young, *supra,* note 22 at 108 and 118. M. Melli, *supra,* note 11.

26. I. Garfinkel, *Child Support: Weaknesses of the Old and Features of a Proposed New System* in I Institute for Research on Poverty, *supra,* note 5 at 5. "The problem of welfare in the United States is, to a considerable extent, a problem of the nonsupport of children by their absent parents." S. Rep. No. 93-1356, *supra,* note 17 at 8145.

27. B. Bernstein, "Shouldn't Low Income Fathers Support Their Children?" 66 *The Public Interest* 56 (Winter 1982).

28. A summary discussion of this proposal can be found in I. Garfinkel, *supra,* note 26 at 1.

29. Wis. Stat. §767.25(4) (1979-1980).

30. J. Cassetty, *Child Support and Public Policy* 63 (1978).

31. J. van der Gaag, *On Measuring the Cost of Children* in III Institute for Research on Poverty, *supra,* note 5 at 1. See also I. Sawhill, *Developing Normative Standards for Child Support and Alimony Payments, Ibid.* at 234.

32. J. van der Gaag, *supra,* note 31 at 21.

33. W. Johnson, Divorce, Alimony, Support and Custody: A Survey of Judges' Attitudes in One State, 3 *Fam. L. Rep.* (BNA) 4001 (1976).

34. J. Cassetty, *supra,* note 30.

35. M. Melli, *supra,* note 7.

36. J. Cassetty, *supra,* note 30 at Table IV-1.

37. The Wisconsin "long arm" statute has a provision for actions affecting the family in which a personal claim is asserted. It is based on residence by the respondent in the state "in marital relationship with the petitioner for not less than 6 consecutive months within the 6 years next preceding the commencement of the action . . ." Wis. Stat. 801.05(11) (1979-80) See also *Kulko v. Calif. Sup. Ct.,* 436 U.S. 84, 98 S. Ct. 1690, 56 L. Ed. 132 (1978).

38. Wisconsin, like all American jurisdictions, has a version of URESA. The Wisconsin version is the 1968 revised act. Wis. Stat. §52.10 (1979-80).

39. This issue is discussed in detail in the report of the research team. I. Garfinkel, *supra,* note 26 at 38.

Chapter Thirty-three

New Zealand's Nonjudicial Parental Income Attachment Scheme

G. J. Thomas

Barrister and Solicitor, Wellington, New Zealand

INTRODUCTION

New Zealand has a comprehensive system of social benefits. For some years prior to 1973 "Emergency Benefits" were paid to solo parents at the discretion of officers of the Social Welfare Department. In 1973 "Domestic Purposes Benefits" for solo parents were given statutory recognition.[1] At the present time the Domestic Purposes Benefit is $126.00 per week for a parent with one child. That compares with an average weekly wage of $237.00 gross or $176.00 after tax.[2] Any woman, whether living apart from her husband or whether unmarried, is entitled, if she has a dependent child, to a Domestic Purposes Benefit. Men's liberation does exist. A man who has a dependent child and has lost his wife is also entitled to a benefit. Since most applicants for the Domestic Purposes Benefit are women the writer assumes for the purposes of this chapter that any applicant and beneficiary is a woman.

Officers of the Social Welfare Department generally required an applicant for benefit to obtain a maintenance order for herself and her child or to enter into an enforceable maintenance agreement which was acceptable to the department. The cost of Domestic Purposes Benefits and related emergency benefits rose greatly through the 1970s, far exceeding the rate of inflation. In 1970, the cost was 2.3 million, $0.3 million recovered by maintenance payments.[3] In 1980, $169.5 million was paid out; $12.3 million was recovered in maintenance payments.[4] In that ten year period, the number of Domestic Purposes beneficiaries increased ten-fold. Seventy-five percent of beneficiaries were involved in marriage breakdown.[5]

Such an increase in social welfare payments caused much public comment. A common suggestion was that the Domestic Purposes Benefit actually encouraged marriage breakdown. The Government became concerned about the increasing drain on public funds. Ninety-three percent of the cost of the Domestic Purposes Benefit in 1980 was carried by the taxpayer at large.[6] However, the public at large thought that people should meet their obligations to support their children. It was always a condition of receipt of a Domestic Purposes Benefit that the beneficiary commence proceedings for a maintenance order or enter into an agreement for maintenance which was acceptable to the department. Most offers by the person from whom maintenance was sought were not acceptable to the department and court proceedings were the order of the day. Delays in instructing a lawyer, delays on the part of the lawyer, delays in serving documents, and delays in obtaining court fixtures meant it was often months or years before a maintenance order was made. The applicant for a maintenance order was almost always legally aided. Three methods were adopted by the Social Welfare Department to overcome the delays inherent in awaiting a court order:

1. The department wrote regularly to the lawyer instructed by the beneficiary, enquiring about progress;
2. It exercised statutory powers[7] to institute and appear in maintenance proceedings brought in the name of the beneficiary; and
3. It instituted a scheme whereby applicants for a benefit were immediately sent for marriage counselling in the hope that if there were no reconciliation there might be agreement on what the husband was to pay for maintenance.

The second method brought criticism from the legal profession and led to questions in Parliament. It was criticized as an improper interruption to the lawyer/client relationship. It was against this background that the Social Security Amendment (No. 2) Bill 1979 was brought before Parliament. It proposed a scheme whereby a liable parent was to make contributions towards the maintenance and support of his child and spouse. The scheme was very similar to the "administrative order" suggested by the Finer Report in the United Kingdom.[8] That report, whose recommendations were never implemented in the United Kingdom, suggested that the Benefits Commission should, after assessing the amount to be paid by a liable relative, make an administrative order to that effect. An underlying premise of that scheme was that "fair assessment and efficient collection are essentially administrative processes."[9] The Finer Report did not suggest that *liability* to pay — an investigation of matrimonial conduct or of paternity — should be fixed other than by the court.[10]

The New Zealand Bill proposed that "liable parents" should make payments to the Social Welfare Department. The Bill was amended substantially before becoming law. Firstly, it dovetailed into the new structure of Family Courts then being considered by Parliament. Secondly, it removed any provision for spousal maintenance. Thirdly, the basis for objecting was widened and the onus of proof removed from the objector. Fourthly, account was taken of a liable parent's own circumstances, in particular, any new family which he might have established. Fifthly, procedures for enforcing the obligations laid down were established, in particular, attachment of wages.

When the Bill was introduced in the form in which it later became law, Parliament was told that it was "a speedy administrative method for recovering the cost of Domestic Purposes Benefits."[11] Fears that the scheme was Draconian and a bureaucratic monster were allayed. The declared aim of the Bill was that people should meet their obligations to support their children by a system which was a cross between a tailor-made system, as provided by the courts, and an automatic assessment system. The Bill became law as the *Social Security Amendment Act 1980,* with effect from 1 April 1981.

THE ACT

An applicant for a Domestic Purposes Benefit is entitled to that benefit if she is caring for a dependent child, or children, and if the father of each dependent child has been identified in law. This means identity in law; it has nothing to do with actual whereabouts. "Liable Parent" is defined as "every person (other than beneficiary) who is liable in law to maintain the dependent child, whether or not that person is also liable in law to maintain the beneficiary."[12] Every parent of a child is liable to maintain that child.[13] Step-parents and foster-parents can be included as liable parents. Various ways of proving paternity for the purposes of identifying a liable parent are provided for. If a beneficiary has no legal proof of identity of the father of her child, then she must bring paternity proceedings. She is not entitled to a Domestic Purposes Benefit until she does, though she will receive emergency assistance.

Any maintenance order or agreement providing for the maintenance of the beneficiary or the child is suspended as soon as a benefit is granted.[14] Accordingly, only benefits granted after April, 1981, are subject to the Act. The Benefits Scheme and Liable Parent Scheme are dealt with by the Social Welfare Department on a data program. Both schemes warrant such an administrative approach as data inputs are simple and massive numbers of persons are involved. The scheme of the Act does not affect a woman who is not receiving a Domestic Purposes Benefit; she must institute maintenance proceedings through the courts in the normal way.

The basis of the new scheme is a procedure for fixing the contribution required from a liable parent towards the costs of the benefit being received by the mother of the child. Every liable parent is required to contribute towards the cost of the benefit an amount calculated in accordance with the Twentieth Schedule of the Act. Once that contribution is calculated the department gives notice of the required contribution to the liable parent. Liability to pay commences on the twenty-eighth day after the date on which the notice is given. If the whereabouts of the liable parent is unknown, it commences on the twenty-eighth day after the contribution is calculated.[15] A liable parent is in fact given about ten weeks from the time he receives notification of an application for a benefit before he must actually start making contributions. Five weeks is allowed to complete the papers and a further five weeks is allowed for service of the Notice of Contributions and for making the first of those contributions. A notice can be served personally or by leaving it at the liable parent's residence or place of business, or by sending it by registered letter to either of those places.[16]

The department looks at what a liable parent can pay in assessing the quantum of his contributions. In order to make its calculations, the department sends a notice to the liable parent, advising that an application for a benefit has been made and advising the liable parent of his consequent liability and requiring him to provide a statement of gross earnings for the last income year. There is a discretion to use current wages, at the choice of the liable parent. One presumes that this election would only be made where the liable parent had suffered a drop in earnings. Use of income for the last income year is a notion favorable to the liable parent. New Zealand's income year finishes on March 31. If a liable parent's income is being looked at in the following December, it would probably be higher than his notional income for the purposes of the Liable Parent Scheme. Inflation of wages is currently at about 15 percent per annum.

If the liable parent does not provide the necessary information, the Social Welfare Department can determine, as best it can on the information available to it, his likely gross income. There is an onus of proof on a liable parent if he wishes to change that determination. One presumes that that is an incentive to the giving of truthful information. In one office of the Social Welfare Department, 70 percent of assessments are default assessments because the information initially requested has not been returned.[17]

Gross earnings is the basis for calculating the contribution of a liable parent. This calculation of his contribution is the focal point of the whole scheme and is made, as indicated, in accordance with the Twentieth Schedule to the Act. There are four possible calculations and it is the lowest sum which is adopted as the contribution required. The possible contributions are:

1. $20.00 per week for each of the beneficiary's dependent children plus a further $20.00 where one or more of those children is under the age of five. Atkin thinks that this is an element of spousal maintenance creeping back into the system and the writer respectfully agrees. The extra sum assumes that preschool children require the attention of a mother or, alternatively, that the mother must pay for day care if she wishes to work;
2. The weekly amount of benefit (this will really be the minimum contribution);
3. The amount of the liable parent's weekly benefit less the following amounts:
   (*a*) Income Tax; and
   (*b*) Either $50.00 towards rent and $60.00 spending allowance or $50.00 towards board and $30.00 spending money; and
   (*c*) The actual cost of travel to and from work; and
   (*d*) An allowance for (other) relatives; and
   (*e*) Anything paid towards occupation of a house by the beneficiary in question;
4. One-third of the liability parent's income after the deduction of tax. Atkin comments that this approach is similar to that used in courts in England as a starting point determining maintenance orders but never accepted by New Zealand courts.

Coloured pamphlets setting out the effects of the scheme, together with self-assessment forms, have been widely distributed. They seem a baffling jigsaw, but give the right sums. Like New Zealand's income tax assessment scheme, the Liable Parent Scheme relies on the honesty of the individual completing the form. Once the department has calculated the least contribution required, it gives notice of the amount to the liable parent.[18]

OBJECTIONS

A liable parent can object and the department will reconsider any contributions. If it does not allow the objection in full, it must file papers in the Family Court so the court can consider the whole matter. Administrative review will generally weed out mathematical errors. In its pamphlet, the department invites review of assessments at any time, even by telephone, in cases like loss of job or remarriage.

The grounds for objection are set out.[19] Apart from obvious grounds like incorrect addition or choice of the wrong calculation under the Twentieth Schedule, there are the following:

1. The objector is not liable in law to maintain the dependent child;
2. The child is not the child of the liable parent;

3. Some other person is liable to contribute to maintenance;
4. Other financial provision for the child has been made;
5. Any matter that could be taken into account in a maintenance application under the *Family Proceedings Act 1980*. This act covers family law matters in general as distinct from maintenance arising from the granting of a benefit.

There are two reported cases on objections. Both those and the only case on the scheme which the writer has argued before a Judge concerned matter 5, the catchall provision. All three cases concerned a father who objected on the grounds that his separated wife was either working or living in a *de facto* relationship where she received financial support. In all three cases, the Social Welfare Department investigated the matter and determined that the wife should still receive a benefit. Liability under the Liable Parent Scheme followed automatically. In all cases, the liable parent could afford to pay the contribution assessed but refused to do so as a matter of principle. In both decided cases[20] the judge conceded there were grounds for objection. In one, a capital payment towards maintenance had been made. In the other, the judge thought the liable parent could earn more than she was doing. In both those cases, the court said it would intervene where a beneficiary was exploiting the system. The Chief District Court Judge said that a heavy burden lay on welfare officers to have regard to the effects of granting a benefit. The writer is still awaiting a decision in the case argued by him.

There is provision for appeal from the Family Court to the High Court and thence, if a point of law is involved, to the Court of Appeal.[21] Proceedings are not open to the public.[22] The court can suspend liability when an objection has been filed.[23] The department has discretionary power to release a liable parent or make necessary alterations to the contribution where exaction of the full contribution would entail various hardships.[24] One officer of the Social Welfare Department has dealt with eight applications under this provision and granted all but one.[25] The department is also obliged to review contributions from time to time.[26] Amounts are backdated. Atkin makes the point that if the department has delays in its administration, then a liable parent could face a demand for substantial arrears arising from a salary increase.

ENFORCEMENT

Where any contribution is unpaid, it can be recovered as a debt. It can also be deducted from any benefit to which the liable parent is entitled, for example, a sickness benefit or unemployment benefit.[27] A Deduction Notice (so-called) can be issued voluntarily by a liable parent. Where payments are in arrears for fourteen days, the department can also issue such a notice. It is addressed to the employer of a liable parent.[28] A copy is also served on the liable parent. A Deduction Notice creates a charge over wages due by the employer. Monies so charged must be paid to the department. Failure to do so makes the money owing a debt due by the employer who also commits an offence punishable by fine. The Act binds the Crown as an employer. The Deduction Notice informs both employer and liable parent of their rights to rectify errors and if either employer or parent is not satisfied, rights of appeal to the registrar of the court to vary or discharge the notice are available.[29] No matter what the contribution required, an employer shall not pay out more than 40 percent of net wages. Accordingly, there is some residual protection of wages.[30]

EFFECT OF SCHEME: CONCLUSION

At the time of this writing, the scheme has been in operation for nearly twelve months. No financial data on the revenue recovered is yet available. One officer of the department[31] considers that the rate of collection will be substantially higher than the 7 percent returned to the revenue before the scheme was implemented. Whether substantially more revenue will be collected from liable parents, remains to be seen. The Department of Social Welfare certainly hopes more revenue will be collected. The writer considers that the scheme is to the financial advantage of many liable parents. Because there is no element of spousal maintenance, many liable parents pay a contribution that is less than the courts would probably have ordered on making a maintenance order. Liable parents can assess their financial position without waiting for a maintenance hearing. A system whereby all liable parents pay, albeit at lower levels, seems inherently fairer than one where some parents paid and others did not pending a maintenance hearing by the court.

Atkin lists what he considers are the important consequences for family law:

a) One can now surmise the end of spousal maintenance. This is in line with the philosophy of the *Family Proceedings Act* which sees spousal maintenance not as a life-long concomitant of marriage but as a transitional mechanism for assisting the parties to a broken marriage to adjust to a new life style;
b) Routine maintenance cases which were clogging up the judicial system have been removed from it;
c) Wives are no longer forced into litigation with their husbands merely to secure their benefits. The liable parent and an arm of government become adversaries, rather than spouse and spouse.

Against that, Atkin considers that the new scheme extracts one aspect of marriage breakdown from the whole package of custody, occupation of home, and division of property. He also considers that there should be a formal reference to counselling as part of the scheme, in view of the importance of counselling and mediation in the present Family Court system. The writer respectfully agrees with the latter view. He respectfully disagrees with the former. If a liable parent knows exactly what his maintenance obligations are, he is more likely to settle other family concerns. He knows where he stands financially and need not attempt to delay a court hearing.

The main benefit of the new scheme, in the opinion of the writer, is in reducing the area of conflict between spouses. Previously, the Social Welfare Department required a wife to commence maintenance proceedings as a condition of her benefit. Proceedings for separation, custody and matrimonial property were generally issued at the same time. Now, the parties know where they stand financially and can resolve other matters by agreement. The reduced tension level means less quibbling over access or valuation of chattels. Matrimonial applications of all sorts have dropped by one-half in the Family Court, where the writer normally practices, since the scheme came into effect. The expertise of Family Court Judges is now being used where it should be used — in areas of custody, access and division of property. Since most beneficiaries were legally aided, the Legal Aid fund will no longer pay for petty maintenance arguments. What the scheme cannot do is provide for the case of a liable parent who is deliberately trying to evade responsibility, by assuming a false name or leaving for Australia.

Constitutional lawyers might balk at the Executive fixing the quantum of maintenance. The Executive fixes the quantum of tax we pay, why not maintenance? This new legislation assumes that determining what the liable parent should pay is essentially an administrative and not a judicial task. Just because a beneficiary receives a benefit she should not be pushed into a dispute with her spouse or boyfriend. Liability of that parent is essentially a dispute between him and the state, as a collector of revenue. The powers of review and appeal on any aspect of the scheme are the citizen's safeguard against abuse of administrative power.

NOTES

1. *Social Security Amendment Act 1973.*
2. R.S. White, Social Welfare Department.
3. W.R. Atkin: "Liable Parents: The New State Role in Ordering Maintenance," (1981) 5 *Otago L.R.* 48–63.
4. N.Z. Parliamentary Debates 1980, 2,258.
5. Atkin, *op. cit.*
6. N.Z. Parliamentary Debates, 1980, 2,558.
7. S. 27F(3) as inserted by *Social Security Admendment Act 1973.*

8. Report of the Committee on One-Parent Families (Lond, 1974, H.M.S.O. Amnd. 5,629, especially Sections 10, 11, 12 of Part 4).
9. Finer, *op. cit.,* Part 4, 209.
10. Finer, *op. cit.,* Part 4, 247.
11. N.Z. Parliamentary Debates, p. 2,554.
12. S. 271 *Social Security Act 1964.*
13. S. 72 *Family Proceedings Act 1980.*
14. S. 27J.
15. S. 27K.
16. S. 27Z1.
17. R.S. White, Social Welfare Department.
18. S. 27N.
19. S. 27P.
20. *Carmine v. Social Security Commission* and *Priston v. Social Security Commission,* I.N.Z.F.L.R. (1981).
21. S. 27R — 27T.
22. S. 27U.
23. S. 270 (2).
24. S. 272G.
25. R.S. White, Social Welfare Department.
26. S. 272H.
27. S. 27X.
28. S. 26Y.
29. S. 272C.
30. S. 272B.
31. R.S. White, Social Welfare Department.

Chapter Thirty-four

Child Support in the United States: Reporting Good News*

Harry D. Krause

University of Illinois College of Law
Champaign, Illinois, U.S.A.

THE FEDERAL CHILD SUPPORT ENFORCEMENT LEGISLATION OF 1975

In 1934, the American Law Institute's *Restatement of the Law of Conflicts* characterized support obligations and their enforcement as "of no special interest to other states and since the duty is not imposed primarily for the benefit of an individual, it is not enforceable elsewhere." In theory, this notion was laid to rest by the widespread enactment of the *Uniform Reciprocal Enforcement of Support Acts* of 1950, 1958, and 1968. In practice, however, American law remained deeply insensitive to the enforcement of child support obligations.

In the last two decades, several social trends merged to change this situation: increasing rates of divorce, family abandonment, and illegitimacy combined to leave unprecedented numbers of children in single-parent homes, typically without adequate or any support from the other parent. In consequence, *attitudes* began to change — and the law followed slowly.

In 1974, child support enforcement still lay in shambles. Inadequate laws still were producing low returns at prohibitive expense. Studies of the subject, even those commissioned by the federal government, still met with apathy. Aggravating the practical neglect was ideological dislike of

---

* Portions of this chapter draw on H. Krause, *Child Support in America: The Legal Perspective* (Michie, 1981) which provides more detail and full citations. Copyright: Harry D. Krause.

support enforcement that sprang from the spreading notion in the welfare community that the state, rather than absent fathers, should support abandoned children. What feeble attempts there were to bring deserting fathers to accept responsibility were discounted with the argument that the funds thus collected would not benefit the children, because collections would be offset against AFDC entitlements. In Congress, the Senate Finance Committee, chaired by Senator Long, had concerned itself with child support legislation since the early 1970s. On several occasions, the Senate had passed significant child support amendments which ultimately failed in the House. Representative Martha Griffiths, in her effort to stimulate Congressional interest in child support enforcement, described the situation:

> Over 12 million American children — almost one child out of every five — does not live with both parents. Most of these children live with their mothers and of those, about half live in poverty. . . . Eighty percent of AFDC [welfare receiving] children have absent parents, and almost one-third of these children are covered by support orders or agreements. However, although these orders represent findings that the parents are able to pay, few are obeyed.

In 1974, Congress finally moved to strengthen enforcement of child support obligations across the nation — thereby, it was hoped, reducing the cost of the Aid to Families with Dependent Children (AFDC) programs significantly. Effective August 1, 1975, sweeping amendments changed the AFDC Title of the *Social Security Act,* and a new Child Support Title (IV-D) was added. A broad base of regulations was soon developed to implement the new legislation.

Today, the resulting program is well on its way to success. Early critics are being convinced of its viability and most now believe that the future will bring greatly increased efficiency and corresponding results. In 1974, the influential *Washington Post* characterized the proposed program as "an unwarranted intrusion of the federal government [into personal lives that] would yield little while costing a great deal . . . the benefits to be derived are minimal at best. The dangers are incalculable." By March, 1978, the *Washington Post* had been converted: "About 1 million parents who otherwise would pay nothing are now making payments. And the more than $1 billion anticipated this fiscal year in child-support payments obtained for welfare mothers or other families where the father has disappeared or refuses to support the children is equal to about 10 percent of the entire national cost of the Aid to Families with Dependent Children program."

Even under the federal initiative, state authority and state laws remain the primary vehicles for the establishment of paternity and child support collection. What is new is that the federal government has become an active stimulator, overseer and financier of state collection systems. Each state enforcement agency — now commonly known as a "IV-D Agency," reflecting its statutory location — must meet standards imposed by the Department of Health and Human Services (HHS) Office of Child Support Enforcement (OCSE) or lose 5 percent of its federal AFDC funding. If, on the other hand, the enforcement program meets federal standards, the state receives 75 percent of the program's cost from HHS.

In summary, the amendments impose on state AFDC programs the additional function of acting as intake agencies for child support enforcement programs, and require them to collect data. Specific new rules include the following: state AFDC agencies must use the social security numbers of all AFDC applicants as identification; the AFDC agency must notify the state child support enforcement agency whenever it grants benefits to deserted children and must open its records to support enforcement officials; applicants must assign their right to uncollected child support to the state and must agree to cooperate in locating the absent parent, establishing paternity, obtaining a support judgment if none is outstanding and securing payments. Limited exceptions are authorized to the duty to cooperate, but not to the assignment requirement. In case of an applicant's unjustified failure to cooperate, AFDC benefits are withheld from the applicant, but not from the child or children.

Each state IV-D agency maintains a "state parent locator service" equipped to search state and local records for information regarding the whereabouts of an absent parent and may call upon the sophisticated, computerized federal parent locator service based in Washington with access to Social Security, Internal Revenue and vast other federal data resources. Once the absent parent (or alleged parent) is located, the state (if necessary and possible) establishes paternity, obtains support judgment, and enforces the obligation through either in-state or interstate proceedings (with access to the federal courts as a last resort). All states are bound to cooperate fully with the enforcement efforts of sister states. *In extremis,* HHS may request the Internal Revenue Service to collect outstanding judgments as though they were a tax liability. Finally, anyone with support rights against a federal employee or beneficiary may garnish the absent parent's federal money under a statutory waiver of sovereign immunity. After collection, the state disburses child support payments, keeping detailed records and reporting to OCSE. To encourage local participation in child support enforcement, a portion of the proceeds is turned over to the collecting unit of local government.

The program also is available to non-AFDC parents who pay an application fee and agree to pay the cost of collection from payments collected for them and also, under certain conditions, for the enforcement of *international* family support (see Cavers, "International Enforcement of Family Support," 81 *Col.L.Rev.* 994, 1981).

Experience is developing rapidly and favorably. The federal parent locator service was initiated in late March, 1975. In its very first year, the new service was able to find addresses for almost 90 percent of the names concerning which the states sought help. During fiscal year 1977, child support enforcement programs yielded IV-D agencies a total of $818 million ($603 million in 1976) composed of $409.5 million for AFDC recipients ($280 million in 1976) plus $408.5 million for non-AFDC claimants ($323.7 million in 1976). The stated cost in 1977 amounted to $258.8 million ($142.6 million in 1976) for an average return of $3.16 for each dollar spent. An additional estimated $21.3 million in support payments went directly to AFDC families and thereby reduced AFDC assistance payments. The fiscal 1977 program (for both AFDC recipients and non-AFDC applicants) located 341,111 persons (181,504 in 1976), established paternity in 68,263 cases (14,706 in 1976), and established support obligations in 183,073 cases (75,008 in 1976).

Later figures show continuing acceleration. In fiscal year 1979, 480,000 absent parents were located (642,000 in 1980), support obligations were established in more than 300,000 cases (373,000 in 1980), paternity was ascertained in more than 117,000 cases (144,000 in 1980) and more than one and one-third billion dollars were collected (one and one-half billion in 1980), including $730 million in non-AFDC collections ($874 million in 1980). In 1977, 20 percent of AFDC families (600,000) were being served by the support enforcement program, and HEW (now HHS) projections in 1978 looked toward 35 percent by 1981. By late 1978, 1.2 million missing parents had been located, $1.3 billion had been collected for children on welfare (as compared to about $10.7 billion paid out in aid) and a further $1.5 million had been collected for children not on public aid.

So far, OSCE has been lenient in allowing the states time to gear up for the program. Federal audits of state programs ultimately will pinpoint problems and help provide solutions, by assistance and by the threat of federal sanctions. Interestingly, two originally controversial remedies had not seen much use. By late 1979, federal court enforcement had not yet been tried and IRS collection had been used sparingly.

If a verdict regarding the support enforcement program may be attempted at this stage, the overall impression is good — even excellent. Enormous progress has been made toward alleviating a serious social problem. However, this verdict is conditional. It relates to what should be seen as the first stage of the program. The initial period of successfully putting the basic program into place, prodding reluctant or indifferent states to cooperate, and improving the mechanics of collecting support at the national, state and local levels, is over. The time has come for a qualitative leap forward. A good program must now become better — not necessarily in dollar-cost-benefit terms, but in cost-benefit terms that reflect more of the underlying social values sought to be realized (see Krause, "Child Support Enforcement: Legislative Tasks for the Early 1980's," 15 *Fam.L.Q.* 349, 1982).

STATE LAWS GOVERNING THE SUPPORT OBLIGATION

A cynic may hypothesize that American (state) child support laws, both in terms of substance and enforcement procedures, have been permitted to survive in their present state of disarray, unevenness and consequent unfairness only because they have *not* been enforced with any degree of regularity. Indeed, the seeming irresponsibility of American fathers may at least in part be explained in terms of unrealistic obligations being imposed and sought to be enforced under unrealistic laws.

It seems reasonable to suggest that the federal initiative that now causes the sudden activation of these laws, imposes a corresponding responsibility on the federal authorities to assure that the states develop more sensible, more uniform and more predictable support laws. So far, the federal government has failed to provide leadership regarding this crucial point which, admittedly, raises "sticky" constitutional problems, less as a matter of power than of policy.

Nevertheless, it is my view that with all reasonable respect for traditional state sovereignty regarding family law, current federal law provides adequate room for Washington to play an important role in defining standards for acceptable state law on these questions. If OCSE believes that this goal requires more specific federal legislation, it should work toward that. At the very minimum, in the context of OCSE-sponsored support enforcement, federal standards ultimately must assure less arbitrary and diverse conceptions of the "needs of the child" and the "father's ability to pay" as well as assuring less counterproductive methods of support enforcement than are now the rule (e.g., wage deduction *to avoid default,* rather than jail — and loss of job — *after default*). From the standpoint of sound policy, it should be an important goal of federal involvement to assure that state enforcement efforts will not reach the point of increasing, rather than reducing, social disorganization. Aside from reasonable enforcement methods, this involves manageable, live and let-live, levels of support. What does present state law provide?

Civil child support obligations generally are statutory. The extent of the obligation, however, remains largely undefined. Aside from the deliberate reluctance of the courts to involve themselves in the day-to-day operation of the functioning family (unless and until the situation is so bad that "child neglect" laws are offended and furnish the basis of intervention), even in the context of divorce, separation or a paternity proceeding, few clear answers appear. The court's discretion regarding the amount of child support usually reigns supreme, the basic criteria being the needs of the child and the father's (and perhaps the mother's and the child's) ability to earn.

Section 15(e) of the *Uniform Parentage Act* summarizes factors commonly used by the courts in the exercise of their broad discretion:

> In determining the amount to be paid by a parent for support of the child and the period during which the duty of support is owed, a court enforcing the obligation of support shall consider all relevant facts, including (1) the needs of the child; (2) the standard of living and circumstances of the parents; (3) the relative financial means of the parents; (4) the earning ability of the parents; (5) the need and capacity of the child for education, including higher education; (6) the age of the child; (7) the financial resources and the earning ability of the child; (8) the responsibility of the parents for the support of others; and (9) the value of services contributed by the custodial parent.

The *Uniform Marriage and Divorce Act* contains a similar listing. It does appear, however, that courts do not adhere consistently to these "common-sense" factors which seek to put some ground under their otherwise unbridled discretion. Principled methods of defining a child support formula — fairly weighing the child's need against the father's ability to pay — are needed, but few judges seem to look kindly at any restraint on their wisdom. The national picture thus remains one of great diversity, divergence and confusion. The most basic questions remain unanswered: just what *are* necessities, how should the child's "need" be defined once necessities are taken care of, what *is* the father's "ability to pay," especially if he chooses not to work or is "underemployed"? The bottom line is that a father must retain enough to live on after making support payments. But how much is enough? At the "welfare level," token awards such as $10 per week have been the rule, although the new federal involvement may change this custom.

Support orders, as well as child support obligations agreed upon in separation agreements, generally remain modifiable to respond to a significant change in circumstances, whether that change be in terms of the parent's ability to pay or the child's need. Rhode Island recently enacted an interesting innovation: any child support order must be reconsidered *de novo* in the event the child becomes a recipient of public assistance. As in the case of defining the initial award, statutory or judicial guidelines defining a "significant change in circumstances" generally are lacking, nor would they be easily conceived. Again, judicial discretion reigns nearly supreme. In an effort to reduce the uncertainty — which often leads to unwarranted harassment of the supporting parent by the custodial parent and wasteful use of court facilities — the *Uniform Marriage and Divorce Act* requires "a showing of changed circumstances so substantial and continuing as to make the terms [previously set] unconscionable." Whether this language will produce significantly greater certainty remains to be seen. As a legal term of art, the word "unconscionable" has had a long and checkered history.

A common question is what effect should be given the father's creation of a new family. Traditionally, the courts have taken the position that the father's prior child support obligations take absolute precedence over the needs of his new family. More recently, however, some courts have considered the interests of both families and have attempted a fair apportionment. This approach seems more realistic. Arguably, the balance of social interest (though not necessarily individual equity) might even weigh in favor of the father's current family because that family might founder if earlier obligations were enforced beyond the father's reasonably available means — with the possible result of two families drawing welfare payments rather than one. Whatever the policy, current equal protection reasoning makes it difficult to defend blanket discrimination in favor of or against the children of one or the other marriage or, for that matter, nonmarital children. In competition with each other for their father's support, all children should stand on an equal footing and have equal legal claims.

Too many important issues remain and cannot be discussed in the limited space available here: Should the father's support obligation be reduced if his former wife remarries and his children receive some support from the mother's new husband? What is the extent of the father's freedom to change his occupation or professional status for one less lucrative or to quit work altogether? Should arrears continue to accrue even when the father loses his employment involuntarily? What should be the role of support judgments with automatic adjustment clauses? Should child support orders be self-reducing or self-terminating: for instance when the father takes over custody or when some or all children reach majority or are emancipated, or where social security benefits are paid to the children? Should a support-delinquent father's arrears be credited with voluntary payments made to or on behalf of his children, especially during visitation or vacations? Should the parental support obligation end at the parent's death or should a liquidated support obligation be enforced against the parent's estate? (For discussion of these and other questions, see H. Krause, *Child Support in America: The Legal Perspective.* 1981, 3–99.)

THE UNIFORM RECIPROCAL ENFORCEMENT OF SUPPORT ACT

The burden in our complex multistate setting of obtaining jurisdiction over absent defendants, recognition of out-of-state judgments and actual collection of child support owed, indicates the need for an efficient method of enforcing child support across American state lines. Fortunately, there exists a greatly simplified alternative to wholly individual enforcement efforts. The *Uniform Reciprocal Enforcement of Support Act* (URESA), or an equivalent, has been enacted in every state and territory of the United States. In addition, several states have concluded reciprocal arrangements with foreign countries, such as Australia, Bermuda, Canada, France, the United Kingdom, the Republic of South Africa, the Federal Republic of Germany and others. Under the Act, an action to secure support from an obligor residing in another state may be initiated in one state and tried in another, thereby relieving the support claimant of the burden of leaving the home jurisdiction. The objective of the Act "is to aid stationary mothers in exacting child support from peregrinating fathers" (*In re Marriage of Ceganovich*, 61 Cal. App. 3d 289, 132 Cal. Rptr. 261, 1976). The Act originated in 1950, was amended in 1958, and revised substantially in 1968. The pre-1968 versions of the Act were popularly referred to as URESA, whereas the 1968 version is referred to as revised URESA or RURESA. Approximately one-half of the states now have enacted RURESA and, as pointed out above, *all* have *some* form of URESA or an equivalent.

Briefly, the Act provides that the person to whom a duty of support is owed may file a petition in her (or his) own state, called the initiating state. The initiating court then makes a preliminary finding as to whether the petition sets forth sufficient facts indicating that the alleged obligor actually owes a duty of support and that an out-of-state-court (called the "responding court") can obtain jurisdiction over the obligor. There need not be a previous court order fixing the amount of support, if the existence of a support obligation is indicated by the facts. After making a brief, preliminary determination of liability, the initiating court certifies and transmits its findings to the responding court having jurisdiction over the obligor, or to any agency in the responding state which will forward the petition to the appropriate court. While RURESA requires that the responding state agency use all available means to locate the obligor, less stringent rules govern locator services in URESA states. The federal child support enforcement act, of course, now offers much more effective means to locate support obligors than had been available before.

Upon receipt of the petition, the responding court dockets the case and notifies the prosecuting attorney whose duty it is to serve the obligor and to prosecute the case diligently. If there is danger that the obligor will flee from the responding court's jurisdiction, he may be arrested or required to post bond. Although the state prosecutor typically represents the obligee in a civil proceeding, URESA does not provide for appointment of counsel for the obligor.

After obtaining jurisdiction over the obligor, the responding court holds a hearing to determine whether a support obligation exists. The duties of support imposed upon an obligor "are those imposed under the laws of any state where the obligor was present for the period during which support is sought." During the hearing, the obligor has an opportunity to present defenses and both parties may submit evidence. After finding a duty of support, the responding court may issue a support order and may subject the obligor's property to the order. The responding court must transmit payments to the initiating court "forthwith."

In general, the responding court's jurisdiction is limited to the support obligation. In most cases, therefore, it has been held that the responding court may not consider collateral issues such as custody or visitation rights and may not condition its support order on the performance of a duty owed by the obligee. This limitation on the jurisdiction of the responding court enables the parties to participate in the support action without risking the adjudication of peripheral matters. The defense of nonpaternity, if there is no judgment establishing paternity and entitled to full faith and credit, has caused courts to disagree on whether paternity may be litigated for the first time in a URESA action. The 1968 RURESA, however, specifically provides that paternity may be litigated under certain conditions.

Among a variety of other matters, the Act also contains important provisions dealing with criminal enforcement (even allowing the extradition of "support-defendants") and allowing the registration at the forum of out-of-state support orders.

CONCLUSION

In these last paragraphs, it is well worth re-emphasizing the significance of the federal support enforcement legislation — above and beyond the welfare context. To date, this legislation represents the most important federal legislative venture into *family* law: The provisions encouraging non-AFDC support enforcement under the program alleviate the all too common lot of the abandoned mother who has sufficient productive capacity and pride to keep herself and her children above the welfare-eligibility line, but whose earning capacity may have been impaired by a role-divided marriage and now is restricted by the custodial services she renders her children. The typical father's earnings enable him to make a reasonable contribution to child support, but he does not earn enough to do that without "pain." Unless "encouraged," many fathers thus are unwilling to make their proper contributions which, though significant in terms of their children's needs, too often are not large enough to make it economical to involve lawyers in repeated enforcement forays under the cumbersome and correspondingly expensive traditional child support enforcement procedures.

When it discussed the controversy over the continuation of federal funding for this important aspect of the program, the Senate Finance Committee summarized the case for non-AFDC enforcement:

> The purpose of the requirement on the States to provide services to nonrecipients is to assure that abandoned families with children have access to child support services before they are forced to apply for welfare. Access to these services may mean the difference between a family's dependence on welfare for support or being supported by a legally responsible parent.

The extension to the "private sector" of the parent locator, paternity establishment and enforcement and collection features may well be the most important single feature of the federal Act and ranks along with the development of equal rights for the nonmarital child under *(federal)* constitutional law, as one of the two most significant items of "good news" in this area. "Good news" in terms of results achieved, but not necessarily in terms of our federal-state structure. Both developments represent significant breaks in the American tradition of federal abstention in the area of family law — traditionally the preserve of state sovereignty.

Part Seven

Family Decisions and Medical Ethics

In this, the final section of the volume, some of the newest and knottiest among family law problems are confronted by two authors. In the Netherlands, Rood-de Boer deals with the current status of minors in regard to medical treatment (Chapter 35). Even today, when physicians are obligated to give their adult patients full information on their medical condition and not to give treatment without the patient's "informed consent," Rood-de Boer points out that adult patients are far from true partners in the relationship; they must rely on the expertise of the physician, and are therefore in actuality dependents. When we move along the line, in spite of the recent Recommendation Concerning a European Statute for the Rights of the Child adopted by the General Assembly of the Council of Europe, we find that the parents of minors in Holland continue to have practically complete authority to make all decisions for their children, including medical decisions — so we have parents dependent on physicians and children on their parents. The Dutch child is still a long way from having any say on medical treatment that may be administered to him or her or on refusing such treatment. One unusual section of the law in the Netherlands, which is relevant here, is that since 1976 there has been no compulsory vaccination. While the government provides every necessary condition to make it as easy and cost free as possible for parents to have their children vaccinated, it is felt that compulsion would reduce the motivation for voluntary compliance and remove the personal responsibility of the parents. The Dutch, it seems, have a very strong distaste for Big Brother, and an equally strong respect for parental autonomy. There do exist various legal exceptions to the absolute parental power in making medical decisions for their minor children, but Rood-de Boer finds that such exceptions are made ever more rarely, and only in emergency cases. She ends her discussion with a set of guidelines which she believes can be used to protect the rights of the minor patient, and stresses that the minor, if capable of discernment, should have the right to be fully informed and to express his or her wishes about the medical treatment to be applied. Except in emergency, or where such a minor is very anxious that the parents should not be informed, as in some cases of abortion, the parents also should receive essential information about the treatment before it is applied. The coordinating measures she suggests, the author is convinced, would help to bring into balance the power of the physician, the power of the parents over their children, and the rights of the child.

But the problems family law faces now and in the foreseeable future are more numerous and more involved than balancing out the powers and rights of family members in traditional medical decisions. In the last chapter in this volume (Chapter 36) the American, Baron, writes of the ethical issues arising from the enormous advances in medical technology, which almost weekly present difficult new choices that somehow must be confronted and decided on, often immediately. "Informed consent" has seemingly placed medical decisions more and more in the hands of patients, although patient autonomy is not yet complete and physicians are lobbying to return the power of decision making to themselves. The courts sometimes seem to "side" with the doctors, and subtly to place the final authority with the medical profession. Nevertheless, the current trend in American law seems to be that a legally competent patient has the constitutional right to reject or accept any or all medical treatment — which, however, carries the question into another thicket of debatable issues: who is to decide for the child, the retarded person, the senile or the patient in coma?

Parental power over day-to-day and general decisions affecting their child is well established in America, but the medical treatment parents want for their child is no longer always accepted by doctors, the courts, or the child itself. The courts have acceded to parents' wishes in refusing treatment for some medical problems of their child and have overridden the parents in others, especially of course where the life of the child is immediately at stake. The courts have intervened particularly where they have doubts about exclusive parental devotion to the patient child, as in organ transplant cases, where genetic similarity between donor and recipient is important for success, and where the donor is preferably a sibling — who may be a minor of very tender years himself. Sterilization of mentally retarded minors is another touchy area, and the courts have been so uneasy about the constitutional rights involved that at times they have overreacted by denying court jurisdiction in such cases. Abortion for minors is of course the most widely publicized area of conflict between the rights of parents and of minors: the recent "squeal rule" promulgated by the Department of Health and Human Services, which requires that the parents of a minor seeking an abortion must be informed, is currently being hotly debated on constitutional grounds.

Baron discusses other medical decisions by families in situations hitherto unheard and undreamed of, surrogate motherhood for instance, or the right to forego extraordinary measures to prolong a life only technically extant. The fairly simple decisions, historically made by the doctor in conjunction with the patient before he lost consciousness, or with some member of the family afterward, have now often become obsolete when confronted by the terrible and terrifying possibilities of the new medical technology. The "living will" adopted by some of the states has cut through part of the tangle of alternatives, but case piles on case where there seems no precedent in law or in ethics on which to formulate a decision. The basic values of Western society are at stake. Leaving the power of decision to the physician is no longer acceptable, yet neither is placing it in the hands of the courts, where there are no clear precedents and where the resulting mountains of dockets could produce chaos.

The world will not grow simpler, the problems fewer, consensus more frequent. From country to country, state to state, province to province, there are different viewpoints on the assuagements that can lighten the burdens of the human condition. But with all the variations in remedies, one underlying concern is present everywhere: the value of the family. Even in countries where the good of the state appears officially at the top of hierarchal values, the family is still recognized as the base and foundation of state and society, as the molder and support of the individual. The role of family law in this cruel and confused world is ever more important. We hope that this collection of articles, ideas and hopes from the four corners of the earth will be of interest and assistance to jurists, lawmakers, social workers, the medical profession — and practicing lawyers!

Chapter Thirty-five

Decision Making About Health Care and Medical Treatment of Minors

Madzy Rood-de Boer

The Netherlands

WHAT ARE THE PROBLEMS TO BE DEALT WITH?

In this chapter, a (narrow) legal aspect of health care is discussed: decision making about the care and treatment of underage patients. How is this decision making arrived at? Who are the ones who make the decisions? Are there possibilities of appeal? The position of the minor, with regard to these questions, is viewed within the framework of curative and individual preventive care. In other words: we shall discuss micro-medical-legal questions.

In the field of collective health protection there are, of course, many regulations — such as rules laid down in environment law, or the so-called motorized-bicycle helmet rule *inter alia* — which is important to minors in general, but also to them individually. In this chapter, however, we have not opted for a macrotreatment, by discussing public or administrative law, but are dealing with decision making about heath care for minors mainly as a problem of private law.

One more preliminary remark: in the chapter we refer regularly to the *physician* responsible for treatment. Whatever is said about the doctor and the minor, applies *m.m.* equally to others working in health care, *e.g.,* in the nursing and paramedical professions when their care concerns minors.

DECISION MAKING IN HEALTH CARE

Generally speaking, the decision on whether a certain medical treatment should be submitted to is made in consultation between physician and (conscious) patient. The times are past when the physician, as medical authority, made the decision alone, and the patient, being ignorant of his bodily condition and/or of his ailments, as well as of the medical possibilities of recovery or improvement, could hardly function as an "interlocutor" in the making of the decision. The increased maturity of all people and the availability of popularized scientific information in the field of health care have contributed to a "new consultative situation." This impels nearly all physicians themselves to give their patients more or less detailed information on their medical situation, as well as on the possibilities for treatment. The decisions are then arrived at by a certain form of consensus: the physician supplies his expert opinion, the patient makes a choice (if possible), and the two reach a joint conclusion. It sounds simple.

This form of decision making, however, is not really simple. Conflicts may still occur. The treatment, decided on by mutual consent, may later lead to differences of opinion. Conflicts may arise about the results of the treatment, or about payment, or about the way the physician deals with his patient before, during or after treatment. A court is sometimes applied to in order to settle such a conflict (the unpaid bill; the operation that failed), or there is recourse to some disciplinary board (*e.g.,* with a complaint about ill or humiliating usage of the patient by the physician). Although judicial intervention remains an exception, feelings of dissatisfaction and annoyance regularly occur.

The basic problem is that it may seem that the parties arrive at a decision on the basis of equality, but that in actuality there is no equality in a medical relationship. The fact that the patient asks for help turns him into an inferior, a dependent; and the exclusive expertise of the physician turns the latter into the superior, the actual decision maker. The legal construct of a contract for providing assistance does not reflect the medical reality. Moreover, in the medical world, a certain fear arises when Parliament wants to deal with medical behaviour:[1] at once there is apprehension of restrictive regulations. The patients, on their side, are loath to push their demands, *e.g.,* by forming groups of interested parties. They fear for their future — they will need their doctor again!

So far we have dealt with decisions about medical treatment of grown-ups, which are to a certain extent influenced by the dependence of the patients. The image becomes far more complex when we focus on decision making concerning underage patients.

MINORITY AND PARENTAL AUTHORITY

The *Civil Code* (BW) leaves small doubt about the limits and the meaning of minority and also about the contents of parental authority. Article 233,

I BW states that those who have not yet reached the age of twenty-one years and are not, nor have been, married, are minors. A person is thus a minor from zero to twenty-one years.

During this period, the minor is subject to parental authority (article 246, I BW); he is incapable of legally valid action (art. 234, I BW). This implies that the minor cannot and may not make independent decisions, and that he must be assisted by his legal representative.

If we were to apply this strict (and, in my opinion, obsolete) statutory law in the medical field, the health care treatment of an underage patient seems again to be a fairly simple matter. The physician, in order to reach a decision, has to deal only with the parents of the child. It is in consultation with them that the decision is made. The child is only indirectly concerned in this, it is not a party. In the "law of reality," the problem of minors in health care is considerably more delicate and difficult. Minors live — legally speaking — in double dependence, on the physician who treats them, and on their parents.

The complication in studying our subject is, firstly, contained in the fact that the legal concepts of *parental authority* and *minority* are not static concepts.[2] In our country an article appeared a few years ago, concerning a "new, reasoned" formulation of parental authority,[3] which has been accepted into general doctrine, without ever having been really contradicted or refuted. The text, drafted by seven "juvenile law experts," for a new article 246, I BW, reads as follows:

- Parents shall be *responsible* for the care and education of their under-age children. To this end they shall have parental authority over these children, in so far as the law does not stipulate differently. Parental authority shall be exericised *reasonably and fairly* and with due regard to the rights and claims of the children.
- Under-age children shall have the right as their personality grows, *to develop* in accordance with their own insight. This right shall comprise *i.a.* the right to choose in the fields of: religion, ethics, education, profession and relaxation, *medical and other provision of aid.* (Chapter M.R.) This right shall be exercised reasonably and fairly and with due regard to the rights and claims of the parents and the other members of the family. . . .
- Disputes concerning the rights and claims, mentioned in this Article between the parents among themselves, or between one parent and his under-age child, shall be decided by the court.

In this newly defined parental authority, the terms responsibility, reasonableness and fairness, and development are the significant words.

It is interesting to note that the trend of thought regarding a modern formulation of parental authority has acquired a European dimension, since, in Recommendation 874 concerning a European Statute for the Rights of the Child, adopted by the General Assembly of the Council of Europe, it is stated, with reference to the legal position of the child (II, subs. b):

The notion of parental responsibility should be substituted for that of parental authority, and the rights of the child as a distinct member of the family should be defined."[4]

Just to put the record straight: The above is part of a plan for the future. In a positivist interpretation of the prevailing rules concerning parental authority, the parents are still the ones who make the decisions (also in medical matters), whether the child be zero or twenty years old. In practice, however, the new concept of parental authority casts its shadow ahead.

Especially with regard to *minority,* during the last twenty years in the Netherlands an abundance of literature[5] has been published in which the contours of a regulation of the legal status of those who have not yet reached the age of majority become visible. Although in the pending bills[6] concerning lowering of the age of majority no such regulation of the legal status is contained, nevertheless the legal authors, as well as those engaged in the practice of giving assistance, and also the parties represented in parliament, keep urging insistently that such a regulation should be made. It is possible that the pending bills will be amended along these lines.

At any rate, what was said above about parental authority applies to minority as well: in a narrow interpretation the child has no say (not even about medical matters concerning itself), but in reality, in a number of cases heed is already being paid to its right to have its say and to share in the decision making.

The way in which these general introductory remarks might apply to health care will be dealt with in the following sections.

PRACTICAL PROBLEMS

What difficulties may arise in the practise of health care with regard to minors? We shall not be able to touch on more than a fraction of the medico-legal problems. Our starting point must be that, in general, what the physician proposes with regard to the minor will carry great weight with the parents. Due to the social position of the physician, to his knowledge, to the great confidence enjoyed by the professional group, to the parents' doubts about their own judgment etc., the decision will nearly always be what the physician has proposed. It has been said before: in the decision making his voice will mostly be the decisive one.

In outlining some problem situation which may nevertheless arise, I shall not speak about the irritation felt by some physicians because the decision making is no longer exclusively in their hands.

Kohlhaas[7] writes that we live in a time of "overextension of the rights of the patients" and of an "already too tiring duty of the physician to inform the patients".

In his view the good old principle *"salus aegroti suprema lex"* has been exchanged for *"voluntas aegroti suprema lex"*.

It seems to me, however, that he exaggerates. After all, the will of the parents with regard to their child will only then be *"suprema lex"* when it coincides with the will of the physician.

The difficulties shart when physician and parents are not on the same wave-length. If they want something particular, and he does not want it, then it probably will not happen. A physician cannot be compelled to give a particular medical treatment, and the parents will have to accept that fact or start looking for another physician who is more attentive to their wishes.

The reverse position produces even worse problems: the parents do *not* want what the physician considers he has to do. Sometimes the parental refusal is based on ethical conviction, at other times the parents consider that they have to withhold their consent on purely humanitarian grounds. They do not wish that the child's chances to live should be extended when there can be no question of a life truly fit for a human being. Or they do not wish that their child's suffering should be prolonged.

In this kind of situation it may unfortunately happen that the physician's *voluntas* is made to prevail. At times in a very subtle way, *e.g.*, by providing incomplete or too vague information, at other times with a direct threat: "You are bad parents if you do not consent," or "If you do not cooperate, I shall see to it that you are deprived of your parental authority."

It may also happen that, when the parents arrive at visiting time, they discover that the operation they objected to has already been performed. "There was no time left to discuss the matter again. . . ." Or it appears that the child has suddenly been transferred to another hospital in which the operation to which the parents did not consent has meanwhile been performed.

In these examples — which could be amplified with many more — the physicians undoubtedly acted from lofty ethical principles. The good of the patient was their supreme law. But the result was that in these cases parental authority was totally disregarded and the will of the physician was decisive. If, in such cases, compulsion or threat has been implicitly or explicitly used, this would seem to be absolutely wrong. It would even have been "better" that the parents were deprived of their parental authority through judicial intervention (see next section). In a situation where the child's life is at stake, it is infinitely preferable that a court should investigate and decide, rather than that the physician should force through his decision. One must hope, of course, that the speed with which in some cases the decision has to be made would not render the recourse to a court nugatory.

The clash between parents and physician need not always be over an immediately necessary health treatment of the child. In a detailed and very well documented article,[8] Wolters describes how unrest has recently been caused in children's clinics by experiments on children.

He mentions *inter alia* the experiment performed in Willowbrook State Hospital on mentally retarded persons, where healthy feeble-minded children were infected with a mild form of jaundice in order that the natural course of the disease might be studied.[9]

The author points out that the most elementary conditions for a medical experiment were not complied with. I would like to add that this research must also have been contrary to the legal rules about parental authority or is it possible that all the parents had agreed to the experiment? Probably they only discovered it afterwards. On the ethical permissibility of nontherapeutic clinical research involving children, Ackerman[10] has written that decisions on such experiments should be participated in by the parents, as part of their parental authority. Literature on these questions is quite extensive; I regret that I cannot say more about it here.

The practical problems may become even more complicated when parents disagree among themselves or when they concern an older minor who has his own opinion about the medical treatment. Whatever factual situation one tries to imagine, in all probability what will happen will be what the physician considers necessary, although he may strive for some form of "informed consent" by the parents and the growing child. If parental consent cannot be obtained, there are some solutions which legal practice has discovered.

"SOLUTIONS" BY MEANS OF A JUDICIAL MEASURE OF CHILD PROTECTION

In this section we shall indicate how decision making concerning a medical problem of the child can be forced by applying a judicial measure of child protection. Sometimes it will be possible to let the family participate in the decision making, as a result of such a measure.

Article 257, I BW provides a possibility for a *Juvenile Court* "to place the child *provisionally under supervision* pending the investigation." The general condition, stated in Article 254, I BW, that the measure must concern a child, "growing up in such circumstances that it is threatened with moral or bodily ruin," must of course be complied with in this case too. In practice what happens most often is that the health care establishment to which the child has been taken — *e.g.,* the hospital — telephones the Council for Child Protection because there is urgent necessity for surgery. Decision making between physician and parents, however, cannot take place, either because the parents cannot be found at such short notice (and the child is already lying on the operating table), or because the parents refuse to give their consent. This refusal may be based on ethical conviction. The medical staff, on the other hand, considers that the child's condition is so serious that further delay or surgery would not be justified. In view of the speed required the Juvenile Court is requested to order a provisional placement under supervision and to appoint a family guardian (article 255, I BW). The family guardian can then give replacing consent to the urgently required operation or blood transfusion of the child. Once the peril to the child's life has receded, the Juvenile Court may, at any time, discontinue the provisional placement under supervision (Article 258, 2 I BW).

It may happen that in a case of emergency temporary "twin measures" are considered, *viz., suspension of parental authority and provisional commitment to the Council for Child Protection.* These two measures can only be envisaged when the refusal by the parents to consent to medical treatment of their child can be interpreted as "serious neglect of the care or education of the child." This neglect can provide the legal ground for depriving the parents of their parental authority (Article 268, I sub a, I, BW). If this ground exists, the *Rechtbank* (normal court of first instance) can pronounce the suspension (Article 271, 1, I BW) and commit the child to the Council for Child Protection, in which case this Council has all the authority over the child which the parents have in normal cases (Article 271, 4, I BW).

On the basis of facts which could provide the grounds for depriving the parents of their authority, the *Public Prosecutor* can, if he considers it necessary in the interest of the children, withdraw them from the parents' authority and commit them provisionally to the Council for Child Protection. Within two weeks, the Public Prosecutor shall request the *Rechtbank* to confirm the committal. When granting this confirmation the *Rechtbank* shall determine a period during which the committal remains in force (Article 272, 1, 2 and 4, I BW). I feel inclined to think that only those situations can be considered sufficient for suspension of parental authority and committal where there is a certain margin for a few days or weeks, without irreparable damage being done to the health of the child.

If there is disagreement between the parents over the decision to be made, and one of them wishes to go along with the physicians's proposal while the other takes a negative attitude towards it, still another legal approach can be imagined. In that case the *Rechtbank* can limit its action *to suspension in the exercise of parental authority of the refusing parent,* while the other parent (who agrees to the medical treatment) exercises the parental authority alone during the suspension. This parent gives consent to the treatment of the child. In this case it is sufficient to suspend the one parent; committal to the Council for Child Protection is not necessary (Article 271, 1 and 2, I BW). Once the operation has been performed, the

Rechtbank revokes its suspension decision and the parental authority of both parents is thus restored.

In what has been said above, a number of possibilities have been mentioned, *viz.*

1. provisional placement under supervision of the child, and
2. suspension of parental authority combined with provisional committal to the Council for Child Protection, or
3. suspension in the exercise of parental authority of one refusing parent as a result of which a number of justicial authorities, *viz.*
    (a) the juvenile court,
    (b) the *Rechtbank,*
    (c) the Public Prosecutor, and
    (d) the Council for Child Protection

cooperate in reaching a decision in the interest of the child, without the cooperation of the household (or almost outside the family circle) and in which the urgent advice of the physician is followed.

Some criticisms on the aforesaid legal possibilities should be made:

1. Using the measures for child protection is inappropriate in these cases; the articles of the law were not — and are not — intended to force through such medical treatments;
2. One can take these roads only in real emergency situations. Only if there is peril to the life of the child will the judicial authorities be willing to lend their cooperation; otherwise the conditions imposed by the law are not fulfilled;
3. The application of child protection measures has become marginal in the legal practice of the last few years. It is only in exceptional circumstances that there is recourse to the packet of legal measures, in particular because of the stigmatizing effect which such decisions have been shown to have on all parties concerned;[11]
4. With regard to medical problems, many people are inclined to assume, almost without thought, that those active in health care must be right. They are experts. They know the latest methods of treatment and the latest medicines. As opposed to that, the parents know hardly anything. But they know their child.[12]
It is almost a forbidden question, but do the people in health care always know what is in the interest of the child? Is it possible that, for physicians (and others in health care), other considerations also play a part? Might it be that the parents were ultimately right, when they refused to consent to yet another operation, e.g., knowing that their child was going to die?
5. The most important criticism is that, with regard to all the above-mentioned measures which in themselves are far from perfect, the

child has no say whatsoever. In our family law the minor has practically no "legal standing," and, in so far as we acknowledge a duty to hear the minor, that duty is very limited.[13] Further in the chapter I shall try to show, from three examples, how it might be possible to change this situation (see section, Examples of Guidelines).

JUDICIAL DECISIONS

Among judicial decisions a very few examples can be found of child protection measures taken in order to make medical treatment possible.

The *Court of Appeal at the Hague* handed down a decision in the following case (NJ 1967 121): In a young child — during the first instance not yet three years old — a congenital abnormality of the eye had been found, which caused a dangerous, increased pressure in the eye. If this were not corrected, the retina would suffer irreparable damage. Observation seemed necessary. The parents would not agree to this. The Council for Child Protection requested the Juvenile Court in Rotterdam to order a placement under supervision on the grounds of the threat of corporal and mental ruin of the girl (Article 254 I BW). The Juvenile Court rejected the request, on the consideration that the parents were not prepared to cooperate and had no understanding of the seriousness of the situation. Within the framework of placement under supervision no relief could be provided, according to the Juvenile Court.

On appeal, the Court of Appeal at the Hague decided differently. In the interest of the minor, the Court of Appeal held that measures should be taken in order to avert the danger, if possible, in spite of the fact that the parents had declared that they refused their consent.

The *Rechtbank in Dordrecht* (NJ 1973 432) rendered a Solomon's judgment in the following case: A child suffered from a serious heart abnormality, which, in the opinion of the child cardiologist, made a speedy operation necessary. Without an operation the child's health would deteriorate and in the long run this would have very serious and permanent consequences. Now, it was still not too late for effective surgery. The risk of the operation was 10 percent. The father refused on the ground of his conviction, based on his religion, that the child would recover anyway. The *Rechtbank* considered that conviction groundless. The mother was prepared to consent to the operation. The father was suspended from exercise of his authority. Further decisions were held over until the result of the medical treatment should be known.

These two cases illustrate what was stated earlier about the choice that might have to be made concerning appeal to the judiciary, when no decision about treatment of the child, which is in accord with the judgment and intention of the physician, can be made within the family circle.

Finally, the following summary account is given of two cases that were dealt with by medical disciplinary boards. They concern mainly older minors, who had their own views about medical treatment.

The *Medical Disciplinary Board in Amsterdam* (no. 7119 a, Stcr. 24-4-1972, nr. 79) was confronted with a complaint, lodged by a guardianship institution against a gynecologist, who had performed an abortion on an underage girl placed under guardianship of the said organization, without having obtained the consent of the plaintiff institution. The girl, eighteen years old, had applied to an assistance institution in Amsterdam, which had referred her to the gynecologist, who, one week later, had performed the abortion. During that period, contacts had taken place between the social workers of the assistance institution and the board and the management of the guardianship institution. The latter were interested only in the whereabouts of the girl and in her return. They were fundamentally opposed to abortion.

The disciplinary board held that, in general, physicians are not at liberty to undertake treatment of minors without the consent of their legal representative. However, circumstances might occur in which a physician can be compelled, in the interest of the patient, to undertake treatment even without consent — or in spite of the refusal to grant it. The board was of the opinion that in this case such circumstances had occurred. The eighteen year old's determination, attesting to her independence, also played a part. Confidence in the medical profession had not been undermined, even if the interest of the underage patient had been placed above the legal authority of the guardianship institution.

I close this section with the decision of the *Central Medical Disciplinary Board* (published in the Periodical for Health-law 1979, pp. 207-209).

The Central Board held that dismissal from a hospital of a sixteen year old patient cannot be prevented, even if the parents were not aware of the dismissal. This was especially so in this case, where the dismissal had taken place without any medical objection. The physician, about whom the parents had complained (because of the unusual hour of the dismissal and the obvious disregard of the parents' wishes), had no authority, on principle, to prevent the patient's departure. The board felt that the physician's action had not been serious enough to have caused any undermining of confidence in the medical profession.

This decision is important because it accepted the independent right of an underage patient to decide about undergoing medical treatment and/or entering a hospital, when the minor is sufficiently capable to evaluate the situation.

LITERATURE

There is an abundance of literature on the legal aspects of medical treatment of children.

Thus, the question has been asked whether *blood transfusion* may be practised on patients who adhere to the creed of Jehovah's Witnesses, or on their babies. "Yes, in certain circumstances," says one writer;[14] "No," says another,[15] "it would be contrary to Article 9 of the European Convention on Human Rights (freedom of religion) to withdraw a child from parental authority, *e.g.*, in order to make it undergo a blood-exchange transfusion."

Hemodialysis of a child has also given rise to publications on the psycho-social accompaniment of families with a child that has to be taken to a dialysis centre. Wolters wrote[16] about the great psychological pressure exerted on parents to give up a kidney for their diseased child. Such an organ transplant has many legal aspects. Family donation in case of *kidney transplantation* has been widely treated in legal literature,[17] including cases where an underage child would be the donor. Rang holds the view that, if a child were to be selected as "family donor," not only would the child (irrespective of its age) have to consent to the operation, but that, although the parents are formally responsible, it would really be better to free them from the burden of having to decide. The point at issue, after all, is that the life of one of the parents, or of one of the other children in the family, is dependent on the organ of that one selected child. In such a case of conflicting interests, Rang would like to see a special curator appointed by the District Court, by analogy to Article 250 I BW, although in this case there is no conflict of property rights between parents and child.

During the last few years much has been written in the Netherlands about *abortion,* in particular about abortion practiced on underage girls. In Rotterdam, it is customary[18] that pregnant underage girls, who cannot, or do not wish or dare to talk to their parents about their pregnancy — far less, ask for their consent to an abortion by the Dr. W.F. Storm Clinic, to which they have applied for an abortion — are referred to the "Fiomburo." Formally, the intent of such referral is to obtain the so-called "second signature" or "social signature." In fact, what is involved is a kind of statement, which is prepared after one or more interviews with the underage client. The background is that abortion is a medical operation and that minors need the consent of their legal representative for it. True, such a "social signature" is no legally valid substitute for the absence of parental consent. But it is a means of achieving careful decision making when the decision cannot be made in the family circle, because the pregnant girl cannot, or does not wish or dare to talk about it with her parents.

An Amsterdam physician-sexologist[19] mentions the dilemma that arises for the physician when the underage girl asks for abortion and, at the same time, stipulates that her parents must not know anything about it. Dr. Wibaut suggests that, in such a case, the physician would be wise not to decide alone. Calling in an *ad hoc* team of assistants to make the decision gives support to the physician in his responsibility and results in more careful decision making.

The *polio* explosion which occurred in the Netherlands in the summer of 1978, again brought to the fore the legal problems around *vaccination*. Because these seem typically Netherlands problems, I shall enter somewhat more fully into the literature concerning vaccination, especially of children. The main difficulty is that, in our country, there are certain (chiefly reformed) population groups, who, for religious reasons, reject all vaccination, including vaccination against polio. The epidemic of 1978 made victims exclusively among these groups. In the rest of the population there was a good "vaccination situation."

What does the law say about compulsory vaccination?

The statutory regulations concerning provisions against infectious disease are piecemeal. In the twenties of the last century, provincial and communal bylaws existed which contained a vaccination obligation for schoolchildren. It referred to vaccination against smallpox. With regard to other diseases, there has never been any legal regulation in our country. A Royal Decree of 1814 had made vaccination compulsory for children of parents who received financial "aid" payments. After the smallpox epidemic of 1871, which caused 15,787 deaths in the Netherlands, a countrywide legal regulation was passed and enforced from 1872 until 1928. Without vaccination against smallpox children were not allowed to attend school. The indirect compulsion contained in this law was sharpened with the enforcement of the *Compulsory Education Act* (1902). This Act regulates the penal liability of parents who do not send their children to school. It was only in 1912 that the *Vaccination Act* was amended to recognize the validity of medical counter-indications in certain cases. During the period of 1928–1939 there was no legal compulsion, or pressure, for parents to have their underage children vaccinated. After 1939 a system prevailed of legally regulated individual pressure, in which objections by the parents, chiefly based on medical and ethical grounds, were taken into account.

In 1975, the *Vaccination Act* was revoked. Since January 1, 1976 the "Act on Control of Infectious Diseases and Detection of Their Causes" has been in force. This law covers more territory than the previous regulation and sets out clearer starting points. The Government shall share in the responsibility for creating appropriate health care for the entire population. To this end, the central Government shall create the necessary conditions by eliminating financial thresholds, by conducting an active policy of stimulation, and by establishing and supervising effective programs of vaccination.

Since the introduction of the new Act, there are provincial vaccination administrations, from which it is precisely known which children, from the birthyear of 1976 onwards, have not been vaccinated. The national system of vaccination administration has a list of all non-vaccinated persons. All this together forms, as it were, the Government's offer and supervision of vaccination. However, we have *no compulsory vaccination*. The reasons for this are:

1. An absolute obligation to be (and cause to be) vaccinated reduces the motivation for voluntary compliance.
2. The personal responsibility of the parents would be removed, which is not in accordance with present-day conceptions concerning maturity of citizens.
3. It is hard, if not impossible, to enforce compliance with a vaccination obligation.

If we translate the aforesaid into legal terms, it can be posited that the powers and obligations of the Government under public and administrative law cease where the powers and obligations of the parents under private law commence. The Government endeavours, by providing information, to convince the greatest possible number of parents of the benefit of complying with vaccination regulations,[20] but the decision must be made by the parents and by the older child himself or herself. The decision making takes place in the family circle.

As was to be expected, after the latest epidemic intense discussion flared up again. "A Government, mindful of upholding human rights, cannot leave any means untried when the rights of the child are violated, in God's name or in anyone's name. God's will is not law," writes Doek.[21] According to him, parents who refuse — and persist in their refusal — to have their children vaccinated against polio, should be stripped of their parental authority. As a preparatory measure to this end, the child should be entrusted to the Council for Child Protection. This Council can have the child vaccinated immediately. Doek is also in favour of an absolute vaccination obligation. This proposal, for compulsory action by the Government, in spite of its — for the Netherlands — very radical nature, met with great interest, kindled by the generally felt indignation against parents who on religious grounds exposed their children to the "devastating peril of polio" (JED). In his desire for introduction of compulsory vaccination, Doek was supported.[22] But his proposal to withdraw nonvaccinated children from parental authority by means of provisional placement in the care of the Council for Child Protection met with some reluctance, as is apparent in professional writings. The question of whether such a medical problem can be solved by legal measures is still moot. But the question remains as to whether a large-scale action, as proposed by Doek, would not endanger public mental health.[23]

Apart from these matters of principle, I wish to point out that the proposal is, in fact, impracticable. Korteling (See Note 22) mentions that in the regions where the polio epidemic was raging in 1978, there were

65,000 unvaccinated persons under twenty-seven years of age. If one should try to entrust the minors amongst them to the provisional care of the Council for Child Protection, this measure would have to be taken for tens of thousands of children. Our judicial apparatus for child protection is not equipped for this — in any respect.

This bird's-eye view of some subjects encountered in recent writings seems to show the wide distance between legal thinking and medical thinking concerning decisions to be made in the interest of the child.

EXAMPLES OF GUIDELINES

In professional literature some examples can be found of guidelines which can assist the medical world and the parents in making decisions concerning their child. Perhaps these three models (without explanatory statements) could serve as subjects for discussion.

First Example of Some Rough and Ready Rules[24]

Information

1. All minors, provided they are able to express themselves, have the right to be informed in advance of treatment in the field of health care, which it is thought that they should undergo.
2. All parents (or guardian), provided they do not suffer from serious mental disorder, have the right to be informed of any health treatment, which it is thought that their children should undergo.
3. The obligation to provide this information in advance is incumbent on the one(s) who carries (carry) responsibility for the treatment.

Decision Making

4. The consent of the parents (or the guardian) of the minor is required for the health care treatment to be applied.
5. The consent of a minor, who is capable of discernment and who must be considered able to express an opinion at that moment, is also required for the health care treatment to be applied to him.

Exceptions to the Obligations to Inform

6. On the strength of very cogent reasons, the information to the parents may be omitted. The request to do so may be made by a minor capable of discernment.

7. On the strength of very cogent reasons, the information to the minor may be omitted. The request to do so may be made by the parents (guardian) of a minor, who is not yet capable of discernment.

Special Forms of Decision Making

8. If the parents refuse to consent to treatment of a minor, who is capable of discernment and who is eighteen years of age or older, the consent of the minor alone is sufficient. This also applies to the case, referred to under 6, where the minor is eighteen years of age or older and is capable of discernment.
9. If, in an emergency situation, the consents, mentioned under 4 and 5, are unobtainable, the competent child protection authorities should be appealed to in order that a substitute consent may be obtained.[25]

Second Example of Some Guidelines[26]

Information

1. The physician should inform the minor of the essential facts of treatment in a manner which the minor can understand and cope with.
2. Barring the exceptions set out hereinafter, the physician is entitled to inform, besides the minor himself, the latter's parents as well.
2.1. The parents may not be informed if the patient is capable of discernment and objects to information to the parents, unless the physician is of the opinion that not informing the parents would seriously harm the patient.
2.2. The parents of a patient who is not capable of discernment may not be informed, if informing them would be against the interest of the child.
3. In those cases where a physician is entitled to inform parents, he is also under the obligation to do so, except when the patient is capable of discernment. The parents, as well, should be informed of the essential facts of treatment in a manner which they can understand and cope with.

Consent

4. Treatment of a minor incapable of discernment needs the consent of the parents.
5. A minor capable of discernment may not be treated without his consent.

6. Treatment of a minor capable of discernment needs, on principle, the consent, not only of the minor himself, but also that of his parents. *However:* *(a)* for treatment of a simple kind the consent of the parents is assumed to have been given; *(b)* for treatment which cannot be postponed until majority is reached, the minor's consent is sufficient in cases where the parents refuse theirs.
7.1. For treatment needed to prevent serious mental or bodily harm — and which does not fall into the category mentioned under 6*(b)* above — a measure of child protection may be attempted in order to break the impasse created by the parents' refusal of consent.
7.2. If, in case of urgent necessity, it is impossible to obtain in time a consent (of parents or minor), action may be taken without such consent.

Third Example of Some Rough and Ready Rules[27]

Medical assistance

1. A minor who is capable of discernment (from fourteen years of age and older) has the right to apply to a general practitioner or a dentist for consultation or treatment and to be treated by them without the previous consent of the parents.
2. For specialized and/or radical medical treatment, besides the consent of the minor who is capable of discernment but is not yet sixteen years old, the consent of the parents is needed as well. If the parents refuse to give their consent, the Juvenile Court may give substitute consent at the request of the minor.
3. A minor sixteen years of age or older can independently, *i.e.* even without his parents' consent, request medical assistance and undergo any treatment, whether specialized and/or radical, or not.
4. The parents have the right to apply to the Court in order to make their underage child undergo necessary treatment, on which he fails to decide himself.
5. The physician has the obligation to inform the minor and his parents as fully as possible concerning intended treatment and its consequences. If the minor is sixteen years of age or older, it is, on principle, incumbent on him to inform his parents concerning treatment he is to undergo.

CLOSING NOTES

In the foregoing I have tried to look at decision making in the field of medical care and treatment of underage patients. It is obvious that, in these kinds of decisions, the physician occupies a central and very powerful position. True, the parents have the right, based on their parental authority, to consent (or not) to treatment of their child; but in cases of emergency the health service can act without the cooperation of the patient by applying to the Court and by eliciting child protection measures. On the other hand, the problems connected with vaccination against polio show that parental authority can prevent a child from being vaccinated, even when, as prophylaxis, it would be highly desirable to have it done. In the striving for balance between medical power and parental authority, it should be evident from what has been said that the child itself may suffer.

NOTES

1. W.B. van der Mijn. "The Lawmakers and Medical Behaviour," *Medical Contact*, 1972, 1,165 *seq.*
2. M. Rood-de Boer. "A Delicate Balance (Parental Authority)," in Wiarda, *Juvenile Law at a Turning Point*, 1974, 129-49.
3. J.E. Doek, G.P. Hoefnagels, W. Jonkers, J. Nota, M. Rood-de Boer, J. de Ruiter, S. Slagter in "Rights of Juveniles and Authority of Parents," in *NJB*, 1975, 95-105.
4. Meetings of 3 and 4.10.1979. Doc. 4,376 Recommendation 874 (1979) on a European Chapter on the rights of the child nr. 9: Text adopted on 4.10.1979 (10th sitting).
5. For a survey, see *i.a.* J.A.C. Bartels: "Reflexions on the Rights of Juveniles and on Incapacity to Perform Legally Valid Actions," *NJB*, 1977, 431 *seq.*
6. Among them: nrs. 15,416, 15,417 and 15,974, 1978.
7. M. Kohlhaas. "Parental Refusal to Consent to Operation in spite of its Necessity in order to Save the Child's Life," *German Medical Weekly*, 1.1.1965, 46 *seq.*
8. W.H.G. Wolters. "Medical Experiments and Research on Children and Young Adolescents," in *Monthly Mental Health*, 1979, 823-43.
9. A.R. Jonsen. "Research Involving Children: Recommendations of the National Comm. for the Protection of Human Subjects of Biomedical and Behavioural Research," in *Pediatris*, 1978, 121 *seq.*
10. T.F. Ackerman. "Moral Duties and Non-therapeutic Clinical Research Procedures Involving Children," in *Bioethics Quarterly*, 1980, 94 *seq.*
11. It is not surprising that, in legal literature, proposals have recently been made for arriving at new kinds of measures of child protection of an *ad hoc* character, which would not entail any labelling. See *e.g.* the papers, submitted in 1980 to the Association for Family and Juvenile law, by M. van Beugen and M. Rood-de Boer (A House for Tomorrow). Periodical for F.J.R. 1980, p. 130-74.
12. For this passage I have in part made use of the paper I submitted in 1974 to the Association for Health Law, "The Position of the Minor in Health Law," 7 and 8.
13. Article 227, 4 and 228, 1 I BW concerning adoption and Article 167 I BW concerning the regulation of custody and visiting rights after divorce.
14. J. Peters. "No Blood transfusion?", *Medical Contact* 1977, 1,595 *seq.*
15. W. Schuurman Stekhoven. "Patient's Rights — Human Rights," *Neth. Periodical for Medicine*, 1979, 55 *seq.*

16. W.H.G. Wolters, "Psychosocial Care at Hemodialysis-Centre and Renal Transplantation for Children and Adolescents," *Acta Paedo Psycho. Europaeica* 1978, and MGV 1979, p. 58 *seq.*

17. J.F. Rang, "Health-law Aspects of Family Donation in Cases of Kidney Transplantation," *Periodical for Health-law,* 1979, p. 14 *seq.* J. Goldstein, A. Freud, A.J. Solnit, "Before the Best Interests of the Child," 1979, p. 106, *seq.*

18. G. Passier, "Assisting Under-age Abortion-Clients," *MGV* 1979, p. 95 *seq.*

19. F.P. Wibaut. "Abortion on Minors without the Consent of the Parents," *Medical Contact,* 1980, 943 *seq.*

20. To this end, in the summer of 1978, the State Secretary appeared twice on television. She also wrote two personal letters (28-6-1978 and 30-6-1978) to the parents of young (nonvaccinated) children and to the religious denominations concerned.

21. J.E. Doek. "Polio, Also a Case for the Judiciary," *Mental Health Monthly,* 1978, 637 *seq.*

22. W. Korteling, Jr. "Government-Action Must Prevent Polioexplosion," in *Per. on Health-law,* 1980, 93 *seq.*

23. A. Hetting. "To whom is the Polio-Child Entrusted?," *MGV,* 1979, 66 *seq.*

24. M. Rood-de Boer. "The Position of the Minor in Health Law," adapted from a paper submitted to the Society for Health Law, 1974.

25. I do not wish to enter here into the exceptionally difficult decisions on whether euthanasia should be applied. See, *e.g.,* "Euthanasia for Newly-Born Defective Babies," *Advice by the Health-Council,* 1975.

26. Working group on the legal position of minors in health care. Guidelines with comments in *Medical Contact,* 1976, 48 *seq.*

27. From J.E. Doek and S. Slagter. "More Rights for Minors," 1976, second impression, 98 and 99. Summary in rough and ready rules.

Chapter Thirty-six

Medicine and Human Rights: Emerging Substantive Standards and Procedural Protections for Medical Decison Making Within the American Family*

Charles H. Baron[†]

Boston College Law School
Newton Centre, Massachusetts, U.S.A.

The American family is increasingly becoming a crucible for testing the great issues of ethics raised by advances in American medical technology. This trend is in part attributable to the fact that the technology itself does not stand still; it increasingly offers new and awesome choices which must be made by someone. For example: Shall an aged and terminally ill parent be kept alive indefinitely by machines that replace the natural functions of lungs and heart? Shall a fetus be carried to term and allowed to be born alive when amniocentesis reveals genetic characteristics that make the child undesirable to the parents? But this trend is also attributable in great part to developments of the last two decades which have seen medical treatment decisions increasingly taken out of the hands of physicians and placed in those of patients who are to make them on the basis of "informed consent." In 1971, the Supreme Court of New Jersey could believe it reflected the then current state of the law when it allowed a hospital to force one of its patients to accept life-saving blood transfusions

---

* This article first appeared in *Family Law Quarterly*, Vol. 17, No. 1, Spring 1983, p. 1.
† The author thanks Linda Bentley, a third-year student at Boston College Law School, for the invaluable research assistance she provided to him in the preparation of this chapter.

despite the fact that such acceptance violated her religious beliefs.[1] But by 1978, the right of a patient to refuse life-saving medical treatment could seem so well-established that all parties to the case agreed that such treatment could be forced upon her only if she could be proved to be legally incompetent:

> The decision of the [lower court] judge, as well as the opinion of Dr. Kelley, predicates the necessity for the appointment of a guardian chiefly on the irrationality (in medical terms) of Mrs. Candura's decision to reject the amputation. Until she changed her original decision and withdrew her consent to the amputation, her competence was not questioned. But the irrationality of her decision does not justify a conclusion that Mrs. Candura is incompetent in the legal sense. The law protects her right to make her own decision to accept or reject treatment, whether that decision is wise or unwise.[2]

As I point out in more detail later, the recognition of autonomy in the patient to make medical decisions is not yet complete, and there are forces at work that would return much decision-making power to the hands of physicians. Among these are lobbying efforts by many leaders of the medical profession. For example, the Editor of the distinguished *New England Journal of Medicine* has answered an earlier article of mine in the following language:

> Contrast my description of medical practice with the recent assertion made by Charles Baron . . . that "our society has never conferred upon its medical community the power to decide which of society's members shall live and which shall die." Now, if by that statement he means that physicians do not have the authority arbitrarily to terminate a patient's life, he is of course correct. But if he means to convey that doctors have no business deciding whether to institute or to withhold treatment, when such decisions may have life or death implications, then he is simply ignorant of the facts of medical practice. As I have tried to show, those kinds of decisions — always with the informed consent of patients or their families, when such consent is reasonably available — are being made all the time. There is nothing more crucial to a physician's professional role than the making of such decisions. *His responsibility for the welfare of his patients often requires that he deal with technical medical issues which are of vital importance to his patients but which they are unable to comprehend fully, if at all, and which they must therefore delegate to him. Unless he is willing to assume this decision-making role in the patient's behalf he is not really doing his job.*[3]

And even the courts have displayed a certain amount of willingness to delegate such life-and-death decisions to doctors in subtle ways. The most prominent examples of this phenomenon are the decisions of the Supreme Court of the United States that recognize a constitutional right to an abortion. In his opinion for the Court in *Roe v. Wade*,[4] Justice Blackmun, who had close associations with the medical profession before his appointment to the Court,[5] recognizes a right to choose an abortion which resides not in the pregnant woman but rather in "the pregnant woman's attending physician." "This holding," he states, ". . . vindicates the right of the physician to administer medical treatment according to his professional judgment up to the points where important state interests provide compelling justifications for intervention. Up to those points, *the abortion decision in all its aspects is inherently and primarily a medical decision, and basic responsibility for it must rest with the physician.*"[6] And, in the later case of *Colautti v. Franklin*,[7] the Court, through Justice Blackmun again, confers upon the individual physician even the power to decide what statistical likelihood of survival outside the mother establishes sufficient "viability" for the state's "compelling interest" in fetal life to come into play.

However, despite the existence of these potentially reactionary lines of force, the current state of the law seems to be that a legally competent patient has the right to refuse medical treatment of any sort — except in the most extraordinary circumstances.[8] And this right is increasingly being recognized as having a constitutional basis. Thus, one of the most recent federal decisions in the area begins its analysis with:

> what seems to us to be an intuitively obvious proposition: a person has a constitutionally protected interest in being left free by the state to decide for himself whether to submit to the serious and potentially harmful medical treatment that is represented by the administration of antipsychotic drugs. The precise textual source in the Constitution of the protection of this interest is unclear, and the authorities directly supportive of the proposition itself are surprisingly few. Nevertheless, we are convinced that the proposition is correct and that a source in the Due Process Clause of the Fourteenth Amendment for the protection of this interest exists, most likely as part of the penumbral right to privacy, bodily integrity, or personal security.[9]

But what about this constitutionally protected right to make one's own medical decisions when the patient is not legally competent — when one is a child, mentally retarded, senile, or in coma? Who should make these decisions then and on what basis? If it is not to be doctors, then one is naturally led to consider the patient's "next-of-kin" as candidates, and it is here that the American family becomes caught up in the tangle of the new medical technology.

The general power of parents to make medical decisions for minor children seems well-established in the United States.[10] In most cases, this would be consistent with the policy bases for allowing parents the power to make legally binding decisions for their children generally. The child is considered not capable of making decisions in his own best interests. The parents are considered capable of making such decisions, and it is presumed that they will be desirous of doing only what is best for their child. Moreover, who else could possibly make decisions for the child? So many decisions must be made for the child on a regular basis that the state, even if it believed that it knew better what the child would or should want for himself, would not have the resources for making all of the decisions that had to be made. Most of these decisions have relatively minor consequences. There is usually no clear "right decision." And the "rightness" of the decision for the child may be complicatedly influenced by the values of the family group and by the fact that the child will have to function as a continuing part of that family group after the decision has been made for him.

Of course, in the area of medical decision making, many of these reasons for recognizing parental power do not carry the same weight that they do for parental decision making in general. For one thing, many medical decisions are likely to have enormous consequences as to the welfare of the child. For another, an objective cost-benefit analysis may make one of the choices seem overwhelmingly right and the other clearly wrong. Finally, decision-making intervention by some agency outside the family would seem feasible if it were restricted to those relatively rare situations in which the parents seemed to be making an objectively wrong and extremely important medical decision. Hence, it is not surprising that American courts seem increasingly inclined to intervene in medical decision making in order to protect the best interests of children. However, even in the medical area, a great deal of deference is accorded to parental discretion — at least where the parents sincerely believe that they are acting in the best interests of their child and evidence indicates that the efficacy or safety of the proposed treatment is open to question. Thus, courts have acceded to parents' wishes in refusing treatment for conditions such as rickets,[11] a disfigured arm,[12] a speech impediment,[13] and the need for a spinal fusion operation.[14] On the other hand, courts have overriden the parents in cases involving vaccination,[15] removal of tonsils and adenoids,[16] and other medical procedures to cure non-life-threatening problems.[17] And the courts have, of course, been much more ready to supplant parental decisions with their own in cases where the life of the child is immediately threatened.[18]

The tension between concern for the welfare of the child and deference to the decision-making power of well-meaning parents is well illustrated by a comparison of two very similar cases in which the courts reached opposite results as to whether parents should be allowed to use the controversial drug laetrile in the treatment of a child's cancer. In the well-publicized *Chad Green* cases,[19] the courts of Massachusetts decided to take legal (but not physical) custody of a child from his parents and grant it to the Massachusetts Department of Public Welfare so that he would be given chemotherapy that had a 50 percent chance of causing remission of his acute lymphocitic leukemia. In the fall of 1977, when Chad was one and a half years old, he had been put on a course of chemotherapy that had brought the disease into remission for a few months. Subsequently, he had become ill and his doctor discovered that Chad's mother had taken him off medication — apparently because she believed it had unpleasant side effects that made the treatment not in his best interest. The doctors then initiated a course of legal proceedings in which they were able to obtain a court order mandating chemotherapy. Some months later, the Greens reopened the proceedings in an attempt to win court approval for a course of "metabolic therapy" — involving laetrile, vitamins, and enzyme treatments — which they had been using to supplement the court-ordered chemotherapy. Presented with evidence that the laetrile treatment had brought about a level of cyanide in Chad's blood that could cause brain damage or death and presented with no testimony from a Massachusetts physician in favor of the laetrile treatment, the court ordered it stopped. Subsequently, the Greens took their child to Mexico for the purpose of continuing their treatment of choice. Chad died there on October 12, 1979.[20] During this same period, *In re Hofbauer,*[21] was wending its way through the courts of New York. Joseph Hofbauer, aged seven, had been taken by his parents to Jamaica for a month of "metabolic therapy" (including laetrile) for treatment of his recently diagnosed Hodgkins Disease. When they returned to New York State, the parents were charged with neglect of their child and the Saratoga County Commissioner of Social Services sought custody for the purpose of having chemotherapy administered. The court refused to find Joseph a neglected child or award custody to the state. But here, unlike the situation in *Chad Green*, there was no finding that laetrile therapy had affected the child deleteriously, there was support from New York licensed physicians for continuing the experiment with laetrile and, perhaps most important, the parents expressed a willingness to resort to chemotherapy if and when that became necessary. There is a sense of court recognition of good faith cooperation from the parents in *Hofbauer* that seems to be missing in *Chad Green*, despite the fact that the courts in neither case ever openly questioned the parents' sincere concern for the welfare of their children.

It is in those cases where they have had doubts about the parents' single-minded devotion to the patient-child that the courts have been most ready to intervene in the making of medical decisions. One situation which raises such doubts is presented by modern organ and tissue transplant technology. Important to the success of most such transplants is genetic similarity between the donor and the recipient patient. As a result, siblings of the potential recipient are very often the preferred or even the only feasible candidates for donation. Where an adult, living sister or brother is asked to contribute one of two functioning kidneys to a sibling who has none or to contribute small amounts of bone marrow for colonization within the bones of a sibling whose own bone marrow has been destroyed, the physicians may proceed only upon the consent of the competent donor.[22] However, in the case of the potential donor sibling who is still a minor (sometimes, in the case of bone marrow transplants, a minor of very tender years), the donor cannot give legally recognized consent and one would normally look to the parents to do so. But, as was recognized very early,[23] the parents in such a situation cannot be expected to concern themselves only with the best interests of the donor child — they are caught in a conflict of interest situation where they must consider trading-off the interests of one child for those of another. Hence, the courts of Massachusetts, and other states in which such transplants have been performed, have made themselves available to give legal authorization for the transplant where that could be shown to be justified.[24] The basis for justifying such consent has not always been easy to work out. In some cases where a consenting donor was near the age of majority, it has been based upon the "mature minor" rule.[25] Most commonly, it has been based upon a theory of psychological benefit to the donor child which leads the court to conclude that the incompetent consenting child would still consent were he competent to do so.[26] However, the courts of Massachusetts have also used as justification a principle which recognizes that the interests of the donor child in such a case cannot be abstracted completely from the interests of the family as a whole and which therefore grants to the parents the primary decision-making responsibility which the court then reviews for possible abuse.[27]

Another area in which courts have circumscribed parental consent to medical treatment because of suspicions regarding parental motivation is that of sterilization of mentally retarded children. Here, worry that the parents have opted for sterilization to serve their own interests rather than those of the child is combined with special concern regarding the right to procreate which is constitutionally protected. Involuntary sterilization of incompetents on eugenic grounds enjoyed great vogue in many parts of the United States in the early part of this century. Although such practices were explicitly held to be constitutional by the Supreme Court of the United States in 1927,[28] later cases have cast grave doubt on the continuing viability of that holding.[29] Since the 1920s, medical and popular opinion in the United States has turned strongly against the notion of compulsory sterilization — in part in reaction to the spectre of eugenics-gone-haywire in Nazi Germany. On the other hand, the same period has seen voluntary sterilization become the birth control method of choice for a growing number of competent adults. Highly publicized concerns over "the pill" and IUD's have made tubal ligations increasingly popular with women, and, by 1975, the Association for Voluntary Sterlization reported that vasectomies had become the second most common operation performed on men — exceeded only by circumcision.[30] As a result, there is a basis for arguing that one discriminates against the mentally retarded by not allowing parents to provide the "proxy consent" necessary for authorizing a birth control method which is available — indeed constitutionally protected in its availability[31] — to all competent adults.

Because of shame over the period of eugenic involuntary sterilization, the courts have been cautious in developing new institutions for "voluntary" sterilization through proxy consent. They have been clearly unwilling to allow such consent to be given by parents without close judicial supervision. The worry is that parents may irreversibly deny their child the fundamental right to procreation by overreacting to their own fears of their child's sexuality and to concerns that they will be burdened with possibly defective grandchildren. Indeed, the judicial worry has been so great that the courts might well be accused of overreacting in this area. During the past twenty years, a number of state courts have taken the unprecedented step of denying jurisdiction to exercise their general *parens patriae* power in such cases, even where substantial evidence could be presented that sterlization would be in the best interests of the retarded child.[32] However, case law now seems to be settling into a pattern under which *parens patriae* jurisdiction will be exercised as in other proxy consent cases — allowing sterlization, but only where the court is convinced that the child's best interests are truly advanced thereby.[33]

The area of medical decision making for children in which parental power has been most circumscribed is that of abortion. Here the issue has not been whether parental consent to an abortion is *sufficient*, it has been whether such consent is *necessary* in those cases where the child herself has decided to abort. In 1976, shortly after the decision in *Roe v. Wade*, the court decided that parents could not constitutionally be authorized by a state to veto their minor daughter's choice to have an abortion.[34] In light of the fact that the parents' refusal might be, in the Court's view, "arbitrary" — based, perhaps, on vindictiveness or an effort to impose the parents' strict moral views on their child — the Court held that alternative procedures for obtaining authorization had to be made available. Three years later, in *Bellotti v. Baird*[35] the Court held that a state which provided such alternative procedures could not require that the parents should first be asked for their consent or even be informed that such procedures were being availed of. Because of the "unique nature of the abortion decision" under these circumstances (among other things, the fact that delay could decide by default the question of whether one child would be forced to take on the responsibilities of raising another), the Court decided that a pregnant minor must be provided the option of going directly to court for approval of her abortion decision without having to inform her parents of the decision. The Court acknowledged the delicate balancing of important interests that was involved:

> There is an important state interest in encouraging a family rather than judicial resolution of a minor's abortion decision. Also, we have observed above, parents naturally take an interest in the welfare of their children — an interest that is

particularly strong where a normal family relationship exists and where the child is living with one or both parents. These factors may properly be taken into account by a court called upon to determine whether an abortion in fact is in a minor's best interests. If, all things considered, the court determines that an abortion is in the minor's best interests, she is entitled to court authorization without any parental involvement. On the other hand, the court may deny the abortion request of an immature minor in the absence of parental consultation if it concludes that her best interests would be served thereby, or the court may in such a case defer a decision until there is parental consultation in which the court may participate. But this is the full extent to which parental involvement may be required.[36]

Clearly, in the realm of family medical decision making, even the power of parents to make medical decisions for their minor children is subject to growing areas of exception. When we look beyond the relationship of parent and minor child, exception becomes the rule. There is scant authority even for one spouse to make a medical decision for the other.[37] Where a spouse, brother, or parent becomes incompetent to make such decisions for himself, developing case law indicates that another family member exercises decision-making authority for him most safely by obtaining court authority to do so as the patient's legal guardian. Until recently, few such cases seem to have been brought to court. In part, this probably reflects the fact that most medical decisions that had to be made for incompetent patients were either of a minor nature or involved an emergency. Frequently the incompetence was as well of a very temporary nature — *e.g.,* the patient was anesthetized or otherwise temporarily unconscious. Under such circumstances, the physician would frequently be authorized by earlier-given consent of the patient or by law to make a "judgment call" on his own.[38] Out of an abundance of caution, the physician might consult and obtain consent from next-of-kin on the scene. Such consultation would provide the doctor in a close case with a sense of what the patient might want for himself. It was also a humane, diplomatic, and sensible thing to do. If the patient regained consciousness, he would be less likely to think that the physician had acted in a "high-handed" fashion. If he did not regain consciousness, the most likely candidates for bringing suit against the doctor would have been made a part of the decision-making process. This simple scenario seems to have passed into history with the advent of the new medical technology and the awesome stakes it presents on each side of so many patient care decisions.

By now, Karen Quinlan's name must be one of the best known in the world. *In re Quinlan,*[39] the lawsuit which brought her to prominence, was filed by Karen's father for the purpose of having this twenty-two year old daughter found legally incompetent and to have himself appointed her guardian with authority to turn off the machines that were keeping her alive. Although not "brain dead," Karen had severe brain damage which had left her in a chronic and persistent vegetative state of coma. There was no known cure for her condition, it was predicted that she would never be restored to cognitive or sapient life, and the prognosis was that even her vegetative state could not continue without life-support machinery. While there was no certainty that she experienced pain, she was intubated, constantly connected to a mechanical respirator, and was described as "emaciated, having suffered a weight loss of at least 40 pounds, and undergoing a continuing deteriorative process. Her posture is described as fetal-like and grotesque; there is extreme flexion-rigidity of the arms, legs and related muscles, and her joints are severely rigid and deformed."[40] When Karen's family, after months of tortured indecision, became reconciled to the fact that her condition was hopeless, they asked her attending physician to remove her life-support apparatus. He refused to do so, unless and until she could be proven to be brain dead, on the ground that such action, in his view, would be contrary to prevailing medical standards, practice, and ethics. It was in the face of this refusal that Mr. Quinlan decided to go to court.

In a landmark decision, the Supreme Court of New Jersey held essentially that Mr. Quinlan had a right to "second opinion" from the medical community on behalf of his daughter. At the outset, the court determined that, on the medical facts presented, Karen's constitutional right of privacy would entitle her to demand "death with dignity" were she competent to do so.[41] Since she was not competent to do so, the court permitted Karen's family to decide that it would be her judgment to decline further intrusive life-prolonging treatment. But, apparently because it was not Karen herself demanding cessation of life support, the court held that the medical community should be accorded some discretion to determine whether life support should in fact be stopped. The lower court had delegated such discretion in extraordinarily broad terms:

> The nature, extent and duration of care by societal standards is the responsibility of a physician. The morality and conscience of our society places this responsibility in the hands of the physician. What justification is there to remove it from the control of the medical profession and place it in the hands of the courts?[42]

While expressing unwillingness to go this far in deferring to physicians, the supreme court was concerned about the fact that it, "a court, having no inherent medical expertise, [might be] called upon to overrule a professional decision according to prevailing medical practice and standards...."[43] It therefore looked at and weighed a developing medical-ethical literature that discussed the question of what should be done in cases like Karen's, and it concluded that it was not clear that Karen's physician had made his decision according to what could be called generally prevailing medical practice and standards. The trend, indeed, seemed to be in the direction of allowing patients such as Karen to "die with dignity." Moreover, it seemed to the court that resistance to this trend on the part of many doctors rested less on medical-ethical considerations than on fear of the law's response to what might be seen as an act of homicide. Here, the court saw it could do a service to the medical profession by clarifying the law in a way that would free the development of medical ethics from the shadow of this fear.

The court ruled that, in cases like Karen's, the "life support system may be withdrawn and said action shall be without any civil or criminal liability therefor on the part of any participant, whether guardian, physician, hospital or others"[44] — but only if certain procedures are followed. First, the family must agree, for the patient, to the act of withdrawal. Second, responsible attending physicians must agree to it. Third, in order to deal with the problem of divergent opinions regarding the developing medical practice and standards in this area, agreement must also be obtained from a hospital "ethics committee."[45] In order to provide Karen's family with an opportunity to avail itself of this process, the court appointed Mr. Quinlan guardian of Karen's person with authority to choose an attending physician agreeable to termination of life support — although it recognized as well that "her present treating physicians may give reconsideration to her present posture in the light of this opinion."[46]

As might be expected, the *Quinlan* decision was received warmly by the medical community. Not only did it give legal sanction to an act of "passive euthanasia" on the facts of the case brought before the court, it seemed to delegate to the medical community and its hospital ethics committee the power to decide what other fact situations might justify termination of life-prolonging treatment. However, as Professor George Annas has pointed out, the medical community and its lawyers may have read *Quinlan* too broadly.[47] Although the court talked in terms of an ethics committee which comprised "physicians, social workers, attorneys, and theologians,"[48] the job it assigned the committee in the *Quinlan* case was merely the medical-prognostic task of agreeing "that there is no reasonable possibility of Karen's ever emerging from her present comatose condition to a cognitive, sapient state...."[49] Although the court says at one point in the opinion:

> We consider that a practice of applying to a court to confirm such decisions would generally be inappropriate, not only because that would be a gratuitous encroachment upon the medical profession's field of competence, but because it would be impossibly cumbersome[50]

it cautions at another:

> [N]otions as to the distribution of responsibility [between physicians and courts], heretofore generally entertained, should however neither impede this Court in

deciding matters clearly justiciable nor preclude a re-examination by the Court as to underlying human values and rights. Determinations as to these must, in the ultimate, be responsive not only to the concepts of medicine but also to the common moral judgment of the community at large. In the latter respect the Court has a nondelegable judicial responsibility.[51]

Finally, once the medical facts of Karen's case could be settled, there seemed little question about what would be best for her from an ethical point of view. As the court had noted, a decision to let Karen die "should be accepted by a society the overwhelming majority of whose members would, we think, in similar circumstances, exercise such a choice in the same way for themselves or for those closest to them."[52] Not every case would implicate only ethical issues as to which there could be said to be such a societal consensus.

In the year following *Quinlan*, the Supreme Judicial Court of Massachusetts decided a case whose facts forced the court to deal directly with value questions that the facts of *Quinlan* had allowed to be left on the sidelines. As a result, the decision seemed to differ from *Quinlan* in ways that threatened the satisfaction of the medical community. *Superintendent of Belchertown School v. Saikewicz*[53] began as an application on the part of doctors at an institution for the mentally retarded for permission to provide chemotherapy to an inmate who had been diagnosed as terminally ill with leukemia. Joseph Saikewicz was sixty-seven years of age but had an I.Q. of only 10. Although he had living relatives, he had had almost no contact with them during a lifetime of institutionalization. In the two weeks between filing a petition for appointment of a guardian for Mr. Saikewicz and the first hearing on the petition before the court, the attending physicians had decided to recommend against chemotherapy. The evidence was that refusing treatment for leukemia might mean death for Mr. Saikewicz within a period ranging from a few weeks to several months, but the death would be relatively comfortable. Giving him chemotherapy might prolong life for as much as thirteen months, but it might shorten it, and it would have side effects including anemia, bleeding infections, "severe nausea, bladder irritation, numbness and tingling of the extremities, and loss of hair."[54] After hearing, the trial court concluded that "not treating Mr. Saikewicz would be in his best interests,"[55] but, because of the importance of the issues involved, the court reported the central questions in the case to the Massachusetts Appeals Court. There was then an application for direct appellate review in the Supreme Judicial Court which was granted. On July 9, 1976, the Supreme Judicial Court affirmed the trial court's decision and promised that an opinion would follow.

In the opinion which was promulgated some sixteen months after the decision, the court mirrored the reasoning in *Quinlan* up to a point. For the first time in Massachusetts, the court recognized a constitutional right on the part of a patient to refuse life-prolonging treatment so long as certain enumerated compelling state interests did not outweigh it in the particular case.[56] It held that, on the facts of the case before it, those state interests were not overwhelming and that Mr. Saikewicz, were he competent, would therefore have the right to refuse chemotherapy. The court then went beyond *Quinlan* in holding that an incompetent person should have the same right to refuse medical treatment as a competent one; the sole question should be one of what the incompetent patient would want for himself were he competent for a moment to make that decision. Of *Quinlan,* the Saikewicz court said:

> The court's observation that most people in like circumstances would choose a natural death does not, we believe, detract from or modify the central concern that the guardian's decision conform, to the extent possible, to the decision that would have been made by Karen Quinlan herself. Evidence that most people would or would not act in a certain way is certainly an important consideration in attempting to ascertain the predilections of any individual, but care must be taken, as in any analogy, to ensure that operative factors are similar or at least to take notice of the dissimilarities.[57]

Under the "substituted judgment" test[58] employed in *Saikewicz,* one of the relevant dissimilarities from other patients faced with chemotherapy which had to be considered was Joseph Saikewicz's profound mental retardation. The court was careful to point out that this was *not* to be considered from the point of view of devaluing the "quality of life" which was at stake. "The [lower court] judge," the court said, "as well as the parties, were keenly aware that the supposed ability of Saikewicz, by virtue of his mental retardation, to appreciate or experience life had no place in the decison before them."[59] However, because of his grave mental disability, Saikewicz was found incapable of understanding the "continuing state of pain and disorientation precipitated by the chemotherapy treatment."[60] As a result, the court concluded that this fact, "together with the other factors properly considered by the judge, [satisfies us] that the decision to withhold treatment from Saikewicz was based on a regard for his actual interests and preferences and that the facts supported this decision."[61]

The major departure from the *Quinlan* opinion was reserved for the last part of the *Saikewicz* opinion where the court discussed the procedures which should be used for deciding such cases in the future. Here the court explicitly rejected Quinlan's delegation of decision-making power to an ethics committee and held that legal protection for termination-of-care participants could be provided only by the courts. Although the court thought it might be desirable for a judge to consider the conclusions of any ethics committee in a given case, it warned:

> We take a dim view of any attempt to shift the ultimate decision-making responsibility away from the duly-established courts of proper jurisdiction to any commit-

tee, panel, or group, ad hoc or permanent. Thus, we reject the approach adopted by the New Jersey Supreme Court in the *Quinlan* case of entrusting the decision whether to continue artificial life support to the patient's guardian, family, attending doctors, and hospital "ethics committee."[62]

We do not view the judicial resolution of this most difficult and awesome question — whether potentially life prolonging treatment should be withheld from a person incapable of making his own decision — as constituting a "gratuitous encroachment" on the domain of medical expertise. Rather, such questions of life and death seem to us to require the process of detached but passionate investigation and decision that forms the ideal on which the judicial branch of government was created. Achieving this ideal is our responsibility and that of the lower court, and is not to be entrusted to any other group purporting to represent the "morality and conscience of our society," no matter how highly motivated or impressively constituted.[63]

Whereas the reaction of the medical community to *Quinlan* had been warm, its reaction to *Saikewicz* was heated. An editorial in the *New England Journal of Medicine* accused the Supreme Judicial Court of wanting to "play doctor" and saw the *Saikewicz* decision as evidencing "total distrust of physicians' judgment" in termination of care cases.

Traditionally, doctors responsible for the care of "incompetent" patients have abided by the wishes of the next of kin, who are, of course, greatly influenced by the doctor's professional opinion. In the absence of relatives, physicians have customarily used their own best judgment, aided by the advice of colleagues and frequently the opinions of other health professionals, ministers and lawyers; sometimes they are also advised by special hospital committees organized for this purpose.[64]

The argument was that these "life and death" decisions were essentially medical in nature and therefore should be left to those who are experts in medicine. But, as a number of commentators, including this author,[65] have pointed out, these decisions are not merely medical in nature. Although it is within the expertise and authority of doctors to make determinations regarding diagnosis, prognosis, and treatment alternatives available to a patient, they have no expertise nor delegated authority to determine what the patient will accept by way of treatment — be he competent or incompetent. Nor do physicians have the training, the authority, or the institutional framework needed for dealing with the issues of societal ethics raised by these decisions.

Cases like *Saikewicz* and *Quinlan* raise questions that implicate basic values in our society, and the answers that are given to these questions can have profound consequences in situations seemingly far removed from the case at hand. If it is justifiable to remove Karen Quinlan from a respirator in order to let her die with dignity, why is it not justifiable to take other steps, such as injecting her with a lethal but painless drug, when she continues to breathe on her own once the respirator is removed? Is it because there is some important difference between acts of omission and those of commission? If so, why is the difference considered important and why is it that "pulling the plug" is considered an act of omission? If we may not consider Joseph Saikewicz's profoundly retarded state in weighing the value of continued life to him, why is that we may take into consideration the minimal value to Karen Quinlan of a future "vegetative" existence? We do, in fact, allow abortions to women who discover that they are pregnant with a child who is likely to be born with some level of mental retardation. Indeed, we allow abortions on all sorts of grounds which relate not to the best interests of the child but to the best interests of the mother and her family. Why should we at the moment of birth suddenly become restricted to considering only the best interests of the individual whose life is in question? If we are not to back into answers to these questions in a way which is ultimately destructive of our society, we must early on see to it that they are answered within a system which forces us, among other things, to face potential consequences as we decide individual cases.

As I have written elsewhere:

> The choice between doctors and courts of law as proxy decision makers for incompetents is not primarily a decision between two kinds of people on the basis of their relative competence as individual decision makers. It is not a question of whether doctors or judges are better trained to make life and death decisions for persons who cannot decide for themselves. Properly viewed, the choice is between, on the one hand, unsystematic determination by individual persons, be they doctors or judges, and, on the other hand, the type of systematic determination of questions which characterizes the ideal of Anglo-American court systems. Hence, in deciding to entrust life and death decision making for incompetents to the court systems rather than to individual doctors, the *Saikewicz* court was not expressing distrust for doctors. Rather the court was expressing its special faith in the judicial system by requiring for the deciding of these very important questions the special qualities of process that characterize the ideal of our courts and give empirical content to the concept of "the rule of law."[66]

One fundamental aspect of this process is the fact that judicial decisions are supposed to be principled. When a judge decides the case before him, he must do so in terms of a principle that is applicable to other cases as well. Unless the court is ready to overrule earlier cases, the principle must be consistent with what has been done before. At the same time, the court must anticipate future cases that may come before it since today's decision will be precedent for tomorrow's. Of course, there is room here for fine-tuning of principles when fact situations arise which are significantly unlike those which may have been earlier anticipated. Thus, a principle which now seems to have been stated in too sweeping form in an earlier case may be cut back so as to exclude a case that comes within the principle's letter but not its spirit. On the other hand, a principle that seems to have been stated in too limited form may be extended to cover a case that comes under the principle's spirit but not its letter. "All occasions do not arise at once," Lord Mansfield once observed, "a statute very seldom can take in all cases, therefore, the common law, that works itself pure by rules drawn from the fountain of justice, is for this reason superior to an act of parliament."[67] Professor Lon Fuller has made much the same point with an example from Wittgenstein:

> Someone says to me: "Show the children a game." I teach them gaming with dice and the other says "I did not mean that sort of game." Must the exclusion of the game with dice have come before his mind before he gave me the order?[68]

A second critical quality of the judicial process is its effort to keep the decision maker impartial. Only those facts that are made relevant by the legal principle that is to be applied are to be considered in reaching a decision. Of course, judges are human, so the law does not rely merely on the judge's self-control to keep him from rendering decisions based in part on prejudicial irrelevancies. As much as possible, the system tries to provide to litigants triers of fact who know nothing about the case before evidence is introduced. Then, at trial, rules of evidence provide advocates with the right to object to the introduction of evidence which is legally irrelevant.

The presence of these advocates introduces a third important element of process — the adversary system. As unsavory as this aspect of Anglo-American procedure may seem to the outsider, it deals sensibly with some inescapable facts about human nature. The first is the fact that judges, like other human beings, prefer to cut short the anxiety of indecision by reaching decisions as quickly as possible. The second is that lawyers, if placed in a competitive situation, will prefer winning to losing and thus will do all they can to counteract any tendency they may detect on the part of the judge to precipitately decide a case against them. "Failure generally attends the attempt to dispense with the distinct roles traditionally implied in adjudication," a body of distinguished American legal scholars and practitioners once warned. "What generally occurs in practice [where advocates have been eliminated] is that at some early point a familiar pattern will seem to emerge from the evidence; an accustomed label is waiting for the case and, without awaiting further proofs, this label is promptly assigned to it."[69] Within prescribed limits, the advocate is encouraged to harness his competitive instincts toward pressing upon the judge all of the evidence and arguments that support the case of his client and to keep out all evidence which would undo the impartiality of the judge toward his client. Moreover, since the advocate's job is not limited to proof of facts, he also plays a critical role in the development of the governing principles. As Justice Holmes has observed:

> The external and immediate result of an advocate's work is but to win or lose a case. But remotely what the lawyer does is to establish, develop, or illuminate rules which are to govern the conduct of men for centuries; to set in motion principles and influences which shape the thought and action of generations which know not by whose command they move.[70]

> Shall I ask what a court would be unaided? The law is made by the Bar, even more than by the Bench.[71]

It is the contending advocates who, in the first instance, force the judge's attention to adjudicative and legislative facts related to the fairness and practical value of the rules which they wish to have him mold to their case. And it is they who force him to consider the consequences in future cases of adopting a principle opposed to the interests of their clients in the present case.

The last, and perhaps most important, element of judicial process which needs to be addressed is its public nature. What the judge does is done for the most part in a goldfish bowl. Sir William Blackstone characterized a trial as an "open examination of witnesses, *viva voce*, in the presence of all mankind."[72] Not only are the hearings open to the public and the press, but decisions involving important questions of law most often end up in the form of published written opinions. As a result, many more minds and mouths than those of the parties' advocates have the chance to participate in the judge's effort at the development of legal principles. The judge knows that his opinion may come under scholarly scrutiny in law reviews and scholarly texts. He knows as well that it may become grist for criticism and even humorous jibes in innumerable law school classes. And through coverage in the popular media, the whole of society may come to play a role in setting limits on judges' rulings. Controversial decisions such as *Quinlan* and *Saikewicz* have in fact provoked continuing and widespread public dialogue. Gradually, such dialogue may develop lines of consensus regarding societal values upon which the courts can draw.

But what makes publicity the most important of the elements of judicial process is its tendency to protect all elements of the process from serious erosion. One need not be a cynic to observe that the operation of the judicial process in the real world endemically departs, in one way or another, from the ideal of "detached but passionate investigation and decision" which was held high in *Saikewicz*. But the public nature of these departures provides the opportunity for discovery and criticism which may force the process back onto course. The judge who renders biased or unprincipled decisions is readily subject to exposure and censure. Failures of advocacy on the part of counsel — whether self-imposed or court-mandated — may lead to public embarrassment. And even the decision to withdraw a particular proceeding from public view is subject to public criticism since that decision itself must normally be made public.[73] It should come as no surprise, then, that Jeremy Bentham, who disagreed with Blackstone on so many other issues, agreed heartily regarding the importance of publicity to public process. "Without publicity," he said, "all other checks are insufficient: in comparison of publicity, all other checks are of small account. Recordation, appeal, whatever other institutions might present themselves in the character of checks, would be found to operate rather as cloaks than checks; as cloaks in reality, as checks only in appearance."[74]

Of course, these elements of process are not present when physicians make decisions for incompetents. Medical personnel are placed under no institutional constraints to make their termination of care decisions consistent with each other under some articulated principle, to base them only upon facts relevant to such a principle, to open them to zealous advocacy of all interests, or to make all aspects of the process available to public scrutiny. As I have observed previously:

> My own experience in working with medical personnel faced with medical-ethical problems suggests that there is no consistency as to principle from doctor to doctor or time to time, and that any given physician may not be able to articulate and defend a principle which justifies his particular decision. This should come as no surprise, of course: Doctors are so preoccupied making the medical decisions for which they *have* been trained, they have neither the time nor training for developing consistently applied [principles for] medical-ethical decisions. As a result, they accommodate these constraints by reaching a decision that will leave them feeling the least misgiving. Nonetheless, these misgivings are still sufficiently great to result in a remarkable degree of "burn out" by staff in intensive care units.[75]

Under the circumstances, one might have expected that physicians would have welcomed *Saikewicz* as an opportunity to give up responsibility for these troubling decisions and turn them over to the courts. However, as we have seen, that was not the reaction. Instead, the reaction was to feel misunderstood, unappreciated, and hurt and to threaten civil disobedience:

> "No-treatment" or "withdrawal of treatment" decisions for incompetent patients are being made all the time throughout the hospitals of Massachusetts, but very few are being brought to judicial attention. The reasons are obvious enough, and are implicit in what has already been said. Neither relatives nor physicians want to go to the trouble or expense of obtaining a court judgment, particularly when they have no confidence that the judgment will be medically or ethically sound. If there is real doubt that the court will consider the quality of life involved, and if the medical recommendations of the physicians in charge of the case, as well as the wishes of the family, are to be examined in an adversarial courtroom proceeding, then most families and physicians would prefer to stay away from the courts. At present, it commonly is believed that they take very little risk in doing so, but that view could of course be changed by future developments.[76]

The gauntlet had been thrown down at the feet of the judiciary, and it is still unclear how the courts will ultimately respond. Even in

Massachusetts, decisions since *Saikewicz* have shown wavering regarding the question of whether termination of care decisions are properly to be brought to the courts. Seven months after the opinion in *Saikewicz*, the intermediate Appeals Court of Massachusetts rendered a decision which seemed to place it on the side of the doctors. That decision, *In re Dinnerstein*,[77] arose out of an action seeking a court declaration as to whether physicians attending an incompetent patient terminally ill with Alzheimer's disease could lawfully "no-code,"[78] the patient — i.e., direct that no efforts be made to resuscitate her in the event of cardiac or respiratory arrest. Plaintiffs argued that the court should find such action lawful on either of two grounds. One was based on the substituted judgment test of *Saikewicz*: that the facts justified a finding that Mrs. Dinnerstein would request a "no-code" if she were competent to do so. The other ground (preferred by the plaintiffs), was that a doctor may lawfully "no-code" a patient without prior court approval. The appeals court held for the plaintiffs on the latter ground by concluding that the case presented "a question peculiarly within the competence of the medical profession of what measures are appropriate to ease the imminent passing of an irreversibly, terminally ill patient in light of the patient's history and condition and the wishes of her family. That question is not one for judicial decision, but one for the attending physician, in keeping with the highest traditions of his profession, and subject to court review only to the extent that it may be contended that he has failed to exercise "the degree of care and skill of the average qualified practitioner, taking into account the advances in the profession."[79] In reaching that conclusion, the court attempted to distinguish *Saikewicz* on grounds which, as I have argued elsewhere,[80] are patently insufficient. But the real grounds for the decision are apparent: the appeals court had openly retreated in the face of the medical community's stance of massive resistance to *Saikewicz*. As the court said:

> [*Saikewicz*] would appear to establish a rule of law that unless such a court determination has been obtained, it is the duty of a doctor attending an incompetent patient to employ whatever life-saving or life-prolonging treatments the current state of the art has put in his hands. *As it cannot be assumed that legal proceedings such as the present one will be initiated in respect of more than a small fraction of all terminally ill or dying elderly patients,* the *Saikewicz* case, if read to apply to the natural death of a terminally ill patient by cardiac or respiratory arrest, would require attempts to resuscitate dying patients in most cases, without exercise of medical judgment, even when that course of action could aptly be characterized as a pointless, even cruel, prolongation of the act of dying.[81]

Dinnerstein, which had gone beyond *Quinlan* by not requiring ethics committee approval of physicians' termination of care decisions, was received by the medical community with a sense of cautious relief. The caution was occasioned by the fact that the decision had not come from the highest court of the state. There was uncertainty about the extent to which *Dinnerstein* could be considered to state the law of the Commonwealth.[82] Thus, it was hoped that the Supreme Judicial Court would clarify matters when it faced the same issues two years later in the case of *In re Spring*.[83] That case had first come before the appeals court which had decided it in a fasion consistent with its decision in *Dinnerstein*. Earle Spring was a seventy-eight year old man who had gone into rapid mental decline contemporaneously with his succumbing to a series of illnesses which had culminated in "end stage kidney disease." His physical condition required that he be taken to a hospital three times a week and connected to a machine for five hour stints of dialysis. There was evidence that Mr. Spring, who had previously led a healthy and active life, was resisting the treatments which were uncomfortable and debilitating. Mr. Spring's son had sought court authority as his guardian to have the dialysis stopped on the ground that, were his father not senile, he would prefer death over continued treatment. The trial court ultimately determined that "the ward's attending physician, together with the ward's wife and son, are to make the decision with reference to the continuance or termination of the dialysis treatment."[84] That decision was affirmed by the appeals court in language which echoed its earlier opinion in *Dinnerstein*:

> The importance of the role of the family and the doctor is highlighted by *the self-evident fact that the vast majority of treatment decisions relative to persons who are incompetent by reason of senility or retardation are made for them by their family and the doctor, without court proceedings*.[85]

The Supreme Judicial Court granted expedited review to the appeals court decision and arguments were heard only three weeks later. Four days after that it issued an order reversing the appeals courts. "[I]t was error," the court said, "to delegate the decision to the attending physician and the ward's wife and son."[86] It seemed a clear setback for the doctors, but, when the court's opinion in the case appeared some four months later, it appeared as if they had actually won something of a victory — albeit a victory stated entirely in the form of dictum rather than holding. "Neither the present case nor the *Saikewicz* case involved the legality of action taken without judicial authority," the court said, "and our opinions should not be taken to establish any requirement of prior judicial approval that would not otherwise exist."[87] As to whether there is any risk of criminal liability for the doctor who acts without such approval before causing the death of a patient, the court hints that the answer is "no" so long as the doctor acts "on a good faith judgment that is not grievously unreasonable by medical standards."[88] The court also hints at a "no" answer to the question of civil liability for battery. "Unless there is an emergency or an overriding state interest, the medical treatment of a competent patient without his consent is *said* to be a battery, but there is *serious question* whether it is *useful* to think about medical treatment of incompetent patients in terms of battery."[89] Besides, *maybe* consent could be given by some person other than the patient — a parent, spouse, or guardian. And, even if not, "[w]ithholding of treatment does not fit neatly into the category of battery"[90] since the doctor need not ever touch the patient in order to withhold treatment. As a result, the standard of liability which would *seem* to apply to a doctor who withholds treatment from an incompetent patient is that merely of whether or not he has been *negligent*, and that standard is not a function of whether or not prior consent has been obtained from a court. "Thus absence of court approval does not result in automatic civil liability for withholding treatment...."[91]

"What, then, is the significance of our disapproval [in *Saikewicz*] of a shift of ultimate responsibility away from the courts?"[92] the court asks. The answer seems to reduce to a piddling, procedural point the court's earlier bold statement of commitment to the process of "passionate but detached investigation and decision making." "When a court is properly presented with the legal question, whether treatment may be withheld," it states, "it must decide that question and not delegate it to some private person or group."[93] In light of the fact that no one had ever suggested such a delegation in *Saikewicz*, it is hard to take seriously the court's suggestion that this was all that it meant to say in that case. As a result, *Spring* seemed to constitute an acceptance of the retreat represented by *Dinnerstein*, and the court hinted as much. "Without approving all that is said in the opinion of the Appeals Court," the court stated, "we think the result reached on the facts shown in that case was consistent with our holding in the *Saikewicz* case."[94]

However, cases decided by the Supreme Judicial Court since *Spring* suggest that its dictum in that case will not prevent it from gradually resuscitating *Saikewicz* as the need for doing so manifests itself. In *Guardianship of Roe*,[95] the court held in 1981 that court approval must be sought before antipsychotic drugs may be forced upon an incompetent mental patient on a nonemergency basis.

> The question presented by the ward's refusal of antipsychotic drugs is only incidentally a medical question. Absent an overwhelming State interest, a competent individual has the right to refuse such treatment. To deny this right to persons who are incapable of exercising it personally is to degrade those whose disabilities make them wholly reliant on other, more fortunate, individuals. In order to accord proper respect to this basic right of all individuals, we feel that if an incompetent individual refuses antipsychotic drugs, those charged with his protection must seek a judicial determination of substituted judgment. No medical expertise is required in such an inquiry, although medical advice and opinion is to be used for the same purposes and sought to the same extent that the incompetent individual would, if he were competent. We emphasize that the determination is *not* what is medically in the ward's best interests — a determination better left to those with extensive medical training and experience. The determination of what the incompetent individual

would do if competent will probe the incompetent individual's values and preferences, and such an inquiry, in a case involving antipsychotic drugs, is best made in courts of competent jurisdiction.[96]

In 1982, the court determined that prior court approval should be required in two additional categories of cases. In the controversial "Baby Billy" case,[97] the court held that the facts justified no-coding a terminally ill infant on a substituted-judgment basis and that the prior court determination which had been sought on the question was mandatory in such a case.

> [W]e conclude that, although this case appears similar to *Dinnerstein* because the entry of a "no code" order is in issue and the child is terminally ill, the principles enunciated in *Saikewicz* are applicable. Absent a loving family with whom physicians may consult regarding the entry of a "no code" order, this issue is best resolved by requiring a judicial determination in accordance with the substituted judgment doctrine enunciated in *Saikewicz*.[98]

And *In re Moe*,[99] the court was presented for the first time with the question of whether "substituted judgment" could be exercised for a mentally retarded ward on the question of whether she should accept sterilization as the birth control method of choice. The answer was "yes," but the court added:

> Since sterilization is an extraordinary and highly intrusive form of medical treatment that irreversibly extinguishes the ward's fundamental right of procreative choice, we conclude that a guardian must obtain a proper judicial order for the procedure before he or she can validly consent to it. Guardians and parents, therefore, absent statutory or judicial authorization, cannot consent to the sterilization of a ward in their care or custody.[100]

Perhaps inadvertently, the court also cited *Saikewicz, Spring,* and *Roe* for the following sweeping proposition: "[O]ur prior cases have established that prior judicial approval is required before a guardian may consent to administering or withholding of proposed extraordinary medical treatment."[101]

While there are cases from other states in which courts have determined that they have jurisdiction to decide questions regarding terminating life support for incompetent patients, there are few decisions other than *Quinlan* and *Saikewicz* as to when court approval is required. A Delaware case, *Severns v. Wilmington Medical Center*,[102] raises the question and then seems to leave it for determination by the state legislature.[103] The "Brother Fox" case, *Eichner v. Dillon*,[104] deals with the issue head-on, answering it differently in the Court of Appeals of New York than it had been answered in the intermediate appeals court of that state. The Appellate Division of the New York Supreme Court had adopted the approach of *Saikewicz* and gone beyond it, laying out a complicated procedure in which the court was to review medical as well as societal questions that were raised in each case.[105] The court of appeals set aside this aspect of the decision of the appellate division, stating that "[i]f it is desirable to enlarge the role of the courts in cases involving discontinuance of life sustaining treatment for incompetents by establishing, as the appellate division suggested in the *Eichner* case, a mandatory procedure of successive approvals by physicians, hospital personnel, relatives and the courts, the change should come from the Legislature."[106]

Of course, it is easy to see why the courts would be reluctant to require that all such decisions should be brought before them. Besides the resistance of the medical community that such a requirement would create, there are, as the physicians are fond of pointing out,[107] so many such decisions that must be made every day that they would threaten to completely overwhelm the courts. However, the "substituted judgment" aspect of such cases could be easily taken care of in many cases. Legislation empowering individuals to write "living wills" — which are designed to handle in advance the question of what the patient would want for himself were he to become incompetent — has been passed in thirteen states and is pending in twenty-two others.[108] Moreover, there is nothing to suggest that the courts do not have the power to create such an institution without express legislative authority. Where such expressions of advance authority were utilized with regularity, the "substituted judgment" questions would remain largely only for children and the mentally retarded. Left for the courts also, of course, would be the difficult job of working out, on a case-by-case basis, all of the difficult societal-ethical issues as to which principles for consistent decision making is so badly needed. But even this task should become less burdensome as time goes on. As I have suggested previously,[109] the courts should be able gradually to carve out classes of cases for which advance court approval is not required. The Appeals Court of Massachusetts did just this in the *Dinnerstein* case.[110] I think they may have been right in doing so, but for reasons other than those primarily relied upon by the court.[111] The courts have done this also with the cases involving refusal of life-saving care by competent patients. The principle of patient autonomy in such situations is sufficiently well-established by now that cases need to be brought only where a novel fact situation raises some doubt under the rationale of the earlier decisions.[112] But such classes of exception cannot be developed in the abstract. The courts can develop substantive principles for such classes of cases and conclude that the principles can be safely applied without court intervention to the facts of each case as it arises, only out of a process that, in the first instance, requires them to confront them all.

Of course, more than the sheer number of such cases makes the courts reluctant to take on this task. It is likely that it is the prospect of being forced continually to confront the "future shock" problems which the cases raise that disturbs judges the most. Difficult as such decisions are for the doctors to make, doctors at least have the luxury of making them in secret and in a fashion which may allow them to believe that they are not even making a decision. As we have seen, the process requirements of the "rule of law" do not allow this luxury to judges. It may well be for this very reason that the United States Supreme Court decisions mentioned earlier, *Roe v. Wade* and *Colautti v. Franklin,* show their distressing tendency to throw a cloak over difficult ethical decisions by calling them "medical questions" and delegating them to doctors. In contrast to this example of unwillingness to take on the difficult tasks of statecraft is the image which has been left by the work of the great American jurist Lemuel Shaw. During thirty years as Chief Justice of the Massachusetts Supreme Judicial Court, Shaw shaped the common law in Massachusetts to respond to such nineteenth-century challenges as the rise of the railroads, the development of steam power, the growing use of the factory system, and the spread of the corporate form of doing business. One contemporary said of Shaw: "If the simplest motion were made, Chief Justice Shaw had to unlimber the heavy artillery of his mind, go down to the roots of the question, consider the matter from all possible relations, and deal with it as if he were besieging a fortress."[113] The forces which were transforming society in the America of the nineteenth century must have been every bit as frightening at the time, as are, today, the forces which threaten to transform comtemporary American society. Yet, Shaw took them on with a courage, creativity, and intelligence which earned him the title: "America's Greatest Magistrate." His landmark decisions in nearly every area of the law earned him a nationwide reputation and provided a foundation for modern American jurisprudence.

Happily, while debate continues on the question of whether *Saikewicz*-type cases *must* be brought to court, enough such cases *are* being brought to court that "future shock" issues are being faced by judges and substantive principles are being developed for dealing with them. As might be expected of any beginning effort, the development is gradual and random and the principles are largely inchoate. On the one hand, very little has been done by way of facing the important question of the significance of distinguishing between acts and omissions to act. For the most part the courts have acted as if common sense makes clear that certain acts under certain circumstances merely "allow nature to take its course" while others are clear acts of homicide.[114] Sometimes they employ the screen of distinguishing medical treatment which is "lifesaving" from that which is merely "life-prolonging."[115] However, on other issues, the courts have mounted a much more forthright attack and seem gradually to be developing a body of ever-refining principle. One such issue is that of the extent to which a competent person may choose death over continued medical treatment. As was earlier mentioned, the courts were slow to recognize such a right at all. In *Quinlan* and *Saikewicz* they recognized such a right, but only where it was not outweighed by certain state interests which included: (1) the preservation of human life, (2) the protection of the interests of innocent third parties, (3) the prevention of suicide, and (4) maintaining the ethical integrity of the medical profession.[116] Although the importance of such state interests is still mentioned in later cases,[117] there appears to be only one recent case in which they were held to outweigh a patient's right to refuse treatment — that being *Commissioner of Correction v. Myers*,[118] an unusual Massachusetts case in which a prisoner refused to submit to kidney dialysis unless the state agreed to transfer him to a minimum security prison. The clear trend seems to be toward recognizing increased personal autonomy over one's physical and psychological health and the length of one's life.

The same trend toward autonomy is evident in cases which deal with the subtle and difficult issues surrounding the notion of "legal incompetence." As we saw earlier, the courts are unwilling to equate incompetence with mere irrationality — even "medical irrationality."[119] They are also unwilling to equate it with insanity.[120] The presumption in every case is in favor of competence, and new notions are developing of "limited incompetence" and "limited guardianships" even for those cases where it can be proved that the proposed ward is incapable of making certain decisions for himself.[121] Finally, the ward, whether he is incompetent by reason of minority or by reason of mental defect, is being looked to more and more as a source of direction to the guardian or court in the effort to make a "substituted judgment."[122] Of course, the courts' use of the "substituted judgment" test and the almost complete exclusion of consideration of interests other than the ward's also represent commitment to the notion of personal autonomy. As we have seen, this seems to have become the dominant, if not exclusive,[123] test for making medical decisions of all sorts for children and other persons held to be legally incompetent.

Obviously, the fact that the courts have relatively consistently stated these high-sounding principles does not mean that they have consistently and impartially applied them in fact. In at least two cases it is rather clear that they have not. In the 1979 California case *In re Phillip B.*,[124] the Court of Appeal for the First District let stand a lower court decision permitting parental veto of an operation to correct a congenital heart defect in a twelve year old mentally retarded child. Without the surgery, Phillip would live at most another twenty years, and, during that time, he would "suffer from a progressive loss of energy and vitality until he is forced to lead a bed-to-chair existence."[125] In part because his parents had refused to consent to medical treatment some six years earlier, Phillip's physical condition created a risk of mortality from the operation of from 5 to 10 percent, but his doctor believed that the risks were clearly outweighed by the potential benefits to him. Despite the fact that the parents had institutionalized Phillip at birth and despite the fact that the court states at one point that "the underlying consideration is the child's welfare and whether his best interests will be served by the medical treatment,"[126] the court allowed the parental decision to stand while observing: "[S]ince the state should usually defer to the wishes of the parents, it has a serious burden of justification before abridging parental autonomy by substituting its judgment for that of the parents."[127] As commentators have noted,[128] it is hard to believe that the court would have reached this same conclusion in a case where the child was not mentally retarded. Therefore, the case seems to have been decided in part on bases other than the substituted judgment of the child, i.e., judicial bias based, presumably, upon the court's sense of the lessened value to the parents and society of the life of a mentally retarded child.

More shocking failures of judicial process than just lack of impartiality were involved in the second, and very recent case. There, the Supreme Court of Indiana undid as well the public nature of the proceedings by condoning a series of secret court hearings and ordering records sealed.[129] Newspaper reports tell us that these secret proceedings authorized the parents of "Infant Doe" to instruct his doctors to allow him to die of starvation rather than to surgically remove an esophageal blockage which prevented him from taking nourishment by mouth. The reason, as with Phillip B., was the presence of Down's syndrome with its prognosis of some degree of mental retardation.[130] The newspaper accounts suggest that the decision purported to be based, at least in part, on a theory of substituted judgment. "These people loved the baby," one county official is quoted as saying. "It was not an act of anything but absolute love. This was a parent's ultimate act of love, given the child's medical condition."[131]

Do these cases, with their failures of basic elements of the judicial process, demonstrate that the process virtues ascribed to the judiciary earlier in this article are illusory? By way of answer, consider the fact that both cases, as a result of having been brought to court, became subject to widespread public discussion and criticism. This has been true even of the "Infant Doe" case which was supposed to have been kept secret, and debate over the case continues on radio, on television, and in the newspapers even as I write. Physicians admit that the "Infant Doe" scenario is quietly acted out every day in obstetrical intensive care units across the United States.[132] Because these nonjudicial decisions are made in secrecy, there is no opportunity for public input into the decision-making process despite the fact that attitudes toward the sanctity of life in American society may well be gradually changed thereby. Where such decisions are made in public, the public has an opportunity to clamor for correction of what it may see as departures from the "rule of law" — whether substantive or procedural. And judges, lawyers, and legal scholars have an opportunity to educate and lead the public in this effort.

The responsibility of the legal profession is especially heavy, it seems to me, to police the system for failures in the basic elements of process. One such failure has been the lack of adequate adversary process in many of these cases. Because the patient in the vast majority of these cases is incompetent, he is unable to retain and direct counsel for the purpose of protecting what he sees as his interests in the case. In the early cases involving kidney transplants from minor donors, it was assumed that the other parties to the case would carry the burden of adversary development of the record.[133] But neither the hospital, on one side, nor the parents, nominally on the other, could be depended upon to carry the burden of arguing against the donation. Both sides were only concerned with seeing the court do "what was right" and were eager to save the life of the recipient child. Later, in the early bone-marrow transplant cases,[134] the courts began to appoint guardians *ad litem* to represent the interests of the ward. However, in most cases, this improved protection of the ward very little. In addition to the fact that such guardians of the interests of the ward were frequently persons associated with the hospital in question rather than independent advocates, their job assignment was that of investigating the case and coming up with a proposal as to what they considered to be in the best interests of the ward. The job of determining this "best interests" question was ultimately for the judge. Instead of ensuring that this determination was made upon a record made full by advocacy on both sides of the donation question, the guardian *ad litem* was simply premasticating the "best interests" question on an information base which itself suffered from lack of adversary development. To counter this problem, an article which I wrote with two co-authors proposed:

> Courts should be required to appoint guardians ad litem to represent prospective minor donors in all transplant proceedings. The guardian's role should be defined as that of an advocate of the child's interest in not acting as a donor; the guardian should be instructed to present all the evidence and arguments against his ward's donation and to oppose the positions taken by the hospital and family, regardless of the guardian's personal perception of the child's actual interests.
>
> In transplant cases there are only two possible dispositions, and the parents and the hospital will provide all the evidence and arguments in support of authorization. What is institutionally necessary if the prospective donor is to be protected adequately is not the guardian's more objective opinion whether the operation is in the child's best interests but a party to present the arguments that support denying authorization.[135]

Subsequently, there was some perceivable increase in the incidence of zealous advocacy on the part of guardians *ad litem,* including the first case in which a guardian *ad litem* was successful in preventing donation from his client — a mentally retarded relative in a family that included other candidates.[136] And, in recent years, guardians *ad litem* performed heroically in a number of "substituted judgment" cases.[137] However, less-than-zealous advocacy is still widespread. It is interesting to note that this appears to have been a basic failing of process in both *In re Phillip B.* and the "Infant Doe" case. One wonders if the other elements of process would have failed if there had been the presence of vigorous advocacy. Even the *Saikewicz* decision suffered from lack of adversariness. There the guardian *ad litem* joined the other parties at the original hearing in recommending to the court that Mr. Saikewicz not be given chemotherapy. Presumably because of that, it fell to advocates who intervened at the appellate level to try to introduce into the record "a number of recent empirical studies which cast doubt on the view [presented at trial] that patients over sixty are less successfully treated by chemotherapy."[138] The Supreme Judicial Court refused to receive the evidence because "[n]one of these authorities was brought to the consideration of the probate judge."[139] However, the court appeared to attempt to head off such problems in future cases by suggesting:

> As an aid to the judge . . ., it will often be desirable to appoint a guardian ad litem, sua sponte or on motion, to represent the interests of the person. Moreover, we think it appropriate, and highly desirable, in cases such as the one before us to charge the guardian ad litem with an additional responsibility to be discharged if there is a finding of incompetency. This will be the responsibility of presenting to the judge, after as thorough an investigation as time will permit, all reasonable arguments in favor of administering treatment to prolong the life of the individual involved. This will insure that all viewpoints and alternatives will be aggressively pursued and examined at the subsequent hearing where it will be determined whether treatment should or should not be allowed.[140]

Even under the procedure suggested in *Saikewicz,* there are still patent problems of absence of advocacy in important ways. First, the procedure assumes the appointment of a guardian *ad litem* before the proposed ward is found to be incompetent. What would seem more appropriate would be the appointment of counsel whose job it is to defend his client from the petitioner's effort to prove him incompetent.[141] Second, the court should have required that a guardian *ad litem* be appointed for every patient found to be incompetent unless he already has an advocate representing him.[142] Third, the procedure provides for advocacy only in those cases where the petition requests that medical care be terminated. Where the petition attempts to force medical care on the patient, the guardian *ad litem* should present the evidence and arguments in favor of termination of care. Fourth, the guardian *ad litem* should be directed to play only the role of an advocate and should not mix this role with that of a neutral investigator reporting or making recommendations to the judge.[143] Finally, in those cases where the petitioner is unwilling to aggressively present either side of the case, (as is the case at times with family members), the court should appoint two advocates — each to be responsible for only one side of the case.[144] However, the *Saikewicz* procedure represented a significant improvement over that which had existed previously. And in the recent *Moe* case, the Supreme Judicial Court improved the procedure still further:

> Upon a guardian's petition for an order authorizing the sterilization of his or her ward, the court must appoint a guardian ad litem to represent the ward. The guardian ad litem is to be charged with the responsibility of zealously representing the ward, and must have full opportunity to meet with the ward, present proof, and cross-examine witnesses at the hearing. . . . In order to guarantee a thorough adversary exploration of the difficult question posed, the guardian ad litem should present all reasonable arguments in favor of the court's denial of the petition so that "all viewpoints and alternatives will be aggressively pursued and examined at the subsequent hearing." . . . This adversary posture will ensure that both sides of each issue which the court must consider are thoroughly aired before findings are made and a decision rendered.[145]

Still more could be asked for the procedure which is under development.[146] But one could do much worse than the process which is developing it — the process of gradual growth of common law which "works itself pure" from case to case.

Winston Churchill is reputed to have once said: "Democracy is the worst of all political systems, except for every other system." Much the same can be said for democracy's companion — the rule of law. Each puts away with "Father Christmas" the notion of an all-wise Platonic philosopher king capable of promulgating and implementing right rules for the government of society. What we are left with then is each other, and the ongoing task of working out for ourselves institutions and principles which make it possible for us to live together with some measure of happiness. For better or for worse, modern medicine has made the American family an arena in which are raised questions fraught with large implications for the rest of society. In the fifth century B.C., a great Athenian politician observed: "Although only a few may originate a policy, we are all able to judge it."[147] That notion seems to have stood the test of time. "In my course I have known and, according to my measure, have cooperated with great men," Edmund Burke said over two thousand years later, "and I have never yet seen any plan which has not been mended by the observations of those who were much inferior in understanding to the person who took the lead in the business."[148] The opportunity to benefit from such observations is maximized when life-and-death questions are answered in our public courts of law; we minimize that opportunity when we leave them to be answered in private by Platonic physician-kings.

NOTES

1. *John F. Kennedy Memorial Hosp. v. Heston,* 58 N.J. 576, 279 A.2d 670 (1971).
2. *Lane v. Candura,* 6 Mass.App. 377, 383, 376 N.E. 2d 1,232, 1,235-36 (1978).
3. Relman, "The Saikewicz Decision: A Medical Viewpoint," *4 Am. J. L. and Med.* 233, 237 (1978) emphasis supplied.
4. 410 U.S. 113 (1973).
5. Before coming to the Court, Justice Blackmun had served for about ten years as general counsel to the famed Mayo Clinic. That experience had left him with an awe of doctors which he acted out in writing the *Roe* opinion:

At Mayo, he had watched as Doctors Edward C. Kendall and Philip S. Hench won the Nobel Prize for research in arthritis. He rejoiced with other doctors after their first successful heart by-pass operation, then suffered with them after they lost their next four patients. He sat up late nights with the surgical staff to review hospital deaths in biweekly meetings, and recalled them in detail. He grew to respect what dedicated physicians could accomplish. These had been terribly exciting years for Blackmun. He called them the best ten years of his life.

If a state licensed a physician to practice medicine, it was entrusting him with the right to make medical decisions. State laws restricting abortions interfered with those medical judgments. Physicians were always somewhat unsure about the possible legal ramifications of their judgments. To completely restrict an operation like abortion, normally no more dangerous than minor surgery, or to permit it only with the approval of a hospital committee or the concurrence of other doctors, was a needless infringement of the discretion of the medical profession.

Blackmun would do anything he could to reduce the anxiety of his colleagues except spurn the assignment [to write the opinion in *Roe v. Wade.*] The case was not so much a legal task as an opportunity for the Court to ratify the best possible medical opinion. (B. Woodward and S. Armstrong, *The Brethren* (1979) 174-75).

6. *Roe v. Wade, supra,* note 4, at 165-66, emphasis supplied.
7. 439 U.S. 379 (1979). Blackmun's tendency to defer continually to the medical profession has not escaped the notice of his colleagues on the court:

Blackmun's 1973 abortion opinion had subjected the Court to a great deal of ridicule. It was as if Blackmun had developed a special constitutional rule for handling medical questions. [Justice] White dubbed it Blackmun's "medical question doctrine." It seemed to hold that, under the Constitution, doctors rather than the Court, had the final authority on certain medical-legal questions. White found that notion ludicrous. Blackmun had created another "political questions" doctrine. The notion that the Court couldn't meddle in the internal affairs of the other branches of government had been broadened to include the medical profession. (Woodward and Armstrong, *supra,* note 5, at 416).

8. A rare recent exception is *Commissioner of Correction v. Myers,* 1979 Mass.Adv. Sh. 2523, 399 N.E.2d 452 (1979), where the Supreme Judicial Court of Massachusetts denied a prison inmate the right to refuse life-saving hemodialysis because the state's interest in preserving order in the prison outweighed the prisoner's right to privacy.

9. *Rogers v. Okin*, 634 F.2d 650 (1st Cir. 1980), *remanded for further proceedings sub. nom. Mills v. Rogers*, 50 U.S.L.W. 4,676 (1982).

10. See W. Prosser, *The Law of Torts*, 102–03 (4th ed. 1971).

11. *In re Tuttendario*, 21 Pa.Dist. 561 (Dist. Ct. 1911).

12. *In re Hudson*, 13 Wash.2d. 673, 126 P.2d 765 (1942).

13. *In re Seiferth*, 309 N.Y. 80, 127 N.E.2d 820 (1955); *In re Frank*, 41 Wash.2d 294, 248 P.2d 553 (1952).

14. *In re Green*, 448 Pa. 338, 292 A.2d 387 (1972).

15. *Mannis v. State ex rel. Dewitt School Dist. No. 1*, 240 Ark. 42, 398 S.W.2d 206 (1966).

16. *In re Karwath*, 199 N.W.2d 147 (Iowa 1972).

17. *In re Cicero*, 101 Misc. 2d 699, 421 N.Y.S.2d 965 (1975) (spinal disorder); *In re Sampson*, 29 N.Y.2d 900, 278 N.E.2d 918, 328 N.Y.S.2d 686 (1972) (disfigurement); *In re Carstairs*, 115 N.Y.S.2d 314 (N.Y. Dom. Rel. Ct. 1952) (emotional illness); *In re Rotkowitz*, 175 Misc. 948, 25 N.Y.S. 624 (N.Y. Dom. Rel. Ct. 1941) (deformity of foot); *In re Weintraub*, 166 Pa.Super. 342, 71 A.2d 823 (1950) (emotional illness).

18. *People ex rel. Wallace v. LaBrenz*, 411 Ill. 618, 104 N.E.2d 769, *cert. denied*, 344 U.S. 824 (1952); *State v. Perricone*, 37 N.J. 463, 181 A.2d 751, *cert. denied*, 371 U.S. 890 (1962); *Hoener v. Bertinato*, 67 N.J.Super. 517, 171 A.2d 140 (Juv. and Dom. Rel. Ct. 1961); *Application of Brooklyn Hosp.*, 45 Misc.2d 914, 258 N.Y.S.2d 621 (Sup. Ct. 1965); *Heinemann's Appeal*, 96 Pa. 112 (1880); *Mitchell v. Davis*, 205 S.W.2d 812 (Tex. Civ. App. 1947).

19. *Custody of a Minor*, 375 Mass. 733, 379 N.E.2d 1,053 (1978) and *Custody of a Minor*, 1979 Mass.Adv.Sh. 2124, 393 N.E.2d 836 (1979).

20. *Boston Globe*, Oct. 14, 1979, at 1, Col. 5.

21. 65 App. Div.2d 108, 411 N.Y.S.2d 416 (1978), *aff'd*, 47 N.Y.2d 648, 393 N.E.2d 1009, 419 N.Y.S.2d 936 (1979).

22. See Baron, Botsford, and Cole, "Live Organ and Tissue Transplants from Minor Donors in Massachusetts," 55 *B.U.L. Rev.* 159, 164–65 (1975).

23. *Id.* at 160.

24. *Id.* at 161–62, nn. 15 and 16.

25. See *Rappeport v. Stott*, Civil No. J 74–57 (Mass., Aug. 28, 1974).

26. See, for example, *Masden v. Harrison*, Eq. No. 68,651 (Mass., June 12, 1957).

27. *Nathan v. Farinelli*, Eq. No. 74–87 (Mass., July 3, 1974).

28. *Buck v. Bell*, 274 U.S. 200 (1927).

29. Cited frequently as having implicitly overruled *Buck v. Bell* is *Skinner v. Oklahoma*, 316 U.S. 535 (1942).

30. *Association for Voluntary Sterilization, A.V.S. NEWS*, March 1975.

31. See *Hathaway v. Worcester City Hosp.*, 475 F.2d 701 (1st Cir. 1973); *Ruby v. Massey*, 542 F. Supp. 361 (D. Conn. 1978); *Voe v. Califano*, 434 F.Supp. 1058 (D. Conn. 1977); *North Carolina Ass'n. for Retarded Citizens v. State of N.C.*, 420 F.Supp. 451 (M.D.N.C. 1976); *Relf v. Weinberger*, 372 F.Supp. 1196 (D.D.C. 1974).

32. *See* LaChance, "In re Grady: The Mentally Retarded Individual's Right to Choose Sterilization," 6 *Am. J. L. and Med.* 559, 570–72 (1981).

33. See, for example, *In re Moe*, 385 Mass. 555, 432 N.E.2d 712 (1982); *In re Grady*, 170 N.J.Super. 98, 405 A.2d 851 (1979).

34. *Planned Parenthood v. Danforth*, 428 U.S. 52 (1976).

35. 443 U.S. 622 (1979).

36. *Id.* at 648.

37. Occasionally cited for this proposition are *Pratt v. Davis,* 224 Ill. 300, 79 N.E. 562 (1906) and *Belger v. Arnot,* 344 Mass. 679, 183 N.E.2d 866 (1962).
38. Prosser, *supra,* note 10, at 103.
39. 70 N.J. 10, 355 A.2d 647 (1976).
40. *Id.* at 26, 355 A.2d at 655.
41. *Id.* at 39, 355 A.2d at 663.
42. *In re Quinlan,* 137 N.J.Super. 227, 259, 348 A.2d 801, 818 (Ch. Div. 1975).
43. *Quinlan, supra,* note 39, at 45, 355 A.2d at 666.
44. *Id.* at 54, 355 A.2d at 671.
45. Here the court was responding to a published suggestion by Dr. Karen Teel that doctors would be wise to establish such committees in order to broaden responsibility for making medical-ethical decisions:

> Physicians, by virtue of their responsibility for medical judgments are, partly by choice and partly by default, charged with the responsibility of making ethical judgments which we are sometimes ill-equipped to make. We are not always morally and legally authorized to make them. The physician is thereby assuming a civil and criminal liability that, as often as not, he does not even realize as a factor in his decision. There is little or no dialogue in this whole process. The physician assumes that his judgment is called for and, in good faith, he acts. Someone must, and it has been the physician who has assumed the responsibility and the risk.
>
> I suggest that it would be more appropriate to provide a regular forum for more input and dialogue in individual situations and to allow the responsibility of these judgments to be shared. Many hospitals have established an Ethics Committee composed of physicians, social workers, attorneys, and theologians, . . . which serves to review the individual circumstances of ethical dilemma and which has provided much in the way of assistance and safeguards for patients and their medical caretakers. Generally, the authority of these committees is primarily restricted to the hospital setting and their official status is more that of an advisory body than of an enforcing body. (Teel, "The Physician's Dilemma: A Doctor's View: What the Law Should Be," 27 *Baylor L. Rev.* 6, 8-9 (1975).)

46. *Quinlan, supra,* note 39, at 54, 355 A.2d at 671.
47. See Annas, "Reconciling Quinlan and Saikewicz: Decision Making for the Terminally Ill Incompetent," 4 *Am. J. L. and Med.* 367 (1979).
48. *Quinlan, supra,* note 39, at 49, 355 A.2d at 668.
49. *Id.* at 54, 355 A.2d at 671.
50. *Id.* at 50, 355 A.2d at 669.
51. *Id.* at 44, 355 A.2d at 665.
52. *Id.* at 41-42, 355 A.2d at 664.
53. 373 Mass. 728, 370 N.E.2d 417 (1977).
54. *Id.* at 773, 370 N.E.2d at 421.
55. *Id.* at 730, 370 N.E.2d at 419.
56. Those state interests were identified as: "(1) the preservation of life; (2) the protection of the interests of innocent third parties; (3) the prevention of suicide; and (4) maintaining the ethical integrity of the medical profession." *Id.* at 741, 370 N.E.2d at 425.
57. *Id.* at 749, 370 N.E.2d at 429.
58. As the court noted, this doctrine had had long-standing legitimacy in the field of administration of the estate of an incompetent person. See *Ex Parte Whitbread in re*

Hinde, a Lunatic, 35 Eng. Rep. 878 (1816). However, there was more recent authority for using it in cases involving medical treatment. See *Strunk v. Strunk,* 445 S.W.2d 145 (KY. Ct. App. 1969). In *Saikewicz,* the court described the test as calling upon the court to "don the mental mantle of the incompetent" and said:

> In short, the decision in cases such as this should be that which would be made by the incompetent person, if that person were competent, but taking into account the present and future incompetency of the individual as one of the factors which would necessarily enter into the decision making process of the competent person. (*Id.* at 752–53, 370 N.E.2d at 431.)

The facts of *Saikewicz* were strange ones for invoking the "substituted judgment" test rather than the "best interests" test. The former was designed for cases, such as *Whitbread,* where the incompetent had been previously competent. In such a case, there is a prior record of competent decision making upon which to draw in donning the incompetent's "mental mantle." Where, as with Joseph Saikewicz, there is no such prior period of competent decision making to draw upon, the "substituted judgment" test would seem to collapse into the "best interests" test. See Baron, Botsford, and Cole, *supra,* note 22, at 170, n. 54.

The court seemed to think that the "substituted judgment" test was required if it was to to be able to take into consideration Saikewicz's inability to understand the purpose of undergoing the pain and disorientation of chemotherapy. But this could have been weighed in the balance even under the "best interests" test. Costs and benefits of treatment are a function of each person's peculiar physical and mental make-up and the circumstances in which he finds himself. Thus, Saikewicz's inability to reduce the rigors of chemotherapy through understanding and gaining hope from its purpose presents a clear cost item. The "substituted judgment" test would come into play only if we knew what his competent decision-making foibles would be and if we were willing to take those into consideration even though they might lead us to a decision that might not fully accord with what we would think would be in his "best interests."

Some evidence that the Supreme Judicial Court has refined its distinction between the two tests since *Saikewicz* is provided by the following language from a more recent decision:

> If the judge feels that the "best interests" of the ward demand one outcome but concludes that the ward's substituted judgment would require another, then in the absence of an overriding State interest, the substituted judgment prevails. In short, if an individual would, if competent, make an unwise or foolish decision, the judge must respect that decision as long as he would accept the same decision if made by a competent individual in the same circumstances. We digress concerning this "right to be wrong" only to establish the relationship between the "best interests" standard and the substituted judgment determination. *(In re Roe,* 1981 Mass.Adv.Sh. 981, 1,017 n. 20, 421 N.E.2d 40, 59–60 n.20 (1981).)

59. *Saikewicz, supra,* note 53, at 754, 370 N.E.2d at 432.
60. *Id.*
61. *Id.* at 754–55, 370 N.E.2d at 432.
62. *Id.* at 758, 370 N.E.2d at 434.
63. *Id.* at 759, 370 N.E.2d at 435.

64. Relman, "The Saikewicz Decision: Judges as Physicians," 298 *New Eng. J. Med.* 508 (1978).
65. Baron, "Medical Paternalism and the Rule of Law: A Reply to Dr. Relman," 4 *Am. J.L. and Med.* 337 (1979).
66. *Id.* at 346-47.
67. *Omychund v. Barker,* 26 Eng. Rep. 15, 22-23 (Ch. 1744).
68. Fuller, "Human Purpose and Natural Law," 53 *J. Philos.* 697,700 (1956).
69. *Report of the Joint Conference on Professional Responsibility of the American Bar Association and the Association of American Law Schools,* 44 A.B.A.J. 1159, 1160 (1958). For an empirical study that supports the conclusions of the Joint Conference Report, see J. Thibaut and L. Walker, *Procedural Justice: A Psychological Analysis* (1975).
70. Holmes, "Eulogy on S. Bartlett," in *Speeches* at 43 (1913).
71. Holmes, "The Law," in *Speeches* at 16 (1913).
72. 3 W. Blackstone, *Commentaries* *373.
73. It was, for example, the order of the Illinois Supreme Court sealing the records in a recent infanticide case that led to furor in the press over that case and the secrecy with which it was surrounded. See "Rights in Conflict: Who Lives, Who Dies, and Who Decides?," *Chicago Tribune,* May 2, 1982, § 1, at 6, col. 1.
74. J. Bentham, *Rationale of Judicial Evidence* 524 (1827).
75. Baron, "To Die Before The Gods Please: Legal Issues Surrounding Euthanasia and the Elderly," 14 *J. Geriatric Psychiatry* 45, 57-58 (1981).
76. Relman, *supra,* note 3, at 241.
77. 6 Mass. App. 466, 380 N.E.2d 134 (1978).
78. The term is one of several items of medical jargon which have grown up around the development of advanced methods of cardiopulmonary resuscitation (CPR). One "codes" a patient when one signals for teams of medical personnel to descend on the patient for the purpose of giving him emergency CPR. This term derives from the "Code 99" or "Code Blue" that would be announced over the hospital intercommunications system for the purpose of mustering all available personnel to the patient's room. One "no codes" a patient when one gives orders (written or verbal) that no CPR or other extraordinary resuscitative measures are to be given the patient in the event of cardiac or respiratory arrest. A "no code" is sometimes called an ONTR (order not to resuscitate) or a DNR (do not resuscitate).
79. *Dinnerstein, supra,* note 77, at 475, 380 N.E. 2d at 139.
80. Baron, *supra,* note 65, at 369 n. 65.
81. *Dinnerstein, supra,* note 77, at 471, 380 N.E.2d at 137.
82. Relman, *supra* note 3, at 236; Baron, "The Dinnerstein Decision and 'No-Code' Orders," 300 *New Eng. J. Med.* 264 (1979).
83. 1980 Mass. Adv. Sh. 1209, 405 N.E.2d 115 (1980).
84. *Id.* at 1211, 405 N.E.2d at 118.
85. *In the Matter of Spring,* 8 Mass.App. 831, 840 n. 9, 399 N.E.2d 493, 499 n. 9 (1979).
86. *Spring, supra,* note 83, at 1210, 405 N.E.2d at 117.
87. *Id.* at 1216, 405 N.E.2d at 120.
88. *Id.* at 1217, 405 N.E.2d at 121.
89. *Id.* at 1218, 405 N.E.2d at 121.
90. *Id.* at 1218, 405 N.E.2d at 122.
91. *Id.* at 1219, 405 N.E.2d at 122.

92. *Id.*
93. *Id.*
94. *Id.* at 1215, 405 N.E.2d at 120.
95. *supra,* note 58.
96. *Id.* at 1001-2421 N.E.2d at 51-52.
97. *Custody of a Minor,* 385 Mass. 697, 434 N.E.2d 601 (1982).
98. *Id.* at 709-10, 434 N.E.2d at 608.
99. 385 Mass. 555, 432 N.E.2d 712 (1982).
100. *Id.* at 559, 432 N.E.2d at 716-17.
101. *Id.* at 559, 432 N.E.2d at 716.
102. 421 A.2d 1334 (Del.1980).
103. *Id.* at 1346.
104. 52 N.Y.2d 363, 438 N.Y.S.2d 266, 420 N.E.2d 64 (1981).
105. *Eichner v. Dillon,* 73 App.Div.2d 431, 426 N.Y.S.2d 517 (1980).
106. *Eichner v. Dillon, supra,* note 104, at 382-83, 438 N.Y.S.2d at 276, 420 N.E.2d at 74. *In re Storar,* a case decided with *Eichner v. Dillon* and sharing its opinion and citation in the court of appeals, is noteworthy for also seeming to leave important questions to the legislature. That case involved a profoundly retarded and terminally ill adult whose mother had refused to give her consent to continued life-prolonging treatment on the ground that it was bothersome, intrusive, and outweighed by the benefits of permitting her son a peaceful death. While allowing a proxy decision for "death with dignity" for Brother Fox, because there was evidence in that case to justify that substituted judgment, the court denied John Storar's mother the opportunity to make such a decision for him. Unfortunately, the short opinion can be read as disallowing, until the New York legislature changes the law, any decision to terminate life-prolonging care in cases where there is no evidence to support a substituted judgment. On the other hand, some of the language in the opinion suggests that the court is merely holding that, in the absence of such evidence, a rigid "best interests" test is to be applied and that Mrs. Storar's decision did not pass that test. *Id.* at 380-81, 438 N.Y.S.2d at 275, 420 N.E.2d at 73.
107. Relman, *supra,* note 3, at 241.
108. As of April, 1982, the Society for the Right to Die reported "right to die" laws having been enacted in Alabama, Arkansas, California, District of Columbia, Idaho, Kansas, Nevada, New Mexico, North Carolina, Oregon, Texas, Vermont, and Washington. It reported bills pending in Alaska, Connecticut, Florida, Georgia, Hawaii, Illinois, Indiana, Iowa, Maryland, Massachusetts, Michigan, Mississippi, Missouri, New Jersey, New York, Ohio, Oklahoma, Pennsylvania, Rhode Island, South Carolina, Tennessee, and West Virginia.
109. Baron, *supra,* note 65, at 359.
110. *Supra,* note 77.
111. What would justify the decision is that the medical facts of the case would have presented Mrs. Dinnerstein with no real choice if she were competent. It is arguable that anyone would prefer no-coding over being kept alive in Mrs. Dinnerstein's hopeless condition. Thus the court could have used the case to carve out an exception to the requirement of advance court approval for those cases whose medical facts present such an open-and-shut issue of substituted judgment. See Baron, *supra,* note 65, at 362, n. 65. The *Quinlan* case arguably presents the same sort of situation and should be read as articulating the same narrow rule. See Annas, *supra,* note 47.
112. For example, *Commissioner of Correction v. Myers, supra,* note 8.

113. L. Levy, *The Law of the Commonwealth and Chief Justice Shaw: The Evolution of American Law:* 1830 to 1860 at 24 (1957).

114. *See,* for example, *Quinlan, supra,* note 39 at 43, 355 A.2d at 665.

115. *Saikewicz, supra* note 53, at 741-42, 370 N.E.2d at 425-26. However, that distinction was implicitly eroded by the Appeals Court of Massachusetts in *Lane v. Candura, supra,* note 2, and seemingly abandoned by the Supreme Judicial Court in *Commissioner of Correction v. Myers, supra,* note 8, in favor of a weighing of the "obtrusiveness" of the treatment which is proposed.

116. *Id.* at 741, 370 N.E.2d at 425.

117. For example, *In re Spring, supra,* note 83.

118. *Supra,* note 8.

119. See *Lane v. Candura, supra,* note 2.

120. In Massachusetts, this is provided for in part by statute, see M.G.L. ch. 123, § 25. However, it is recognized as well by case law. See *Boyd v. Board of Registrars of Voters,* 368 Mass. 631, 334 N.E.2d 629 (1975).

121. See *Guardianship of Bassett,* 7 Mass. App. 56, 385 N.E.2d 1,024 (1979).

122. See *Doe v. Doe,* 377 Mass. 272, 278-79, 385 N.E.2d 995, 999-1000 (1979).

123. For one exception, see *Nathan v. Farinelli, supra,* note 27.

124. 92 Cal.App. 3d 796,156 Cal.Rptr. 48, (1979).

125. *Id.* at 800, 156 Cal.Rptr. at 50.

126. *Id.* at 802, 156 Cal.Rptr. at 51.

127. *Id.*

128. See Annas. *Denying the Rights of The Retarded: The Phillip Becker Case,* The Hastings Center Report, December 1979, at 18.

129. *Rights in Conflict: Who Lives, Who Dies, and Who Decides?, supra,* note 73.

130. *Id.*

131. *Id.*

132. See Duff and Campbell, "Moral and Ethical Dilemmas in the Special-Care Nursery," 389 *New Eng. J. Med.* 890 (1973), and Robertson, Involuntary Euthanasia of Defective Newborns: A Legal Analysis, 27 *Stan. L. Rev.* 213, 214 (1975).

133. Baron, Botsford, and Cole, *supra,* note 22, at 181-86.

134. *Id.*

135. *Id.* at 186-87.

136. *In re Pescinski,* 67 Wis.2d 4, 226 N.W.2d 180 (1975).

137. Perhaps most notable was the performance of Mark I. Berson of the Greenfield, Massachusetts Bar as guardian *ad litem* in the *Spring* case. Despite pressure from all other parties to the case and vilification from the Massachusetts press, he provided his client with all of the protection the situation seemed to require. This included (1) a successful appeal of the case-in-chief to the Supreme Judicial Court from an adverse decision in the Appeals Court of Massachusetts and (2) a separate successful appeal to a single justice of the Supreme Judicial Court of the probate judge's subsequent order disallowing the introduction of newly discovered evidence on the question of Mr. Spring's competency. See *In re Spring,* No. 80-37 (S.J.C., Suffolk County, February 4, 1980).

138. *Saikewicz, supra,* note 53, at 732 n.4, 370 N.E.2d at 421 n.4.

139. *Id.*

140. *Id.* at 757, 370 N.E.2d at 433-34.

141. See Baron, "The Mixed Roles of The Guardian Ad Litem: Part II — The Critical Role of Counsel," *Guardianship News,* April 1981, at 1.

142. See Baron, "Assuring Detached But Passionate Investigation and Decision: The Role of Guardians Ad Litem in Saikewicz-type Cases," *4 Am. J.L. and Med.* 111, 127–130 (1978).

143. See Baron, "The Mixed Roles of the Guardian Ad Litem," *Guardianship News,* March 1981, at 1 (Part 1), *Guardianship News,* April 1981, at 1 (Part 2).

144. Baron, *supra,* note 142, at 128–29.

145. *Supra* note 99 at 566–67, 432 N.E.2d at 721.

146. For one thing, the court still envisions the guardian *ad litem* as serving the inconsistent "mixed roles" of advocate and something else:

> The guardian ad litem, *in his recommendation,* should attempt to ascertain the ward's actual preference for sterilization, parenthood, or other means of contraception.

Id. at 570, 432 N.E.2d at 722. Emphasis supplied. In making this "recommendation," does the guardian *ad litem* function as fact investigator, or expert witness, or master? Does he make these recommendations subject to the rules of evidence in open court? If he is a lawyer, does he warn his ward-client that he may breach the attorney-client confidence by testifying regarding the substance of his conversations with his ward-client? See Baron, *supra* note 143.

147. Pericles, "Funeral Oration," in *Thucydides, History of the Peloponnesian War,* Book II, § 40.

148. 1 K. R. Popper, *The Open Society and its Enemies* vi (4th rev. ed. 1962).